*L*earners
with Disabilities

Learners
with Disabilities
A Social Systems Perspective of Special Education

Thomas M. Shea
Southern Illinois University—Edwardsville

Anne Marie Bauer
University of Cincinnati

WCB **Brown &**
Benchmark
PUBLISHERS
Madison, Wisconsin • Dubuque, Iowa

Book Team

Managing Editor *Sue Pulvermacher-Alt*
Production Editor *Diane Clemens*
Photo Editor *Carol A. Judge*
Permissions Coordinator *Mavis Oeth*
Art Processor *Joyce Watters*
Visuals/Design Developmental Consultant *Marilyn A. Phelps*
Visuals/Design Freelance Specialist *Mary L. Christianson*
Publishing Services Specialist *Sherry Padden*
Marketing Manager *Pamela S. Cooper*
Advertising Manager *Jodi Rymer*

WCB Brown & Benchmark

A Division of Wm. C. Brown Communications, Inc.

Executive Vice President/General Manager *Thomas E. Doran*
Vice President/Editor in Chief *Edgar J. Laube*
Vice President/Sales and Marketing *Eric Ziegler*
Director of Production *Vickie Putman Caughron*
Director of Custom and Electronic Publishing *Chris Rogers*

Wm. C. Brown Communications, Inc.

President and Chief Executive Officer *G. Franklin Lewis*
Corporate Senior Vice President and Chief Financial Officer *Robert Chesterman*
Corporate Senior Vice President and President of Manufacturing *Roger Meyer*

Photo Research by Carol Smith

Cover Photo © David Young-Wolff/Tony Stone World Wide, LTD.

Cover and interior design by David Lansdon

Illustrations by Precision Graphics unless noted otherwise.

Copyedited by Nikki Herbst

The credits section for this book begins on page 473 and is considered an extension of the copyright page.

*T*his book is dedicated to

Dolores, my best friend and wife, and
Keith, Kevin, and Jane
and to Riley and our children,
Demian, Tarie, Christopher, Sarah, and Mickey

Brief Contents

Expanded Contents

Section

1

The Social Systems Contexts of Learners with Disabilities   1

Human Development and Learners with Disabilities   3

Families and Learners with Disabilities   73

Transitions between Social Subsystems   97

Family and Community Issues in Contemporary Society   115

Section

3

Learners Who Vary in Accessing the Environment   203

Learners with Communication Disorders   205

10

Learners with Physical and Other Health Impairments   229

Learners with Visual Impairments   257

Learners with Hearing Impairments   285

Section

4

Learners Who Vary in Their Learning Styles and Rates   313

13

Learners Identified as Learning Disabled   315

Learners with Severe and Multiple Disabilities   387

Learners Who Are Gifted, Talented, or Creative   413

Section

5

A Look Toward the Future 443

18

Issues, Trends, and Directions 445

List of Figures

List of Tables

List of Boxes

Preface

In 1979, Urie Bronfenbrenner posited what he described as an "unorthodox" theoretical perspective of human development. His perception challenged current theory with its concept of the developing person and the environment, and most dramatically with its description of the evolving nature of interactions between the individual and the environment. In the past decade this theoretical perspective has not been refuted as too unorthodox; rather, it has been used to provide a framework to study the impact of divorce (Kurdek, 1981), day care placement (Belsky, 1980a), child abuse (Belsky, 1980b), and family adaptation to learners with disabilities (Bauer & Shea, 1987; Shea and Bauer, 1987).

In this text, Bronfenbrenner's ecological theory provides the framework for understanding the vast amount of information we have about learners with disabilities. Through the social systems perspective, learners with disabilities are suggested to be human learners first, who then vary in learning style and developmental rates, interaction styles, and ability to access the environment through communication, mobility, vision, and audition. Using this perspective, it is impossible to understand disabilities without examining the nested contexts (family, classroom, school, community, and society) in which the individual is developing. To fail to do so, to paraphrase Bronfenbrenner's description of developmental psychology, would be to continue the "study of the strange behavior of children in strange situations with strange adults for the briefest possible periods of time."

Audience and Purpose

This text serves to introduce undergraduate and beginning graduate students in both general and special education to the basic concepts of human diversity and its impact on self, family, education, community, and society. As an introduction to that subsystem we refer to as "special education," we emphasize information that will assist future professionals in their efforts to facilitate the development of those children, youth, and adults who are perceived as different from their peers. Unlike the authors of other texts, we have dared to espouse a theoretical basis for our discussions; without this theoretical framework we feel that working with individuals with special needs is a series of independent strategies and techniques rather than an integrated effort to enhance an individual's potential through interactions and relationships with others. We reflect the current emphasis of the Carnegie Report (1986) and the Holmes Group (1986) reforms in assuring that teachers function from a theory base and knowledge of child development and instructional methodologies.

Organization

The text begins with a discussion of the social systems contexts of learners with disabilities. Chapter 1 discusses the nature of human development from the social systems perspective and the implications of this ecological development perspective for working with learners with disabilities. The following chapters in this section address issues that impact on learners with disabilities regardless of the variations they demonstrate. Chapters are included on societal perceptions of learners with disabilities (Chapter 2), schooling and learners with disabilities (Chapter 3), and families with members with disabilities (Chapter 4). The final chapters in this section address transitions learners with disabilities make between social systems (for example, home and school, or school and work, as in Chapter 5) and family and community issues in contemporary society (Chapter 6).

The next three sections of the text discuss the variations in human development that are usually referred to as "disabilities," "exceptionalities," or "handicapping conditions." Using a social systems perspective, we are able to discuss the full range of each variation, rather than just those learners who are disabled by the variation. We are able to communicate the need for all teachers to recognize and celebrate the diversity among children, youth, and adults.

In Section Two, we discuss learners who vary in their interactions, including learners from diverse cultures and ethnic groups (Chapter 7) and learners identified as behaviorally disordered (Chapter 8). Learners who vary with regard to accessing the environment are discussed in Section Three. Chapters are devoted to learners with communication disorders (Chapter 9), orthopedic disabilities and health impairments (Chapter 10), visual impairments (Chapter 11), and hearing impairments (Chapter 12).

In Section Four, we discuss learners who vary in learning style and rate. Chapters are devoted to learning disabilities (Chapter 13), mild or moderate mental retardation (Chapter 14), mild disabilities (Chapter 15), severe and multiple disabilities (Chapter 16), and learners who are gifted, creative, or talented (Chapter 17). The fifth section and final chapter of the text discusses emerging issues, trends, and directions in special education (Chapter 18).

Within each chapter, we support your learning through the use of objectives, key words and phrases, and figures mapping the information in the learners' developmental contexts. The reader will find a glossary of terms at the end of the text.

We have chosen our language carefully to communicate our belief system regarding learners who vary from their peers. We will not say "the retarded" or "visually impaired students"; we will refer to learners *with* mental retardation or learners with visual impairments. We especially recognize those students whose variations may be based on clinical judgement or the nature of instruction and schooling: we will refer to learners "identified as behaviorally disordered" and learners "identified as learning disabled." We will describe ways to mediate the environment to provide equal benefit for these learners, rather than techniques or strategies to make the learner match the system. We fully recognize and apologize for any awkwardness of style this may pose to readers. We hope, however, that such awkwardness results in reader recognition of the learner, rather than the variation that learner presents.

Teaching Supplements

To help you teach your course, several teaching supplements are available. First we have an Instructor's Manual (IM) written by us and a Test Item File (TIF) written by Annie Hawkins and Michele Roszmann-Millican of the University of Cincinnati.

The Test Item File is also offered on MicroTest III, a powerful but easy-to-use test generating program by Chariot Software Group. MicroTest is available for DOS, Windows, and Macintosh personal computers. With MicroTest, you can easily select the questions from the test item file and print a test and answer key. You can customize questions, heading, and instructions; add or import questions of your own; and print your test in a choice of fonts. You can obtain a copy of MicroTest III by contacting your local Brown & Benchmark sales representative.

We also have a transparency set available to adopters of our text which includes thirty 1-color and full-color transparency acetates.

Finally, qualified adopters can choose from several excellent videotapes that are available. Contact your Brown & Benchmark sales representative for more details about the videotapes.

Learning Supplement

In order to help your students grasp the material, a Student Study Guide is available. The Study Guide was written by Sheila Dove Jones and Ann Marie Cook, both of Bloomsburg University. Each chapter contains objectives, an outline, guided review (key terms and fill-in-the-blank questions), a self test (multiple choice, true/false, matching, and short answer questions), and critical thinking exercises. All questions are page-referenced to this text and include an answer key at the end of the study guide.

Acknowledgments

This book is about social systems, and we must acknowledge those individuals in our personal social systems for their support in our efforts. To Dolores and Riley, a thanks for their constant support, and a thanks to our children Keith and Kevin, daughter-in-law Jane, Demian, Tarie, Christopher, Sarah, and Mickey, for their patience and understanding of time at the computer. We must recognize Paul Tavenner and the staff of Brown & Benchmark for their understanding and support, and their willingness to take a chance with an introductory text that is a deviation from the commonplace, as well as the reviewers who provided insights to our work:

Annette R. Clem-Robinson
Seattle Pacific University

Gail M. Dummer
Michigan State University

Valerie Owen
National-Louis University

Jack Joseph Hourcade
Boise State University

Sally M. Todd
Brigham Young University

Donald Stauffer
Slippery Rock University

Robbie Ludy
Northwest Missouri State University

Ann Cranston-Gingras
University of South Florida

Iva Dene McCleary
University of Utah

Curt Dudley-Marling
York University
Ontario, Canada

Janet Jamieson
University of British Columbia
Vancouver

Ruth Violet
Vancouver Community College

Finally, we must thank the learners who vary from their peers, and who challenge the educational system, for what they have taught us.

Thomas M. Shea
Anne M. Bauer

1

The Social Systems Contexts of Learners with Disabilities

Chapter

1

Human Development and Learners with Disabilities

After completing this chapter, you will be able to:

1. describe the social systems perspective of human development.
2. describe the impact of the social systems approach on learners who vary from their peers.
3. describe the application of the social systems perspective in the text.

*K*ey Words and Phrases————————————————

accommodation	microsystem
behavior	milieu
behavioral perspective	norm
biophysical perspective	ontogenic system
congruence	psychoeducational perspective
development	reciprocal association
ecology	social systems perspective
ecological context	special education
exosystem	transactions
macrosystem	transition
mesosystem	

*J*AMIE IS A 7-YEAR-OLD BOY WITH DOWN SYNDROME. HIS BIRTH WAS UNPLANNED. AT THE TIME OF HIS BIRTH, HIS mother was the single parent of two school-aged children. When Jamie was an infant, she was unable to find affordable child care service in the community. Because it was necessary that she return to work, she had to leave Jamie in the care of a young cousin.

A young man who was visiting the cousin's home physically abused Jamie because he would not stop crying. Jamie's mother, seeing her son bruised when she picked him up after work, took him to the hospital. As required by law, hospital personnel reported the case of suspected abuse to the authorities. The case was investigated by the Department of Human Services and authorities prohibited Jamie's mother from leaving him in the cousin's home. During the 3 weeks that a caseworker was seeking appropriate day care for Jamie, his mother remained home from work. When she called her employer at the end of the third week to say she must remain out of work yet another few days, she was informed to return to work immediately or lose her job.

With no other resources (her family refused to help because she had "turned in" her cousin), Jamie's mother signed a voluntary agreement for her son to enter foster care. After Jamie spent 30 days in an emergency foster home, the courts ruled a temporary commitment to the custody of the Department of Human Services. Jamie left his emergency home for a long-term foster home. Because of his delayed development and behavioral problems, Jamie frequently changed foster homes.

When Jamie was five, his mother remarried. Her husband assumed responsibility for her two other children but did not want to attempt to parent a child with a disability. He urged Jamie's mother to terminate parental rights to Jamie. Jamie was placed in the permanent custody of the courts, and a social worker was assigned to find an adoptive home.

By the time Jamie was 7 years old, he had lived in five different foster homes. No family has yet come forward to adopt him. At present, Jamie is socially withdrawn, has frequent temper outbursts, engages in limited play with a few toys, and has a speaking vocabulary of two words: "no" and "more."

● Jack is a 7-year-old boy with Down syndrome. His birth was unplanned. His mother, with two school-age children, put her career on hold when Jack was born. This would enable her to care for him full-time and participate in infant stimulation and early intervention services with him.

While still in the hospital, upon learning that Jack had Down syndrome, his mother immediately contacted the local Down syndrome Association and was assigned a parent partner who not only provided social and emotional support but also information on Jack's disability and available community services. Jack's paternal grandparents, thrilled to have yet another grandchild, willingly cared for Jack at least one weekend a month so that other family members could have time for themselves and mother and father could have a "night out."

Jack has been in a variety of infant stimulation and early intervention programs since birth. He has participated in educational programs and communication therapy since he was 6 months old. At this time, Jack is an active and healthy boy who attends regular school with special education services. He has several friends and is on the swimming team with age-peers at the local YMCA. He communicates his needs effectively ■

Introduction

This book is about learners with disabilities and special education. Learners with disabilities are individuals who are seen by others as "different." For various reasons, as learners, these children and young persons are not perceived to be the same as other learners. They may vary from their peers in appearance, how they communicate, and how they move. They may vary in the manner in which they interact or relate with others, in the way they gain access to the environment, or in the rate and manner with which they learn.

Special education is essentially a subsystem of regular education. It is responsible for the education of learners with disabilities. In other words, **special education** is a part of general education that assumes responsibility for individuals who do not fit the system; that is, children who vary from the norm or standard. Learners with disabilities are a challenge to an educational system designed to accept young children in preschool and kindergarten and, during the next thirteen to fourteen years, move them through high school into college, vocational training, or the workplace. Unlike the majority of children, learners with disabilities often do not move as quickly and unobtrusively through the system as their peers. More specifically, they challenge the system.

"Learners with disabilities" are first and foremost human learners. However, as learners with disabilities, they are often perceived to vary from peers to such an extent that something beyond that which usually occurs at home, in the classroom, and in the community must be provided to them if they are to be successful. In the educational system, that "something" is frequently special education. In the home and community, that "something" may be any one of a broad range of educational, therapeutic, and rehabilitation services offered by public and private medical and human service agencies.

Any consideration of learners who are perceived to vary from their peers must begin with a discussion of the **norm,** or that which is considered to be normal, commonly occurring, or typical—that which sets a standard.

In this text, we apply a social systems perspective to address the unique development experienced by each learner, typical or disabled. A **social systems perspective** is one in which the individual is seen as developing in a dynamic relationship with and as an inseparable part of the social contexts in which the individual functions over her or his life span. The particular perspective we apply is Bronfenbrenner's ecology of human development (1979). This perspective was first presented by Bronfenbrenner in the 1960s and further developed in the 1970s. Since that time it has been researched, analyzed, discussed, and enhanced by many theoreticians and practitioners in special education, psychology, and the social sciences. You will become familiar with these persons and their contributions to social systems or ecological theory in the first section of the text. This section is the basis for the analysis and discussion of the various groups of learners with disabilities presented in the remainder of the text.

A social systems or ecological perspective is not the only perspective through which human development and learners with disabilities can be viewed. There are many others, a few of which will be discussed briefly. However, it is important to understand that the authors selected social systems theory as a framework because it is broad in scope and allows the integration of much of the information derived from other theories. It is a perspective that allows us to study and utilize all facets of the individual and the environment when explaining human development and learners with disabilities. The selection of a more restrictive theory would have limited our discussion of various individual, behavioral, and environmental factors.

Among the other perspectives available for the study of development and learners with disabilities are the behavioral, psychoeducational, and biophysical theories. From the **behavioral perspective,** an individual's behavior is viewed as being maintained by the stimuli in the immediate environment in which the individual is functioning. Teaching involves manipulating those stimuli and managing the immediate environment to facilitate change in the individual's behavior. In this perspective, little consideration is given to factors within the individual and factors in the individual's extended environment. For example, if a student fails to turn in homework assignments, the teacher would arrange for a reward following each time an assignment is turned in.

From the **psychoeducational perspective,** factors within the individual are seen as the primary cause of behavior. Emphasis is focused on the dynamic equilibrium of intrapsychic phenomena such as the id (basic instinct), ego (manager), and the superego (conscience). In addition, emphasis is placed on the impact of the immediate and extended environments. Teaching involves accepting and interpreting the individual's behavior and encouraging new and more effective modes of interacting. An interview would be held with the student who fails to bring in homework assignments, to explore the reasons the work is not returned. The student's feelings about the work and the relationship with the teacher and those who supervise the homework would be examined.

The **biophysical perspective** emphasizes neurological and other organic factors as the cause of behavior. Teaching involves providing ordered, controlled environments to assist the individual to neurologically process stimuli. In addition, this perspective involves concern for nutrition, medication, and other medical interventions. Failure to bring in homework assignments may be viewed as a short-term memory problem, and strategies to improve retention may be employed.

The authors believe that these competing theories, though they do make a significant contribution to the understanding of human development and the learner with disabilities, are limited in scope and restrict our view of human development, of learners with disabilities, and of the factors involved in learning.

The Social Systems Perspective

The following four terms occur throughout the literature regarding the social systems perspective: ecology, development, behavior, and congruence. We shall define each term as it is used in the literature, in order to provide readers with a common frame of reference.

Ecology is the study of the relationship of humans with their environment, which involves reciprocal association (Thomas & Marshall, 1977). An individual's ecology is all the surroundings or the milieu of the behavior (Scott, 1980). From an ecological perspective it is assumed that an individual is an inseparable part of the ecological unit, which is composed of the individual, the school, the home, the neighborhood, and the community. **Reciprocal association** means that the individual and the environment affect each other; both are actors and reactors.

Development is the continual adaptation or adjustment of the individual and the environment to each other. It is a progressive mutual accommodation that takes place throughout the life span between growing individuals and their changing environments. It is based on "the person's evolving conception of the ecological environment and his [or her] relationship to it, as well as the person's growing capacity to discover, sustain, or alter its properties" (Bronfenbrenner, 1979, p. 9).

Thomas and Marshall (1977), relating this continual adaptation or development to the function of special education, stated:

> The environment seldom adapts, and never completely to the specific needs of an individual with a handicap. Therefore, the ultimate purpose of any special education program is to assist that individual in adapting to the environment to [her or] his maximum capacity (p. 16).

Behavior is the expression of the dynamic relationship between the individual and the environment (Marmor & Pumpian-Mindlin, 1950). Behavior occurs in a setting that includes specific time, place, and object "props" as well as previously established patterns of behavior (Scott, 1980). By "previously established patterns of behavior," we mean those ways of behaving that are characteristic of an individual and that he or she develops over time and brings to the setting in which the behavior is occurring. Understanding behavior requires more than the simple observation of an individual's behavior by one or two persons in a specific setting; it requires an examination of the systems of interaction surrounding the behavior and is not limited to a single setting. In addition, to understand behavior one must take into account those aspects of the environment beyond the immediate situation in which the individual is functioning that may impact on the behavior (Bronfenbrenner, 1979).

Congruence is the "match" or "goodness of fit" between the individual and the environment. Thurman (1977) suggests that individuals who we judge to be normal are operating in an ecology that is congruent. The "normal" individual's behavior is in harmony or congruence with the norms of the environment. Thurman further maintains that when there is a lack of congruence, the individual is viewed as either deviant (being out of harmony with the norms) or incompetent (lacking the necessary behaviors). Congruence between the individual and the environment results in maximum competence and acceptance. According to Poplin and Stone (1992), an individual may be identified as disabled when there is a mismatch between past and present experiences.

In summary, from the social systems perspective, human development is the progressive, mutual **accommodation** (adaptation and adjustment) between an active, growing human being and the ever-changing settings in which the individual functions, as well as the relationships between those settings and the broader ecological contexts (the environments in which the individual develops) in which they are imbedded. These relationships are emphasized, rather dramatically, in the cases of "Jamie" and "Jack" at the beginning of the chapter. The reader is urged to reread the two cases and note the significant disparity between the ecological circumstances to which "Jamie" and "Jack" were exposed and the potential impact these differences may have had on their development.

This systems perspective has many implications for the way in which we perceive individuals identified as learners with disabilities and, thus, describe them in this text. We accept the proposition that human development implies change in the characteristics of an individual and that this change implies reorganization over time and space. We accept the contention that human development is grounded in the **ecological contexts** or settings in which it occurs. In this manner, development is an individual's evolving concept of the environment and her or his relationship to it, as well as the person's increasing ability to discover, maintain, or change certain aspects of that environment.

The social systems approach is distinguished by its concern with the ongoing and progressive accommodation between the growing human learner and his or her

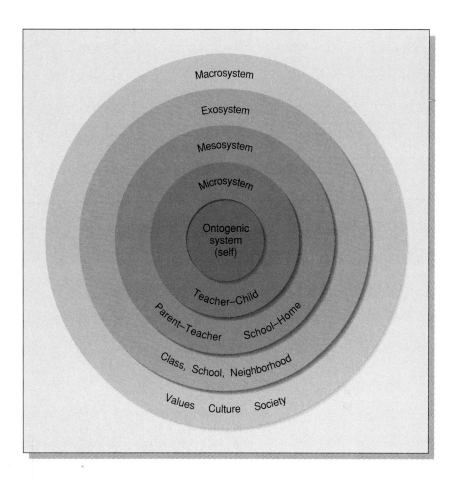

Figure 1.1
Developmental contexts. From Anne M.
Bauer and Thomas M. Shea, *Teaching
Exceptional Students in your Classroom.*
Copyright © 1989 by Allyn and Bacon.
Reprinted with permission.

immediate environment, and the way in which this relationship is formed and rec-
onciled by forces coming from more distinct aspects of the individual's social
milieu (the individual's social surroundings).

Human Development from a Social Systems Perspective

Objective One: To describe the
social systems perspective of
human development.

Bronfenbrenner suggests that the ecological contexts, or settings, in which an individual develops are nested, one inside the other, like a set of Russian dolls (see Figure 1.1). He argues that the nested nature of the contexts are decisive in the individual's development as events take place within them. For example, he suggests that
a child's ability to read may be related to the nature of the relationship between the
child's home and school as well as the methods used in school to instruct reading.

Riegel (1975) suggests that any individual change must be viewed within the
context of the larger social and cultural system. From a special education perspective, the specific settings of most relevance to the development of the learner with
disabilities are school, family, neighborhood, and community.

In the systems perspective, all individuals are viewed as growing, dynamic persons who progressively move into and restructure the settings in which they find
themselves. As previously stated, these systems are nested. Kurdek (1981) calls the
systems interdependent and states that the nature of this interdependence is
dynamic. Bronfenbrenner refers to the ecological contexts as the microsystem, the
mesosystem, the exosystem, and the macrosystem (see Figure 1.1).

Microsystems include the one-to-one relationship between the developing individual and teacher/care giver.

The Mesosystem includes interrelationships between the home and school of the developing individual.

Decisions by the school system affect the individual indirectly.

The Microsystem

The **microsystem** is the pattern of activities, roles, and interpersonal relationships experienced by a developing individual in the setting in which he or she is functioning. In the home, the microsystem includes relationships between either parent and the child, the child and each sibling, and between other pairs of family members. In the school, the microsystem includes the relationships between the child and teacher as well as the child and each of her or his peers. Referral to special education usually begins when there is a problem or lack of congruence in child-teacher or child-peer interaction within the microsystem.

The Mesosystem

The **mesosystem** represents the interrelations among two or more settings (microsystems) in which the individual actively functions. This may include the interrelations among home and school, home and service agency, home and neighborhood, and school and peer group. For example, nonmajority culture students may be challenged by the interrelationships between their home culture and the

Each individual contributes personal traits to a classroom.

Accommodations make once-challenging tasks accessible to persons with disabilities.

school culture and, as a consequence, be overrepresented, as a group, in special education. Parent-teacher collaboration and family-community service involvement are included within the mesosystem. The mesosystem also includes a consideration of **transitions**, or the movement of the learner with disabilities from one microsystem to another.

The Exosystem

The **exosystem** represents those settings that do not involve the individual directly. However, events occurring within the exosystem affect, or are affected by, what happens in settings (microsystems) in which the individual functions. Exosystem settings include, for example, a parent's workplace, a sibling's classroom, and the school system. The exosystem includes such factors as the availability of special education service programs, the goals of educational programs in the community, and the selection of school system-wide instructional materials and textbooks.

The Macrosystem

The **macrosystem** involves the majority culture's belief system. These are broad social factors that impinge on the settings within which the individual is contained. Society's general perspective of learners with disabilities, teachers, special education, the social role of students, and community values, for example, all impact on each student's education (Riegel, 1975).

The Ontogenic System

Belsky (1980) suggests that though Bronfenbrenner's ecological contexts provide an essential recognition of the complexity of human development, using only those contexts fails to take into account the individual differences or variations that each learner brings to his or her primary microsystems. He argues for the inclusion of the ontogenic system suggested by Tinbergen (1951) within the social systems perspective.

The **ontogenic system** includes the personal characteristics of the individual. Among these characteristics are the cognitive, communicative, social, and physical competencies that individuals bring to the settings in which they are functioning. Each individual has personal factors for coping with the environment, including personality attributes, skills, abilities, and competencies. As Gatlin (1980) so adroitly suggests, individuals do not deliberately make inappropriate behavioral decisions, but "attempt to satisfy their needs as they best understand them, while attempting to maintain some sense of personal and social integrity" (p. 252).

By including the ontogenic system in our perspective, we are forced to look at human development not as a series of cause and effect relationships between the individual and the environment, but as transactions among the individual and the environment. Sameroff (1975) contends the contact between the individual and the environment is a **transaction** (or communicative exchange) in which each is altered by the other. For example, the infant is influencing her or his caregiving environment at the same time that the caregiving environment is influencing the infant. Mothers with similarly behaving children may vary in their responses toward each child and thus cause different developmental outcomes. A child's development cannot be explained entirely by either biological or environmental factors. Rather, developmental and behavioral outcomes are due to the ongoing reciprocal interactions between the individual organism and the environment (Sameroff & Chandler, 1975).

Impact of the Social Systems Approach

Objective Two: To describe the impact of the social systems approach on learners who vary from their peers.

As a result of our professional experiences in education and special education, we conclude, as Bronfenbrenner asserted, that as currently understood and practiced, developmental psychology is "the study of the strange behavior of children in strange situations with strange adults for the briefest possible periods of time" (1979, p. 19). Kauffman (1984) suggests that in their work with children, special educators have been willing partners in telling the public that we can do things we simply cannot do. For example, we cannot mainstream all learners with disabilities, teach all children to read, or assure that every child attains his or her potential. Kauffman maintains that any time a child becomes known as a special education student, we must balance the likely outcomes of our available strategies with the harm we do her or him simply by identification.

The use of a social systems framework forces us, as professionals, to seek above and beyond relationships between causes and instructional strategies. Rather, the social systems perspective insists that we recognize the complexity of the many issues related to individuals who are perceived as varying from their peers. Taking into account the transactions between the developing child and the environment, we can recognize how predictions resulting from the child's early assessment may be inadequate (Sameroff, 1975). For example, if a child is identified as demonstrating a disability, the parents may treat the child in a manner that creates a self-fulfilling prophecy, thus limiting the child by their subconscious interaction style. Parents' perceptions of their child influence their behavior toward their child. Parents who perceive the child as limited interact with the child in a way which supports that perception. The same is true of the influence of teachers' perceptions of learners.

The Social Systems Perspective in the Text

Objective Three: To describe the application of the social systems perspective in this text.

The social systems perspective provides the framework for this text. It is used to organize the vast amount of information provided to college and university students in introductory courses in special education.

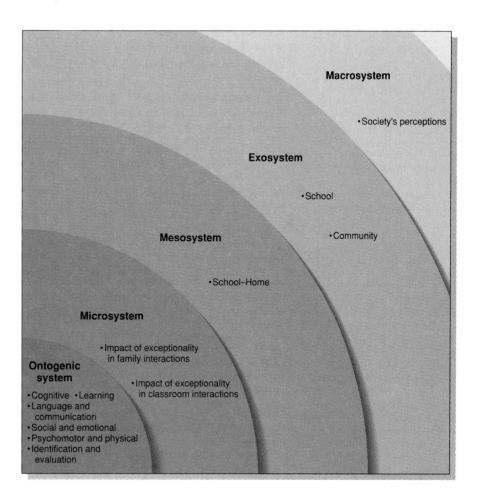

Figure 1.2
Chapter content and the systems perspective.

The first section of the text addresses, in detail, Bronfenbrenner's ecological contexts introduced in this chapter. Information is provided on families and learners with disabilities (the microsystem), transitions between the various contexts (the mesosystem), and schooling and learners with disabilities (the macrosystem).

The next three sections of the text (Chapters 7 through 17) address primarily the individual learners or the ontogenic system. Sections are devoted to discussions of learners with disabilities who vary from their peers in how they interact with the environment, how they access the environment, and how they learn. However, as the systems perspective implies, it is impossible to discuss individuals without also describing the contexts in which they develop. Thus in each chapter information specific to individual variations is provided. To assist the reader, a standard format is used for these chapters.

Each chapter begins with an introduction which sets the stage for the information provided in the chapter. The introduction presents basic issues with regard to the specific group of learners with disabilities under discussion. Next, each chapter address the ecological contexts of development as they apply to the group of individuals. A schemata depicting the developmental contexts as discussed in each chapter is presented in Figure 1.2.

The first part of each chapter describes the ontogenic system or the personal characteristics of the group of individuals being discussed. These include cognitive and learning characteristics, language and communication skills, social and emotional characteristics, and psychomotor and physical characteristics. The second part of each chapter discusses the "professional" context applied to considerations of the characteristics discussed under the first objective, that is definition, classification, prevalence and incidence, screening and identification, and assessment and evaluation.

The third part of each chapter describes the impact of the disability within the microsystem, that is, the home and classroom. Strategies and techniques for enhancing the individual's development within and among these settings, the microsystem and the mesosystem, are described in the fourth part of each chapter. This is followed by a discussion of the impact of the disability on participation in the larger social system of the school and the community (the exosystem). Each chapter concludes with a discussion of society's (the macrosystem's) perceptions of individuals with the disability under discussion.

Summary

In this chapter, learners with disabilities and special education were defined and discussed. Learners with disabilities are individuals who are perceived by others as varying from their peers. They may differ in appearance, how they communicate, and how they move. They may vary in the ways in which they interact and relate to others, gain access to the environment, or the rate and manner in which they learn. In this chapter, the authors emphasized that learners with disabilities are first and foremost learners, and these learners vary from their peers in some manner. Special education is presented as the subsystem of general education that is responsible for learners with disabilities. Learners with disabilities are those individuals who challenge the general education system, which is designed primarily for learners who can move quickly and unobtrusively through the system.

The social systems perspective of disabilities and several terms essential to effective communication between reader and authors were presented. The social systems approach was defined as a perspective in which the individual is seen as developing in a dynamic relationship with and as an inseparable part of the social contexts in which the individual functions over her or his life span. The definitions of terms (ecology, development, behavior, congruence) essential to understanding the social systems perspective were presented. Ecology is the study of the relationship of humans with their environment and involves reciprocal association. Behavior is the continuous adaptation of the individual and environment to each other, the expression of the dynamic relationship between the individual and the environment. Congruence represents the "match" between the individual and the environment.

The social systems perspective was differentiated from other perspectives of human development and learning. It is applied in the text because it is broad in scope and allows the integration of much of the information derived from other theories (behavioral, psychoeducational, and biophysical).

The ecology of human development, originally presented by Bronfenbrenner, and enhanced by others, was discussed. Each of the ecological contexts (ontogenic system, microsystem, exosystem, mesosystem, and macrosystem) was defined and exemplified. The pattern of activities, roles, and interpersonal relationships experienced by the individual in the setting in which she or he is functioning is the microsystem. The mesosystem represents the interrelationships among two or more microsystems in which the individual functions. Those settings in which the individual does not directly function, but which have an impact on the individual, comprise the exosystem. The culture's general belief system is the macrosystem. The ontogenic system represents the personal characteristics of the individual and accounts for the individual differences or variations that each learner brings to his or her microsystems. The five ecological contexts are dynamically interdependent.

The implications of the ecological perspective for the study of learners with disabilities and special education were discussed. The social system perspective requires the recognition of the complexity of the many issues related to individuals who are seen as differing from their peers.

The chapter concludes with an overview of the text and its chapters and their relationships to the ecological perspective. Essentially, the text is a blending of the social systems perspective (Chapters 1 through 6) with more traditional information on learners with disabilities and special education (Chapters 7 through 17). The information in Chapters 7 through 17 are presented using the ecological contexts as a framework.

The following five chapters are devoted to a detailed discussion of each of the ecological contexts introduced in this chapter. Chapter 2 focuses on the macrosystem, or societal perceptions of learners with disabilities.

References

Belsky, J. (1980). Child maltreatment: An ecological integration. *American Psychologist, 35*, 320–335.

Bronfenbrenner, U. (1979). *The ecology of human development.* Cambridge, MA: Harvard University.

Gatlin, H. (1980). Dialectics and family interaction. *Human Development, 23*, 245–253.

Kauffman, J. M. (1984). Saving children in the age of Big Brother: Moral and ethical issues in the identification of deviance. *Behavioral Disorders, 10*, 60-70.

Kurdek, L. A. (1981). An integrative perspective on children's divorce adjustment. *American Psychologist, 36*, 856–866.

Marmor, J., & Pumpian-Mindlin, E. (1950). Toward an integrative conception of mental disorders. *Journal of Nervous and Mental Disease, 3*, 19–29.

Poplin, M. S., & Stone, S. (1992). Paradigm shifts in instructional strategies. In W. Stainback & S. Stainback (Eds.), *Controversial issues confronting special education.* Boston: Allyn & Bacon.

Riegel, K. F. (1975). Toward a dialectical theory of development. *Human Development, 18*, 50–64.

Sameroff, A. (1975). Transactional models in early social relations. *Human Development, 18*, 65–79.

Sameroff, A., & Chandler, M. J. (1975). Reproductive risk and the continuum of care-taking causality. In F. D. Horowitz, M. Heatherington, S. Scarr-Salapatek, & G. Siegel (Eds.), *Review of child development research, Volume IV.* Chicago, IL: University of Chicago Press.

Scott, M. (1980). Ecological theory and methods of research in special education. *Journal of Special Education, 4*, 279–294.

Thomas, E. D., & Marshall, M. J. (1977). Clinical evaluation and coordination of services: An ecological model. *Exceptional Children, 44*, 16–22.

Thurman, S. K. (1977). Congruence of behavioral ecologies: A model for special education programming. *Journal of Special Education, 11*, 329–333.

Tinbergen, N. (1951). *The study of instinct.* London: Oxford University Press.

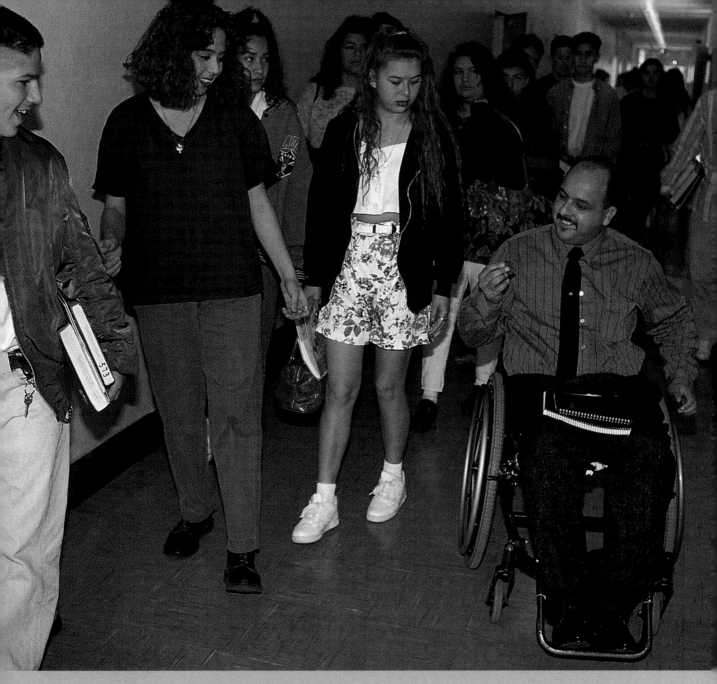

Chapter

2

Societal Perceptions of Learners with Disabilities

17

*O*bjectives _____

After completing this chapter, you will be able to:

1. describe the macrosystem in which learners with disabilities develop.
2. describe the evolution of current professional practices with individuals who vary from their peers.
3. describe issues related to societal perceptions that impact on the individual's development.

*K*ey Words and Phrases _____

Americans with Disabilities Act of 1990 (ADA)
compensatory education
disability
handicap
stigma
the wild boy of Aveyron

*A*FTER FIFTEEN YEARS AS A PROFESSIONAL EDUCATOR I WAS LOOKING FOR WORK. AN M.ED. PLUS 30 ADDITIONAL HOURS OF graduate work in the area of guidance/counseling and pupil personnel work gave me what I thought [was] an impressive background. I became a regular visitor to area social service agencies, rehabilitation services, employment and job placement services. For reasons never fully understood by me I came away empty handed: no job placement prospects, insufficient or inadequate training programs. I was 40 years old, well educated, and highly overqualified for most of the work positions for which I could be considered. Over the years our society has made great strides in providing assistance and opportunities to persons with disabilities. However, the business world is slow to accept the premise that "disability does not mean inability" (a statement by an individual with a hearing impairment) (Zepf, 1990, p. 32) ■

Introduction

This chapter focuses attention on the macrosystem, an ecological context in which the learner with disabilities develops. This system includes the given society's values and beliefs. The macrosystem has an impact on the individual's opportunities to learn in school and function in society. The macrosystem includes the belief system supported by the majority culture, and it includes broad social factors that impinge on the settings within which the individual with disabilities functions. This context includes society members' general perceptions of individuals with disabilities, teachers, educational administrators, schools (including special education programs), and business and industry. According to Riegel (1975), society's general perspective of teachers, the social role of students, and community values all affect each student's education.

This chapter provides an overview of society's perceptions of individuals with disabilities, their status in society, their education, and their functioning in the workplace. Much of the information presented is derived from survey research conducted by individual researchers and research groups such as Louis Harris and Associates and the Gallup Organization. The evolution of current professional practices or treatment of individuals who vary from their peers is discussed. The chapter concludes with a discussion of the impact of societal perceptions on individual development.

Objective One: To describe the macrosystem in which learners with disabilities develop.

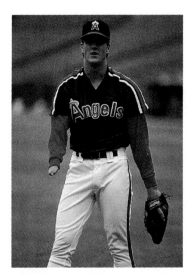

A person with a physical handicap can lead a productive life. Jim Abbott plays professional baseball.

The Macrosystem of Learners with Disabilities

"Disability" versus "Handicap"

In 1975, Public Law 94–142 defined "handicapped children" as those who are mentally retarded, hard of hearing, deaf, speech impaired, visually handicapped, seriously emotionally disturbed, orthopedically impaired, other health impaired, deaf–blind, or multihandicapped, or who have specific learning disabilities. [In 1990, Public Law 101–476, the Individuals with Disabilities Education Act (IDEA) added learners with autism and traumatic brain injury to the disability categories.] To be considered handicapped according to Public Law 94–142, students had to require special education and related services as a consequence of their disabilities.

This prerequisite for identification as handicapped, that is, the need for special education and related services, drew a careful line of demarcation between disability and handicap. **Disability** referred to a reduction of function or the absence of a particular body part or organ, such as the loss of a limb (Blackhurst, 1985). A **handicap** was viewed as a disadvantage resulting from a disability that limits or prevents fulfillment of a role (McCarthy, 1984). This differentiation is consistent with Bronfenbrenner's position with regard to development in the macrosystem, that is, "The direction and degree of psychological growth are governed by the extent to which opportunities to enter settings conducive to development in various domains are open or closed to the developing person" (1979, p. 288). This premise is reflected by Zepf (1990), who has a hearing impairment, in the opening statement of this chapter: opportunities are frequently closed to developing persons simply because they have a disability.

In an effort to remove the stigma of the term "handicapped," Congress changed the terminology to "disabilities" with the passage of Public Law 101–476. These amendments to Public Law 94–142 changed the name of the legislation from the

"Education for All Handicapped Children Act" to the "Education of Individuals with Disabilities Act." Public Law 94–142, Public Law 101–476, and other legislation, as well as several judicial decisions having significant impact on the education of learners with disabilities, are discussed in Chapter 3.

In the remainder of this section, we will explore society's general beliefs and values regarding disabilities, including acceptance of persons with disabilities in the workplace and in the educational system as well as by professionals who work with them.

General Beliefs and Values

Yoshida, Wasilewski, and Friedman (1990) studied the content of five metropolitan area newspapers for a 2-year period to determine the news coverage allowed to persons with disabilities. They found that the most frequently presented topic was the cost of developing community-based programs and providing services to persons with emotional disabilities. Budget expenditures, taxes, and housing for persons with disabilities as well as normalization and treatment in institutional settings were the topics next most likely to appear. Yoshida and associates found a paucity of articles on the actual education or instruction of individuals with disabilities. The vast majority of articles concerned adults with disabilities.

The International Center for the Disabled (ICD) Survey of Disabled Americans (1986) was the first national survey designed to study the attitudes and experiences of disabled Americans. It sought to determine the impact of the individuals' disabilities on the quality of their lives, including work, social life, daily activities, education, and personal life. It explored the barriers persons with disabilities confront in their efforts to lead full and productive lives.

The survey, conducted through telephone interviews with one thousand persons with disabilities, focused on life changes in the past 10 years, the personal meaning of disability, types of work available, barriers to work, social life and services, and government and employer benefits and policies. The survey also explored the perceptions of persons with disabilities as an underprivileged group and the emerging consciousness of persons with disabilities as a group.

The vast majority of persons with disabilities reported that they believed their lives had improved within the past 10 years. They reported that their disabilities had broad and varied repercussions. As a group, persons with disabilities had far less education than other Americans. They were poorer than other Americans. Persons with disabilities stated that they are generally unable to travel as they would like and have difficulty attending social events outside of the home such as theater, concerts, and sports events. They participate less than persons without disabilities in going to the movies, eating in restaurants, grocery shopping, and general community life. Barriers to a full social life include fear that the disability will cause the individual to become sick, hurt, or victimized by crime; the need for help from other persons in getting around; lack of access to public transportation or someone to drive them; and a lack of access to public buildings and restrooms.

According to the survey results, there are definite indications of an emerging group consciousness among persons with disabilities. They perceive themselves as a minority and believe that equal rights legislation should be applied to persons with disabilities in the same way as it is applied to other minorities.

People with disabilities are more mobile now than ten years ago.

Acceptance in the Workplace

Schafer, Rice, Metzler, and Haring (1989) surveyed both nondisabled co-workers of persons with disabilities and other nondisabled employees who worked in the same business but not with persons with disabilities. Co-workers of persons with disabilities expressed more comfort and acceptance about working with persons with mental retardations, and more respondents strongly agreed that such persons are friendly on the job and socially and vocationally competent than did nondisabled employees who did not work with persons with disabilities. The surveyors found that perceptions of co-workers of the social and vocational competencies of workers with severe disabilities are equal, and in many instances superior, to the perceptions of co-workers of workers with mild and moderate levels of mental retardation. Schafer and associates reported that co-workers expressed relative comfort and willingness to work with individuals identified as mentally retarded. However, the majority of the contact between workers who were and were not disabled was related to task performance; very little contact was reported among these groups of employees during work breaks and after work.

In 1986, Louis Harris and Associates conducted a nationwide survey of 920 employers for the ICD on the employment of Americans with disabilities (ICD, 1987). The survey was based on telephone interviews with 210 top managers or corporate executives, 301 equal opportunity employment managers, 210 department heads or line managers, and 200 top managers of very small companies. The survey results may not be generalized to particular groups, but they do provide a general picture with regard to persons with disabilities in the workplace.

The 1986 survey was a consequence of a survey conducted in 1985 for the ICD and the National Council on the Handicapped (ICD, 1986) in which it was found that two-thirds of all working-age persons with disabilities were not working, even

Some of the general public may be uncomfortable interacting with someone with a disability.

though a large majority stated a willingness to work. The survey results indicated that work makes a considerable difference in the lives of persons with disabilities. Workers with disabilities are more satisfied with life, less likely to consider themselves disabled, and less likely to perceive their disability as a barrier to realizing their full potential as a person.

In the 1986 survey, the overwhelming majority of the managers gave employees with disabilities a good or excellent rating on overall job performance. Less than one percent of the managers rated the job performance of employees with disabilities as poor. In addition, the managers stated that nearly all employees with disabilities do their job as well or better than other employees with similar positions. Employees with disabilities were rated to be as punctual and reliable as other employees or more so. They were as productive or more productive than employees without disabilities and demonstrated better than average leadership on the job. They were ambitious and had a desire to be promoted. In general, they were an asset to their employers.

Eighty percent of the department heads and line supervisors stated that employees with disabilities were not more difficult to supervise than other employees. There was little difference in the rating of overall job performances of supervisors who did and did not supervise persons with disabilities. Approximately sixty percent of the top managers reported that their companies can provide training for persons with disabilities in company facilities.

The survey results suggest that cost should not be a barrier to employing persons with disabilities. Three-fourths of the managers stated that the cost of employing a person with disabilities is about the same as employing a person without disabilities. The managers indicated that making accommodations for employees with disabilities is not expensive. The cost of accommodations is within the range of the cost of accommodations for all employees. About fifty percent of the managers stated that their company has made accommodations for employees with disabilities including the removal of architectural barriers, purchase of special equipment, adjusting of work hours, and restructuring of jobs.

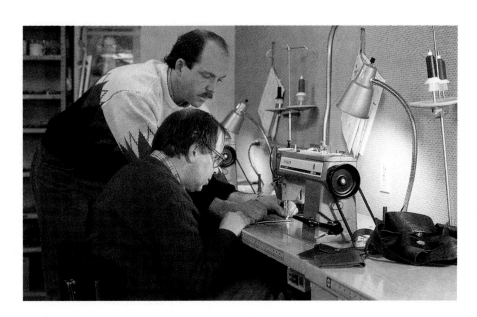

With proper training, individuals with disabilities are competent employees.

Even though persons with disabilities have demonstrated excellent job performance, and employing them appears to involve limited additional cost, companies have not employed persons with disabilities in large numbers. Only forty-three percent of the 301 equal employment opportunity managers surveyed stated that their company had hired a worker with disabilities in the year prior to the survey. Large companies and companies with federal contracts, which mandate the employment of persons with disabilities, were more likely to employ such persons than were smaller companies.

The survey results indicate that the barriers to employing persons with disabilities are (a) lack of qualified applicants, (b) few company programs or policies with regard to employing those with disabilities, (c) a lack of consciousness among middle management employers with regard to employing persons with disabilities and company policies with regard to employing persons with disabilities, and (d) managers' lack of consciousness with regard to persons with disabilities as a group. The survey revealed that discrimination on the job is a major barrier to the employment of persons with disabilities. Three in four managers feel that persons with disabilities will encounter discrimination on the job.

Approximately seven in ten managers believed that their company was making a sufficient effort to employ persons with disabilities and should not make a greater effort to employ them. Interestingly, the managers also thought that their companies would make a greater effort to employ workers with disabilities in the next three years but anticipated that rehabilitation and placement agencies would assume responsibility for training qualified applicants. Managers were very supportive of proposed initiatives and policy changes suggested by employers, state and federal agencies, legislatures, and private rehabilitation and placement agencies and foundations. They favored (a) cooperative company and school or agency training programs, (b) part-time jobs and internships prior to full employment, (c) functional job descriptions presented by the employer rather than a teacher or vocational program personnel, (d) tax deductions for company expenses required to accommodate workers with disabilities, (e) salary subsidies for trial employment of persons with severe disabilities, (f) technical assistance and counseling for employees with disabilities, and (g) voluntary employment targets. All managers support the concept that civil rights laws which protect minorities against discrimination should apply to persons with disabilities. Equal employment opportunity managers were most supportive of this concept; top managers were the least supportive.

The acceptance of learners with disabilities in the workplace is marked with paradox. Though both co-workers and employers report comfort and willingness to work with individuals with disabilities, two-thirds of individuals with disabilities, according to one survey, are not working. Though managers report good or excellent job performance, employment of persons with disabilities is limited. Though managers and employers express an openness to employing persons with disabilities, that openness apparently is rarely put into practice.

Perceptions of Professionals

Professionals' perceptions of persons with disabilities and their families are affected by the roles which those professionals assume. Marsh, Stoughton, and Williams (1985) found that the ratings of the impact of the disability on the individual and the family by clinical psychologists, school psychologists, teachers, and parents were significantly different. Clinical and school psychologists tend to imbue many childhood behaviors with greater psychological significance than do either teachers or parents. According to Marsh and associates, both the role and the age of the professionals rating a child's behavior can significantly influence their assessment of a child's mental health status.

Professionals may make unwarranted inferences with regard to the magnitude of the challenges that confront the families of children with disabilities. Blackard and Barsch (1982) examined to what extent professionals were able to accurately predict parents' responses to questionnaire items on the impact of the child with disabilities on the family, and they found significant differences in the responses of parents and professionals. When compared to parents, professionals tended to overestimate the negative impact of the child with a disability on family relationships. They overestimated the extent to which parents reported community rejection and lack of support and the parents' ability to use appropriate teaching and behavior management techniques in the home. Professionals magnified the impact of the child with disabilities on all aspects of family functioning presented in the questionnaire: changes in marital relationships, changes in family goals, restrictions of family activities, effects on other children in the family, and financial considerations. Blackard and Barsch cautioned professionals that, though direct assessment of the family is necessary, they should avoid unwarranted assumptions with regard to the negative impact of the child with disabilities on the family.

Perceptions of Peers

With regard to students, Condon, York, Heal, and Fortschneider (1986) found girls to be more accepting of learners with disabilities than boys. Respondents from schools with students with disabilities were more accepting than respondents from schools without students with disabilities. Older students were more tolerant of students with disabilities than were younger students; this was especially true in schools with students with disabilities. However, increased acceptance appeared to dissipate when contact between students with and without disabilities was interrupted.

Berryman (1989) develops a picture of the general acceptance of students with disabilities in the educational mainstream by measuring the attitudes of 377 adults at a shopping mall in a small city. The results of the survey suggest a positive attitude concerning the general concept of mainstreaming and the mainstreaming of learners with disabilities with a normal potential for learning. The respondents had a less favorable attitude toward students who were likely to have difficulty functioning in the general classroom setting. The most favorable attitudes were expressed toward mainstreaming students with speech disorders and chronic medical problems. The least favorable attitudes were expressed towards students who exhibited disruptive behavior. An interesting finding was that the respondents who had not had a child in school since 1975 were less favorable towards mainstreaming than respondents who did have a child in school after that year. Younger persons had a more favorable attitude toward the mainstreaming of students with normal learning potential than did older persons.

Perceptions of Educators

In 1987, Louis Harris and Associates conducted a survey on the status of special education in the United States for the ICD and the National Council on Disability (ICD, 1989). This was the first survey designed to assess the perceptions of public school educators, students with disabilities, and parents of students with disabilities with regard to the effectiveness of special education in meeting the needs of students with disabilities. Educators, parents, and students with disabilities were interviewed by telephone and asked to assess changes in the educational system and give a "report card" on present-day educational and related services, including evaluation of the instructional quality and methodology, educational placements and mainstreaming, the impact of the integration on students without disabilities, social interaction among students with and without disabilities, the Individualized Education Plan, transition from the school to employment or further education, and future projections.

The survey population included 702 educators, 1000 parents, and 200 youth with disabilities. The educators included four representative subsamples of special education district directors, principals, and regular and special education teachers. The parent sample was weighted to be representative of the ten handicapping conditions defined in Public Law 94–142. Survey results, in general, suggested that students with disabilities are receiving better services today than they were ten or twelve years ago. Parents suggested that they fought hard to obtain appropriate services for their children but are reasonably satisfied at the present. However, the survey results indicate that schools remain inadequately prepared to serve students with disabilities and prepare them for employment and higher education.

Both educators and parents agreed that services in the public schools for students with disabilities have improved since the passage of Public Law 94–142 in 1975. The majority of principals and teachers, however, do not have adequate training in special education and are not confident making decisions with regard to the education of students with disabilities. Only forty percent of regular teachers had any training in special education; however, on average, they have three or four students with disabilities in their classrooms. The majority of educators reported that they modified teaching and testing procedures to accommodate students with disabilities. Educators maintained, however, that they are less successful with persons with disabilities than with persons without disabilities.

Americans with Disabilities Act

With the enactment of the **Americans with Disabilities Act** (ADA) in July 1990 (Public Law 101–336), full participation of individuals with disabilities in American society was recognized (Council for Exceptional Children, 1990). This act is patterned after Section 504 of the Rehabilitation Act of 1973, which has guaranteed the civil rights of individuals with disabilities for two decades. Among the provisions of the ADA are a modification of the definition of individuals with disabilities, and requirements in the areas of transportation, telecommunications, employment, and public accommodations for persons with disabilities, as well as protections for persons with Acquired Immune Deficiency Syndrome (AIDS) and Human Immunodeficiency Virus (HIV) (Kendrick, 1990; Johns, 1990).

A person with disabilities is broadly defined in the ADA as someone who has a physical or mental impairment (or has a record of such an impairment, or is regarded as having such an impairment) that substantially limits that person's participation in some major life activity. The definition covers three groups of individuals with disabilities: (1) persons with actual physical or mental impairment (such as persons with learning disabilities, visual impairments, or mental retardation); (2) persons who are discriminated against as a consequence of their past experience with a disabling condition (for example, persons with a record of impairment such as a previous medical disability or mental illness); (3) persons who are not actually impaired but who are regarded as impaired as a result of disfigurement.

Public, private intercity, and rail transportation are all affected by the ADA. All new public transportation buses must be accessible to individuals with disabilities; retrofitting of existing public buses is not required. Paratransit services for persons with disabilities are required, unless the provision of these services would cause undue financial burden. Rural and small communities must make a "good faith" effort to comply with transportation requirements. Private transit providers must make their buses accessible within a period of 6 or 7 years, depending on the size of the company. All new rail transit vehicles must be built to be accessible, and one car per train must be accessible within 5 years. Key rail stations must be accessible within 3 years with exceptions to 20 years in extraordinary cases. Amtrak stations must be made accessible within 20 years.

The ADA requires all common telecommunications carriers to provide intrastate and interstate relay services for telephone calls made by users of telecommunications devices for the deaf (TDDs) and users of voice telephones. Relay system requirements state that an intermediary be available 24 hours a day, 7 days a week, at regular service rates, to transmit messages to and from persons with and without a TDD.

The act also includes protection against discrimination for persons with AIDS and HIV. This protection is viewed as an essential public health tool in the fight against the increased incidence of AIDS and HIV.

The ADA employment mandates apply to all employers with fifteen or more employees. Employers may not refuse to employ a person with disabilities, due to the disability, if the person is qualified to perform the job. The employer is required to make reasonable accommodations in the workplace for the individual with a disability, unless such accommodations would impose undue hardship on the employer. The dates on which employment provisions take effect vary with the number of employees in the company.

Persons with disabilities cannot be discriminated against in access to public accommodations. Public accommodations are defined as the businesses and services that are used every day by all people, for example, department stores and restaurants. New buildings must be accessible when constructed. Public accommodations in existing buildings are required only if such changes are "readily achievable." Public accommodations being renovated must be made accessible. Auxiliary goods and services such as braille signs and visual signals must be available within accommodations to make them accessible to persons with disabilities.

The ADA provides various remedies for violations of the law. These are similar to those provided under the Civil Rights Act of 1964.

In summary, the macrosystem continues to present challenges to individuals with disabilities. Efforts have been made, however, to enable individuals with disabilities to access the community on a more equal basis with their peers. Language has changed to attempt to address the issue of stigma. Though underemployment remains an issue, the perceptions of employers and co-workers are becoming more positive. Educational services for individuals with disabilities have improved. Equal access is approaching reality through legislation, specifically the Americans with Disabilities Act. The evolution of more specific practices with regards to individuals with disabilities is described in the following section.

Evolution of Professional Practices

Objective Two: To describe the evolution of current professional practices with individuals who vary from their peers.

Although treatment for persons with disabilities may have occurred earlier, the first documented attempt to treat and educate persons with disabilities is the establishment of a public hospital for the blind in 1260 (Juul, 1981). During the Middle Ages, with the exception of the reports of religious orders in Switzerland which administered routine and systematic assistance to persons with disabilities, references to the treatment and education of persons with disabilities are scarce.

In 1749, accounts of educator Jacob Rodreques Pereire's (1715–1780) demonstrations before the Academy of Science in Paris were published. These reports described his success in teaching persons with severe hearing impairments to speak and read.

According to Juul, the real impetus for the education of persons with disabilities was generated by the social and philosophical teachings of Jean Jacques Rousseau (1712–1778). In 1762, Rousseau, a philosopher and theorist, published "Emile," a plea for the direct study of children rather than the application of results from the study of adults to children.

Rousseau's optimism about the potential for goodness in both the individual and society inspired Jean-Marc-Gaspard Itard (1774–1838), a physician and educator, in his efforts to teach Victor, the "wild boy of Aveyron." Victor was a young boy discovered in the woods near Aveyron, France. He was thought to be a feral child, untouched by civilization. At that time, Victor's socialization was considered by most persons to be hopeless. Itard's study of Victor, published as a report of the French Academy of Science in 1801 and supplemented in 1806, is the first systematic documentation of efforts to teach a child with disabilities.

Forness and Kavale (1984) discuss three points they believe are significant about the publication of Itard's notes. First, if the publication is carefully examined, it becomes apparent that Itard applied the basis of nearly every educational technique that is applied today in the teaching of persons with disabilities. Second, special education in the United States is a direct beneficiary of Itard's work, in that his student, physician and educator Edouard Sequin (1812–1880), was invited by Samuel Gridley Howe to lecture and work in North America during the mid-nineteenth century. Finally, Itard and Sequin, both physicians, unwittingly established a legacy of medical influence on special education practices which has, in the words of Forness and Kavale, "plagued [the profession of special education] to this day." Their emphasis on etiology (finding the cause or causes of a condition), symptomatology (identifying a cluster of symptoms or the symptoms by which a condition is recognized), exclusionary diagnosis (differential diagnosis or a diagnosis which differentiates a condition from other conditions), and hospitalization for persons with mental retardation left special education, much like medicine, with an intervention system that was usually implemented only after symptoms became sufficiently severe to necessitate referral and extensive evaluation. Because of special education's adherence to this legacy, the courts have entered into the special education decision-making processes in an effort to facilitate change. At present, special education policies are being decided largely outside the profession, by the courts and legislatures. As a result, decisions with regard to the education of learners with disabilities are often based in legal and legislative considerations rather than education and psychological theory and best practice.

A significant, but perhaps a less well recognized contributor to special education, and more specifically early childhood special education, Friedrich Wilhelm August Froebel (1782–1852), educator and founder of the kindergarten, began his work with children during the mid-nineteenth century. With the founding of the Froebel Society in 1873, **compensatory education,** that is, working with children to develop skills commensurate with their more advantaged peers, was established as a goal. This goal is apparent in the work of the Headstart and Chapter One programs of the 1960s and 1970s. Head Start and Chapter One programs are essentially compensatory and remedial education programs for preschool and school-age children whose parents' income is at or below the federally designated poverty level. The purpose of these programs is to give these children the opportunity to compete more equally with their more affluent peers.

In the late 1800s, Alexander Graham Bell became a leading advocate for the normalization of persons with disabilities, particularly individuals with hearing impairments. In his early call for the inclusion of students with disabilities rather than their segregation in more restrictive settings, Bell stated:

> It should be recognized as a fundamental thing, that the collection of defective children exclusively together, is a thing to be avoided as much as possible. Exclusive association with one another only aggravates and intensifies the peculiarities that differentiate them from other people, whereas, it is our object, by instruction, to do away with these differences to the greatest possible extent . . . believing as I do, in the policy of decentralization in dealing with defective children—the policy of separating them from one another as much as practicable during the process of education—and keeping them in constant personal contact with their friends and relatives and ordinary normal people—I would say that it would be better to send the teachers to the children, than to bring the children themselves together (in Blatt, 1985, p. 407).

During the early twentieth century, Europe was the leader in the education of children and youth with disabilities. In an effort to make schools more responsive to the needs of students, Alfred Binet, in Paris, conducted a series of studies about children who varied from their peers in learning style and rate. During this same time, Maria Montessori, working in Italy, developed new educational principles, methods, and materials for the instruction of children with mental retardation and children who were economically disadvantaged. Also during this period, American Alfred Adler established the first "children guidance centers" in an effort to improve the treatment of children with behavioral disorders. At the onset of World War II, many prominent psychoanalysts, such as Rudolf Dreikurs and Fritz Redl, fled Europe and organized treatment centers in the United States.

Juul reports that after World War II, the United States became the undisputed leader in theory, research, and writing in the field of special education. Zirpoli and associates (1989) suggest that advocacy for persons with disabilities and their families evolved from the provision of public protective services organized in the late nineteenth century to private and independent advocacy service groups to the present-day emphasis on self-advocacy.

Professional practices with regard to individuals with disabilities have evolved, yet they continue to represent the legacy of the medical doctors who first worked with individuals with disabilities. Leadership in addressing the needs of learners with disabilities has traveled from Europe to the United States, and has moved from the medical to the educational profession. Individuals with disabilities, with the development of self-advocacy, are assuming greater ownership of and participation in the development of professional practices.

Issues Related to Societal Perceptions

Objective Three: To describe issues related to societal perceptions that impact on the individual's development.

There are several issues related to societal perceptions that impact on an individual's development. These include membership in a minority or ethnic group, gender, stigma, and socioeconomic status. Issues specific to membership in a minority or ethnic group are described in detail in several chapters in this section and elsewhere in the text. In this chapter we will introduce discussion of issues related to gender, stigma, and socioeconomic status.

Gender

In her exploration of feminine psychology, Gilligan (1982) remarks that at this time when efforts are being made to eradicate discrimination between the sexes in the search for social justice, the differences between the sexes are meanwhile being rediscovered and examined in the social sciences. Gilligan describes the nature of relationships, which, when examined with the related issues of dependency, are experienced differently by women and men. For men, separation and individual identity are tied to gender identity, since separation from the mother is necessary for the development of masculinity. For girls and women, issues of feminine identity do not depend on the achievement of separation from the mother or on the process of individuation.

Lyons (1985) contrasts male and female perspectives in several areas. Whereas women tend to perceive others in their own terms and in context, men see others in terms of equality and reciprocity. Whereas women are typically interdependent in relationships to others, men are autonomous, equal, and independent in relationships. Women attach through response, and are concerned with the responsiveness and isolation of others; men attach through roles, obligation, and duty, and are concerned with equality and fairness in relationships. Women tend to emphasize discussion and listening in order to understand others; men emphasize the need to maintain fairness and equality in dealing with others.

Responses to the differential treatment of males and females, such as those noted by Lyons, have been studied with regard to the teaching and learning of mathematics. In a report on classroom interactions in twenty-two geometry classes, Stallings (1985) supports the hypothesis that differential treatment of boys and girls occurs in mathematics classes. Boys exhibited a higher frequency of interactions with teachers on thirteen of the factors studied, including teacher and student questioning, teacher acknowledgement, teacher praise, instruction, and corrective feedback. Research by Luchins and Luchins (1980) supports Stallings' findings. In their survey large differences were found when males and females were asked if they recalled receiving different treatment as mathematics students and professionals because they were male or female. Women report being treated by their peers as though they were strange and being told that boys do not like or are afraid of smart girls. They also reported receiving less attention from teachers who they felt had lower expectations for them than for their male peers.

These differences in classroom behavior have been supported by the findings of studies related to students' goals and aspirations. Gifted females in elementary schools report interests similar to those of gifted males. However, by secondary school, gifted females develop lower career aspirations than those of gifted males (Kerr, 1985). The "cultural underachievement" of women is described by Davis and Rimm (1985) as a result of women's needs to balance professional interests and higher education while fulfilling traditional sex roles. Through recognizing developmental gender issues, it is possible this "cultural underachievement" of women may be avoided by instructors and by women themselves.

Stigma

Goffman (1963), in his classic work on the subject of **stigma,** defines it as an attribute that is deeply discrediting. By definition, he maintains, those who do not depart from the usual expectations perceive persons with the stigma as not quite human. Acceptance is the primary problem confronting an individual with a stigma. In social situations in which an individual is perceived to have a stigma, categorizations that do not fit are usually applied and uneasiness is experienced by both parties. In addition to stigma, itself, Goffman discussed the "courtesy stigma" which is attributed to persons who are related in some way to persons with stigma. Many parents and brothers and sisters of persons with disabilities suffer from the "courtesy stigma." This topic is discussed further in Chapter 4, "Families and the Learner with Disabilities."

Socioeconomic Status

Kozol (in Rohlk, 1990) suggests that if an upper-class student succeeds and enters college, society perceives the student as succeeding because he or she wanted to succeed. For the lower-class student, not attending college is seen as a sign of apathy and lack of motivation, rather than a result of unequal precollege education. Kozol views the educational systems as generating and maintaining a serious gap between the poorest and the richest. He presents the analogy of a baseball game, in which the losing team takes the field without gloves, bats, and uniforms, and the winning team, well-equipped, perceives the game as equal.

Socioeconomic status may serve as a gatekeeper for capable students in several ways. Deschamp and Robson (1984) believe that high-achieving students who attend disadvantaged schools are isolates who are limited by programs aimed at their less capable peers. Consequently, teachers may not recognize the potential of very poor children and fail to provide them with additional help. In school, disadvantaged students may also struggle with attitudes towards school and achievement expectations that are unlike those of their ethnic group. In addition, culturally diverse students may be limited simply because of their membership in their cultural group. This may increase the potential for overidentification of learners from various cultures as requiring special education services.

Stereotypes about individuals living in poverty impact a personal life.

Summary

In this chapter, the macrosystem in which persons with disabilities function was described. Through contrasting the terms "disability" and "handicap," a case was made for the use of language that puts the "person first" and recognizes the uniqueness of each individual. The results of a series of studies sponsored by the International Center for the Disabled were discussed to present an overview of society's values and beliefs about individuals with disabilities. Individuals with disabilities indicated in the surveys that though their lives had improved within the past 10 years, they still face challenges to having a full social life, continuing their education, and accessing transportation and buildings. A group consciousness was felt to be emerging.

Individuals with disabilities are perceived by employers and co-workers as being capable; both groups report comfort and willingness to work with individuals with disabilities. However, two-thirds of the individuals with disabilities, according to one ICD survey, are not working. Employment remains a challenge.

Professionals may make unwarranted inferences with regard to the magnitude of the challenges that confront the families of children with disabilities. Professionals tend to overestimate the negative impact of a child with a disability on family relationships. Students from schools with disabilities, however, were found to be accepting of their peers with disabilities.

The Americans with Disabilities Act was discussed in detail. Through this act, the right to full participation of individuals with disabilities in American society was recognized. With a broader definition of "disability" to include a person who has a physical or mental impairment that substantially limits that person's participation in a major life activity, individuals previously excluded from support and protection through other laws are now provided for.

The evolution of professional practice from the work of medical doctors such as Itard and Sequin through the use of the American legal system to establish educational practice was discussed. The evolution from protective services, to private and public advocacy, to self-advocacy by individuals with disabilities was described.

Three additional issues which have a strong impact on the quality of life of individuals with disabilities were described. These were developmental gender issues, including the cultural underachievement of women; stigma, the assignation of a discrediting attribute; and the role of socioeconomic status as gatekeeper for capable students. The issue of a "courtesy stigma," attributed to persons who are related in some way to persons with stigma, was introduced.

In the next chapter, we proceed from the macrosystem to the mesosystem, which includes school, a common experience for all children. The theme of human development within nested contexts will be explored in the classroom setting. The chapter will conclude with a discussion of services and service delivery systems for learners with disabilities.

References

Berryman, J. D. (1989). Attitudes of the public toward educational mainstreaming. *Remedial and Special Education, 10,* 44–49.

Blackard, M. K., & Barsch, E. T. (1982). Parents' and professionals' perspectives of the handicapped child's impact on the family. *The Journal of the Association of the Severely Handicapped, 76* (2), 62–70.

Blackhurst, A. E. (1985). The growth of special education. In W. H. Berdine & A. E. Blackhurst (Eds.), *An introduction to special education* (2nd ed.). Boston: Little, Brown.

Blatt, B. (1985). Friendly letters on the correspondence of Helen Keller, Anne Sullivan, and Alexander Graham Bell. *Exceptional Children, 51,* 405–410.

Bronfenbrenner, U. (1979). *The ecology of human development.* Cambridge, MA: Harvard University.

Condon, M. E., York, R., Heal, L. W., & Fortschneider, J. (1986). Acceptance of severely handicapped students by nonhandicapped peers. *Journal of the Association for Persons with Severe Handicaps, 11,* 216–219.

Council for Exceptional Children (1990). Precis: Americans with Disabilities Act of 1990: What you should know. Supplement to *Exceptional Children, 57,* 1–2.

Davis, G. A., & Rimm, S. B. (1985). *Education of the gifted and talented.* Englewood Cliffs, NJ: Prentice Hall.

Deschamp, R., & Robson, G. (1984). Identifying gifted-disadvantaged students: Issues pertinent to system-level screening procedures for the identification of gifted children. *Gifted Education International, 2,* 91–99.

Forness, S. R., & Kavale, K. A. (1984). Education of the mentally retarded: A note on policy. *Education and Training of the Mentally Retarded, 19,* 239–245.

Gilligan, C. (1982). *In a different voice.* Cambridge, MA: Harvard University.

Goffman, E. (1983). *Stigma.* Englewood Cliffs, NJ: Prentice Hall.

ICD (1986). Louis Harris and Associates, Inc. (March, 1986). *The ICD survey of disabled Americans: Bringing disabled Americans into the mainstream.* (Conducted for the International Center for the Disabled, New York, and the National Council on the Handicapped, Washington, DC.)

ICD (1987). Louis Harris and Associates, Inc. (March, 1987). *The ICD survey II: Employing disabled Americans.* (Conducted for the International Center for the Disabled, New York, the National Council of the Handicapped, and the President's Committee on Employment of the Handicapped, Washington, DC.)

ICD (1989). Louis Harris and Associates, Inc. (June, 1989). *The ICD survey III: A report card on special education.* (Conducted for the International Center for the Disabled, New York, and the National Council on Disability, Washington, DC.)

Johns, B. (1990). Federal update. *ICEC Quarterly, 39* (3), 23–29.

Juul, K. (1981). Special education in Europe. In J. F. Kauffman & D. P. Hallahan (Eds.), *Handbook of special education.* Englewood Cliffs, NJ: Prentice Hall.

Kenrick, D. (1990). Disabled cheer as Bush signs landmark bill. *Cincinnati Enquirer* (Friday, 27 July, A1, A16).

Kerr, B. A. (1985). Smart girls, gifted women: Special guidance concerns. *Roeper Review, 8,* 30–33.

Luchins, F., & Luchins, R. L. (1980). Women and mathematics: Fact or fiction. *American Mathematical Monthly, 88,* 413–419.

Lyons, N. (1985). *Visions and competencies: Men and women as decision-makers and conflict managers.* Cambridge, MA: Harvard University.

Marsh, D. T., Stoughton, N. L., & Williams, T. A. (1985). Effects of role, gender, age, and parental status on perception of childhood problems. *Exceptional Children, 52,* 170–179.

McCarthy, E. A. (1984). Is handicap external to the person and therefore man made? *British Journal of Mental Subnormality, 30,* 3–7.

Riegel, K. F. (1975). Toward a dialectical theory of development. *Human Development, 18,* 50–64.

Rohlk, L. (1990). Equal education for all? *Beyond Behavior, 1* (1), 2–3.

Schafer, M. S., Rice, M. L., Metzler, H. M. D., & Haring, M. (1989). A survey of nondisabled employees' attitudes towards supported employees with mental retardation. *Journal of the Association for Persons with Severe Handicaps, 14,* 137–146.

Stallings, J. (1985). School, classroom, and home influences on women's decision to enroll in advanced math. In S. F. Chipman (Ed.), *Women and mathematics.* Hillsdale, NJ: Erlbaum.

Yoshida, R. K., Wasilewski, L., & Friedman, D. L. (1990). Recent newspaper coverage about persons with disabilities. *Exceptional Children, 56* (5), 418–423.

Zepf, C. (1990). Overqualified and underutilized: A career disruption. *Hearsay* (Spring-Summer), 32.

Zirpoli, T. J., Hancox, D., Wieck, C., & Skarnulis, E. R. (1989). Partners in policy making. Empowering people. *Journal of the Association for Persons with Severe Handicaps, 14,* 163–167.

Chapter

3

Schooling and Learners with Disabilities

*O*bjectives

After completing this chapter, you will be able to:

1. describe the development of special education in the United States.
2. describe the implications of the systems theory of classroom management.
3. describe the special education evaluation and placement processes.
4. describe the continuum of services and related services provided through special education.

*K*ey Words and Phrases

appropriate education	mainstreaming
cascade of services	norm-referenced evaluation
criterion-referenced evaluation	placement
diagnostic evaluation	prereferral activities
diagnostic evaluation team	Public Law 94–142
General Education Initiative (GEI)	Public Law 99–457
inclusion	Public Law 101–476
Individualized Educational Program (IEP)	referral
Individualized Family Service Plan (IFSP)	related services
individual-referenced evaluation	screening
least restrictive environment	transition services

● July 24, 1930. Joseph, a premature infant with poorly developed lungs, is born at home with the assistance of the neighborhood midwife. He isn't breathing normally and is blue about the face, fingertips, and toes. The midwife, alarmed, sends Joseph's father to get the doctor, who lives three blocks from the family home. The doctor comes immediately. When he enters the bedroom, he is told the baby has stopped breathing. The doctor and midwife comfort the grieving parents by stating that had he lived, Joseph would "never have been right."

● July 24, 1950. Joseph, a premature infant with poorly developed lungs, is born in the hospital maternity wing. He is not breathing normally and is blue about the face, fingertips, and toes. The doctor immediately orders the child placed in a incubator with oxygen. The oxygen content is kept at a high level with the hope that it will help Joseph. After 6 months in the hospital, Joseph is blind as a result of the high levels of oxygen in the incubator and is having trouble eating. His grieving parents are urged to "put him in a home" and go on with their lives. Joseph enters a nursing home at 8 months of age, where he resides until his death from pneumonia at 4 years of age.

- July 24, 1970. Joseph, a premature infant with poorly developed lungs, is born in the hospital maternity wing. He is not breathing normally and is blue about the face, fingertips, and toes. He is immediately rushed to the neonatal unit and placed in an incubator. His parents visit him daily, and volunteers are assigned to massage him and talk to him. After 8 months, he is released from the hospital and goes home. A social worker from United Cerebral Palsy Association visits the family monthly to discuss Joseph's problems. At 3 years of age, Joseph begins physical therapy. When he is 4 years old, Joseph enters the United Cerebral Palsy Association program for children "excused from the public schools." At age 6, he is fitted with an adapted wheelchair and enters the special education district program for students with severe and profound disabilities. Joseph travels to and from school in a van provided by the special district. His parents are thankful for the new law which allows Joseph and others with disabilities to attend the public school.

- July 24, 1990. Joseph, a premature infant with poorly developed lungs, is born in the hospital maternity wing. He is not breathing normally and is blue about the face, fingertips, and toes. He is immediately rushed to the neonatal unit and placed in an incubator. His parents visit him daily, and volunteers are assigned to massage him and talk to him. He receives both physical and occupational therapy, and an early intervention coordinator is assigned to the family. When Joseph is 3 years old he enters the public preschool, where he is one of three children with disabilities in a group of eight. The group is team taught by a general teacher and a special education teacher. Joseph receives daily language therapy and weekly physical and occupational therapy. Joseph scoots about on the floor and enjoys playing and working with other children. His parents are looking forward to Joseph's fifth birthday, when he will join his brother and sister in the neighborhood school ■

Introduction

The systems perspective of human development has profound implications for the conduct of special education. From this perspective, human development is perceived as the process through which the growing person acquires a more extended, differentiated, and valid conception of the environment (Bronfenbrenner, 1979). As children develop, they become increasingly motivated and more capable of engaging in activities to change their environment. From this point of view, then, efforts to control behaviors applied by some special educators, rather than helping students develop self-regulation appear to be inappropriate. The goal of special education should not be to control individuals but to help them develop self-management and decision-making capabilities.

Breme (1975) contends that what we teach is so fundamental and, often, so taken for granted that it never occurs to us, as educators, to seriously question whether or not we should be teaching it. He suggests that every human group has one curriculum—itself: there is no way in which we can participate in any group unless we learn the ways of the group. What are the implications of this proposition for the special educator? Because students must, for better or worse, learn to survive in the school, we have a duty to teach them its social and organizational structure. Educators should recognize that, in school, students are asked to behave in ways that do not have a counterpart outside of the school, in the home and community. The nature of the school itself, then, is an issue for learners with disabilities. In special education, we face the dilemma of helping students survive in school while simultaneously helping them to develop the self-management and decision-making skills they need to function during adulthood in the community.

In this chapter, we will review the development of special education in the United States. We will continue to explore our theme of human development from the social systems perspective by examining its implications for classroom management. Next, we examine diagnostic evaluation and placement processes. The chapter concludes with discussions of the continuum of services needed to address the diverse needs of learners with disabilities, including educational environments that are the least restrictive and most inclusive.

Objective One: To describe the development of special education in the United States.

The Development of Special Education in the United States

From 1875 to 1914, the American public school system was the most significant socialization agent for educating a diverse student population in the "American way of life" (Hoffman, 1975). In the school, acceptable behaviors were explicitly defined by a strict code of conduct. During this time, compulsory school attendance became law. As a result, special programs were initiated in the schools, including ungraded classes for students considered to be mentally deficient, and classes for students who were "incorrigible" in their behavior, deaf, or physically handicapped (Kauffman, 1981). During this period, the National Education Association formed a Department of Special Education. The public school system was seen as the gatekeeper of the social order (Kauffman, 1981; Hoffman, 1975), serving to modify the behavior and beliefs of urban immigrants in ways that would assure the status quo of American society (Sarason and Doris, 1979).

Kauffman (1981) reports several factors (the development of intelligence tests, the flood of immigrants, the rise of organized labor, and developments in psychological theories) that affected the school system during the initial decades of the present century. Interaction among these factors led to the measuring and defining

Congress mandated programs for all children with disabilities in response to greater awareness of individual needs and abilities.

of individual differences and potential. With the economic depression of the 1930s, society became increasingly aware of the potential impact of federal intervention for education. Federal intervention increased after World War II, particularly with the implementation of the G.I. Bill, which provided funds for the education and training of millions of Americans who served in the military service during the war. At this time, in addition to being responsible for socializing students into American society, the educational system was charged with preparing citizens to preserve the American way of life in the "Cold War." In the late 1950s, largely as a result of the panic in America engendered by the launching of the Sputnik satellite by the Soviet Union, Congress mandated programs for the teaching of science and mathematics to the most able students.

The general social unrest of the 1960s resulted in many changes in special education (Kauffman, 1981). For example, the notion arose, and was encouraged by special educators, that the schools were to blame for children's failure. The social systems perspective (Mercer, 1970; 1971) suggested that many students who were seen as incompetent in school were competent in other social systems, that is, in their home, neighborhood, and, frequently, after they left school either voluntarily or through age-based graduation, suspension, or expulsion. Teacher accountability and competency-based instruction emerged and reached fruition in Public Law 94–142 (Education for All Handicapped Children's Act) and its commitment to the Individualized Education Program (IEP). This emphasis on meeting the needs of the individual student was endorsed and furthered in Public Law 99–457 to include individualized programs for families of young children with disabilities. This tradition continued with the enactment of Public Law 101–476, the Individuals with Disabilities Education Act (IDEA) in 1990. These laws are discussed in detail later in this chapter.

Progressive Inclusion in Regular Education

Reynolds (1989) portrays the history of special education as progressive inclusion of learners with disabilities in general education. He suggests that special education has moved from a distal (a point far from) to a proximal (a point near to) arrangement with general education. Special education programs began in residential and separate schools which frequently required the placement of children away from

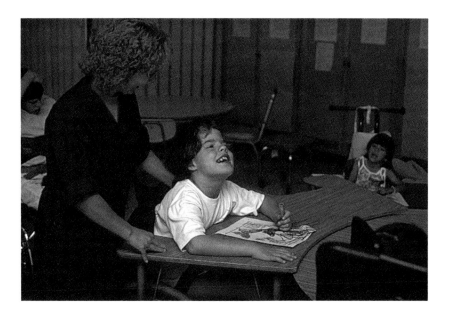

It is important that all children are provided the support needed to be successful.

their families and communities. Today, the vast majority of learners with disabilities attend neighborhood schools except in situations where appropriate services cannot be provided. There has been a dramatic and continuing trend from segregated to integrated school programs and classes for learners with disabilities. As this integration evolves towards full inclusion, however, conflict is occurring both within and among professional and advocacy groups.

As it developed as a discipline, special education moved from making primarily selection or rejection decisions to making placement decisions with regard to the characteristics of individual students (Reynolds, 1989). Poor test scores, poor achievement, and disruptive behaviors were once used by special educators as criteria to select or reject children. Those selected were exiled to special education. Such removal did have some advantages for the teacher and, perhaps, the other students in the general education class, but it was not generally advantageous for learners with disabilities. Today, decisions are made on the criteria of placing and serving learners with disabilities where they will have the best opportunity to achieve and have an educational experience most like that of their peers.

Current emphasis on the General Education Initiative (GEI) (originally called the Regular Education Initiative, or REI) is an effort to continue the movement of learners with disabilities into general classes and thus full inclusion of the learner with disabilities within regular education. This initiative receives its impetus from the failure of research to demonstrate that separate programs for learners with disabilities have merit, especially for learners with mild disabilities. The General Education Initiative gained momentum as a consequence of the recognition of the unreliability of the methods used to classify and place students in special education, the growing number of students at risk for school failure, and the stigma attached to the various labels and terminology used in special education. In his discussion of the research data, Reynolds (1989) suggests that improving regular education would reduce the number of students referred to special education, and that programs offered to students in several categories of disability and at-risk students are not distinctive. In addition, he believes that there is increasing and broad interest in restructuring the schools to include all learners.

This interest in restructuring schools to include all learners is referred to as inclusion. **Inclusion** is the organization of a school so that all students who would usually be assigned to it are educated with their age peers. This concept subsumes integration, in which learners with disabilities attend the same schools, but not necessary the same classes, and **mainstreaming,** in which learners with disabilities are included in general education classes to increase their social interaction opportunities, but not to address their educational goals.

Inclusive schools are schools that educate all students in neighborhood classrooms and schools. This shift from mainstreaming or integration to inclusion has occurred for several reasons. Stainback, Stainback, and Jackson (1992) state that:

1. Inclusion accurately and clearly communicates that all children need to be included in the educational and social life of their neighborhood school.
2. Inclusion, unlike integration, means including someone from the start, rather than "putting them back in."
3. The focus in inclusive schools is to build a system that meets everyone's needs.
4. In inclusive schools, all children, not only those with disabilities, are provided the supports needed to be successful, secure, and welcome.

The Mandate to Educate All Children with Disabilities

Public Law 94–142, the Education for All Handicapped Children's Act, became law in 1975. This law, innovative and challenging for its time, mandates that school districts provide a free, appropriate, public education to all children with disabilities. It includes a legal definition of special education, the specific categories of disabilities, and the related services to be provided to learners with disabilities and their families. In addition, regulations related to the law mandate an **Individualized Education Program** (IEP) for each learner, mutually developed and agreed upon by parents and educators, to be implemented in the least restrictive educational environment in which the student can function successfully. The regulations of Public Law 94–142 outline due process procedures mandated to ensure nondiscrimination in testing and the confidentiality of records and privacy of the individual.

The most controversial provision in the law is the definition of "**appropriate education.**" According to Osborne (1988), educators complained that the term "appropriate" was not clearly defined by Congress. Lower courts ruled that the Education for All Handicapped Children's Act requires a school to maximize the potential of each learner with disabilities commensurate with the opportunity provided to nonidentified students. The Supreme Court, in its review known as the Rowley decision, ruled that a school district satisfied the mandate to provide a free appropriate public education if it provided personalized instruction and services that were reasonably calculated to bring about educational benefit to the child and if all the procedural provisions of the law were adhered to in the formulation of the Individualized Education Program. For students who received the majority of their instruction in the regular class, instruction was to be sufficient to allow the student to earn passing grades and be promoted annually. The specific ruling in the Rowley decision was to deny a sign language interpreter to a high school student with a hearing impairment because the student was able to perform better than average and easily advance from grade to grade without an interpreter. The implication of the ruling was to make the term "appropriate" less robust than originally understood. The Rowley decision implies allowing learners with disabilities to achieve commensurate with their peers rather than attain their fullest potential.

The Education for All Handicapped Children's Act became a law in 1975 mandating school districts provide free, appropriate, public education to all children with disabilities.

The interpretation of the term "appropriate" has become an issue in the education of preschool children with disabilities as well. Edminster and Ekstrand (1987) stated, in view of the Rowley decision, that programs for preschool children are appropriate if they are reasonably calculated to enable the child to progress educationally. Some parents of preschool children with disabilities, however, maintain that a full-day program would be more beneficial to their children than a half-day program. Edminster and Ekstrand, however, found that the amount of time actually engaged in learning in a full-day program was not significantly greater than in the half-day program. This was due to frequent breaks, lunch, and naps. For many preschool children with disabilities, the research appears to demonstrate that the half-day program meets the requirements for an "appropriate" education.

The appropriateness requirement was tested in an administrative hearing in the State of Maryland (Rothstein, 1990). The case involved a 4-year-old child with Down syndrome whose parents requested that the child be enrolled in nonpublic school services for 5 days a week for 5 hours each day rather than a half-day public school program. The hearing officers concluded that the half-day program did constitute an appropriate education. Edminster and Ekstrand suggest that each child's past and present progress be reviewed when determining the appropriateness of a full-day or half-day program for a preschool student. Research presently does not support the conclusion that a full-time program necessarily results in additional educational benefit to the child.

Public Law 99–457

During the 1980s, research on early intervention with children with disabilities moved from inquiring "is early intervention effective?" to examination of which factors and interactions are most productive in early intervention programs. Kochanek, Kabacoff, and Lipsitt (1990) report that the literature and research

Educators are stressing parent collaboration in their child's education.

results were so persuasive that the reauthorization of the Education of the Handicapped Act of 1986 (**Public Law 99–457,** Part H) included provisions for states to initiate major program developments, underwritten by the federal government, so that by 1991 a comprehensive national early intervention system would be in place. The states were given considerable latitude in the conceptualization and implementation of their system. Essential components, however, were prescribed. Each state was required to (a) define the population to be served, and develop reliable and valid procedures to promptly and accurately identify children and families to be served, (b) develop policies to ensure the identification and service of children who experience significant developmental delay or who have established conditions which result in developmental delay, and (c) consider the option of serving children at risk (Federal Register, 1986).

Kachanek and associates researched one of the state requirements, that is, defining the population to be served and developing reliable and valid procedures to promptly and accurately identify those to be served. They found that early identification models which focus on developmental delays or adverse medical events from birth to 3 years of age are inadequate to fully identify children eventually judged to have learning problems. They contend that screening procedures must be multivariate, focusing on both the child and the family and differentially weighing risk over time.

Public Law 99–457 reauthorized Public Law 94–142 and extended its rights and protections to children from 3 to 5 years of age in the 1991 school year. New state grant programs for infants and toddlers (birth through 2 years of age) with disabilities are provided by the law. Parents are to be involved in their child's program through a written **Individualized Family Service Plan** (IFSP). The plan is developed by a multidisciplinary team and the parents (Trohanis, 1986). Public Law 99–457 is the federal government's commitment to a free, appropriate, public education for all learners with disabilities. In Public Law 99–457, an IFSP rather than an IEP is mandated for very young children, emphasizing the importance of the family as the focus of service and its essential nature to the development and education of young children.

Public Law 101–476, The Individuals with Disabilities Education Act

Through **Public Law 101–476** (the Individuals with Disabilities Education Act, or IDEA), several shortcomings of the general and special education services for learners with disabilities were recognized. It was recognized that:

1. The special education needs of children with disabilities were not always met; more than half of these children did not receive the services they need.
2. One million of the children with disabilities do not attend school with their peers.
3. Many children in general education continue to fail because of undetected disabilities.
4. Because of inadequate services, many children have to find services outside the public school system.

The essential purpose of IDEA was to ensure that all children with disabilities and their families receive the services they need and to support the states in the provision of these services. The significant changes in the law with regard to the learner with disabilities are described in the following paragraphs (Council for Exceptional Children, 1990).

The 1990 reauthorization and amendments to Public Law 94–142 reflected changes in the language used with regard to learners. Rather than "handicapped children," the law refers to "children with disabilities." Two new categories were added to the definition of disability: "autism" and "traumatic brain injury." Autism had been previously classified as "other health impaired." The definition of "related services" was expanded to include rehabilitation counseling and social work services. The latter was previously in the federal regulations but not in the law.

Transition services were added and defined as a coordinated set of activities for a student, designed with specific outcomes in mind. These services are to promote movement from school to post-school activities, including post-secondary education, vocational training, integrated employment (including supported employment), continuing and adult education, adult services, independent living, or community participation. Activities are to be based on the individual student's needs and should consider the student's preferences and interests. Activities may include instruction, community experiences, the development of employment and other post-school adult living objectives, and, when appropriate, acquisition of daily living skills and functional vocational evaluation.

Public Law 101–476 added two provisions to the IEP mandate: (1) a statement of the needed transition services, and (2) the requirement that the educational agency reconvene the IEP team to identify alternative strategies to meet student transition objectives when a participating agency, other than the educational agency, fails to provide agreed upon services. The statement of needed transition services is mandated for students when they reach 16 years of age (or earlier when appropriate) that lists the interagency responsibilities or linkages before the student leaves school. In addition, the Bureau of Indian Affairs of the Department of the Interior and tribally controlled schools, funded by the department, are included in the definition of "public or private nonprofit agency or organization."

Table 3.1 summarizes the legislative initiative regarding education of individuals with disabilities from 1975 through 1990. This table suggests trends towards greater participation of parents and inclusion of learners with disabilities in the community.

*T*able 3.1   Legislation Related to the Education of Individuals with Disabilities

Number	Title	Mandates
Public Law 94–142	Education for All Handicapped Children Act	Free, appropriate, public education for all handicapped children Individualized Education Program Due process Least restrictive environment
Public Law 99–457	Education of the Handicapped Act	Included provisions to initiate major program development for early intervention by 1991 Extended rights and protections from 3 to 5 years of age Individualized Family Service Plans
Public Law 101–476	Education of Individuals with Disabilities Act	"Person first" language Transition plans

Objective Two: To describe the implications of the systems theory of classroom management.

Systems Theory and Classroom Management   Jones (1986) suggests that in special education there is a recursive nature to the use of classroom management interventions. During the 1940s and 1950s, emphasis in classroom management was on biological causes and interventions through the reduction of extraneous environmental stimuli, routine, drill, and the sequencing of instruction. During the 1960s, counseling and psychoeducational interventions were predominant. Emphasis was on individualized interventions, inferring the reasons for inappropriate behavior, and improving interpersonal relations. This period was followed by an emphasis on the use of behavioral interventions which focused on the principles of learning and the control or modification of student behavior. Teachers learned to state precise behavioral and instructional objectives and to persistently and consistently intervene in students' behavior. They provided individual and group reinforcement for desired behavior. Organization and management skills were emphasized. Simple, often superficial, control-oriented classroom management techniques were predominant.

With the application of the systems perspective, we are seeing a shift from the application of a single approach to management to an integration of the biophysical, counseling and psychoeducational, and behavioral perspectives within the systems framework. In the systems perspective, learning principles are applied (the behavioral perspective), with consideration of interpersonal relationships (the counseling and psychoeducational perspective) and with recognition of the impact of neurological and physical factors (the biophysical perspective) on children's functioning in the classroom.

The systems perspective has significant implications for classroom management, particularly with regard to interaction between teacher and student. As Bronfenbrenner (1979) suggests, learning and development are facilitated by the participation of the developing person in progressively more complex patterns of reciprocal activity with someone with whom that person has developed a strong and enduring personal relationship. Learning occurs as the balance of power gradually shifts to the developing person. Teachers, then, must relate to students as capable persons, able to make choices and manage their own behavior. More specifically, they must trust in their students' abilities.

Mother Fights Special Classes of Autistic Son
After Years, Court May Decide Isolation Of Mentally Disabled

By Brian Wallstin
Post-Dispatch Special Correspondent

Every day, Chris Atkinson, 11 years old and mildly autistic, walks from one classroom in Hallsville Elementary School to another to spend 70 minutes with mentally handicapped students.

A four-year dispute over that 70 minutes has taken the fifth-grader's mother, Nancy, and his educators, the Boone County R-IV School District from the rural mid-Missouri school to the federal district court in Jefferson City.

Nancy Atkinson says her son belongs in a regular classroom full time. The school district thinks otherwise. Atkinson says that is costing her son a better education, not to mention nearly half his IQ.

"Before the educable mentally handicapped classroom, his IQ was 73," Nancy Atkinson said. "After, by [the school's] own testing, it was down to 39. That kind of proves my point. He's just not getting anything out of this."

Atkinson's attorney, John Murray of Missouri Protection and Advocacy Services,

said the case, which has yet to be scheduled for hearings, could affect the course taken by other parents of autistic children.

"The real issue is placement and where he will be educated," he said. "We feel he should be in a regular classroom with the help of a trained support system."

The school district maintains that Chris—the town's only autistic student—belongs in a classroom with other "educable mentally handicapped" students. The financially strapped district has paid $75,000 in legal costs on the case and recently was forced to lay off two teachers and a middle school principal because of budget problems.

At the center of the dispute is a conflict between two worthy goals: the classroom integration of regular education students and those with special needs, and an educational reform movement that stresses tougher standards and higher scores.

"The tensions seem to arise from the reform movement on one side and on the other is the right of individuals that basically says you can't discriminate," said Michael

Pullis, a professor of special education at the University of Missouri at Columbia. "Whose rights are more important? It's just a dilemma."

Kathy Boos is a psychological examiner for the Judevine Autism Project in Columbia, a pilot project for the Judevine Center for Autistic Children in St. Louis. Boos said: "It's become a philosophical thing. [The schools] want to raise the test scores, and then they see a student entering the classroom with the potential to lower the mean."

The case began four years ago when Nancy Atkinson fought to have Chris removed from a behavior disorder class. Under federal law, school districts must work with parents to develop an Individualized Education Program for special education students. The school developed a program for Chris that included daily time in a classroom for educable mentally handicapped.

Nancy Atkinson has been fighting that program ever since. She also has found herself in a battle of wills with district

According to Bickel and Bickel (1986), there are three characteristics associated with effective instruction: (a) teacher behavior, (b) the organization of instruction and academic learning time, and (c) instructional supports, such as class size and teacher in-service training. From the systems perspective, appropriate teacher behavior would encourage and facilitate interpersonal transactions rather than one-way communication. The appropriate organization of instruction and academic learning time would involve emphasis on student choice and self-management skills, whenever possible. Finally, instructional support through class size and teacher in-service training would be represented in the systems perspective by limited class size, thus encouraging the development of relationships, and recognition of teachers as lifelong learners through frequent in-service training. Unfortunately, as Bickel and Bickel report, classroom and teacher effectiveness research, designed to judge the worth of particular instructional and management procedures, focuses primarily on basic skills achievement. There is a need for research that considers students' conceptual learning and problem-solving and interaction skills as a central outcome measure for judging teacher and classroom effectiveness.

superintendent Ralph Powell, who has met each challenge from Atkinson with one of his own.

"I just think it's a matter of a superintendent who is not going to have a parent telling him what to do," she said. "But if he's messing up Chris' life by making him take the EMH class, will he care in 10 years?"

Privacy laws prohibit Powell from discussing specifics of the case. But he said he has no information about a child's Individualized Education Program until it is appealed and then only to make sure the plan meets state and federal guidelines and the needs of the child.

Atkinson thought she had finally won in December 1990 when a state Department of Education review officer ruled that the school—like most schools—had no one qualified to teach Chris. The state ruled that Chris should be removed from the special class and gave the school 60 days to bring in an outside expert on autism to assess his education program.

The district appealed the state's decision, claiming that it strips the district of "its power to contract with personnel for services and hands that power to private citizens."

Powell said that Chris' full-time aides all had received training in autism through a state-sponsored program called Project Access.

Boos said Project Access was "excellent information, but it's more like an in-service presentation as opposed to hands-on practice." Chris' current aide refused the Judevine Center's offer for more practical training, she said.

"She said she wasn't making enough money," Boos said.

Because socialization and communicative skills are the main deficiencies of autistic children, many special education experts believe the best preparation for life would be exposure to non-handicapped peers.

Boos describes Chris as "mild-mannered, with no tremendous risk possibilities. He has taken on the nuances of the regular classroom in the past and tolerated it. To me it would make more sense to keep him there and train the aide."

She points to a school in Auxvasse that has a student with a much more extreme case of autism. The school has developed what Boos says is a model program to deal with the unique needs of the autistic child, without spending more money on a specialized aide.

Pullis says that, more and more, schools like the one in Auxvasse are finding benefits for all students in requiring exposure of handicapped and non-handicapped students to each other.

"There is this whole group of idealists for full inclusion that say this is how the world ought to be," Pullis said. "They're trying to get more kids integrated and not at the expense of the regular education kids."

As to why the district has fought so long and hard to keep one child from getting the education his parents believe is best for him, Boos suggests that superintendents are "between a rock and a hard place." ∎

Reprinted with permission of *St. Louis Post-Dispatch.*

The systems perspective emphasizes the interaction between the setting, the student, the teacher, and all the other "actors" within the setting. Blom, Lininger, and Charlesworth (1987) propose that disability, then, may be seen as a mismatch between the child and the environment. In this mismatch, not only is the child not able to cope with the setting as well as his or her peers are, but others are not coping with the child as well as they are coping with the child's peers. As Green and Weade (1988) believe, what occurs in classrooms, such as constructing knowledge, occurs during interaction with others. Communication that occurs in the classroom setting affects (a) what students have an opportunity to learn, (b) what they actually learn, and (c) which students have an opportunity to display their knowledge and learning.

The teaching-learning behaviors that occur in any classroom are largely a product of the interaction of the persons in that classroom with one another and the environment. Copeland (1982) contends that classrooms take on characteristics as teachers and students influence and are influenced by one another. It must be remembered that classroom events are affected by students as well as teachers.

Pinnel and Galloway (1987) summarize the developmental approach to classroom management as follows:

- Teachers must recognize that students make a significant contribution to the educational process.
- Learning occurs when students feel a need to change or learn.
- Learning is holistic, rather than a series of individual pieces of information or skills.
- Teachers must recognize the power of the social context of the classroom on learning.
- Teachers must develop a personal understanding of learning and development.
- Teachers must care about what takes place in their classrooms.

The role of the teacher, then, is to facilitate the development of each student, rather than to simply intervene in behaviors deemed inappropriate (Bauer and Sapona, 1991).

In work with students with disabilities, we must, as Hood, McDermott, and Cole (1980) suggest, describe the social organization of situations in which abilities and disabilities are exhibited by specific individuals. In their description of one day in the educational life of a student with learning disabilities, they found that the student's disability was as much a product of interactions in the classroom as it was a product of the student's personal limitations. Though not the only setting, the classroom can serve as a "display board" for the weaknesses of the environment in which a student is functioning. When assessing a student, teachers must take into account how both the learner and the classroom are dynamically involved in behavior. If conclusions are to be made about a learner's behavior on the basis of this assessment, then classroom variables should be defined in terms of how the student is using them to organize his or her behavior and environment.

Objective Three: To describe the special education evaluation and placement processes.

Evaluation and Placement

The evaluation and placement process in special education, structured in part by the mandates of Public Law 94–142 and its amendments, include screening, referral, diagnostic evaluation, and placement. In recent years, regular education and prereferral procedures have been implemented before initiating formal referral to special education.

Prereferral activities

Prereferral activities are also known as "prereferral interventions" (Graden et al., 1985) and "intervention assistance" (Graden, 1989). The goal of prereferral activities is to provide the student with needed assistance within the regular classroom. These activities are not considered to be the initial step in the special education evaluation and placement processes. Prereferral strategies are developed with general education personnel through collaborative consultation and problem-solving activities. Prereferral interventions are developed through team-based collaborative efforts. They are interventions designed to assist general educators in work with specific students who are presenting academic or behavioral problems. The intervention is implemented before the student is formally identified as at risk for a disability and referred to special education.

Box 3.1

Prereferral Intervention

Louise was doing well in Mr. Raphael's fourth grade classroom until December, when her behavior changed. Louise no longer completed her homework, did not participate in games during recess, and had, on two occasions, pinched children who were swinging in "her" swing on the playground. After receiving no response to notes to Louise's mother regarding concerns about these behaviors, Mr. Raphael telephoned Louise's home. Louise's 19-year-old aunt, who was "helping out with the kids," reported that Louise's mother had entered a hospice program for terminal cancer patients. Louise's father was spending a great deal of time at the hospice, but "just couldn't bring himself to take the kids to visit."

Mr. Raphael approached Ms. Turner, the school principal, to discuss Louise's behavior. Mr. Raphael and Ms. Turner agreed that an Intervention Assistance Team should be formed to discuss Louise's behavior. Mr. Raphael recommended that Ms. Holt, the art teacher, with whom Louise had particular rapport, be included in the team. Ms. Turner suggested that Ms. Michael, the school counselor, and Ms. Wang, who had recently worked with her classroom when one of her student's mother died in an automobile accident, also be included.

The Intervention Assistance Team met and discussed Louise's behavior. A plan was formulated which included:

1. Weekly meetings for Louise with the school counselor.
2. Increased efforts to encourage Louise to participate appropriately during recess, while recognizing her feelings; Louise was to be cued: "I know it's hard to have fun when you're worried about someone. Would you like to talk about how you're feeling before you go join the game?" or "I know you're feeling hurt and worried right now, but the rule is to keep your hands to yourself on the playground. How could you ask [child's name] to move to another swing? Could you swing on another one?"
3. Review of materials Ms. Wang had received from the local children's hospital regarding dealing with death, separation, and loss in the classroom.
4. Continued communication attempts with the home, recognizing that the family was in crisis and all contacts should be supportive rather than reports of negative behavior.
5. Meeting again in 4 weeks to evaluate the plan and Louise's progress. ∎

Pugach and Johnson (1989) discuss several assumptions which underlie prereferral interventions. First, prereferral activities are a function of general education. The purpose of the interventions is to identify and implement strategies for working with students in the general classroom and thus avoid classification as disabled. Second, consultation is a multidirectional activity, in which all educational professionals within the school, at one time or another, serve as consultants to each other. Third, classroom teachers, given time and structure, are capable of solving many of the classroom problems of their students without the direct intervention of specialists. Finally, Pugach and Johnson maintain that all problems do not require the same configuration (or group) of educators to develop interventions, and that fluid membership in the prereferral teams increases schoolwide commitment and involvement. An example of the prereferral process is presented in Box 3.1. The process varies with the student's problem and personnel involved.

In a study by Carter and Sugai (1989) thirty-four states were found to recommend or require prereferral activities. The most common activities were instructional modifications, counseling, and behavior management strategies.

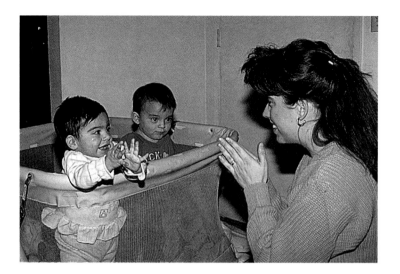

Children are screened for possible communication disorders.

Screening and Referral

Children are identified for further study for special education services in two ways: screening and referral. **Screening** is the process of identifying students who may potentially demonstrate a disability and need further study. Screening may take place in the community, through private physicians and health clinics, for example, or in a more formal and systematic manner, such as when children enter preschool or kindergarten. Screening may also occur in the school, when groups of children are administered specific screening instruments to determine if further evaluation is warranted. Frequently used screening instruments are listed in Box 3.2.

The second way children are identified for further study is referral. **Referral** is the process of soliciting and accepting nominations for evaluation from others. Before the child enters school, referral may originate with a parent, physician, social worker, or case manager. When the child attains school age, referral to special education may begin when the prereferral process fails to ameliorate the child's problem. At this point in the evaluation and placement processes, the special educator assumes significant responsibility. White and Calhoun (1987) interviewed experienced, "expert" special educators to determine their perceptions of their responsibilities during the evaluation and placement processes. The results of this study are presented in Table 3.2.

Simply being referred to special education has an impact on the student and her or his future in the school system. Algozzine, Christenson, and Ysseldyke (1982) found that ninety-two percent of the students referred to special education were evaluated, and of those evaluated seventy-three percent were placed in special education. Teachers' direct observations, it appears, are reliable criteria for referral and consequent placement.

To initiate referral, the teacher completes a referral form. This form indicates the nature of the teacher's concern and the interventions that have been attempted to ameliorate the student's problem. Information from screening instruments and the student's records are included on the form. A sample referral form is presented in Box 3.3.

Box 3.2

Sample Screening Instruments

Expressive language

Bankson, N. W. (1977). *Bankson language screening test.* Baltimore, MD: University Park Press.

Zimmerman, I. L., Steiner, V. G., & Evatt, R. L. (1982). *Preschool language scale.* Columbus, OH: Merrill.

Reading (group screening)

Balow, I., Farr, R., Hogan, T., & Prescott, G. (1979). *Metropolitan achievement test: Survey battery.* NY: Psychological Corporation.

CTB/McGraw-Hill (1977). *California achievement tests.* Monterey, CA: McGraw-Hill.

Gardner, E., Rudman, H., Karlsen, B., & Merwin, J. *Stanford achievement test (7th ed.).* NY: Psychological Corporation.

Written expression

Educational Testing Service (1979). *Circus.* Princeton, NJ: Educational Testing Service.

Hieronymus, A. N., Lindquist, E. F., & Hoover, H. D. (1982). *Iowa tests of basic skills.* Chicago: Riverside.

Mathematics

Dunn, L. M., & Marjwardt, F. C. (1970). *Peabody individual achievement test.* Circle Pines, MN: American Guidance Service (AGS).

Behavior

Bruininks, R. H., Weatherman, R. F., Woodcock, R. W., & Hill, B. K. (1984). *The scales of independent behavior.* Allen, TX: Developmental Language Materials.

Lambert, N. M., Bower, E. M., & Hartsough, C. S. (1979). *Pupil behavior rating scale.* Monterey, CA: Publishers Test Service.

Quay, H. C., & Peterson, D. R. (1967). *Behavior problem checklist.* Champaign, IL: University of Illinois.

The completed referral form is usually forwarded to the principal. If, after review, the principal determines that further action is necessary, the form is forwarded to the school referral team. A conference, attended by selected members of the referral team, the parents, the teacher, and the principal, is scheduled. During the conference, a collaborative decision is made whether or not to refer the student for diagnostic evaluation. Regardless of the decision of the majority of the team members, the parents must consent to have their child evaluated.

Diagnostic Evaluation

Diagnostic evaluation is the process of studying a student and the student's developmental contexts to determine the cause, nature, and circumstances of the student's problem if, in fact, there is a problem. Diagnostic evaluation is not an end in itself; rather, it is conducted to identify appropriate activities to assist the student to become more successful in school (Bender, 1988). According to Lambert (1988), a

Table 3.2   Responsibilities of Special Educators During the Screening/Referral, Diagnostic Evaluation, and Placement Process

Responsibilities during referral:
1. Making the initial contact positive and productive
2. Evaluating the referral
3. Providing instructional recommendations
4. Facilitating the formal referral process

Responsibilities during and following screening:
1. Obtaining parent permission to screen
2. Observing the student in the current placement
3. Conducting academic screening
4. Advising whether to proceed with diagnostic evaluation
5. Conferring with the referring teacher and parents

Responsibilities during and following diagnostic evaluation:
1. Coordinating activities with the school psychologist
2. Acting upon recommendations of the diagnostic evaluation
3. Conferring with the referring teacher and parents
4. Collaborating on the development of the IEP

Responsibilities during the IEP conference:
1. Encouraging collegial participation
2. Encouraging parent attendance
3. Obtaining parent consent for placement

National Academy of Science panel on ability testing and the testing of persons with disabilities proposed the following guidelines for the conduct of a diagnostic evaluation:

1. Before referring children for special education diagnostic evaluation, the general education teacher should attempt several interventions and note the effects of those interventions on the child's performance.
2. Assessment specialists should demonstrate that the measurement instruments employed validly assesses the student's needs and are related to the interventions.
3. Placement teams should demonstrate that different labels or classifications of disability are related to a specific prescription for intervention which is likely to lead to improved student functioning.
4. Special education staff should demonstrate, at least annually, that a child should remain in special education service.

Bender (1988) recommends that an evaluation of the learning environments in which the student is currently functioning be completed in addition to the diagnostic evaluation of the student. He contends that present procedures, which focus almost exclusively on the student, may not provide the most useful information on which to base educational decisions and may fail to provide special educators

Box 3.3

Sample School Referral Form

Student: DOB:
Address:
Telephone: Sex:
Parent or guardian:
Person initiating referral:
  1. Reason for referral
  2. Has an Intervention Assistance Team been involved? Summarize the efforts of the IAT.

  3. Parent contacts (attach log):
  4. Information from cumulative record:
      Hearing Screening: Vision Screening:
      Speech & Language: Medical/Health History:
      Attendance: Patterns in Grades:
      Test Scores:
          Achievement:
          Intelligence:
          Others:
  5. Further information for referral:
      Social Skills Screening:
      Observations (attach)
      Anecdotal records (attach)
      Parent communication (attach)
  6. Comments
Teacher Signature   Date
Reviewed by Principal: Date
Reviewed by School Referral Team:

and related service personnel with the knowledge needed to make meaningful intervention decisions. In addition, he suggests, the discussion of the special education placement of a student often focuses exclusively on the special education aspects of the placement and ignores the educational opportunities, or lack of them, available to the child in various general education settings. Bender contends that assessment of the student's current learning environment by the team of professionals evaluating the student would provide useful information with regard to the student's needs and how best to respond to them. This information may be obtained from self-reports from the general educators involved or through direct observation of the settings.

Public Law 94–142 requires that all diagnostic evaluation instruments (a) be administered in the child's native language, (b) be valid for the purpose for which they are being administered, and (c) be administered by qualified personnel. In addition, no single instrument may be used as the basis of the decision with regard to the child's eligibility for special education services.

Direct observation is helpful in determining learners interaction.

Tindal (1990) differentiates three types of diagnostic evaluation: **norm-referenced evaluation** compares learners to a specific group or sample, **criterion-reference evaluation** focuses on the learner's mastery of specific skills, and **individual-referenced evaluation** focuses on the learner's progress over time. In addition, Tindal discusses three sources of evaluation information: observations, interviews, and tests. Tests are designed to elicit information about the student's knowledge and skills. Tests frequently administered during the diagnostic evaluation process are presented in Table 3.3. The specific tests used will vary with the student's problem, the setting in which the student is functioning, and the qualifications of the professional administering the instrument.

The evaluation of young children (infants, toddlers, and preschoolers) presents several unique challenges. Tindal (1990) believes that the reliability and validity of tests for preschool children suffer due to the limited behaviors of young children and the unevenness of the development that occurs in young children within relatively brief periods of time. Tests of developmental milestones, which are most frequently administered, pose difficulties because young children are so individualistic in the ways in which they move through developmental stages. Preschool children may demonstrate inconsistent development, which may occur in bursts, making testing even more difficult (Shepard & Smith, 1983).

Another factor that complicates diagnostic evaluation is cultural diversity. For example, although Caucasian students perform similarly with familiar and unfamiliar examiners, African-American and Hispanic children score dramatically higher when evaluated by familiar examiners (Fuchs & Fuchs, 1989). This finding compels us to ask, "Does the lack of familiarity with the examiner bias the evaluation of minority students?" An additional bias may be the standardization sample on which the norms of the test are based. More specifically, is the instrument being administered normed on a population comparable to the cultural and socioeconomic status of the student being evaluated so that if avoids a majority culture bias?

Public Law 94–142 requires that a group of individuals be assembled and involved as a **diagnostic evaluation team.** The regular educator provides information on the child's current functioning in the classroom. The special educator provides information from systematic observation of the child. Parents, active and contributing members of the team, provide information on the child's development, behavior in the home and community, and their perceptions of the child's strengths

Table 3.3   Some Tests of Skills and Knowledge

Reading

Karlsen, B., Madden, R., & Gardner, E. (1977). *Stanford diagnostic reading test.* NY: Harcourt, Brace, Jovanovich (HBJ).
Spache, G. (1981). *Diagnostic reading test.* Monterey, CA: McGraw–Hill.
Woodcock, R. W. (1987). *Woodcock reading mastery tests revised.* Circle Pines, MN: American Guidance Service (AGS).

Mathematics

Beatty, L., Madden, R., Gardner, E., & Karlsen, B. (1976). *Stanford diagnostic mathematics test.* NY: HBJ.
Enright, W. (1980). *Enright inventory of basic arithmetic skills.* North Billerica, MA: Curriculum Associates.

General Information and Achievement

Boehm, A. E. (1986). *Boehm test of basic concepts—revised.* San Antonio: Psychological Corporation.
Karlsen, B., Madden, R., & Gardner, E. (1977). *Stanford diagnostic reading test.* New York: HBJ.
Kaufman, A., & Kaufman, N. (1986) *Kaufman test of educational achievement.* Circle Pines, MN: AGS.
McCarthy, D. (1972). *McCarthy scales of children's abilities.* Circle Pines, MN: AGS.
Woodcock, R. (1978). *Woodcock-Johnson psychoeducational battery.* Boston: Teaching Resources.

and weaknesses. The psychologist collects and presents diagnostic information on the child's functioning as measured by standardized tests and inventories, projective techniques, observations, and interviews. The social worker, serving as a liaison between home and school or school and community agencies, develops and presents the child's social history. Others who may be members of the diagnostic evaluation team are the communication specialist, audiologist, occupational and physical therapist, vision specialist, correctional personnel, and so on. The specific makeup of the team depends greatly on the problem the child presents and the availability of specialized personnel. Diagnostic evaluation team members have two responsibilities: to develop a child study report and to write an Individualized Education Plan (IEP).

Placement

During its deliberations, the diagnostic evaluation team reviews all the information gathered on the student and determines on the basis of that information if the student is eligible for **placement,** that is, the assignment of a student to special education services. If the student is deemed to be eligible, the team writes an IEP. According to the Federal Register (1977, 121a. 346), the IEP includes the following:

1. A statement of the child's present level of performance.
2. Annual goals and short-term objectives.
3. The specific education and related services to be provided to the child, including the amount of time to be spent with nonidentified peers.
4. Projected dates for the initiation of services and anticipated duration of services.
5. Criteria for determining, at least annually, progress made towards the goals and objectives.

*T*able 3.4   Sample IEP

---

*Metropolitan*____ School District

INDIVIDUAL EDUCATION PROGRAM

Student's Name *Michael Riley*_____ Birth Date *7/6/83*

School *Metropolitan Elementary*_____ Date of IEP Conference *9-15-92*

Date of Initial Placement Program ____*9-5-90*

Summary of Present Levels of Performance – Strengths & Weaknesses

Strengths: *Enthusiastic and within grade equivalent limits of achievement, verbalizes his behavioral problems, can express steps of problem resolution*	Weaknesses: *Difficulty managing behavior in large groups; verbally aggressive when not responded to immediately; physically aggressive when children enter his personal space; difficulty playing cooperatively on playground*

Annual Goals	Description & Amount of Time in Regular Education Program	Special Consideration and Comments	Committee Members Present Signature/Position
1) Michael will work cooperatively in his classroom *2) Michael will play cooperatively on the playground*	*100%*	*Work with behavioral consultant to implement and evaluate plan*	*Sally Striker* (Chairperson) *Jo Ann Riley* (Parent) *Katty Sanders* (Teacher)

Committee Recommendation for specific Procedures/Techniques, Materials, Etc.	Objective Evaluation Criteria for Annual Goal Statements
1) daily parent-teacher journal *2) immediate reward of praise; behavioral contracts*	*Weekly conferences with teacher and Michael — Anecdotal records and self recorded data*

Placement Recommendation:
White Copy: *Referring School*
Yellow Copy: *Director of Special Education*   *In general education classroom*
Pink Copy: *Parents*

As required in Public Law 101–476, "a statement of the needed transition services" is to be included in IEPs for students beginning no later than age 16 (in some cases earlier) and annually thereafter. A sample IEP is presented in Table 3.4. A sample transition plan is presented in Table 3.5. Gerber (1981) characterizes the IEP as a resource management tool. It serves as a means of allocating services and determining appropriate placement for the child.

Placement in special education has a profound impact on the remainder of the child's school career. Walker and associates (1988) studied "who leaves and who stays in special education." They found that termination of special education

*T*able 3.4   (Cont.)

Short Term Objectives	Specific Ed and/or Support Service	Person(s) Responsible	Amount of Time	Beginning & Ending Date	Review Date
1a) Michael will make no more than 3 verbal comments during each period with cues from teacher	BD Resource	Teacher – BD Resource	100%	9-15-92	9-15-93
1b) Michael will self-record verbal comments	Teacher	Teacher	100%	9-15-92	9-15-93
2a) Michael will play cooperatively with his class with his classroom aide available		Teacher – BD Resource	100%	9-15-92	9-15-93
2b) Michael will play cooperatively with his class, meeting weekly with BD resource room teacher to discuss progress	BD Resource	BD Resource	100%	9-15-92	9-15-93

services was strongly associated with the child's initial primary classification of disability. Students classified as speech impaired were the most likely to be terminated (33.1 percent), followed by students classified as learning disabled (14.9 percent), behaviorally disordered (9.1 percent), and visually impaired (8.6 percent). Those classified as hearing impaired, physically/multiply handicapped, or mentally retarded were rarely, if ever, terminated from special education services.

For the infants and toddlers with disabilities, described in Public Law 99–457 as individuals from birth to their third birthday, the IFSP replaces the IEP. The IFSP is reviewed semiannually and evaluated annually. The content of the plan is similar to that of the IEP:

1. A statement of the infant's or toddler's present level of functioning.
2. A statement of the family's strengths and needs as related to the development of the family's infant or toddler with disabilities.
3. A statement of the major anticipated outcomes for the infant or toddler and the family, and the criteria, procedures, and timeliness used to determine the degree to which progress is being made and whether revisions of the anticipated outcomes are necessary.
4. A description of the specific early intervention services necessary to meet the unique needs of the infant or toddler and the family.

*T*able 3.5   Sample Individualized Transition Plan

Metropolitan School District
Early Childhood and Special Education

Individualized Transition Plan

Date Initiated: *9-30-93*   Review Date: *9-30-94*

Name: *Tara Trainer*   DOB: *1-5-77*   Sex: *F*   Grade: *10*

School: *Metro High School*

Placement at time of ITP: *Self Contained; Three "out" classes*

♦ ♦ ♦ ♦ ♦ ♦ ♦ ♦ ♦ ♦ ♦ ♦ ♦ ♦ ♦ ♦ ♦ ♦

Participants:

Name:	Role:	Signature:
Sue Trainer	Parent/Guardian	*Sue Trainer*
Mark Trainer	Parent/Guardian	*Mark Trainer*
Barry Martinez	District/Rep.	*Barry Martinez*
Sandy Sharkins	Teacher	*Sandy Sharkins*
Tara Trainer	Student	*Tara Trainer*

Community Living Goals:

Objective	Activities	Responsibility
① To initiate and continue a way of managing personal finance	a) open checking account b) maintain checking account	Parent
② To use public transportation to job and home	a) using a phone to determine schedule b) Transportation Training	Special Ed Teacher
③ To maintain reading periodicals/newspaper for information	a) subscribe to magazine b) newspaper available daily	Parent/Spec. Ed Teacher

---

5. The projected dates for initiation of services and the anticipated duration of the services.
6. The name of the case manager from the service most relevant to the infant's or toddler's and family's needs who is responsible for the implementation of the plan and coordination with other agencies and persons.
7. A plan for the transition of the toddler to preschool services.

A sample IFSP is presented in Table 3.6. When the toddler enters preschool at 3 years of age, the IEP becomes the document used for service and placement descriptions.

*T*able 3.5 (Cont.)

Employment Goals:

Objective	Activities	Responsibility
① To work two periods each day in Metro elementary Day Care Co-Op as aide	a) Bi-weekly visits	Teacher
② To complete child care course	a) attend course	Child care course instructor
③ To expand work time to 5 - ½ days a week	a) work with job site	Teacher

Comments:

Tara has worked as a volunteer in child care settings. She is very interested in gaining employment as a preschool aide. Her time receiving educational instruction will gradually decrease until she is working ½ day, five days a week.

Krauss (1990) suggests that unlike the IEP, the IFSP defines the service recipient as the family rather than just the child. It requires specific judgments with regard to the family's service needs and reconstitutes the decision-making team by mandating family representation. Unlike Public Law 94–142, Public Law 99–457 formally acknowledges that services to family members can and should be provided independent of the child's educational program. This, as can be readily understood, is a significant departure from the IEP process.

The Continuum of Services and Related Services

Objective Four: To describe the continuum of services and related services provided through special education.

Placement in special education services cannot occur without parental consent. Due process hearings are conducted if either party, local education agency or parent, disagrees with the placement decision. Due process hearings may be held on whether the learner may be evaluated, on the results of the evaluation, on the content of the IEP, and on the placement.

*T*able 3.6   Sample IFSP

Metropolitan School District
Early Childhood and Special Education

Individualized Family Service Plan (IFSP)

Date Completed: *10-4-92*   Evaluated: *9-8-92*

Reviewed: *1-4-93*   *4-4-93*   *7-4-93*   *10-4-93*

Child's Name: *Elizabeth Barrett*   DOB: *5-16-91*   Sex: *F*

Family Address: *214 Tampa Rd, Defiance, Ohio*

Telephone: (H) *(555)555-9214*   (W) *(555)555-5672*

Parent(s) or Guardian(s): *John Barrett, Marcia Hoskins*

◆ ◆ ◆ ◆ ◆ ◆ ◆ ◆ ◆ ◆ ◆ ◆ ◆ ◆ ◆

IFSP Team

Name:	Role:	Signature:
Marcia Hoskins	*Parent*	*Marcia Hoskins*
John Barrett	*Parent*	*John Barrett*
Sally Schwartz	*Case Manager*	*Sally Schwartz*
Kelly Kristofer	*OTR*	*Kelly Kristofer*
Michael Brinkley	*MSW*	*Michael Brinkley MSW*
Jill Traber	*Audiologist*	*Jill Traber*
Sarah Logan	*Speech/Lang*	*Sarah Logan*

Services (Frequency, Intensity, and Duration):

Services will begin immediately and continue through 5-16-94 when Beth will be eligible for public school preschool programming. Frequency and intensity are goal dependent.

Signatures of Parent(s) or Guardian(s):

I/we have had the opportunity to participate in the development of this IFSP. I/we understand the plan, and give permission for the implementation of this plan with my/our cooperation.

Marcia Hoskins   Date *October 4, 1992*

John Barrett   *4 Oct 92*

A student is placed in a special education service after the diagnostic evaluation team has determined that she or he has special educational needs and has written an IEP. The team bases its decision to place the student on the following guidelines, mandated in Public Law 94–142:

1. To maximum extent appropriate, children with disabilities, including children in public and private institutions or other care facilities, are educated with children who are not disabled.

Table 3.6   (Cont.)

Assessment Instruments and Procedures:
Receptive Expressive Language Scale (RELS)
Real Time Observation
Language Sample
Ecological Interviews

Medical Information:
Elizabeth has a bilateral profound hearing loss. Except for frequent respiratory infections, Elizabeth is physically healthy. She wears a body-aid to amplify sounds.

Developmental Levels:
Elizabeth's motor skills are developmentally appropriate. With her hearing aids, she turns to loud environmental sounds (Stereo on high); the amount of information she receives is unknown. She gives eye contact to adults and makes some gestures.

Child's Strengths and Needs:
Elizabeth's social and motor skills are clearly her strength. She needs to begin to develop a conventional communication system.

Family's Strengths and Needs:
The Hoskins-Barrett family feels that their greatest need is to have a way to communicate with Elizabeth. They are also very interested in her learning verbal language. The family is motivated, and Elizabeth's three older siblings are very supportive. The family is concerned about the effectiveness of the hearing aid.

Outcomes:

Objectives	Strategies	Duration	Responsibility
① To increase Elizabeth's expressive language	Conversation; interaction and play	10-1-92 — 10-4-93	Speech/Lang; Parent
② To monitor Elizabeth's hearing aid and provide more effective instrument	Contact Children's Hospital	10-92	Audiologist; Parent
③ Provide sign language instruction to family	Contact Community Service for the deaf	11-92	Parent; Caseworker

---

2. Special classes, separate schooling, or other removal of children with disabilities from the regular educational environment occurs only when the nature or severity of the disability is such that education in regular classes with the use of supplementary aids and services cannot be achieved satisfactorily (Federal Register, 1977, 121.550).

In essence, the guidelines mandate that the student be placed in the least restrictive educational environment in which she or he can function effectively. As a consequence of the application of these guidelines, the General Education Initiative has emerged. This initiative is discussed in detail in the next section of this chapter.

The application of the least restrictive environment mandate also applies in preschool programs. The **least restrictive environment** clause requires that the learners be placed in the setting which provides the maximum amount of interaction with learners without disabilities while providing enough support for the learner with disabilities to be successful. Edminster and Ekstrand (1987) suggest that Public Law 99–457 mandates opportunities for preschool children with disabilities equal to those for school-aged children. A problem emerges, however, in that most states that provide preschool programs for children with disabilities do not provide "general education programs" for nonidentified preschool-aged children. The United States Office of Education maintains that if there are programs for nonidentified preschoolers available within a jurisdiction, then mainstreaming opportunities are automatically required. The Office of Education has determined that if nonidentified programs are not provided within a jurisdiction, local education agencies, if possible, must coordinate preschool special education programs with other existing public service programs, such as Headstart, and make them available for mainstreaming purposes. If, however, coordination efforts fail, school systems are not required to create preschool programs for children without disabilities or enter into contracts with private facilities for the sole purpose of implementing the mainstreaming requirement.

Due to the family intervention focus of Public Law 99–457, the least restrictive environment mandate is not an issue for infants or toddlers with disabilities. A statement of participation with peers without disabilities is not included in the IFSP.

Taylor (1988) describes several "pitfalls" in the least restrictive environment principle. First, it legitimizes restrictive environments; as long as services are conceptualized with regard to the "restrictiveness of environments," some individuals will be placed in restrictive environments simply because they are available for placement. In addition, the principle equates separating learners with disabilities from their peers with the most intensive services and integration with the least intensive services. However, intensive services can be provided in inclusive or integrated settings. Taylor also argues that professionals, though allegedly following the principle of the least restrictive environment, continue to dominate decision making, emphasizing the economical provision of services rather than the provision of services in the least restrictive environment. The least restrictive environment, according to Taylor, tends to support separate programs rather than inclusion.

An ongoing dialogue has occurred between proponents of full inclusion and those who wish to preserve the concept of the least restrictive environment. Stainback and Stainback (1992) argue that schools should be "inclusive communities" in which each student is provided the support necessary to learn in his or her neighborhood school. Vergason and Anderegg (1992) contend that a commitment to full inclusion is tantamount to uniform placement, which violates each child's rights to an appropriate education.

There has not yet been a great deal of research regarding the attitudes of practitioners towards inclusion. Feelings concerning mainstreaming, a more restrictive concept, have, however, been explored through research.

Garver-Pinhas and Schmelkin (1989) found significant differences among groups of special education teachers, general education teachers, principals, and special education administrators in attitudes towards mainstreaming. In academic concerns, regular teachers exhibited the least positive attitudes, followed by special education teachers; principals and special education administrators had more positive attitudes. In the area of administrative concerns, special education administrators and teachers had the least positive attitudes. The special educators consistently reported that they failed to believe that support will be given by principals to youngsters with disabilities who are mainstreamed.

In the efforts towards keeping learners with disabilities with their age-peers to the greatest extent possible, the General Education Initiative emerged.

The General Education Initiative

The **General Education Initiative** (GEI) gained momentum through the work of Ms. Madeline Will (1986), former assistant U.S. secretary of education, who suggested that special educators should seriously question the effectiveness of "pull-out" services for many students with disabilities. "Pull out" services are outside services provided to learners with disabilities which removes them from general education classes during the school day. Gersten and Woodward (1990) discussed several factors which led to the emergence of the GEI. First, there is a concern that special education has become a haven for students who are difficult to teach, rather than those with observable disabilities. This concern is supported by the large number of students who are classified as learning disabled, though research has demonstrated a significant overlap between students classified as learning disabled and general education students in remedial programs (Jenkins, Pious, & Peterson, 1988). Second, there is a concern that once placed in special education services, students are rarely terminated from them. The General Education Initiative is a professional effort by some special educators to reform general and special education to maximize the provision of special education services in the general education classroom.

Jenkins, Pious, and Jewell (1990) report that the literature regarding the GEI makes five assumptions about the role of the regular education teacher. The literature infers that regular education teachers are responsible for: (a) educating all students assigned to them; (b) making and monitoring major instructional decisions for all students assigned to them; (c) providing instruction that follows a normal developmental curriculum; (d) managing instruction for diverse populations; and (e) seeking, using, and coordinating assistance for students who require more intense services than those provided to their peers. Currently, these responsibilities are not assigned to many regular educators. In addition, general educators are not trained to assume these responsibilities, and the support necessary to make the GEI successful is not necessarily available in many schools.

There has been considerable controversy in special education with regard to the GEI. Braaten and associates (1988) express the concern that the GEI was merely "patent medicine," dealt out to meet a wide range of needs without prescriptive and professional support. They contend that the GEI will only serve to reduce services to populations of students (for example, the behaviorally disordered) who are already underserved. Algozzine and associates (1990) counter that special education cannot afford to accept only prescribed interventions that have been

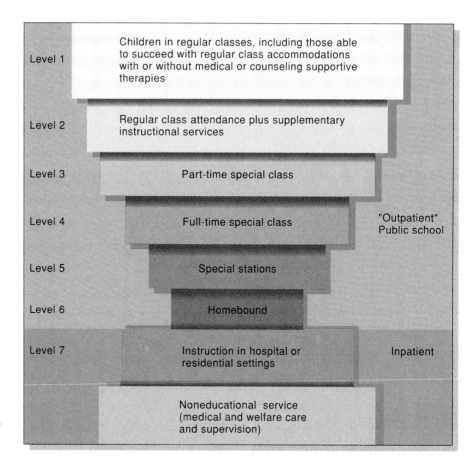

Figure 3.1
The cascade system of special education services. From E. Deno, "Special Education As Developmental Capitol," in *Exceptional Children*, 37 (3), 1970. Copyright © 1970 The Council for Exceptional Children. Reprinted by permission.

demonstrated to be effective; in fact, this would make much of what has and is occurring in special education unacceptable. The purpose of the initiative is to cause general educators, special educators, and parents to adopt a shared responsibility for students with disabilities, and to attempt innovative, experimental efforts to develop a coherent administrative organization and teacher alternatives to support students with disabilities within regular education. The most widely accepted and applied administrative organization of services for learners with disabilities is the "cascade of services" discussed in the following section.

The Cascade of Services

The concept of a **cascade of services,** first proposed by Reynolds (1962), is most widely recognized in its amended form, which was presented by Deno (1970). This cascade or continuum of services is presented in Figure 3.1. The continuum provides a framework for tailoring services to meet the needs of individual students. The seven levels of service in Figure 3.1 range from the least restrictive services, in which most students are served (the base of the triangle), to more restrictive services, in which fewer students are served (the apex of the triangle). The services in Levels 1 through 6 are provided by the school. Level 7 services are provided by community mental health and welfare and family service agencies.

In the remainder of this section, the general functions of the various levels are presented, and selected research findings regarding the efficacy of these services are reviewed. Specifics for planning, organizing, and conducting services at the various levels of the cascade are presented in Chapters 7 through 17.

Level 1: Students in Regular Classes   Students served at this level are able to function in the regular class with or without medical and counseling support therapies. Typically, the services these students receive are provided through private and public medical, mental health, and social service agencies.

Level 2: Students in Regular Classes with Supplementary Instructional Services
Stainback, Stainback, and Harris (1989) state that the emerging role of the special educator is as a support facilitator. In this role, the special educator has three functions. First, the special educator, in consultation with the general education teacher and the student with disabilities, identifies the types of assistance and support needed. Next, the special educator collaborates with the general education teacher and student to determine what specific assistance is most applicable in the setting in which they are functioning. In this step, general class teacher, special educator, and student jointly gather information, define the specific problem, and identify possible support interventions. Finally, the special educator assists in organizing and implementing the agreed upon support service. This model recognizes the responsibilities of the general educator as encouraged by the GEI.

The most common Level 2 service is the resource room, which is a special education placement alternative in which the students receive specific support through specialized services while continuing to receive the majority of their instruction in the general education classroom. Bak, Cooper, Dobroth, and Siperstein (1987) report that resource room service had advantage with regard to peers' perceptions of the student with disabilities. In written vignettes, nonidentified fourth-through-sixth graders perceived students assigned to resource rooms as more capable than students assigned to special education classes. It was found in the population studied that older students had higher expectations of the capabilities of students with disabilities regardless of placement than did younger students.

In an interview study of 686 students with mild disabilities, Jenkins and Heinen (1989) gave the students a choice between receiving additional assistance from their classroom teacher or a specialist in either their classroom or a pull-out program. The students overwhelmingly expressed preference for receiving the assistance in their classroom and from their general class teacher. The principle reason for the selection of the general class teacher was that the students believed that their teacher knew what they needed. Embarrassment about being removed from their classroom and receiving assistance from a specialist played a major role in the students' choice of their general teacher and classroom. Students also indicated that they wanted to remain with their classmates and that staying with their teacher was more convenient.

Level 3: Students in General Education Classes Part-Time and Special Education Classes Part-Time   In this level of service, students attend both general classes and self-contained special education classes. The transition between these two settings, however, is frequently problematic for the student with disabilities. Tymitz-Wolf

(1984) found that students with mild mental retardation worried about partial placement in the general class. They reported more stress concerning social and transitional demands than academic demands.

Level 4: Students in Full-Time Special Class   At this level, students spend all of their school time in special class. Algozzine, Morsink, and Algozzine (1988) studied forty self-contained special classes for students with various disabilities. They found few differences in teacher communication patterns, learner involvement, and instructional methods among classes serving students with learning disabilities, emotional disturbances, and educable mental retardation. Teachers of the three groups were similar with regard to how they structured student time, provided feedback to students, and gave directions. The teachers worked infrequently with groups, used inquiry rather than lecture, assisted in the development of problem-solving skills, or facilitated transfer of learning. Instruction for students identified as mildly mentally retarded, learning disabled, or behaviorally disordered was more similar than different, though teachers of students who are mildly mentally retarded modified instruction to respond to individual learner needs about half as frequently as teachers of students with learning disabilities or behavioral disorders.

Level 5: Students in Special Schools   The number of special schools has decreased significantly with the trend towards the inclusion of children with disabilities into the general education system. Special schools are usually separate facilities, which severely restrict interaction between students with disabilities and students without disabilities. In most districts a few students with severe disabilities are educated in special schools.

Level 6: Students Receiving Homebound Services   Homebound services are usually short-term intervention for students who are physically unable to attend school. Homebound placement is the most restrictive of all placements. It prohibits interaction with other students, both with disabilities and nonidentified. The hours of instruction are severely limited, in some cases 1 hour a day or 5 hours a week, and not equivalent to that of students attending school.

Terminating Special Education Services

As indicated previously, students initially classified as hearing impaired, physically/multiply handicapped, or mentally retarded rarely, if ever, are terminated from special education services (Walker and associates, 1988). Students who remain in special education, then, must either graduate from school as a special education student or age-out of the program.

Kortering, Julnes, and Edgar (1990) describe the legal considerations involved in the graduation of special education students. They report that judicial review, though limited in scope, does provide specific guidelines to local districts. First, local districts have the discretion to restrict the awarding of a standard high school diploma. They may award either a standard or nonstandard diploma to special education students. Second, legal precedents require that procedures resulting in the differentiation of special education students should be based on standards that are fair and have been articulated to the student and his or her parents. School district procedures must give all special education students the opportunity to satisfy the standards as established or through the provisions of a reasonable accommodation.

Local district personnel should keep in mind that though the court does intervene in procedural matters, it is inclined to leave the responsibility of substantive academic matters to the expertise of professional educators. Finally, the goals and objectives on each student's IEP should provide a proper means for evaluating whether a student can graduate. These goals and standards can be used in place of standard district requirements.

Often, learners with disabilities, if they are to benefit fully from the special education services discussed above, require additional support services. These "related services" are discussed in the next section.

Related Services

Public Law 94–142 defines **related services** as "transportation, and such developmental, corrective, and other supportive services as are required to assist the handicapped child to benefit from special education" (Federal Register, 1977, Section 121.550). Related services include:

- Transportation: providing travel to and from school and between schools, as well as across gravel around school buildings. Special equipment that is needed, such as ramps, elevators, or lifts for buses, must be provided.
- Speech pathology: identifying diagnosing, and appraising speech or language disorders, referral to other professionals specializing in speech and language services, and counseling and guidance of parents, children, and teachers regarding speech and language disorders.
- Audiology: identifying students with a hearing loss; determining the range, nature, and degree of that loss; language, auditory, and speech reading training; prevention programs and counseling and guidance for students, parents, and teachers regarding hearing loss; determining the need for, selecting, fitting, and evaluating hearing aids.
- Psychological services: administering and interpreting psychological and educational tests and assessments; obtaining and interpreting information about learning styles and consulting with other staff.
- Physical therapy: providing services as needed by a qualified physical therapist.
- Occupational therapy: conducting activities to improve independent functioning skills and prevent further loss of function.
- Recreation: assessing leisure functioning and conducting therapeutic recreation, leisure education, and recreation programs by school and community agencies.
- Early identification: creating and adhering to formal plans for identifying disabilities in children as early as possible.
- Medical services: providing services by a licensed physician to determine the child's medically related disabling condition which results in the child's need for special education and related services.
- School health services: providing services by a qualified school nurse or other qualified person.
- Counseling services: providing services by qualified social workers, psychologists, guidance counselors, or other qualified personnel.
- Social work services: preparing social or developmental histories and group and individual counseling services for children and their families.
- Parent counseling and training: helping parents understand the special needs of their child and providing them with information about child development.

Rehabilitation counseling was included as a related service in Public Law 101–476. At this time the legal definition of rehabilitation counseling has not occurred in the federal regulations.

Two related services that have generated controversy are psychotherapy and school health services. Osborne (1984) suggests that if a state requires that psychotherapy be provided by a licensed psychiatrist, then it is an exempt medical service. In regard to school health services, Osborne (1988) indicates that school health and medical services must be provided if they help to ensure the child's ability to profit from the educational program. If the student, however, is already benefiting from educational services without related services, then school health and medical services do not have to be provided by the school district.

Few districts have all the professional personnel available to provide the entire range of related services. Huntze and Grosenick (1980) stress that when a service is not available within the district, the child's needs are generally not met in the district or through the purchase of services from another district or private agency.

Summary

Several topics essential to understanding special education and the relationships between special education and general education were discussed in this chapter. The development of special education and general education in the United States was reviewed, and its impact on services for children with disabilities at various times in history was emphasized. As a result of compulsory school attendance laws passed during the second half of the nineteenth century, special programs were initiated in the schools. Schools, as the primary socialization agent to "the American way of life," served to modify the behavior and beliefs of urban immigrants in ways that assured the continuation of American society. The general social unrest of the 1960s fed the interest to meet individual needs, culminating in mandated free, appropriate, public education for all learners with disabilities through Public Law 94–142. Subsequent amendments to this law have increased efforts to serve students in less restrictive environments, to increase services to students at younger ages, and to support them in their transition to adult life.

The significance of social systems theory for classroom management was discussed and exemplified. Through the systems perspective, learning principles are applied with consideration of interpersonal relationships, and with recognition of the impact of neurological and physical factors on children's functioning in the classroom. Teachers must relate to students as capable persons, and trust in their abilities. The interaction between the setting, the student, the teacher, and all the other "actors" within the setting are emphasized.

Diagnostic evaluation and placement processes were described, including screening and referral procedures. Prereferral activities were discussed, and the importance of these activities for preventing the misidentification and premature classification of children as disabled was emphasized. The Individual Education Program is characterized or described as a resource management tool. The Individual Family Service Plan, defining the family rather than the child as the service recipient for children younger than three years of age, requires specific judgements with regard to the family's service needs.

The chapter included discussions of two concepts that are currently of great concern in special education: the least restrictive environment and the General Education Initiative. Challenges to the concept of the least restrictive environment, in the form of the movement towards inclusion, were described. The "cascade" or continuum of services generally available to students with disabilities was presented.

The chapter concluded with a section on the related services authorized by Public Law 94–142 and its amendments which should be available to students with disabilities as needed.

In the next chapter, we turn our attention to the learner with disabilities and the family. The family is discussed as a social system which is a continuation of our social systems perspective. The adaptation of the family and its members to the member with disabilities is discussed in detail. The chapter includes practical suggestions and activities to facilitate collaboration between families and educators for the benefit of the learner with disabilities.

References

Algozzine, B., Christenson, S., & Ysseldyke, J. E. (1982). Probabilities associated with the referral to placement process. *Teacher Education and Special Education, 5* (6), 15–20.

Algozzine, B., Maheady, L., Sacca, K. C., O'Shea, L., & O'Shea, D. (1990). Sometimes patent medicine works: A reply to Braaten, Kauffman, Braaten, Polsgrove, and Nelson. *Exceptional Children, 56,* 552–557.

Algozzine, B., Morsink, C. V., & Algozzine, K. M. (1988). What's happening in self-contained special education classrooms. *Exceptional Children, 55,* 259–265.

Bak, J. J., Cooper, E. M., Dobroth, K. M., & Siperstein, G. N. (1987). Special class placements as labels: Effects on children's attitudes toward learning handicapped peers. *Exceptional Children, 54,* 151–155.

Bauer, A. M., & Sapona, R. H. (1991). *Managing classrooms to facilitate learning.* Englewood Cliffs, NJ: Prentice Hall.

Bender, W. N. (1988). The other side of placement decisions: Assessment of the mainstream learning environment. *Remedial and Special Education, 9* (5), 28–33.

Bickel, W. E., & Bickel, D. D. (1986). Effective schools, classrooms, and instruction: Implications for Special Education. *Exceptional Children, 52,* 489–500.

Blom, S. D., Lininger, R. S., & Charlesworth, W. R. (1987). Ecological observation of emotionally and behaviorally disordered children: An alternative method. *American Journal of Orthopsychiatry, 57,* 49–59.

Braaten, S., Kauffman, J. M., Braaten, B., Polsgrove, L., & Nelson, C. M. (1988). The regular education initiative: Patent medicine for behavior disorders. *Exceptional Children, 55,* 21–27.

Breme, J. (1975). *A matrix for modern education.* Toronto, Canada: McClelland & Stewart.

Bronfenbrenner, U. (1979). *The ecology of human development.* Cambridge, MA: Harvard University.

Carter, J., & Sugai, G. (1989). Survey on prereferral practices: Responses from state departments of education. *Exceptional Children, 55,* 298–302.

Copeland, C. D. (1982). Teaching-learning behaviors and the demands of the classroom environment. In W. Doyle & T. L. Good (Eds.), *Focus on Teaching 1,* 83–97.

Council for Exceptional Children (1990). Precis: Americans with Disabilities Act of 1990: What should you know. Supplement to *Exceptional Children, 57,* 1–2.

Deno, E. (1970). Special education as developmental capital. *Exceptional Children, 37,* 229–237.

Edmister, P., & Ekstrand, R. E. (1987). Preschool programming: Legal and educational issues. *Exceptional Children, 54* (2), 130–136.

Federal Register (1977). Public Law 94–142, Sec. 111–550.

Fuchs, D., & Fuchs, L. S. (1989). Effects of examiner familiarity on Black, Caucasian, and Hispanic children: A meta-analysis. *Exceptional Children, 55,* 303–308.

Garver-Pinhas, A., & Schmelkin, L. P. (1989). Administrators' and teachers' attitudes toward mainstreaming. *Remedial and Special Education, 10* (4), 38–43.

Gerber, M. M. (1981). Economic considerations of "appropriate" education for exceptional children. *Exceptional Education Quarterly, 2,* 49–58.

Gersten, R., & Woodward, J. (1990). Rethinking the Regular Education Initiative: Focus on the classroom teacher. *Remedial and Special Education, 11* (3), 7–16.

Graden, J. (1989). Redefining "prereferral" intervention as intervention assistance: Collaboration between general and special education. *Exceptional Children, 56,* 227–331.

Graden, J. L., Casey, A., & Christenson, S. L. (1985). Implementing a prereferral intervention system: Part I: The model. *Exceptional Children, 51,* 377–384.

Green, J. L., & Weade, R. (1988). Teaching as conversation and the construction of meaning in the classroom. Paper presented at the Annual Meeting of the American Educational Research Association, April, 1988.

Hoffman, E. (1975). The American public school and the deviant child: The origins of their involvement. *The Journal of Special Education, 9,* 414–423.

Hood, L., McDermott, R., & Cole, M. (1980). "Let's try to make it a good day"—some not so simple ways. *Discourse Processes, 3,* 155–168.

Huntze, S. L., & Grosenick, J. (1980). *National needs assessment in behavior disorders: Resource issues in behavior disorders.* Columbia, MO: University of Missouri.

Jenkins, J. R., & Heinen, A. (1989). Students' preferences for service delivery: Pull-out, in-class, or integrated models. *Exceptional Children, 55,* 516–523.

Jenkins, J., Pious, C. G., & Peterson, D. L. (1988). Categorical programs for remedial and handicapped students: Issues of validity. *Exceptional Children, 55,* 147–158.

Jenkins, J. R., Pious, C. G., & Jewell, M. (1990). Special education and the Regular Education Initiative: Basic assumptions. *Exceptional Children, 56,* 479–491.

Jones, V. (1986). Classroom management in the United States: Trends and critical issues. In D. P. Tattum (Ed.), *Management of disruptive pupil behavior in schools* (pp. 69–90). Chichester, England: John Wiley.

Kauffman, J. M. (1981). Historical trends and contemporary issues in special education in the United States. In J. M. Kauffman & D. P. Hallahan (Eds.), *Handbook of special education* (pp. 3–23). Englewood Cliffs, NJ: Prentice Hall.

Kochanek, T. T., Kabacoff, R. I., & Lipsitt, L. P. (1990). Early identification of developmentally disabled and at-risk preschool children. *Exceptional Children, 56,* 528–538.

Kortering, L., Julnes, R., & Edgar, E. (1990). An instructive review of the law pertaining to the graduation of special education students. *Remedial and Special Education, 11* (4), 7–13.

Krauss, M. W. (1990). New precedent in family policy: Individualized Family Service Plan. *Exceptional Children, 56,* 388–395.

Lambert, N. M. (1988). Perspectives on eligibility for and placement in special education programs. *Exceptional Children, 54,* 297–301.

Mercer, J. R. (1970). Sociological perspectives on mild mental retardation. In H. C. Haywood (Ed.), *Social-cultural aspects of mental retardation.* NY: Appleton-Century-Crofts.

Mercer, J. R. (1971). The meaning of mental retardation. In R. Koch & J. C. Dobson (Eds.), *The mentally retarded child and family.* NY: Brunner/Mazel.

Osborne, A. (1984). How the courts have interpreted the related services mandate. *Exceptional Children, 51,* 249–252.

Osborne, A. (1988). The Supreme Court's interpretation of the Education for All Handicapped Children's Act. *Remedial and Special Education, 9* (3), 21–25.

Pinnell, G. S., & Galloway, C. M. (1987). Human development, language, and communication: Then and now. *Theory into Practice, 26* (Special Issue), 353–357.

Pugach, M., & Johnson, L. J. (1989). Prereferral interventions: Progress, problems, and challenges. *Exceptional Children, 56,* 217–226.

Reynolds, M. (1962). A framework for considering some issues in special education. *Exceptional Children, 28,* 367–370.

Reynolds, M. (1989). An historical perspective: The delivery of special education to mildly disabled and at risk students. *Remedial and Special Education, 10* (6), 7–11.

Rothstein, L. (1990). *Special education law.* New York: Longman.

Sarason, S. B., & Doris, J. (1979). *Educational handicap, public policy, and social history.* New York: The Free Press.

Shepard, L. A., & Smith, M. L. (1983). An evaluation of the identification of learning disabled students in Colorado. *Learning Disabilities Quarterly, 6* (2), 115–127.

Stainback, S. B., Stainback, W. C., & Harris, K. C. (1989). Support facilitation: An emerging role for special educators. *Teacher Education and Special Education, 12,* 148–153.

Stainback, S. W., & Stainback, W. (1992). Schools as inclusive communities. In S. Stainback & W. Stainback (Eds.), *Controversial issues confronting special education* (pp. 29–44). Boston: Allyn & Bacon.

Stainback, S., Stainback, W., & Jackson, H. J. (1992). Toward inclusive classrooms. In S. Stainback & W. Stainback (Eds.), *Curriculum considerations in inclusive classrooms* (pp. 3–18). Baltimore: Paul H. Brookes.

Taylor, S. (1988). Caught in the continuum: A critical analysis of the principle of the least restrictive environment. *The Journal of the Association for Persons with Severe Handicaps, 13,* 41–53.

Tindal, G. (1985). Investigating the effectiveness of special education. *Journal of Learning Disabilities, 18,* 101–117.

Tymitz-Wolf, B. (1984). An analysis of EMR children's worries about mainstreaming. *Education and Training of the Mentally Retarded, 19,* 157–168.

Vergason, G. A., & Anderegg, M. L. (1992). Preserving the least restrictive environment. In S. Stainback & W. Stainback (Eds.), *Controversial issues confronting special education* (pp. 45–54). Boston: Allyn & Bacon.

Walker, D. K., Singer, J. D., Palfrey, J. S., Orza, M., Wenger, M., & Butler, J. A. (1988). Who leaves and who stays in special education: A two-year follow-up study. *Exceptional Children, 54,* 393–402.

White, R., & Calhoun, M. L. (1987). From referral to placement: Teachers' perceptions of their responsibilities. *Exceptional Children, 63* (5), 460–468.

Will, M. C. (1986). Educating children with learning problems: A shared responsibility. *Exceptional Children, 52,* 411–415.

4

Families and Learners with Disabilities

*O*bjectives

After completing this chapter, you will be able to:

1. describe the family as a social system.
2. discuss the adaptation of families to members with disabilities.
3. describe family collaboration in special education.

*K*ey Words and Phrases

collaboration	information-giving activities
collaborative support for school programs	information-sharing activities
	nonparticipation
criteria of the least dangerous assumption	parent training
	stage theory

*M*ICHAEL, 11 YEARS OLD, HAD BEEN CONSISTENTLY CHALLENGED BY THE ACTIVITIES PRESENTED BY HIS TEACHERS IN school. Though described as likeable, pleasant, and eager to please, Michael had a limited reading vocabulary and decoded words with a whole-word rather than a phonics strategy. In addition, his progress in mathematics was affected by his tendency to transpose numbers, writing, for example, 14 as 41.

Michael had been retained in second grade and tutored throughout third grade. Fourth grade presented several new challenges which put Michael at risk for failure. He was expected to change classrooms to attend his various classes because the fourth grade was departmentalized. As a result, he had several teachers to interact with instead of one with whom he could establish a relationship. His weakness in reading caused him to have difficulties using instructional materials.

Following a series of classroom interventions applied in an effort to help Michael, he was evaluated and an IEP was written for placement in a part-time program for children with learning disabilities. Michael's parents were "glad to have a name for his problems," and excited about the potential of Michael receiving "real help." The psychologist questioned their motives and asked Mr. Nolan, Michael's special education teacher, "What is wrong with them? Who would ever want their child in special education?" ■

Introduction

In recent decades, there has been a dramatic change in the complex relationship between families and schools. Coleman (1987) suggests that families at all economic levels are becoming increasingly ill-equipped to provide the family setting that schools are designed to complement and augment in the effort to prepare students for the next generation. Coleman contends that the following indicators demonstrate the reduced incentive of parents to assume responsibility for their children:

- Prior to the 1960s, there was a general assumption that parents would pay for their children's college education; presently, college costs are seen increasingly as a government responsibility.
- The growth of afterschool and summer school activities reflects a decrease in parents' responsibility for children and an increase in parent concern for personal fulfillment.
- Parental authority over their college and high school age children has relaxed.
- Parents delegate an increasingly wide range of socialization activities to the school, including family and sexuality instruction, afterschool activities, and life skills instructions.

These indicators appear to be paralleled in special education. For example, the cost of post-secondary special education is increasingly assumed to be the responsibility of publicly funded vocational rehabilitation agencies. The extended school year, afterschool activities, and respite care programs are becoming more readily available at public expense. The parents of children with complex, challenging behaviors are increasingly relying on the schools and special educators to decrease these behaviors and instruct the children in socially appropriate behaviors. Special education has assumed the teaching of basic self-care, survival, and life skills to children. In recent decades, advocacy for persons with disabilities and their families has evolved from the provision of public protective services to the development of private and independent advocacy service groups and self-advocacy (Zirpoli, Hancox, Wieck, & Skarnulis, 1989).

In this chapter, we will explore the family as a social system and discuss the implications for families with members with disabilities. Using Bronfenbrenner's (1979) developmental contexts, we will summarize recent research findings with regard to families with members with disabilities. We conclude the chapter with a discussion of family collaboration in the education of children with disabilities.

Objective One: To describe the family as a social system.

The Family as a Social System

The family is not simply a collection of individuals; it is a social system. Minuchin (1974) offers several principles of social systems which apply to families:

- The family, itself, is a structured whole, a complete unit, with interdependent elements.
- As in a social system, interactions in the family are reciprocal and represent continuous give and take, accommodation and adaptation, rather than linear cause and effect interaction patterns.
- The family attempts to maintain stability. In the effort to maintain stability, the behavior of family members is perceived as purposeful. Resistance to change appears to be a natural occurrence.

When the family is perceived as a social system, it becomes apparent that linear cause and effect explanations of family members' behavior are inadequate to explain family operation (Johnston & Zemitsch, 1988). In the family, each person's functioning within the system helps maintain and change the behavior of other family members. Effecting change in one member provides the opportunity for effecting change in other members.

When a family member is born with or diagnosed as having disabilities, other family members assume new roles and the family system reorganizes (Bronfenbrenner, 1986). This reorganization changes the expectations and attitudes of family members. In addition, it affects other major settings or ecological contexts in which the individual with the disability functions, such as the school.

It must be noted that the family has changed dramatically in the latter part of this century. Families are no longer typically comprised of a married mother and father, with two or more children. Today, most children live in one-parent families, reconstituted or blended families, foster homes, extended families with relatives, or in a variety of other family arrangements (Epstein, 1988).

Objective Two: To discuss the adaptation of families to members with disabilities.

Adaptation of Families

Traditionally, the adaptation of families to members with disabilities has been perceived as the progression through a series of psychological stages: shock, denial, bargaining, anger, depression, and acceptance (Kroth and Otteni, 1985; Creekmore, 1988). Parents of children with disabilities are understood to experience chronic sorrow, a grieving process that persists throughout the life of the parent and child (Kroth and Otteni, 1985). Grieving is viewed by some professionals as necessary for parents in order to free themselves of the dream of the "perfect" child (Hinderliter, 1988).

Although **stage theory,** progression through a series of psychological phases, is accepted by many professionals, there is little empirical evidence to support it and the inferences drawn from it. As a result of an extensive review of the literature, Blacher (1984) concludes that the stages are a result of clinical judgments based on interviews with parents of children with disabilities, rather than analysis of objective data. Allen and Affleck (1985) report in their analysis of the literature that they found no support for any stagelike arrangement or grouping of parents' reactions.

Kratochvil and Devereux (1988) discuss another problem with regard to the application of stage theory which is that it presupposes a final stage: closure, with adjustment to or acceptance of the situation. In interviews with parents, however, they found that despite overall adjustment, all parents experience "down periods." These recurring feelings of grief were triggered by unreached milestones, worries about the future, and introspection.

Recently, two alternative explanations of the adaptation of families to the birth or diagnosis of a child with disabilities have been suggested. Bauer and Shea (1987) present an integrated perspective on family adaptation in which adjustment becomes a developmental process, an effort to meet both the parents' and the child's needs. Family adaptation is seen as occurring within several personal, familial, social, and cultural ecological contexts. In her explanation, Kamfe (1989) discusses the adjustment of the family to the birth or diagnosis of a child with a disability as a transition in the family's development. These alternative explanations are discussed in the following sections.

Parents are encouraged to visit their child's school to learn ways to support the child's educational program.

An Integrated Perspective

In the integrated perspective (Bauer & Shea, 1987; Shea and Bauer, 1991), Bronfenbrenner's ecological contexts form a framework for the simultaneous consideration of (a) what is taking place within the immediate household (microsystem), (b) the factors at work in the larger social system in which the family is functioning (exosystem), (c) the interaction of these settings with one another (mesosystem), and (d) the overriding cultural beliefs and values that influence the microsystem and exosystem (macrosystem). The integrated framework also includes the ontogenic system originally proposed by Kurdek (1981).

The Ontogenic System: Personal Factors for Coping with a Child with Disabilities   The ontogenic system was proposed by Kurdek as a complement to Bronfenbrenner's ecological contexts. The ontogenic system includes the personal factors that influence an individual's ability to cope with stress. Ontogenic development represents what an individual brings to the family setting and the parenting role. In the discussion of the ontogenic system which follows, consideration is given to parent gender and personality and the characteristics of the child with the disability. A summary of the recent research with regard to these factors is presented in Table 4.1.

The literature suggests that parents' stress is primarily a function of their personality and physiology and not a consequence of the nature of the disability. It would appear that programs designed to relieve family stress by providing goods, services, and other resources are of questionable effectiveness (Bradshaw, 1978). Successful collaboration involves helping family members in their efforts to develop more effective ways of managing stress. The literature also reports that mothers and fathers vary in their needs and perceptions of the child with disabilities. Successful collaboration programs must then be designed to respond to the unique needs of both mothers and fathers.

Table 4.1   Research Concerning the Ontogenic System

Authors	Findings
Gender	
Cummings (1976)	Fathers of children with mental retardation differed from fathers of typical children with regard to depression and preoccupation with the child, as well as diminished self-esteem. Fathers, unlike mothers, have fewer opportunities to do something directly helpful to the child, which would provide concrete evidence for their loving, caring, and benevolent concern.
Erickson and Upshur, 1989	Fathers of children with developmental delays do not perform more child-care tasks than fathers of typical children; when the child is more seriously disabled, fathers assumed fewer tasks than did the mothers.
Golderg, Marcovitch, MacGregor, and Lojkasek (1986)	Fathers of preschoolers with developmental delays reported fewer distress symptoms, higher self-esteem, and more internal locus of control than did mothers; fathers experience less support.
Holroyd, 1974	When compared with fathers, mothers of children with disabilities describe themselves as less able to experience personal development or freedom, more limited in how they can use their time, poorer in health or mood, more sensitive with regard to how the child fits into the community, and more aware of disharmony within the family.
Personality factors	
Cantwell, Baker, and Rutter (1979)	Failed to identify any abnormalities of personality in the parents of children with even severe disabilities such as autism.
Darling (1979)	Parental traits which may affect acceptance of the birth or diagnosis of a child with disabilities include social class (parents of lower socioeconomic status appear to be more accepting), religion (Roman Catholics appear to be the most accepting), personal self-acceptance, prior experience with children, and parents' age (younger parents are more tolerant than other parents).
Rees, Strom, and Wurster (1982)	The parents of children with mental retardation resembled parents of children with normal intelligence in self-perception as teachers of their children and child rearers.
The nature of the child's disability	
Bradshaw, 1978	Stress in mothers with severely disabled children was higher than in mothers of children without disabilities; little of the variation in stress could be ascribed to the external social and physical conditions of the family and the child; stress scores did not vary with the child's disabilities, mobility, capacity to communicate, or personal independence. Stress levels appeared to be a function of parents' personality and physiology.
Frey, Greenberg, and Fewell (1989)	Greater stress was reported by parents of boys with disabilities and parents of children with limited communication skills.
Gath, 1977	The mental health of mothers of children with Down syndrome is similar in type and degree to that experienced by other mothers raising small children under difficult circumstances, and is not significantly greater than the stress indigenous to raising a healthy baby.
Harris and McHale (1989)	Parents of children with developmental delays reported stress related to more time for caregiving, concern over present and future needs, and uncertainty over the child's prognosis.
Holroyd (1974)	Mothers of children with autism were found to be more upset and disappointed about the child's condition, more aware and concerned about the child's dependency, more concerned about the effect of the child on the family, more concerned about the lack of recreational and community activities for the child, and more aware of the child's personality and behavior problems than mothers of children with Down syndrome. Mothers of children with Down syndrome were more concerned about their tendencies to be overprotective and encourage dependence and about the limited school or occupational opportunities available for their child.
Holroyd, Brown, Wikler, Simmons (1975)	Parents of children with fewer physical disabilities tend to be less pessimistic. Stress ratings were higher for mothers of older and children living at home than mothers of younger children.
Holroyd and Guthrie (1979)	Parents of children with neuromuscular disabilities were more pessimistic, while parents of children identified as having behavioral disorders reported more problems in integrating the child into the family. Parents of children in wheelchairs had significantly higher stress factors related to excessive time demands, overcommitment and martyrdom, limits on family opportunities, physical incapacitation of the child, and lack of activities for the child.
Irvin, Kennel, and Klaus (1982)	Parental reactions to their child's disability were dependent on medical characteristics of the disability.
Wikler, Wasow, and Hatfield (1981)	The intensity of parental stress is a function of the child's developmental stage as well as the parents' individual abilities to cope with difficulties.

The Microsystem: Intrafamilial Relationships   The microsystem focuses on complex relationships within the immediate family, that is, mother-father, parent-child, and sibling-child relationships. Family interactions before and after the birth or diagnosis of a child with disabilities have been explored in several research studies. These studies are summarized in Table 4.2.

*T*able 4.2   Research Concerning the Microsystem

Authors	Findings
Mother-father relationships	
Drotar, Baskiewicz, Irvin, Kennel, and Klaus (1975)	Parents emphasized the typical aspects of their families in self-reports and suggested that maintaining a satisfactory relationship with each other was crucial to their adaptation to the child's disability.
Friedrich, Wilturner, and Cohen (1985)	Marital satisfaction was a significant predictor of the parents' coping with their child's disability.
Germain and Maisto, 1982	The presence of both parents in the home is a major source of emotional support to the family.
Parent-child relationships	
Beckman-Bell (1981)	The best predictors of the amount of stress reported by mothers were caregiving demands, the child's responsiveness, and the existence of self-stimulatory behaviors.
Cantwell, Baker, and Rutter (1979)	Mothers spent as much as twice the amount of time in concentrated interaction with their child with a disability as with their children without disabilities.
Harper (1984)	Mothers of children with multiple disabilities reported on positive relationships, detachment, obedience, independence, and management problems; a positive relationship is contingent upon a combination of compliant child behaviors in association with general child competence.
Levy-Shiff (1986)	Having a child with mental retardation was reflected more in mothers' than fathers' behavior, with mothers having fewer positive interchanges with their children. Mothers performed most of the caregiving for their children, even when fathers were at home.
Schell (1981)	The development of reciprocity and a bond between parent and child are difficult to attain when parents are unable to interpret the infant's signals or if the infant seems unresponsive to the parents' activities.
Sibling-child relationships	
Dyson, Edgar, and Crnic (1989)	The effect of the child with disabilities on the siblings is mediated by the family's psychological and personal resources. Self-concept was influenced by the perceived family and parent problems, and variations in social competence were accounted for by the emphasis parents placed on personal growth and independence.
Featherstone (1980)	Siblings of children with disabilities may feel that they live in two cultures: the world of typical classmates and the world of the "exceptional" family; siblings are accepting and helpful to the child with disabilities.
Menke (1987)	Children and parents agreed that both worried about the ill child but disagreed on the nature of their worries and concerns. Specific worries and concerns depended on the siblings' age and the ill child's diagnosis.
Sydney and Minner (1984)	Teachers indicated that placement in programming for students identified as having behavioral disorders was more appropriate for students with siblings identified as behaviorally disordered than for an identically described student with a sibling without disabilities; information regarding a student's sibling may influence the placement recommendations of special class teachers.
Family functioning	
Byasee and Murrell, 1985	There is no relationship between the severity of behavioral differences and abnormality in family functioning.
Cantwell, Baker, and Rutter (1979)	Families of children with autism were not characterized by abnormality in family life or interaction.
Gallagher, Beckman, and Cross (1983)	Two factors that may influence stress levels in families with a child who is disabled are: (a) the child growing older and (b) the parents' view of the cause of the disability may have a significant impact. The strongest predictor of both child progress and maternal performance was the mother's perception of whether or not she could be effective with her child.
McAllister, Butler, and Lei (1973)	Interaction between parent and child was less frequent in families with a child identified as having behavioral disorders than in families without such children.
Significant others	
Lowenthal and Haven (1986)	Families with members with disabilities experience decreased social interaction outside of the family, the impact of which is considerably reduced if the parents have a close personal relationship with each other, giving each other social support.

The stress experienced by families of children with disabilities is a result of an ongoing process of interaction between personal characteristics and environmental influences (Beckman-Bell, 1981). Collaboration between parents and teachers on behalf of the child with disabilities is enhanced when professionals consider (a) the interaction of personal characteristics and environmental influences, (b) those family characteristics which may change, and (c) those family characteristics which are not likely to change. If these factors are considered in decision making then programs can be designed to respond to an individual family's issues and concerns.

Individuals with disabilities need social activity outside the home.

The Exosystem: External Social Supports   The exosystem is the context in which events occurring outside the individual's immediate environment (the microsystem) affect it (Bronfenbrenner, 1979). Settings within the exosystem may include work, church, neighborhood, school, and community. In this section, consideration is given to the amount of change caused in the exosystem by the birth or diagnosis of the child with disabilities as well as the formal and informal support systems available to the family. Significant factors within the exosystem are professionals who may interact with the family, social interactions, and external support systems. The research regarding adaptation and the exosystem is summarized in Table 4.3.

Friends, relatives, and self-help organizations may provide social and other support to parents of children with disabilities. Social support appears to be significant in the positive adaptation of families to members with disabilities.

The Mesosystem: Interrelationships among Contexts   The mesosystem involves the interrelationships of the developmental contexts in which the individual actually participates. These contexts vary at different times during the individual's lifetime and may include the relationships between school and family and social agency and family. The research related to this context is summarized in Table 4.4.

McAfee and Vergason (1979) make three recommendations to further the coordination of school and home efforts on behalf of the child with disabilities. First, a written or unwritten contract should be drawn between school and home to increase the potential that each contributes towards the common goals they have for the child. Second, parents must assume some responsibility for their children's education. Finally, both school and family should seek ways to regain community support for the educational system.

*T*able 4.3   Research Concerning the Exosystem

Authors	Findings
Abrams and Kaslow (1977)	Families with limited resources have difficulty redirecting resources to alleviate service needs.
Blackard and Barsch (1982)	Parents reported restrictions in family activities.
Donnellan and Mirenda (1984)	Professionals may encourage shopping behavior (seeking numerous professional opinions) by initially denying the existence of the child's problem, suppressing information, and disagreeing among themselves.
Dunlap and Hollingworth (1977)	Parents reported that the presence of a child with a disability had little effect on the family.
Farber (1975)	Families with an abundance of personal, social, and financial resources are better able to adjust to the problems of raising a child with a disability because they have resources to obtain needed services.
Holroyd, Brown, Wikler, and Simons (1975)	Mothers who demonstrated a high level of stress lacked social support, family cohesion, family opportunities, and financial independence.
Kiern, 1971	"Shopping," that is pursuing other professionals' evaluations after receiving at least two earlier opinions, occurred in only three percent of the families, and these parents were usually making specific requests for information.
Korn, Chess, and Fernandez (1978)	In three-fourths of the families studied, the child with disabilities did not impair marital quality or family patterns.
Marcus (1977)	Parents are often discouraged or misled by professionals.
McAllister, Butler, and Lei (1973)	Parents of children identified as having behavioral disorders are less likely than parents of other children to visit relatives, neighbors, friends, or co-workers or participate in social clubs or organizations.
Schell (1981)	Professionals overestimate the extent to which parents report community rejection and lack of support, while underestimating the parents' ability to use appropriate teaching and behavior management techniques in the home. Support systems within the extended family increase the family's ability to cope with having a child with disabilities.

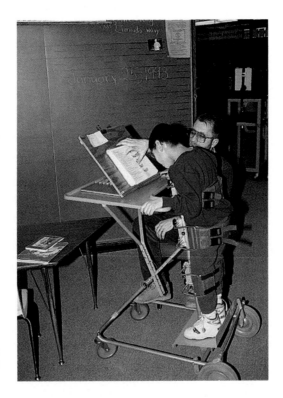

Although parents are partners in their child's education, parents' choice to not participate should be respected.

*T*able 4.4   Research Concerning the Mesosystem

Author	Findings
School/family	
Karnes and Zehrbach (1972)	Services for individuals with disabilities can be improved if parents are meaningfully involved in their child's educational program.
O'Connell (1975)	Parents may change their behavior and improve the educational value of the family environment for the child as a consequence of school/family involvement.
Ross (1964)	School/family involvement may reduce personal and family problems related to the child's difficulties.
Social Agencies/family	
Clark and Baker (1983)	In families with children with mental retardation, families who were less proficient in the skills being taught (a) were of lower socioeconomic status, (b) anticipated greater problems in training, and (c) were less experienced in behavior modification techniques. The parents who had difficulty implementing the techniques they learned during training were those who were less likely to have taught their children before training, to have achieved proficiency during training, and to have intact marriages.
Levinson (1969)	Families that received assistance for longer periods were more likely to have children with serious emotional problems; parents perceive agency roles as confusing and inadequate.
Winton and Turnbull (1981)	The factors of greatest importance in parents' selection of preschool services for their child were (a) logistics, i.e., location and transportation, (b) respite (65% stated that they needed relief), (c) parent-professional relationships, (d) parent involvement activities (all parents liked informal contact with teachers, yet nearly twenty percent expressed that they would like having the opportunity to have no role in their child's formal education), and (e) the availability of a peer group for discussion and support.

Though the provision of appropriate services for the child is a critical issue, school (and, perhaps, social agency) personnel may oversimplify the issue of parent involvement by equating parents' involvement in formal programs with parents' involvement with their child. According to MacMillan and Turnbull (1983), a decision not to be involved in educational programming with their child does not mean that the parents are not involved with their child in the larger context of home and community. Parents have a right to choose not to be involved in a formal program when they feel noninvolvement is beneficial to them, the family, and the child. Decisions about the degree of involvement should grow out of parents' individual needs and preferences rather than the generalized expectations of professionals.

Bronfenbrenner (1979) indicates that the developmental potential of a setting within the mesosystem is enhanced if the person's initial transition into that setting is not made alone, but with one or more persons with whom they have participated in prior settings. For example, when Jerry made the transition from his special education class to a general education class for mathematics instruction, he was placed in the fifth grade in which George, his peer tutor, was taking mathematics instruction. Development is enhanced if, prior to entry into a new setting, individuals are provided with appropriate information, advice, and vicarious experiences. The developmental potential of settings within the mesosystem is enhanced to the extent that there exist direct and indirect links to power so that participants can influence the allocation of resources and make decisions that are responsive to their needs. Transitions between developmental contexts are explored in Chapter 5.

Meeting the needs of individual parents should be the goal of any collaborative program. In a discussion of parents of children identified as mentally ill, Marcus (1977) suggests that a thorough understanding of the range of pressures and bewildering daily events affecting the lives of these families will enable professionals to deliver services based on parents' real needs rather than presumed needs. In this

manner, strategies for intervention can be designed to respond to the family's expressed needs and concerns, and their style of adaptation. The impact of the child with disabilities on family relationships and the family, itself, needs to be carefully assessed if professionals are to successfully assist the family (Blackard and Barsch, 1982).

The Macrosystem: Societal Beliefs and Values about the Family and Disability   The macrosystem, that is, societal beliefs and values about disabilities, is discussed in Chapter 2. In this section, we discuss societal beliefs and values concerning the family.

Society views marriage as a continuing union of two persons which produces healthy, perfect children (Greer, 1975). Families not producing perfect children are considered "different" (Darling, 1979). This difference creates a stigma for the parents. As a consequence, the parents may exhibit a loss of self-esteem, shame, defensiveness, aloneness, feelings of insignificance, or loss of belief in immortality, that is, carrying on a part of you in your children.

Darling (1979) further defines stigma as a form of social reaction to members who are different and do not conform to an arbitrary set of expectations. Parents may, in addition, acquire a "courtesy stigma" by association with their child (Birenbaum, 1970). The parents' former social identity is not fully retained with the birth or diagnosis of a child with a disability. The social factors of inclusion, which will reduce intimacy with parents of similar children, may increase parents' stress (Gallagher, Beckman, and Cross, 1983). Dealing with the public means that parents must confront ignorance and callousness, explain behaviors, suppress anger and shame, and develop a thick skin, a sense of humor, or indifference (Marcus, 1977).

Voysey (1975) suggests that parents use various strategies to deal with societal expectations with regard to their child's disability and their role as parents. These strategies are characterized by the following verbalizations:

- "It could happen to anyone."
- "We take it day by day."
- "We didn't deserve this—it just happened."
- "We appreciate little successes more."
- "We understand other people's problems better."
- "Each person makes a special contribution."

Voysey suggests that parents of children with disabilities manage the impressions they project to others. They may convey to others how successful the child is, by simply mentioning the disability informally, by supplying only partial information, or by trying to "tell it like it is."

Positive and realistic changes in society's beliefs, attitudes, and values with regard to families and disabilities will provide the support parents need to help them adapt to the birth or diagnosis of a child with a disability. As professionals working with families with members with disabilities, it is essential to recognize our personal presumptions and biases towards them. Open acceptance of family members as individuals rather than as a stereotyped group (for example, parents of children with mental retardation or siblings of children identified as behaviorally disordered) is essential.

Clouded Minds
Parents renew struggle to help attention-deficit children succeed in their schools

By Janet Filips
Newhouse News Service

His parents always knew Johnny was different. As a toddler, he was strangely prone to accidents, constantly bumping into walls, taking risks.

"He's all boy," the pediatrician said. "He'll outgrow it."

Later, his teachers asked why Johnny wouldn't sit still, follow the rules, behave. "He's a gifted student," they told his parents. "He could do it if he wanted to."

Finally, school administrators recommended a child psychiatrist. After three months of counseling and testing, the doctor provided an answer to the teachers' string of whys: Johnny, 11, suffered from attention-deficit hyperactivity disorder.

For parents of children like Johnny, a new school year means more than a rush of shopping for sneakers and pencils. It is time to resume a crusade with a valuable prize: a year in their child's bruised life.

It is time to fight for the attention and understanding of principals and teachers so they will do as much as possible to help such children absorb information, succeed with assignments, make friends and feel good about themselves.

The parents try to devise ways to keep home life predictable, calm and positive.

They weigh the merits and risks of putting their child on a medicine such as Ritalin to help achieve improved behavior.

Attention-deficit hyperactivity disorder, often abbreviated to ADHD, wears many faces. It may also be called attention deficit syndrome. According to the American Psychiatric Association, it afflicts from 3 percent to 5 percent of schoolchildren. But other estimates range from 1 percent to 20 percent. Some experts and parents believe the disorder often goes undiagnosed.

ADHD children's mental strength encompasses gifted, average, learning disabled and retarded. Far more boys are diagnosed than girls, though some people wonder if girls just slip through the cracks.

Attention-deficit children can be quiet souls who keep their eyes locked on the teacher as their minds roam light-years away. They can be wiggle bugs who wander the classroom, shouting answers and throwing tantrums.

A common cause underlies the extremes: a snag in the chemistry in the front of the brain, the part that filters distractions, controls impulses and calms arousal.

Because of that glitch, competing information confuses the attention-deficit child. The drone of a lawn mower, a kid at the next desk making faces, jitters about a test—all such internal and external stimuli glob together. The brain doesn't put out enough of the neurotransmitters that help other children screen the distractions and zero in on the teacher's explanation of tonight's homework.

"As the children get older, the hyperactivity tends to fade," says Dr. David Willis, a behavioral pediatrician in Portland, Ore. "But the difficulty in concentration continues."

Stimulants—Ritalin, Dexedrine and Cylert—are the most commonly prescribed medicine to temporarily improve a child's conduct and performance at school.

The stimulants wake up the part of the brain responsible for inhibition. Three-quarters of the children who try stimulants find they help them focus their attention, control their behavior and get along with others.

If one stimulant doesn't work, another might. Two other types of drugs, anti-depressants and high-blood-pressure medicine, also are used.

In the 1980s, controversy about such medication was sparked by criticism from the Church of Scientology's Citizens Commission on Human Rights.

Adaptation as Transition

Kamfe (1989) discussed family adaptation to the birth or diagnosis of a child with disabilities as transition. The transition model assumes that the discovery of the child's deafness, mental retardation, or other disability represents a significant event or transition in the life of the family. In her model, Kamfe suggested several variables that influence the family's adaptation, including:

- the child's specific condition or disability
- the family's perceptions, or the meaning they attach to the event, including its degrees of importance, disruptiveness, manageability, and stress-creating impact

That criticism was unfounded, according to Russell A. Barkley, a professor of psychology and neurology at the University of Massachusetts Medical Center who often is cited as the nation's foremost authority on ADHD.

In his book, "Attention-Deficit Hyperactivity Disorder: A Handbook for Diagnosis and Treatment," Barkley recounts, "Ritalin, it was claimed, was a dangerous and addictive drug often used as a chemical straitjacket to subdue normally exuberant children because of intolerant educators and parents and money-hungry psychiatrists." He says those reports included no evidence and reflected no major controversy in medical or scientific circles.

But as a result, doctors became more thorough in assessing the disorder, and more diligent in tracking their patients' response to medication. ADHD experts emphasize that effective treatment doesn't stop with a prescription but nearly always requires counseling and a variety of approaches at home and school.

ADHD children need structure, but not rigidity; frequent reinforcement; learning that doesn't rely solely on listening skills; small-group and hands-on projects; discussion; a variety of approaches; consistency in discipline; a dynamic teaching style; a minimum of distractions.

Hints that the disorder is a possibility can show up in preschool and sometimes toddlerhood. But ordinarily, kindergarten is the earliest it's caught.

Some teachers know the signs of the disorder. Others don't, and they may decide the child is simply uncooperative.

Today's rallying cry is for early identification and treatment. "When you go through three years of school being treated like a dummy or a bad egg," says one parent, "you're going to have a lasting bad attitude."

The longer the disorder is undiagnosed, the more problems can fester. The children may become depressed and angry. They feel they can't do anything right. Home life is tumultuous.

Parents are often relieved to pinpoint the cause of their child's behavior, but the diagnosis is the beginning of much work.

"The parent has a great responsibility to advocate," says one school administrator who recommends that parents make an appointment with their child's teacher within the first two weeks of school to express their concerns, share information and make a plan.

Collaboration, the experts agree, is the best way to help ADHD children. The team might include the principal, teacher, parents, pediatrician, psychiatrist or psychologist—and, if old enough, the student.

"The No. 1 risk factor is the impact on their self-esteem," says clinical psychologist Jeffrey Sosne. "You need to distinguish between your child being responsible for his behavior and being to blame."

The symptoms

Recognizing attention-deficit hyperactivity disorder is the first step to getting help. According to psychologist Claudia Hoffman, of Children's Hospital Medical Center's Psychology Service:

- Not all children who seem "hyperactive" have attention-deficit hyperactivity disorder, she cautions.
- Hyperactivity also can be symptomatic of other problems, such as anxiety, depression or mental illness.
- A child must be correctly evaluated and diagnosed. (Dr. Hoffmann performs such evaluations at the medical center. Call 559–4336 for more information.)
- Adults also suffer from attention-deficit hyperactivity disorder ∎

- conditioning variables, including the individual or situational factors that moderate perception, response, or outcome of the transition, including social status indicators, experiences, resources, and social supports
- responses, including the mourning process
- outcomes, which ideally are constructive actions towards the child's development

By viewing family adaptation to the birth or diagnosis of a child with a disability as transition, the complex interactions of the many variables involved become apparent. The family's adaptation is highly individualized and multivariate, and includes an extremely complex set of perceptions, social status indicators, experiences, personal resources, social supports, and characteristics of the disability. According to Kamfe, the complexity and interactions of these variables account for some of the differences in parental responses to the birth and diagnosis of a child with a disability and the conflicting reports in the literature on parents' adaptation.

Objective Three: To describe family collaboration in special education.

Family Collaboration and Special Education

According to Public Law 94–142 and its amendments, parents have the right to:

- inspect and review all their child's educational records.
- have an independent evaluation made of their child.
- receive written notice of any change in the identification, evaluation, or placement of their child, or any change in the child's Individualized Education Program (IEP).
- receive an impartial due process hearing if they disagree with the school's decision.
- participate equally with school personnel in developing, reviewing, and revising their child's IEP.

Public Law 99–457, as previously discussed, reauthorized these rights and added the Individual Family Service Plan (IFSP) for children with disabilities between birth and three years of age. In the IFSP, a case manager is designated who is responsible for implementing the plan and coordinating services. The family, rather than only the child, is the client of the educational program. The philosophical position underlying the IFSP is consistent with the Syracuse University Center on Human Policy's (1987) position statement on families, which indicates that:

- families should receive the supports necessary to maintain their children in the home.
- supports should serve the entire family.
- supports should maximize the family's control over the services they receive.

Donnellan and Mirenda (1984) propose several standards to serve as a foundation for all parent collaboration programs in special education. They suggest that all interventions be based on the assumption that parents are not the cause of their child's disability, and that professionals should recognize the danger of blaming parents for the child's disability. In addition, professionals should be aware of their personal and professional strengths and weaknesses. They should apply the **criteria of the least dangerous assumption,** which states that if a parent program was ineffective, it is because the program was ineffective and not because the family is defective or incapable. Donnellan and Mirenda further contend that a full explanation of the child's disability is essential to the parents. Professionals should be sensitive to the unique emotional and practical problems of living with an individual with disabilities and ensure that support services are made readily available to parents who wish them.

Donnellan and Mirenda state that under no circumstances should parents be told by professionals that "nothing can be done" for their child. All intervention programs should involve families to the maximum extent possible and should be designed to meet the needs of the child in the broader context of the needs of the family. Parents should be recognized as the experts in all areas related to their child's unique history, behavior, and needs. They should have full access to all diagnostic and educational information.

The unique strengths of each family should be recognized.

The following four principles are suggested by Dunst, Trivette, and Deal (1988) to govern assessment and intervention activities in response to the needs of families:

1. Intervention efforts should be based on family-identified needs, aspirations, and personal projects to promote positive child, parent, and family functioning.
2. The strengths and capabilities of the family should be the basis for promoting the family's ability to mobilize resources.
3. The major emphasis of programming should be on strengthening the family's personal social network as well as untapped but potential sources of informal aid and assistance.
4. Helping behaviors should promote the family's acquisition and use of competencies and skills necessary to mobilize and secure resources.

Several researchers have described the nature of family collaboration in special education and compared special and regular education in various cultural groups. Yanok and Derubertis (1989) found comparable patterns of responses between parents of students with disabilities and nonidentified students in the areas of school involvement, quality of instruction, and equality of educational opportunity. In a comparison of parents of regular education students and special education students, Salisbury and Evans (1988) found that the parents of students in special education were presented more opportunities for involvement, were more satisfied with their involvement, and felt more able to influence their child's education. The involvement of parents of students in regular education was reported to decrease as the students grew older. The involvement of the parents of students in special education, however, remains constant throughout the child's educational career. Lynch and Stein (1987), in a study contrasting African-American, Hispanic-American, and majority culture families reported that Hispanic-American families were satisfied with their children's special education programs but were less knowledgeable and less involved than were Anglo and African-American families. The comments of parents from Hispanic-American families with reference to their involvement seemed to convey the message "teacher knows best."

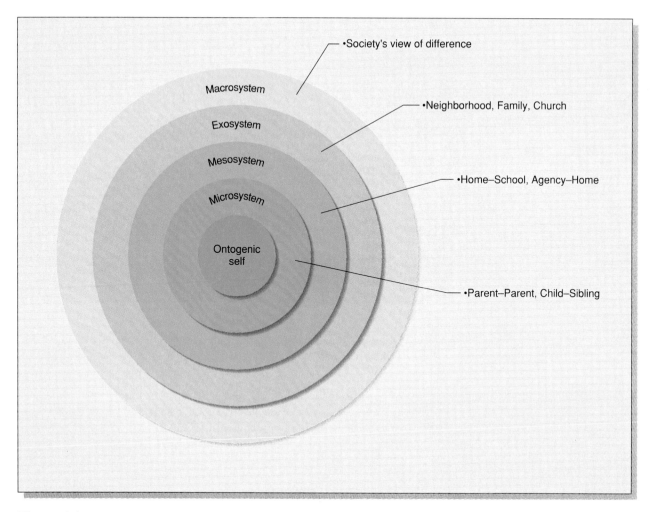

Figure 4.1
Developmental contexts as related to parent and family adaptation.

A Model for Collaboration with Families

The ecological perspective recognizes that families are complex and unique social systems. Because families vary so greatly, professionals must have an understanding of individual parents' current level of development when assisting their child. Olson (1988) suggests that models for working with families should consider that services and needs may range, developmentally, from a crisis level, in which it is difficult to address other than immediate needs, through a need for information and education, to the need for skill training. Throughout these stages, parents and families need emotional support and practical assistance in performing task-oriented activities such as developing, with others, the child's IEP or IFSP and accessing community services in response to family and child needs.

Recognition of the uniqueness of each family necessitates the application of a model for collaboration that emphasizes individualized programming. Shea and Bauer (1991) describe such a model as a recursive system, in which the steps in the model are revisited as family collaboration develops over time (see Figure 4.1). The phases in the model for collaboration include (a) introductory activities and assessing parent/family needs, (b) selecting goals and objectives, (c) planning and implementing activities, and (d) evaluating activities.

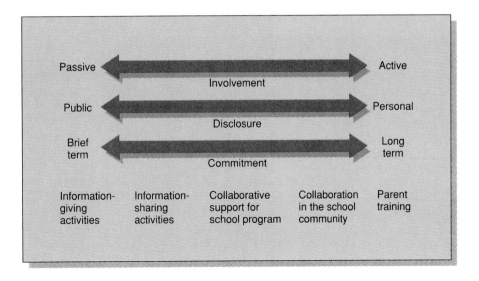

Figure 4.2
A continuum of family collaboration.

In the model, family collaboration is an ongoing process that terminates only after the student leaves the school or program. Is the first phase, introductory activities and assessing parent/family needs, the teacher contacts the parents, explains the program, and invites their participation. Next, assessment is conducted to ascertain the parent/family needs and priorities with regard to collaborating with others, including professionals, on behalf of their child. During the second phase, the information obtained as a result of the needs assessment is used to collaboratively select goals and objectives for collaborative parent-teacher activities.

In the third phase, activities responsive to the objectives selected in phase 2 are either designed or selected from those available in the classroom, school, or community. Activities should reflect the level of personal involvement the parent desires, rather than the level of involvement the professional wishes the parent to have. The final phase, evaluation, is conducted both during and at the conclusion of the collaborative activities. Both the availability of the activities and the effectiveness of the activities are evaluated. Programming should include activities and supports designed to facilitate family and child transitions between placements within a special education program, between special education programs and general education programs, and to post-secondary education programs including higher education, employment, and independent and supervised living arrangement.

A Continuum of Activities

Collaborative activities may include information-giving activities, information-sharing activities, collaborative program support activities, collaborative school community activities, and parent training activities. These activities may be viewed as a continuum based on (a) the time commitment that can be made, (b) the amount of personal involvement desired, and (c) the amount of personal disclosure the parents desire and can attain. For example, reading a classroom newsletter requires much less time, personal involvement, and personal disclosure for both parents and teacher than does participation in a discussion group on "reactions to the birth or diagnosis of a child with disabilities." An example of a continuum is presented in Figure 4.2.

Parent-teacher conferences are a way to keep parents aware of their child's progress.

Information-Giving Activities   In **information-giving activities,** the family is a passive recipient of information. Information is typically objective and the professional-parent contact is brief. Examples of activities in this area are written notes, telephone calls, periodic report cards, notices, meeting and program announcements, and newsletters.

Information-Sharing Activities   The most common **information-sharing activity** is the parent-teacher conference. In special education, a parent conference is conducted at least annually in the form of an IEP conference. In addition, conferences may be conducted to plan and implement collaborative activities, such as behavior management and problem-solving programs. Information also may be shared through notebooks the child carries to and from home and school and in which parents and teacher share written information about the child's performance and other common concerns. Information may be shared in the form of checklists on which the parents and teacher comment about the child's daily and weekly performance. Group meetings, either on specific topics or in the form of parent-teacher organization meetings, are examples of information-sharing activities.

Collaborative Support for School Programs   Activities in the area of **collaborative support for school programs** require increased activity and commitment on the part of the family members. A common activity in the area of support for the school program is a home-school intervention, in which family members work together to implement the IEP goals and objectives. In addition, parents may serve as teachers of their children or may supervise their child's home study to support the school program.

Collaboration in the School Community   **Collaboration,** that is, working together to accomplish a task, in the school community generally requires a significant time commitment on the part of family members. In school community collaboration, family members may serve as paraprofessionals, instructors, volunteers, or committee members. Other school community activities in which family members may

A field trip is a school activity in which parents can participate.

be involved are functioning as a roomparent, tutor, instructor of mini-courses, assistant on field trips, and acting as an aide in preparing instructional materials and equipment.

Parent Training   **Parent training** requires both parents and professionals to make a substantial time commitment. Parent training is the most intrusive of the collaborative activities because it involves the learning of knowledge and skills that may require parents to change current behaviors and interaction patterns. Both commercial and teacher-made materials may be used in parent training. Sensitivity to parents' goals, abilities, and culture is essential to successful parent training programs.

Families Who Choose Not to Collaborate   If we accept that each family is a unique social system, then it is logical that the factors that influence family involvement in their child's education are also unique to each family (MacMillan & Turnbull, 1983). With the many complex problems that confront contemporary families, collaboration in the education of their child is not always a major priority.

In a study of sixty minority families and twenty-nine teachers, Leitch and Tangri (1988) reported "work" as the major reason given by working parents for **nonparticipation** in their child's education program. For the unemployed parents, poor health was the most frequently reported reason for not participating. In addition, many parents felt their participation would not be helpful to the child. Teachers who did not pursue active collaboration with parents most often reported their own family responsibilities as their reason for nonparticipation.

Teachers suggested that the barriers to collaboration with parents included the parents' unrealistic expectations of the school and responsibilities for a large family. Teachers suggested that parents did not collaborate because (a) parents held the attitude that school isn't important enough to take time from work; (b) parents were unable to help with school work; (c) parents were jealous of teachers' upward mobility; (d) parents felt that long-time teachers were apathetic and not responsive to them; (e) there was an absence of activities to attract parents to the schools; and (f) teachers resented and suspected the motives of parents who were involved. According to the teachers, the most frequent barrier to collaboration was the parents' attitude towards the school. Teachers indicated that the school contributed to the parents' nonparticipation by exhibiting apathy towards parents, by requiring an overabundance of paperwork, by not reducing the cumbersomeness of the system for anyone trying to initiate a program, and by intimidating parents' from a position of authority.

These perceptions of parents and teachers on collaboration may increase the professional's feelings of anxiety and helplessness with regard to parent collaboration. These feelings may be exhibited by professionals through (Bloom, 1983):

- helpless anger, becoming punitive and confused when working with students.
- anger at the student's parents ("When I finally get something going he or she screws it up.").
- complexity shock, becoming either anxious for more constructive efforts or angry, frustrated, and desirous of a simpler situation.
- paranoic sellout, feeling that they are somehow responsible for the child's problem.
- anger at a child's success and subsequent "time-warp" ("He somehow forgets how to do it between the classroom and home.").
- implementation despair ("I've tried it all, nothing works.").
- retreat into professional neutrality.

In work with parents with problems, Bemporad, Ratey, and O'Driscoll (1987) report that there are three sets of issues the professional must confront. First, there are the parents' innate problems, such as the physical stamina needed to live with a child with a disability. Second, there are psychological defenses parents use to cope with the exhaustion, anger, and pain experienced as a result of the disability. Finally, there is the change in the parents' socializing experiences as a result of the disability and the psychological defenses. Recognizing the complexity of the parents' personal issues may increase teacher sensitivity to parent needs.

There are, however, some parents whose personal difficulties are such that parent-teacher collaboration is not feasible or not adequate to meet their needs. Coleman (1987) suggests that there are times when parents' needs are beyond the teacher's ability and training. These parents must be referred to other qualified professionals. Referral is appropriate when parents:

- are experiencing financial difficulties.
- are involved in marital discord or other crisis.
- routinely express feelings of helplessness, hopelessness, and desperation.
- express the feeling that they are out of control with regard to their child.
- report that the child is habitually involved with the juvenile court system.
- appear to be constantly under high levels of stress and duress.
- consistently initiate discussions regarding personal problems rather than issues related to the student and the student's program.

Through referral to the appropriate school or community agency professional, the intense needs of these parents can sometimes be met.

Summary

In this chapter, attention was focused on the families of learners with disabilities. The dramatic changes that occurred in the relationships between families and schools and families and special education in recent decades were discussed.

The family as a social system was discussed, and its characteristics and reorganization as a consequence of the birth or diagnosis of a member with a disability were described. Using the ecological theory of human development, we discussed the process of family adaptation to the member with a disability. We reviewed the traditional psychological stage theory and grieving theories of adaptation and suggested that research evidence could not be found to support their premises. Two other theories of adaptation were introduced: the integrated perspective (Bauer & Shea, 1987; Shea & Bauer, 1991) and transition theory (Kamfe, 1989).

In the discussion of the integrated perspective, we reported the empirical research evidence to support each of the ecological contexts (ontogenic system, microsystem, exosystem, mesosystem, macrosystem) which impact on family adaptation. Next, the principles and variables underlying Kamfe's transition theory of adaptation were discussed.

In the final section of the chapter, attention was given to family collaboration in special education. It was stated that Public Law 94–142, Public Law 99–457, and Public Law 101–456 all give parents of learners with disabilities the right to collaborate with others in their child's educational program. The Donnellan and Mirenda (1984) criteria of the least dangerous assumption was discussed and recommended for application in programming.

A model for collaboration was presented and each of its four phases discussed. Using a continuum, we reviewed the various collaborative activities and their impact on parents' and professionals' time, level of involvement, and degree of personal disclosure. Five kinds of collaborative activities were discussed and exemplified: information-giving, information-sharing, program support, collaboration in the school community, and parent training. The chapter concluded with a discussion of the reasons some parents and professionals choose not to participate in collaborative programming.

Throughout the chapter, we emphasized that it is essential that the uniqueness of each individual family be recognized and that programs be available to respond to individual family needs and desires.

References

Abrams, J. C., & Kaslow, F. (1977). Family systems and the learning disabled child: Interventions and treatment. *Journal of Learning Disabilities, 10* (2), 86–90.

Allen, D. A., & Affleck, G. (1985). Are we stereotyping parents: A postscript to Blacher. *Mental Retardation, 23,* 200–202.

Bauer, A. M., & Shea, T. M. (1987). An integrative approach to parental adaptation to the birth or diagnosis of an exceptional child. *School Social Work Journal, 9,* 240–252.

Beckman-Bell, P. (1981). Child related stress in families of handicapped children. *Topics in Early Childhood Special Education, 1,* 45–52.

Bemporad, J. R., Ratey, J. J., & O'Driscoll, G. (1987). Autism and emotion: A theological theory. *American Journal of Orthopsychiatry, 57,* 477–484.

Birenbaum, A. (1970). On managing a courtesy stigma. *Journal of Health and Social Behavior, 11,* 196–206.

Blacher, J. (1984). Sequential stages of parental adjustment to the birth of a child with handicaps: Fact or artifact. *Mental Retardation, 22* (2), 55–68.

Blackard, M. K., & Barsch, E. T. (1982). Parents' and professionals' perspectives of the handicapped child's impact on the family. *The Journal of the Association for the Severely Handicapped, 76* (2), 62–70.

Bloom, R. B. (1983). The effects of disturbed adolescents on their teachers. *Behavioral Disorders, 8,* 209–216.

Bradshaw, J. (1978). Tracing the causes of stress in families with handicapped children. *The British Journal of Social Work, 8,* 181–192.

Bronfenbrenner, U. (1979). *The ecology of human development.* Cambridge, MA: Harvard University.

Bronfenbrenner, U. (1986). Ecology of the family as a context for human development: Research perspective. *Developmental Psychology, 22,* 723–742.

Byasee, J. E., & Murrell, S. A. (1985). Interaction patterns in families of autistic, disturbed, and normal children. *American Journal of Orthopsychiatry, 4,* 473–478.

Cantwell, D. P., Baker, L., & Rutter, M. (1979). Families of autistic and dysphasic children: Family life and interaction patterns. *Archives of General Psychiatry, 36,* 682–687.

Clark, D. B., & Baker, B. L. (1983). Predicting outcomes in parent training. *Journal of Consulting and Clinical Psychology, 51,* 309–311.

Coleman, J. (1987). Families and schools. *Educational Researcher, 16* (6), 32–38.

Creekmore, W. N. (1988). Family-classroom: A critical balance. *Academic Therapy, 24* (2), 202–207.

Cummings, S. T. (1976). The impact of the child's deficiency on the father: A study of mentally retarded and chronically ill children. *American Journal of Orthopsychiatry, 46,* 246–255.

Darling, R. B. (1979). *Families against society.* Beverly Hills, CA: Sage.

Donnellan, A. M., & Mirenda, P. (1984). Issues related to professional involvement with families of individuals with autism and other severe handicaps. *The Journal of the Association for Persons with Severe Handicaps, 9,* 16–26.

Drotar, D., Baskiewicz, A., Irvin, N., Kennell, J., & Klaus, M. (1975). The adaptations of parents to the birth of an infant with a congenital malformation. *Pediatrics, 56,* 710–717.

Dunlap, W. R., & Hollingsworth, J. S. (1977). How does a handicapped child affect the family? *Family Coordinator,* July, 286–293.

Dunst, C. J., Trivette, C. M., & Deal, A. G. (1988). *Enabling and empowering families: Principles and guidelines for practice.* Cambridge, MA: Brookline Books.

Dyson, L., Edgar, E., & Crnic, K. (1989). Psychological predictors of adjustment by siblings of developmentally disabled children. *American Journal of Mental Retardation, 94,* 292–302.

Epstein, J. (1988). How to improve programs for parent involvement. *Education Horizons, 66* (2), 58–60.

Erickson, M., & Upsher, C. C. (1989). Caretaking burden and social support: Comparison of mothers and infants with and without disabilities. *American Journal of Mental Retardation, 94,* 250–258.

Farber, B. (1975). Family adaptations to severely mentally retarded children. In M. Begab & S. Richardson (Eds.), *The mentally retarded in society: A social science perspective* (pp. 247–266). Baltimore: University Park Press.

Featherstone, H. (1980). *A difference in the family.* New York: Basic Books.

Frey, K. S., Greenberg, M. T., & Fewell, R. R. (1989). Stress and coping among parents of handicapped children: A multidimensional approach. *American Journal of Mental Retardation, 94,* 240–249.

Friedrich, W. H., Wilturner, L. T., & Cohen, D. S. (1985). Coping resources and parenting mentally retarded children. *American Journal of Mental Deficiency, 90,* 130–139.

Gallagher, J. J., Beckman, P., & Cross, A. (1983). Families of handicapped children: Sources of stress and its amelioration. *Exceptional Children, 50,* 10–19.

Gath, A. (1977). The impact of an abnormal child upon parents. *British Journal of Psychiatry, 130,* 405–410.

Germain, M. L., & Maisto, A. A. (1982). The relationship of a perceived family support system to the institutional placement of mentally retarded children. *Education and Training of the Mentally Retarded, 17,* 17–33.

Goldberg, S., Marcovitch, S., MacGregor, D., & Lojkasek, M. (1986). Family response to developmentally delayed preschoolers: Etiology and the father's role. *American Journal of Mental Deficiency, 90,* 610–617.

Greer, B. G. (1975). On being the parent of a handicapped child. *Exceptional Children, 41,* 519.

Harper, D. C. (1984). Child behavior toward the parent: A factor analysis of mothers' reports of disabled children. *Journal of Autism and Developmental Disorders, 14,* 165–182.

Harris, V. S., & McHale, S. M. (1989). Family life problems, daily caregiving activities, and psychological well-being of mothers of mentally retarded children. *American Journal of Mental Retardation, 94,* 231–239.

Hinderliter, K. (1988). Death of a dream. *Exceptional Parent, 18* (1), 48–49.

Holroyd, J. (1974). The questionnaire on resources and stress: An instrument to measure family response to a handicapped family member. *Journal of Community Psychology, 2,* 92–94.

Holroyd, J., Brown, N., Wikler, L., & Simmons, J. Q. (1975). Stress in families of institutionalized and noninstitutionalized autistic children. *Journal of Clinical Psychology, 35,* 734–739.

Holroyd, J., & Guthrie, D. (1979). Stress in families of children with neuromuscular disease. *Journal of Clinical Psychology, 35,* 734–739.

Irvin, N. A., Kennel, J. H., & Klaus, M. H. (1982). Caring for parents of an infant with a congenital malformation. In M. H. Klaus & J. H. Kennel (Eds.), *Parent infant bonding.* St. Louis: Mosby.

Johnston, J. C., & Zemitsch, A. (1988). Family power: An intervention beyond the classroom. *Behavioral Disorders, 14* (1), 69–79.

Kampfe, C. M. (1989). Parental reaction to a child's hearing impairment. *American Annals of the Deaf, 134,* 255–259.

Karnes, M. B., & Zehrbach, R. R. (1972). Flexibility in getting parents involved in the school. *Teaching Exceptional Children, 5* (1), 6–19.

Kiern, W. C. (1971). Shopping parents: Patient problem or professional problem? *Mental Retardation, 9* (4), 6–7.

Korn, J., Chess, S., & Fernandez, P. (1978). The impact of children's physical handicaps on marital quality and family interaction. In R. M. Lerner & G. B. Spanier (Eds.), *Child influence on marital quality and family interaction.* New York: Academic Press.

Kratochvil, M. S., & Devereaux, S. A. (1988). Counseling needs of parents of handicapped children. *Social Casework, 69* (7), 420–426.

Kroth, R. L., & Otteni, H. (1985). *Communicating with parents of exceptional children: Improving parent-teacher relationships* (2nd ed.). Denver: Love.

Kurdek, L. A. (1981). An integrative perspective on children's divorce adjustment. *American Psychology, 36* (8), 856–877.

Leitch, R. M., & Tangri, S. S. (1988). Barriers to home-school collaboration. *Educational Horizons, 66* (2), 70–75.

Levinson, P. (1969). The next generation: A study of children in AFDC families. *Welfare in Review, 7,* 1–9.

Levy-Shiff, R. (1986). Mother-father-child interactions in families with a mentally retarded young child. *American Journal of Mental Deficiency, 91,* 141–142.

Lowenthal, M. F., & Haven, C. (1986). Interaction and adaptation: Intimacy as a critical variable. *American Sociological Review, 33,* 20–30.

Lynch, E. W., & Stein, R. C. (1987). Parent participation by ethnicity: A comparison of Hispanic, Black, and Anglo families. *Exceptional Children, 54,* 105–111.

McAfee, J. K., & Vergason, G. A. (1979). Parent involvement in the process of special education: Establishing the new partnerships. *Focus on Exceptional Children, 11* (2), 1–15.

McAllister, R. L., Butler, E. W., & Lei, T. P. (1973). Patterns of social interaction among families of behaviorally retarded children. *Journal of Marriage and the Family, 35,* 359–370.

MacMillan, D. L., & Turnbull, A. P. (1983). Parent involvement in special education: Respecting individual differences. *Education and Training of the Mentally Retarded, 18,* 4–9.

Marcus, L. M. (1977). Patterns of coping in families of psychotic children. *American Journal of Orthopsychiatry, 47,* 388–398.

Menke, E. M. (1987). The impact of a child's chronic illness on school-aged siblings. *Children's Health Care, 15* (3), 132–140.

Minuchin, S. (1974). *Families and family therapy.* Cambridge, MA: Harvard University Press.

O'Connell, C. Y. (1975). The challenge of parent education. *Exceptional Children, 41,* 554–556.

Olson, D. G. (1988). A developmental approach to family support: A conceptual framework. *Focal Point, 2* (3), 3–6.

Rees, R. J., Strom, R. D., & Wurster, S. (1982). A profile of childrearing characteristics for parents of intellectually handicapped children. *Australia and New Zealand Journal of Developmental Disabilities, 8,* 183–186.

Ross, A. E. (1964). *The exceptional child in the family.* New York: Grune & Stratton.

Salisbury, C., & Evans, I. M. (1988). Comparison of parent involvement in regular and special education. *The Journal of the Association for Persons with Severe Handicaps, 13,* 268–272.

Schell, G. S. (1981). The young handicapped child: A family perspective. *Topics in Early Childhood Special Education, 1,* 21–28.

Schild, S. (1982). Beyond the diagnosis: Issues in recurrent counseling of parents of the mentally retarded. *Social Work in Health Care, 8,* 81–93.

Shea, T. M., & Bauer, A. M. (1991). *Parents and teachers of children with exceptionalities: A handbook for collaboration* (2nd ed.). Boston: Allyn & Bacon.

Sydney, J., & Minner, S. (1984). The influence of sibling information on the placement recommendations of special class teachers. *Behavioral Disorders, 10,* 43–45.

Syracuse University Center on Human Policy (1987). *A statement in support of families and their children.* Syracuse, NY: Author.

Voysey, M. (1975). *A constant burden: The reconstitution of family life.* London: Routledge and Keagan Paul.

Wikler, L., Wasow, M., & Hatfield, E. (1981). Chronic sorrow revisited: Parent vs. professional depiction of the adjustment of parents of mentally retarded children. *American Journal of Orthopsychiatry, 51,* 63–70.

Winton, P. J., & Turnbull, A. D. (1981). Parent involvement as viewed by parents of preschool handicapped children. *Topics in Early Childhood Special Education, 1,* 11–19.

Yanok, J., & Derubertis, D. (1989). Comparative study of parental participation in regular and special education programs. *Exceptional Children, 56,* 195–199.

Zirpoli, T. J., Hancox, D., Wieck, C., & Skarnulis, E. R. (1989). Partners in policymaking: Empowering people. *The Journal of the Association for Persons with Severe Handicaps, 14* (2), 163–167.

Chapter

5

Transitions between Social Subsystems

*O*bjectives

After completing this chapter you will be able to:

1. describe the transitions confronting individuals who vary from their peers.
2. describe strategies for facilitating transitions.

*K*ey Words and Phrases

Civil Rights Act of 1964
Education of the Handicapped Act
  of 1983
generalization
Individuals with Disabilities Education
  Act of 1990

Perkins Vocational Education Act
  of 1973
transition
Vocational Education Act of 1963

● Two-thirds of all Americans with disabilities between the ages of 16 and 64 are not working (ICD Survey of Disabled Americans, 1986).

● Adults with disabilities who do work average over $2000 less in annual wages than their co-workers who are not disabled (U.S. Department of Education, 1983).

● Most of the 1978 graduates of Colorado special education programs were employed in jobs at minimal wages and were living with parents on whom they were financially dependent (Mithaug and associates, 1985).

● The National Council on the Handicapped (1986) indicated that attitudes, physical and communication barriers, and lack of appropriate training inhibit the ability of persons with disabilities from all age groups to reach independence ■

Introduction

In the social systems perspective, the mesosystem represents the interaction among the subsystems in which an individual functions. In special education, these interactions generally involve the transitions (a) from early childhood intervention programs to school-age programs, (b) between educational settings, usually from a more restrictive to a less restrictive setting, such as from special class to resource room and regular class, and (c) from school to work, vocational training, or higher education and independent or supported living arrangements. Social systems theory suggests that an individual's developmental potential is enhanced if that individual's initial transition into a new setting is not made alone, that is, if the individual enters the new setting in the company of one or more persons with whom he or she participated in prior settings.

In this chapter, we explore the transitions that occur during the educational career of individuals with disabilities. The implications of the social systems approach for enhancing the developmental potential of transitions for individuals with disabilities are discussed.

Bronfenbrenner (1986) suggests that there are three steps in the **transition** or movement of a child from one setting to another. The first step involves the intersetting relationships that exist prior to the actual transition. Preexisting relationships are powerful factors in forming attitudes and expectations about the child's anticipated performance in the new environment. During the second step, which follows the transition into the new setting, the family system reorganizes. Reorganization involves changes in the family members' expectations and attitudes towards the child. The final step occurs after the transition and results in changes in the relationship between the family and school, or the child, school, and family.

To facilitate the transition process, Bronfenbrenner suggests focusing efforts on enhancing the interrelationship between each of the child's present environments and the environment into which the child is making the transition. For example, if a child was to make a transition between a preschool program and a school-based special education program, an effort would be made to enhance the interrelationships among persons from the preschool program, the school-based program, and the family. The child either actively participates, or will actively participate, in each of these environments.

Objective One: To describe the transitions confronting individuals who vary from their peers.

The Transition Process

A transition is not an event; it is a process. Lazzari and Kilgo (1989) write that for families with a member with a disability, the transition process includes three phases: preparation, implementation, and follow-up. Professionals should recognize that, consistent with the social systems perspective, both the child and the family are making the transition and, as a consequence, feel the stress of change. This stress is exacerbated by the fact that subsystems or environments are involved in the process which are unfamiliar to the parents and child.

During the transition process, parents may have to interact with unfamiliar private and public agencies which vary with regard to eligibility criteria and quality of available services (Smith & Strain, 1988). In addition, the focus of the interventions to be implemented with child and family often changes from program to program. These and similar issues arise whether the transition is between an early childhood intervention or preschool program to a school-based program, between various school programs, or between a school program and adult life in the community.

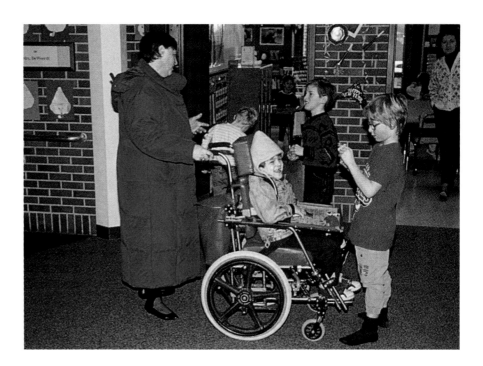

A visit to the school the child will attend supports the transition for parents and students.

Ferguson, Ferguson, and Jones (1988) state that transitions are socially constructed processes and therefore are responsive to planning. When planning a transition, the professional must assess the family's historical and cultural contexts as these relate to the transition. Though the study by Ferguson and associates was conducted with the parents of individuals with disabilities who were entering adulthood, their findings are relevant to the transitions of students during their school careers.

Rather than a single transition process, the parents studied by Ferguson and associates reported three distinct, simultaneous transition processes associated with their child's movement into adulthood. The processes included (a) a bureaucratic transition, (b) a family life transition, and (c) a status transition.

Bureaucratic transition is the process whereby agencies and professionals become involved with the child and family. The specific agencies and professionals involved in a transition varies with the particular transition being made by the child and family. These may include, among others, representatives of agencies delivering early childhood or preschool services, representatives of various school-based programs, and representatives of the special education district and adult service agencies. The absence of planned bureaucratic transition processes can be a disruptive force and lead to unsatisfactory outcomes. With regard to their bureaucratic transitions, some parents reported that they "surrendered to professionals." By "surrendered to professionals," the parents meant that they deferred to the opinions and explanations of professionals with regard to services for their child even though these services appeared to them to be inadequate.

Other parents reported "abandonment by professionals." They received little assistance from professionals who chose not to help or who gave up on the child and family. A third group of parents felt they were forced to assume the role of "pseudo-professionals" in order to obtain the services their child needed. Finally, some parents reported they could interact with some professionals in a positive and constructive manner, but with others they had to assume a negative and adversarial stance.

The second type of transition, as reported by Ferguson and associates, is the family life transition. Some parents reported that they met this transition with both passive resignation and self-reliance. They perceived the problems related to the transition into the new setting and the problems encountered in the new setting itself as just one more phase in their never-ending isolated struggle to obtain appropriate services for their child. They had to rely on their own ability to obtain stable and secure services. Another group of parents felt that they were forced to rely on personal resources and resented being put in such a position by professionals. They reported active feelings of being unjustly treated when they found it necessary to assume the added responsibilities of ensuring that their child received appropriate services. Finally, the parents reported a natural, collective sense of self-reliance, that is, a strong sense of social support from and mutual reliance on other parents of children with disabilities.

The third form of transition reported by the parents was related to changes in the status of the child. In some of the families Ferguson and associates studied, for example, the issue of the adult status of the individual with the disability became an issue of control of the individual rather than the independence of the individual. To be more specific, the issue of the individual's independence, which is a child-or-adult question, became a parent-or-professional question of who would control the individual.

Ferguson and associates urge professionals to understand that transition is not a single process, but several simultaneous processes which the child and family must negotiate successfully. Throughout these processes communication is essential. Communication, and thus transition, is facilitated by family collaboration in decision making and the facilitation of appropriate services in a timely manner.

Transition from Early Intervention and Preschool to School

Several issues surrounding the transition from early childhood intervention and preschool programs to school-based programs became apparent with the implementation of the mandates of Public Law 99–457. Diamond, Spiegel-McGill, and Hanrahan (1988) remind us that the transition from an early childhood intervention or preschool program to a public school program sometimes involves considerable upheaval for the child and the family. The familiar faces of the preschool program are replaced by the more "businesslike" affect of grammar school. They suggest that separation from the preschool experience may be the most abrupt and permanent break with past experiences that the child makes before leaving home as an adult. Turnbull and Turnbull (1986) note that early childhood transitions are important because they set the stage for all future transitions.

Diamond and associates report that there are several changes that occur during the transition to a school-based environment. The demands of school differ greatly from the demands of the preschool. The skills needed to function successfully in kindergarten include social skills, self-help skills, and the ability to function independently. In addition, the transition to a school-based program has a direct effect on the family in the areas of personal and family schedules, transportation, family support services, and communication strategies between the home and the school.

In a survey of parents of young children with disabilities, Hanline (1988) found the parents had informational needs, service needs, and concerns about the child's transition into the public school special education program. The major concerns expressed by the parents were the need for information about services offered by the school district, discomfort regarding working with unfamiliar individuals with regard to the child, and concerns about whether their child would actually receive needed services. The parents were also concerned about being excluded from the decision-making process and losing control over their child's daily activities. Hanline suggests that a major goal for professionals working with parents during a transition should be to help them to identify actual and potential problems and assist them in carrying out the task of solving or mitigating those problems.

Transition between School-Age Programs

The transition between school-age programs, as with all transitions, impacts on both the child and the family. The secure, protected environment of the segregated classroom is difficult to leave behind. Hanline and Halvorsen (1989) interviewed the parents of fourteen children with disabilities in an effort to evaluate the support they received during the child's transition to an integrated educational placement from a segregated special education setting. Prior to the transition, the parents reported concerns about their child's safety, the nonaccepting attitudes of the regular teachers and students, a decrease in program quality, transportation problems, lack of district commitment to the integration of students with disabilities, and the child's potential failure in the new environment. After the child's integration into the less restrictive program, however, the parents reported several positive changes. The primary benefit they cited was the child's skill enhancement, including their child's demonstration of more appropriate social skills. Parents were pleased that their child was developing friendships with nonidentified peers which often extended beyond school hours. In addition, the parents reported that their personal expectations for their child had risen. The brothers and sisters of the children with disabilities reported that they were less concerned about their responsibilities for the long-term care of their brother or sister with the disability.

According to the parents interviewed by Hanline and Halvorsen, the transition to the less restrictive environment was facilitated by parent representation on planning teams and observations of model integrated school settings. Parents reported that it was helpful to link up with other parents and consistently communicate with special and regular education personnel involved with the child and family.

Another strategy for easing the transition to less restrictive settings is referred to by its developers as "exit assistance" (George & Lewis, 1991). This strategy involves four stages which allow special educators and parents to make data-based decisions about readiness to move to less restrictive settings. In the first phase, long-range planning must take place. George and Lewis contend that at the initial IEP meeting, in which the child enters special educational services, goals, and objectives that address the reasons for the student's placement into special education should be included. Academic and behavioral issues that must be addressed for the child to be successful in less restrictive placements should serve as long-range student goals.

When the student begins to achieve the goals that address issues related to the restrictiveness of his or her placement, pre-exit activities may begin. In this phase, three steps should be completed. First, the materials, setting, schedule, student evaluation, behavioral management, and student responsibilities of the less restrictive setting should be assessed. In the next step of this phase, the special educator approximates the requirements of the new, less restrictive setting in the student's current, supported placement. As the student becomes successful, the third step, the assessment of the student's readiness, takes place. In this step the academic and behavioral skills the student is demonstrating should be compared with those of his or her peers in the less restrictive setting.

Children learn to interact with each other if given the opportunity.

The third phase, the transition itself, involves final preparations for the student, staff, and parents to deal successfully with the change. During the IEP meeting, decisions should be made about the types of accommodations, adaptations, and support services needed. George and Lewis suggest an "exit coordinator" be appointed to ensure that the required activities and services take place. Finally, in the follow-up and evaluation phase, information is gathered on the student's performance in the new setting. Consultative services are delivered as necessary, and a gradual reduction of teacher support takes place.

Generalization   One issue that has emerged with regard to the transition of students between school-based programs is the generalization of skills and behaviors from one environment to another. **Generalization** refers to the individual's ability to apply a skill learned in one setting to another setting. The value of interventions in more restrictive environments is lost if the skills and behaviors learned in that environment are not generalized to the new environment (Brown, Kiraly, & McKinnon, 1979). Skills and behaviors learned in special education settings are frequently highly individualized and completed independently. Skills learned in this manner may not transfer to group instructional settings such as the regular classroom (Bauer & Shea, 1989). To be successful in the less restrictive environment of the regular classroom, students need to learn to interact positively with others, obey class rules, and display proper work habits (Salend & Lutz, 1984). The lack of these behaviors, less evident in the more restrictive environment of the special education classroom with fewer children and vigilant special education teachers, may be very apparent in the less restrictive setting of the regular classroom. Plans should be implemented to facilitate the generalization of skills learned in the more restrictive environment to the less restrictive environment.

Transition from School to Community

In the transition from school life to adult life in the community, there are many challenges that confront young adults with disabilities. According to Rusch and Phelps (1987), the general public first became aware of the challenges confronting these young adults following World War I when thousands of American veterans with physical disabilities were found to require assistance in their effort to return to the workforce. In 1918, the first vocational rehabilitation act became law. This law provided assistance to veterans with disabilities and translation services for individuals with visual impairments. During the 1920s and 1930s programs such as the Civilian Conservation Corps (CCC) were implemented to provide employment opportunities to youth, many of whom were mildly disabled. In the 1950s work-study programs were instituted to assist individuals with mild disabilities.

A major event in the history of the United States was the **Civil Rights Act of 1964,** which banned discrimination in education on the grounds of race, ethnic origin, or religion. During the 1970s nondiscrimination assurances were extended to individuals with disabilities. The **Vocational Education Act of 1963,** as amended in 1968 and 1976, set aside 10 percent of the funds allocated to vocational education for programs for persons with disabilities. The **Perkins Vocational Education Act of 1973** included a major emphasis on services for individuals with severe disabilities. In addition, the Perkins Act mandated that the states improve services by requiring client involvement in the design and delivery of vocational rehabilitation services.

In the 1983 amendment to the **Education of the Handicapped Act** (Public Law 98–199), Congress sought to address directly the major educational and employment transition difficulties confronting young adults in special education services. The United States Office of Special Education and Rehabilitation Services was authorized to spend $6.6 million annually in grants and contracts to strengthen and coordinate education, training, and related services to assist youth with disabilities in the transition to post-secondary education, competitive employment, or adult services.

In Public Law 101–476, the **Individuals with Disabilities Education Act,** "transition services" were mandated for the movement of individuals with disabilities from school to post-school, including post-secondary education, vocational training, integrated employment (including supported employment), continuing and adult education, adult services, and independent living or community participation. Transition services were based on individual needs, preferences, and interests. Individualized Education Programs prepared for individuals 16 years of age, and in some cases younger, must include a transition service plan. The transition place must be designed to include instruction, community experiences, the development of employment and other post-school adult living objectives, and, when appropriate, acquisition of daily living skills and functional vocational evaluation (see Chapter 3 for an example of a transition plan). The law authorized "rehabilitation counseling" and "social work services" to facilitate the transition process. Finally, the law provided for and authorized interagency responsibilities or linkages with appropriate community and adult services before the individual with disabilities leaves school.

Secondary School Programming and the Least Restrictive Environment   Edgar (1987) reports on two trends that have prompted criticism of current secondary school programs for individuals with mild disabilities. First, salary data indicates that only 18 percent of the individuals with mild disabilities who were studied earn more than minimum wage, and, if individuals with learning disabilities and behavioral disorders were removed from the sample, only 5 percent of this population were making more than the minimum wage. Second, special education students are more likely to drop out of school than were their regular class peers. In addition, students with learning disabilities and behavioral disorders drop out of school more frequently than do their disabled peers and make poorer use of post-secondary school educational opportunities.

Increased academic standards for graduation from high school challenges inclusion.

Edgar suggests that the least restrictive environment concept, currently in broad use in special education, has translated into high levels of mainstreaming in secondary education programs. Though the practice of mainstreaming was questioned when originally suggested, it appears to be effective because academic education is the core of most secondary special education programs.

The current "excellence in education" movement in the United States has resulted in increased academic standards and consideration of proficiency tests for graduation from high school. Even a cursory glance at secondary special education curriculum indicates the curriculum is nonfunctional as it relates to the goals of secondary special education. Edgar suggests that a radical shift in curriculum is needed if it is to serve the needs of secondary special education students. The curriculum must focus on functional, vocational, and independent living skills.

In addition to the content of the secondary curriculum for individuals with disabilities, concern has been expressed regarding the manner in which functional activities are conducted. Chadsey-Rusch (1990), in her observational study, found that students with disabilities typically (a) were more involved in task-related than nontask-related interactions; (b) engaged in more interactions with teachers than with peers; (c) engaged in interactions that were similar across contexts, rather than a wide range of social contacts characteristic of those which occur in the community; and (d) were dependent on contrived or extra cues and feedback from the teachers or trainers in their vocational settings to facilitate performance. Chadsey-Rusch argues that teachers need to increase the frequency of nontask interactions among secondary school students and consciously decrease the frequency of directions and praise. More interactions are needed with nondisabled peers to encourage interactions with nonidentified individuals after leaving the special education setting.

The Transition from School to Work   The emphasis in intervention programs for youth in transition from school to adult life is frequently on "finding a job." Neubert, Tilson, and Iancone (1989), however, argue that transition outcomes should be viewed in terms of economic self-sufficiency, not simply as an individual's ability to access an initial job. In their study, Neubert and associates found that during the first 3 months of employment, 74 percent of the individuals experienced problems that necessitated the intervention of a staff member. During the first year of employment over one-half of the participants changed jobs and requested additional assistance. It is evident that the outcome of the transition from school to adult life should be viewed in terms of obtaining a job, keeping a job, and becoming a self-sufficient adult member of the community.

Objective Two: To describe strategies for facilitating transitions.

Strategies to Facilitate Transitions

Transition from School to Post-secondary Education and Training

Youth with disabilities participate in post-secondary education and training programs at only one-fourth the rate of their nonidentified peers and at only one-third the rate of economically disadvantaged youth (Fairweather & Shaver, 1991), yet a major factor in the transition from high school to adulthood is access to and success in post-secondary training. Only a small proportion of youth with disabilities—those with speech, visual, hearing, or health impairments—are more likely than their nonidentified peers to receive additional training after high school. Even among those who receive a high school diploma (in contrast to a certificate of attendance or other indicator of participation in but not completion of high school content area units required for graduation), participation remains far less likely than that of nonidentified peers.

It is evident from this discussion that there is a need for a plan or strategy to enhance an individual's transition to a new environment. For children moving from an early intervention or preschool program to a school-based program, a transition plan is required as a part of the Individualized Family Service Plan mandated in Public Law 99–457. As previously discussed, the Individuals with Disabilities Education Act (Public Law 101–476) mandates "transition services," and a transition plan must be included in the IEP for learners 16 years of age, and in some cases, as young as 14 years of age. According to Wolery (1989), the literature indicates that carefully planned transitions are essential to (a) ensure continuity of services; (b) minimize disruptions to the family system by facilitating the family's adjustment to the changes that occur; and (c) ensure that children are prepared to function in the receiving program.

In a national survey of 1,549 local educational agencies, stratified by enrollment, geographic region, and socioeconomic status, Fairweather (1989) found that more than 50 percent of the agencies provided at least one of four vocational programs: counseling, vocational education, occupational/physical therapy, or vocational rehabilitation. Less than one percent of the agencies, however, had some type of transition program, and only one-third had a staff member whose main function was to help students find employment. Fairweather found that the size of the local educational agency was strongly related to the likelihood that secondary-aged students with disabilities would have vocational preparation programs available to them. Students in large districts are more likely to have access to vocational preparation programs than are students in smaller districts. Transition-oriented programs directed essentially at assisting students with disabilities to find employment, enroll in post-secondary educational programs, and live independently in the community are uncommon.

In a follow-up report, Fairweather, Stearns, and Wagner (1990) write that the opportunities for special education students in transition-related programs are influenced by the size of the district and wealth of the community. These findings may have significance because transition-oriented programs tested on a few students in a limited number of locations may not be replicable in other settings. The writers suggest that program requirements should take into account variations in opportunities by type of district in which the student resides.

There are several roles special educators and parents fulfill in order to optimize the transition process (Everson & Moon, 1987). Special educators should be responsible for:

- organizing and attending meetings related to planning the transition.
- coordinating the development and implementation of the transition plan.
- identifying the need to refer and ensuring referral to other appropriate agencies and services.
- ensuring parent, family, and student participation in transition planning and implementation processes.

To optimize the process, parents should be responsible for:

- attending meetings related to planning the transition.
- providing information on the needs of the family and the individual, as well as the responsibilities the family is able and willing to assume.
- focusing the team's planning on individual student and family needs.
- providing informal home and community skill training and behavioral interventions that support the student's development.

Several barriers to effective planning and coordination of services may emerge including service fragmentation and duplication, unsystematic transition planning, and limited parental involvement (Johnson, Bruininks, & Thurlow, 1987). Johnson and associates contend that each educational system needs a coherent policy framework that incorporates greater consistency across programs in philosophy, goals, standards, and practices to guide the ongoing management of planning for transition.

Transition from Early Intervention and Preschool Programs

The goals of transition for infants and children are to provide a program that meets their needs more effectively and efficiently and minimizes the adjustment difficulties during the transition (Wolery, 1989). Transition planning for a move from an early intervention or preschool program to a school-based program should be initiated 6 to 12 months prior to the anticipated change in placement (McDonald, Kysela, Siebert, McDonald, & Chambers, 1989). Parents should be informed of the projected transitions and consulted as to how they would like to be involved in the process. In addition, the family should be assisted in planning for future environments and transitions beyond the change in placement presently under consideration. Finally, follow-up support services should be provided to the parents. McDonald and associates suggest a four-step process to facilitate the transition process. The steps are presented in Box 5.1.

An alternative transition process begins in the fall prior to the child's entrance into kindergarten and continues throughout the first term of kindergarten year (Diamond, Spiegel-McGill, & Hanrahan, 1988). This process is summarized in Box 5.2. During the preliminary planning phase, the child's IEP is written to reflect goals and objectives that will enable the child to enter the least restrictive environment during the upcoming kindergarten school year. During this phase, the parents are encouraged to observe kindergarten and preschool programs for nondisabled children. The observations will facilitate their development of a frame of reference for

---

Box 5.1

Transition Facilitation Process*

Step 1   Determine the time frame in collaboration with parents (minimum of 6 months prior to anticipated transition).

Step 2   Add specific transition goals and activities to the Individualized Family Service Plan or Individualized Education Program.

Step 3   Establish a time-line which includes activities for both parents and staff, such as visitations, observations, reviewing program descriptions.

Step 4   Provide follow-up services ■

* Adapted from McDonald, Kysela, Siebert, McDonald, and Chambers (1989).

Box 5.2

Phases in Preschool to Kindergarten Transition *

Phase	Time
Preliminary planning	One year prior to kindergarten entry
Initial contacts with accepting school district	November through February
Exploring placement options	February through June
Implementing the transition process	June through August
Follow-up in school district	First term in receiving kindergarten ■

* Adapted from Diamond, Spiegel-McGill, and Hanrahan (1988).

---

the discussions of their child's placement. A liaison person from the preschool who will monitor the transition process is identified. A liaison person is responsible for assisting the parents in efforts to gain information about placement options, accessing services in the community, and the transition process itself.

The second phase in the transition process involves making the initial contact with the school district in which the child will be served. The contact is made through a referral to the school district's child study team. At this time, it is helpful to conduct a parent conference to discuss the child's current functioning and the parents' expectations for school placement. This conference may evolve into a series of meetings to help the parents develop realistic expectations for their child and the placement. Members of the child study team may begin informal contact with the preschool or early intervention program to familiarize themselves with the child and the environment. Assessment information appropriate for planning the transition are provided to both parents and child study team members.

The third phase of the transition planning process suggested by Diamond and associates involves the exploration of placement options. A meeting is conducted with a member of the child study team who recommends various programs for parents' consideration. Parents are encouraged to visit the recommended programs. At this time, if not prior to it, the parents must be informed of their legal rights under both state and federal law, and these rights must be explained to them. Finally, in this phase, the child study team meets to recommend an appropriate placement by developing, and then writing, an IEP.

Before the end of the child's final preschool year and during the summer, the public school teacher makes visits to the preschool and the child visits the school and program he or she will attend. Preschool records and parent information are provided to the receiving program so that the child will be "ready to go" as soon as the school year begins. The final phase, follow-up, takes place throughout the first term of the school year. Through follow-up, early intervention of preschool program personnel demonstrates a continuing commitment to the child and the family. During the follow-up, the parents are provided assistance, if needed.

Transition between School-Based Settings

When addressing the issues of transitions between school-based programs, two factors must be considered: (a) the transition decision, which must match the student's needs to the new environment, and (b) obtaining services needed to facilitate the transition.

Making the Transition Decision   Students entering new, less restrictive educational settings generally confront increased class size, less individual attention, a more rapid instructional pace, and different evaluation standards from those they have experienced in the special education setting. Wood and Miederhoff (1989) explain that there is a need to compare the characteristics of the original setting with the setting into which the student is moving. To facilitate this comparison they developed a transition checklist which includes three subsections: (a) requirements for functioning successfully in the classroom, (b) requirements for successful interpersonal and social relations, and (c) requirements for functioning in related environments. The classroom subsection includes consideration of physical and instructional variables, dominant teaching techniques, materials, content, and evaluation strategies. In the interpersonal and social relations subsection, consideration is given to student interactions, dress and appearance, and attitudes. In the section on related environments, the student's ability to self-manage in the cafeteria, during physical education, and in specialized classes such as art and music are assessed. The characteristics of the more inclusive setting are compared with the student's present functioning to determine in which areas the student needs assistance and instruction to function successfully in the new setting.

Services to Facilitate the Transition   Adamson, Matthews, and Schuller (1990) propose five procedures to bridge the gap between special education services and the regular education classroom program. These services are consultation, collaborative teaching/co-teaching, structured recess, work completion groups, and contract checkouts.

During consultation, the special educator assists the general educator in the selection of methods and techniques designed to assist the student. The special educator models the methods or techniques and facilitates and monitors their implementation by the general educator. In addition, the special educator assists the general educator in obtaining, adapting, and supplementing instructional materials, evaluating selected methods or techniques, developing other techniques if the selected ones are ineffective, and providing positive reinforcement to the general educator. In collaborative teaching/co-teaching, the special educator serves as a model for the general educator, engaging in collaborative planning for implementation of specific strategies that may have been used previously by either

And Baby Makes Controversy
A couple breaks new ground for disabled parents

Natalie Earl is only 5 weeks old, but one day, like most kids, she'll probably ask her parents how they met. It was 1978, Leigh and Bill Earl might tell her, at a nursing home in Grand Rapids, Mich. They were 15. They had cerebral palsy and they lived there.

In recent years, through advances in technology, changing social attitudes and new legislation, people with severe handicaps have achieved independence unimaginable a generation ago. Both the Earls went to college. In 1988, they moved to an East Lansing apartment, assisted 17 hours a week by social-service aides. Though unemployed (Bill is looking for a job), they were a model, mainstream couple.

All that changed last year, when Leigh got pregnant and decided not to have an abortion. Who, concerned friends asked, would care for the child? The Earls were convinced that, with some extra help from the aides, they could. "All we're asking for," says Bill, "is a chance to have a family." As soon as she became pregnant, Leigh says, she started asking Ingham County Department of Social Services (DSS) exactly what they would provide but never got an answer. It took Mark Cody, an attorney from a nonprofit advocacy agency, to discover that, since the Earls didn't work outside the home, they didn't qualify for state-funded child care. (By then, Leigh was in her seventh month.) Since Leigh delivered a healthy daughter on May 5, volunteer nannies have moved in to help. The DSS aides who come to the Earls' home aren't permitted to help at all, even to pick the baby up. Natalie's parents cannot lift or bathe her, but Leigh is able, with assistance, to breast-feed. "The system has not been set up to handle this kind of a case that is so different," says DSS spokesman Chuck Peller. "It's just not equipped."

Many Americans with disabilities are deciding that if they can live and work in the mainstream, they can also have children. But if they need extra child care, who pays? If the state does, says Janet Strope, DSS director for Ingham County, there are bound to be problems. Any parents with some sort of impairment, as well as parents who abuse drugs or their kids, "could keep their children if we would provide someone in the home 24 hours a day. That carries it to an extreme, but we would then have to draw a line as to when we would provide [help] and when we wouldn't. That would be very, very difficult to do." The Earls are willing to challenge the state. "What Bill and Leigh are doing is really breaking new ground for people with severe disabilities to be parents," says Marsha Morse, a project coordinator at United Cerebral Palsy of Michigan. "There currently are no programs that support people with disabilities to do parenting." She thinks Bill and Leigh "deserve the opportunity to try. They can be parents, but not in the traditional role." In the last 20 years, the definition of family has changed radically. Clearly, it's also time to rethink the definition of parent ■

Katrine Ames with Frank Washington and Nichole Christian in East Lansing

of the educators. The teachers may choose to team teach, divide the class into two groups for instruction, teach small groups, or engage in individual instruction.

The third strategy, structured recess, is implemented to help students to learn appropriate game playing, self-structuring, that is, the skills needed to organize themselves for play, the use of time, skills for coping with difficulties, and appropriate interaction with peers. As the structured recess program progresses over time, the external supports, provided by the teacher, are faded as the students increase their skills and ability to play independently. The next strategy, work completion groups, is a daily 30-minute work period used to monitor student performance. During the work completion period, the regular educator sends the special student to the resource room to work on incomplete classroom assignments. Students who have completed their assignments may be sent to the resource room for a reinforcement period. The final strategy, the daily checkout, is implemented to monitor student-teacher contingency contracts or agreements. For example, the student may have an agreement (a contract) with the teacher to complete an

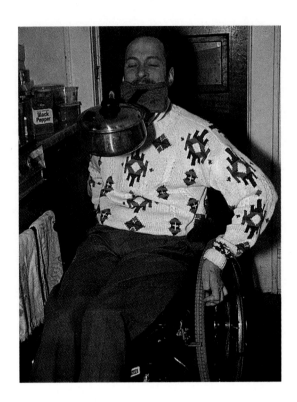

Educational plans should enable persons'
life-skill goals and objectives.

assignment during reading class. The teacher checks the assignment and provides an
agreed-upon reward. The checkout period is used to evaluate progress on the contract and distribute reinforcers for appropriate work and behavior. A daily checkout
form may be used to report performance to parents and concerned teachers.

Transition to Work and Community

Individual transition planning is necessary to increase the access of students
enrolled in high school programs to community services (McDonnell, Wilcox, &
Boles, 1986). Planning for the transition into the community must begin early in the
student's high school career and focus on the development of the skills, opportunities, and services that will be necessary to support the individual in the community.
The writers suggest that transition activities should be a part of the IEP and should
culminate during the last year of high school with a formal plan that identifies
and establishes the specific services required to meet the individual's needs upon
graduation.

Goals of the transition plan for the move from school to community should be
very broad, such as (a) to learn what transition is and why it is important to the
family; (b) to identify the information and skills needed by the family for transition
into the new program; (c) to identify the transitions that will take place during the
next 5 years (Lazzari & Kilgo, 1989). Planning for transition from school to work
must occur 3 to 5 years prior to the time at which the student leaves school.

D'Alonzo, Owen, and Hartwell (1985) suggest several goals appropriate for
the transition of young adults as they approach departure from school-based programs. First, the educational plans should address the development of appropriate
life-skill educational goals and objectives. Second, employment seeking and

maintenance skills should be emphasized as well as community survival skills training. In addition, transition plans should provide for supervised on-site employment training. Support should be provided to special and regular educators as they address transition issues with students. Finally, the plan should address increased collaboration between community agencies and special education as well as vocational education and special education.

Three transition preparation stages may be designed to meet goals, such as suggested by D'Alonzo and associates (Wehman, Kregal, & Barcus, 1985). First, school instruction is presented to the student. Second, the transition plan is developed, and third, the student is placed in meaningful employment, which is the desired final outcome of the transition.

Summary

In this chapter, the mesosystem and the transitions learners with disabilities make during their educational careers were discussed. Bronfenbrenner's three steps in the transition process, intersetting relationships, family system reorganization, and changes among the learners' various environments, were reviewed.

The literature and research on transitions from early childhood intervention and preschool programs to school-based programs, between school-based programs, and from school programs to adult life in the community were presented. We noted, in agreement with Ferguson and associates, that a typical transition is more appropriately described as three distinct, simultaneous transitions: a bureaucratic transition, a family life transition, and a status transition.

Transitions between early intervention and preschool programs to school-based programs may be the most abrupt and permanent break with past experiences that the child makes before leaving home as an adult. This transition has a direct effect on the family in terms of schedules, transportation, support services, and communication strategies between home and school. The transition between school-age programs can be facilitated by parent observations and participation in planning. Generalization of skills plays an important role in transitions between programs.

The transition from school to community presents unique challenges to the learner and family. Tension exists between academic and functional curricula for learners in secondary programs. The transition from school to work should be viewed as a transition towards self-sufficiency, not merely "finding a job."

In the final section of the chapter, attention was focused on specific strategies for facilitating transitions between various environments. Emphasis was placed on the need for long-range planning and collaboration among the student with disabilities, parents, family members, special educators, and social agency personnel. The role of the special educator and the parents in transition planning and implementation were discussed. Specific strategies for planning and implementing transitions from early childhood intervention and preschool programs to school-based programs, between school programs, and from school programs to adult life in the community were presented.

In the next chapter, we continue the discussion of the social systems contexts in which learners with disabilities develop by focusing attention on family and community issues in contemporary society. We discuss family issues which impact on child development, the impact of substitute care on development, juvenile delinquency, and the effects of poverty on children.

References

Adamson, D. R., Matthews, P., & Schuller, J. (1990). Five ways to bridge the resource-room-to-regular-classroom gap. *Teaching Exceptional Children, 22* (2), 74–78.

Bauer, A. M. , & Shea, T. M. (1989). *Teaching exceptional students in your classroom.* Boston: Allyn & Bacon.

Bronfenbrenner, U. (1986). Ecology of the family as a context for human development: Research perspectives. *Developmental Psychology, 22*, 723–742.

Brown, L., Kiraly, Jr., J., & McKinnon, A. (1979). Resource rooms: Some aspects for special educators to ponder. *Journal of Learning Disabilities, 12*, 56–58.

Chadsey-Rusch, J. (1990). Social interactions of secondary-aged students with severe handicaps: Implications for facilitating the transition from school to work. *The Journal of the Association for Persons with Severe Handicaps, 15* (2), 69–78.

D'Alonzo, B. J., Owen, S. D., & Hartwell, L. K. (1985). Transition models: An overview of the current state of the art. *Techniques, 1* (6), 429–436.

Diamond, K. E., Spiegel-McGill, P., & Hanrahan, P. (1988). Planning for school transition: An ecological-developmental approach. *Journal for the Division of Early Childhood, 11*, 245–253.

Edgar, E. (1987). Secondary programs in special education: Are many of them justifiable? *Exceptional Children, 53*, 555–561.

Everson, J. M., & Moon, M. S. (1987). Transition services for young adults with severe disabilities: Defining professional and parental roles and responsibilities. *The Journal of the Association for Persons with Severe Handicaps, 12* (2), 87–95.

Fairweather, J. S. (1989). Transition and other services for handicapped students in local education agencies. *Exceptional Children, 55*, 315–320.

Fairweather, J. S., & Shaver, D. M. (1991). Making the transition to postsecondary education and training. *Exceptional Children, 57* (3), 264–270.

Fairweather, J. S., Stearns, M. S., & Wagner, M. M. (1990). Resources available in school districts serving secondary special education students: Implications for transition. *The Journal of Special Education, 22* (4), 419–432.

Ferguson, P. H., Ferguson, D., & Jones, D. (1988). Generalizations of hope: Parental perspectives on the transitions of their children with severe retardation from school to adult life. *The Journal of the Association for Persons with Severe Handicaps, 13* (3), 177–187.

George, N. L., & Lewis, T. J. (1991). EASE: Exit assistance for special educators—helping students make the transition. *Teaching Exceptional Children, 23* (2), 34–39.

Hanline, M. F. (1988). Making the transition to preschool: Identification of parent needs. *Journal of the Division for Early Childhood, 12*, 98–107.

Hanline, M. F., & Halvorsen, A. (1989). Parent perceptions of the integration transition process: Overcoming artificial barriers. *Exceptional Children, 55* (6), 487–492.

ICD (1986). *Survey of disabled Americans: Bringing disabled Americans into the mainstream: A nationwide survey of 1,000 disabled people.* New York: International Center for the Disabled.

Johnson, D. R., Bruininks, R. H., & Thurlow, M. L. (1987). Meeting the challenge of transition service planning through improved interagency cooperation. *Exceptional Children, 543*, 522–530.

Lazzari, A. M., & Kilgo, J. L. (1989). Practical methods for supporting parents in early transitions. *Teaching Exceptional Children, 22* (1), 40–43.

McDonald, L., Kysela, G. M., Siebert, P., McDonald, S., & Chambers, J. (1989). Parent perspectives: Transition to preschool. *Teaching Exceptional Children, 22* (1), 4–9.

McDonnell, J., Wilcox, B., & Boles, S. M. (1986). Do we know enough to plan for transition? A national survey of state agencies responsible for services to persons with severe handicaps. *The Journal of the Association of Persons with Severe Handicaps, 11* (1), 53–60.

Mithaug, D., Horiuchi, C., & Fanning, P. (1985). A report on the Colorado statewide follow-up survey of special education students. *Exceptional Children, 51*, 397–404.

National Council on the Handicapped (1986). *Towards independence*. Washington, DC: Author.

Neubert, D. A., Tilson, G. P., & Iancone, R. N. (1989). Postsecondary transition needs and employment patterns of individuals with mild disabilities. *Exceptional Children, 55*, 494–500.

Rusch, F. R., & Phelps, L. A. (1987). Secondary special education and transition from school to work: A national priority. *Exceptional Children, 53*, 487–492.

Salend, S. J., & Lutz, G. L. (1984). Mainstreaming or mainlining: A competency based approach to mainstreaming. *Journal of Learning Disabilities, 17* (1), 27–29.

Smith, B. J., & Strain, P. (1988). Early childhood special education in the next decade: Implementing and expanding PL 99–457. *Topics in Early Childhood Special Education, 8* (1), 37–47.

Turnbull, A., & Turnbull, R. (1986). *Families, professionals and exceptionality: A special partnership*. Columbus, OH: Merrill.

U.S. Department of Education (1983). SSA publishes major work disability survey. *Programs for the Handicapped, 1*, 7–8.

Wehman, P. H., Kregel, J., & Barcus, J. M. (1985). School to work: Vocational transition for handicapped youth. In P. Wehman & J. H. Hewitt (Eds.), *Competitive employment for persons with mental retardation: From research to practice*. Richmond, VA: Commonwealth.

Wolery, M. (1989). Transitions in early childhood special education: Issues and procedures. *Focus on Exceptional Children, 22* (2), 1–15.

Wood, J. W., & Miederhoff, J. W. (1989). Bridging the gap. *Teaching Exceptional Children, 21* (2), 66–68.

Chapter

6

Family and Community Issues in Contemporary Society

*O*bjectives

After completing this chapter you will be able to:

1. describe the impact of divorce on the learner's development.
2. describe the impact of child abuse, neglect, and maltreatment on the learner's development.
3. describe the impact of substitute care on the learner's development.
4. describe the issue of learners raised in poverty.
5. describe the effects of prenatal drug and alcohol exposure on the learner's development.

*K*ey Words and Phrases

Adoption Assistance and Child Welfare Act of 1980
child abuse
Child Abuse Prevention and Treatment Act of 1974
child maltreatment

child neglect
fetal alcohol syndrome
foster care
possible fetal alcohol effect
prenatal drug and alcohol exposure
substitute care

● In 1979 there were 49.1 million married couples, and 49 percent of the women worked; in 1989 there were 52.3 million married couples, and 58 percent of the women worked.

● In one large metropolitan area, there was a 48 percent increase in the number of single parent families with children under 18 in the 10 years between 1980 and 1990.

● During the same 10-year period, there was also a 79 percent increase in the number of single male parent families with children under 18 years of age. (Summary statements of data presented by the University of Cincinnati Institute for Policy Research, 1991) ■

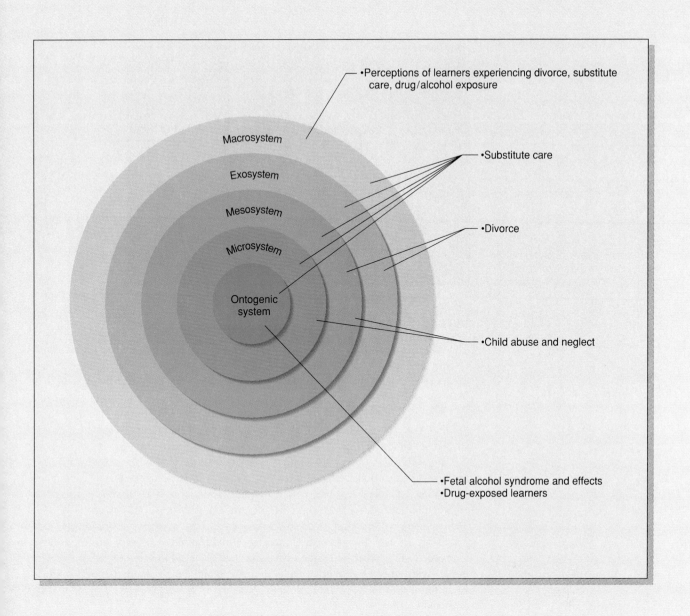

•Perceptions of learners experiencing divorce, substitute care, drug/alcohol exposure

Macrosystem

Exosystem

Mesosystem

Microsystem

Ontogenic system

•Substitute care

•Divorce

•Child abuse and neglect

•Fetal alcohol syndrome and effects
•Drug-exposed learners

Young mothers are more likely to have low-birth-weight infants with the potential for medical and developmental complications.

Introduction

The American family is no longer comprised of "mom, dad, and two children." During the past several decades, there have been significant and dramatic changes in family style and structure in America. These changes continue at the present and will continue into the foreseeable future. As a result of these changes and changes in contemporary society, many children are developing in environments that place them at risk for varying from their less-challenged peers and, thus in need of special education services.

Dubowitz, Newberger, Melnicoe, and Newberger (1988) discuss several factors that have caused changes in the American family: high incidence of divorce, adolescent parenthood, single parent families, formation of stepfamilies, maternal employment outside of the home, lack of child care services, and poverty. The frequency of divorce has increased to approximately one in every two marriages. It is generally agreed that divorce generates considerable stress for children. The increase in adolescent parenthood has increased the number of low-birth-weight infants whose birth frequently results in medical and developmental complications. In addition, the increase in adolescent parenthood has increased infant mortality rates and family instability.

Dubowitz and associates also discuss the single parent family. If the current trend in single parent families continues, nearly 60 percent of all children born in 1982 will spend at least 1 year of their life living in a single parent home before they reach the age of 18. Single parent households, particularly those headed by a female, are at a significant economic disadvantage. Families headed by women are likely to be poor. In addition, children living in single parent families have been found to be at greater risk for maltreatment than children from two parent families. Being raised in a single parent household places the children at risk for stress and may impact on the children's future educational accomplishments and economic status.

Concurrent with the increase in divorce is an increase in the number of stepfamilies. Dubowitz and associates suggest that each year one-half million adults become stepparents. Researchers have reported conflicting results in studies of children raised in stepfamilies. This family arrangement is not necessarily negative, especially if an absent parent is replaced and the remaining biological parent gains the love and support he or she needs and if the family's economic difficulties are alleviated. However, in all probability, the children will remain divided between their loyalty to the biological parent and the stepparent.

Due to financial need, increased societal pressure to attain career satisfaction and achievement in the workplace, and desire by women for greater involvement with and autonomy in the world at large, maternal employment outside of the home has increased significantly in recent decades. No direct causal relationship between the mother working outside of the home and particular child problems has been established. The quality and consistency of child care during infancy and early childhood may be a more valid predictor of the child's development than whether or not the mother works outside of the home. Children of mothers employed outside of the home have a less rigid stereotypic perception of the female sex role. This is true, particularly, if their mother performs work that has not been traditionally associated with the female sex role. In addition, maternal employment has been shown to be beneficial for adolescent sons and daughters because it provides a positive model for them.

Dubowitz and associates report several other factors that consistently confront families in contemporary society. There is a shortage of quality and affordable child care services and uncertainty surrounding the effects of raising children in substitute care settings, such as an infant or child care center. The nation's low birthrate and the increase in the child mortality rate are significantly correlated with poverty. There is a dramatic increase in the number of homeless families in America, and homelessness generates enormous stress and special health and psychological vulnerabilities in children.

Objective One: To describe the impact of divorce on the learner's development.

The Impact of Divorce

When individuals end a marriage through divorce, they do so in the hope of improving the quality of life for themselves and their children. Wallerstein and Blakeslee (1989), in an extensive study of families 10 years following a divorce, report several issues that had an impact on child development. They describe several differences between the impact of divorce and other life crises such as death, illness, and unemployment. Divorce more often involves anger, which may be expressed physically or verbally, or both. Rather than striving to ensure their children's safety and emotional security, parents in the process of seeking a divorce frequently give priority to their adult problems. This diminishes their capacity to parent. In addition, during the process of divorce, the usual social supports available to parents and children are less available because relatives and friends tend to withdraw from the conflict occurring within the family.

According to Guidubaldi and Perry (1985), divorce is the most pervasive severe psychological stressor for children. Wiehe (1984) studied sixty-two children, 9 to 14 years of age, who had experienced divorce in their families and sixty matched children who had not experienced divorce. He found that the children from divorced families had poorer social and academic skills and lower self-esteem, more negative attitudes towards both of their parents, and a more external locus of control, that is, they viewed personal life events as occurring outside of their control.

The effects of divorce on the learner's development endures over time. In one study, children from divorced families were found, 2 years after the divorce, to perform more poorly on a multifactored mental health index than their intact-family

Children with parents who have divorced may experience a loss of self-esteem and fewer social supports.

peers. This effect was more evident among boys than girls (Guidubaldi & Perry, 1985). Six years following divorce, children in divorced families encountered more negative life changes than did children from intact families. The boys demonstrated externalizing behavior problems, such as fighting or inappropriate language; the girls demonstrated internalizing behavior problems, such as withdrawal and depression. In addition, girls experienced more disruption than the boys when their parents remarried (Hetherington, Cox, & Cox, 1985). After 10 years, a significant number of adolescent and young adults remained burdened by vivid memories of the parents' divorce, feelings of sadness, resentment towards their parents, and a sense of being deprived of their childhood (Wallerstein, 1985).

Though divorce is common in contemporary society, social sanctions and the stereotyping of children of divorce continue to affect the children's development. Guttman, Geva, and Gefen (1988) found that the knowledge that a child's parents are divorced has an adverse effect on evaluations of the child's academic, social, and emotional functioning. The "child of divorce" stereotype was present in both teachers' and students' perceptions and became an organized theme in their perceptions of the child. The strongest effect was in the area of emotional disturbance, in that teachers assumed the child's problems arose from the parents' unfriendly divorce.

Wallerstein and Blakeslee (1989) describe a series of dilemmas present in contemporary society with regard to the frequency of divorce. Just because the parents are divorced does not necessarily mean that the child's psychological needs change. Family structures have become asynchronous with emotional needs. Rather than serving as an "oasis," a place where the individual can relax and repair, the home has become a place of significant stress. In addition, the economic burden of divorce is falling on women and children, with women with minor children experiencing, on the average, a 73 percent decline in their standard of living in the first year of divorce. Following a divorce, parent-child relationships are permanently altered.

In the conclusion of their 10-year study of families and divorce, Wallerstein and Blakeslee summarized the impact of divorce on children's development. Cooperative parenting by both parents, difficult in adoptive families, is vital to the child's proper development. The process of divorce results in a diminished capacity to parent which continues and permanently disrupts the child developmental process. New, unfamiliar parent-child relationships may develop in which the child is overburdened by responsibility for a parent's psychological welfare or by serving as an instrument of parental rage. Frequently, the children bear the psychological, economic, and moral brunt of the divorce.

Objective Two: To describe the impact of child abuse, neglect, and maltreatment on the learner's development.

The Impact of Maltreatment

In 1985, there were nearly two million official reports of child maltreatment made in the United States (American Humane Association, 1987). **Child maltreatment,** a term used to describe both abuse and neglect as well as their complex interactions, from a developmental organizational perspective is not a single or fixed incident, but rather ongoing transactions or patterns of behavior wherein the individuals involved reciprocally influence one another to cause disturbances in the caretaking process (Cicchetti, Toth, & Hennessy, 1989). Public Law 93–247, the **Child Abuse Prevention and Treatment Act,** which became law in 1974, uses the terms **child abuse** and **child neglect** to refer to physical or mental injury, sexual abuse, or

Home should be a place where children can be safe, not a stressful setting that will damage them physically and mentally.

neglect of a child under the age of eighteen, by a person responsible for the child's welfare under circumstances which indicate that the child's health or welfare is harmed or threatened.

In an extensive review of the literature on the effects of child maltreatment on child development, Youngblade and Belsky (1989) conclude that child maltreatment is associated with dysfunctional parent-child relations, as evidenced by the children's increased likelihood of forming, during infancy, an insecure attachment for the maltreating parent. In addition, they concluded that the effects of child maltreatment are not limited to familial relations, as there are repeated indications that maltreatment is associated with dysfunctional peer relations.

In a detailed description of the effects of child maltreatment on children's development, Cicchetti, Toth, and Hennessy (1989) report that the formation of a secure attachment relationship with the primary caregiver(s) during the first year of life is one of the most important developmental tasks of infancy. During this critical period, children who have sensitive caregivers come to view themselves as acceptable and lovable, whereas children with insensitive and/or irresponsible caregivers learn to see themselves as unacceptable and unlovable. Children who have not developed an attachment with a primary caregiver may display a preoccupation with attachment concerns that may interfere with their ability to adapt to the preschool environment.

Cicchetti and associates found that as early as 30 months of age, maltreated children use proportionately fewer words to describe their internal psychological states than did their nonmaltreated peers. In older elementary school students, maltreatment is reflected in a negative self-image which leaves students feeling less competent and less academically motivated than their peers. Children who have been maltreated exhibit more avoidance and aggressive behavior towards peers. They exhibit limited social skills and a greater frequency of withdrawal. As a group, these children are more anxious, inattentive, and apathetic than other children and rely more heavily on teachers for encouragement and approval.

Crittenden (1989) discusses a combination of deficits and distortions in the development of maltreated children that can be expected to affect both their class-room behavior and academic achievement. Maltreated children often exhibit disruptive, defiant, bullying aggression which results in interpersonal confrontations with peers and teachers. Defiant abused children appear to spend too much time fighting to learn well. Or, maltreated children may become so compliant and overly concerned with meeting others' standards that they rarely experience the joy of discovery or the satisfaction of achievement. Over-compliant abused children are so concerned with finding the right answer that they are frequently unable to attend to and manipulate ideas and concepts.

The underlying issues for all maltreated children are predictability and control in their life. It is generally agreed that most maltreated children have experienced unpredictable and uncontrollable environments (Crittenden, 1989). Crittenden describes the following hierarchy of needs of maltreated children. These children need to learn:

1. To predict events in their environment; without this skill they cannot organize their behavior.
2. To achieve their desired objectives in socially appropriate ways.
3. To communicate openly with others and use developmentally appropriate cognitive and language skills.
4. To develop trust through carefully regulated, unambiguous, and consistent affective experiences.
5. To develop the self-confidence, self-motivation, and self-control necessary to enjoy and benefit from the intellectual stimulation of education programs.

There is a broad range of transaction patterns that occur among parents and children. In their work at the Marlborough Family Service Agency, Asen, George, Piper, and Stevens (1989) found that the identification of the typical pattern of abuse was a helpful first step in planning the management of families engaged in physical abuse. They found a broad range of transaction patterns that occur among abusing parents and abused children: helpless and help-recruiting, professional, transgenerational, stand-in, distance-regulating, transferred, cultural, and denied. These patterns, which are described in detail in the remainder of this section, are not separate entities, and in many families more than one pattern can be identified. Those administering treatment, however, are encouraged to assume that one pattern predominates and treatment should focus on that pattern.

The first pattern Asen and associates describe is helpless and help-recruiting abuse. Families exhibiting this form of abuse appear to have a limited range of skills for dealing with everyday issues and thus resort to abuse. To help resolve the problems of abuse, those in the family's extended social systems contexts, for example, school personnel, relatives, and therapists, attempt to help the inexperienced family develop more appropriate ways of behaving. Repeated offers of help and its acceptance by the family may lead to a situation wherein the helper, knowingly or unknowingly, becomes involved in the problem of abuse to a point of

Brothers Would Like to Live Together

Matthew, 8, Jason, 7, and Adam, 3, are bright, lively brothers who are looking forward to being reunited in a new family.

Matthew and Adam have been together in one foster home for more than two years; Jason is in another foster home, but sees his brothers often. When they get together, they may squabble a bit, but they're still glad to see each other, their caseworker, Carla Winning, says.

In their birth home, Matthew had responsibilities beyond his years, Winning says, and this probably accounts for him being the most serious of the three. He still tries to look out for his brothers' well being.

Matthew enjoys school

Matthew's in third grade now. He enjoys school and gets along well with teachers and classmates.

He's an excellent reader who likes all of his subjects. His grades have slipped a bit this fall because he's thinking about adoption, but his foster mother expects his grades to improve when he's settled, if not before.

At home, he enjoys outdoor play—baseball, kickball, biking and climbing trees—as well as building with Legos and playing Nintendo. When Jason comes to visit, the boys frolic in a field nearby.

Matthew is well-mannered and respectful, and does his chores well when reminded. "He's a great little boy," says his foster mom. "I wouldn't change anything about him. He's a pleasure to be around."

Adam learns quickly

When Adam moved into his foster home, he was old enough to be walking and talking, but he did neither because of neglect in his birth home. But with love and stimulation, he caught up fast.

He talks well, rides a two-wheeler with training wheels, plays outdoor games with the bigger boys and has learned to swim. He also can dress himself and almost can tie his shoes.

The challenge now, says his foster mom, is keeping up with his curiosity. "He gets into things because his mind is just working all the time."

Because there are no other little ones around for him to play with, he goes to preschool now, and is thriving there.

His teacher showed each child seven objects on a plate for a short time recently and then hid the objects and asked the child to name them. Adam got all seven right two different times, his foster mom said proudly.

Not long ago, when a grown foster sister got a blister on her foot, he chided her gently, saying, "Sissy, if you wore socks, that wouldn't have happened."

Adam is mildly allergic to chocolate and also has some hay fever symptoms and a history of ear infections. His doctor is considering removing Adam's tonsils when he is 5 or so.

Making his bed, picking up his toys and pushing the vacuum sweeper are Adam's favorite chores.

Jason likes to make things

Jason is a lot like both his brothers in personality and interests, his foster mom says.

He is in second grade and also likes school, reads well and gets good grades. He shares their enthusiasm for Nintendo and Legos, as well as outdoor sports and games.

His special interest is in making things—especially holiday cards and notes for those he cares about. "He's so thoughtful," his foster mom adds. "On Saturdays, he sometimes writes out a menu, takes my order and brings me breakfast.

"He's a very caring, giving, sharing little boy. He had no qualms about sharing his room and toys" when a younger foster child moved into the home.

He's a bit worried about adoption, his foster mom says, but she believes he will adapt well.

A two-parent home with no other young children, at least for now, is Winning's goal for the boys. She would prefer residents of a small town or rural area, but would consider any family that has enough space for the boys to run and play.

They will need a family that can provide both love and structure. They also may need to remain in counseling for a while after placement ■

Reprinted with permission of *The Indianapolis Star.*

assuming parenting responsibilities. As a consequence, the outside help becomes a problem in itself. Such families, then, require additional help to decrease their dependency on the helping relationship.

The second pattern of abuse, described by Asen and associates, is professional abuse. In this pattern, the professional becomes overinvolved in the family's problem and assumes parenting duties. As a general rule in helping relationships, professionals work with an individual or family only as long as they have a problem, and service is terminated when the problem is resolved. In the professional abuse pattern, the family demonstrates just enough progress to keep the professional motivated, engaged, and interested in maintaining a relationship with the family. To resolve this situation, the professional must separate from the family situation sufficiently to conduct an objective evaluation of the relationship.

Transgenerational abuse can occur when the grandparents become involved in raising their grandchildren, by accepting the caretaking role or as a consequence of sharing a residence with their son's or daughter's family. In some cases, transgenerational abuse results in a repetition of the cycle of poor parenting and abuse that occurred when the grandparents were raising their children. In other cases, the fact that the child's biological parents remain dependent on the grandparents gives the grandparents a second opportunity to parent. In this situation, unresolved problems related to the parent's own childhood may be reactivated. To assist these families, authority and responsibility within the family must be shifted from the grandparents to the child's biological parents.

The fourth pattern of abuse is stand-in abuse. If one parent has a close relationship with the child and the relationship between the parents is distant, then maltreatment of the child may represent a means of punishing the partner without undermining the marriage. The family may adopt a pattern of behavior in which, at times of crisis, one child is singled out and punished or the child learns to behave in a manner that elicits abuse. In this situation, the child serves as a conflict regulator between the parents. Stand-in abuse may also occur in situations where one parent is "overengaged" with the child and the other is "disengaged." The primary issue for the professional working with these families is to find a way to help the parents resolve their conflicts without using the child as the focus of anger.

In some families, there is a pattern of distance-regulating abuse. The child learns that the only way to achieve close physical contact with mother or father is to behave in such a way as to evoke punishment. In these cases, closeness is experienced in the act of punishment and the subsequent hugs and comforting that are a consequence of the parent's feelings of guilt about the abuse of the child. In other families who regulate personal distance through child abuse, there is a predictable sequence of outbursts of violence. The violence serves the purpose of stabilizing the family at a point where there is neither too much closeness nor too much distance between the members. In working with these families, enjoyable experiences which enhance cohesion among the family members are essential.

Transferred abuse is another pattern found among families. It is difficult to understand the processes underlying this particular pattern of abuse. It appears that intense experiences from the parent's past are transferred to the present and the child becomes the target of the feelings associated with these past experiences. These families need help differentiating between the past and the present and understanding that they are superimposing the past on the present.

Cultural abuse occurs in some families. When these families are challenged with regard to their disciplinary practices, they state that their behavior towards their children is appropriate from the perspective of their cultural origins, even though their behavior is not accepted in the culture in which they presently live or by authorities within that culture. The parent may state that a particular way of disciplining their child is an inherited family practice. To assist these families it is often necessary to involve other families with the same cultural background who manage their children without abusing them. The essential message to be communicated to families involved in cultural abuse is: "We recognize that your culture

The traditional family unit has been changed by adoption and fostering.

may have different disciplinary practices, but in this community the law and the authorities take a firm stand against those practices." The parents are urged to rethink their interactions with their children because they risk losing their child if the abuse continues.

The final pattern of abuse, which may include any of the previously discussed patterns, is denied abuse. In this situation, the child is injured but the cause of the injury is denied by the abusing parent. In order to work effectively with these families, the focus of intervention must shift from "Who did this?" to an analysis of the pattern of interaction within the family. The family must demonstrate that their parenting is "good enough" to keep their child rather than children's service authorities demonstrating that the parenting is "bad enough" to remove the child from the family's custody.

These various patterns of abuse emphasize the functions of abuse within the child's family and extended social systems context. The teacher's primary role in child abuse is not to treat abusive families or to attempt the interventions suggested for each type of abuse, but to refer any evidence or suspicion of abuse to the proper authorities and to cooperate with professionals working with the family.

Objective Three: To describe the impact of substitute care on the learner's development.

The Impact of Substitute Care

Children are described as being in **substitute care** when their primary caregivers are individuals other than their biological parents, including relatives, informal foster parents, licensed foster parents, adoptive families, or group residential facility personnel.

Schor (1988), in a detailed discussion of **foster care** (care in foster homes), reports that since 1983 the foster care population in the United States has grown in absolute size and contains higher proportions of older children and children with disabilities. Today, foster children have more serious physical and emotional problems than in the past.

According to Schor, foster care placement is intended to be a planned, temporary service implemented for the purpose of strengthening families. Ideally, if after studying the family and providing appropriate services, reuniting the child and the family is not deemed possible or is considered not to be in the best interest of the child, parental rights are terminated and the child is placed with an adoptive family. There are, however, some children for whom neither reunion with their family nor adoption is feasible. Frequently, these children remain with foster care families, in various settings and on a temporary basis, until they reach their majority.

According to the Schor report, the current foster care population is composed of approximately equal numbers of males and females. Forty percent of the population is children from minority cultures. Twenty-five percent of the population is disabled. Approximately three-quarters of the children are in foster placement because of maltreatment; most of these children return to their biological family within 1 year. Twenty percent of the children reenter foster care within a year of discharge. Twenty-five percent of the children are likely to remain in foster care after a 2-year placement. The number of children entering foster care and the severity of their physical, emotional, and social problems is increasing. Social service agencies are having increasing difficulties recruiting and retaining foster care parents.

Children in foster care have been found to demonstrate more frequent and serious health care problems than children living with their biological families. Schor reports that these children may have chronic medical disorders, dental needs, prenatal exposure to drugs, and congenital infections. The children demonstrate variations from their peers in growth, decreased visual and auditory acuity, elevated rates of developmental delays and educational problems, and serious emotional problems. Hochstadt, Jaudes, Zimo, and Schachter (1987) found that learners in foster care, ranging in age from 10 days to 17 years of age, had significantly greater delays and major deficits in adaptive behavior. In addition, these learners demonstrated behavioral problems often associated with psychiatric disorders.

Substitute care is a challenge to both child and family. Normal developmental family processes are challenged by a distortion in the family cycle (Elbow, 1986). Biological families begin with dependent relationships and progress towards individuation, as the children assume more and more responsibility for their personal lives. The members of the substitute family begin as independent individuals and progress towards attachments. The process is further limited by the temporary nature of the placement.

The **Adoption Assistance and Child Welfare Act of 1980** (Public Law 96–272) was a consequence of national concern for children who were "adrift in foster care" (Seltzer & Blocksberg, 1987). The law emphasized the need to develop plans for the permanent placement of children in need of out-of-home placement for either a short or extended period of time. Maluccio and Fein (1983) describe permanency planning as the process of designing and implementing a set of goal-directed activities aimed at helping children live in families that offer ongoing relationships with nurturing individuals and at giving children the opportunity to establish lifetime relationships. The process of permanency planning is intended to (a) protect the child, (b) support stable relationships between the child and caregivers, (c) preserve the biological family, and (d) enhance the psychosocial and behavioral adjustment of the child. Selzer and Blocksberg (1987) report a higher rate of adoption from foster care when social service workers and agencies accept the philosophy of permanency planning.

Brodzinsky and associates (1986) summarize the behavior of older adopted children in a manner that is perhaps applicable to all foster and biological families. They suggest that attempts by school-age children to understand the basis of their relinquishment by their parents, that is, through sadness and anger, are actually normal, age-appropriate, inevitable components of the experience. The children's reactions are similar to those associated with a parent's death or divorce. The reactions represent children's grief and mourning in response to parental loss. Unlike children of divorce, however, many children in substitute care are struggling with the loss of parents for whom they may have only vague, distorted memories. Their loss is more pervasive, and potentially more problematic, as they enter adolescence and begin to struggle with the issues of personal identity.

Objective Four: To describe the issue of learners raised in poverty.

The Impact of Poverty

Baumeister, Kupstas, and Klindworth (1990) report on the significant reversals that are occurring in the specific and general health indicators that affect children. They contend that a new, multifactored model is needed to explain the increased prevalence of children's health disorders. The model takes into consideration the wide array of contemporary psychosocial problems such as adolescent pregnancy, suicide, substance abuse, and developmental disorders. Without specific prevention efforts, they suggest that a "biologic underclass" of children will emerge whose problems are related to poverty, lack of adequate and timely prenatal care, and prevalence of human immunodeficiency virus (HIV) and other chronic illnesses.

The impact of poverty on children's development has been referred to as "double jeopardy," since the factors of biologic vulnerability, secondary to prematurity, maternal depression, temperamental passivity, and inadequate environmental stimulation and the insufficient social support available to the poor serve to potentiate each other (Parker, Greer, and Zuckerman, 1988). This increased biologic vulnerability is related to teenage pregnancy, limited prenatal care, poor maternal nutrition, and maternal depression.

Parker and associates state that the interaction of biological factors and poor social support put children at serious risk. They argue that intervention should involve strengthening relationships and social supports for children in poverty, suggesting that even in stressed families, the presence of a good relationship with one parent reduces the risk for children. For older children, the presence of a close, enduring relationship with an external support figure (for example, a schoolteacher) may likewise serve a protective function. One goal of social support and therapeutic interventions must be to establish environments and relationships for the child that promote a positive self-concept.

Early intervention for children living in poverty is essential; the House Select Committee on Children, Youth, and Families estimates that every $1.00 spent on preschool education saves at least $4.75 in later educational and social costs.

Objective Five: To describe the effects of prenatal drug and alcohol exposure on the learner's development.

The Impact of Parental Substance Abuse

When a family is involved in substance abuse, two things happen to the children. First, the interactions that usually occur between parents and young children may not occur because the parents are preoccupied with obtaining and using drugs. Second, parents involved in substance abuse frequently do not have the same priorities as other parents. Their primary concern is to acquire and use their substance of choice, not to care for their children. As a result, the children's needs are neglected. Children living with parents who are substance abusers live in unstable, often dangerous environments and are cared for inconsistently by parents who frequently have psychological and physical complaints.

When discussing children from families in which there is substance abuse, Weston and associates (1989) stress the importance of carefully considering the mother's behavior. Maternal behaviors associated with drug-induced organic mental disorders, such as seizures, paranoid and suicidal ideations, violent or aggressive behavior, harming self and others as a consequence of delusions, and impaired motor coordination, present significant dangers to children. In addition, the effects of the mother's drug of choice are frequently intensified by the use of other health-impairing substances, such as alcohol, tobacco, alternate drugs, and drug substitutes.

Conducting research with families who engage in substance abuse is problematic. Research subjects are difficult to locate largely due to the nature of substance abuse, which is illegal and frequently requires abusers to participate in illicit activity to sustain their habit. It is difficult to collect research data because the subjects typically lead disorganized daily lives and are preoccupied with activities associated with their addiction (Howard, Beckwith, Rodning, & Kropenske, 1989).

There are two groups of children associated with substance abuse in families who are of great significance to educators and the educational system. Due to the potentially serious effects of *any* maternal use during pregnancy, children whose mothers used any drugs or alcohol of any kind during any time of the pregnancy are referred to as **prenatally exposed.** This includes far more children than those born addicted to a controlled substance. The first group is composed of children prenatally exposed to cocaine, usually in the form of alkaloidal cocaine (crack). The second group is composed of children prenatally exposed to alcohol.

Children Prenatally Exposed to Cocaine

There are several reasons why cocaine has become known as the "first substance of abuse." First, it is readily available and thus does not require the user to seek drugs in the so-called "underclass" society. Second, it does not require injection for use and effect; in the form of crack, it can be smoked. Finally, it is cost-competitive with similar quantities of alcohol purchased in public establishments (Keith and associates, 1989). Crack cocaine is sold in the form of small, cream-colored chunks that resemble rock salt. Its use leads to a 5 to 15 minute reaction or "high" within less than 10 seconds and has a far more powerful effect than that of powdered cocaine (Gold, 1987). The use of crack results in an intense, but fleeting, feeling of competence, which is quickly replaced with feelings of irritability, restlessness, and depression. Cocaine use is frequently part of a multidrug or polydrug abuse syndrome. Its use is not restricted to those persons usually perceived as "drug addicts." Farrar and Kearns (1989) urge medical personnel not to dismiss the possibility of cocaine use solely on the basis of a patient's appearance, age, and socioeconomic status. In fact, in one study, 25 percent of cocaine users denied use at the time of their hospital admission interview. Cocaine use is reported to be associated with a greater risk for sexually transmitted diseases, and increased use of alcohol, tobacco, marijuana, opiates, and increased illicit drugs during pregnancy (Frank and associates, 1988).

When a woman uses cocaine 1 or 2 days prior to delivery, it can be detected in the urine of the newborn child for as long as 96 hours after the birth. In contrast, in adults, cocaine is apparent in the urine for approximately 60 hours. The slower metabolism of the cocaine by the newborn is due to the relative immaturity of the infant's liver (Van de Bor, Walther, & Sims, 1990). Although the exact risk of

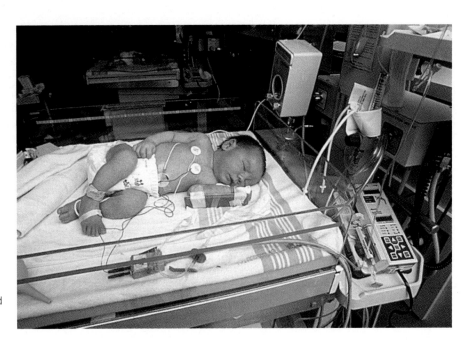

Infants who have been exposed to drugs and alcohol may have delayed motor, cognitive, and perceptual performance.

cocaine exposure during human pregnancy is unknown, physicians are urged to counsel patients with regard to possible risks to the fetus and to carefully monitor their patients (Hoyme and associates, 1990).

The most frequently reported characteristic of cocaine-exposed infants is low birth weight, also known as prenatal growth retardation (Bingol and associates, 1987; Chasnoff, 1988a; Farrar & Kearns, 1989; Frank and associates, 1988). In a follow-up study of 3- to 7-year-old infants exposed to cocaine, growth retardation was found to be related to delayed cognitive, motor, and perceptual performance (Harvey and associates, 1982).

Neurobehavioral abnormalities are well documented in cocaine-exposed infants (Chasnoff, 1988a). According to Hadeed and Siegel (1989), 10 percent of babies exposed to cocaine exhibit unexplained jitteriness. Using the Brazelton Neonatal Behavioral Assessment Scale, Chasnoff and associates (1985) found that infants exposed to cocaine exhibited serious depression in interactive behaviors and poor organizational responses to environmental stimuli. In a comparison of the motor development of cocaine-exposed infants to non-drug exposed infants, Schneider and Chasnoff (1987) found infants exposed to cocaine to feel stiff when their limbs were moved and exhibit excessively extreme postures. They exhibited tremors, especially in their arms and hands when reaching for objects. As they grow older, the primitive reflexes must be replaced by more mature movement patterns if the children are to develop a normal body image.

Children who have been prenatally exposed to cocaine may demonstrate various physical abnormalities, for example, extremely small head size (Hadeed & Siegel, 1989) and malformations of limbs (Bingol and associates, 1987). In a study by Hoyme and associates (1990), seven of ten cocaine-exposed infants had limb defects, such as the absence of arms below the elbow, missing digits, or missing forearm bones. Due to an increase in cerebral blood flow, infants exposed to cocaine are at risk for intracranial hemorrhaging after birth (Van de Bor, Walther, & Sims, 1990).

When interacting with their environment, Howard and associates (1989) found infants exposed to cocaine to be disorganized. They were less responsive to their mothers and more difficult to both engage in interaction and to console. In addition, they exhibited unpredictable fluctuations in emotional responses (Chasnoff, 1988b). These infants do not experience the normal processes of mother-child attachment, which are essential to the early relationship between mother and infant.

Children prenatally exposed to cocaine have developmental scale scores which are in the low average range (Howard and associates, 1989). Their most striking deficits are in unstructured free play situations which require self-organization, self-initiation, and independent follow-through in play activities. For their age, the children demonstrated significantly less representational play than expected. Their play activities were characterized by scattering, batting, and picking up and putting down toys.

Dixon and Bejar (1989) report what is, to date, the most alarming results of research on infants exposed to cocaine. Using cranial ultrasonography, they contrasted cocaine-exposed and drug-free yet clinically ill children. They found that the type, location, and distribution of brain lesions in cocaine-exposed infants suggests that neural damage may not be clinically evident during infancy or early childhood. Rather, such neural damage may become evident only after the child's first year of life, when more complex visual-motor and social cognition tasks are required such as during preschool and school activities. Dixon and Bejar suggest that even among drug-exposed "normal neonates," there is grave concern for abnormal neurologic, cognitive, and behavioral development as they approach school age.

Children Prenatally Exposed to Alcohol

The effects of the unborn child's exposure to alcohol were first described by Jones and Smith in 1973. They suggest that exposure to alcohol, in utero, could be the primary cause of children's growth deficiencies, birth defects, and mental retardation. Streissguth (1977) reported that prior to 1973, most health care professionals attributed the learning and developmental problems of children from alcoholic families to chaotic homelife and poor parenting. However, children from alcoholic families raised in foster homes, characterized by a consistent and nurturing environment, were found to demonstrate similar problems (Streissguth, 1976). Discussions and research led professionals to the conclusion that, in children of alcoholic mothers, the primary damage to the child may occur in utero. This condition is called the **fetal alcohol syndrome.**

In 1980, the Fetal Alcohol Study Group of the Research Society on Alcoholism (Rossett & Weiner, 1984) presented minimal criteria for the diagnosis of fetal alcohol syndrome. The diagnosis of the syndrome is recommended when the child has symptoms in each of the following categories:

1. Prenatal and/or postnatal growth retardations: weight, length, and/or head circumference below the tenth percentile when corrected for gestational age.
2. Central nervous system involvement: signs of neurologic abnormality, developmental delay, or intellectual impairment.
3. Common facial characteristics with at least two of these three symptoms: (a) microcephaly, (b) microophthalmia and/or widely spaced eyes, (c) poorly developed median groove between the upper lip and the nose, thin upper lip, or flattening of the upper jaw.

Abel (1984) suggested that if only one or two of these symptoms are evident, and if the mother is suspected of alcohol use during pregnancy, then diagnosis of **possible fetal alcohol effect** may be made. Cooper (1987) suggests that the option of diagnosing possible fetal alcohol effect broadens the view of alcohol effects on the fetus, emphasizing that alcohol may not only cause the fetal alcohol syndrome but may be associated with a wide range of adverse outcomes. Fetal alcohol effect children, who are far more numerous than fetal alcohol syndrome children, represent a significant challenge to teachers and health care professionals (Rossett & Weiner, 1984). Nadle (1985) suggests that three to five children per one thousand have fetal alcohol effect.

Children with fetal alcohol effects or fetal alcohol syndrome present a broad range of intelligence test scores. A significant relationship has been found between intellectual functioning and the physical symptoms of these syndromes: children with more predominant facial characteristics and slower skeletal growth demonstrate more severe brain dysfunction (Streissguth, Herman, & Smith, 1978). Infants as young as 8 months of age with prenatal alcohol exposure exhibit lower weight, shorter length, smaller head circumference than normal, minor physical anomalies, and feeding problems (Day and associates, 1990).

The most common anomaly associated with prenatal exposure to alcohol is growth retardation, with the child's length being more severely affected than its weight (Rossett & Weiner, 1984). Of perhaps greater concern, however, is that most of these children demonstrate persistent hyperactivity and distractibility which contributes significantly to poor educational performance (Spohr & Steinhausen, 1987). Cooper (1987) contends that these children display a variety of school problems that are characteristic of central nervous system impairment.

In a series of carefully controlled empirical studies, Streissguth and associates (1984, 1987, 1989) and Sampson, Streissguth, Barr, and Bookstein (1989) documented the neurobehavioral effects of prenatal alcohol exposure. They found that as little as 1.5 ounces of alcohol per day is significantly related to an average intelligence quotient decrement of almost five points. In longitudinal studies controlled for birth order and maternal education, nutrition, and use of caffeine, alcohol, and nicotine, Sampson and associates found that their 4-year-old subjects had significantly poorer attention spans and orientation, and longer reaction times than did nonexposed children. By school age, analysis revealed a pattern of neurobehavioral deficits in the areas of memory, problem solving, focusing and maintaining attention, and regulating impulsivity across three settings: (a) on standardized intelligence and achievement tests, (b) on laboratory vigilance tasks, and (c) in the classroom, as reported by teachers. Though the children exhibited auditory, spatial, and verbal memory deficits, impulsivity was found to be the most significant characteristic in the laboratory and classroom.

In a sample of primarily middle class, majority culture mothers who reported occasional multiple drinks in the period prior to realizing they were pregnant, Sampson and associates (1989) found alcohol use significantly correlated with a lowered intelligence quotient, poor academic achievement, school behavior problems, and deficits in attention and vigilance. The children's fetal alcohol effects included poor short-term memory, impulsivity, problems with quantitative functioning, and difficulties with sustaining attention. In a study by Streissguth (1976), alcohol-effect children demonstrated hyperactivity and fine motor problems, such as tremulousness, weak and primitive grasp, poor finger articulation, and delay in establishing hand dominance. As Van Dyke and Fox (1990) report, a

Tiny Babies Struggle for Better Mental Footing

By Richard Whitmire

Two years ago Kim Snowden, then 17, went into labor two months early and delivered a son, Deries, weighing only 2 pounds, 9 ounces.

For a time, everything seemed OK. But when Deries turned 2 and was still not talking, she knew something was seriously wrong. "It hurts," Snowden says. "Everyone wants to have a normal baby."

Snowden sought out Dr. Pat Casey, who runs an intervention program out of the University of Arkansas to correct problems arising from babies born too early or too small, or damaged by moms who smoked, drank or used drugs while pregnant.

The program leads specially trained teachers through a minute-by-minute choreographed curriculum that more resembles a computer repair manual than a guide to teaching toddlers. And it works: 20 years of testing shows it can raise IQs of damaged kids from 6 to 20 points.

Researchers say this curriculum could be part of the answer to a troubling trend building in the USA, with more women giving birth to tiny babies and doctors using new technology to save them.

Increasingly, those babies come home to families in poverty unable to help their children overcome the obstacles of being born too small.

In a four-month investigation, Gannett News Service found this cycle of low birth weight babies already spilling into schools. More kids—and more with multiple problems—are showing up in the nation's special education classes.

Intelligence quotient is one of life's more brutal calculations. If Deries scores less than 70, he faces a life of full-time special education. Push his IQ to 80, and with good education he can be literate; push it into the 90s, closer to the average ranges around 100, and he can work in the world of high tech.

Contrary to popular belief, IQ is not fixed at birth, but expandable within a range of about 30 points, experts say.

"Mental retardation is not necessarily something a child is born with, and when it's caused by environmental factors, it's particularly reversible," says Craig Ramey, University of Alabama at Birmingham psychologist. He led the team that developed the curriculum used here.

The federal Centers for Disease Control was so impressed that in July it announced a nationwide program using the curriculum to prevent mild mental

significant number of children who were diagnosed with fetal alcohol exposure in the 1970s exhibited learning problems, behavioral problems, and attention deficits in the 1980s.

Shaywitz, Caparulo, and Hodgson (1981) describe the behavior and language disorders among their patients with prenatal exposure to alcohol. These children had adequate nonverbal skills, yet had difficulty in verbally expressing themselves. They were found to perseverate, that is, repeat beyond the usual end point of a behavior, on familiar routines and play themes and topics, as well as apparently blocking some concepts their teachers reported they knew. The children were anxious, had poor peer relationships, and played immaturely or inappropriately. The language of these children was unusual; they used adequate articulation but displayed poor knowledge of the rules of dialogue, reduced sentence length, a failure to appreciate the communicative functions of language, and diminished or inappropriate spontaneous language. The children were hypervigilant, distractible even in normal levels of auditory and visual stimulation, and behaviorally disorganized.

Streissguth, Herman, and Smith (1978) report that school was a particular challenge to the alcohol-exposed children they studied. Their most significant problem appeared to be hyperactivity. None of the children was described as rebellious, antisocial, or negative. Considerable difficulty, however, was noted in regard to both learning and classroom management. Younger alcohol-exposed children were found to be generally cooperative and friendly, yet difficult to work with due to their hyperactivity. In some cases, hyperactivity decreased as the children grew older, but they continued to have difficulties focusing their attention (Streissguth, Clarren, & Jones, 1985).

retardation among poor children. It has just released bids for a 15-site program that would serve 6,000 children, if Congress provides the $200 million to pay for it.

Cost is a major obstacle that could prevent the help Deries is getting from reaching the thousands of other children who need it: At $6,000 to $10,000 a child, the program does not come cheap.

Even typical special education classes cost more than twice that of regular classes. The cost in 1988 for these special classes: $371 million.

But answers must be found. Researchers tracking the connection between low birth weight babies and education problems are turning up some grim statistics.

University of Miami psychologist Keith Scott linked medical and school records of children born at Miami's inner-city Jackson Memorial Hospital and found that nearly 40% of the very low birth weight babies born there—those under 3 pounds, 4 ounces—ended up in special education classes.

"We're going backward," Scott said. "As a larger number of people fall into poverty, it will steadily get worse."

It has long been known that up to one-fifth of very low birth weight babies will suffer major handicaps: cerebral palsy, blindness, deafness and severe mental retardation. Now experts are discovering that an additional 15% to 25% will suffer other disabilities: behavior problems, lowered IQ and developmental problems.

As many as 21,000 babies born each year under that weight will suffer either serious physical handicaps or subtle learning problems.

The smallest babies suffer the most. Of the children born less than 1 pound, 14 ounces, nearly 85% will suffer problems in school, says Dr. Maureen Hack of Cleveland's Rainbow Babies and Childrens Hospital, an expert on the tiniest babies. For those less than 1 pound, 11 ounces, school problems are an inevitability, she says. "We are producing a group of children with inferior intelligence," Hack says. "I am pessimistic about these small babies" ■

Shaywitz, Cohen, and Shaywitz (1980) suggest that behavioral and learning problems may be the most significant, yet most frequently overlooked, deficits of children exposed to alcohol. Though the children in their sample had intelligence quotients well within the normal range, all experienced school failure. Hyperactivity, usually controlled with medication, was found to be present in all but one of the students. The students were described as being unable to function without one-to-one or small group instruction. Statements by school personnel such as "cannot sit still" and "seems to have the skills yet is not learning" were noted in all of the students' records. By third grade, all the students were recommended for special education services.

Other medical disorders are also apparent in alcohol-exposed children. In a 10-year follow-up study, Streissguth, Clarren, and Jones (1985) reported intra-oral problems including poor dental alignment, malocclusions, and cleft palate; eye problems ranging from strabismus to sever myopia; heart murmurs; and skeletal problems such as scoliosis and dislocated hips. Chronic otitis media and permanent hearing loss, which also have serious impact on language learning, were noted in over half of the children.

Summary

In this chapter we described various family and community factors that place children at risk for disabilities. The impact of divorce, child abuse, neglect, and maltreatment, and prenatal drug and alcohol exposure were explored. In addition, issues related to children growing up in substitute care or poverty were presented.

Divorce is perhaps the most pervasive psychological stressor for children. The process of divorce diminishes the parents' ability to provide for the child's emotional needs; the child's developmental process is disrupted.

Child maltreatment is associated with problematic parent-child interactions and insecure attachment. Children who have been maltreated are more anxious, inattentive, and anxious than are their peers. The underlying issues for these children are predictability and control in their life. These children may be removed from their biological families and placed in substitute care. Though foster care is ideally a temporary, planned service, some children cannot be united with their families, and they may either remain in foster care or placed in adoptive homes.

Poverty places the child's development in "double jeopardy"; there are both biologic vulnerability and limited resources for children living in poverty. Prenatal drug and alcohol exposure places children at even greater risk. These children are low in birth weight and may demonstrate a pattern of physical and behavioral challenges.

Though the complex interaction of these factors does have a serious impact on children's development, the teacher's role in assisting in the mitigation of their effects cannot be overemphasized. Parker, Greer, and Zuckerman (1988) indicate that even in stressed families, the presence of one close, enduring relationship with an external support figure (such as a school teacher) may serve as a protective function. Through this relationship children may develop a positive self-concept, and children with positive self-concepts seek, establish, and maintain the kind of supportive relationships and experiences that promote successful outcomes.

References

Abel, E. L. (1984). Prenatal effects of alcohol. *Drug and Alcohol Dependence, 14*, 1–10.

American Humane Association (1987). *Highlights of official child neglect and abuse reporting.* Denver: The American Humane Association.

Asen, K., George, E., Piper, R., & Stevens, A. (1989). A systems approach to child abuse: Management and treatment issues. *Child Abuse and Neglect, 13*, 45–57.

Baumeister, A. A., Kupstas, F., & Klindworth, L. M. (1990). New morbidity: Implications for prevention of children's disabilities. *Exceptionality, 1*, 1–16.

Bingol, N., Fuchs, M., Diaz, V., Stone, R. K., & Gromisch, D. S. (1987). Teratogenicity of cocaine in humans. *Journal of Pediatrics, 110*, 93–96.

Brodzinsky, D. M., Schechter, D., & Brodzinsky, A. B. (1986). Children's knowledge of adoption: Developmental changes and implication for adjustment. In R. D. Ashmore & D. M. Brodzinsky (Eds.), *Thinking about the family: Views of parents and children* (pp. 205–232). Hillsdale, NJ: Lawrence Erlbaum.

Chasnoff, I. J. (1988a). Drug use in pregnancy: Parameters of risk. *The Pediatric Clinics of North America, 35*, 1403–1412.

Chasnoff, I. J. (1988b). Newborn infants with drug withdrawal symptoms. *Pediatrics in Review, 9*, 273–277.

Chasnoff, I. J., Burns, N. J., Schnoll, S. H., & Burns, K. A. (1985). Cocaine use in pregnancy. *New England Journal of Medicine, 313*, 666–669.

Cicchetti, D., Toth, S., & Hennessy, K. (1989). Research on the consequences of child maltreatment and its application to educational settings. *Topics in Early Childhood and Special Education, 9* (2), 33–55.

Cooper, S. (1987). The fetal alcohol syndrome. *The Journal of Child Psychology and Psychiatry and Allied Professionals, 28*, 233–227.

Crittenden, P. M. (1989). Teaching maltreated children in the preschool. *Topics in Early Childhood Special Education, 9* (2), 16–32.

Day, N. L., Richardson, G., Robles, N., Sambamoorthi, U., Taylor, P., Scher, M., Stoffer, D., Jasperse, D., & Cornelius, M. (1990). Effect of prenatal alcohol exposure on growth and morphology of offspring at eight months of age. *Pediatrics, 85,* 748–752.

Dixon, S. D., & Bejar, R. (1989). Echoencephalographic findings in neonates associated with maternal cocaine and methamphetamine use: Incidence and clinical correlates. *Journal of Pediatrics, 115,* 770–778.

Dubowitz, H., Newberger, C. M., Melnicoe, L. H., & Newberger, E. H. (1988). The changing American family. *The Pediatric Clinics of North America, 35,* 1291–1311.

Elbow, M. (1986). From caregiving to parenting: Family formation with adopted older children. *Social Work, 31,* 366–370.

Farrar, H. C., & Kearns, G. L. (1989). Cocaine: Clinical pharmacology and toxicology. *The Journal of Pediatrics, 115,* 665–675.

Frank, D. A., Zuckerman, B. S., Amaro, H., Aboagye, K., Baucher, H., Cabral, H., Fried, L., Hingson, R., Kayne, H., Levenson, S., Parken, S., Reece, H., & Vinci, R. (1988). Cocaine use during pregnancy: Prevalence and correlates. *Pediatrics, 82,* 888–895.

Gold, M. S. (1987). Crack abuse: Its implications and outcomes. *Resident and Staff Physician, 33* (8), 3–6.

Guidubaldi, J., & Perry, J. D. (1985). Divorce and mental health sequelae for children: A two-year follow-up of a nationwide sample. *Journal of the American Academy of Child Psychiatry, 24,* 531–537.

Guttman, J., Geva, N., & Gefen, S. (1988). Teachers' and school children's stereotypic perception of "the child of divorce." *American Educational Researcher Journal, 25,* 555–571.

Hadeed, A. J., & Siegel, S. R. (1989). Maternal cocaine use during pregnancy: Effect on the newborn infant. *Pediatrics, 84,* 205–210.

Harvey, D., Prince, J., Burton, J., Parkinson, D., & Campbell, S. (1982). Abilities of children who were small for gestational age babies. *Pediatrics, 69,* 296–300.

Hetherington, E. M., Cox, M., & Cox, R. (1985). Long-term effects of divorce and remarriage on the adjustment of children. *Journal of the American Academy of Child Psychiatry, 24,* 518–530.

Hochstadt, N. J., Jaudes, P. K., Zimo, D. A., & Schachter, J. (1987). The medical and psychosocial needs of children entering foster care. *Child Abuse and Neglect, 11* (1), 53–62.

Howard, J., Beckwith, L., Rodning, C., & Kropenske, V. (1989). The development of young children of substance abusing parents: Insights from seven years of intervention and research. *Zero to Three, 9* (5), 8–12.

Hoyme, H. E., Jones, K. L., Dixon, S., Jewett, T., Hanson, J. W., Robinson, L. K., Msall, M. E., & Allanson, J. E. (1990). Prenatal cocaine exposure and fetal vascular disruption. *Pediatrics, 85,* 743–747.

Jones, K. L., & Smith, D. W. (1973). Recognition of the fetal alcohol syndrome in early infancy. *Lancet, 2,* 999–1001.

Keith, L. G., MacGregor, S., Friedell, S., Rosner, M., Chasnoff, I. J., & Sciarra, J. J. (1989). Substance abuse in pregnant women: Recent experience at the perinatal center for chemical dependence of Northwestern Memorial Hospital. *Obstetrics and Gynecology, 73,* 715–723.

Maluccio, A. N., & Fein, E. (1983). Permanency planning: A redefinition. *Child Welfare, 63,* 197.

Nadle, M. (1985). Offspring with fetal alcohol effects: Intervention and identification. *Alcoholism Treatment Quarterly, 2* (1), 105–116.

Parker, S., Greer, S., & Zuckerman, B. (1988). Double jeopardy: The impact of poverty on early child development. *The Pediatric Clinics of North America, 35,* 1227–1240.

Rossett, H. L., & Weiner, L. (1984). *Alcohol and the fetus.* New York: Oxford Press.

Sampson, P. D., Streissguth, A. P., Barr, H. M., & Bookstein, F. L. (1989). Neurobehavioral effects of prenatal alcohol. Part II: Partial least squares analysis. *Neurotoxicology and Teratology, 11,* 477–491.

Schneider, J., & Chasnoff, I. J. (1987). Cocaine abuse during pregnancy: Its effects on infant motor development: A clinical perspective. *Topics in Acute Care and Trauma Rehabilitation, 2,* 59–73.

Schor, E. L. (1988). Foster care. *The Pediatric Clinics of North America, 35* (6), 1241–1252.

Seltzer, M. M., & Blocksberg, L. M. (1987). Permanency planning and its effects on foster children: A review of the literature. *Social Work, 37,* 65–68.

Shaywitz, S. E., Cohen, D. J., & Shaywitz, B. A. (1980). Behavior and learning difficulties in children of normal intelligence born to alcoholic mothers. *The Journal of Pediatrics, 96,* 978–982.

Shaywitz, S. E., Caparulo, B. K., & Hodgson, E. S. (1981). Developmental language disability as a consequence of prenatal exposure to ethanol. *Pediatrics, 96,* 978–982.

Spohr, H. L., & Steinhausen, H. C. (1987). Follow-up studies of children with fetal alcohol syndrome. *Neuropediatrics, 18,* 13–17.

Streissguth, A. P. (1976). Psychologic handicaps in children with the fetal alcohol syndrome. *Annals of the New York Academy of Sciences, 273,* 140–145.

Streissguth, A. P. (1977). Maternal drinking and the outcome of pregnancy: Implications for child mental health. *American Journal of Orthopsychiatry, 47,* 422–431.

Streissguth, A. P., Barr, H. M., Sampson, P. d., Darby, B. L., & Martin, D. C. (1989). IQ at age four in relation to maternal alcohol use and smoking during pregnancy. *Developmental Psychology, 25,* 3–11.

Streissguth, A. P., Bookstein, F. L., Sampson, P. d., & Barr, H. M. (1987). Neurobehavioral effects of prenatal alcohol: PLS analysis of neuropsychologic tests. *Neurotoxicology and Teratology, 11,* 492–507.

Streissguth, A. P., Clarren, S. K., & Jones, K. L. (1985). Natural history of the fetal alcohol syndrome: A ten-year follow-up of eleven patients. *Lancet* (Part 2), *47,* 422–431.

Streissguth, A. P., Herman, C. S., & Smith, D. W. (1978). Intelligence, behavior, and dysmorphogenesis in the fetal alcohol syndrome: A report on 20 patients. *Journal of Pediatrics, 92,* 262–267.

Streissguth, A. P., Martin, C. D., Barr, H. M., Sandman, B. M., Kirchner, G. L., & Darby, B. L. (1984). Intrauterine alcohol and nicotine exposure: Attention and reaction time in four-year-old children. *Developmental Psychology, 20,* 533–541.

University of Cincinnati Institute for Policy Research (1991). A comparison of family structure. Unpublished manuscript.

Van de Bor, M., Walther, F. J., & Sims, M. E. (1990). Increased cerebral blood flow velocity in infants of mothers who abuse cocaine. *Pediatrics, 85,* 733–736.

Van Dyke, D. C., & Fox, A. A. (1990). Fetal drug exposure and its possible implications for learning in the preschool and school-age population. *Journal of Learning Disabilities, 23* (3), 160–163.

Wallerstein, J. (1985). Children of divorce: Preliminary report of a ten-year follow-up of older children and adolescents. *Journal of the American Academy of Child Psychiatry, 24,* 545–553.

Wallerstein, J., & Blakeslee, S. (1989). *Second changes: Men, women and children a decade after divorce.* New York: Ticknor & Fields.

Weston, D. R., Ivins, B., Zuckerman, B., & Lopez, R. (1989). Drug-exposed babies: Research and clinical issues. *Zero to Three, 9* (5), 1–7.

Wiehe, V. R. (1984). Self-esteem, attitude towards parents, and locus of control in children of divorced and nondivorced families. *Journal of Social Service Research, 8* (1), 17–28.

Youngblade, L. M., & Belsky, J. (1989). Child maltreatment, infant-parent attachment security, and dysfunctional peer relationships in toddlerhood. *Topics in Early Childhood Special Education, 9* (2), 1–15.

Section

2
Learners Who Vary in Their Interactions

Learners Identified as Behaviorally Disordered

Learners from Diverse Ethnic, Cultural, and Linguistic Groups

137

*P*ERHAPS NO GROUP OF LEARNERS GREATER REFLECTS THE SYSTEMS PERSPECTIVE OF HUMAN DEVELOPMENT THAN that of those who vary in their interaction patterns. In this section, we discuss both learners identified as behaviorally disordered and learners from various ethnic, cultural, and linguistic groups. We discuss these learners as varying from the behavioral expectations of school, yet frequently competent in other social systems.

Since the turn of the century, the American public school has emerged as the main socialization agent of diverse students for learning the "American way of life." Appropriate behavior and normalcy has been explicitly defined by the schools through the expected and accepted behaviors and interactions (Hoffman, 1975). The social systems perspective assumes that as social beings, students in schools are socialized to act in specific ways (Kugelmass, 1987). Conflicts occur when the values and expectations of the school contradict those the child has learned, or when the same behavior has different meanings to the child and those in authority. Mercer (1965, 1973) argues that in regard to applying the social systems perspective to the educational system, it is primarily the expectations of the teacher that determine who will be identified and referred as possible candidates for special education. In public school, students are considered normal if not visibly defective, and they remain there until they fail to meet the role expectations of teachers.

Students identified as different represent a discordance with the regular education system, demonstrating a lack of fit with expectations (Hobbs, 1980). Due to this lack of fit, the regular education system assumes that the "problem" lies exclusively within the child. Mehan and associates (1986) suggest that it is not the students' characteristics or behavior that leads to success or failure, but the expectations that teachers have for students' behavior that causes these academic outcomes. The reasons students are successful or unsuccessful is not because of the inherent characteristics of their actions, but because they are labeled successful or unsuccessful. What is "normal" then, is socially constructed by the educational system and is a consequence of educators' and students' interactions. These interactions generate an original designation such as "problem student," and the student's actions are taken into account as different.

One model of the interactions that generate the student's identification is presented by Wood (1981). In this model, a teacher's attention is drawn to the behavior of a student. The teacher then judges whether the behavior is pleasing or disturbing. If the teacher is disturbed by the behavior, he or she must decide whether some action should be taken. Depending on an appraisal of social and political factors, the teacher may decide not to react, to respond immediately, to seek support in acting to change the student's behavior, or to escape from the setting. If action is taken, the teacher puts in motion the system to label the student disordered, disruptive, or problematic. If the teacher infers that the disturbing behavior has been learned and is maintained by the environment, the student is then labeled behaviorally disordered. If the behavior is inferred to be a function of past experiences and the student's inner emotional state, the student is then labeled emotionally disturbed.

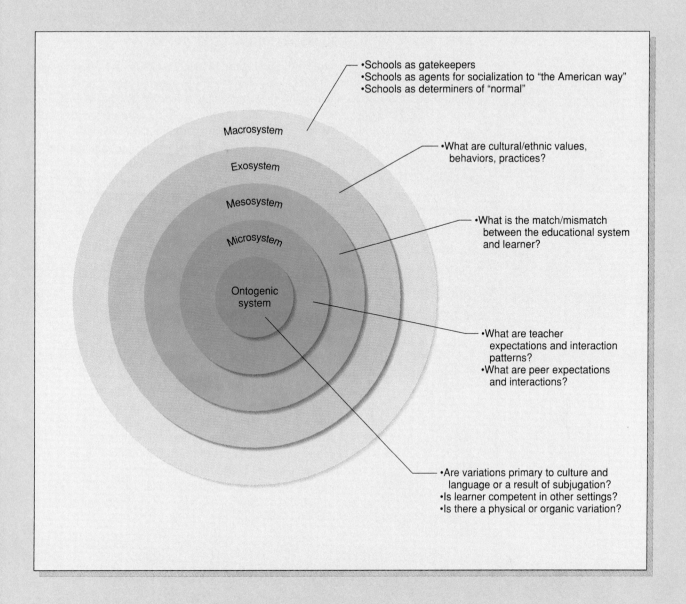

The social system's perspective attempts to view the definition of the individual's behavior as a function of the values of the social system within which he or she is being evaluated (Mercer, 1965). In this view, no clear consensus regarding which behaviors represent a norm violation exists; behaviors that may be considered appropriate in one setting may be perceived as deviant in another. Kugelmass (1987) asserts that majority culture, middle-class children may, in fact, have less difficulty in conforming to their behavioral expectations of school than other children, not because they are never disobedient, aggressive, or overtly defiant, but because they have been exposed to more of a variety of social situations and have learned a fact of life essential for survival: different social situations demand different behaviors.

Learners Identified as Behaviorally Disordered

Kugelmass (1987) suggested that the procedure by which students are referred and placed in special programs for behavioral disorders is generally thought of as an event that assures that students with special needs will receive an education that is appropriate. The outcome of this procedure is believed to be a proper educational response; yet, she found that more than the students' condition was responsible for placement. The school district's definition of deviant behavior contributed significantly. Psychologists presented an official and sanctioned definition of students' behaviors. Their perspective an the power attached to their professional role identity caused the school district to remove difficult-to-manage students without questioning any prior assumptions about how the classrooms in which they were attempting to function were being operated.

Developmental Contexts of Learners Identified as Behaviorally Disordered and from Various Ethnic, Cultural, and Linguistic Groups

According to Sarason and Doris (1979), the public school system has, in the past, served as a means to mold successive groups of urban immigrants arriving in the country in a manner that would propagate the existing control of society. The educational system continues to be responsible for this function in our society.

As social beings, children in schools are socialized to act in a specific way. A conflict occurs when the values and expectations of the school contradict those the child has learned, or when the same behavior has different meanings to the child and those in authority. Labeling children depends on the conformity of the child's behavior and school achievement to some criteria. However, the subjectivity of these criteria impacts on students' opportunities. Many of these learners may function competently outside of the school and may be indistinguishable from the general population once they leave the educational system. Questions generated by the systems perspective concerning these two groups are depicted in the figure on page 139.

Competencies emerge not as the properties of persons, but as the properties of situations presented in the educational system (Mehan and associates, 1986). In these two chapters, we focus on learners who, as suggested by the social system perspective, challenge the general educational system, yet may be seen as competent in other settings ■

References

Hobbs, N. (1980). *The futures of children.* San Francisco: Jossey Bass.

Hoffman, E. (1975). The American public school and the deviant child: The origins of their involvement. *The Journal of Special Education, 9,* 414–423.

Kugelmass, J. W. (1987). *Behavior, bias, and handicaps.* New Brunswick, NJ: Transaction, Inc.

Mehan, H., Hertweck, A., & Meihls, J. L. (1986). *Handicapping the handicapped.* Stanford, CA: Stanford University.

Mercer, J. (1965). Social system perspective and clinical perspective: Frames of reference for understanding career patterns of persons labelled as mentally retarded. *Social Problems, 13,* 18–34.

Mercer, J. (1973). *Labeling the mentally retarded.* Berkeley: University of California Press.

Sarason, S. B., & Doris, J. (1979). *Educational handicap, public policy, and social history.* New York: The Free Press.

Wood, F. (1981). *Perspective for a new decade.* Reston, VA: Council for Exceptional Children.

Chapter

7

Learners Identified as Behaviorally Disordered

*O*bjectives

After completing this chapter, you will be able to:

1. describe the personal characteristics of learners identified as behaviorally disordered.
2. describe the identification and evaluation of learners identified as behaviorally disordered.
3. describe the impact of behavioral disorders on interactions in the home and school.
4. describe ways to mediate the environment for learners identified as behaviorally disordered.
5. describe the impact of behavioral disorders on participation in larger social systems—the school, community, and society.

*K*ey Words and Phrases

aggression
behavioral disorders
depression
Diagnostic and Statistical Manual of
  Mental Disorders
disturbed behaviors
disturbing behaviors

externalizing behaviors
internalizing behaviors
levels systems
life space interview
seriously emotionally disturbed
token economy

*H*AVE YOU EVER FELT WEIRD, BUT COULDN'T FIGURE OUT WHY? SOMETIMES I FEEL LIKE THAT. MAYBE IT'S A PART of growing up. I don't know, but I keep moving away. Things have been smooth sailing. I have nothing to think about or worry over. That's for grownups, and my parents do that well. All I have to do is make sure my room is cleaned, put my bike away, stay out of trouble and get fair grades. Fair grades, sometimes that's hard to do, but I keep moving.

"One day something happened and things began to change. I began to feel really weird, like a yo-yo, swirling around and round. I didn't get it, but I keep moving anyway. At times the swirling would be strong like a swift wind passing by, but I keep moving anyway. Some days the swirling would be smooth as the flowing sea, but I keep moving anyway. Ask me how I feel. Fine, I guess. How should a kid my age feel? I have nothing to worry about. Besides, that's for grownups.

"As time went on, things really got rough. Remember the swirls, remember the wind, I found myself within, being tossed to and fro, feeling like I had no place to go. I have parents, what did they care, I found myself alone. My life seemed to drag, there was no hope. My only thought was to give up the ghost, but I keep moving. Now, what will I do? Where will I go?"

(Excerpted with permission from *Patrick* by J. A. Johnson. Copyright © 1991 J. A. Johnson.) ▪

144

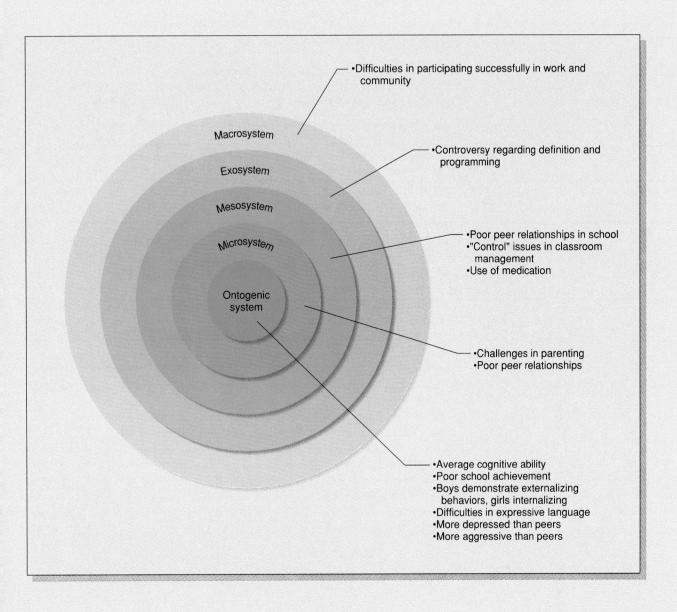

•Difficulties in participating successfully in work and community

•Controversy regarding definition and programming

•Poor peer relationships in school
•"Control" issues in classroom management
•Use of medication

•Challenges in parenting
•Poor peer relationships

•Average cognitive ability
•Poor school achievement
•Boys demonstrate externalizing behaviors, girls internalizing
•Difficulties in expressive language
•More depressed than peers
•More aggressive than peers

Macrosystem

Exosystem

Mesosystem

Microsystem

Ontogenic system

Introduction

Rhodes (1967) states that behavioral disorders are as much a function of where and with whom a child interacts as the child's behavior itself. Algozzine (1980) reaffirms this position when he states:

> . . . it is not simply the level and type of behavior that the child exhibits which may result in being identified as "disturbed," but the fact that that particular set of characteristics which make him/her an individual results in differential reactions (or degrees of disturbingness and intolerance) from others within the child's ecosystem (p. 112).

A systems perspective of programming for learners identified as behaviorally disordered within schools can serve to assist staff in understanding the various subsystems that have interactive effects upon an individual learner (Johnson & Zemitzsch, 1988). Though an extremely heterogeneous group, learners identified as having behavioral disorders challenge the school systems and professionals who serve them in their interactions.

During the 1990–91 school year, 392,559 learners age 6–21 were identified as behaviorally disordered in the United States. The proportion of school-aged population this represents ranged from 1.66 percent in Connecticut to .03 percent in Mississippi. The 1990–91 school year marked the sixth year of slow growth in numbers of learners identified as behaviorally disordered (U.S. Department of Education, 1992). The actual prevalence of learners identified as behaviorally disordered, however, may vary greatly from the numbers of those served. Because of the subjective nature of definitions of behavioral disorders, accurate data on the prevalence of behavioral disorders among children and youth are difficult to obtain. Shifts toward more educationally focused definitions, consistently applied from state to state, may facilitate the development of prevalence data. Huntze and Grosenick (1980) estimated between 1 and 35 percent of the school population may demonstrate behavioral disorders. Since only 0.69 percent of the school-age population is currently receiving services (U.S. Department of Education, 1992), this group of learners may be the most underserved of all those with disabilities.

Objective One: To describe the personal characteristics of learners identified as behaviorally disordered.

Personal Characteristics

Cognitive Functioning and Academic Achievement

Morse, Cutler, and Fink's (1964) early work suggested that learners identified as behaviorally disordered had above average cognitive ability. More recent studies, however, suggest that these learners exhibit average or lower than average measured cognitive abilities when compared to their typical peers (Colman, 1986). Learners with more severe behavioral disorders exhibit intelligence quotients in the mentally retarded range (Freeman & Ritvo, 1984).

During the 1989–90 school year, 44.6 percent of the learners identified as behaviorally disordered in the United States failed one or more courses in their most recent year of high school, far more than students in the other closest disability areas (speech impaired—35.0 percent, learning disabilities—34.8 percent). The average grade point of learners identified as behaviorally disordered was the lowest among students in all disability areas at 1.7 of a possible 4.0; in addition, these students were integrated into the fewest general education courses in high school (an average of 1.9). Learners identified as behaviorally disordered are also the most likely to drop out of high school: 40.14 percent of these learners dropped out nationally, and, in New York, 66.4 percent dropped out.

In a study exploring the concomitance of learning disabilities and behavioral disorders, Fessler, Rosenberg, & Rosenberg (1991) find the proportion of learners identified as behaviorally disordered who also have learning difficulty to be surprisingly large. Over 37 percent of the learners were identified as learning disabled, and an additional 17.8 percent were found to have learning problems and academic deficiencies sufficient enough to impede normal rates of achievement.

A primary characteristic of these learners is difficulty in demonstrating changes through academic instruction (Epstein, Kinder, & Bursuck, 1989). In comparing reading performance of learners identified as behaviorally disordered to that of their peers, reading achievement was significantly below (about 1.5 to 2 grade levels) that of their peers in elementary school; by secondary school the discrepancy was about 3.5 grade levels (Coutinho, 1986).

A challenging set of data are presented by Scruggs and Mastropieri (1986), who found that there was no real difference between the academic achievement of learners identified as behaviorally disordered and learners with learning disabilities. In a later study which used teacher ratings, learners identified as behaviorally disordered and learners with learning disabilities were rated as equally, significantly below normal levels in academic achievement (Luebke, Epstein, & Cullinan, 1989). In this study, no difference was found in subject area or by gender.

Social Skills, Interaction, and Behavior

Schloss, Schloss, Wood, and Kiehl (1986) in a critical review of social skills research with learners identified as behaviorally disordered find that research has failed to build a comprehensive body of knowledge due to the absence of an underlying theory base. In addition, social skills training has not been individualized in response to learners' needs or characteristics. The social significance of social skills training has not been studied.

In a role-playing test of social competence which focused on positive and negative statements, learners identified as behaviorally disordered and their nonidentified peers demonstrated significantly different responses (Hughes & Hall, 1985). Both the content and voice quality of the learners' responses to role-play scenes of positive and negative assertion differentiated the two groups.

The general education classroom behaviors of learners identified as behaviorally disordered and their peers have also been explored. In a study of male third, fourth, and fifth graders, ten behaviors accounted for over 80 percent of the variance in group measurement and included social interaction with teacher, following directions, out-of-seat behavior, teacher-group approach to schoolwork, seeking approvals, responding to disapprovals, attending to schoolwork, raising of hands for attention, teacher-group approach to other activity, and calling out in class without raising a hand. Only teacher and child behaviors combined produced these significant results, again calling to mind the need to assess the context in which behaviors occur (Slate & Saudargas, 1986).

More than half the referrals for learners as potentially demonstrating behavioral disorders are typically enrolled in third through sixth grade, and almost three-fourths of these are male (Hutton, 1985). The most frequently stated reasons for referral are in the area of conduct disorders: a) poor peer relationships, b) frustration, c) below academic expectations, d) shy and withdrawn behavior, e) disruptive behavior, f) fighting, g) refusing to work, and h) short attention span. Poor peer relationships was the most frequent reason for referral among both boys and girls.

Edelbrock (1984), in an analysis of data from the Child Behavior Checklist he developed with his associates, found two broad clusters of behaviors among learners identified as behaviorally disordered: internalizing and externalizing. **Externalizing behaviors** included stealing, lying, disobedience, and fighting, for example, and **internalizing behaviors** included physical complaints, phobias, worrying, social withdrawal, and fearfulness, among others. The clusters of behavior by sex and age, as derived by Edelbrock, are presented in Table 7.1

Language   There is a significant difference in the expressive language characteristics in conversations of learners identified as behaviorally disordered and their nonidentified peers (McDonough, 1989). The learners identified as behaviorally disordered used shorter utterances than did their peers. In their discourse, learners identified as behaviorally disordered made errors in relations, failing to identify new information or repair responses when there were communication breakdowns. For example, a learner identified as behaviorally disordered may approach a teacher and state, "Man, he's going to get busted for doing that," failing to recognize the need to identify both the individual or the activity for the teacher. These learners demonstrated poor topic maintenance, inappropriate responses, situational inappropriateness, and inappropriate speech style.

In a study of learners identified as demonstrating mild to moderate behavioral disorders, Camarata, Hughes, and Ruhl (1988) found that 97 percent of the children fell a minimum of one standard deviation before the normative mean on an individually administered test of language. The pattern of language problems these learners demonstrated was consistent with the pattern of learners identified as learning disabled.

Adolescents placed in a psychiatric hospital were found to be significantly less informative and less effective in their communication than were nonidentified peers (Rosenthal & Simeonsson, 1991). In yet another study, 54 percent of a group of learners identified as behaviorally disordered were found to demonstrate speech or language difficulty (Trautman, Giddan, & Jurs, 1990).

Depression   The diagnostic criteria for **depression** are the same for adults and children. These criteria require that there be a dysphoric mood, that is a loss of interest or pleasure, for at least 2 weeks. At least four of the following symptoms must also be present: appetite disturbance, sleep disturbance, psychomotor agitation (excitability, hyperactivity) or retardation, loss of energy, feelings of worthlessness or guilt, diminished ability to think, and thoughts of suicide or death. Depression in children is not a rare occurrence; from 30 to 60 percent of child psychiatry outpatients fulfill the criteria for depression. This depression, without intervention, can last for months and lead to impaired school performance, poor peer and family interaction, and even suicide (Weller & Weller, 1986).

Though the symptoms of depression are similar among adults and children, the ways in which these symptoms are expressed vary (Weller & Weller, 1986). Some depressed children present problems such as a conduct disorder, which often is mistaken for the problem rather than a symptom. In addition, differences in cognitive and language functioning makes assessment of depression in children difficult.

***T*able 7.1**   Behavioral Problem Syndromes Derived for
Boys and Girls Aged 4–5, 6–11, and 12–16

Internalizing	Mixed	Externalizing
Boys 4–5		
1. Social Withdrawal	5. Sex Problems	6. Schizoid
2. Depressed		7. Aggressive
3. Immature		8. Delinquent
4. Somatic Complaints		
Girls 4–5		
1. Somatic Complaints	5. Obese	6. Aggressive
2. Depressed		7. Sex Problems
3. Schizoid		8. Hyperactive
4. Social Withdrawal		
Boys 6–11		
1. Schizoid	6. Social Withdrawal	7. Hyperactive
2. Depressed		8. Aggressive
3. Uncommunicative		9. Delinquent
4. Obsessive-Compulsive		
5. Somatic Complaints		
Girls 6–11		
1. Depressed		6. Sex Problems
2. Social Withdrawal		7. Delinquent
3. Somatic Complaints		8. Aggressive
4. Schizoid-Obsessive		9. Cruel
5. Hyperactive		
Boys 12–16		
1. Somatic Complaints	6. Hostile-Withdrawal	7. Delinquent
2. Schizoid		8. Aggressive
3. Uncommunicative		9. Hyperactive
4. Immature		
5. Obsessive-Compulsive		
Girls 12–16		
1. Anxious-Obsessive	5. Immature-Hyperactive	6. Delinquent
2. Somatic Complaints		7. Aggressive
3. Schizoid		8. Cruel
4. Depressed, Withdrawal		

From Thomas H. Ollendick and Michel Hersen, *Child Behavioral Assessment: Principles and Behaviors.*
Copyright © 1984. Reprinted by permission of Allyn & Bacon.

Learners identified as behaviorally disordered can be distinguished from their nonidentified peers in terms of characteristics associated with depression (Cullinan, Schloss, & Epstein, 1987). Depression among these learners was only related to lack of acceptance by peers, unlike the nonidentified children, in whom depression was also related to educational performance. Females were significantly at greater risk for falling into severe depression than were their male counterparts identified as behaviorally disordered (Maag & Behrens, 1989).

Aggression is fairly pervasive among learners identified as behaviorally disordered.

Working with families of depressed children is essential (Cytryn & McKnew, 1986). Individual psychotherapy for the child should be used after parent counseling and family therapy has not made a change in the child's behavior. The use of medication is justified only when a depressive illness has been reliably diagnosed, and the child has failed to respond to psychotherapy and environmental manipulation. Side effects, blood pressure, and electrocardiograms must be screened at regular intervals, and careful monitoring is essential in medication for children.

Aggression   Aggression (behavior intended to dominate others) has been found to be fairly pervasive among learners identified as behaviorally disordered. In Ruhl and Hughes' (1985) study using teacher surveys, 84 percent reported having encountered extreme physical aggression among their students; 64 percent indicated that students, teachers, and aides had all been targets of these actions. Over half indicated that severe aggressive acts, such as choking or hitting, occur at least once a month, and 29 percent reported weekly occurrences. Most commonly, between one and three times a month, mild physical aggression occurred. Learners' physical aggression towards themselves was reported by 73 percent of the teachers, and 94 percent noted destruction of property. This pervasiveness of aggression and disruption was also reported by Epstein, Kauffman, and Cullinan (1985) in their study of behavior patterns among learners identified as behaviorally disordered. The most consistent, persistent pattern they found among the learners they assessed was that of aggression demonstrated as disobedience, negativism, boisterousness, temper tantrums, disruptiveness, fighting, profane language, jealousy, irresponsibility, attention-seeking, uncooperativeness, irritability, and impertinence.

Aggressive behaviors have been found to follow interactions in which the students identified as behaviorally disordered initiated greetings or made requests of peers and the peers ignored the greetings, denied the requests, or made a derogatory comment to the students. Knapczyk (1988) used videotape exemplars of social situations to model, rehearse, and provide directed feedback of appropriate alternatives. The intervention was effective, and peers were more willing to interact with students identified as behaviorally disordered.

Identification and Evaluation

Objective Two: To describe the identification and evaluation of learners identified as behaviorally disordered.

Since the term "seriously emotionally disturbed" was first defined in Public Law 94–142, there has been controversy relating to the terminology used with these learners, the definition itself, and the assessment of learners identified as having behavioral disorders.

In a general sense, learners identified as having **behavioral disorders** are those whose behavior varies in frequency, intensity, and duration from their general education peers to such an extent that it comes to the attention of authority figures, usually teachers, and results in their being labeled as behaviorally disordered. Kauffman (1985) suggests that identifying learners as behaviorally disordered is the process of comparing them to the nebulous standard of "normal," which is in itself difficult, if not impossible, to define. Shea and Bauer (1987) contend that it is normal for all learners to have periods during their lives that are characterized by ineffective decision-making, inadequate learning of accepted behavior, crisis, conflict, depression, and stress. At such times, behaviors similar to those exhibited by learners identified as behaviorally disordered are not uncommon.

Kauffman (1981) discussed another difficulty when defining behavioral disorders. He stated that some behavior may be deemed inappropriate in one setting and not in another simply due to differences in expectations in the settings. This means that there are both "disturbed" and "disturbing" behaviors. **Disturbing behaviors** are those that occur at a certain place and time and in the presence of certain individuals. **Disturbed behaviors** are those that occur in many settings and are a part of the individual's habitual behavior pattern. Disturbing behaviors, though difficult to accept under specific circumstances, are not indicative of a behavioral disorder.

Public Law 94–142 uses the term **seriously emotionally disturbed** to identify the learners referred to in this chapter as "identified as behaviorally disordered." According to the definition in the law, this term means:

(i) . . . a condition exhibiting one or more of the following characteristics over a long period of time and to a marked degree, which adversely affects educational performance:
   (a) an inability to learn which cannot be explained by intellectual, sensory, and health factors;
   (b) an inability to build or maintain satisfactory interpersonal relationships with peers and teachers;
   (c) inappropriate types of behavior or feelings under normal circumstances;
   (d) a general pervasive mood of unhappiness or depression; or
   (e) a tendency to develop physical symptoms or fears associated with personal or school problems.
(ii) The term includes children who are schizophrenic or autistic. The term does not include children who are socially maladjusted unless it is determined that they are seriously emotionally disturbed (Federal Register, 1977, 42, 162).

Some behavior may be deemed inappropriate in one setting and not in another due to differences in expectations.

Children classified as autistic were excluded from the federal definition of "seriously emotionally disturbed" in the 1981 regulations and reclassified as "other health impaired." In 1990, through Public Law 101–456 (Individuals with Disabilities Education Act), learners with autism were again reclassified, and a separate category of disability was delineated.

In 1985, the Council for Children with Behavioral Disorders (Huntze, 1985) argued that the term "behaviorally disordered" should replace the term "seriously emotionally disturbed" because (a) the term is not associated exclusively with any particular theory of causation or intervention techniques, (b) the term would afford a more comprehensive assessment of the population, (c) "behaviorally disordered" is far less stigmatizing, (d) the term is more representative of the students who are disabled by their behavior, and (e) the change in terminology is representative of a focus on the educational responsibility delineated in the law.

In 1987, the Executive Committee of the Council for Children with Behavioral Disorders urged that:

1. The federal definition of "seriously emotionally disturbed" be revised, with a functional *educational* definition taking its place.
2. "Socially maladjusted" children and youth should not be excluded from the definition.
3. Any new definition should focus on the sources of data collection necessary to determine whether a student is behaviorally disordered.
4. Any new definition should require documentation of prior attempts to modify a targeted student's deviant behavior within regular education setting and the use of intervention models that exemplify the least restrictive alternative.
5. Priorities within the field of behavioral disorders include leadership training on a national basis, teacher training, research, and training for general education personnel.

The task force on definition of the National Mental Health and Special Education Coalition (Editor, 1990) completed its work on the draft definition that it is promoting as a substitute for the current definition of seriously emotionally disturbed in the Education for All Handicapped Children Act. The definition includes the following points:

- Emotional or behavioral disorder refers to a condition in which behavioral or emotional responses of an individual in school are so different from his/her generally accepted, age-appropriate, ethnic, or cultural norms as to result in significant impairment in self care, social relationships, educational progress, classroom behavior, or work adjustment. This category may include children or youth with schizophrenia, depression, anxiety disorders, attention deficit disorders, or with other sustained disturbances of conduct or adjustment.
- Emotional or behavior disorder is more than a transient, expected response to stressors in the individual's environment and persists despite individualized interventions, such as feedback to the individual, consultation with parents or families, and/or modifications of the educational environment.
- The eligibility decision must be based on multiple sources of data about the individual's behaviors or emotional function. Emotional or behavioral disorder must be exhibited in at least two different settings, at least one of which is educational.

Public Law 98–199, the Education of the Handicapped Act Amendments of 1983, mandated a study to determine the potential impact that changing the terminology and definition used with learners identified as behaviorally disordered would have. Arguments were that the federal label of "seriously emotionally disturbed" was stigmatizing and educationally irrelevant; others argued that any change would cause an incredible influx of students with purely behavioral problems into the category, which would strain states' financial resources.

The federal definition and the definition proposed by the Task Force on Definition of the Mental Health and Special Education Coalition, discussed above, are but two of the many definitions that have been applied to differentiate learners identified as behaviorally disordered from other learners. Definitions tend to vary with the purpose of their authors. In the literature, we find definitions written by authorities in the field based on their experience and theoretical point of view, by researchers to delineate a specific population for study, and by administrators for the purpose of planning and managing programs.

In their 1985 study, Talmadge, Gamel, Munson, & Hanley (1985) found considerable variation from state to state of the numbers of learners identified as behaviorally disordered who are served. Differences in definition from state to state account for 35 percent of the variation amount the numbers of students served (Wright, Pillard, & Cleven, 1990). Roughly two-thirds of the variance among the numbers of students served remained unaccounted for. Wright and associates proposed that this variation could be accounted for at three levels: (a) state definitions and identification procedures, which are not directed by federal guidelines, (b) school district procedures, which, depending on the state, may not be directed by state guidelines, and (c) the training and practices of prereferral intervention teams, evaluation teams, and team members.

Issues Related to Assessment of Learners Identified as Behaviorally Disordered

The most widely used classification system for learners identified as behaviorally disordered is the *Diagnostic and Statistical Manual of Mental Disorders of the American Psychiatric Association—Revised* (3rd edition, revised, 1987). This is a classification system based on the clinical expertise of hundreds of mental health practitioners. It includes seventeen major diagnostic categories, including one specifically for infants, children, and adolescents. Within this category ten major syndromes and forty-five subsyndromes are described. The ten major syndromes and subsyndromes are presented in Table 7.2. In the manual, each diagnostic syndrome is described in detail, such as the attention deficit disorder with hyperactivity, shown in Table 7.3.

The Revised Problem Behavior Checklist (Quay & Peterson, 1987) as part of the screening process is a good example of issues of reliability and validity in identifying learners identified as behaviorally disordered. Simpson (1989), in a comparison of two groups of teachers' ratings of the same 95 children, found little agreement between the two groups of teachers in identifying children who were described as either mildly or highly deviant. He concludes that the rating of the behavior of children is extremely subjective. The issue of the context is very relevant in these findings; situations may differ markedly from one regular education

TABLE 7.2   Classification System-DSM III-R

I. Developmental Disorders
  A. Mental Retardation
    1. Mild Mental Retardation
    2. Moderate Mental Retardation
    3. Severe Mental Retardation
    4. Profound Mental Retardation
    5. Unspecified Mental Retardation
  B. Pervasive Developmental Disorders
    1. Autistic Disorder
    2. Pervasive Developmental Disorder Not Otherwise Specified
  C. Specific Developmental Disorders
    1. Academic Skill Disorders
    2. Language and Speech Disorders
    3. Motor Skills Disorder
II. Disruptive Behavior Disorders
  A. Attention-Deficit Hyperactivity Disorder
  B. Conduct Disorder
  C. Oppositional-Defiant Disorder
III. Anxiety Disorders of Childhood or Adolescence
  A. Separation Anxiety Disorder
  B. Avoidant Disorder of Childhood or Adolescence
  C. Overanxious Disorder
IV. Eating Disorders
  A. Anorexia Nervosa
  B. Bulimia Nervosa
  C. Pica
  D. Rumination Disorder of Infancy
V. Gender Identity Disorders
  A. Gender Identity Disorder of Childhood
  B. Transsexualism
  C. Gender Identity Disorder of Adolescence or Adulthood, Nontranssexual Type
VI. Tic Disorders
  A. Tourette's Disorder
  B. Chronic Motor or Vocal Tic Disorder
  C. Transient Tic Disorder
VII. Elimination Disorders
  A. Functional Encopresis
  B. Functional Enuresis
VIII. Speech Disorders Not Elsewhere Classified
  A. Cluttering
  B. Stuttering
IX. Other Disorders of Infancy, Childhood, or Adolescence
  A. Elective Mutism
  B. Identity Disorder
  C. Reactive Attachment Disorder of Infancy or Early Childhood
  D. Stereotypy/Habit Disorder
  E. Undifferentiated Attention Deficit Disorder

American Psychiatric Association: *Diagnostic and Statistical Manual of Mental Disorders,* Third Edition, Revised, Washington, DC, American Psychiatric Association, 1987.

***T*ABLE 7.3**   Diagnostic Criteria for Attention Deficit Disorder with Hyperactivity

The child displays, for his or her mental and chronological age, signs of developmentally inappropriate inattention, impulsivity, and hyperactivity. The signs must be reported by adults in the child's environment, such as parents and teachers. Because the symptoms are typically variable, they may not be observed directly by the clinician. When the reports of teachers and parents conflict, primary consideration should be give to the teacher reports because of greater familiarity with age-appropriate norms. Symptoms typically worsen in situations that require self-application, as in the classroom. Signs of the disorder may be absent when the child is in a new or one-on-one situation.

The number of symptoms specified is for children between the ages of eight and ten, the peak age range for referral. In younger children, more severe forms of the symptoms and a greater number of symptoms are usually present. The opposite is true of older children.

A. Inattention. At least three of the following:
  (1) often fails to finish things he or she starts
  (2) often doesn't seem to listen
  (3) easily distracted
  (4) has difficulty concentrating on schoolwork or other tasks requiring sustained attention
  (5) has difficulty sticking to a play activity
B. Impulsivity. At least three of the following:
  (1) often acts before thinking
  (2) shifts excessively from one activity to another
  (3) has difficulty organizing work (this not being due to cognitive impairment)
  (4) needs a lot of supervision
  (5) frequently calls out in class
  (6) has difficulty awaiting turn in games or group situations
C. Hyperactivity. At least two of the following:
  (1) runs about or climbs on things excessively
  (2) has difficulty sitting still or fidgets excessively
  (3) has difficulty staying seated
  (4) moves about excessively during sleep
  (5) is always "on the go" or acts as if "driven by a motor"
D. Onset before the age of seven
E. Duration of at least six months
F. Not due to Schizophrenia, Affective Disorder, or Severe or Profound Mental Retardation

American Psychiatric Association: *Diagnostic and Statistical Manual of Mental Disorders,* Third Edition, Revised, Washington, DC, American Psychiatric Association, 1987.

class to another, and raters may vary markedly, even when attempting to identify learners whose behavior is very different from their peers.

Skiba (1989) reviewed eighty-nine correlations between classroom observations and behavioral ratings drawn from sixteen studies. He found very low correlations between what was actually observed and what was rated by teachers using formal rating scales. He suggests that there are serious problems with the validity of assessments that look for the problems within the students themselves. He maintains that the recognition of the "problem situation" rather than the "problem student" should be used to identify and describe behavior problems in schools.

The lack of consensus regarding designation and description of learners identified as behaviorally disordered extends to researchers in the field. Kavale, Forness, and Alper (1986) found in their survey of 323 research studies in behavioral disorders and emotional disturbance that the research literature presents a divergent picture in regards to the nature and prevalence of behavioral disorders, and reflects a lack of consensus regarding standard identification criteria. The Executive Committee of the Council for Children with Behavioral Disorders (1989) argues that until definition, classification, and measurement criteria for learners identified as behaviorally disordered are made more objective and verifiable, assessment of behavioral disorders will continue to be highly subjective and open to multiple sources of bias.

Cultural Diversity and Assessment

Many factors may contribute to the misclassification of learners from diverse cultures as behaviorally disordered. Some of these factors include:

1. Language, which affects how the educational community interacts and perceives the learner's behavior.
2. Faulty teacher perceptions and lowered expectations.
3. The higher rates at which learners from cultural minorities enter the referral-to-placement process, which increases their likelihood of identification. (Executive Committee of the Council for Children with Behavioral Disorders, 1989.)

In order to address these issues and reduce the overrepresentation of learners from minority cultures in programs for learners identified as behaviorally disordered, the Executive Committee of the Council for Children with Behavioral Disorders recommends that assessment must include a recognition of the context in which the behavior occurs. This more functional means of assessment assumes that learning is an interactive process, which occurs within a context. In addition, it assumes that learners from minority cultures will respond to "good teaching" and that this programming may be provided without labeling or classifying the child. Finally, this functional assessment assumes that early, collaborative intervention is preferred to entering the referral-to-placement process.

Carlson and Stephens (1986), in their study of the Social Behavior Assessment Scale, conclude that bias was not found in the instrument itself; rather, differential scores on the rating forms were either an indication of teacher bias or of real cultural differences.

Objective Three: To describe the impact of behavioral disorders on interactions in the home and school.

The Impact of Behavioral Disorders in the Home and School

Ramsey and Walker (1988) studied the family management practices of male, fourth grade learners identified as antisocial. Though they found no differences between these learners and their nonidentified peers in the area of involvement, significant differences were found in discipline, monitoring, positive reinforcement, and problem solving. They concluded that learners identified as antisocial were exposed to far more negative and less competent family management practices than were their peers.

Parent Involvement in Interventions

Reimers and Wacker (1988) find that though the amount of disruption an intervention causes and the willingness of parents to participate in the intervention initially had an affect on its acceptability, once the treatment was in place the effectiveness of the treatment as rated by the parents had the largest influence on acceptability.

Parents are equal partners in their child's education.

Parents' Needs   Simpson (1988), in his exploration of parents' needs, finds that the most widely used and/or requested service by parents is that of information exchange, through informal feedback, progress reports, conferences, and program information. Parents also request parent-coordinated service programs, counseling, therapy and consultation, consumer and advocacy training, and home program training. Teachers perceive parents as needing parent-coordinated service programs, home program training, consumer and advocacy training, and counseling, therapy, and consultation. According to Simpson, there is a significant difference between teachers' perceptions of parents' needs and parents' expressed needs.

Relationships in the Classroom

As indicated earlier, one of the most pervasive indicators of identification as behaviorally disordered is poor peer relationships. In addition, relationships with teachers are challenging for these learners. Teachers rated extreme social withdrawal (lack of communication) and deficiencies in specific academic learning strategies and skills as the most difficult to manage in the classroom (Safran, Safran, & Barcikowski, 1988).

Objective Four: To describe ways to mediate the environment for learners identified as behaviorally disordered.

Mediating the Environment

In mediating the environment for learners identified as having behavioral disorders, strategies and interventions have been historically tied to several competing perspectives. The psychodynamic perspective maintained that the cause of behavior is within the individual, and thus interventions must deal with the learner's dynamic, intrapsychic life. The biophysical perspective postulates a relationship between physical conditions and the behavior exhibited by the learner. The behavioral perspective defines behaviors as all human acts that are observable and measurable, and maintained by variables in the environment. The systems or ecological perspective, such as that in which this text is grounded, focuses on the reciprocal relationship between the learner or group of learners and the contexts in which they are interacting.

Though these perceptual fields argue strongly for significantly different strategies, very few comprehensive program descriptions for learners identified as behaviorally disordered are available in the literature (Grosenick, George, & George, 1988). McConnell (1987) suggests a reemphasis on the careful selection of which behaviors should be addressed. She argues that to maximize the likelihood that the behaviors and skills on which we work become "entrapped," that is kept under the control of naturally occurring reinforcement, that behaviors are selected which: (a) will be maintained after the intervention is terminated, (b) will generalize across other settings or other behaviors, and (c) will covary with specific social behaviors of peers. When behaviors such as these are selected, we would be more likely to expect that newly acquired social behaviors will continue at high rates and generalize to new settings after the specific intervention stops.

In their 3-year study of programs and policies regarding learners identified as behaviorally disordered, Knitzer, Steinberg, and Fleisch (1990) sought to explore the scope of policy, program possibilities, and the experiences of parents with children identified as behaviorally disordered, and to review current information to underscore the data gathered. Knitzer and associates describe seven typical placement possibilities for learners identified as behaviorally disordered. These include regular classrooms, resource rooms in the regular school, self-contained classrooms in regular schools, special schools and day schools, day treatment programs, residential treatment centers, in-patient psychiatric hospitals, and homebound instruction. Enormous variation was found in placement. For example, in seven states, between 10 and 20 percent of all learners identified as behaviorally disordered are in residential placements; in seven others, under one percent are in residential placements. In seven states, more than half of all learners identified as behaviorally disordered are served in resource rooms, whereas eleven states rely heavily on self-contained classrooms or separate facilities.

The placement that emerged as most problematic is residential placement. Evidence suggested that decisions for residential placement were driven by factors other than student needs, such as a lack of services in the school or the need for respite for the family. Children were often placed far from their homes, making case monitoring and parent contact difficult. In some states, parents were required to relinquish custody in order to obtain residential treatment for their child. Rather than supporting the child's development, residential placement further isolated the child from family and peers.

In their observations of programs throughout the nation, Knitzer, Steinberg, and Fleisch found several pervasive themes in the educational programs of learners identified as behaviorally disordered, as follows:

- Control of learners served as a central part of the nature of the learners' school experience.
- Academics, what was being taught and how it was being taught, were secondary to behavior control. They suggested a haphazard nature of curricula activities.
- Social skills curricula were held to be important, but classrooms were structured so that no social interaction could take place.
- Physical activity was rare; students were sometimes expected to sit at their desks without talking or interacting for hours on end. Physical activity was sometimes regarded as a reward rather than a right for the children.

- In many programs, there was a limited mental health presence, with little access to therapy for the children and little consultation and support for teachers.
- Parents often experienced difficulties in ensuring appropriate placements, and teachers often experienced a sense of isolation and lack of support.
- Transitions were frequently ignored, in particular transitions from one placement to another.

In a study of how students perceived their educational environments, Leone, Luttig, Zlotlow, and Trickett (1990) describe data that support the work of Knitzer and her associates. They found that students in special schools for learners identified as behaviorally disordered perceive order and organization lower and teacher control higher than did students in traditional school programs. Student satisfaction, however, was related to greater levels of perceived involvement, affiliation, and teacher support for learners with special needs.

Preschool   Beare and Lynch (1986) contend that there are substantial numbers of preschool children who demonstrate behaviors indicative of behavioral disorders but who are not being served by mandated public school programs nor consultative programming. Public schools are apparently unaware of these children despite screening efforts. Scruggs, Mastropieri, Cook, and Escobar (1986) conducted a meta-analysis of single subject research conducted on young children. They found that reinforcement produced the most positive outcomes, followed by punishment/time-out, and differential attention, and that learners' characteristics such as sex, disability, and target behavior generally bore little relation to treatment outcome. They concluded that positive results were found for home-based interventions and for younger subjects, though these findings were somewhat inconsistent.

Impact of Placement Options   During the 1989–90 school year, the largest percentage of learners identified as behaviorally disordered were served in separate classes (34.6 percent), with slightly fewer in resource rooms (32.9 percent), and far fewer in regular classes (12.6 percent), separate schools (14.3 percent), residential settings (3.5 percent), and homes or hospitals (2.2 percent). Only two categories of disability have more students served in separate facilities: learners with multiple handicaps and learners who are deaf and blind (U.S. Department of Education, 1990).

It comes as no surprise that learners identified as behaviorally disordered exhibited more problem behaviors than did their peers with learning disabilities, and secondary students exhibited more rule-breaking than did elementary students (Sindelar, King, Gantland, Wilson, & Meisel, 1985). More anxious, fearful behavior and rule-breaking were exhibited in special classes than in resource rooms.

Referral of Learners Identified as Behaviorally Disordered   Sevcik and Ysseldyke (1986) found that prior to referral for evaluation for identification as behaviorally disordered, teachers proposed and actually used interventions that involved teacher-directed actions, such as specific behavioral methods, nonspecific methods, structure change, and changing grouping. When teachers employed specific interventions, however, it was found that just slightly over a third involved positive reinforcement, while punishment and unspecified interventions comprised slightly

Learners who choose to cooperate are granted more and more privileges such as field trips.

under two-thirds of the interventions. When given a choice, teachers selected using the services of a consultant almost as readily as teacher-directed actions, but consultative options were only actually used in 10 percent of the cases.

Classroom Management

The selection of techniques and strategies for classroom management is viewed through the lens of the individual implementing the strategy. A practitioner who views the learner from a psychodynamic perspective will focus on counseling techniques, expressive media, and surface management techniques to deal with the "here and now" of behaviors. The behaviorist will manipulate the immediate environment and apply social learning theory, including modeling, desensitization, and various self-management and self-instruction interventions. Biophysical interventions may include diet or medication. In the systems perspective, however, each of the wide range of interventions available may be applied after careful consideration of the learners and the context in which the behavior occurs.

Bauer and Sapona (1988) argue that with the increasing recognition of child development within context, behavioral models of behavior management will be used as only one part of comprehensive management frameworks. With the emphasis on control implicit in the behavioral model of management, learners identified as behaviorally disordered may be limited in their ability to achieve by the restrictive classroom environment. The emerging concept of schooling is to "bring to students the skills that will widen for each of them the spectrum of learning environments in which they can relate" (Joyce, 1987, p. 427). In the emphasis on controlling behaviors, many incidental opportunities for learning may be lost. Bauer and Sapona (1988) suggest that instead the teacher should be a proactive facilitator who exercises a facilitative stance. This stance supports co-learning in a meaningful context, with mutual negotiation between teacher and student and greater opportunities to interact.

When working with learners identified as behaviorally disordered, the student's interaction pattern is usually viewed as a problem in itself. Brooks (1991) relates some of these behavior patterns, however, to the power relationship which is evident in classroom or treatment settings. Hubbell (1981) describes first and second order changes in addressing these behavior problems. Hubbell describes first order changes as management strategies that change the environment, such as putting contingencies in place, providing a rationale for rules and rewards, or modifying attitude and activity. All of these strategies occur with the teacher remaining in charge. These first order changes may, however, fail among learners for whom behavior represents the relationship tactic of challenging the power and authority of adults. When the student's problem is with authority itself, any action taken by the teacher will be met with opposition.

In second order changes, Hubbell describes the need for the teacher to relinquish authority. The learner is allowed to choose among several alternatives. Brooks (1991) describes the ultimate choice, of participating or doing nothing. He indicates, however, that several conditions are necessary for the successful use of this approach. For example, activities must be inherently appealing, and they must be accompanied by materials reinforcing to those who choose to cooperate. If the learner spontaneously joins in the activity at any point, he or she should be included without comment as long as behavior is appropriate.

Levels systems, organizational frameworks within which various behavior management interventions are applied to shape students' social, communicative, and academic behaviors to preestablished levels, are frequently used with learners identified as behaviorally disordered. A levels system includes: (a) a description of each level, (b) criteria for movement from one level to another, and (c) behavioral expectations, restrictions, and privileges for each level. As students proceed through each of the levels, the behavioral responsibilities and privileges increase (Bauer, Shea, & Keppler, 1986). Levels systems may vary in many ways, as to:

1. How students proceed through the levels. Options include student negotiation of level, moving lock-step through the system, group consensus on each student's level, or teacher designation of level depending on an assessment of the student's behavior.
2. The amount of time students remain on each level. A specific amount of time may be designated as a minimum stay.
3. Who reviews the student's status and monitors the learner's behavior. Students, peers, teacher, or any combination of these may be involved in the evaluation process. Self-monitoring or teacher monitoring may be used.

The advantages of a well-developed, individualized levels system include offering security, structure, and routine. Teachers are delivered from the "me against them" position, and structures and procedures enhance self-management. An example of a levels system is shown in Table 7.4.

Students' survey responses suggest that they attribute positive behavior change to the implementation of levels systems (Mastropieri, Jenne, & Scruggs, 1988). However, this finding in itself is of concern when the use of such systems is only to provide a framework for students. If students attribute the change to the system rather than themselves, they remain externally controlled instead of attributing change to enhanced self-management.

TABLE 7.4   Sample Levels System

Behavior Management System
Severe Behavior Handicap Class
Aiken Senior High School (Murphy, 1991)

Level I

Responsibilities
  1. Follow classroom rules.
  2. Earn at least 53 points daily.
  3. Goal set by staff.
  4. Supervised by staff at all times.
  5. Attend group meetings.

Consequences
  1. Points are earned when responsibilities are met.
  2. If 53 points are not earned for three days in a row, you drop to the beginning of Level I.

Privileges
  1. Participate in goal activity.
  2. 50 bonus points are given for earning all 70 daily points.

Level II

Responsibilities
  1. Follow classroom rules.
  2. Earn at least 56 points daily.
  3. Participate in group meetings.
  4. Set own goal.

Consequences
  1. Points are earned when responsibilities are met.
  2. If 56 points are not earned for three days in a row, you drop to the beginning of Level II.
  3. Three more consecutive days of minimum points not earned will result to a drop to the beginning of Level I.

Privileges
  1. Participate in goal activity.
  2. Buying time.*
  3. Participate in field trips.
  4. 75 bonus points for earning all 70 daily points.
  5. Self-escort.

Level III

Responsibilities
  1. Follow classroom rules.
  2. Earn at least 59 points daily.
  3. Participate in group meetings.
  4. Make honest "I" statements.

Consequences
  1. Points are earned when responsibilities are met.
  2. If 59 points are not earned for three days in a row, you drop to the beginning of Level III.
  3. Three more consecutive days of minimum points not earned will result in a drop to the beginning of Level II.
  4. If you are unable to be honest about your behavior and continue to blame others for your actions, you will be required to go to Level II.

Privileges
  1. Lead group meetings.
  2. Keep own point record.
  3. 100 bonus points for earning maximum points.
  4. Buying time.
  5. Participate in field trips.

Level IV

Responsibilities
  1. Follow classroom rules.
  2. Earn at least 63 points daily.
  3. Make honest "I" statements.

  * A time to purchase items such as pencils, tablets, chewing gum, and hygiene items, with points earned. Buying time takes place at a designated time each week.

4. Turn in homework.
5. Complete class assignments.
6. Participate in all out classes.
7. Come to school with supplies.

Consequences
1. Points are earned when responsibilities are met.
2. If 63 points are not earned for three days in a row, you drop to the beginning of Level IV.
3. Three more consecutive days of not earning 63 points will result in a level drop to the beginning of Level III.
4. If you are unable to meet the responsibilities of this level, you will be required to move to Level III.

Privileges
1. Set goal activity in collaboration with other students.
2. Earn a "no homework pass" (1 per week if all days count).
3. Run buying time.
4. 125 bonus points for earning all 70 points.
5. Lead group meetings.

Level V

Responsibilities
1. Follow classroom rules.
2. Earn at least 66 out of the possible 70 daily points.
3. Put forth effort and maintain passing grades in all classes.
4. Turn in homework.
5. Make honest statements about your behavior and put forth effort to change areas needing improvement.
6. Successfully participate in all out classes.
7. Come to school with supplies.

Consequences
1. Points are earned when responsibilities are met.
2. If 66 points are not earned for three days in a row, you will drop to the beginning of Level V.
3. Three more consecutive days of minimum points not earned will result in a level drop to the beginning of Level IV.
4. If you are unable to meet the responsibilities of this level, you will be required to move to Level IV.

Privileges
1. Lunch with a staff member once a month at the Overlook or a restaurant.
2. Earn a free period once a month if all days are counted.
3. Earn 175 bonus points for earning all 70 points daily.
4. Lead group meetings.
5. Keep own point record.
6. Run buying time.
7. Participate in field trips.

Maintenance

Responsibilities
1. Follow school and classroom rules.
2. Put forth effort in all classes and maintain passing grades.

Privileges
1. No point chart will be maintained for maintenance level students, however, a student on maintenance is given all of the above privileges.
2. 200 bonus daily for meeting all the required responsibilities.

Note: A referral to an administrator or skipping a class will result in a drop to the beginning of the level you are on. A suspension or expulsion will result in a drop to the beginning of the previous level.

Courtesy E. Susanne Murphy, Aiken Senior High School, Cincinnati, Ohio.

Rosenberg (1986) reports that structured classroom managements systems such as token economies and level systems are common, yet may not achieve maximum effectiveness. In his study, daily review of classroom rules resulted in an overall time-on-task improvement and a reduction in disruption.

A **token economy** is an exchange system that provides individuals or groups whose behavior is being changed with nearly immediate feedback cues of the appropriateness of their behavior. These cues (tokens) are at a later time exchanged for backup reinforcers (items and activities). Tokens are usually valueless to the students initially. However, their value becomes apparent when the students learn that the tokens can be exchanged (traded) for backup reinforcers.

When developing a token economy, the educator must first select the specific behavior or behaviors to be changed. These behaviors, referred to as target behaviors, must be discussed and clarified with the individual or group whose behavior is to be changed. Next, a token is selected. Then, a menu or list of backup reinforcers is developed and posted in the classroom. Finally, the economy is implemented.

During the course of the intervention, time must be provided during the school day for the exchange of tokens. As the school year progresses, the teacher must revise the reward menu and backup reinforcers to avoid satiation.

The properly managed token economy is effective because individuals are only competing with themselves and the reinforcer menu provides a variety of desirable items and activities.

In a day treatment program, the child's functioning at entry was found to be the best predictor of the family's ability to work well as a unit, with younger, nontruant children and involved families of less disturbed children (Baenen, Glenwick, Stephens, Neuhaus, and Mowrey, 1986). Children with behavioral problems such as poor concentration, passivity, and daydreaming tended to have comparatively positive outcomes, though research has demonstrated that children with such problems progress with no intervention. Children with conduct disorders had more severe problems and more changes in family structure during treatment, such as moves in foster care.

Self-management Programs   Self-management through self-evaluation has been demonstrated to reduce students' off-task and disruptive behaviors in a resource room. However, even when trained to make judgements about their own behavior and to solve social problems, students had difficulty applying these skills in the general education classroom (Smith, Young, West, Morgan, & Rhode, 1988). In an attempt to increase generalization, strategies such as the group meeting (see Box 7.1) and "Think Aloud" (Box 7.2) have been used.

In a review of self-management outcome research with learners identified as behaviorally disordered, Nelson, Smith, Young, and Dodd (1991) report that the procedures did indeed promote productive social and academic behaviors among learners identified as behaviorally disordered. In addition, the procedures appeared to be durable. Spontaneous generalization, however, was not noted. Treatment effects, however, were found to generalize if the generalization was part of the systematic program.

Transition   The issue of transition frequently emerges in discussions of programs for learners identified as behaviorally disordered. Swan, Brown, and Jacob (1987) found that over half of the preschool group and over a third of the elementary, middle, and high school groups were reintegrated directly into general education. Of

Box 7.1

Class Meetings

Class meetings are frequently used in programs serving learners identified as behaviorally disordered. The purpose of the meeting is for teachers and students to collaboratively discuss behavioral, personal, and academic problems. Meetings can assist students in developing their own goals, thinking about their own behavior in contexts, and becoming more attentive to the class environment (Morris, 1982). A typical class meeting agenda follows (Bauer, personal observation, 1993):

1. Meeting called to order.
2. Rules for class meeting read (for example, statements should be positive; listen while others talk; everyone has a say).
3. Goals stated (students state their weekly goals and progress made towards those goals. Other students may assist the student in evaluating his or her behavior).
4. Group business attended to (any issues affecting the group may be discussed).
5. Personal business attended to (personal issues may be discussed).
6. Gripes aired (concerns about situations, events, or interpersonal problems may be discussed; gripes must be stated as an issue, and problem solving strategies are applied to support the individual presenting the gripe).
7. Positives stated (each individual makes a positive statement about himself or herself or another).
8. Meeting adjourned ■

Courtesy E. Susanne Murphy, Aiken Senior High School, Cincinnati, Ohio.

Box 7.2

"Think Aloud"

Camp and Bash (1981) developed a general problem-solving strategy which they refer to as "Think Aloud" to assist students in improving interpersonal interactions. In "Think Aloud," students are taught a series of self-instructional questions, such as:

1. What is the problem?
2. What is my plan?
3. Am I using my plan?
4. How did I do?

Through teacher modeling and role playing problem situations, "Think Aloud" can be used to deal with impulsive responding of learners identified as behaviorally disordered, such as verbally or physically aggressive behavior ■

Source: B. W. Camp and M. S. Bash, (1981). *Think Aloud: Increasing Social and Cognitive Skills.* Champaign, Illinois: Research Press.

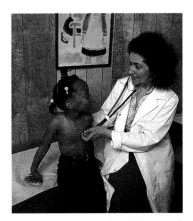

Preventive medicine includes maintenance of doctor checkups.

those reintegrated into less restrictive special education settings, over half continued as learners identified as behaviorally disordered, suggesting that most students are not reclassified when they are reintegrated into less restrictive settings.

Medical Intervention   Medication is the most common medical intervention for behavioral disorders (Cullinan, Epstein, & Lloyd, 1983). In their review of the use of medication with learners identified as behaviorally disordered, Epstein and Ollinger (1987) recommend that: (a) school personnel should be well informed about the drug therapy, (b) teachers should follow school policy for the administration and management of prescribed medications, (c) the school should ensure that a physician-school-parent communication link is established in every case where medications have been prescribed, (d) teachers should collect data on target behaviors during and after the use of medication. Through direct observation, more careful and profitable use of medication may emerge.

Life Space Interviews   The **life space interview** is a technique developed by Redl (1966) in which the teacher and student interact in a guided interview, allowing the learner to describe an incident that occurred and the feelings related to the incident, and discuss how to respond more effectively in the future. Though the literature on life space interviewing is "fragmented, out of date, and lacks any conclusive evidence about the efficacy of this strategy" (Long, 1990), the strategy is one which very aptly fits a systems or contextual model of development: teachers need to understand a crisis from the student's point of view, while also promoting the student's active choice and responsibility for the behavior. Box 7.3 provides descriptive information about life space interviews.

Psychiatric Hospitalization   Feinstein and Uribe (1986) contend that hospitalization should be considered for learners identified as behaviorally disordered only after all outpatient alternatives have been ineffective or refused, or when the problem is severe enough to necessitate a comprehensive inpatient program. Problems judged severe include being overtly or potentially dangerous to self, family, or others; self-destructive behavior through drug or alcohol abuse or self-inflicted injuries; or repetitive running away, violence, truancy, promiscuity, social isolation, extreme mood swings, or a psychotic disorder. Hospitalization is reasonable when there are problems in all life support areas (family, community, and school) and efforts to mobilize the individual to change have failed.

   The use of short-term hospitalization (periods up to 3 months) has been abused by some programs since short-term care fits many insurance plans (Feinstein & Uribe, 1986). Problems with short-term hospitalization occur when individuals are rapidly discharged back to families, special education programs, or loosely organized programs when the learner shows evidence of superficial compliance but has not resolved problems.

Objective Five: To describe the impact of behavioral disorders on participation in larger social systems—the school, community, and society.

The Impact on the School, Community, and Society

Individuals identified as behaviorally disordered demonstrate difficulties in interacting with their peers in positive ways. These difficulties present challenges to these learners that are pervasive throughout their school careers and as they enter the community.

   In data generated from 145 special education administrators in 27 states, Grosenick, George, George, & Lewis (1991) find that the identification of students

Box 7.3

Life Space Interviews

Purpose:

To change behavior, enhance self-esteem, reduce anxiety, and increase understanding and insight into behavior and feelings

Steps:

1. focus on the behavioral incident
2. identify the central issue and select a therapeutic goal
3. select a solution grounded in values
4. develop a plan for success
5. resume activity

Student Prerequisite Skills:

Adequate attention, expressive language, comprehension, reasoning, and trust in the adult-interviewer

Adult Prerequisite Attributes:

Involvement with the student, self-control, sensitivity, belief in the student's need for protection, gratification, relationships, and responsibility

Outcomes:

Resolution of the incident, as well as increased student understanding, problem-solving ability, and self-esteem ■

From M. M. Wood and N. J. Long, *Life Space Intervention: Talking with Children and Youth in Crisis.* Copyright © 1991 Pro-Ed, Austin, TX. Reprinted by permission.

---

identified as behaviorally disordered seems fairly well developed. The ways in which students exited programs and the ways in which these programs were evaluated were less formalized. In this study, teachers continued to play the central role in program implementation, with general education teachers considerably less involved. The self-contained classroom remained the most prevalent setting for these students, but a great deal of variability among programs was noted. The behavioral perspective continues to dominate, with the primary focus on determining eligibility, curriculum and programming, and exit criteria based on the tenets of the behavioral perspective. A lack of communication and collaboration with agencies external to the schools continued to be evident.

Learners identified as behaviorally disordered have lower status in the classroom, though they are known as well by their peers as are their nonidentified peers (Sabournie & Kauffman, 1985). The learners identified as behaviorally disordered rated their fellow learners identified as behaviorally disordered in the same class higher than their peers in social status. Learners identified as behaviorally disordered, in comparison with matched nonidentified peers, assigned higher social rejection to their nonidentified peers, and received far less acceptance and more rejection from them (Sabournie, 1987). No differences in assigned acceptance or assigned and received familiarity among same and opposite gender classmates were found between learners identified as behaviorally disordered and their nonidentified peers.

Grade level differences in degrees of behavioral tolerance occur; children demonstrate increased tolerance as they progress into upper elementary grades (Safran & Safran, 1985). The total group of learners studied, however, agreed that the most disturbing behaviors were outer-directed—negative aggressive, and poor peer cooperation—which held definite interpersonal consequences. Consistent with Voeltz's (1980) study of peer acceptance, learners feel justified in rejecting rule breakers when social rules are violated. The learner identified as behaviorally disordered, with limited strategies for approaching peers in positive ways, is rejected when his or her efforts result in breaking socially accepted rules.

Leone (1984) assessed adolescents who had been judged to have successfully left a residential day treatment program for students identified as behaviorally disordered 2 to 4 years earlier. These students were found to be seriously deficient in reading, spelling, mathematics, and written language. The students were, for the most part, living with their families. In a later study of more specific characteristics, Leone, Fitzmartin, Stetson, and Foster (1986) found that the more successful adolescents were those who were enrolled in day rather than residential treatment programs and who had lower rates of absenteeism. The most successful learners were also able to name specific characteristics that others liked about them and were likely to be working and/or attending school. Both successful and unsuccessful former students held generally positive attitudes towards the program in which they had been enrolled, though more successful students tended to disassociate themselves from enrollment in the program.

Positive perceptions were also reported in a study that used telephone interviews. Nearly two-thirds of students contacted reported having a job and were generally adjusted to the satisfaction of their parents (Neel, Meadows, Levine, & Edgar, 1988). However, fewer than one in five were involved in post-secondary programs, whereas about 50 percent of their nonidentified peers were in post-secondary programs. The rate of unemployment for these learners, however, was nearly three times as high as that of national figures. About one-third of the learners identified as behaviorally disordered were not engaged in structured activities outside the home and were not receiving the training and support necessary to enable them to participate in the adult world.

In their survey of students 1 year after their class was scheduled to be graduated, Frank, Sitlington, and Carson (1991) report that of those who graduated, about two-thirds of the males and one-third of the females were living with parents or relatives. Only slightly over half (58 percent) of the graduates were currently employed full- or part-time. Only an additional 14 percent of the graduates were "otherwise meaningfully engaged" (as homemakers or students or in on-the-job training). Among the dropouts, 81 percent reported their marital status as single, and 30 percent were employed at least part-time. An additional 14 percent were "otherwise meaningfully engaged." Only a small proportion of these individuals were receiving help from a community agency or school personnel.

Summary

Identification of a learner as behaviorally disordered depends on the context in which the learner is participating. There is great variation in the numbers of learners identified from school system to school system, and state to state. Nationally, it is generally felt that learners identified as behaviorally disordered are under-identified.

Learners identified as behaviorally disordered demonstrate lower academic achievement than do their nonidentified peers. In addition, they frequently have poorer communication skills and, as a consequence, have great difficulty in social settings.

The definition of behavioral disorders and identification of learners as behaviorally disordered is controversial. The need to assess behavior in the context in which it occurs has emerged as an essential part of the identification of behavioral disorders.

There is also great controversy related to the provision of programs for learners identified as behaviorally disordered. Recent studies have demonstrated that programming emphasizes control rather than the development of social interaction and communication skills, often to the neglect of other curriculum areas. Learners who leave programs for learners identified as behaviorally disordered are frequently behind their peers in academic skills and are underemployed.

References

Algozzine, B. (1987). The disturbing child: A matter of opinion. *Behavioral Disorders, 5* (2), 112–115.

American Psychiatric Association (1987). *Diagnostic and statistical manual of mental disorders* (3rd ed.); revised. Washington, DC: American Psychiatric Association.

Baenen, R. S., Glenwick, D. S., Stephens, M. A. S., Neuhaus, S. M., & Mowrey, J. D. (1986). Predictors of child and family outcome in a psychoeducational day school program. *Behavioral Disorders, 11*, 272–279.

Bauer, A. M. (1993). Personal observation: Aiken Senior High School, E. S. Murphy, teacher.

Bauer, A. M., & Sapona, R. H. (1988). Facilitating communication as a basis for intervention for students with severe behavioral disorders. *Behavioral Disorders, 13*, 280–287.

Bauer, A. M., Shea, T. M., & Keppler, R. (1986). Levels systems: A framework for the individualization of behavior management. *Behavioral Disorders, 12*, 28–25.

Beare, P. L., & Lynch, E. C. (1986). Underidentification of preschool children at risk for behavioral disorders. *Behavioral Disorders, 11*, 177–183.

Brooks, A. P. (1991). Behavior problems and the power relationship. *Language, Speech and Hearing Services in the Schools, 22*, 89–91.

Camarata, S. M., Hughes, C. A., & Ruhl, K. L. (1988). Mild/moderately behaviorally disordered students: A population at risk for language disorders. *Language, Speech, and Hearing Services in the Schools, 19* (2), 191–200.

Camp, B. W., & Bash, M. S. (1981). *Think aloud: Increasing social and cognitive skills.* Champaign, IL: Research Press.

Carlson, P. E., & Stephens, T. M. (1986). Cultural bias and identification of behaviorally disordered children. *Behavioral Disorders, 11*, 191–199.

Coleman, M. C. (1986). *Behavior disorders: Theory and practice.* Englewood Cliffs, NJ: Prentice Hall.

Coutinho, M. J. (1986). Reading achievement of students identified as behaviorally disordered at the secondary level. *Behavioral Disorders, 11*, 200–207.

Cullinan, D., Epstein, M. H., & Lloyd, J. W. (1983). *Behavior disorders of children and adolescents.* Englewood Cliffs, NJ: Prentice Hall.

Cullinan, D., Schloss, P. J., & Epstein, M. H. (1987). Relative prevalence and correlates of depressive characteristics among seriously emotionally disturbed and nonhandicapped students. *Behavioral Disorders, 12*, 90–98.

Cytryn, L., & McKnew, D. H. (1986). Treatment issues in childhood depression. *Pediatric Annals, 15* (12), 856–860.

Edelbrock, C. (1984). Developmental considerations. In T. H. Ollendick & M. Hersen (Eds.), *Child behavioral assessment principles and procedures* (p. 230–237). New York: Pergamon.

Editor (1990). Coalition finalizes definition. *CCBD Newsletter,* August, 1990, 1.

Epstein, M. H., Kauffman, J. M., & Cullinan, D. (1985). Patterns of maladjustment among the behaviorally disordered. II: Boys aged 6–11, Boys aged 12–18, Girls aged 6–11, Girls aged 12–18. *Behavioral Disorders, 10,* 125–135.

Epstein, M. H., Kinder, D., & Bursuck, B. (1989). The academic status of adolescents with behavioral disorders. *Behavioral Disorders, 14,* 157–165.

Epstein, M. H., & Ollinger, E. (1987). Use of medication in school programs for behaviorally disordered pupils. *Behavioral Disorders, 12,* 138–145.

Executive Committee of the Council for Children with Behavioral Disorders (1987). Position paper on definition and identification of students with behavioral disorders. *Behavioral Disorders, 13,* 9–19.

Executive Committee of the Council for Children with Behavioral Disorders (1989). White paper on best assessment practices for students with behavioral disorders: Accommodation to cultural and individual differences. *Behavioral Disorders, 14,* 263–278.

Federal Register (August 23, 1977) *42* (162), 478.

Feinstein, S. C., & Uribe, V. (1986). Hospitalization of the young: Rationale and criteria. *Pediatric Annals, 15* (12), 861–866.

Fessler, M. A., Rosenberg, M. S., & Rosenberg, L. A. (1991). Concomitant learning disabilities and learning problems among students with behavioral/emotional disorders. *Behavioral Disorders, 16* (2), 97–106.

Frank, A. R., Sitlington, P. L., & Carson, R. (1991). Transition of adolescents with behavioral disorders: Is it successful? *Behavioral Disorders, 16,* 180–191.

Freeman, B. M., & Ritvo, E. R. (1984). The syndrome of autism: Establishing the diagnosis and principles of management. *Pediatric Annals, 13,* 284–296.

Grosenick, J. K., George, N. L., & George, M. P. (1988). The availability of program descriptions among programs for seriously emotionally disturbed students. *Behavioral Disorders, 13,* 108–115.

Grosenick, J. K., George, N. L., George, M. P., & Lewis, T. J. (1991). Public school services for behaviorally disordered students: Program practices in the 1980s. *Behavioral Disorders, 16,* 87–96.

Hubbell, R. (1981). *Children's language disorders: An integrated approach.* Englewood Cliffs, NJ: Prentice Hall.

Hughes, J. N., & Hall, D. M. (1985). Performance of disturbed and nondisturbed boys on a role play test of social competence. *Behavioral Disorders, 11,* 24–29.

Huntze, S. L. (1985). A position paper of the Council for Children with Behavioral Disorders. *Behavioral Disorders, 10,* 167–174.

Huntze, S. L., & Grosenick, J. K. (1980). *National needs analysis in behavior disorders: Human resources issues in behavior disorders.* Columbia, MO: University of Missouri.

Hutton, J. B. (1985). What reasons are given by teachers who refer problem behavior students? *Psychology in the Schools, 22,* 79–82.

Johnston, J. C., & Zemitzsch, A. (1988). Family power: An intervention beyond the classroom. *Behavioral Disorders, 14* (1), 69–79.

Joyce, B. R. (1987). Learning how to learn. *Theory into Practice, 26,* 416–428.

Kauffman, J. M. (1981). *Characteristics of children's behavior disorders* (2nd ed.) Columbus, OH: Merrill.

Kauffman, J. M. (1985). *Characteristics of children's behavior disorders* (3rd ed.) Columbus, OH: Merrill.

Kavale, K. A., Forness, S. R., & Alper, A. E. (1986). Research in behavioral disorders/emotional disturbance: A survey of subject identification criteria. *Behavioral Disorders, 11,* 159–167.

Knapczyk, D. R. (1988). Reducing aggressive behaviors in special and regular class settings by training alternative social responses. *Behavioral Disorders, 14* (1), 27–39.

Knitzer, J., Steinberg, Z., & Fleisch, B. (1990). *At the schoolhouse door: An examination of problems and policies for children with behavioral and emotional problems.* New York: Bank Street College of Education.

Leone, P. (1984). A descriptive follow-up of behaviorally disordered adolescents. *Behavioral Disorders, 9,* 207–214.

Leone, P., Fitzmartin, R., Stetson, F., & Foster, J. (1986). A retrospective follow-up of behaviorally disordered adolescents: Identifying predictors of treatment outcome. *Behavioral Disorders, 11,* 87–97.

Leone, P. E., Luttig, P. G., Zlotlow, S., & Trickett, E. J. (1990). Understanding the social ecology of classrooms for adolescents with behavioral disorders: A preliminary study of differences in perceived environments. *Behavioral Disorders, 16,* 55–65.

Long, N. J. (1990). Comments on Ralph Gardner's article "Life space interviewing: It can be effective, but don't . . ." *Behavioral Disorders, 15,* 119–124.

Luebke, J., Epstein, M. H., & Cullinan, D. (1989). Comparison of teacher-rated achievement levels of behaviorally disordered, learning disabled, and nonhandicapped adolescents. *Behavioral Disorders, 15,* 1–8.

Maag, J. W., & Behrens, J. T. (1989). Epidemiologic data on seriously emotionally disturbed and learning disabled adolescents: Reporting extreme depressive symptomatology. *Behavioral Disorders, 15,* 21–27.

Mastropieri, M. A., Jenne, T., & Scruggs, T. E. (1988). A level system for managing problem behaviors in a high school resource program. *Behavioral Disorders, 13,* 202–208.

McConnell, S. R. (1987). Entrapment effects and the generalization and maintenance of social skills training for elementary school students with behavioral disorders. *Behavioral Disorders, 12,* 252–263.

McDonough, K. M. (1989). Analysis of the expressive language characteristics of emotionally handicapped students in social interactions. *Behavioral Disorders, 14,* 127–139.

Morris, S. M. (1982). A classroom process for behavior change. *The Pointer, 26* (3), 25–28.

Morse, W. C., Cutler, R. L., & Fink, A. H. (1964). *Public school classes for the emotionally handicapped.* Washington, DC: Council for Exceptional Children.

Murphy, E. S. (1991). *Behavior management systems.* Cincinnati, OH: Aiken Senior High School.

Neel, R. S., Meadows, N., Levine, P., & Edgar, E. G. (1988). *Behavioral Disorders, 13,* 209–216.

Nelson, J. R., Smith, D. J., Young, R. K., & Dodd, J. (1991). A review of self-management outcome research conducted with students who exhibit behavioral disorders. *Behavioral Disorders, 16,* 169–179.

Quay, H. C., & Peterson, D. R. (1987). *Manual for the revised behavior problem checklist.* Unpublished manuscript available from H. C. Quay, Box 248704, University of Miami, Coral Gables, FL 33124.

Ramsey, E., & Walker, H. M. (1988). Family management correlates of antisocial behavior among middle school boys. *Behavioral Disorders, 13,* 187–201.

Redl, F. (1966). The life space interview: Strategy and techniques. In F. Redl, *When we deal with children* (pp. 35–67). New York: Free Press.

Reimers, T. M., & Wacker, D. P. (1988). Parents' ratings of the acceptability of behavioral treatment made in an outpatient clinic: A preliminary analysis of the influence of treatment effectiveness. *Behavioral Disorders, 14* (1), 7–15.

Rhodes, W. C. (1967). The disturbing child: A problem of ecological management. *Exceptional Children, 33,* 449–455.

Rosenberg, M. S. (1986). Maximizing the effectiveness of structured classroom management programs: Implementing rule-review procedures with disruptive and destructible students. *Behavioral Disorders, 11,* 239–248.

Rosenthal, S. L., & Simeonsson, R. J. (1991). Communication skills in emotionally disturbed and nondisturbed adolescents. *Behavioral Disorders, 16,* 192–199.

Ruhl, K. L., & Hughes, C. A. (1985). The nature and extent of aggression in special education settings serving behaviorally disordered students. *Behavioral Disorders, 10,* 95–104.

Sabournie, E. J. (1987). Bidirectional social status of behaviorally disordered and nonhandicapped elementary school pupils. *Behavioral Disorders, 13,* 45–57.

Sabournie, E. J., & Kauffman, J. M. (1985). Regular classroom sociometric status of behaviorally disordered adolescents. *Behavioral Disorders, 10,* 191–197.

Safran, J. S., & Safran, S. P. (1985). A developmental view of children's behavioral tolerance. *Behavioral Disorders, 10,* 87–94.

Safran, S. P., Safran, J. S., & Barcikowski, R. S. (1988). Assessing teacher manageability: A factor analytic approach. *Behavioral Disorders, 13,* 245–252.

Schloss, P. J., Schloss, C. N., Wood, C. E., & Kiehl, W. S. (1986). A critical review of social skills research with behaviorally disordered students. *Behavioral Disorders, 12,* 1–14.

Scruggs, T. E., & Mastropieri, M. A. (1986). Academic characteristics of behaviorally disordered and learning disabled students. *Behavioral Disorders, 11,* 184–190.

Scruggs, T. E., Mastropieri, M. A., Cook, S. B., & Escobar, C. (1986). Early intervention for children with conduct disorders: A quantitative synthesis of single-subject research. *Behavioral Disorders, 11,* 260–271.

Sevcik, B. M., & Ysseldyke, J. E. (1986). An analysis of teachers' prereferral interventions for students exhibiting behavioral problems. *Behavioral Disorders, 11,* 109–117.

Shea, T. M., & Bauer, A. M. (1987). *Teaching children and youth with behavior disorders.* Englewood Cliffs, NJ: Prentice Hall.

Simpson, R. L. (1988). Needs of parents and families whose children have learning and behavior problems. *Behavioral Disorders, 14* (1), 40–47.

Simpson, R. L. (1989). Agreement among teachers in using the Revised Behavior Problem Checklist to identify deviant behavior in children. *Behavioral Disorders, 14,* 151–156.

Skiba, R. J. (1989). The importance of construct validity: Alternative models for the assessment of behavioral disorder. *Behavioral Disorders, 14,* 175–185.

Slate, J. R., & Saudargas, R. A. (1986). Differences in the classroom behaviors of behaviorally disordered and regular class students. *Behavioral Disorders, 12,* 45–53.

Smith, D. J., Young, K. R., West, R. P., Morgan, D. P., & Rhode, G. (1988). Reducing the disruptive behavior of junior high students: A classroom self-management procedure. *Behavioral Disorders, 13,* 231–239.

Swan, W. W., Brown, C. L., & Jacob, R. T. (1987). Types of service delivery models used in the reintegration of seriously emotionally disturbed/behaviorally disordered students. *Behavioral Disorders, 12,* 99–103.

Talmadge, D. K., Gamel, N. M., Munson, R. G., & Hanley, T. M. (1985). *Special study on terminology: Comprehensive review and evaluation report.* (Contract No. 300–84–0144). Mountain View, CA: SRA Technologies.

Trautman, R. C., Giddan, J. J., & Jurs, S. G. (1990). Language risk factor in emotionally disturbed children within a school and day treatment program. *Journal of Childhood Communication Disorders, 13* (2), 123–133.

United States Department of Education (1990). *Twelfth annual report to Congress on the implementation of the Education of the Handicapped Act.* Washington, DC: Author.

United States Department of Education (1992). Fourteenth annual report to Congress on the implementation of the Individuals with Disabilities Education Act. Washington, DC: Author.

Voeltz, L. M. (1980). Children's attitudes toward handicapped peers. *American Journal of Mental Deficiency, 84,* 455–464.

Weller, E. B., & Weller, R. A. (1986). Clinical aspects of childhood depression. *Pediatric Annals, 15* (12), 843–850.

Wood, M. M., & Long, N. J. (1991). *Life space intervention: Talking with children and youth in crisis.* Austin, TX: Pro-ed.

Wright, D., Pillard, E. D., & Cleven, C. A. (1990). The influence of state definitions of behavior disorders on the number of children served under PL 94–142. *Remedial and Special Education, 11* (5), 17–22.

Learners from Diverse Ethnic, Cultural, and Linguistic Groups

After completing this chapter, you will be able to:

1. describe the largest minority cultural and ethnic groups and the personal traits generally attributed to each.

2. describe issues related to the assessment of learners from various cultures and ethnic groups.

3. describe the impact of various cultures and ethnic groups on classroom interactions.

4. describe ways to mediate the environment for learners from various cultures and ethnic groups.

5. describe the impact of membership in various cultures and ethnic groups in the larger social systems of the community and society.

Key Words and Phrases

African American	**Hispanic**
Anglo	**migrant**
Appalachian	**minority**
Asian American	**Native American**
ethnicity	

S AN EXPERIENCED FIRST-GRADE TEACHER, I AM CONVINCED THAT A CHILD NEEDS TO BE FAMILIAR WITH A significant number of these concepts [standard English, print as communication] to be able to assimilate so much new knowledge in one sitting . . . I do not advocate a simplistic 'basic skills' approach for children outside of the culture of power . . . Rather, I suggest that schools provide these children the content that other families from a different cultural orientation provide at home [e.g., experience with books, visits to museums, trips to the library]. This does not mean separating children according to family background, but instead, ensuring that each classroom incorporates strategies appropriate for all the children in its confines" (Delpit, 1988, p. 286). [Comments made with reference to teaching learners representing minority cultures and ethnic groups by a professional who represents a minority culture . . .] ▪

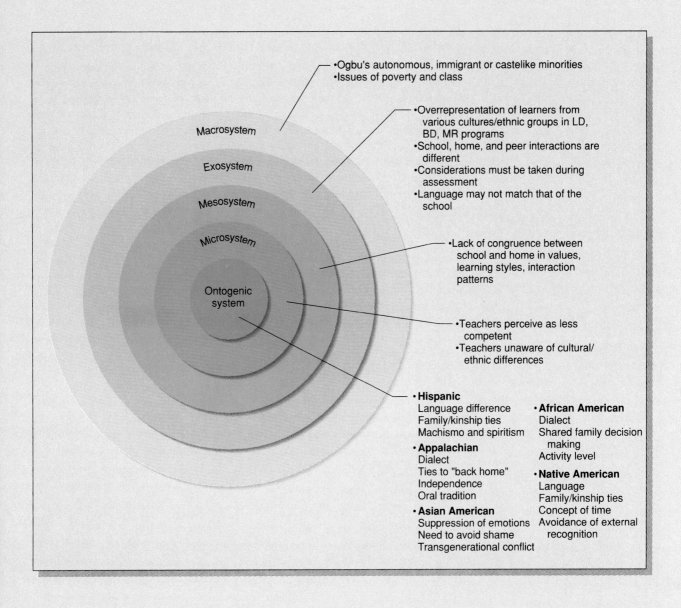

Macrosystem

Exosystem

Mesosystem

Microsystem

Ontogenic
system

•Ogbu's autonomous, immigrant or castelike minorities
•Issues of poverty and class

•Overrepresentation of learners from
 various cultures/ethnic groups in LD,
 BD, MR programs
•School, home, and peer interactions are
 different
•Considerations must be taken during
 assessment
•Language may not match that of the
 school

•Lack of congruence between
 school and home in values,
 learning styles, interaction
 patterns

•Teachers perceive as less
  competent
•Teachers unaware of cultural/
  ethnic differences

• **Hispanic**
  Language difference
  Family/kinship ties
  Machismo and spiritism
• **Appalachian**
  Dialect
  Ties to "back home"
  Independence
  Oral tradition
• **Asian American**
  Suppression of emotions
  Need to avoid shame
  Transgenerational conflict

• **African American**
  Dialect
  Shared family decision
    making
  Activity level
• **Native American**
  Language
  Family/kinship ties
  Concept of time
  Avoidance of external
    recognition

Introduction

Mindel and Habenstein (1981) define **ethnicity** as membership in a group of people who share a unique social and cultural heritage that is transmitted from one generation to the next. In North America, race and ethnicity may overlap (as with Chinese Americans or African Americans) or be independent of each other (Hispanics may be white, black, native American, or all three). Ethnic identity is a particular challenge when individuals also represent a racial minority. These individuals are generally easily distinguishable from the members of the mainstream of society. Many Caucasian ethnic groups may practice their cultural customs in their homes and places of worship but blend into the mainstream of society at their pleasure. This is often not possible for racially distinguishable groups.

Minority groups are those groups who have unequal access to power, and are, for the most part, considered by the majority group to be inferior or less worthy of sharing power in some way (Mindel & Habenstein, 1981). However, by the year 2000, one in three Americans will be African American, Hispanic, or Asian American (Yates, 1987). Applying this prediction to practice, Hodgkinson (1985) suggests that the motive for addressing diversity can no longer be liberalism or obligation, but a question of societal self-interest. Society must recognize the contributions of various minority groups and implement procedures to permit them equal access to power within society.

Changes in society, and a new kind of pluralism, also support the need to address diversity. Pluralism suggests that members of diverse ethnic, cultural, and linguistic groups continue their participation in their traditional custom while participating in society on the whole. Kochman (1991) contrasts the old "melting pot" pluralism and the new "salad bowl" pluralism. Whereas in the past, individuals were expected to assimilate into society, individuals are now expected to demonstrate their individual uniqueness.

In this chapter, an effort is made to represent the unique experiences of the many children in our schools from various cultures and ethnic groups. In this effort, we will discuss five significant minority and ethnic groups: Asian Americans, Hispanics, African Americans, Native Americans, and Appalachians. As Gibbs and Huang (1989) suggest, the discussion of cultural and ethnic groups must be done within the frame of reference of the great diversity of the individuals within these groups. However, individuals within a culture and ethnic group typically share some history, cultural tradition, and social experiences when compared with the Anglo or majority culture. It is this shared cultural experience that we will discuss in this chapter, while recognizing the uniqueness of each individual within each group. At no time do we suggest that all members of a cultural or ethnic group demonstrate the characteristics described. Rather, we again defer to the impact of the context in which the learner develops, and the impact of interpersonal differences on the development of each learner.

Though we recognize that each child is unique, several general trends have been identified in persons from the different cultural groups which may help us to understand members of culturally diverse groups (Olion & Gillis-Olion, 1984). In addition to cultural and ethnic identity, the issues of class and poverty frequently impact on the individual values and behaviors of members of minority cultures.

An additional issue for students from diverse ethnic, cultural, and linguistic groups is a lack of congruence between what happens in and out of school. Resnick (1987) suggests that school learning is discontinuous in several important ways

It is important to celebrate everyone's culture and ethnic identity.

with daily life of learners from various cultural and ethnic groups. First, in schools individual rather than shared cognition is valued. Students ultimately are judged by what they can do themselves. Work, personal life, and recreation, on the other hand, take place within social systems, and each person's ability to function successfully depends on what others do and how several individuals' mental and physical performances mesh. Schools also vary from personal life in that in school pure mentation (mental activity) rather than tool manipulation is emphasized. School is an institution that values thought that proceeds independently. In schools, symbols are manipulated rather than the contextualized reasoning that takes place outside of school. Finally, in schools all children are required to be generalists; outside of school specific competencies and skills are emphasized.

Cultural and Ethnic Minorities

Objective One: To describe the largest minority cultural and ethnic groups and the personal traits generally attributed to each.

In this discussion of Hispanics, African Americans, Native Americans, Asian Americans, and Appalachians we remind the reader of the unique developmental context, experience, and personal characteristics of each learner. To suggest that all learners represent all the characteristics presented is racial, cultural, or ethnic stereotyping. This section and those that follow describe potentially common threads through the cultural or ethnic experience of these learners. Throughout this discussion we will use the term **Anglo** to describe the mainstream Caucasian, male, middle-class ways of knowing and being.

Hispanic Americans

Hispanics are those learners of all races whose cultural heritage is tied to the use of the Spanish language and Latino culture (Fradd, Figueroa, & Correa, 1989). The Hispanic population has entered a tremendous period of growth, which may result in an American demographic picture composed of 47 million Hispanics out of 265 million Americans by the year 2000 (Hodgkinson, 1985).

Hyland (1989) describes the American Hispanic population as highly concentrated in urban areas, and highly isolated in housing and schooling. This isolation is reputedly related to linguistic skills, in that Hispanic children are usually placed in classrooms or schools where children of limited English proficiency are in the majority. Hispanic students may belong to any of a large number of ethnic subgroups: Mexican American, Chicano, Puerto Rican, Cuban, or Central or South American.

Mexican Americans   Mexican Americans tend to be the youngest among Hispanic groups, with a median age of 23.3 years. In 1984 the reported median income of Mexican-American families was $19,200. Mexican Americans tend to be young, poor, and living in large families while confronting problems of illiteracy and lack of facility in English (Ramirez, 1990).

The contemporary Mexican-American family is a mixture of traditional and contemporary patterns. Traditional values such as the primacy of the family and extended kinship ties remain strong. The kinship system is highly integrated, including "compadres" (godparents) for emotional and social support, help with child rearing, financial support, and assistance in problem solving (Ramirez & Arce, 1981).

The concept of "machismo" (male dominance) continues to influence the role of the male in Mexican-American culture. Trankina (1983) indicates that this concept traditionally requires men to be forceful and strong and to be without tender emotions. This traditional masculine aggressiveness also encompasses a strong sense of personal honor and belief in the importance of the family and the need to care for children. Ramirez and Arce (1981) found that the concept of machismo and absolute patriarchy have diminished, with joint decision-making and greater equality apparent.

Ramirez (1990) indicates that the parent-child relationship overshadows the marital relationship in Mexican-American culture. The home is usually child centered, with parents being indulgent and passive with younger children. Parents are nurturing and protective, and they accept the child's individuality. As children grow older, they are often assigned greater tasks and responsibilities. The father's role with older children is as strict disciplinarian, with the father serving as an authoritarian and the mother often serving as mediator between father and children.

In comparison with Anglo culture, Mexican Americans expect less physical distance in personal interactions and are accustomed to frequent physical contact. These interaction patterns often create discomfort in others not of the Mexican-American culture.

In Mexican-American culture, there is an emphasis on cooperation and respect for authority (Ramirez, 1990). A Mexican-American student may appear to accept the teacher's directions and suggestions even though they are covertly resistant. Guinn (1977) suggests that Mexican Americans are more oriented to the here and now, rather than the future, than are Anglo students. In addition, Mexican-American learners emphasize "doing" rather than "being" and depend on group cooperation. Whereas members of the Anglo culture assume that an individual can master adversity, Mexican Americans are more fatalistic and accommodate themselves to problems.

Puerto Rican Americans   The majority of mainland Puerto Ricans reside in the greater metropolitan New York area (Inclan & Herron, 1989). As American citizens, Puerto Ricans have voting privileges and have ease of travel between the mainland and the island. However, Puerto Ricans have no congressional representatives, speak Spanish, maintain an Hispanic culture, and experience racial and political discrimination. This juxtaposition of cultures makes self-definition of Puerto Ricans residing on the mainland particularly challenging (Inclan & Herron, 1989).

Mass migration did not begin from Puerto Rico to the United States until after World War II (Sowell, 1981). By 1970, the mainland Puerto Rican population was 1.5 million, about half of the island population. Typical of Hispanic cultures, machismo is considered a virtue, and personalism calls for the development of inner qualities to attain self-respect and gain the respect of others. Catholicism, with its stress on a personal relationship with God, is the predominant religion. In addition, Puerto Ricans often demonstrate spiritism, which is a belief in good and evil spirits than can affect one's life (Garcia-Preto, 1982).

Generational change is apparent in Puerto Ricans. First-generation migrants exhibit predominantly traditional values, with "barrios" serving to recreate and preserve the native culture. Second and third generations cope with and adapt to the language and values of the mainstream culture, sometimes generating personal stress and feelings of failure due to the tension between cultures (Inclan, 1985).

African Americans

Since 1900, the **African-American** population (individuals whose ancestry can be traced to Africa) of the United States has remained between 10 and 12 percent. By the year 2000, there will be approximately 35 million African Americans in the United States (Allen & Majidi-Ahi, 1989). According to McAdoo (1978), the lifestyles, values, and experiences of African Americans vary, but, as a group, they share the common experience of economic isolation, prejudice, and legally reinforced racism. Long-established cultural patterns and a high level of maternal employment has led to shared decision-making processes in many African-American families.

An important socialization issue for African-American learners is coping with racism. African-American parents, in efforts to combat racism, emphasize the development of achievement motivation, self-confidence, and high self-esteem (Peters, 1981). In addition, there may be a cultural difference in attitudes towards time, which may be perceived as resistance or apathy by Anglo individuals.

Communication styles among African Americans vary from that of Anglo culture in that it is possible to converse without constant eye contact (Allen & Majidi-Ahi, 1989). In addition, Smith (1981) indicates that African Americans are less likely to verbally reinforce one another in conversation.

Native Americans

Once estimated at 10 million, the population of **Native Americans** (any member of the indigenous peoples of North and South America) has been reduced through "cultural genocide" to between 1.5 and 1.8 million (LaFromboise & Low, 1989). Native Americans were victims of war with the majority culture. Those who

The family remains the center of many Native American tribal cultures.

survived were then systematically deprived of access to their way of life. In further efforts to dilute the Native American culture, rather than accepting tribally defined memberships or community consensus, federal programs require one-quarter genealogically derived Native American ancestry to be legally recognized as Native American and therefore eligible for many federal, state, and indian nation benefits. There are, in the United States, 517 federally recognized native entities (196 of which are in Alaska) and 36 state-recognized Native American tribes. Each of these tribes maintains unique customs, traditions, social organizations, and ecological relationships (Leap, 1981).

The median income of Native Americans living on reservations is $9,942, approximately one-third of the median income of Caucasian-American households, and far below the median income of $17,786 for African-American families (U.S. Bureau of Census, 1986).

Economic and educational challenges for Native Americans are pervasive. About one-third of adult Native Americans are illiterate, and only 20 percent have a high school education (Brod & McQuiston, 1983). An overriding problem for Native American youth is alcohol and substance abuse. The use of alcohol among Native American teenagers is three times that of adolescents in the population at large (Bobo, 1985).

Native American cultures are complex and diverse. One common thread among the various Native American cultures is the collective interdependence of tribes and nations, with family members responsible to each other, to the clan, and to the tribe (LaFromboise & Low, 1989). Relationships between family members and the community are complex. Some nations, such as the Navaho, are matriarchal with women taking primary responsibility for the children, while others are patriarchal. The family, however, has remained the forum for problem solving and support in Native American communities.

Native Americans represent an extremely diverse group of cultures. Pepper (1976), in his general review of Native American culture and schooling, reports that more than half of the school-age Native Americans use their native language, with over 300 languages having been documented.

Pepper offers a description of the general trends in Native American cultures. Among Native Americans, age and experience are greatly respected and elders are revered. Personal glory is avoided, while contributions to the group and its continued existence are praised. Native Americans live in extended families. Positive and cooperative relationships are emphasized, and competition is avoided. Native Americans place great emphasis on the sharing of material goods and community property. Feelings and thoughts are expressed through actions and efforts. The harmony of human life with nature is a primary focus.

In Native-American culture, time is present oriented. As a consequence, members of this culture may have difficulty in the areas of future planning and clock-time with regard to work. Work is understood to be that which is necessary for the common good.

Children are trained through participation in adult life. The extended family or kinship groups accept responsibility for child rearing. School is required for knowledge, but generally excelling is avoided. Childhood is relatively brief, and by age 16 a young person is expected to assume adult responsibilities.

Brendtro, Brokenleg, and Bockern (1990) present a holistic Native-American philosophy of child development, which, they suggest, emerges from the wisdom of the people. They contend this philosophy is appropriate for all children in our complex society. The basic premise underlying this Native-American philosophy is that to develop successfully, children must have or feel the spirit of belonging (trust, attachment, love, friendship), mastery (success, achievement, motivation, creativity), independence (autonomy, confidence, responsibility, self-discipline, inner control), and generosity (self-sacrifice, caring, sharing, loyalty). Examples of the characteristics of Native-American child development are presented in Box 8.1. The authors believe that all children should be reared in an environment that encourages and supports these basic philosophical principles.

Asian Americans

Asian Americans have roots in any of the Asian countries. They can be Chinese Americans, Japanese Americans, or Southeast Asians.

Chinese Americans The Chinese Exclusion Act of 1882 was the first legislation to ban a particular race from entering the United States. This law was followed 60 years later by the Oriental Exclusion Act, which banned all immigration from Asia. These acts came about largely due to economic depression and the fear that Chinese immigrants would take jobs from majority culture individuals. During the period from 1890 to 1945, more Chinese left than entered the United States, with the remaining living under the constraints of the exclusion laws (Huang and Ying, 1989).

Chinese family structure, Huang and Ying report, is based on Confucian ethics. Sons remain more highly valued than daughters, with the first-born son perceived as the most valued child. Fathers, removed from the everyday tasks of the family, are often the figurative heads of families, while the mothers may in fact be the driving force in the family.

The expression of emotion is highly frowned upon in Chinese-American families, and the ability to suppress undesirable thoughts or emotions is highly valued. These communication patterns sharply contrast with mainstream American values of expression (Shon & Ja, 1982). In addition, Shon and Ja describe the essential need to avoid shame and loss of face. The ability to place the group's or family's

Box 8.1

Characteristics of Native-American Child Development

In their discussion of the characteristics of Native-American child development, Brendtro, Brokenleg, and Bockern (1990) provide excellent examples of the spirits of belonging, mastery, independence, and generosity.

Belonging: "The days of my infanthood and childhood were spent in surroundings of love and care. In manner, gentleness was my mother's outstanding characteristic. Never did she, nor any of my caretakers, ever speak crossly to me or scold me for failures or shortcomings" (Standing Bear, 1933).

Mastery: "There was always one, or a few in every band, who swam the best, who shot the truest arrow, or who ran the fastest, and I at once set their accomplishments as the mark for me to attain. In spite of all this striving, there was no sense of rivalry. We never disliked the boy who did better than the others. On the contrary, we praised him. All through our society, the individual who excelled was praised and honored" (Standing Bear, 1933).

Independence: "I can remember . . . a toddler trying to open a door to a cabin. He could not make it. This was a big, heavy door, and he was shoving and shoving. Well, Americans would get up and open the door for him. The Blackfoot Indians sat for half an hour while the baby struggled with that door, until he was able to get it open himself. He had to grunt and sweat, and then everyone praised him because he was able to do it himself" (Hoffman, 1988).

Generosity: "A high school boy will spend his last coins in buying a pack of cigarettes, walk into a crowded recreation room, take one cigarette for himself and pass out the rest to the eager hands around him ... Another high school boy will receive a new coat in the mail and wear it proudly to the next school dance. For the next three months the same coat will appear on cousins and friends at the weekly dances, and it may be several months before the original owner wears his new coat again" (Bryde, 1971) ■

---

wishes above individual desires is held as a virtue. In this way, everything an individual does is viewed as a reflection on the family. In view of this desire to save face, Chinese Americans rarely approach formal psychological helpers except as a last resort (Huang and Ying, 1989).

Japanese Americans   Specific Japanese terms are usually applied to identify the various generations of Japanese Americans. The "issei" are the first generation of Japanese to come to the United States; the "nisei," second-generation Japanese Americans, are born here. The third generation are often called the "sansei," while the fourth and fifth generations are referred to as "yonsei" and "gosei."

The second generation of Japanese Americans (the nisei) are typically raised with a mixture of Japanese and American values. In the early 1900s the nisei associated primarily with other Japanese Americans and were exposed to pressures to conform to the issei experience. Laws preventing Japanese from marrying Caucasians existed in most states, and until 1952 the issei were not allowed to apply for citizenship. During World War II all persons of Japanese ancestry were forcibly removed from their homes, businesses, and communities on the west coast of the United States and placed in internment camps in the interior of the country. In

Asian family culture holds that an individual's behavior reflects on the family.

recent years, the federal government has apologized for this act and has remunerated members of the Japanese-American population for the injustice of internment.

Yamamoto and Kubota (1989) describe the Japanese-American family structure as one which emphasizes the family over the individual, hierarchical relationships, conformity, and social control based on shame, guilt, and duty. Japanese culture values being "reserved," that is, not expressing one's wishes or preferences, and deferring to those in authority and repressing or internalizing emotion.

Southeast Asian Refugees   Today's Southeast Asian refugee children and youth have spent a large amount of their lives living in violence, experiencing great personal loss, anxiety, and discontinuous education and health care. The extended family, so vital in Asian cultures, is not accessible to these children and youth. In addition to relocation, families undergo sociocultural changes, in which children view their parents as changing from previously competent, independent individuals into persons who acculturate more slowly than they do. Yet, as in other Asian cultural groups, self control and repression of emotions are highly valued. Post-traumatic stress disorder, marked by night terrors, numbing of the emotions, and flashbacks to violent incidents, may be apparent in southeast Asian refugees (Huang, 1989).

Appalachians

Sullivan and Miller (1990) suggest that Appalachians in urban areas are a distinct cultural group who are not easily identifiable as a minority, since race, sex, or surname do not identify them. **Appalachians** are those individuals who were born, or whose ancestors were born, in the federally defined Appalachian region of 397 counties and 5 independent cities in portions of 13 states, including New York, Pennsylvania, Maryland, Ohio, Virginia, West Virginia, Kentucky, Tennessee, North Carolina, South Carolina, Georgia, Alabama, and Mississippi (McCoy & Watkins, 1980). The challenge confronting these individuals is exemplified by Appalachians living in Cincinnati. In the Cincinnati area, first- and second-generation Appalachian migrants constitute about a fourth of the population (Obermiller, Borman, & Kroger, 1988). Of the ten neighborhoods in Cincinnati with the highest school dropout rates, eight are predominantly Appalachian. Urban Appalachian students perform poorly on the standardized tests used to classify students throughout their academic careers (Borman, Mueninghoff, & Piazza, 1989). Berlowitz and Durand (1977) identify high absenteeism, high suspension, and low reading and math achievement as variables linked with high dropout rates of Appalachian students enrolled in public secondary schools. The use of Appalachian dialect and the cultural emphasis on individualism are in conflict with standard English and the conformity emphasized in many public schools.

Migrant Families

One of the most seriously underserved and inappropriately served groups of learners with disabilities are the children of migrant families (Interstate Migrant Council, 1984). **Migrants** are individuals or groups who move frequently to find work. In the United States, there are an estimated 800,000 migrant students. Of this number, 8,000 (1 percent) are receiving special education services, compared to approximately 10 percent of students in the general student populations (Perry, 1982). According to Salend (1990), California and Oregon, among the states employing the largest number of migrant workers, serve 1.37 percent and 3 percent of their migrant students, respectively, in special education. These percentages may be compared to 8.33 percent (California) and 10 percent (Oregon) of the general student population receiving special education services (Bird, 1985; McCoy, 1986).

Among the factors that place this group of learners at risk for disabilities are (Baca & Harris, 1988):

- high mobility. Migrant families change residence frequently, moving from state to state with the harvest seasons and the availability of employment.
- low socioeconomic status. Migrant families are generally employed in low wage, unskilled jobs. Most frequently these jobs do not provide adequate housing and employee benefits, such as health care.
- language and cultural differences. The vast majority of migrant families are members of cultural and ethnic minorities, especially Spanish-speaking minorities. Because they move in groups, they often lack the opportunity for exposure to the English language and majority American culture.
- poor general health and nutrition. Due to mobility, low wages, lack of health insurance, lack of an understanding of how to use community medical and social services, and the hazards of their employment, migrant families frequently are in poor health and lack proper nutrition. The fact that children begin working in the field with parents at a young age contributes to the general lack of health and nutrition.

Objective Two: To describe issues related to the assessment of learners from various cultures and ethnic groups.

Assessment of Learners from Diverse Cultural and Ethnic Groups

An overrepresentation of learners from various cultures and ethnic groups in the special education population often leads to discussions of assessment of these learners. In 1968, Dunn described the "six hour mentally retarded child." "Six hour mentally retarded children" were those who were only considered to be "different" in school during the school day and year. At other times and in other settings such as at home, in the community, at church, and at work, these children could not be differentiated from their peers without disabilities. Using United States Office of Education statistics, Dunn reported that one-third of all special educators were teachers of students with mental retardation, and between 60 and 80 percent of their students were minority children from low socioeconomic status homes. Mercer (1973) reported similar overrepresentation in her study of special education classes in California, with Hispanics constituting only 11 percent of the school population yet 45.3 percent of the students in classes for individuals with mild mental retardation. In her findings, white students constituted 81 percent of the public school population, but only 32.1 percent of the individuals placed in classes for students with mental retardation.

In a review of the Office of Civil Rights Elementary and Secondary Schools Civil Rights surveys published between 1980 and 1986, Chinn and Hughes (1987) confirm that representation of some minority groups continues to be disproportionately high in certain categories. They find that the overrepresentation of African Americans in classes for students who are mentally retarded or who have behavioral disorders remains at twice the level that would be expected from the percentage of African Americans in the school population. Dramatically fewer Hispanics are now being placed in classes for students who are mentally retarded than Mercer reported in 1973—an indication of recognition that Hispanic representation was disproportionately high and that many learners were misdiagnosed. Disproportionately low numbers of African Americans, Hispanics, and Native Americans were found in classes for the gifted and talented. When the intelligence quotient was the same across groups, African-American children were found to perform better on visual spatial tasks of the Wechsler Intelligence Scale for Children (Revised) while Caucasian children performed better on tasks of abstract thinking and general knowledge (Taylor & Richards, 1991). These findings offer some insight into the disproportionately high numbers of referrals and placements from diverse cultures and ethnic groups.

The United States Department of Education (1992) reported that African-American youth are more highly represented in every disability category. This overrepresentation is most evident in the categories of speech and language disorders, mental retardation, and behavioral disorders. Though 12 percent of the school-aged population is African American, 24 percent of all individuals with disabilities are African American.

In a migrant population, Barresi (1984) found that (a) approximately 10.7 percent of migrant students with mild disabilities were identified; (b) the identification of these students' disabilities occurred late in their school career; (c) there were significant delays in the transfer of students' special education records from jurisdiction to jurisdiction; (d) students' assessment data was duplicated in the various districts; (e) there were significant gaps in the services provided to the students due to the differences in services provided by the various schools the learners attended; (f) placements were often inappropriate due to language barriers which also appeared to delay the referral process; and (g) services were impeded by a lack of awareness and consistent and purposeful coordination between migrant education service personnel and special education service personnel.

In a discussion of the assessment of individuals from various cultures and ethnic groups, Gibbs and Huang (1989) suggest that culture may have a significant impact on five major domains of functioning: (a) individual psychosocial adjustment, (b) family relationships; (c) school adjustment and achievement, (d) relationships with peers, and (e) adaptation to the community.

During the assessment process, consideration must be given to *individual psychosocial adjustment.* Physical appearance, particularly variations from the Anglo norms in height, weight, or physique, should be considered. Culturally appropriate ways of expressing emotion or participating in social interaction can be confused with lack of affect or depressed affect. For example, eye contact, which is discouraged in some ethnic groups, is demanded in mainstream cultural communication. In order to assess self-concept and self-esteem, which are grounded in self-evaluation, the examiner should understand cultural standards. Other issues that emerge with regard to individual assessment include the culture or ethnic group's perceptions of interpersonal competence, attitudes towards autonomy, attitudes toward achievement, management of aggression and impulse control, and coping and defense mechanisms.

When assessing *family relationships,* professionals should recognize that role and functions vary according to families. Subtle issues, such as who is addressed first, mother or father, and to whom correspondence should be addressed, may have an impact on the teacher's relationship with the family. Male children may have culturally based difficulties complying with the requests of a female teacher. In some cultures and ethnic groups, age and sex-role hierarchies emerge, and traditional family interaction patterns may not be compatible with the demands of the American educational system which stresses verbal fluency and competition.

During the assessment of *school adjustment and achievement,* professionals should recognize that there may be a significant transition for the student between home and school. In dealing with achievement, minority culture individuals rarely achieve as well as majority culture students on tests. Relationships with peers in school become more difficult as the student matures; as students grow older they are more likely to become aware of their particular ethnic or minority status and its associated degree of desirability.

In *relationships with peers,* minority students frequently have two distinct sets of peer relationships and interaction patterns in and out of school. In viewing and understanding their *adaptation to the community,* professionals should recognize that minority children are sometimes token members of groups or the group's scapegoat. Children from minority cultures may view the world of work quite differently than do children from the majority culture. These perceptions may impact on the way in which children of minority cultures view education, the purpose of education, preparation for work, and work as a significant factor in their lives.

Alternative instructional strategies must be used prior to referring learners from diverse ethnic, cultural, and linguistic groups to special education services, in order to eliminate the unnecessary assessment of children challenged by cultural mismatch with a teacher or other professional (Olion & Gillis-Olion, 1984). Olion and Gillis-Olion emphasize that all professionals should recognize that assessment should document assets as well as deficits. In addition, the collection of multi-source data is especially important, and gathering this data in assessment should be an ongoing process. The active involvement of parent and teachers is emphasized.

Olion and Gillis-Olion argue that professionals must be culturally aware. Cultural awareness can indeed impact on the interpretation of results. Dana (1988), in his study of the Minnesota Multiphasic Personality Inventory, found culturally distinct patterns of results that may be identified as problems. For example, African Americans demonstrate symptoms of alienation, which, rather than demonstrating a problem, reflect a cultural variance. Annis and Corenblum (1988) report that among Canadian Native American children, fluent in both English and their native language (Ojibwa), significant differences occurred in self-identification depending on the language used in assessment.

Recommendations for Nonbiased, Functional Assessment

The Executive Committee of the Council for Children with Behavioral Disorders (1989) offers the following recommendations for the conduct of a nonbiased, functional assessment of learners from diverse ethnic, cultural, and linguistic groups:

1. Attention should be focused on classroom and school learning environments rather than medical or mental health based models.
2. Learner, teacher, and administrator culture, expectations, tolerance, learning and reinforcement history, and family situations should be considered.
3. Attention should be focused on student and teacher behaviors and the contexts in which they occur.
4. The conditions under which behaviors are observed, taught, and required should be studied.
5. Specific, measurable, instructionally based standards for academic and social behaviors should be established.
6. An assessment of the student's current learning environment, with documentation of prereferral interventions, should be implemented prior to referral.
7. Effective and efficient instructional procedures should be applied.
8. Teaching behaviors, instructional organization, and instructional supports should be assessed.
9. The responsibility for learning or performance failure should not be placed on the student.
10. Teachers should be prepared in a functional assessment perspective that focuses on children at risk for academic and/or behavioral difficulties.
11. Professionals should be realigned towards a functional assessment perspective ■

In a position paper on the assessment of children from various cultures and ethnic groups, the Executive Committee of the Council for Children with Behavioral Disorders (1989) states that misdiagnosis often occurs as a result of (a) language differences, (b) teachers' faulty perceptions and low expectations of the academic and social competence of learners from various cultures and ethnic groups, and (c) the fact that more learners from various cultures and ethnic groups are classified as behaviorally disordered because a disproportionate number of students from these groups are referred for assessment. Further recommendations for nonbiased assessment of learners from diverse ethnic, cultural, and linguistic groups appear in Box 8.2.

Objective Three: To describe the impact of various cultures and ethnic groups on classroom interactions.

The Impact of Various Cultural and Ethnic Groups on Classroom Interactions

Though considerable variation exists within and across cultures, the interactions which many of the cultural or linguistic minority children engage in prior to entering school are context-imbedded situations in which children have been able to negotiate meaningfully. However, when they enter the classroom, they find that the context is very different. They are provided with limited feedback from their efforts to learn and understand the Anglo school culture.

Hispanic Americans

According to Hyland (1989), Hispanic learners are significantly behind the general population in academic attainment. They enter school with a significantly different social, economic, and cultural background than do their peers who understand Anglo culture. Delgado-Gaitan and Trueba (1985) found, by carefully observing and recording the classroom interactions of seven Mexican-American students under four different participation structures (group response, individual called response, silent work, and instructional group work) that copying was a legitimate activity among the students. This behavior appeared to be based on home socialization patterns that stress collectivity and social cohesiveness. Rather than representing low ability and lack of motivation, copying is considered by Mexican students to be a constructive approach to intellectual exchanges and the acquisition of new knowledge in a social unit composed of peers.

Commins and Miramontes (1989) report the results of an ethnographic study that explored the relationship of Mexican-American students' achievement and language abilities. Students were perceived by teachers to have limited language abilities in Spanish and English; yet, across all settings, students displayed strengths in both languages. The organization of instruction in the classroom tended to limit the students' abilities to demonstrate their full range of competence in two languages. The students' lack of English structural proficiency and lack of vocabulary in Spanish was interpreted by teachers as a lack of conceptual ability; over a variety of contexts, however, students showed the ability to use language as a vehicle for effective self-expression both socially and cognitively.

African Americans

Hanna (1988) suggests that individuals belong to both speech and movement communities. As a consequence of the differences between the African-American children's and Anglo teachers' speech and movement communities, six important areas of potential problems emerged: achievement, disruption, family cooperation, interpersonal negotiation of relationships, motor movement, and the expression of anger.

In the area of achievement, Hanna found that many African-American inner city children considered academic book learning to be "white." She found that African-American children who operated in a dual system of standard English dialect and Black English Vernacular carried a more demanding cognitive burden than individuals operating in a single system in which there are fewer translations necessary.

In reference to disruption, Hanna suggests that students may set into motion forces to eliminate a poor self-image. These students may play to a peer audience for recognition when they don't receive recognition from the teacher. Hanna speaks of a culture of disruption rather than cooperation among some young, frustrated learners.

Other cultural variations emerge as problems for Anglo teachers. The African-American practice of familial cooperation was interpreted by some teachers as cheating. New children in the classroom negotiate interpersonal relationships, and participants probe for common experiences with their peers. They seek cues in how to act or what to expect from the teacher. These behaviors are problematic if they differ from the teacher's expectations of behavior, if the teacher does not understand that these are cultural ways of behaving. African-American children demonstrate more motor activity and wear clothing which accents body movement. Touch is initiated sooner and is more common among black children.

Lower socioeconomic status African-American learners appear to be socialized to greater aggression and expression of anger. Aggression or acting out is related to the development and maintenance of friendships and personal defenses. These friendships exist on several levels and emerge into kinships. In defending these ties, African-American learners were found to strike out with less restraint.

Native Americans

The performance of Native American learners in the public schools is influenced by the anxieties, mores, aspirations, and behavior patterns of their culture (Pepper, 1976). These children tend to withdraw when unfamiliar with a situation. They are taught to listen and wait until they attain an age at which it is perceived that their years of experience have prepared them to learn enough and be influential enough to attract listeners. Rather than announcement or verbal recognition, Native Americans rely on quiet recognition and silence as expressions of respect.

According to Gilliland and Rehner (1988), professionals teaching Native Americans have two major areas of concern: (a) understanding the Native American culture, which varies from the Anglo culture with regard to self-image, learning styles, discipline, and motivation, and (b) making the subject matter presented in schools, such as language arts, social studies, mathematics, science, and art, culturally relevant.

Appalachians

Lewis, Messner, and McDowell (1985) describe Appalachian culture (especially the isolation and reliance on folk remedies) as an unchanging culture. There are two particular segments of this culture: those who remain in the Appalachian region and Appalachian migrants who have moved to urban areas seeking employment.

Appalachians in the Region   In Heath's (1983) ethnographic study of two working-class Appalachian communities, the contrast of school and home play and communication patterns became evident as a mismatch challenging for teachers. She observed these patterns as early as preschool. One group of children found the concept of play centers in which specific toys were used for designated time periods puzzling; teachers' attempts to maintain schedules and encourage play activities were met with student frustration.

In terms of communication style, Heath found that the use of indirect questions rather than commands (for example, "could we have some air in here?" rather than "open the window") was difficult for the children to understand. When gathered for group story time, one group of children interrupted and spoke with other children while the teacher was reading.

Hensen and Resick (1990) believe that even Appalachians who have remained in the region are in a cultural transition. The traditional remedies appropriate to the care and prevention of health problems have been lost, and new ways of the mainstream culture have not yet been learned by the surviving generation, generating a void in knowledge.

In terms of the relationship with their children, Appalachian mothers were found to have unrealistically high expectations of their infants. They were restrictive of their older children's activities, and used physical punishments, paired with reasoning and rewards, as discipline (Kennedy, 1985). Though low-income, Appalachian Caucasian mothers value self-direction and internalization, they acknowledge the need for conformity as an adaptive mechanism and maintain a desire for their children to rise above their current status (Peterson & Peters, 1985).

Urban Appalachians Relocated Appalachian families have been described as suffering from "existential depression," reactive to separation from the meanings found in both nature and the family's extended network "back home" (Lantz & Harper, 1989). Those families who left the Appalachian region were more highly motivated to follow the goals set by mainstream society, whereas those who stayed behind placed greater importance on their continued association with family and familiar surroundings, and the lifestyle of the region (Daniel, 1985).

A study exploring a Caucasian mainstream-culture female teacher and her interactions with a Caucasian mainstream-culture male, an Appalachian male, and an African-American male first grade student, found that, in terms of recognition of discourse differences, the Appalachian student was most challenged: he finished the year in the lowest reading group (Pepinsky & DeStefano, 1983).

Migrant Families

Migrant children with disabilities have several unique educational needs in addition to their need for special education services. These include (Baca & Harris, 1988):

- native language development and instruction. These services must be provided either by a bilingual educator in consultation with a special educator or by a bilingual special educator.
- English as a second language (ESL) instruction, provided by the special educator or in cooperation with an ESL teacher. Instruction should be meaningful and appropriate to the child's age and development level. Caution must be taken to assure that the child's culture is not denigrated.
- self-concept enhancement. Mobility, poverty, and the general life-style of the migrant child appear to have a negative impact on the self-concept (Henggeler & Tavormina, 1979). Self-concept enhancement is an important part of the curriculum for migrant students.
- acculturation enhancement. Migrant learners can be helped greatly through instruction and experiences that familiarize them with the majority culture. Caution must be taken to assure that the child's culture is not denigrated.
- family and community involvement. The family appears to be the one constant social unit in the life of the migrant student. It is important that the family be involved to the extent possible in the learner's educational program. Family involvement is enhanced through home visits and the use of the family's primary language.
- coordination of services. The special educator or other service provider should assume the role of consultant to the family.
- use of the Individualized Education Program. Involve the migrant educator, ESL educator, and other community and school service providers in the development of the comprehensive IEP. In addition, use available services for the transfer of information from jurisdiction to jurisdiction.

Teachers and students in a classroom with obvious efforts to recognize and integrate the students' cultures (bulletin boards, flags, maps, objects of art and interest).

Objective Four: To describe ways to mediate the environment for learners from various cultures and ethnic groups.

Mediating the Environment

Cummins (1989) suggests that learners from minority cultures and ethnic groups are disempowered educationally in much the same way that their communities are disempowered by interactions in society. In short, these learners are either "empowered" or "disabled" as a direct result of their interactions with educators in the schools. He links empowerment to the extent to which the following occur:

1. Language and culture are a part of the school program.
2. Community participation is an integral component of the children's education.
3. Instruction promotes intrinsic motivation on the part of students to use language and generate their own knowledge.
4. Assessment focuses on the ways in which academic difficulties are a function of interactions within the school context rather than problems within the students.

In working with learners from different cultures, Au (1980) suggests developing a social context that is comfortable for the teacher and for the learners. Through interweaving text-derived content and personal experience, a more comfortable social context should evolve. In addition, a level of comfort must be negotiated between teachers and parents of the learners whom they teach. Lightfoot (1981) contends that territoriality exists between parents and teachers because of stereotypes about minority parents and teachers. Schools, she argues, organize public "rites" such as PTA meetings, open houses, or newsletters which delineate rather than explore collaboration. These interactions are institutionalized means of establishing boundaries under the guise of "partnership."

Cross (1988) proposes a five-part framework for providing culturally competent services that would enhance true collaboration. The following elements would be essential:

1. An awareness and acceptance of ethnic difference. Celebrating diversity, rather than arguing that everyone is really the same, enhances collaboration.
2. Self-awareness of one's personal culture. Teachers must examine their own values and beliefs regarding family, goals, and schooling.
3. Recognition of the dynamics of differences. The culturally transmitted patterns of communication, etiquette, and problem solving should be recognized.
4. Knowledge of the family's culture.
5. Adaptation of skills, that is, modifying the teacher-child interaction and teaching/learning process to support cultural differences.

Beyond academic competence there is a need for students to demonstrate interactional competence in social settings in order to do well in school; the major identified literacy/achievement problem was called an "attitude" problem. Gilmore (1987) found that students who frequently displayed stylized "sulking and stepping" were usually described by teachers as having a "bad attitude."

For effective learning, the role of the culture must be recognized and used in the activity settings during the actual learning process (Trueba, 1988a). Culture appears to be at the heart of academic success regardless of the learner's ethnicity or culture. An effective learning environment must be constructed in which the learner is assisted through meaningful and culturally appropriate relationships in the internalization of the Anglo values embedded in our school system. Trueba (1988b) believes that at the heart of academic failure may be a profound cultural conflict, and that there are ways to socialize minority children for academic success. Culturally based instructional models can help in the acquisition of English literacy for academic success.

Language

As suggested by the quotation that opened this chapter, Delpit (1988) believes that students must be taught the language codes needed to participate fully in the mainstream of American life, not by being forced to attend to low, inane subskills, but rather within the context of meaningful communicative endeavors. Learners must be allowed the resource of the teacher's expert knowledge while being helped to acknowledge their own "expertness." An appropriate education for poor children and children of color can only be devised in consultation with adults who share their culture. Teachers need to not only "help students to establish their own voices, but to coach those voices to produce notes that will be heard clearly in the larger society" (p. 296).

Dialects serve to identify speakers in either geographical or social space (Farr, 1986). Different rules distinguish different dialects. Learners who have rules in their linguistic competence that produce nonstandard features have difficulty editing their writing so that it reflects written grammatical standards. Bidialectalism is based on the assumption that nonstandard dialects are as valid as standard English; if one acquires a second dialect, two linguistic systems are available for oral and written communication.

In his study of English language learning among Hispanic children, Trueba (1988b) followed twelve children across school and home settings. Trueba found that cultural conflict may help explain problems in the acquisition of English literacy. English literacy school activities presuppose cultural knowledge and values that children and family have not acquired. To address these challenges, he recommends that:

1. Students should be placed in learning environments in which there are opportunities for educators to evaluate and analyze failure and degradation incidents related to academic performance.
2. Learning skills and levels students have achieved in specific subjects should be identified.
3. Learning experiences should be constructed that are more congruent with a child's cultural and linguistic backgrounds, and in which children play a major role in determining or negotiating the level and content of what they want to learn.
4. Learning experiences should be expressed in clear goals, well understood and internalized by the children, and supported by a creative reward system.

Trueba states that two factors must be addressed simultaneously: (1) the school system should be sensitized to develop culturally based instructional models that are effective for minorities, and (2) children representing minorities should be socialized to achieve academically.

Migrant Families

Through the states, the federal government provides migrant education services. The migrant educator is the primary service provider; she or he has a diverse role, which includes (Salend, 1990):

- certification of the migrant family as eligible for service
- assisting parents to enroll their children in school and serving as parent advocate
- identifying and contacting community agencies, organizations, and other resources that can offer assistance to the family, such as medical and dental services
- providing supplemental instruction to the student, including bilingual instruction, ESL instruction, and career education
- consulting with special and general educators
- providing parent training
- serving as interpreter
- providing transportation for families

Migrant students should be entered into the Migrant Student Record Transfer System (MSRTS) as soon as possible after school enrollment. MSRTS is a computerized communications system which collects and maintains and transfers academic and health records for migrant children throughout the United States. The system includes information about special education services required by individual children entered into the program. It lists information on the child's disability, assessment, related services, and IEP. Information is provided on how to contact the child's previous school.

The Impact of Larger Social Systems on Diverse Cultural and Ethnic Groups

Ogbu (1985) explored why cultural and language dissonance appears temporary for some minority groups and more persistent for others. He suggests that minorities are characterized by at least two types of cultural/language differences. One is a primary cultural difference, which existed before the group became a minority. The other is a secondary difference, which arose after the group became subordinate to others, as cultural ways of behaving in order to cope with their subordination and exploitation, protect their identity, and maintain their boundary. Ogbu describes three kinds of minority groups: (1) autonomous minorities, who are not usually victims of stratification, (2) immigrant minorities, who have not had time to internalize the effects of discrimination, and (3) castelike or subordinate minorities, who are denied true assimilation into the mainstream. Castelike minorities may demonstrate school difficulties due to their forced incorporation and subordination, the cumulative effects of being denied access to a good education, early discrimination experienced in white schools, limited opportunities, and school behavior of accommodation and assimilation being seen as "buying out."

Another issue in the discussion of cultural diversity is social class. Turner (1973) reports clear evidence of the relevance of social class to the child's definition of the control situation and his or her own choice of control. In discussing control, working-class children mention control by threats. Control in the schools seems to maintain social differences, in that middle-class children may have an orientation to an elaborated code such as that found in schools, while other children may be less comfortable with such codes.

In an analysis of lower-track classes in a secondary school, Page (1987) finds that these classes were neither specific to the individual needs of the students nor were they determined by social order. Teachers made explicit references to the children's socioeconomic classes concurrently with academic and behavioral characteristics to form a constellation of traits by which teachers identified the students. The curricula used in these "terminal education classes" recreated the educational norm of each institution and translated teachers' perceptions of students' social class characteristics and made them visible in the classroom. Being "low class" emerged as a culture in itself in the school, cutting across race and ethnicity.

Self-Perception and Society's Perceptions of Racial and Ethnic Differences

In the earliest studies of racial preference, Clark and Clark (1939) found that racial identification occurs between the third and fourth year of the child's life. Yet in terms of racial preference (in the selection and description of dolls representing different races as "pretty" or "nice"), African-American children typically chose the Caucasian doll to play with. These findings have been confirmed in more recent studies with not only African-American children, but Native Americans, Asian Americans, Hispanics, and New Zealand Moaris, with what is called a "white bias" consistently demonstrated (Aboud & Skerry, 1984).

Clark and Clark (1939) in their explanation of the "white bias" write that learners are distressed by the conflict between personal racial identity and the perceived value of that race in society. The selection of Caucasian dolls or pictures indicates an attempt to identify with the dominant group. Williams and Morland (1976) contend that what is actually in place is a "light-color bias," with children acting according to learned behavior that light is good, clean, and nice, and dark is bad, dirty, or mean.

Though these are probably not the only possible theories for the so-called "white bias," this bias can also be viewed in terms of the context of the assessment. Trent (1964) found that African-American assessors elicited different preferences for pictures of Caucasian and African-American persons from children who were African American or Caucasian. Corenblum and Wilson (1982) found that Native American children were more likely to select a Native American doll as looking like themselves when the dolls were presented by a Native American. In addition to race, the language used may also impact on preferences children report. Gibbons (1983) believes that language acts as another contextual cue that enhances personal group identification and helps learners define the situation.

Several independent variables contribute to the "white bias." Its very existence raises some questions about racial and ethnic minorities in North American society. Aboud and Skerry (1984) suggest that when the power or status of a minority group is low, preferences emerge for the majority group. Dana (1988) states that group consciousness, the restoration of an original cultural identity as a means of making sense out of life experiences and dealing with the effects of racism, emerges in situations such as the "white bias" to increase positive self-affirmation and cultural identity. Learners from various cultures and ethnic groups are simultaneously, and in various degrees, dealing with the social and economic reality of Anglo culture.

Perceptions Regarding Family

Chavkin (1989) argues that although minority parents want to be involved in their children's education, appropriate structures and strategies do not exist for involving them. Communication does not occur because of lack of resources and time. Professionals must, however, debunk the myth that minority parents don't care about their children's education.

In their survey of 1,118 Black and Hispanic parents, Williams and Chavkin (1985) demonstrated that these parents, regardless of ethnicity or minority status, were concerned about their children's education. Parents expressed strong interest in a variety of roles and activities, and were interested in being involved in school decisions, going to school performances, helping their children at home, and assisting at school events.

The Metropolitan Life Survey of the American Teacher (1987) results indicated that parents in inner city districts were less satisfied than were suburban parents with the frequency of their contacts with the teacher. Minority parents reported that they were intimidated by the staff and institutional structures of the school.

Impact of Segregation

Coleman, Campbell, Hobson, McPartland, Mood, Weinfeld, and York (1966) conducted an extensive series of national studies regarding the impact of segregated facilities on the educational life of learners. Predominantly African-American schools were found to have lower quality and quantity of facilities and curricular choices for students. These learners were found to score as much as one standard deviation below Anglo pupils' scores at first grade. Coleman and associates found

Schools should recognize that learners from minority cultures and ethnic groups are often challenged by the Anglo culture of schools.

that the most important variable in improving the education of African-American learners who had been educated in segregated settings was the educational backgrounds and aspirations of their school peers.

As Coleman and his associates were studying segregated facilities, Rosenberg (1965) presented the concept of contextual dissonance, which he described as a sense of not belonging with the people or to the environment in which one finds oneself. He reported that African-American learners in integrated schools had lower self-esteem than those in primarily African-American schools. When a group of African-American students who had not been dislocated for purposes of integration was examined, they held higher self-esteem than Caucasians.

While de facto segregation continues to exist, some means of creating heterogeneous groups to prepare learners to exist in a pluralistic society remains necessary (Streitmatter, 1988). Schools have, in Streitmatter's opinion, been deemed the primary means of implementing this goal. He argues that care must be taken to consider all of the ramifications of implementing this goal; the individual learner's self-esteem and healthy progression through the identity development process is an important consideration for policymakers working toward more effective and positive school integration.

Summary

In this chapter five major ethnic, cultural, and linguistic groups are discussed: Asian American, African American, Hispanic, Native American, and Appalachian. The material in this chapter is written with the recognition that within each ethnic and cultural group there is vast diversity and individuality.

By the year 2000, one in every three Americans will be African American, Hispanic, or Asian American. This change in population requires that the school be reorganized to respond to the individual and group needs of learners from diverse ethnic and cultural groups and, at the same time, respect and protect the uniqueness of the members of these groups as individuals and groups having common history, traditions, and experiences. In addition, attention should be given to the unique challenges presented to the children of migrant families.

Ethnic and minority groups are overrepresented in special education. Assessment is not sensitive to the cultural uniqueness of the members of these minorities. A greater emphasis on assessment within cultural context is suggested in this chapter. Assessment must be responsive to individual psychological adjustment, family relationships, school adjustment and achievement, and relationships with peers.

Learners from various cultures and ethnic groups must be helped to adjust to a difficult transition from their familiar cultural context to the unfamiliar context of the classroom and school. This may be accomplished through educator sensitivity to learners' culture and language, the integration of minority community leaders and parents into the education process, and the use of learners' personal experiences and perceptions in the educational process.

Finally, society and, especially, educators, must develop an awareness of and sensitivity to diverse cultural and ethnic backgrounds.

References

Aboud, F. E., & Skerry, S. A. (1984). The development of ethnic attitudes: A critical review. *Journal of Cross-Cultural Psychology, 15,* 3–34.

Allen, L., & Majidi-Ahi, S. (1989). Black American children. In J. Gibbs & L. Huang (Eds.), *Children of color* (pp. 148–178). San Francisco: Jossey Bass.

Annis, R. C., & Corenblum, B. (1988). Effect of test language and experimenter race on Canadian Indian children's racial and self-identity. *The Journal of Social Psychology, 126,* 761–773.

Au, H. K. (1980). Participation structures in a reading lesson with Hawaiian children: Analysis of a culturally appropriate instructional event. *Anthropology and Education Quarterly, 11,* 91–115.

Baca, L., & Harris, K. C. (1988). Teaching migrant exceptional children. *Teaching Exceptional Children, 20* (4), 32–35.

Barresi, J. (1984). *Interstate Migrant Council: National workshop on special education needs of migrant handicapped students. Proceedings report.* Denver: Education Commission of the States.

Berlowitz, M. J., & Durand, H. (1977). School dropout or school pushout? A case study of the possible violation of property rights and liberties by the de facto exclusion of students from the public schools. Working Paper #8. Cincinnati: Urban Appalachian Council.

Bird, B. (1985). Comparisons of the total school population with migrant students in special education. Unpublished manuscript, California Task Force on Migrant Education, Sacramento.

Bobo, J. K. (1985). Preventing drug abuse among American Indian adolescents. In L. D. Gilchrist & S. P. Schinke (Eds.), *Preventing social and health problems through life skills training.* Seattle: University of Washington School of Social Work.

Borman, K. M., Mueninghoff, E., & Piazza, S. (1989). Urban Appalachian girls and young women: Bowing to no one. In L. Weis (Ed.), *Class, race, and gender in U.S. schools* (pp. 230–248). Albany, NY: Sage.

Brendtro, L. K., Brokenleg, M., & Bockern, S. V. (1990). *Reclaiming youth at risk: Our hope for the future.* Bloomington, IN: National Education Service.

Brod, R. L., & McQuiston, J. M. (1983). American Indian adult education and literacy: The first national survey. *Journal of American Indian Education, 1,* 1–16.

Bryde, J. (1971). *Indian students and guidance.* Boston: Houghton Mifflin Company.

Chavkin, N. F. (1989). Debunking the myth about minority parents. *Educational Horizons, 67* (4), 119–123.

Chinn, P. C., & Hughes, S. (1987). Representation of minority students in special education classes. *Remedial and Special Education, 8,* 41–46.

Clark, K., & Clark, M. (1939). The development of consciousness of self and the emergence of racial identification in Negro preschool children. *Journal of Social Psychology, 10,* 591–599.

Coleman, J. S., Campbell, E. Q., Hobson, C. J., McPartland, J., Mood, A. M., Weinfeld, F. D., & York, R. L. (1966). *Quality of educational opportunity.* Washington, DC: Government Printing Office.

Commins, N. L., & Miramontes, O. B. (1989). Perceived and actual linguistic competence: A descriptive study of four low-achieving Hispanic bilingual students. *American Educational Research Journal, 26* (4), 443–472.

Corenblum, B., & Wilson, A. E. (1982). Ethnic preferences and identification among Canadian Indian and white children: Replication and extension. *Canadian Journal of Behavioral Science, 14,* 50–59.

Cross, T. (1988). Services to minority populations: What does it mean to be a culturally competent professional? *Focal Point, 2* (4), 1–3.

Cummins, J. (1989). A theoretical framework for bilingual special education. *Exceptional children, 56* (2), 111–119.

Dana, R. H. (1988). Culturally diverse groups and MMPI interpretation. *Professional Psychology: Research and Practice, 19,* 490–495.

Daniel, B. P. (1985). Cultural influences on moving or staying: An Appalachian case study. *Journal of Applied Social Sciences, 10* (1), 51–61.

Delgado-Gaitan, C., & Trueba, H. T. (1985). Ethnographic study of participant structures in task completion: Reinterpretation of "handicaps" in Mexican children. *Learning Disability Quarterly, 8,* 67–75.

Delpit, L. D. (1988). The silenced dialogue: Power and pedagogy in educating other people's children. *Harvard Educational Review, 58,* 280–298.

Dunn, L. (1968). Special education for the mildly retarded: Is much of it justifiable? *Exceptional Children, 7,* 5–24.

Executive Committee of the Council for Children with Behavioral Disorders (1989). White paper: Best assessment practices for students with behavioral disorders: Accommodation to cultural diversity and individual differences. *Behavioral Disorders, 14,* 263–278.

Farr, M. (1986). Language, culture, and writing: Sociolinguistic foundations of research on writing. In E. Z. Rothkopf (Ed.), *Review of research in education, Volume 13* (pp. 195–223).Washington, DC: American Educational Research Association.

Fradd, S., Figueroa, R. A., & Correa, V. I. (1989). Meeting the multicultural needs of Hispanic students in special education. *Exceptional Children, 56,* 102–104.

Garcia-Preto, N. (1982). Puerto-Rican families. In M. Goldriek, J. K. Pierce, & J. Gordano (Eds.), *Ethnicity and family therapy.* New York: Guildford.

Gibbons, J. P. (1983). Attitudes towards languages and code-mixing in Hong Kong. *Journal of Multilingual and Multicultural Development, 4,* 129–147.

Gibbs, J. T., & Huang, L. N. (1989). A conceptual framework for assessing and treating minority youth. In J. T. Gibbs & L. N. Huang (Eds.), *Children of color.* San Francisco: Jossey Bass.

Gilliland, H., & Rehner, J. (1988). *Teaching the native American.* Dubuque, IA: Kendall/Hunt.

Gilmore, P. (1987). Sulking, stepping, and tracking: The effects of attitude assessment on access to literacy. In D. Bloome (Ed.), *Literacy and schooling* (pp. 98–119). Norwood, NJ: Ablex.

Guinn, R. (1977). Value clarification in the bicultural classroom. *Journal of Teacher Education, 28,* 46–47.

Hanna, J. (1988). *Disruptive school behavior: Class, race, and culture.* New York: Holmes and Meyer.

Heath, S. B. (1983). *Ways with Words.* New York: Cambridge University Press.

Henggeler, S. W., & Tavormina, J. B. (1979). The children of Mexican-American migrant workers: A population at risk? *Journal of Abnormal Child Psychology, 6* (1), 97–106.

Hensen, M. M., & Resick, L. (1990). Health beliefs, health care, and rural Appalachian subcultures from an ethnographic perspective. *Family and Community Health, 13* (1), 1–10.

Hodginkinson, H. (1985). *All one system.* Washington, DC: Institute for Educational Leadership.

Hoffman, E. (1988). *The right to be human: A biography of Abraham Maslow.* Los Angeles: Jeremy P. Tarcher, Inc.

Huang, L. N. (1989). Southeast Asian refugee children and adolescents. In J. T. Gibbs & L. N. Huang (Eds.), *Children of color: Psychological interventions with minority youth* (pp. 278–321). San Francisco: Jossey Bass.

Huang, L. N., & Ying, Y. (1989). Chinese American children and adolescents. In J. T. Gibbs & L. N. Huang (Eds.), *Children of color* (pp. 30–66). San Francisco: Jossey Bass.

Hyland, C. R. (1989). What we know about the fastest growing minority population: Hispanic Americans. *Educational Horizons, 67* (4), 124–130.

Inclan, J. (1985). Variations in value orientations in mental health work with Puerto Ricans. *Psychotherapy, 33* (2S), 324–334.

Inclan, J. E., & Herron, D. G. (1989). Puerto Rican adolescents. In J. T. Gibbs & L. N. Huang (Eds.), *Children of color* (pp. 251–277). San Francisco: Jossey Bass.

Interstate Migrant Council (1984). *National policy workshop on special education needs of migrant handicapped students. Proceedings report.* Denver: Education Commission of the States.

Kennedy, J. H. (1985). Childrearing attitudes in Appalachia today: A preliminary look. *Psychological Reports, 56,* 677–678.

Kochman, T. (1991). Culturally based patterns of difference. Paper presented at the University of Cincinnati.

LaFrambroise, T. D., & Low, K. G. (1989). American Indian children and adolescents. In J. Gibbs & L. Huang (Eds.), *Children of color* (pp. 114–147). San Francisco: Jossey Bass.

Lantz, J. E., & Harper, K. (1989). Network intervention, existential depression, and the relocated Appalachian family. *Contemporary Family Therapy: An International Journal, 11,* 213–223.

Leap, W. L. (1981). American Indian language maintenance. *Annual Review of Anthropology, 10,* 271–280.

LeVine, E. S., & Padilla, A. M. (1980). *Crossing cultures in therapy: Pluralistic counseling for the hispanic.* Pacific Grove, CA: Brooks/Cole.

Lewis, S., Messner, R., & McDowell, W. A. (1985). An unchanging culture. *Journal of Gerontological Nursing, 11* (8), 20–25.

Lightfoot, S. (1981). Toward conflict resolution: Relationships between families and schools. *Theory into Practice, 20* (2), 97–104.

McAdoo, H. P. (1978). Minority families. In J. H. Stevens & M. Matthers (Eds.), *Mother-child, father-child relationships.* Washington, DC: The National Association for the Education of Young Children.

McCoy, C. B., & Watkins, V. M. (1980). Drug use among urban ethnic youth. *Youth and Society, 11,* 83–106.

McCoy, J. L. (1986). The migrant handicapped student: Strategies for involving the migrant parent in the IEP process. Salem, OR: COPE Project.

Mercer, J. (1973). *Labeling the mentally retarded.* Los Angeles: University of California Press.

Mindel, C. H., & Habenstein, R. W. (Eds.) (1981). *Ethnic families in America: Patterns and variations* (2nd ed.). New York: Elseview.

The Metropolitan Life Survey of the American Teacher—Strengthening links between home and school (1987). New York: Louis Harris and Associates.

Obermiller, P., Borman, K., & Kroger, J. (1988). The Lower Price Hill Community School. *Urban Education, 23,* 123–132.

Ogbu, J. U. (1985). Research currents: Cultural-ecological influences on minority school learning. *Language Arts, 62,* 860–869.

Olion, L., & Gillis-Olion, M. (1984). Assessing culturally diverse exceptional children. *Early Child Development and Care. 15,* 203–232.

Page, R. (1987). Teachers' perceptions of students: A link between classrooms, school cultures, and the social order. *Anthropology and Education Quarterly, 18,* 77–99.

Pepinsky, H. B., & DeStefano, J. S. (1983). Interactive discourse in the classroom as organizational behavior. *Advances in Reading/Language Research, 2,* 107–137.

Pepper, F. (1976). Teaching the American Indian child in mainstream settings. In R. L. Jones (Ed.), *Mainstreaming and the minority child.* Reston, VA: The Council for Exceptional Children.

Perry, J. (1982). The ECS interstate migrant education project. *Exceptional Children, 48,* 496–500.

Peters, M. (1981). Parenting in Black families with young children. In H. McAdoo (Ed.), *Black families.* Newbury Park, CA: Sage.

Peterson, G. W., & Peters, D. F. (1985). The socialization values of low-income Appalachian White and rural Black mothers: A comparative study. *Journal of Comparative Family Studies, 16* (1), 75–91.

Ramirez, O. (1990). Mexican American children and adolescents. In J. T. Gibbs & L. N. Huang (Eds.), *Children of color* (pp. 224–250). San Francisco: Jossey Bass.

Ramirez, O., & Arce, C. H. (1981). The contemporary Chicano family: An empirically based review. In A. Baron, Jr. (Ed.), *Explorations in Chicano psychology.* New York: Praeger.

Resnick, L. B. (1987). Learning in school and out. *Educational Researcher, 16* (9), 13–20.

Rosenberg, M. (1965). *Society and the adolescent self-image.* Princeton, NJ: Princeton University Press.

Salend, S. J. (1990). A migrant education guide for special educators. *Teaching Exceptional Children, 22* (2), 18–21.

Shon, S., & Ja, D. (1982). Asian families. In M. McGodrick, J. K. Pearce, & J. Giordano (Eds.), *Ethnicity and family therapy.* New York: Guilford Press.

Smith, E. (1981). Cultural and historical perspectives in counseling Blacks. In D. W. Sue (Ed.), *Counseling the culturally different: Theory and practice.* New York: Wiley.

Sowell, T. (1981). *Ethnic America.* New York: Basic Books.

Standing Bear, L. (1933). *Land of the spotted eagle.* New York: Houghton Mifflin.

Streitmatter, J. L. (1988). School desegregation and identity development. *Urban Education, 23,* 280–293.

Sullivan, M., & Miller, D. (1990). Cincinnati's Urban Appalachian Council and Appalachian identity. *Harvard Educational Review, 60* (1), 106–124.

Taylor, R. L., & Richards, S. B. (1991). Patterns of intellectual differences of black, Hispanic, and white children. *Psychology in the Schools, 28,* 5–9.

Trankina, F. (1983). Clinical issues and techniques in working with Hispanic children and their families. In G. J. Powell, J. Yamamoto, A. Romero, & A. Morales (Eds.), *The psychosocial development of minority group children.* New York: Brunner/Mazel.

Trent, R. (1964). The colour of the investigator as a variable in experimental research with Negro subjects. *Journal of Social Psychology, 40,* 280–284.

Trueba, H. T. (1988a). Culturally based explanations of minority students' academic achievement. *Anthropology and Education Quarterly, 19,* 270–287.

Trueba, H. T. (1988b). English literacy acquisition: From cultural trauma to learning disabilities in minority students. *Linguistics and Education, 1,* 125–152.

Turner, G. J. (1973). Social class and children's language of control at age five and age seven. In B. Bernstein (Ed.), *Class, codes, and control* (pp. 135–201). London: Routledge & Kegan Paul.

U. S. Bureau of Census (1986). *Money income and poverty status of families and persons in the United States—1985.* Washington, DC: U.S. Government Printing Office.

Williams, Jr., D. L., & Chavkin, N. F. (1985). *Final report of the parent involvement in education project.* Washington, DC: National Institute of Education.

Williams, J. E., & Morland, J. K. (1976). *Race, color, and self-concept.* College Hill, NC: University of North Carolina Press.

Yamamoto, J., & Kubota, M. (1989). The Japanese American family. In G. Powell, J. Yamamoto, & A. Morales (Eds.). *The psychosocial development of minority group children.* New York: Bruner-Mazel.

Yates, J. R. (1987). Current and emerging forces. *Counterpoint, 7* (4), 4–5.

3

Learners Who Vary in Accessing the Environment

*T*EACHING AND LEARNING IN CLASSROOMS IS A COMMUNICATIVE PROCESS (PURO & BLOOME, 1987). SPOKEN language is the medium for most teaching and the way most students demonstrate what they have learned (Cazden, 1986). For learners whose communication, physical, and sensory systems are intact, the communicative process that occurs in teaching is automatic. For those who vary in these ways, the communicative process is a challenge.

Learners who vary in their communication, physical, and sensory systems are confronted with the challenge of accessing the vast amount of information and interaction that occurs in the environment. Those with communication disorders have difficulty in either comprehension or expression of language, the primary mode of communication. Those with orthopedic handicaps or health impairments are challenged in accessing the physical environment and are limited in the experiences common to others in interaction with objects, places, and positions, or in their mobility. Learners with visual impairments are challenged in their acquisition of concepts which others learn vicariously through observation. Learners with hearing impairments are challenged in their acquisition of verbal language, an essential mode of instruction and interaction.

Though these challenges have a serious impact on all interactions within the learner's developmental context, technology is emerging that assists in mediating them. However, this technology does not give these learners the equivalent experience of their peers. Rather, this technology provides an even further challenge of sense-making to individuals whose developmental contexts have varied due to their inability to access the environment.

In this section, we will explore learners with communication disorders, with an emphasis on the issue of language and its impact on exploiting the developmental context. We will discuss learners with orthopedic and health impairments, and the variations in their experiences. Finally, we will explore the experiences of learners with visual and hearing impairments. In our discussions, we urge you to recognize that the impairment itself must be viewed in terms of the impact it has on the learner's ability to gain access to the information, interactions, and options available to their peers ■

References

Cazden, C.B. (1986). Classroom discourse. In M. C. Wittrock (Ed.), *Handbook of research on teaching* (3rd ed., pp. 432–463). New York: Macmillan.

Puro, P., & Bloome, D. (1987). Understanding classroom communication. *Theory into Practice, 26* (Special Issue), 26–31.

9

Learners with Communication Disorders

*O*bjectives

After completing this chapter, you will be able to:

1. describe the personal characteristics of learners with communication disorders.
2. describe the identification and evaluation of learners with communication disorders.
3. describe the impact of communication disorders in the home and classroom.
4. describe ways to mediate the environment for learners with communication disorders.
5. describe the impact of communication disorders on participation in the larger social systems—the school, community, and society.

*K*ey Words and Phrases

articulation disorders	phonology
augmentative systems	pragmatics
cluttering	receptive language
cognition	semantics
communication	speech
disfluency	speech disorders
expressive language	stuttering
language	symbols
language disorders	syntax
morphology	transactional model
phonemes	voice disorders

*I*N CONSEQUENCE OF AN ATTACK OF APOPLEXY A SOLDIER FOUND IT IMPOSSIBLE TO EXPRESS IN SPOKEN LANGUAGE HIS feelings and ideas. His face bore no signs of a deranged intellect. His mind (espirit) found the answer to questions addressed to him and he carried out all he was told to do . . . He could not articulate on the spot a word pronounced for him to repeat . . . It was not his tongue which was embarrassed, for he moved it with great agility and could pronounce quite well a large number of isolated words. His memory was not at fault, for he signified his anger at being unable to express himself concerning many things which he wished to communicate" (Head, 1926, p. 11) ■

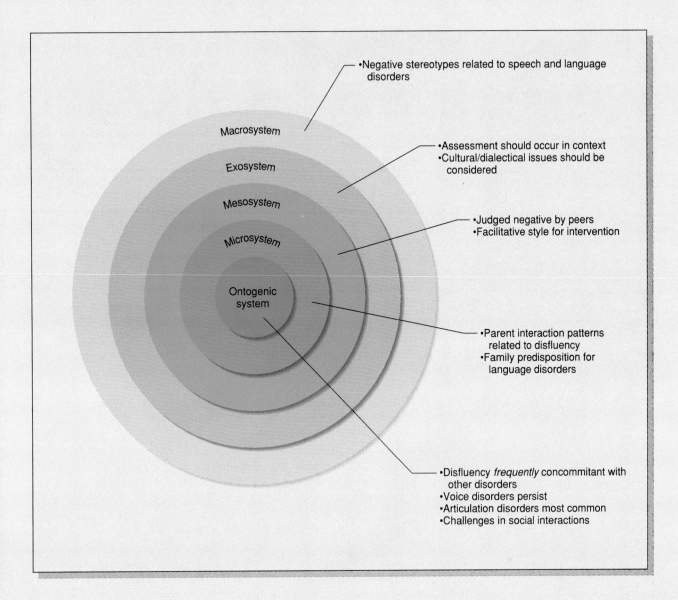

Macrosystem •Negative stereotypes related to speech and language disorders

Exosystem •Assessment should occur in context
•Cultural/dialectical issues should be considered

Mesosystem

Microsystem •Judged negative by peers
•Facilitative style for intervention

Ontogenic system •Parent interaction patterns related to disfluency
•Family predisposition for language disorders

•Disfluency *frequently* concommitant with other disorders
•Voice disorders persist
•Articulation disorders most common
•Challenges in social interactions

Introduction

Language is the ability to communicate complex ideas through an organized system of meaning (Sameroff & Fiese, 1988). This ability to communicate not only supports every social interaction that takes place throughout the day, but it plays a major role in the learner's cognitive development. Sameroff and Fiese (1988) state that language is best described in a developmental context where performance is viewed as the outcome of a learner interacting within human social environments.

Language develops from the learner's need to be understood and to understand. The learner's system relies on rules that are generated out of social interaction and the need to maintain contact and shared understanding (Sameroff & Fiese, 1988). This model is known as the **transactional model** of language development. Within this model, the development of the child is seen as the product of the continuous interactions of the learner and the experiences provided by the caregivers in the social context (Sameroff & Chandler, 1975). There is, in this model, an equal emphasis placed on the effect of the child on the environment and that of the environment on the child. Sameroff and Fiese provide the example of a complicated childbirth which may have made an otherwise calm mother anxious. The mother's anxiety may have caused her to be uncertain and interact inappropriately with the child. The infant, in response to this inconsistency, may develop difficulties in feeding and sleeping patterns that give the appearance of a difficult temperament. This apparent difficult temperament decreases the pleasure that the mother obtains from being with the child, and thus she spends less time with the child. Less time with the child again alters the mother's interaction with the child, making early language development even more difficult. This transactional development of a communication difficulty is depicted in Figure 9.1.

Communication is the verbal and nonverbal means of transmitting and decoding messages from one individual with the intention of stimulating meaning in the mind of another. **Symbols** are the media through which communication occurs. They are the tools with which we think. Symbols, which comprise language, serve as internal representations of the external world (Richards & Richards, 1988). Kaiser and Warren (1988) describe a series of assumptions related to the development of the symbols system we call language. First, language is behavior, which both affects and is affected by the environment. Second, the meaning of language is not only in the words themselves, but in how they are used; that is, language cannot be understood outside of its particular context. Finally, form usually follows function. Form develops as the learner's needs, wants, and intentions become more specific and require a more sophisticated system of communication. Language, voice, and hearing, then, are used to influence others.

Language is described as **expressive** (developing and sending messages) and **receptive** (receiving and interpreting messages). **Speech** is the vocal response mode of language (Schiefelbush & McCormick, 1981). Speech integrates breathing, producing sounds, and controlling the quality and articulation of those sounds to form words. The mechanisms involved in speech production are illustrated in Figure 9.2.

When an individual wishes to speak, the brain sends a message to activate the speech mechanism which includes respiratory, vocal, vibrating, resonating, and articulation or speech mechanisms. The primary function of the respiratory system (diaphragm, lungs, chest, and throat muscles) is to inhale oxygen and expel gases. When air is expelled the voice mechanism is activated. Voice or sound is produced by the larynx, which is located at the top of the trachea and contains the vocal folds

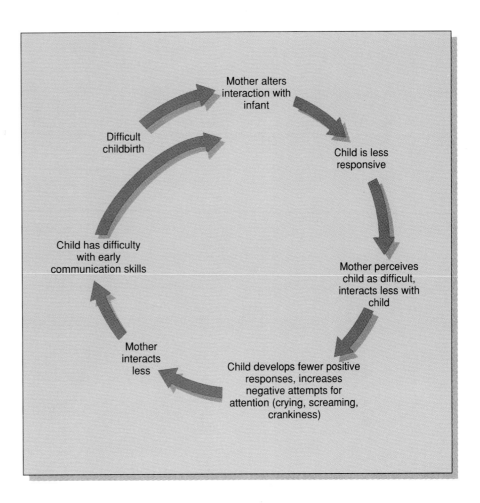

Figure 9.1
Transactional development of a
communication problem.

or cords. The larynx and vocal cords are referred to as the vibrating system. As air is pushed from the lungs, its flow causes the vocal cords to vibrate and produce sound. As the sound passes through the throat, mouth, and nasal cavities (the resonating system), it is shaped into speech sounds by the articulation system (tongue, soft and hard palate, teeth, lips, and jaw). All of these systems must be intact and functioning effectively for the proper production of speech.

Language and Speech Development

The cries, coos, and gurgles of the infant are the beginnings of language and speech development and production. Both the sounds of comfort and distress provide the infant with the exercise needed to develop the complex muscles needed for speech. The child's babbling gradually begins to take form as if the child were practicing consonants and vowel sounds.

At approximately the sixth month, the child begins to use sounds to gain the attention of others and appears to make an effort to respond to others as if in conversation. Vocal play which contains inflection and apparent syllables becomes evident. The child begins to imitate the sounds of others, and to make new sounds.

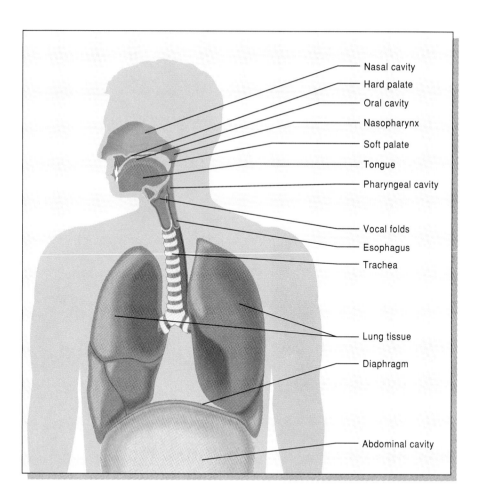

Figure 9.2
The speech mechanism.

As early as 8 to 9 months of age, children use prelinguistic gestures and vocalizations to communicate for a variety of reasons. Bruner (1981) suggests that in the first year of life, children use gestures and vocalizations for three communicative intentions: (a) regulating another's behavior for obtaining or restricting environmental goals; (b) social interaction; and (c) joint attention, directing another's attention for purposes of sharing the focus on some thing or event. Even before words, children use signals intentionally to communicate (Wetherby and associates, 1988).

At about 9 months of age, children use gestures to give an object, show an object, or push an adult's hands, and by 11 months they begin to reach, point, and wave. At about 13 months, children begin using a small number of words that are truly symbolic, referring to objects, events, or classes of objects or events. Between 12 and 18 months, new words are acquired at a slow rate, but children steadily increase their rate of communicating, using sounds in coordination with gestures and using consonants in utterances comprised of many syllables (Kent & Bauer, 1985). Around 18 months of age children experience a surge in vocabulary growth, and rather than learning one new word a week learn several words in a day (Ingram, 1978). Children begin to request information, talk about events, and maintain topics over several turns (Prutting, 1979).

Infants use gestures to communicate.

Communication Disorders

Learners with communication disorders account for the second largest group of learners served under the special education services mandate of Public Law 94–142. According to the U.S. Office of Education (1992), 990,186 children and youth ages 6–21 were served as speech or language impaired during the 1990–91 school year. This represents a 16.4 percent decrease since the 1976–77 school year. Across states, a low of 0.51 percent of the school population was served in the District of Columbia, to a high of 2.61 percent of the school population in Illinois. Over three-fourths of these learners were served in general education classes, and about 18 percent received resource room services. Approximately 5.3 percent attended separate classes or schools, and very few were in other placements (U.S. Department of Education, 1992). The provision of services for learners with communication disorders is the largest service function of special education (Casby, 1989).

In addition to those learners served as primarily communication disordered, it is estimated that approximately one-fourth of learners with other disabilities (for example, mental retardation, learning disabilities, behavioral disorders) receive speech and language services as a related service. In addition, there is frequent association between communication disorders and psychiatric disorders in children (Kotsopoulos & Boodoosingh, 1987). A significant interrelationship has also been found between behavioral disorders and attention deficit disorders and communication disorders (Love & Thompson, 1988).

Personal Characteristics

Objective One: To describe the personal characteristics of learners with communication disorders.

Kretschmer and Kretschmer (1988) report that the consensus of the literature produced in the last decade is that the learner's development and the use of communication (spoken, signed, or written) must be seen in a socially interactive context. In

Verbal activity is important in obtaining communication competence.

other words, learners must have both communication models and opportunities to communicate to construct their own communication competence. This shift in emphasis in the study of language has been termed by some as the "pragmatics revolution." **Pragmatics** are those rules a learner knows and uses in determining who says what to whom, how, why, when, and in what setting (Muma, 1978). Kaiser and Warren (1988) assert that pragmatics assume that:

1. Communicative language is grounded in other behaviors, specifically cognitive skills and social interaction patterns of the learner.
2. Utterances are given contextually relevant meanings by their intentions.
3. There are rules for the use of intention in conversational intercourse.
4. Meaning is determined by function in context.

Pragmatics, however essential, is but one component of language. In addition, there are several other components which contribute to the communication of meaning. Smith (1991) defines these components as follows:

1. **Phonology,** which is the study of the individual speech sounds, or **phonemes,** characteristic of a language and the rules governing the distribution and sequences of phonemes within a language. Phonemes (there are forty-three in American English) do not have meaning unto themselves.
2. **Morphology,** which is the study of the smallest units of meaning. Free morphemes can stand alone, such as "cat," "dog," "out." Bound morphemes contribute to the meaning of free morphemes, and include tense, plurality, possession, or ways of deriving new words (as in the use of prefixes and suffixes).
3. **Syntax,** which is the rule system for constructing sentences. Rather than words randomly strung together, English is characterized by a subject-verb-object sentence order.

4. **Semantics,** which is the meaning of individual words, words in relationship to each other, and the network of meaning.

There are two general categories of communication disorders: speech disorders and language disorders. **Speech disorders** are impairments in the production of oral or spoken language. Disfluency, voice disorders, and articulation disorders are classified as speech disorders. **Language disorders** are deviant or delayed development of comprehension and/or the use of the signs or symbols applied to express or receive ideas in a spoken, written, or other symbol system. The absence of language, delayed language, deviant and interrupted development of language, and post language development disorders are examples of language disorders. Learners may demonstrate receptive (receiving and interpreting), expressive (developing and sending), or mixed (both receiving and sending) language disorders.

Learners Who Are Disfluent   Fluency refers to the smooth flow and rhythm of speech. **Disfluency** includes repetitions or prolongations of sounds, words, or phrases; hesitations or long pauses; struggle behaviors including distortions of lips and mouth, facial grimaces, eye blinks, and extraneous body movements (Rice, 1988). Stuttering and cluttering are examples of disfluency. **Stuttering** is a disruption in the timing of speaking; **cluttering** is a running together in rapid, jumbled speaking of sounds, words, and phrases. According to Van Riper and Emerick (1984) two million persons in the United States exhibit these problems.

Nippold (1990) reviewed the literature since 1920 concerning concomitant speech and language disorders in learners who are disfluent. He found that though the evidence is not convincing, these learners, as a group, are more likely than those who are not disfluent to have other problems in speech and language. Some may have problems that bear relationship to their stuttering. Byrd and Cooper (1989) found that 5- to 9-year-old learners who are disfluent were not delayed in their receptive language skills but were delayed in their expressive language skills. They suggest that young children who are disfluent may appear to have expressive language delays because they attempt to simplify verbal responses as a means of coping with their stuttering. St. Louis and Hinzman (1988), however, found that learners who were disfluent were more likely to have difficulty in articulation.

Disfluency has also been related to learners' personal perception of control. Madison, Budd, & Itzkowitz (1986) found that as learners increased ability to manage their disfluency, they gained a sense of internal rather than external control.

Learners with Voice Disorders   **Voice disorders** are present when a learner has difficulty modulating the resonant quality of speech. Voices vary widely in pitch, volume, and timbre. Moods, emotional states, and attitudes can be identified by the listener through voice quality. Great variations in voice quality are tolerable. However, some voice qualities interfere with effective communication. Learners may have too much nasality in the voice (hypernasal) or too little nasality (denasal). Learners may use an unnaturally high pitch (falsetto), or be harsh, breathy, or throaty (Van Riper, 1978).

Voice disorders appear to persist. Powell, Filter, & Williams (1989) found that almost 40 percent of the learners identified as showing a voice disorder retained that disorder after one year. Four years later, of the learners available in the same school system, 38 percent still demonstrated a voice disorder. They contend that without intervention, voice disorders will persist in children.

Learners with Articulation Disorders   **Articulation disorders,** or phonologic disorders, occur when the learner has difficulty with the sound system of oral language or speech. Articulation disorders are a consequence of the faulty production of phonemes, or the sounds of language. Articulation disorders are the most common of speech disorders served by communication specialists in the schools. There are four types of articulation errors (Van Riper & Emerick, 1984): (a) substitution of one phoneme for another, as "mudder" for mother, (b) disorder of a phoneme, as "shoup" for soup, (c) omission of a sound, as in "mik" for milk, and (d) additions, an extra sound inserted within a word, as "warsh" for "wash."

Among learners with articulation disorders, voice disorders, deficits in expressive language, and hearing problems have been found to occur more frequently than in their typical peers.

Learners with Language Disorders   There is a broad range of language disorders which interfere with a learner's development and communication. Among the most common are the absence of language, delayed language, deviations and interruptions in language development, and language disorders acquired after language has been developed.

Cognition   **Cognition** is the process of knowing and thinking. Several studies have been conducted to determine potential patterns in cognitive skills among learners with language disorders. Condino, Im-Humber, and Stark (1990) find that learners with language disorders have significantly more problems in coding, memory, hypothesis generation, hypothesis evaluation, and deduction than their typical peers. Difficulty in encoding information was also found in solving discrimination-learning problems (Nelson, Kamhi, & Apel, 1987). Learners with language disorders may have difficulty in sustaining and manipulating nonlinguistic symbols as well as linguistic symbols (Snyder, 1987).

Language   Not surprisingly, the most broadly researched characteristic of learners with language disorders is language itself. Learners with language disorders have difficulty with syntactic comprehension (Adams, 1990) and do not monitor their own comprehension as well as do their peers with typical language skills (Dollaghan, 1987). Conversations may be interrupted because of an inappropriate response by a learner with language disorders, which may, in fact, occur because the learner with language disorders misunderstood the literal or implicit meaning of the utterances of the person with whom they were conversing (Bishop & Adams, 1989). Learners with language disorders have been found to rely heavily on semantic expectations or the sequence of content words in comprehending sentences (Van der Ley & Deward, 1986).

When a breakdown in communication occurs, learners with language disorders are more likely to blame the listener than are their peers, who are more likely to blame the speaker (Meline & Bracklin, 1987). Significantly more communication breakdowns are found in the conversation and narration of learners with language disorders than that of their age-matched peers (MacLachlan & Chapman, 1988). Learners with language disorders have significantly more unrepaired sentences in their conversation, and they tend to overlap on their own speech, beginning a new thought before completing the first one (Fujiki, Brinton, & Sonnenberg, 1990). The number of errors in taking turns while having a conversation, interruptions, turn switch times, and poorly timed responses is significantly greater among learners with language disorders (Craig & Evans, 1989). Learners with language disorders are less able to identify the errors in word order in sentences than are their age-matched peers (Fujiki, Brinton, & Dunton, 1987).

Social and Emotional Characteristics   Language disorders impact on social behaviors as well as on the more commonly recognized area of academic achievement (Goldman, 1987). Learners with language disorders demonstrate a high prevalence of anxiety disorders as described in the Diagnostic Statistical Manual of Mental Disorders (DSM III) (Cantwell & Baker, 1987). Learners with language disorders demonstrate significantly poorer understanding of humor, as related to their inability to grasp the nature of multimeaning words. These learners tend to segment and redefine phrases involved, losing meaning of that which is perceived as funny (Spector, 1990). Learners with language disorders demonstrate significant problems in symbolic, adaptive, and integrative play as compared to their peers (Roth & Clark, 1987).

Fine Motor Skills   Learners with language disorders have been found to have difficulty copying simple figures when compared to their age peers (Moore & Law, 1990). In a study examining the relationships between fine motor skills and linguistic abilities of developmentally delayed learners, Sommers (1988) found that language disorders were strongly associated with poor fine motor skills.

Medical Issues   Localized brain damage has been posited as one potential cause of language disorders (Bishop, 1987). Otitis media (middle ear infection) has been suggested as interacting with risk factors occurring at the time of birth in the etiology of language disorders (Bishop & Edmundson, 1986).

Objective Two: To describe the identification and evaluation of learners with communication disorders.

Identification and Evaluation

Public Law 94–142 defines students with communication disorders as "speech impaired." The definition includes communicative disorders such as impaired articulation, language or voice disorders, and fluency disorders (such as stuttering) which adversely affect a child's educational performance. The American Speech-Language-Hearing Association (ASHA) describes communicative disorders as impairments in the ability to perceive and/or process a symbol system, represent concepts, and/or transmit and use symbols systems (National Joint Committee for Learning Disabilities, 1982).

ASHA describes both communication disorders and communication variations (1982).* In communication disorders, ASHA defines:

1. Speech disorders, which are impairments of voice, articulation of speech sounds, and/or fluency, observed in the transmission and use of the oral symbol system. Included in speech disorders are voice disorders (the absence or abnormal production of voice quality, pitch, loudness, resonance, and/or duration), articulation disorders (abnormal production of speech sounds), and fluency disorders (impaired rate and rhythm).

---

* Reprinted by permission of the American Speech-Language-Hearing Association.

Communication specialists may identify subtle language disorders in children.

2. Language disorders, which are impairments or atypical development of comprehension and/or use of spoken and/or written symbol system. Included are disorders of the form, content, or function of language.

Communication variations include:

1. Communicative differences or dialects, which are variations of a symbol system, used by a group of individuals which reflects and is determined by shared regional, social, or cultural and ethnic factors.
2. **Augmentative systems** (such as sign language, gestures, or technological devices), which are used to supplement the communicative skills of individuals for whom speech is temporarily or permanently inadequate to meet communicative needs.

As can be understood from the previous discussion of communication disorders, the number and intricacy of these disorders makes the processes of identification and assessment complex. Learners with obvious speech and language disorders are readily identified by parents, physicians, and day care and preschool professionals. These children are generally referred to the communication specialist prior to entering kindergarten and the primary grades. Learners with more subtle speech and language disorders are not as readily identified.

The assessment of communication disorders is conducted through a comprehensive diagnostic evaluation, appropriate to the learner's age and overall level of development. The evaluation is conducted by the communication specialist in cooperation with other professionals and the parents. It may include the administration of formal standardized instruments to measure intelligence, language, behavior, and achievement. During the initial phase of the assessment process, the presence of a physical problem or hearing impairment is ruled out as the cause of the communication disorder. If a physical or hearing impairment is discovered, it is the primary target of intervention. Also during this initial phase of assessment, the learner's primary language and the language used in the home is determined.

In general, standardized language tests have been found to have limited value in the task of developing an individualized therapeutic program for the learner. To augment standardized tests, language samples are obtained and analyzed with regard to the learner's use, content, and form of expressive and receptive language. Such samples are most useful if obtained in the various contexts in which the learner is functioning. The learner is observed in interaction with peers and teachers. Information is obtained from the parents and teachers about the learner's school work, developmental history, and use of free time (Wood, 1982). The purpose of the diagnostic evaluation is to obtain a comprehensive picture of the learner and his or her communicative strengths and deficits and to write and implement a remedial or therapeutic program. Both what the child is doing, or not doing, and what the environment is doing, or not doing, must be analyzed before intervening with children (Calvert & Murray, 1985). The child's current functional language and what events stimulate language use must be documented.

Assessment is an attempt to understand the performance of an individual in the environments in which that individual functions (Broen, 1988). Craig (1991) proposes that the best professional practice of assessment include:

1. examination of the child's conversational knowledge while controlling the linguistic demands of the task, and, conversely, linguistic knowledge while controlling the conversational demands of the task.
2. examination of the child's ability to integrate conversational and linguistic skills.
3. examination of both expressive and receptive language.

A model for the evaluation of communication disorders is presented in Box 9.1. Box 9.2 presents a contextual analysis of classroom behaviors as related to communication disorders.

Learners with Articulation Disorders   Of all the forms of communications disorders, articulation disorders are the problem for which children are most frequently referred for assessment and service (Edwards, Cape, & Brown, 1989). Care must be taken in assessing the articulation of learners representing various ethnic, cultural, and linguistic groups. In a study of working-class African-American children who use Black English Vernacular, Cole and Taylor (1990) found that African-American children performed differently on standardized tests of articulation as a function of the linguistic norms used to score items. Failure to consider dialect substantially increased the likelihood of mislabeling normally speaking African-American children as having articulation disorders. More naturalistic strategies, such as that proposed by Shriberg and Kwiatowski (1980), may be useful. In the Natural Process Analysis Test, conversational samples of the child's language are gathered. At least one hundred of these utterances are then used to identify and note changes in the individual's sound system.

Assessing Very Young Learners   Several issues emerge in the assessment of very young children. Crais and Roberts (1991) state that there are a limited number of standardized instruments for the birth to 5-year-old population, with even fewer standardized instruments for learners from birth to 3 years of age. In addition, the available standardized instruments tend to be narrow in scope and omit important assessment areas. They suggest that using a series of decision trees may be helpful for providing a nonstandard assessment method for collecting and organizing information. A decision tree is a sequenced set of questions posed by the examiner either to the child directly or to an informant such as a parent or teacher. Responses

---

Box 9.1

Areas of Assessment for a Model for Communication Assessment (Based on Simon, 1985)

Form

Does the student demonstrate:
- a flexible vocabulary (varies with person or setting)
- regular grammar
- tense and subject/verb agreement
- clear use of referents
- appropriate use of subordinators

Function

Does the student:
- sustain topics
- phrase for intent
- support points of view
- use elaborated codes (school, peer, and home language codes)
- use social and cognitive language
- use varied functions and intents of language
- use tactful deviousness
- modify his or her utterance when needed

Style

Does the student:
- take into account the listener's needs
- plan the content of responses
- have adequate word finding
- express himself or herself fluently
- speak intelligibly
- use distinct speech
- speak at a comfortable rate
- speak audibly ▪

---

to the questions may also be obtained by the examiner through observation of the child. For example, if the child does not imitate three-word combinations (a negative response to an assessment question), intervention in increasing word combinations is suggested.

Objective Three: To describe the impact of communication disorders in the home and classroom.

Communication in the Home and Classroom

Learners Who Are Disfluent   Mothers of 5- to 9-year-old learners who were disfluent made significantly more demands, commands, and requests when talking with their children than mothers of fluent children (Langlois, Hanrahan, & Inouye, 1986). Langlois and associates also found that learners who were disfluent were more verbal. They contend that parent-child interactions may be critical to the onset, development, and maintenance of stuttering. In another study, mothers of

Box 9.2

Observation Guide for Classroom Interactions and Communication (adapted from Creaghead and Tattershall, 1985)

Knowledge about the school routine:
- knows routine for activities (starting the day, going to lunch, ending the day)
- knows routine for participating in activities (where to go for reading group, setting up paper for spelling tests)
- deviates from the routine when appropriate (adapts to reading group in a different area of the room, different sized papers)
- reads the teacher's strategies for cuing a given routine (anticipates transitions from the teacher's cues)
- participates effectively in peer routines (playing games in and out of the classroom, sitting with someone at lunch or on the bus)

Knowledge about communicative routines:
- knows when to raise hand, when to join in
- takes turns appropriately, doesn't interrupt
- initiates conversation
- has more than one style of interaction (interacts with formal language with teacher, peer or "in group" language with classmates)
- uses appropriate greetings and closings

Giving and following directions:
- specifies locations and objects adequately, doesn't use pronouns until the listener knows the topic (e.g., walking up to the teacher and saying, "it's broken" rather than "my pencil is broken")
- watches listener to check communication, responds to puzzled looks
- revises directions when necessary
- takes responsibility when directions do not work

Comprehension and use of figurative language:
- restates figurative meaning of idioms
- uses idiomatic expressions that are used by peers
- uses idiomatic expressions appropriately for context and listener
- comprehends material containing figurative language ■

learners who are disfluent were found to talk significantly faster than mothers of fluent children, though their disfluent children spoke more slowly than their peers (Meyers & Freeman, 1985). In fact, Meyers and Freeman's correlational analysis indicated that the more the child stuttered, the more slowly he talked during fluent speech. And, the more slowly the child talked during fluent speech, the faster the mother interacting with him talked. Meyers and Freeman believe that there is an interactive and complex relationship between mother and child speech rates.

Learners with Language Disorders   Strong evidence has been found that language disorders are not randomly distributed across families but tend to concentrate within families (Tomblin, 1989). All family members of learners with language disorders are more likely to have language disorders than are members of families in which there are no members with language disorders. Though birth order was at one time presumed to make a difference, neither first borns nor last borns are more at risk for language disorders (Tomblin, 1990).

Bishop (1987) states that familial variables may impact on the presence of language disorders in either auditory-verbal deprivation (due to home environment or hearing loss) or genetic influences. Two family patterns have been related to language disorders. Learners with fetal alcohol syndrome have been found to vary from their peers in grammatical, semantic, language, articulation, and language structuring abilities (Becker, Warr-Leeper, & Leeper, 1990). Learners who have been maltreated or severely physically abused are also at risk for language disorders.

Though the speech and language of parents of learners with expressive language delays have been found to be less complex, Whitehurst, Fischel, Lonigan, and Valdez-Manchaca (1988) believe that this is due to the sensitivity of parents to their child's level of expressive ability rather than a cause of the problem itself. These mothers have been found to recast their children's utterances more often than the mothers of learners with typical language in an effort to clarify and give information (Conti-Ramsden, 1990).

In a study of parents' attitudes towards family involvement in speech and language services, Andrews, Andrews, and Shearer (1989) found that over half of the parents desired family involvement in their child's therapy. Twenty-eight percent, however, were satisfied without family involvement.

Learners with Articulation Disorders   Learners with articulation disorders are judged more negatively by their peers with regard to both intelligence and personality. Among the raters, girls were more positive in their ratings of others than were boys. Girls with articulation disorders were judged more positively than were boys (Freeby & Madison, 1989).

Learners with Voice Disorders   In a study in which college undergraduate students reviewed audiotapes of normal speaking individuals and individuals with voice disorders, the listeners were found to form negative attitudes towards speakers with voice disorders. Listeners' perceptions of characteristics such as kindness, cleanliness, honesty, and pleasantness were adversely affected by the presence of voice disorders (Ruscello, Lass, & Podbesek, 1988).

Objective Four: To describe ways to mediate the environment for learners with communication disorders.

Mediating the Environment

Traditionally, learners with speech and language disorders were removed from the classroom for individual and small group intervention with a communication specialist. The specialist assessed the learner's communication disability, established objectives for intervention, and planned and implemented the intervention. The communication specialist determined whether the learner's language problem was a primary or secondary disability.

Currently, emphasis is placed on the remediation of the learner's communication disorder in the regular and special education classroom in collaboration with the teacher, whenever possible. Schiefelbush and McCormick (1981) propose that the best place to learn and practice communication skills is in the context in which those skills naturally occur. The generalization of remedial techniques should improve both the learner's speaking performance and social interaction.

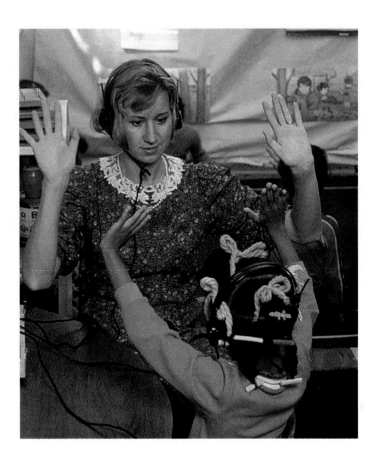

Special educators must have a responsive relationship with the learner.

There are several placement options available for learners with communication disorders: indirect service through consultation with teacher or parent, itinerant services, resource room, and self-contained class. Consultation is the provision of indirect services to the learner by the communication specialist through the learner's teacher. This option is also used when the communication specialist works indirectly with the learner through the parents.

One of the more traditional options for learners with communication disorders is the provision of therapy by an itinerant communication specialist. In an itinerant program, the communication specialist travels from school to school during the day or week to serve the learners on his or her caseload. This option is minimally disruptive to the classroom program. However, it creates scheduling problems and reduces the probability of teacher-specialist consultation.

In the resource room program, the communication specialist is located in a single school. This service is especially valuable in a school with large numbers of learners with multiple disabilities. The final placement option is the self-contained program. This is useful and appropriate for learners with severe communication disorders, very young children, and children making a transition from one program to another, such as day care or preschool to kindergarten. The self-contained program is frequently a half day and includes parental involvement.

The emphasis on remediating learners with communication disorders in the classroom places demands on the general and special education teacher. According to Seibert and Oller (1981), a positive, responsive relationship between learner and teacher is needed so that the learner can risk engagement in the communication process. The learner's willingness to communicate is enhanced when the teacher uses a facilitative style as described by Peck and Schuler (1983) and Peck (1985). The facilitative teacher:

- allows the learner to control and initiate conversation topics
- allows the learner to assume the lead in conversation
- encourages the learner to contribute to the ongoing conversation in many ways
- investigates the communicative environment of the learner and identifies language that is useful to the learner
- develops communicative competence within the context of social interaction
- provides frequent opportunities for learner initiation and control of social interaction
- provides choices and other communicative opportunities to the learner
- responds to learner-initiated social/communicative behavior
- imitates and elaborates on learners' social/communicative behavior

Very Young Learners   Jones and Warren (1991) state that current knowledge about language learning can be used to increase the engagement of young children in intervention concerning their language. They suggest following the child's attentional lead in topic and content, as well as providing novelty. They emphasize that with very young children, activity-based therapy is essential. The communication specialist should avoid asking too many questions, giving too many instructions, and giving the child too little time to respond.

Learners Who Are Disfluent   Starkweather (1990) describes several trends in therapy for learners who are disfluent. Children are receiving treatment at earlier ages, and the communicative environments in which the child is developing are assessed as well as the child himself or herself. Additional emphasis is being placed on the parents in the treatment process and on environmental and behavioral management. The role of language and the relationship between language skill or language use and the development of disfluency, as well as the emotional components of disfluency, are also being addressed.

Technology   For some learners for whom verbal communication does not emerge to a point of being strategically effective and communicative, augmentative systems may be devised to facilitate communication. The purpose of such systems is to promote and facilitate, not replace, the communication modes available to the learner (Russel, 1984). As discussed later in the section concerning learners with hearing impairments, there are several manual systems, such as signing systems and fingerspelling, to facilitate communication. In addition, there are technological aids to help facilitate communication which are generally dependent on the computer and other electronic hardware.

Though microcomputer applications are in their infancy with regard to providing assistance to those with communication disorders, they can be helpful to both the learner and the communication specialist. The specialist can use the computer to manage records, store and analyze speech samples, and make therapeutic programs available to the learner. The microcomputer, as the basis of various kinds of

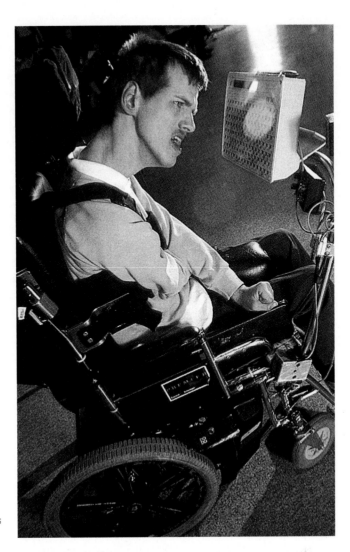

Great care must be taken in selecting any technological device to respond to the needs of the learner with communication disorders.

talking machines, can be used to facilitate the learner's communication. Augmentative communication systems can provide visual, printed, and verbal messages to the individuals with whom the learner is interacting.

Television, the videocassette recorder, and the videodisc can be used to facilitate the learning of communication skills. These devices can be used to collect assessment information and to record and analyze speech samples, and for the presentation of instructional programs and interventions for learners and parents. Other devices, though less technically complex, such as the voice light and delayed feedback devices, can be of assistance to learner and communication specialist. The voice light, controlled by voice intensity, provides the learner feedback with regard to voice control. The delayed feedback device provides the learner with delayed feedback through earphones and thus facilitates the control of disfluency.

Great care must be taken by the communication specialist to individualize any technological device to respond to the specific needs and desires of the learner with communication disorders.

Objective Five: To describe the impact of communication disorders on participation in the larger social systems—the school, community, and society.

The Impact on Participation in Larger Social Systems

Horsley and FitzGibbon (1987) investigated the stereotype applied to learners who are disfluent. In their study, a negative stereotype was found to exist towards individuals who stuttered, particularly towards school-age boys. Boone (1987) believes that adult stutterers frequently determine the kinds of activities they participate in and the occupations they select on the basis of their stuttering. In another study, unsophisticated listeners judged individuals from speech samples with adult articulation problems as "dumb," less likely to be hired, and slow, and in other negative ways (Langhans & Boone, 1975). Though the articulation distortions of a preschool child may be seen as amusing, the persistence of articulation problems in adulthood is not tolerated well in society (Boone, 1987).

Summary

Communication not only supports every social interaction that takes place throughout the day, but it plays a major role in the learner's cognitive development. Learners with communication disorders account for the largest single group of learners served under the special education services mandate of Public Law 94–142. In addition to those learners served as primarily communication disordered, it is estimated that approximately one-fourth of learners with other disabilities (e.g., mental retardation, learning disabilities, behavioral disorders) demonstrate communication disorders.

Communication disorders may involve speech, language, or voice. Assessment and evaluation of learners with communication disorders must include examination of: (a) the child's conversational knowledge, (b) the child's ability to integrate conversational and linguistic skills, and (c) both expressive and receptive language skills. Family variables may impact on the presence of communication disorders.

There are several placement options available for learners with communication disorders. Consultation or indirect services for the learner through teacher or parents and itinerant, resource room, and self-contained programs are all options for learners with communication disorders.

During the 1980s, there has been a decrease in the number of learners identified with communication disorders (U.S. Department of Education, 1992). This decrease is attributed to several factors, including (a) a current trend to identify students with language disorders as having specific learning disabilities, rather than having speech and language impairments; (b) increased availability of speech and language services within general education, and (c) more accurate identification of learners with communication disorders.

References

Adams, C. (1990). Syntactic comprehension in children with expressive language impairment. *British Journal of Communication, 25,* 149–171.

American Speech-Language-Hearing Association (1982). Definitions: Communication disorders and variations. *Journal of the American Speech-Language-Hearing Association, 24,* 949–950.

Andrews, J. R., Andrews, M. A., & Shearer, W. M. (1989). Parents' attitudes toward family involvement in speech-language services. *Language, Speech, and Hearing Services in the Schools, 20,* 391–399.

Becker, M., Warr-Leeper, G. A., & Leeper, H. A. (1990). Fetal alcohol syndrome: A description of oral motor, articulatory, short-term memory, grammatical, and semantic abilities. *Journal of Communication Disorders, 23* (2), 97–124.

Bishop, D. V. (1987). The causes of specific developmental language disorder. *Journal of Child Psychology and Psychiatry and Allied Disciplines, 28* (1), 1–8.

Bishop, D. V., & Adams, C. (1989). Conversational characteristics of children with semantic-pragmatic disorder: II. What features lead to inappropriacy? *British Journal of Disorders of Communication, 24,* 241–263.

Bishop, D. V., & Edmundson, A. (1986). Is otitis media a major cause of specific developmental language disorders? *British Journal of Disorders of Communication, 21,* 321–338.

Boone, D. R. (1987). *Human communication and its disorders.* Englewood Cliffs, NJ: Prentice Hall.

Broen, P. A. (1988). Plotting a course: The ongoing assessment of language. In R. L. Schiefelbusch & L. L. Lloyd (Eds.), *Language perspectives* (2nd ed.) (pp. 299–320). Austin, TX: Pro-Ed.

Bruner, J. (1981). The social context of language acquisition. *Language and Communication, 1,* 155–178.

Byrd, K., & Cooper, E. B. (1989). Expressive and receptive language skills in stuttering children. *Journal of Fluency Disorders, 14,* 121–126.

Calvert, M. B., & Murray, S. L. (1985). Environmental communication profile: An assessment procedure. In C. S. Simon (Ed.), *Communication skills and classroom success* (pp. 135–164). San Diego: College Hill Press.

Cantwell, D. P., & Baker, L. (1987). The prevalence of anxiety in children with communication disorders. *Journal of Anxiety Disorders, 1* (3), 239–248.

Casby, M. W. (1989). National data concerning communication disorders and special education. *Language, Speech and Hearing Services in the Schools, 20,* 22–30.

Cole, P. A., & Taylor, O. L. (1990). Performance of working class African American children on three tests of articulation. *Language, Speech, and Hearing Services in the Schools, 21* (3), 171–176.

Condino, R., Im-Humber, K., & Stark, R. E. (1990). Cognitive processing in specifically language impaired children. *Journal of Psychology, 124,* 465–478.

Conti-Ramsden, G. (1990). Maternal recasts and other contingent replies to language-impaired children. *Journal of Speech and Hearing Disorders, 55* (2), 262–274.

Craig, H. K. (1991). Pragmatic characteristics of the child with specific language impairment: An interactionist perspective. In T. M. Gallagher (Ed.), *Pragmatics of language: Clinical practice issues* (pp. 163–198). San Diego, CA: Singular.

Craig, H. K., & Evans, J. L. (1989). Turn exchange characteristics of SLI children's simultaneous and nonsimultaneous speech. *Journal of Speech and Hearing Disorders, 54,* 334–347.

Crais, E. R., & Roberts, J. E. (1991). Decision making in assessment and early intervention planning. *Language, Speech and Hearing Services in the Schools, 22,* 19–30.

Creaghead, N., & Tattershall, S. S. (1985). Observation and assessment of classroom pragmatic skills. In C. S. Simon (Ed.), *Communication skills and classroom success* (pp. 105–134). San Diego: College Hill.

Dollaghan, C. A. (1987). Comprehension monitoring in normal and language-impaired children. *Topics in Language Disorders, 7,* 45–60.

Edwards, M., Cape, J., & Brown, D. (1989). Patterns of referral for children with speech disorders. *Child Care, Health, and Development, 15,* 417–424.

Federal Register (1977), *42,* 42659–42668.

Freeby, N., & Madison, C. L. (1989). Children's perceptions of peers with articulation disorders. *Child Study Journal, 19,* 133–144.

Fujiki, M., Brinton, B., & Dunton, S. (1987). The ability of normal and language-impaired children to produce grammatical corrections. *Journal of Communication Disorders, 20,* 413–424.

Fujiki, M., Brinton, B., & Sonnenberg, E. A. (1990). Repair of overlapping speech in the conversations of specially language impaired and normally developing children. *Applied Psycholinguistics, 11,* 201–215.

Goldman, L. G. (1987). Social implications of language disorders. *Journal of Reading, Writing, and Learning Disabilities International, 3,* 119–130.

Head, H. (1926). *Aphasia and kindred disorders of speech.* London: Cambridge University Press.

Horsley, I. A., & FitzGibbon, C. T. (1987). Stuttering children: Investigation of a stereotype. *British Journal of Disorders of Communication, 22,* 19–35.

Ingram, D. (1978). *Phonological disability in children.* New York: Elsevier.

Jones, H. A., & Warren, S. F. (1991). Enhancing engagement in early language teaching. *Teaching Exceptional Children, 23* (4), 48–50.

Kaiser, A. P., & Warren, S. F. (1988). Pragmatics and generalization. In R. L. Schiefelbusch & L. L. Lloyd (Eds.), *Language perspectives* (2nd ed.) (pp. 393–442). Austin,TX: Pro-Ed.

Kent, R., & Bauer, H. (1985). Vocalizations of one-year-olds. *Journal of Child Language, 12,* 491–526.

Kotsopoulos, A., & Boodoosingh, L. (1987). Language and speech disorders in children attending a day psychiatric programme. *British Journal of Disorders of Communication, 22* (3), 227–236.

Kretschmer, R. R., & Kretschmer, L. W. (1988). Communication competence and assessment. *Journal of the Academy of Rehabilitative Audiology, 21,* 5–17.

Langhans, J., & Boone, D. R. (1975). *Attitudes towards the communicatively handicapped.* Tucson: University of Arizona.

Langlois, A., Hanrahan, L. L., & Inouye, L. L. (1986). A comparison of interactions between stuttering children, nonstuttering children, and their mothers. *Journal of fluency disorders, 11,* 263–273.

Love, A. J., and Thompson, M. G. (1988). Language disorders and attention deficit disorders in young children referred for psychiatric services. *American Journal of Orthopsychiatry, 58* (1), 52–64.

MacLachlan, B. G., & Chapman, R. S. (1988). Communication breakdowns in normal and language learning-disabled children's conversation and narration. *Journal of Speech and Hearing Disorders, 53,* 2–7.

Madison, L. S., Budd, K. S., & Itzkowitz, J. S. (1986). Changes in stuttering in relation to children's locus of control. *Journal of Genetic Psychology, 147,* 233–240.

Meline, T. J., & Brackin, S. R. (1987). Language-impaired children's awareness of inadequate messages. *Journal of Speech and Hearing Disorders, 52,* 263–270.

Meyers, S. C., & Freeman, F. J. (1985). Mother and child speech rates as a variable in stuttering and disfluency. *Journal of Speech and Hearing Research, 28,* 436–444.

Moore, V., & Law, J. (1990). Copying ability of preschool children with delayed language development. *Developmental Medicine and Child Neurology, 32,* 249–257.

Muma, J. (1978). *Language handbook, concepts, assessment, intervention.* Englewood Cliffs, NJ: Prentice Hall.

National Joint Committee for Learning Disabilities (1982). Learning disabilities: Issues on definition. *American Speech and Hearing Association, 24,* 945–949.

Nelson, L. K., Kahmi, A. G., & Apel, K. (1987). Cognitive strengths and weaknesses in language-impaired children: One more look. *Journal of Speech and Hearing Disorders, 52,* 36–43.

Nippold, M. A. (1990). Concomitant speech and language disorders in stuttering children: A critique of the literature. *Journal of Speech and Hearing Disorders, 55,* 61–60.

Peck, C. A. (1985). Increasing opportunities for social control by children with autism and severe behavior handicaps: Effects on student behavior and perceived classroom climate. *Journal of the Association for Persons with Severe Handicaps, 10,* 182–193.

Peck, C. A., & Schuler, A. L. (1983). Classroom-based language interventions for children with autism: Theoretical and practical considerations for the speech and language specialist. *Seminars in Speech and Language, 4,* 93–103.

Powell, M., Filter, M. D., & Williams, B. (1989). A longitudinal study of the prevalence of voice disorders in children from a rural school division. *Journal of Communication Disorders, 22,* 375–382.

Prutting, C. (1979). Process: The action of moving forward progressively from one point to another on the way to completion. *Journal of Speech and Hearing Disorders, 47,* 123–134.

Rice, M. L. (1988). Speech and language impairments. In E. L. Meyen & T. M. Skrtic (Eds.), *Exceptional children and youth: An introduction* (3rd ed.) (pp. 233–261). Denver: Love.

Richards, M. M., & Richards, L. G. (1988). The development of language and imagery as symbolic processes. In R. L. Schiefelbusch & L. L. Lloyd (Eds.), *Language perspectives* (2nd ed.) (pp. 35–68). Austin, TX: Pro-Ed.

Roth, F. P., & Clark, D. M. (1987). Symbolic play and social participation abilities of language-impaired and normally developing children. *Journal of Speech and Hearing Disorders, 52,* 17–29.

Ruscello, D. M., Lass, N. J., & Podbesek, J. (1988). Listeners' perceptions of normal and voice disordered children. *Folia Phoniatrica, 40,* 290–296.

Russel, M. (1984). Assessment and intervention issues with nonspeaking children. *Exceptional Children, 51,* 64–71.

St. Louis, K. O., & Hinzman, A. R. (1988). A descriptive study of speech, language, and hearing characteristics of school-aged stutterers. *Journal of Fluency Disorders, 13,* 331–355.

Sameroff, A. J., & Chandler, M. J. (1975). Reproductive risk and the continuum of caretaking casualty. In F. D. Horowitz, M. Hetherington, S. Scarr-Salapatek, & G. Siegel (Eds.), *Review of child development research* (Volume 4). Chicago: University of Chicago.

Sameroff, A. J., & Fiese, B. H. (1988). The context of language development. In R. L. Schiefelbusch & L. L. Lloyd (Eds.), *Language perspectives* (2nd ed.) (pp. 3–19). Austin, TX: Pro-Ed.

Schiefelbush, R. L., & McCormick, L. (1981). Language and speech disorders. In J. Kauffman & D. Hallahan (Eds.), *Handbook of special education.* Englewood Cliffs, NJ: Prentice Hall.

Seibert, J. M., & Oller, D. K. (1981). Linguistic pragmatics and language intervention strategies. *Journal of Autism and Developmental Disorders, 11,* 75–88.

Shriberg, L., & Kwiatowski, J. (1980). *Natural process analysis.* New York: Wiley.

Simon, C. S. (1985). Presentation of communication evaluation information. In C. S. Simon (Ed.), *Communication skills and classroom success* (pp. 255–317). San Diego: College Hill.

Smith, C. (1991). What's in a word? On our acquisition of the term "language learning disability." *Teacher Education and Special Education, 14,* 103–109.

Snyder, L. S. (1987). Symbolization in language impaired children. *New Directions for Child Development, 36,* 87–108.

Sommers, R. C. (1988). Prediction of fine motor skills of children having language and speech disorders. *Perceptual and Motor Skills, 67,* 63–72.

Spector, C. C. (1990). Linguist humor comprehension of normal and language impaired adolescents. *Journal of Speech and Hearing Disorders, 55,* 533–541.

Starkweather, C. W. (1990). Current trends in therapy for stuttering children and suggestions for future research. *ASHA Reports Series,* #18, 82–90.

Tomblin, J. B. (1989). Familial concentration of developmental language impairment. *Journal of Speech and Hearing Disorders, 54,* 287–295.

Tomblin, J. B. (1990). The effect of birth order on the occurrence of developmental language impairment. *British Journal of Disorders of Communication, 25,* 77–84.

U.S. Department of Education (1990). *Twelfth annual report to Congress on the implementation of the Education of the Handicapped Act.* Washington, DC: Author.

Van der Ley, H., & Deward, H. (1986). Sentence comprehension strategies in specifically language impaired children. *British Journal of Disorders of Communication, 21,* 291–306.

Van Riper, C. (1978). *Speech correction: Principles and methods.* Englewood Cliffs, NJ: Prentice Hall.

Van Riper, C., & Emerick, L. (1984). *Speech correction: An introduction to speech pathology and audiology.* Englewood Cliffs, NJ: Prentice Hall.

Wetherby, A., Cain, D., Yonclas, D., & Walker, V. (1988). Analysis of intentional communication of normal children from the prelinguistic to the multi-word stage. *Journal of Speech and Hearing Research, 31,* 240–252.

Whitehurst, G. J., Fischel, J. E., Lonigan, C. J., & Valdez-Manchaca, M. C. (1988). Verbal interaction in families of normal and expressive language delayed children. *Developmental Psychology, 24,* 690–699.

Wood, L. M. (1982). *Language disorders in school-age children.* Englewood Cliffs, NJ: Prentice Hall.

Chapter

10

Learners with Physical and Other Health Impairments

229

*O*bjectives

After completing this chapter, you will be able to:

1. describe the personal characteristics of learners with physical and other health impairments.
2. describe the identification and evaluation of learners with physical and other health impairments.
3. describe the impact of physical and other health impairments on interactions in the home and classroom.
4. describe ways to mediate the environment for learners with physical and other health impairments.
5. describe the impact of physical and other health impairments on participation in the larger social systems—the school, community, and society.

*K*ey Words and Phrases

acquired immune deficiency syndrome (AIDS)	juvenile rheumatoid arthritis
adapted physical education	lead poisoning
allergy	muscular dystrophy
cancer	occupational therapy
catheterization	orthopedic disability
cerebral palsy	orthotic
cystic fibrosis	other health impairments
epilepsy (seizure disorder)	physical impairments
heart condition	physical therapy
hemophilia	prosthetics
HIV (human immunodeficiency virus)	sickle cell disease
hydrocephaly	spina bifida (neural tube defect)
juvenile diabetes	spinal cord injury
	traumatic brain injury

*Y*OSEMITE NATIONAL PARK, CALIF. (AP) A ROCK CLIMBER PREVIOUSLY PARALYZED IN A FALL COMPLETED HIS SECOND major climb using only his arms Monday when he and his partner struggled to the 2,200 foot summit of Half Dome . . . Wellman, a park ranger, was paralyzed from the waist down during a climb of another Yosemite peak in 1982. He and Corbett gained international fame in 1989 when they climbed 3,300 foot El Capitan. (*Cincinnati Enquirer,* 17 October, 1991.) ▪

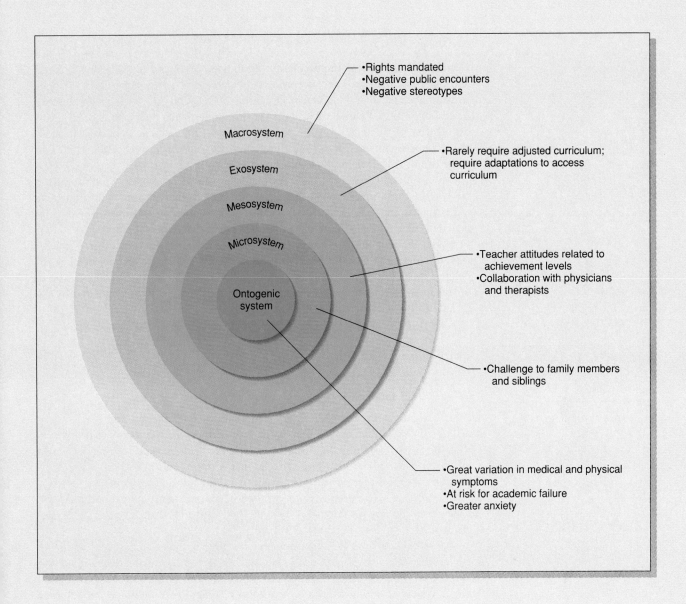

•Rights mandated
•Negative public encounters
•Negative stereotypes

Macrosystem

Exosystem

Mesosystem

Microsystem

Ontogenic
system

•Rarely require adjusted curriculum;
require adaptations to access
curriculum

•Teacher attitudes related to
achievement levels
•Collaboration with physicians
and therapists

•Challenge to family members
and siblings

•Great variation in medical and physical
symptoms
•At risk for academic failure
•Greater anxiety

Introduction

Learners with **physical impairments** (disabilities involving physical functioning) and other health impairments represent 2.2 percent of the population of students served under the Individuals with Disabilities Education Act (U.S. Department of Education, 1992). Learners with other health impairments demonstrated the greatest increase of students served between 1988 and 1989, with a 7.8 percent increase (U.S. Department of Education, 1990). Both learners with orthopedic and with other health impairments were most likely to be served in the general education classroom, though almost 20 percent of those identified as other health impaired were served in hospitals or at home. Almost half of the learners with orthopedic impairments and 35 percent of the learners with other health impairments who exited the educational system did so through graduation with a diploma.

With the number and variety of physical and other health impairments identified, it is impossible to thoroughly discuss them all in a single chapter of an introductory text. For this reason, the physical and other health impairments reviewed in this chapter are selected on the basis of those most frequently encountered by the general and special education teacher.

Objective One: To describe the personal characteristics of learners with physical and other health impairments.

Personal Characteristics

Orthopedic Disabilities

As in all the categories of disability, environmental interaction and the developmental context influence the development of learners with orthopedic disabilities (Sigmon, 1986). **Orthopedic disabilities** include a wide range of disabilities which are severe enough to challenge the learner's participation in daily activities. Lawrence (1991) argues that physical ability is crucial to self-concept development. As a consequence, persons with orthopedic impairments may be challenged through difficulties in mobility, managing body functions, social interaction, and achieving life goals (Lawrence, 1991).

Cerebral palsy is the most frequently occurring orthopedic disability among young learners, with its presence in between 1.5 and 5 of every 1,000 births (Verhaaven & Connor, 1981). Cerebral palsy refers to a dysfunction of the neurological motor system resulting from a nonprogressive brain abnormality which occurred before, during, or shortly after birth (Hardy, 1983). Any condition which adversely impacts on the brain may result in cerebral palsy, *including maternal infection, chronic disease, fetal infection, and birth injury.*

Cerebral palsy is, in fact, several conditions, which are grouped into seven categories (see Table 10.1).

The impact of cerebral palsy on the individual varies with the extent to which the individual is affected. In addition to difficulties in the area of motor functioning, learners with cerebral palsy may have mild to severe communication disorders, hearing impairments, visual impairments, intellectual deficits, seizure disorders, and perceptual difficulties. Many learners with cerebral palsy have multiple disabilities.

Another sort of orthopedic disability is **spina bifida,** or **neural tube defect.** Spina bifida is a defect of the spinal column in which the spine fails to close properly around the column of nerves it is designed to protect. Figure 10.1 differentiates between the normal spine and the spine of an individual with spina bifida.

The disabilities presented by cerebral palsy vary from learner to learner.

Spina bifida results in varying degrees of paralysis, a loss of sensation in the legs, and various degrees of bowel and bladder incontinence (Pieper, 1983). This defect may cause:

a. weakness or diminished sensation in the feet, ankles, and/or legs.
b. incontinence.
c. **hydrocephaly** (fluid accumulated in the ventricles of the brain: a surgically implanted valve may be needed to divert excessive fluid from the brain cavities).
d. learning disabilities and perceptual difficulties.
e. motor difficulties in the arms and hands.
f. seizure disorders.

Due to complications which affect bladder control, individuals with neural tube defect and those with spinal cord injury, discussed later, may require assistance with **catheterization,** or the insertion of a tube into the bladder for the withdrawal of urine. Neural tube defect is found in approximately 0.3 to 0.9 of every 1,000 births in the United States. The female to male ratio of occurrence is approximately 3:1.

Table 10.1   Categories of Cerebral Palsy

Category	Neuromuscular Characteristics
Spasticity	Excessive muscle tone; involuntary contractions; difficulties in movement and motion.
Athetosis	Continual involuntary, slow, writhing movements which occur during voluntary actions; contortions in wrists, fingers, and face which prevent well-controlled motion.
Ataxia	Poor balance and equilibrium; poor control of gross and fine motor functions; coordinated movement difficult to impossible.
Rigidity	Rigid, essentially immobile limbs; movement extremely difficult.
Tremor	Repetitive, rhythmic contractions of muscles; constant, uncontrollable involuntary motion.
Atonicity	Decreased muscle tone.
Mixed	Combinations of the above categories.

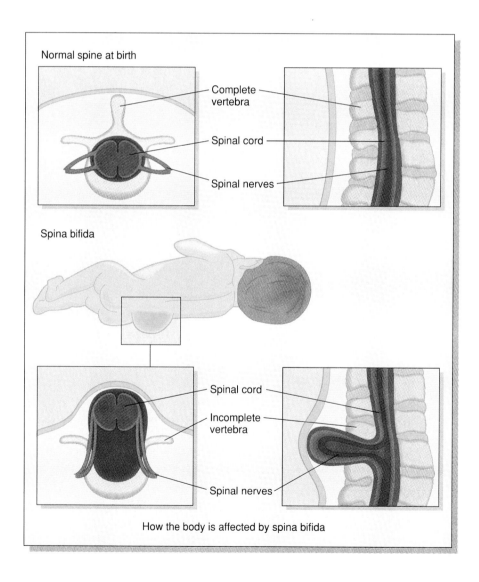

Normal spine at birth

Complete vertebra

Spinal cord

Spinal nerves

Spina bifida

Spinal cord

Incomplete vertebra

Spinal nerves

How the body is affected by spina bifida

Figure 10.1
Neural tube defects (spina bifida).

Traumatic brain injuries and **spinal cord injuries** may present a variety of symptoms depending on the extent and location of the injury. Learners with traumatic brain injuries may require retraining in areas as simple as focusing, or as sophisticated as formulating concepts. The effects of spinal cord injuries, depending on the extent and location of the injury, are similar to the effect of neural tube defect. Traumatic brain and spinal cord injuries may be caused by disease or as a result of accidents or injuries. According to Yashon (1986), the prevalence of spinal cord injuries is 3 in 100,000 individuals. Both traumatic brain and spinal cord injuries are most frequently caused by falls, automobile accidents, and sports injuries.

Traumatic brain injury is a category of disability in Public Law 101–476 (Individuals with Disabilities Education Act of 1990). It is defined as severe trauma to the head that impairs learning, behavior, and motor functioning. The National Head Injury Foundation estimates that there are one-half million cases of traumatic brain injury annually that require hospital admission. Of this group, 100,000 of the victims die, and 100,000 of the victims have permanent disabilities. Traumatic brain injury is the number one killer of people under 34 years of age (Smith & Luckasson, 1992).

Scoliosis, a lateral curve in the spine, is characterized by a prominent shoulder (usually on the right), unlevel shoulders and hips, poor posture, and a flattening of the back. Scoliosis rarely impacts on the learner's educational functioning. A back brace may be used or surgery may be performed to stabilize the spine (Boos, Garlonsky, MacEwen, & Steg, 1984).

Talipes, or clubfoot, involves one or both feet which are turned at an incorrect angle at the ankle. Other physical disabilities include Legg-Calvé-Perthes disease, a hip disorder, and osteomyelitis, a bacterial bone infection. Also included under the general heading of physical disabilities are arthrogryposis, in which the muscles are small and weaker than normal or missing completely, and osteogenesis imperfecta, in which the bones are improperly formed and brittle (Hallahan & Kauffman, 1986).

Amputations, either congenital or acquired, may impact on the learner's educational functioning. Congenital amputations involve the partial or total absence of limbs. Acquired amputations occur as a consequence of trauma (approximately 70 percent) and malignancy (approximately 30 percent) (Verhaaven & Connor, 1981). Learners with amputations may be fitted with prostheses or receive training which allows other parts of the body to assume the functions of the missing part. These children usually attend general education classes.

Gon, Boyce, and Advani (1983) found no significant differences between learners with orthopedic disabilities and their peers. Variations have been found, however, in the defense mechanisms used by learners with or without orthopedic disabilities. When frustrated or confronted with a problem, male learners without orthopedic disabilities turned against the object involved more frequently than learners with orthopedic handicaps, who more frequently turned against themselves. Significantly more anxiety and introversion has been reported among persons with orthopedic disabilities than among those without disabilities (Bandyopadhyay, Roy, Basum, and Chattopadhyay, 1987).

Chronic Illnesses and Other Health Impairments

Learners who are chronically ill or medically fragile are concerned about their
autonomy, their ability to explore the environment, and the effects of the intrusion
of treatments on their bodies and their activities (Ritchie, Caty, & Ellerton, 1984).
In a study of learners with various health issues, similar emotional functioning for
empathy, emotional responsiveness, and depression was found in children with and
without chronic illness. Children who were actively ill demonstrated higher levels
in each of these areas than did children who were well (Nelms, 1989). Learners
with chronic illness are at risk for academic failure even in the absence of a known
cognitive problem (Schlieper, 1985).

Human Immunodeficiency Virus (HIV) and Acquired Immune Deficiency Syndrome (AIDS)

HIV, human immunodeficiency virus, which often develops into AIDS,
is a virus that affects the immune system and impairs the individual's ability to
fight infection. There are no treatments or preventative interventions, such as vacci-
nation, for HIV, though some medications are available which appear to delay the
development of HIV into AIDS. **AIDS, acquired immune deficiency syndrome,**
is characterized by the body's inability to fight infection and is fatal.

Approximately 6,000 children are born each year to mothers infected with
HIV. Of those infants born to these mothers, only 20 to 35 percent become infected
with HIV. However, up to 2 years is necessary to determine whether the children's
own antibodies have replaced their mother's, at which time one can determine
whether they are infected with HIV (Olson, Huszti, Mason, & Seibert, 1989). Pediatric human immunodeficiency virus infection is a growing medical problem, with
a broad range of psychological implications (Task Force on Pediatric AIDS, 1989).
Young children who are HIV positive, for example, have been found to frequently
demonstrate conductive hearing loss (Hopkins, Grosz, Cohen, & Diamond, 1989).
Hopkins and associates state that as HIV positive children are living longer than
previously expected, many will have serious neurological and developmental
deficits and psychosocial stressors.

Seizure Disorders

Epilepsy, or **seizure disorders,** marked by recurrent, unpro-
voked seizures, occurs in approximately 4 percent of school children. Seizures,
which may involve only parts of the body or be generalized throughout the individual's system, are sudden, brief, temporary states of abnormal brain functioning due
to uncontrolled electrical discharges in the brain (Chee & Clancy, 1984). A description of the types of seizures, their appearance, and immediate treatment is provided
in Table 10.2.

Though usually mainstreamed, learners with seizure disorders often have special physical and emotional needs that challenge learning and socialization (Frank,
1985). Learners with epilepsy were found to vary from their peers in higher anxiety
levels and higher dissatisfaction in their self-concept (Margalit & Heiman, 1983).
Those learners with seizure disorders with abnormalities in their electroencephalo-
grams and/or complex partial seizures were found to demonstrate significantly
more psychiatric disorders than did other school children (Hoare, 1984b). These
psychiatric disorders were frequently found to be related to the learner's
inappropriate dependency on parents and other adults (Hoare, 1984a). Children
with epilepsy were more likely than their peers to attribute the success or failure of
their school performance to unknown sources of control. They hold less positive

Table 10.2   Types of Seizures and Appropriate Action

Type of Seizure	Appearance	Appropriate Action
Generalized tonic-clonic (grand mal)	Sudden cry, fall, rigidity, and muscle twitching and jerking; frothy saliva from lips; irregular breathing; possible loss of bladder and/or bowel control; confusion or fatigue may follow when individual regains consciousness	Look for medical identification; protect from hazards. Loosen clothing; pad head if possible; turn on side to keep airway clear; place nothing in the mouth. If seizure lasts longer than 5 minutes, or if multiple seizures occur, call for emergency assistance.
Absence (petit mal)	Blank stare; begins and ends abruptly; may be accompanied by chewing movements or blinking	None apart from reassurance if the individual is under medical supervision for seizures.
Simple partial (Jacksonian)	Individual remains aware; jerking begins in toes or fingers; may proceed to hand, arm; may become convulsive	None apart from reassurance if the individual is under medical supervision for seizures.
Complex partial	Blank stare, followed by chewing and random activity; movement undirected; may pick at clothing; may run or appear afraid; may struggle at restraint; usually follows a typical pattern; no memory of event afterwards	Reassure the individual; gently guide from hazards; stay with the individual. Stay with the individual until completely recovered.
Atonic	Seen in children or adults; sudden collapse; recovery after about 10 seconds to a minute	None apart from reassurance if the individual is under medical supervision and was not injured in a fall.
Myoclonic	Sudden, brief, massive muscle movements that may involve all or part of the body	None apart from reassurance if the individual is under medical supervision.

© Epilepsy Foundation of America, 1991—Adapted with permission.

feelings about school and about their personal worth (Matthews, Barabas, & Ferrari, 1983). It is essential that persons working with learners with seizure disorders project a positive attitude and avoid becoming a "terrified observer." The teacher must have reliable information about the learner and his or her seizures and treatment.

Sickle Cell Disease   **Sickle cell disease,** an inherited blood disorder, affects one in every 650 African Americans. Sickle cell disease causes chronic anemia because red blood cells are unable to survive in circulation in the blood stream for the usual period of time. These red blood cells become rigid and deformed and are not sufficiently pliable to circulate through small blood vessels. Painful crisis periods of bleeding can lead to extended absences, interrupting the educational experience of learners with sickle cell disease (Kim, Gaston, & Fithian, 1984).

Learners with sickle cell disease were not found to vary from their matched peers in self-concept or depression. Rather, consistent patterns of behavior were linked to socioeconomic status rather than presence of the disease (Lemanek, 1986). Variations in personal adjustment and behavioral problems were not found to be related to illness severity (Hurtig, Koepke, & Park, 1989). In a study related to satisfaction with their bodies, adolescents with sickle cell disease were found to be less satisfied than were their healthy peers, and to experience less social involvement (Morgan & Jackson, 1986). In addition, sickle cell disease may be related to subtle neuropsychological and learning problems that may contribute to decreased school performance.

Other Health Impairments

Other health impairments is a generic term used to refer to several physical conditions or diseases which have an impact on the individual's functioning. Descriptions of several of the conditions follow. Learners with these health impairments are disabled only to the extent that the health condition restricts their participation at home, in the school, and in the community.

Heart conditions, congenital or acquired through bacterial or viral infection, occur in as many as 8 in 1,000 learners. The degree of impairment ranges from mild to severe. These learners typically engage in general education curricula and participate in activities within the limits prescribed by their physical condition (Woolf, 1984).

Hemophilia, a sex-linked inherited condition, occurs in approximately 1 in 10,000 male children. Children with this condition, due to problems with coagulation of the blood, may be frequently absent from school. They may have difficulties with mobility and participation in physical education (Gill & Butler, 1984).

Cancer, a group of diseases of unknown cause which produce abnormal cell growth, is diagnosed in approximately 7,000 children each year. The two most frequently diagnosed cancers in children are leukemia and brain tumors. These learners may be frequently absent from school (Ross, 1984).

Allergies, abnormal reactions to specific substances, occur in approximately 20 percent of the general population. The most common allergy among children is seasonal allergic rhinitis which is caused by inhaled pollen. Learners may experience a variety of symptoms, including nasal obstruction; discharge of clear, thin mucus; sneezing; eye and nose itching; and tearing. They may experience swelling of the nasal tissues which blocks drainage of the nasal passages and results in fluid in the ears. This fluid may cause hearing impairments (Kolski & Burg, 1984). Symptoms of allergies are treated with antihistamine, decongestants, eyedrops, and injections. A small number of children are diagnosed with chronic perennial allergic rhinitis. The symptoms of this disorder are similar to the symptoms of seasonal rhinitis noted above. Other common allergies include reactions to insect stings and gastrointestinal reactions. Students with allergies may have difficulties attending and concentrating in school.

Juvenile diabetes is a metabolic disorder caused by the inadequate production of insulin by the body. It occurs in about 1 in every 500 to 1,000 children. Though the specific cause of juvenile diabetes is unknown, an inherited predisposition is suspected. The symptoms of juvenile diabetes include frequent urination and thirst. These children are often tired, irritable, and moody, and they may have achievement problems. Diabetes is treated with insulin, diet, and exercise. The type, timing, and quantities of food these children ingest is essential to controlling diabetes.

The delay or omission of a snack or meal can be dangerous for the student and result in hypoglycemia (an overdose of insulin). These students must avoid prolonged and strenuous exertion which lowers their blood sugar levels. Fluctuations in blood sugar levels result in hypoglycemia and ketoacidosis (an elevation of blood sugar).

Cystic fibrosis occurs in 1 in 2,000 Caucasian Americans and 1 in 17,000 African Americans. Persons with cystic fibrosis have abnormally thick and sticky mucus and highly concentrated glandular secretions. The disorder is terminal and is often complicated with secondary respiratory infections. These learners have a persistent cough. Frequent urination and thirst are common.

Muscular dystrophy is the most frequent cause of progressive muscular weakness in children. Muscular dystrophy is a group of disorders characterized by the wasting and progressive weakness of skeletal muscles. This disorder is inherited and usually shortens the individual's life span. The four most frequently identified types of muscular dystrophy are:

- Duchenne, which develops rapidly between the ages of 2 and 6. Students require the use of a wheelchair by age 12 years. They often die from heart failure or pneumonia in their late teens or early adulthood.
- Facioscapulohumeral, which progresses slowly beginning in the teens. There are long periods during which symptoms do not progress. This form of the disorder begins in the muscles of the face, shoulders, and upper arms.
- Limb-girdle, which is diagnosed in late childhood or early adolescence. Its variable progression begins in either the muscles of the lower trunk or upper legs.
- Myotonic, which progresses steadily, beginning in early adulthood. Initially, weakness is noted in the fingers, hands, forearms, feet, and legs.

Juvenile rheumatoid arthritis, a joint inflammation, is a chronic disorder which affects between 50,000 and 250,000 children. According to the Arthritis Foundation (1983) approximately 36 million children and adults in the United States are affected by arthritis. Systemic juvenile rheumatoid arthritis is one of the major types of arthritis. It affects children of any age and accounts for 20 percent of all cases (Athreya & Ingall, 1984). Symptoms vary from day to day; soreness and stiffness of the joints in the late afternoon is the most common problem for learners with juvenile rheumatoid arthritis. Learners appear to be most comfortable from midmorning to early afternoon.

Lead poisoning is a consequence of the ingestion of lead (usually from lead-based paints) which produces neurological damage. In an extensive review of the literature, Marlowe (1985) concludes that lead, at levels far below those accepted for clinical lead poisoning, is associated with a wide range of behavioral symptoms, including reduced scores on measures of intellectual ability, decreased efficiency in auditory, visual, and language processing; reduced fine-motor performance; attention problems; and inappropriate classroom behavior.

Learners' Understanding of Their Disabilities

Young children develop from having a general understanding of their limitations at about age 6, to realizing the implications of their disability at around age 8 (Minde, Hackett, Killon, & Silver, 1972). Teplin, Howard, and O'Connor (1981), in their study of learners with cerebral palsy, reported that children vary in their willingness to discuss their disabilities. Though all of the 4- to 8-year-old children they interviewed were aware that their arms and legs were different from those of their peers, all of the younger children and about half of the older children denied their difficulty in running. The age of the learner is significantly related to the child's awareness of differences and disability (Dunn, McCartan, & Fuqua, 1988). Children whose orthopedic disabilities are openly discussed at home were significantly more aware of their disability and its implications. Discussion at school about disabilities has not been statistically related to a child's knowledge about being different or about his or her specific disability.

Objective Two: To describe the identification and evaluation of learners with physical and other health impairments.

Identification and Evaluation

Three groups of learners with physical and other health impairments are included in Public Law 94–142: those who are orthopedically impaired, those with other health impairments, and those with multiple disabilities.

Public Law 94–142 identifies learners who are orthopedically impaired as those with a severe skeletal deformity which adversely affects their educational performance. These learners may have congenital anomalies (such as clubfoot, hip displacement, or neural tube defects), disabilities attributed to disease processes (such as poliomyelitis or bone tuberculosis), or impairments from other causes (such as cerebral palsy, amputations, and fractures or burns which cause contractures).

Learners who have other health impairments may have limited strength, vitality, or alertness due to chronic or acute health problems such as heart conditions, tuberculosis, rheumatic fever, nephritis, asthma, sickle cell disease, hemophilia, seizure disorders, lead poisoning, leukemia, or diabetes, any of which could adversely affect a child's educational performance. Of these, heart conditions, asthma, sickle cell disease, seizure disorders, and lead poisoning are the most common. Under the amendments of Public Law 94–142, learners with autism were classified as "other health impaired" from 1981 to 1990. In 1990, under Public Law 101–476 (the Individuals with Disabilities Education Act), learners with autism were classified in a separate category of disability. Prior to 1981, these learners were classified as "seriously emotionally disturbed." These learners, however, are frequently served in programs for learners with multiple disabilities and will be discussed in Chapter 16. Efforts to include learners with attention deficit disorders in this category failed with the passing of Public Law 101–476. However, notice to solicit public comment regarding the appropriate components of an operational definition of "attention deficit disorder" is given in Public Law 101–476. These learners will be discussed in Chapter 15, Learners with Mild Disabilities.

"Multihandicapped," or having multiple disabilities, as described in Public Law 94–142, means experiencing concomitant impairments (such as being mentally retarded and visually impaired, or mentally retarded and orthopedically impaired), the combination of which causes such severe educational problems that these learners cannot be accommodated in special education program soley for one of the disabilities. These learners are discussed in Chapter 17.

The identification of learners with physical and other health impairments is typically completed by medical professionals. Depending on the particular physical disability or health impairment, the learner will be given a series of general and specialized medical examinations. Evaluation is conducted by a variety of general and specialized medical personnel and allied health professionals.

Though the vast majority of learners with physical and other health impairments are served in the general education classroom and study the typical curriculum, it is frequently necessary to make some educational accommodations to effectively respond to these learners' individual needs. Due to a learner's disability, it may be difficult to obtain valid educational assessment information from standardized measurement instruments. For example, learners with motor involvement or communication disorders may not be effectively evaluated on instruments requiring motor coordination or verbal communication. For the effective educational evaluation or assessment of learners with physical and other health impairments, criterion-referenced instruments, task analysis, and direct observation of functioning are recommended. Sirvis (1988) and Gleckel and Lee (1990) recommend assessment of the following areas of functioning: (a) daily living activities, (b) mobility, (c) physical abilities and limitations, (d) psychosocial development, (e) communication, (f) academic potential, (g) adaptations for learning, and (h) transition skills.

Objective Three: To describe the impact of physical and other health impairments on interactions in the home and classroom.

The Impact on Interactions in the Home and Classroom

Interactions in the Home

Chronic Illness   Kazak (1989) emphasizes the need to view children's chronic illness through a family systems approach. The interactions among the various family contexts must be recognized in working with children who have a chronic illness. This concept is particularly evident in Williams, Williams, and Landa's (1989) work regarding the developmental performance of children with chronic illness. They found that family makeup (including higher levels of maternal and paternal education, residing in an urban area, and having fewer children) and being an only child contributed to children's resilience to the challenges of a chronic illness.

Among children with sickle cell anemia, diabetes, and leukemia, children whose general functioning was relatively good were found to come from families that had more resources to cope with the condition (Jessop & Stein, 1985). In addition, their mothers reported that their conditions had less impact on the family. Though mothers of children with chronic illness reported greater stress than mothers of children with no known medical problems, no differences were found between the two groups in marital satisfaction (Kazak, 1987, 1989). Mothers of children with chronic illness who had greater social support demonstrate less psychological distress (Hobfoil & Lerman, 1988). In addition, Hobfoil and Lerman (1988) report that mothers who experienced greater distress received greater social support at the time of crisis, and intimacy with spouse was related to better stress resistance. Social support, however, has been shown to decrease over time (Kazak & Meadows, 1989). Mothers of children with chronic diseases such as sickle cell disease, diabetes, and leukemia with more resources judged their functioning more positively and tended to have children with better psychological adjustment than did families with fewer sources of support (Jessop & Stein, 1985).

The children with fewer previous surgeries, and whose parents exhibited the extremes of parenting stress and an overinvolvement with their child, were found more likely to become disturbed by hospitalization and surgery. When compared with their typical peers, however, children with chronic illness responded much the same when confronted with hospitalization and surgery (Wells & Schwebel, 1987). Poor social functioning of children with chronic illnesses has been related to

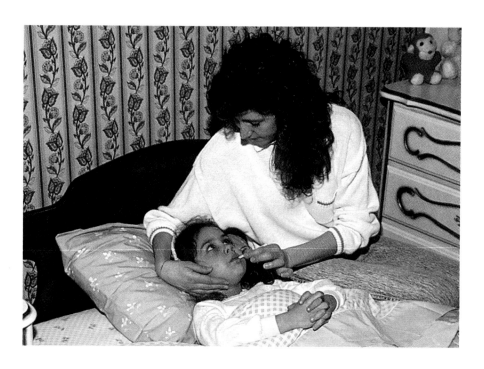

Parents worry when their child is sick.

parental overprotection, while in children with no known illnesses, poor social functioning was related to a lack of parental care (Capelli, McGrath, McDonald, & Katsanis, 1989).

Fathers of children who are ill are less likely to perceive social support in their environment than are fathers of children with no known medical problems or disabilities (Ferrari, 1986). Fathers of children with chronic illnesses are less likely than mothers to report that they feel the challenges strengthen them and their understanding of the medical situation (Powers, Gaudet, & Powers, 1986).

No consistent relationship has been found between the presence of a chronic illness and risk for psychological problems among siblings; rather, the quality of family functioning and relationships has both direct and indirect effects on siblings (Drotar & Crawford, 1985). Wood, Boyle, Watkins, and Noqueira (1988) explored the relationship between disease type, disease activity, and the psychological status of school-aged siblings of children with chronic illnesses. The more psychologically healthy siblings displayed more externalizing rather than internalizing behaviors.

Though young children are able to understand information about another child's illness, this information base does not necessarily facilitate acceptance of the child with the illness (Potter & Roberts, 1984).

Seizure Disorders   Parents of children with seizure disorders varied from those of healthy children in their perceptions of epilepsy. Parents of children with epilepsy, though far more knowledgeable about the educational and behavioral problems of children with epilepsy, often regarded epilepsy as a sign of serious disease (Hoare, 1986). Mothers of children with seizure disorders have been found to use fewer verbal directions and fewer positive responses with the children, using more negative feedback (Chavez & Buriel, 1988).

Sickle Cell Disease   The presence of a child with sickle cell disease presents stress in a family. Single mothers who had a child with sickle cell disease estimated their child's behavior traits and their relationship with the child less positively than did two-parent families, who also reported stress (Evans, Burlow, & Oler, 1988). Dilworth-Anderson (1989), finding varied family structure and overlapping systems of functioning among families of children with sickle cell disease, suggested that families need both broad-based and problem-specific interventions. Self-help groups for individuals with sickle cell disease and their families have been found valuable, and capable of enhancing family and learner personal goals (Nash, 1989).

The healthy siblings of learners with sickle cell disease, when compared with their ill siblings, were found to be at increased risk of psychological adjustment problems. Treiber, Mabe, & Wilson (1987) report that these distress levels are associated with reports of problems in the home and maternal depression and anxiety.

Learners Who Are Positive for HIV   As indicated earlier, most babies born to women with HIV infection, though they test positive for the virus, will not develop AIDS (Levine & Dubler, 1990). An estimated one-third of the children who are HIV positive are currently in foster or adoptive placements. For these children, specialized foster homes with specific training and medical support systems have evolved (Gurdin & Anderson, 1987).

Interactions in the Classroom

When asked who they would rather help first, why, and how much, young school-age children selected persons with orthopedic impairments most frequently over either children with Down syndrome or those with no known disability (Kennedy & Thurman, 1982). In a study in which they were asked to rank "who they liked best," learners with visible orthopedic disabilities and learners with no disabilities ranked wheelchair users and nonidentified persons high and persons with facial marks and obese persons low (Giancoli & Neimeyer, 1983). De Apodaca, Watson, Mueller, and Isaacson-Kailes (1985) offer three possible explanations for significantly higher ratings in some areas of peer rating scales: (a) the persons were truly liked, (b) the children were admired because of their ability to deal with their disability, or (c) peers have a defensive inability to express negative feelings towards persons with disabilities.

Teachers have been found to hold negative attitudes (as indicated by placements in more restrictive environments) towards learners with orthopedic disabilities only when the level of achievement was low (Pliner & Hannah, 1985). Johnson (1986) indicates that teachers may require a broad range of supports and resources when working with learners with chronic illnesses, including in-service training sessions, classroom visits by health professionals, programs for parents, contact with national organizations, and use of computer, local, and regional networks.

A particularly challenging group of learners are those who are medically dependent on technology. Educational placements for these learners range from homebound tutoring, to segregated special education classes, to mainstreamed regular education. Taylor and Walker (1991) indicate that when these learners are in the public school system, they are typically provided the assistance of either a private duty nurse or other trained individual. Court decisions related to technology-assisted learners indicate that because some services are truly medical and not related to the

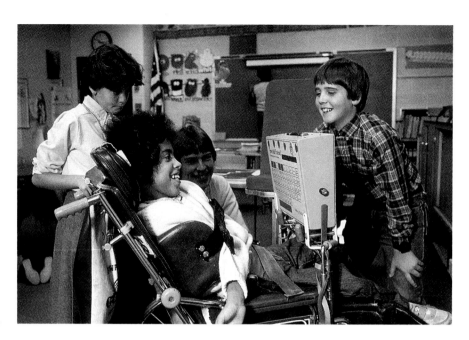

Accommodations needed to mediate the environment are highly individualized for learners medically dependent on technology.

learner's education, and therefore not covered by Public Law 94–142, such services may be covered by Medicaid. Medicaid services required by the learner's individualized education program must be provided (Taylor and Walker, 1991).

Bennett-Levy and Stores (1984) explored teachers' perceptions of classroom behavior relevant to learning difficulties of learners with epilepsy. Four variables—concentration, processing, confidence, and alertness—were found to identify learners with epilepsy. Teachers have been found to perceive learners with epilepsy as having poorer concentration and mental processing ability, as well as being less alert than their peers. Even when matched for educational attainment, teachers perceived learners with epilepsy to be less alert. Bennett-Levy and Stores suggest that the effects of drugs on the learner may explain these findings and may be related to teachers' perceptions.

Objective Four: To describe ways to mediate the environment for learners with physical and other health impairments.

Mediating the Environment

The effect of a learner's disability in the environment and the accommodations needed to help the learner mediate the environment are highly individualized. Accommodations needed to mediate the environment are determined by the individual's age and degree of the disability, the visibility of the disability, the availability of family and other support systems, the attitude of the learner toward the disability, the individual's social status among peers, the presence of architectural barriers, and the need for and availability of transportation (Lewandowski & Cruickshank, 1980; Hardman, Drew, Egan, & Wolf, 1990).

Learners with physical and other health impairments seldom need variations in the curriculum itself; however, the learner's physical condition may require the presence of medical equipment. Mediating the environment, then, in addition to collaborating with medical professionals, may involve administering medication or using assistive devices and equipment. A teacher's role with learners taking medication includes documenting changes in behavior and, in some cases, the severity of symptoms. The most common medications used by learners and their potential side effects are included in Table 10.3.

Table 10.3   Common Medications Used by Learners with
Physical or Other Health Impairments

Medication	Condition or Problem	Potential Side Effects
Aspirin (Ascriptin, Bufferin, Ecotrin)	Juvenile rheumatoid arthritis	Nausea, vomiting, rapid breathing, ringing ears, drowsiness
"Chemotherapy" (Adriamycin, Actinomycin, Cytoxan)	Leukemia, cancer	Hair loss, nausea, vomiting, weight loss, anemia, mouth sores
Corticosteroids	Asthma, leukemia, nephritis, arthritis	Moon-shaped face, increased appetite, euphoria, spontaneous fractures, insomnia, growth retardation, visual disturbances
Cotazym, Pancrease	Cystic fibrosis	Indigestion
Dantrium	Cerebral palsy	Drowsiness, dizziness, weakness, fatigue
Digitalis	Heart conditions	Nausea, vomiting, slowed heart rate
Factor VIII	Hemophilia	Problems related to injections
Insulin	Diabetes	Overdose: personality change, confusion, shakiness, headaches, coma, convulsions
Motrin	Juvenile arthritis	Nausea, stomach pain, indigestion, diarrhea
Phenobarbital, Dilantin	Seizure disorders	Drowsiness, loss of balance, dizziness, headaches, nausea
Ritalin	Attention deficit disorder	Nervousness, insomnia, loss of appetite, dizziness, headache, weight loss
Tegretol	Seizures	Drowsiness, dizziness, unsteadiness, urinary frequency, dry mouth
Zarontin	Seizures	Loss of appetite, nausea, vomiting, drowsiness, headaches, loss of balance, inability to concentrate

Based on information from Lindsey, Leibold, Ladd, & Ownby, 1980.

With some learners, diet control is important. For example, the timing, type, and quantity of food is essential to the continued functioning of learners with diabetes. Learners with seizure disorders may also be on a specialized diet (Scherer, 1983).

Three related services frequently required by learners with physical and other health impairments are (a) occupational therapy, (b) physical therapy, and (c) adapted physical education. The occupational therapist's role is to assist learners, infants through adults, in the development of needed work, recreation, and self-care skills. Concern may be for the initial learning or the restoration or relearning of skills related to everyday life. The focus of **occupational therapy** is on functional outcomes and practical solutions to problems challenging the individual. The therapist may use various tools, toys, appliances, and utensils to help learners with physical disabilities use their bodies more effectively. The learner may have difficulty in balance, posture, tactile discrimination, motor planning, coordination, eye-hand coordination, and so on. Assistance may also be given with the social-emotional concerns related to physical disabilities. Services provided by the occupational therapist may range from consultation with teacher and parents to direct service and may be provided in the home, private office, school, or hospital.

A physical therapist focuses on increasing the individual's strength, endurance, and range of motion.

The physical therapist focuses on increasing the learner's strength, endurance, and range of motion. **Physical therapy** is used to prevent, correct, and relieve physical conditions. The physical therapist uses various forms of therapy including heat, cold, massage, and exercise. Physical therapy may be provided directly or through consultation with teacher and parents and in the home, private office, school, or hospital.

The teacher of **adapted physical education** is concerned primarily with the learner's successful participation in physical education. Attention is focused on the physical education curriculum and activities. Consideration is given to the learner's strength, endurance, and coordination, as well as the learner's safety. Services are generally delivered at school and usually in a small group setting. Services may be offered either directly or through consultation with the learner's teacher.

For very young children with chronic illnesses, medically supervised early intervention programs in either health care settings or in settings closely associated with a medical center or hospital may be necessary (Kahn & Battle, 1987). In these settings, the philosophy of care should develop trust in caregivers and consistency in caregivers, with a goal of increasing interaction with the environment (Jansen, DeWitt, Meshul, & Krasnoff, 1989).

Box 10.1

Seizures: When to Seek Immediate Assistance

- if you are unaware of the individual ever having had a seizure (persons with seizure disorders frequently wear a medical warning necklace or bracelet)
- if the individual's seizure lasts longer than 10 minutes
- if the individual experiences a series of seizures without regaining consciousness
- if the individual is injured during the seizure
- if normal breathing does not resume
- if the individual requests medical assistance ■

Learners with Seizure Disorders   Colandro, Dominguez-Granados, Gomez-Rubio, and Molina-Font (1990) found that learners with seizure disorders who were on therapeutic levels of phenobarbital demonstrated greater differences between their medicated and nonmedicated verbal, performance, and total intelligence quotient scores. These differences were not noted among children receiving valproic acid, another common medication for epilepsy. Box 10.1 provides guidelines for those persons unfamiliar with but confronted with seizures.

Learners Who Are Positive for HIV   Wetterau and Stegelin (1991) report that the likelihood of HIV positive learners being in educational settings increases annually. In their study of the knowledge and attitudes of licensed day care workers with regards to HIV and AIDS, they found that care providers had a generally strong knowledge base related to the virus and the disease. However, there seemed to be little relationship between an individual's knowledge and his or her attitudes about AIDS. Professionals reported that they felt ill-prepared in helping to control infection and a lack of confidence in their ability to work with individuals who have tested positively for HIV.

The recommendations of the American Academy of Pediatrics (Newschwander, 1987) concerning students who test positive for HIV supports unrestricted school attendance, with strict maintenance of the child's confidentiality. Teachers and other learners are not at risk by working and learning in close proximity to these children.

Transitional Services   Care must be taken when learners with physical disabilities or other health impairments are making transitions between programs in the school system (day care or preschool to the primary grades, elementary to secondary school) and from school to independent living in the community, higher education, or work. Transition planning should begin well in advance of the time when the transition is to occur and should be a team effort involving the learner and the learner's parents as well as sending and receiving professionals.

Assistive Equipment, Prosthetics, and Orthotics   There are three categories of devices that may be used to facilitate the effective functioning of learners with physical disabilities and other health impairments: assistive equipment, prosthetics, and orthotics. Assistive equipment includes ordinary devices that are specially designed or modified and applied to facilitate the daily living of learners with disabilities in the home, classroom, school, and office. Among the devices that may be

Orthotic devices enhance individual mobility.

of assistance are uniquely designed cups, spoons, plates, bookholders, pencils, positioning devices, chairs, tables, computer keyboards, and computer screens. These devices must be individually modified to respond to the needs of each learner.

Prosthetics are artificial replacements for missing body parts such as an artificial arm, hand, or leg. Though the effective use of a prosthetic is dependent on residual functioning, it is essential that the prosthetic not interfere with residual functioning and be acceptable for use by the individual. Some individuals with disabilities prefer not to use prosthetics. An **orthotic** device is an assistive device designed to enhance the partial functioning of a part of an individual body such as braces, crutches, canes, or walkers.

Section 504 of the Rehabilitation Act of 1973 mandated that facilities be accessible to individuals with disabilities. During the past two decades, great progress has been made in making buildings and transportation accessible. In 1990, Public Law 101–336 (the Americans with Disabilities Act) required accommodations be made for individuals with disabilities (see Chapter 3).

Adults with physical disabilities are confronted with greater challenges in both employment and society perception of their usefulness and ability to contribute.

Objective Five: To describe the impact of physical and other health impairments on participation in the larger social systems—the school, community, and society.

The Impact on Participation in the School, Community, and Society

Bohan and Humes (1986) interviewed adults with orthopedic disabilities, all of whom used a wheelchair as either their primary or only means of mobility. These adults felt that able-bodied individuals abridged their social rights through continual staring, intrusive questioning, unsolicited assistance, or public humiliation. Those interviewed also indicated that they were dissatisfied with the way they responded to public encounters. They felt that they did not respond appropriately for the circumstances. University students reported that they participated less in extracurricular activities than their peers (Bohan & Humes, 1986). Though social interactions posed few problems, the physical environment often challenged university students with orthopedic disabilities (Burbach & Babbitt, 1988). Automatic doors, elevators, desks at the proper height, and the like were not available.

Pfeiffer (1991) reports that although a physical disability may have an impact on an individual's employability, the social class structure which enables Caucasian males in the United States to have access to education, jobs, and higher income is in place within the disabled community. Caucasian males are far more likely to be employed and to receive higher income than their peers who are female or from minority cultures. Hanna and Rogovsky (1991) suggest that women with disabilities have "two handicaps plus," and are confronted with greater challenges in both employment and in society's perception of their usefulness and ability to contribute.

In their study of the post-secondary experiences of learners with physical disabilities, Liebert, Lutsky, and Gottlieb (1990) found that about two-thirds of the individuals were employed at least part-time. The majority of jobs were in competitive employment, though about one-half could be classified as semiskilled. Personal networks, such as families and friends, were the ways in which individuals found employment, rather than through rehabilitation or other placement agencies. Almost all of the individuals remained single, and most remained living with their parents.

Summary

With the number and variety of physical and other health impairments identified, it is impossible to thoroughly discuss them all in a single chapter of an introductory text. For this reason, the physical and other health impairments reviewed in this chapter are selected on the basis of those most frequently encountered by the general and special education teacher. This chapter provides an overview of the nature of accommodations for these learners. In most cases, learners with orthopedic and other health impairments are most likely to be served in the general education classroom.

Learners with physical and other health impairments vary with the symptoms and intensity of their impairments. These learners are at risk for academic failure even in the absence of a known cognitive problem.

The identification of learners as physically or other health impaired is typically a medical task. Standardized instruments may not provide an accurate picture of the learner. Because of the problems standardized instruments present to these learners, criterion referenced measures provide a more accurate picture of what they are able to achieve.

In the home, parents of learners with physical or other health impairments may experience more stress. No consistent relationship has been found between the presence of a chronic illness and risk for psychological problems among siblings. In the classroom, teachers' negative attitudes have been linked to the learner's achievement rather than his or her impairment itself. A particular challenge for teachers and school systems are learners who are dependent on medical technology.

The accommodations necessary for learners with physical and other health impairments are highly individualized. Seldom do these learners require changes in the curriculum itself. Mediating the environment, in addition to collaborating with medical professionals, may involve administering medication or using assistive devices and equipment. Learners may require related services such as occupational therapy, physical therapy, or adapted physical education.

In the community, adults with physical impairments who use wheelchairs report that others abridged their social rights through staring and questioning. Although social interactions may pose few problems, the opportunity for social interactions and employment may be hindered by the lack of accessibility.

John Hockenberry: Journalist First, Disabled Second

By Roxanne Roberts

National Public Radio correspondent John Hockenberry, soon to join ABC, is determined not to become solely known as the "disabled" journalist, although it's a role in which he is becoming increasingly comfortable and visible.

At age 19, Hockenberry was in a car accident in which his spinal cord was damaged and he was paralyzed from the chest down. In 1980, he began working as a volunteer at NPR affiliate KLCC-FM in Eugene, Ore. Within a year, he was filing reports for NPR and was in the middle of the biggest story of the year—the eruption of Mount St. Helens.

His bosses in Washington didn't realize he used a wheelchair until he missed a deadline—because he couldn't fit his wheelchair into a phone booth to file his story. He didn't discuss his disability with listeners until years later when he returned from two years based in Jerusalem.

"In the Middle East, I was expecting architectural barriers, but I found psychological access," he said. "I found incredible openness about physical helplessness in the Third World that doesn't exist in the United States."

He returned to the Middle East during the Persian Gulf War. Hockenberry left his wheelchair at a Kurdish outpost and spent eight hours on the back of a donkey to get to a story on the thousands of refugees pouring into the mountains.

"Kurds would come by and say, 'Why are we wasting a perfectly good donkey with a journalist on top?' I would explain or a Kurd would explain that I can't walk. Then these starving, dying Kurds would say, 'Then why are you here? You could die up there'—which was the story I was trying to get."

Hockenberry went into journalism thinking he and the chair were two separate entities; today he is one of the leading spokesmen for the disabled and an active proponent of enforcement of the Americans With Disabilities Act, which went into effect this year. As host of the Peabody Award-winning show "Heat," he explored the issues with other disabled people and took his audience through the New York subway system—in a wheelchair.

"I've gone through a very personal transformation on that," he said. "From 'Leave me alone. I have a real job'—which is a bitter, awful way to be—to really understanding that I have a role."

In June, Hockenberry filed a lawsuit against Jujamcym Theaters in New York after being denied access to "Jelly's Last Jam" at the Virginia Theatre. He had purchased a $60 ticket the previous day and was told the house manager would seat him. But at curtain time, the manager allegedly refused to help and turned him away.

He wrote an essay for The New York Times about the incident. But, he said, don't look for him to use his television job primarily to report on the disabled. The fact is, he said, he's "too close" to do those stories effectively.

"The fact that he's in a wheelchair made us ask, 'Can he do the job?' " said ABC executive producer Tom Yellin. "I asked around. When I heard about him being dragged across Turkey on a camel, I figured the guy could get from one place to another reasonably efficiently. The real issue is what you do when you get there. What he does is very exciting. Nothing gets in John's way, as far as I know" ∎

© 1992, *The Washington Post*. Reprinted with permission.

References

Arthritis Foundation (1983). *Arthritis: Basic facts*. Atlanta, GA: Author.

Athreya, B. H., and Ingall, C. G. (1984). Juvenile rheumatoid arthritis. In J. Fithian (Ed.), *Understanding the child with a chronic illness in the classroom*. Phoenix, AZ: Oryx.

Bandyopadhyay, S., Roy, D., Basum, A., & Chattopadhyay, P. (1987). Emotional status of orthopedically handicapped subjects and neurotic patients. *Indian Psychological Review, 32* (8–9), 1–6.

Bennett-Levy, J., & Stores, G. (1984). The nature of cognitive dysfunction in school-children with epilepsy. *Acta Neurologica Scandinavica, 59*, 79–82.

Bohan, D., & Humes, C. W. (1986). Assessment of the integration of physically handicapped college students into extracurricular activities. *Journal of College Student Personnel, 27* (1), 55–57.

Boos, M., Garlonsky, R. M., MacEwen, G. D., & Steg, N. (1984). Orthopedic problems. In J. Fithian (Ed.), *Understanding children with a chronic illness in the classroom*. Phoenix, AZ: Oryx.

Burbach, H. J., & Babbitt, C. E. (1988). Physically disabled students on the college campus. *Remedial and Special Education, 5* (2), 12–15.

Cappelli, M., McGrath, P. J., McDonald, N. E., & Katsanis, J. (1989). Parental care and overprotection of children with cystic fibrosis. *British Journal of Medical Psychology, 62* (3), 281–289.

Chavez, J. M., & Buriel, R. (1988). Mother-child interactions involving a child with epilepsy. *Journal of Pediatric Psychology, 13,* 349–351.

Chee, C. M., & Clancy, R. R. (1984). Epilepsy. In J. Fithian (Ed.), *Understanding the child with a chronic illness in the classroom.* Phoenix, AZ: Oryx.

Colandra, E. P., Dominguez-Granados, R., Gomez-Rubio, M., & Molina-Font, J. A. (1990). Cognitive effects of long-term treatment with pentobarbital and valproic acid in school children. *Acta Neurologica Scandinavica, 81,* 504–505.

de Apodaca, R. F., Watson, J. D., Mueller, J., & Isaacson-Kailes, J. (1985). A sociometric comparison of mainstreamed, orthopedically handicapped high school students and nonhandicapped classmates. *Psychology in the Schools, 22* (1), 95–101.

Dilworth-Anderson, P. (1989). Family structure and intervention strategies: Beyond empirical research. *Annals of the New York Academy of Sciences, 565,* 183–188.

Drotar, D., & Crawford, P. (1985). Psychological adaptation of siblings of chronically ill children: Research and practice implications. *Journal of Developmental and Behavioral Pediatrics, 6* (6), 355–362.

Dunn, N. L., McCartan, K. W., & Fuqua, R. W. (1988). Young children with orthopedic handicaps: Self-knowledge about their disability. *Exceptional Children, 55,* 249–252.

Epilepsy Foundation of America (1983). *Epilepsy: Recognition and first aid.* Landover, MD: Author.

Evans, R. C., Burlow, A., & Oler, C. H. (1988). Children with sickle cell anemia. *Social Work, 33,* 127–130.

Ferrari, M. (1986). Perceptions of social support by parents of chronically ill versus healthy children. *Children's Health Care, 15* (1), 26–31.

Frank, B. B. (1985). Psychosocial aspects of educating epileptic children: Roles for school psychologists. *School Psychology Review, 14,* 196–203.

Giancoli, D. I., & Neimeyer, G. J. (1983). Liking preferences toward handicapped persons. *Perceptual and Motor Skills, 57* (3), 1005–1006.

Gill, F. M., & Butler, R. (1984). Hemophilia. In J. Fithian (Ed.), *Understanding the child with a chronic illness in the classroom.* Phoenix, AZ: Oryx.

Gleckel, L. K., & Lee, R. J. (1990). Physical disabilities. In E. L. Meyen (Ed.), *Exceptional children in today's schools* (2nd ed.) (pp. 359–393) Denver: Love.

Gon, M., Boyce, B., & Advani, K. (1983). Locus of control in orthopedically handicapped and nonhandicapped persons. *Journal of Psychological Research, 27* (2), 75–80.

Gurdin, P., & Anderson, G. R. (1987). Quality care for ill children: Aids specialized foster family homes. *Child Welfare, 66,* 291–302.

Hallahan, D. P., & Kauffman, J. M. (1986). *Exceptional children.* (3rd ed.). Englewood Cliffs, NJ: Prentice Hall.

Hanna, W. J., & Rogovsky, B. (1991). Women with disabilities: Two handicaps plus. *Disability in America, 6* (2), 312–325.

Hardman, M. L., Drew, C. J., Egan, M. W., & Wolf, B. (1990). *Human exceptionality: Society, school, and family* (3rd ed.). Boston: Allyn & Bacon.

Hardy, J. C. (1983). *Cerebral palsy.* Englewood Cliffs, NJ: Prentice Hall.

Hoare, P. (1984a). Does illness foster dependency? A study of epileptic and diabetic children. *Developmental Medicine and Child Neurology, 26,* 20–24.

Hoare, P. (1984b). The development of psychiatric disorder among school children with epilepsy. *Developmental Medicine and Child Neurology, 26,* 3–13.

Hoare, P. (1986). Adults' attitudes to children with epilepsy: The use of visual analogue scale questionnaire. *Journal of Psychosomatic Research, 30,* 471–479.

Hobfoil, S. E., & Lerman, M. (1988). Personal relationships, personal attributes, and stress resistance: Mothers' reactions to the child's illness. *American Journal of Community Psychology, 16,* 565–589.

Hopkins, K. M., Grosz, J., Cohen, H., & Diamond, G. (1989). The developmental and family services unit: A model AIDS project serving developmentally disabled children and their families. *Aids Care, 1* (3), 281–285.

Hurtig, A. L., Koepke, D., & Park, K. (1989). Relation between severity of chronic illness and adjustment in children and adolescents with sickle cell disease. *Journal of Pediatric Psychology, 14* (1), 117–132.

Jansen, M. T., DeWitt, P. K., Meshul, R. J., & Krasnoff, J. B. (1989). Meeting psychosocial and developmental needs of children during prolonged intensive care unit hospitalization. *Children's Health Care, 18* (2), 91–95.

Jessop, D. J., & Stein, R. E. (1985). Uncertainty and its relation to the psychological and social correlates of chronic illness in children. *Social Science and Medicine, 20,* 993–999.

Johnson, B. H. (1986). Resources available to teachers working with chronically ill children and their families. *Topics in Early Childhood Special Education, 5* (4), 92–104.

Kahn, N. A., & Battle, C. U. (1987). Chronic illness: Implications for development and education. *Topics in Early Childhood Special Education, 6* (4), 25–32.

Kazak, A. E. (1987). Families with disabled children: Stress and social networks in three samples. *Journal of Abnormal Child Psychology, 15* (1), 137–146.

Kazak, A. E. (1989). Families of chronically ill children: A systems and social-ecological model of adaptation and challenge. *Journal of Consulting and Clinical Psychology, 57* (1), 25–30.

Kazak, A. E., & Meadows, A. T. (1989). Families of young adolescents who have survived cancer: Social-emotional adjustment, adaptability, and social support. *Journal of Pediatric Psychology, 14* (2), 175–191.

Kennedy, A. B., & Thurman, S. K. (1982). Inclinations of nonhandicapped children to help their handicapped peers. *Journal of Special Education, 16,* 319–327.

Kim, H. C., Gaston, G., & Fithian, J. (1984). Sickle cell anemia. In J. Fithian (Ed.), *Understanding the child with a chronic illness in the classroom.* Phoenix, AZ: Oryx.

Kolski, G., & Burg, I. (1984). Allergies. In J. Fithian (Ed.), *Understanding the child with a chronic illness in the classroom.* Phoenix, AZ: Oryx.

Lawrence, B. (1991). Self-concept formation and physical handicap: Some educational implications for integration. *Disability, 6* (2), 240–245.

Leibert, D., Lutsky, L., & Gottlieb, A. (1990). Postsecondary experience of young adults with severe physical disabilities. *Exceptional Children, 57,* 56–53.

Lemanek, K. L. (1986). Psychological adjustment of children with sickle cell anemia. *Journal of Pediatric Psychology, 11,* 397–410.

Levine, C., & Dubler, N. N. (1990). HIV and childbearing. *Milbank Quarterly, 68,* 321–351.

Lewandowski, L. J., & Cruickshank, W. M. (1980). *Psychological development of crippled children and youth.* Englewood Cliffs, NJ: Prentice Hall.

Lindsey, C. N., Leibold, S. R., Ladd, F. T., & Ownby, R. (1980). Children on medication: A guide for teachers. *Rehabilitation Literature, 41,* 124–126.

Margalit, M., & Heiman, T. (1983). Anxiety and self-dissatisfaction in epileptic children. *International Journal of Social Psychiatry, 29,* 220–224.

Marlowe, M. (1985). Low lead exposure and learning disabilities. *Research Communications in Psychology, Psychiatry, and Behavior, 10,* 153–169.

Matthews, W. S., Barabas, G., & Ferrari, M. (1983). Achievement and school behavior among children with epilepsy. *Psychology in the Schools, 20,* 10–12.

Minde, K. K., Hackett, J. D., Killon, D., & Silver, S. (1972). How they grow up: Physically handicapped children and their families. *American Journal of Rehabilitation Research, 5,* 235–237.

Morgan, S. A., & Jackson, J. (1986). Psychological and social concomitants of sickle cell anemia in adolescents. *Journal of Pediatric Psychology, 11,* 429–440.

Nash, K. B. (1989). Self-help groups: An empowerment vehicle for sickle cell disease patients and their families. *Social Work with Groups, 12,* 81–97.

Nelms, B. C. (1989). Emotional behaviors in chronically ill children. *Journal of Abnormal Child Psychology, 17,* 657–668.

Newschwander, G. E. (1987). Update on AIDS for teachers and policy makers. *Educational Horizons, 65,* 110–113.

Olson, R., Huszti, H. C., Mason, P. J., & Seibert, J. M. (1989). Pediatric AIDS HIV infection. *Journal of Pediatric Psychology, 14,* 1–21.

Pfeiffer, D. (1991). The influences of the socio-economic characteristics of disabled people on their employment status and income. *Disability in America, 6* (2), 210–215.

Pliner, S., & Hannah, M. E. (1985). The role of achievement in teachers' attitudes towards handicapped children. *Academic Psychology Bulletin, 7* (3), 327–335.

Potter, P. C., & Roberts, M. C. (1984). Children's perceptions of chronic illness: The roles of disease symptoms, cognitive development, and information. *Journal of Pediatric Psychology, 9* (1), 13–27.

Powers, G. M., Gaudet, L. M., & Powers, S. (1986). Coping patterns of parents of chronically ill children. *Psychological Reports, 59* (2), 519–522.

Ritchie, J. A., Caty, S., & Ellerton, M. L. (1984). Concerns of acutely ill, chronically ill, and healthy preschool children. *Research in Nursing and Health, 7* (4), 265–274.

Ross, J. W. (1984). The child with cancer in school. In J. Fithian (Ed.), *Understanding the child with a chronic illness in the classroom.* Phoenix, AZ: Oryx.

Scherer, A. (1983). *Epilepsy: You and your child.* Landover, MD: Epilepsy Foundation of America.

Schlieper, A. (1985). Chronic illness and school achievement. *Developmental Medicine and Child Neurology, 27* (1), 75–79.

Sigmon, S. B. (1986). The orthopedically disabled child: Psychological implications with an individual basis. *Individual Psychology: Journal of Adlerian Theory, Research, and Practice, 42* (2), 274–278.

Sirvis, B. (1988). Physical disabilities: In E. L. Meyer & T. M. Skrtic (Eds.), *Exceptional children and youth: An introduction* (3rd ed.) (pp. 387–411). Denver, Love.

Smith, D. D., & Luckasson, R. (1992). *Introduction to special education: Teaching in an age of challenge.* Boston: Allyn & Bacon.

Task Force on Pediatric AIDS (1989). Pediatric AIDS and human immunodeficiency virus infection: Psychological issues. *American Psychologist, 44,* 259–264.

Taylor, S., & Walker, P. (1991). Where there is a will, there is not always a way: Psychology public policy, and the school programming of children who are technology assisted. *Children's Health Care, 20,* 115–120.

Teplin, S. W., Howard, J. A., & O'Connor, M. J. (1981). Self-concept of young children with cerebral palsy. *Developmental Medicine and Child Neurology, 23,* 730–738.

Treiber, F. A., Mabe, P., & Wilson, G. (1987). Psychological adjustment of sickle cell children and their siblings. *Children's Health Care, 18,* 82–88.

U.S. Department of Education (1990). *Twelfth annual report to Congress on the implementation of the Education of the Handicapped Act.* Washington, DC: Author.

U.S. Department of Education (1992). *Fourteenth annual report to Congress on the implementation of the Individuals with Disabilities Education Act.* Washington, DC: Author.

Verhaaven, P. R., & Connor, F. P. (1981). Physical disabilities. In J. Kauffman & D. Hallahan (Eds.), *Handbook of special education* (pp. 248–290). Englewood Cliffs, NJ: Prentice Hall.

Wells, R. D., & Schwebel, A. I. (1987). Chronically ill children and their mothers. *Journal of Developmental and Behavioral Pediatrics, 8* (2), 83–89.

Wetterau, P., & Stegelin, D. (1991). Child care professionals' knowledge and attitudes towards AIDS: A needs assessment. *Children's Health Care, 20,* 21–25.

Williams, P. D., Williams, A. R., & Landa, A. R. (1989). Factors influencing performance of chronically ill children on a developmental screening test. *International Journal of Nursing Studies, 26* (2), 163–172.

Wood, B., Boyle, J. T., Watkins, J. B., & Noqueira, J. (1988). Sibling psychological status and style as related to the disease of their chronically ill brothers and sisters: Implications for models of biopsychosocial interaction. *Journal of Developmental and Behavioral Pediatrics, 9* (2), 66–72.

Woolf, P. K. (1984). Cardiac disease. In J. Fithian (Ed.), *Understanding the child with a chronic illness in the classroom.* Phoenix, AZ: Oryx.

Yashon, D. (1986). *Spinal injury* (2nd ed.). NY: Appleton-Century-Crofts.

Chapter

11

Learners with Visual Impairments

*O*bjectives

After completing this chapter, you will be able to:

1. describe the personal characteristics of learners with visual impairments.
2. describe the identification and evaluation of learners with visual impairments.
3. describe the impact of visual impairments on interactions in the home and classroom.
4. describe ways to mediate the environment for learners with visual impairments.
5. describe the impact of visual impairments on participation in the larger social systems—the school, community, and society.

*K*ey Words and Phrases

amblyopia	partially sighted
astigmatism	peripheral vision
blind	presbyopia
cataracts	retinitis pigmentosa
diabetic retinopathy	retinopathy of prematurity
glaucoma	stereotypies
hyperopia	strabismus
macular degeneration	visual acuity
myopia	visual impairment
nystagmus	visually handicapped

*M*ANY OF HISTORY'S GREATEST ARTISTS WERE KNOWN TO HAVE VISION IMPAIRMENTS. THESE INCLUDE MONET, Pissarro, Degas, Daumier, Renoir, Goya, Cassatt, and others. It is no paradox that artists with little or no vision can actually create works of art in visual media which are rich and varied, and which tell of a continued participation in a visual world. For each artist, including those with no light perception who work in purely tactile media, inner vision becomes activated and is fueled by necessity and translated into shape, form, and color by drawing upon visual and spatial memory, imagination, and dreams. (From the catalog for the art exhibit "Art of the Eye," a collection of works by artists with visual impairments. Delta Gamma Foundation, 1991.) ■

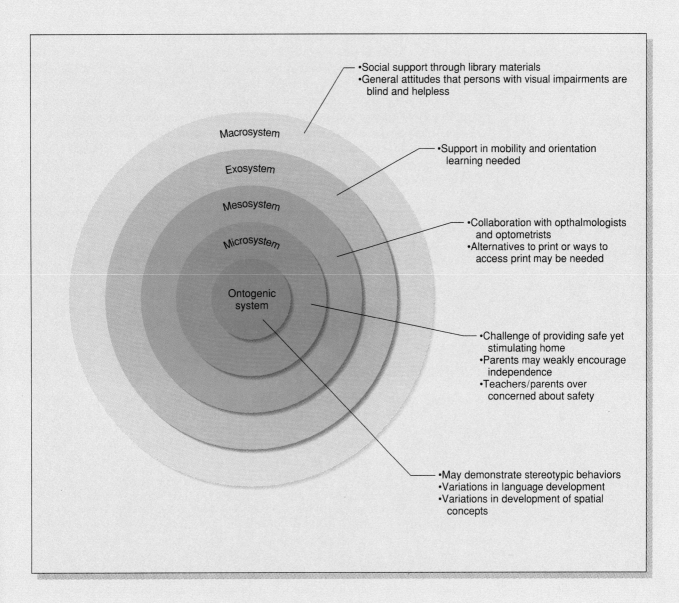

•Social support through library materials
•General attitudes that persons with visual impairments are blind and helpless

Macrosystem

•Support in mobility and orientation learning needed

Exosystem

Mesosystem

•Collaboration with opthalmologists and optometrists
•Alternatives to print or ways to access print may be needed

Microsystem

Ontogenic system

•Challenge of providing safe yet stimulating home
•Parents may weakly encourage independence
•Teachers/parents over concerned about safety

•May demonstrate stereotypic behaviors
•Variations in language development
•Variations in development of spatial concepts

Introduction

Learners with **visual impairment** include those learners whose sight is limited in any way to the extent that special services are required. Many of these persons have sight that is useful for some purposes (Finkelstein, 1989). Others are **blind,** or have profound visual impairment that prohibits the use of vision as an educational tool. Finkelstein suggests that public misinformation about the impact of blindness is evident in surveys conducted on visual impairment: for example, the public fears blindness more than any condition except cancer; children fear only the death of a parent more than they fear becoming blind.

Visual impairment is a low incidence disability—during the 1990–91 school year, only .5 percent of the learners with disabilities served had visual impairments (U.S. Department of Education, 1992). Only the category of individuals who are deaf-blind had fewer learners receiving services. The largest number of these individuals were educated in general education classrooms (37.7 percent), yet 10 percent were served in residential facilities (as compared with 8.6 percent of those who are hearing impaired). The only category of individuals served in residential facilities larger than the category of individuals with visual impairments is individuals who are deaf-blind (U.S. Department of Education, 1990).

Personal Characteristics

Objective One: To describe the personal characteristics of learners with visual impairments.

Finkelstein (1989) contends that because as much as 85 or 90 percent of what we learn comes through our vision, it is often presumed that learners with visual impairments are less capable or have less potential than those who see. However, vision is only one source of information, and learners with visual impairments are as varied as any other group of individuals. These learners' visual impairments have equally varied effects on their personal characteristics.

The mannerisms of learners who are visually impaired have been studied fairly extensively. Stereotypic behaviors, or **stereotypies,** repetitive behaviors with no apparent effect on the environment, and "blindisms," behaviors apparent in learners who are visually impaired, cover a broad range of verbal and motor behavior. Leonhardt (1990) found that stereotypic behaviors occur more frequently in conditions under which the learner has little or no control, in demanding situations, in situations that refer to the visual world, or in situations of loneliness or isolation. Eye and head movements have been related to the onset and severity of the visual impairment, with the more severely and congenitally visually impaired individuals demonstrating more of these behaviors (Jan, Farrell, Wong, & McCormick, 1986). In a study comparing school-age children with visual impairments in Nigeria and England, blindisms such as rocking, spinning, twitching thumbs, and rolling back the eyes were observed more frequently in Nigerian children, and were felt to be related to cultural difference and amount of physical contact the children received (Abang, 1983). These behaviors can have a significant impact on learners. Raver-Lampman (1990) found that when individuals with visual impairments used gaze direction toward the questioner, they were evaluated as being more intelligent and more socially competent than those who did not use gaze direction.

Language Development

Though studies have been conducted on the language development of learners with visual impairments, findings only reemphasize the heterogeneous nature of these learners. Bigelow (1987) noted that the early vocabulary of learners with visual impairments paralleled that of their sighted peers in age and speed of acquisition and in the underlying characteristics of what the children selected to label. Their early words differed, however, and were found to be a function of a combination of the lack of vision and the learner's particular language learning context. In a longitudinal study of the development of function of language in learners with congenital visual impairments, Orwin (1984) found that learners demonstrated limited use of object names and requests, relied heavily on routine phrases and people's names, imitated a great deal, and infrequently referred to objects and events beyond their reach or touch. She felt, however, that given the fact that their language development followed that of peers in other ways, it was unlikely that the children had any general cognitive delay or impairment in representation processes. Anderson and Fisher (1985) reported that young learners with visual impairments tended to cling to nominal realism (assigning animistic qualities to objects and concretely using labels) longer than did their sighted peers, possibly due to the limitations the visual impairment imposed on children's interactions with objects.

McConachie (1990) found that though some learners with visual impairments showed an early facility with expressive language, greater than their true level of comprehension, many showed a lag in expressive speech relative to comprehension, with first words appearing as late as 4 years of age. Erin (1990) generated language samples from learners who were both blind and partially sighted, using common household objects. She found that partially sighted learners had slightly greater complexity of utterances. The learners who were visually impaired had a higher frequency of inappropriate pronoun use than did those who were partially sighted, and they employed less variation in sentence types. However, Erin states that there was a greater variation in the level of language maturity among learners with visual impairments than among those who were partially sighted, suggesting that the developmental context of the learners may influence language development.

In a study of 13- to 17-year-old adolescents with visual impairments and their sighted peers, Civelli (1983) asked the subjects to define twenty words representing objects, movements, animals, and expressions. He found that the learners with visual impairments performed better than the sighted group on all categories except material objects. Persons with more severe visual impairments have been found to ask more frequent questions about objects and events (Erin, 1986).

Children with visual impairments engage in as much emotional facial display as do individuals who are sighted, though they are less likely to refer spontaneously to their facial expression in explaining how the examiner knew how they felt (Cole, Jenkins, & Shott, 1985).

Cognitive Development

Research studies of cognitive development have generally demonstrated variations of development in learners with visual impairments when compared to their peers who are sighted. Ittyerah and Samarapungavan (1989) report that though the cognitive development of individuals who are visually impaired and those who are sighted is not identical, the differences in performance between groups are content or task specific and do not take the form of global deficits across groups of tasks. They hypothesize that these variations in performance are a function of absence of experience and absence of visual information. The development of object permanence in children with visual impairments parallels that of children who are sighted; however, the modalities (touch, sound) used to organize information are necessarily different (Bigelow, 1986). The mental images or concepts of objects that children with visual impairments develop through nonvisual experiences are not significantly different from those acquired by children who are sighted (Anderson, 1984).

The development of spatial concepts by learners with visual impairment has received a great deal of attention. These concepts are of particular importance to learners with visual impairments because of their relationship to personal mobility. In terms of their own bodies in space, learners with visual impairments have been found to vary from their sighted peers in that they had a poorer ability to balance (Mereira, 1990). Though learners with visual impairments are as able as learners who are sighted to discriminate right and left in tasks related to themselves, they have difficulty relating right and left to others. Learners with visual impairments have difficulty projecting positions in space, including recognition of shapes, construction of a projective straight line, and conceptualization of right and left in absolute and mirror image orientation (Birns, 1986).

Learners with visual impairments have demonstrated the ability to reproduce the extent of movements accurately. They have difficulty, however, reproducing movements in their orientation to space or a specific reference point (Dodds & Carter, 1983). Differences have also been found between learners with visual impairments and their sighted peers, with the former demonstrating poorer posture and cardiovascular endurance. In tests of obstacle perception, learners with visual impairments were able to, at above-chance levels, demonstrate distal perception of objects. As a consequence, Ashmead, Hill, and Talor (1989) hypothesize that children with little or no visual experience or formal training use nonvisual information, presumably auditory, to perceive objects.

Social-Emotional Development and Behavior

The social adaptation of learners with visual impairments have been found to be a consistent challenge throughout their development. Van Hasselt (1983) reports consistent patterns of problems in social adaptation in children, adolescents, and adults with visual impairments. He attributes some of these problems to inadequately formed attachments as early as infancy. The most marked problems in social adaptation have been reported among learners who attended residential schools (Hirshoren & Schnittjer, 1983). In addition, problem behavior has been found to be most marked among learners in residential placements (Van Hasselt, Kazdin, & Hersen, 1986). Specific problems have been reported in verbal and nonverbal social skills, but the broad measures of social adaptation have not demonstrated serious problems (Van Hasselt, 1983). If learners with visual impairments have had significant verbal interaction with others, such as participating in games and friendships, they do not differ from their sighted peers in social cognitive tasks (Schwartz, 1983). Learners with visual impairments have been found to be more externally controlled, though social adaptation improved with age and intellectual achievement (Parsons, 1987).

The self-concept of learners with visual impairments has not been found to be less sound than that of their sighted peers (Ubiakor & Otile, 1990). In addition, though specific fears related to concern for bodily injury have been noted, the fears and anxiety levels of learners with visual impairments have not been found to vary from those of their sighted peers (Wilhelm, 1989). Even young learners with visual impairments, however, realize that they see differently than do sighted persons, and that learners with visual impairments need to feel objects to gain a sense of them and that sighted individuals do not.

Objective Two: To describe the identification and evaluation of learners with visual impairments.

Identification and Evaluation

Public Law 94–142 defined **visually handicapped** as having "a visual impairment which, even with correction, adversely affects a child's educational performance. The term includes both partially seeing and blind children" (*Federal Register,* 1977, 300.05). Public Law 101–476 (passed in 1990) modified the term to reflect changes in language, referring to these learners as "visually impaired."

Educational and legal definitions for visual impairment vary. Educationally, students considered blind require alternatives to print and visual materials, and **partially sighted** students may use print and visual materials with the help of large print, optical aids, technological aids, and education in using their residual vision (Orlansky & Rhyne, 1981).

How well an individual can see, visual efficiency, is measured by acuity and peripheral vision. **Visual acuity** is a measure of how well the individual can see at various distances. **Peripheral vision** is a measure of the width of the individual's field of vision or the ability to see outside a direct line of vision. Learners are legally blind if central vision acuity does not exceed 20/200 in the better eye with corrective lenses or if the visual field is less than an angle of 20 degrees (normal vision acuity is defined as 20/20). Learners with 20/200 vision see at 20 feet that which the learner with normal vision sees at 200 feet. Partially sighted individuals are those whose visual acuity is between 20/70 and 20/200 in the better eye with the best correction possible (Finkelstein, 1989). Learners whose impairment is in the angle of vision have a restricted visual field which makes participation in activities such as reading, driving, and similar activities difficult. Problems in the angle of vision are known as tunnel vision, pinhole vision, and tubular vision.

In 1986, Barrage proposed the following educationally relevant classification of visual impairments:

Profound: Most gross visual tasks are very difficult; vision generally not used for detail tasks.

Severe: Visual tasks demand considerable time and energy; performance less accurate than that of learners with normal vision even with visual aids and other modifications.

Moderate: Tasks performed with the use of aids and lighting; performance comparable to learners with normal vision.

Visual impairments may be the consequences of various factors. The most frequent causes are prenatal influences and heredity, injuries, poisoning, tumors, infectious diseases such as rubella and German measles, and general systemic disorders such as central nervous system disorders.

The Vision System

The discussion of the various visual impairments and their impact on the learner's development is best understood with some comprehension of the way in which the vision system functions. The vision system is composed of three parts: (a) the eye, (b) the optic nerve, and (c) the vision center of the brain.

What we see begins as light reflected on the external covering of the eye, or the cornea. The light reflected by the cornea pass through the pupil, an opening in the iris, the colored part of the eye. As the pupil expands and contracts, it controls the amount of light entering the eye. Rays of light pass through the lens, which focuses the light through the transparent, gel-like vitreous humor onto the retina. As light passes through the lens, it is reversed, much like light passing through the lens of a camera. The retina, like the film in a camera, receives the upside-down light "picture," which, to use Finkelstein's (1989) analogy, is then developed by the brain. The photoreceptors of the retina are rods and cones: the rods are responsible for vision in darkness and for peripheral vision and the cones are responsible for color vision, vision in bright light, and central vision (see the diagram of the eye, Figure 11.1).

The outer coat, or "white of the eye," is the sclera, a strip of tendon. Just below the cornea is a chamber containing a continuously flowing clear fluid called the aqueous humor, which is contained by the front and back chambers between the cornea and the lens, and separated by the iris. Since the lens and the cornea have no blood vessels, they receive their nourishment from the aqueous humor, which flows through small channels located at the angle where the iris and cornea meet. If this outlet of aqueous humor is impeded in any way, then the pressure of the eye rises, and a condition known as **glaucoma** may result.

Muscles on the outside of the eye "aim" the eye at an object. When looking at close objects, the eyes converge and the lens focuses. By the time most individuals reach about 45 years of age, this ability to focus for close work is usually lost or impaired, a condition called **presbyopia.**

When we see something clearly, our eyes are aimed in such a way as to place the object's image onto a depression in the central portion of the retina, known as the fovea, which is surrounded by the macula lutea. The concentration of cones in this part of the eye makes it useful for the most acute vision. The retina, however, has both the visual property of resolution (central vision) and detection (peripheral vision). Each of these properties comes into play when discussing visual impairments.

Though the most common visual problems confronting children are those of visual acuity, there is a broad range of visual impairments, each of which varies in degree of impact on the individual. The most common of these visual problems and their impact on the individual are presented in Table 11.1.

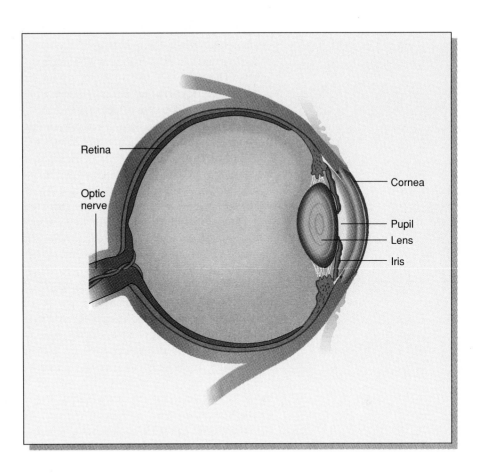

Figure 11.1
Diagram of the eye.

Table 11.1   Common Visual Impairments and Their Impact on Vision

Visual Impairment	Impact on Vision
Amblyopia	"Lazy eye"; may report poor vision in one or both eyes
Hyperopia (Farsightedness)	Blurry near vision; headaches after close work; discomfort
Myopia (Nearsightedness)	Blurry far vision; missing distant details
Cataracts	Lens of the eye becomes cloudy or opaque, obstructing vision
Macular degeneration	Deterioration of the central part of the retina; retain peripheral vision
Diabetic retinopathy	Blood vessels of the retina hemorrhage, causing blurred or distorted vision
Glaucoma	Increased pressure in the eye; gradual vision loss, beginning with peripheral vision
Retinitis pigmentosa	Dark pigment layer of the retina is slowly lost, causing a gradual reduction of the visual field
Retinopathy of prematurity	Deterioration of the retina, formerly caused by high levels of oxygen administered to premature infants

Sources: Grayson, 1984; Rouse & Ryan, 1984; Scott, 1982; National Association for the Visually Handicapped, 1978.

The major refractive visual impairments include myopia, hyperopia, and astigmatism. Each of these impairments is the result of refractive errors due to the shape of the eye and can be corrected with glasses or contact lenses. **Myopia** is nearsightedness. The individual has difficulty seeing distant objects but near or close vision is unaffected. **Hyperopia,** or farsightedness, impairs the individual's ability to see close objects but does not affect seeing distant objects. **Astigmatism** is a refractive error which prevents the light rays from coming to a sharp focus on the retina, causing blurred or distorted vision at any distance.

Cataracts, a clouding of the lens, block the passage of light through the eye, causing blurred vision. Although some cataracts are congenital, their likelihood increases with age. Surgical removal and replacement of the lens results in regained sights in as high as 95 percent of cases (Finkelstein, 1989).

Three visual impairments affecting the muscle functioning of the eyes are strabismus, amblyopia, and nystagmus. These impairments make it difficult for individuals to use their eyes efficiently and effectively. **Strabismus** is the inability to focus on the same object with both eyes. This is a result of the inward or outward deviation of one or both eyes. **Amblyopia** is the reduction or loss of vision in an individual's weaker eye. This loss is due to a lack of use of the eye; no disease is present. **Nystagmus** is the involuntary rapid movement of the eyes. This impairment may be a result of an inner ear disorder or a malfunction of the brain.

Several conditions causing visual impairment involve the retina. **Diabetic retinopathy** is a leading cause of visual impairments, and it has had increased incidence as a result of the increased life span of diabetics. Long-term diabetes changes the tiny blood vessels in the retina. These changes may cause aneurysms in the retinal capillary blood vessels, or it may cause the blood vessels to become engorged with too much blood and burst, or detach the retina. Laser treatment to seal broken vessels or a detached portion of the retina can often slow the course of this impairment.

Macular degeneration, or breakdown, another retinal problem, may come from many causes. Some cases are hereditary, and others are caused by viruses (such as histoplasmosis) or arteriosclerosis. Usually the individual keeps good peripheral vision, though central vision is blurred. Retinal breaks and detachment may occur as part of the aging process or from other causes, with noticeable symptoms such as "floaters," haziness or smokiness, or light flashes in the eye. **Retinitis pigmentosa,** a hereditary disease characterized by degeneration of the retina, involves an abnormal development of excess pigment. With this disorder, the learner's visual field begins to narrow, with a progressive visual loss. The field of vision decreases to the extent that the individual usually becomes legally blind by young adulthood, and gradually loses residual vision thereafter.

Retinopathy of prematurity, which at times advances to a condition known as retrolental fibroplasia, was thought for a long time to be caused by exposing the newborn (and frequently premature) infant to a high concentration of oxygen in an incubator. Presently, researchers disagree regarding the cause of the impairment. An abnormal proliferation of blood vessels in the eye occurs, with the potential for subsequent development of scar tissue and bleeding and detachment of the retina. Blindness may result. Strabismus and myopia are commonly associated with cases in which the blood vessels partially heal. In the large majority of retinopathy of prematurity cases (about 80 percent) the abnormal blood vessels heal completely in the first year of life. In other cases, scarring results in either mild or severe retrolental fibroplasia (Finkelstein, 1989).

Corneal problems may result in either blurred vision or blindness. Scarring or perforation due to corneal ulceration is a major cause of visual impairment throughout the world (Finkelstein, 1989). Ulceration may be caused by streptococcus bacteria, herpes virus, vitamin A deficiency, or other disorders. The cornea may degenerate due to age. When the cornea becomes scarred, hazy, or opaque, or when there is danger of perforation of a corneal ulcer, an ophthalmic surgeon may remove the affected cornea and replace it with a healthy one taken from a donor. Probabilities of rejecting the new cornea are rated by most authorities at 1 to 5 percent (Finkelstein, 1989).

Figure 11.2 presents artworks depicting vision by persons with visual impairments. This artwork offers the reader some understanding of how persons with the various visual impairments see their world. These original artworks are reprinted here with permission from Delta Gamma Center for Children with Visual Impairments.

Visual impairments affect adults, especially older adults, with greater frequency than children. According to the National Society to Prevent Blindness (1983), vision problems impact on 25 percent of the school-age population and one in every twenty children between the ages of 3 and 5 years. Scott (1982) stated that 1 in 500 students are sufficiently visually impaired to affect school functioning. In 1984, Grayson reported the following data on the prevalence of visual impairments: 11.4 million persons in the United States are visually impaired, and 1.4 million persons are severely visually impaired.

Screening and Assessment

Screening for visual impairments usually begins with a measure of visual acuity using the Snellen chart. This chart, presented in Figure 11.3, consists of rows of letters or symbols (Es). The use of letters or symbols is largely dependent on the child's developmental level. The size of the letters on the chart corresponds to normal vision at various distances (15, 20, 30, 40, 50, 70, 100, and 200 feet). The learner, seated 20 feet from the chart, is directed to read the letters in the various rows, and visual acuity is calculated by the examiner. It is important to remember that the Snellen chart is only a measure of visual acuity.

Eye problems are often identified by parents and teachers through observation. Table 11.2 lists several common symptoms to alert parents and teachers about possible visual impairments. Persons observing these symptoms should refer the child for examination by a vision specialist.

Learners with visual impairments are assessed in four general areas: medical, psychological, social, and educational. Medical assessment is conducted by a vision specialist, primarily an ophthalmologist or an optometrist. The ophthalmologist, a medical doctor specializing in disorders of the eye, conducts a physical examination of the eye, prescribes medication and corrective lenses, and performs surgery. The optometrist measures vision and prescribes corrective lenses.

The assessment to be used for educational placement or instructional decision-making purposes includes the evaluation of (a) functional vision; (b) intelligence

Figure 11.2

Right: Mary Solbrig, Our Home, 1985, watercolor on paper, 14 × 21 1/4. Copyright © ART OF THE EYE, and FORECAST PUBLIC ARTWORKS. Macular degeneration is a condition in which the central part of the retina or "macula" undergoes degenerative changes causing loss of vision in that central area of sharpest visual acuity.

Above: Laurel Cazin, As a child, I played hide and seek, as an adult, I hide my fears, 1985, black and white photograph, 22 × 18. Copyright © ART OF THE EYE, and FORECAST PUBLIC ARTWORKS. Diabetic retinopathy occurs as a result of diabetes. Diabetes has damaging effects on almost all the organ systems in the body, including the eyes. Its effect on the eyes is gradual and insidious starting with hemorrhages in the retina and leading to eventual blindness.

Above: Don Pearson, Flamingos, 1984, pastel on paper, 11 1/4 × 15 1/2. Copyright © ART OF THE EYE, and FORECAST PUBLIC ARTWORKS. Retinitis pigmentosa is a condition that is manifested early on by nightblindness and in advanced cases, complete loss of all vision starting with the peripheral or side vision and affecting central vision last. It tends to run in families and is often associated with hearing loss. There is no effective form of treatment known.

Above: Arlene Innmon, (Left) 1. Before Eye Drops with Left Eye; (Right) 2. After Eye Drops with Both Eyes, 1985, acrylic on canvas, two panels each 30 × 24. Copyright © ART OF THE EYE, and FORECAST PUBLIC ARTWORKS.

Glaucoma is a condition of the eyes in which the fluid inside the eye, normally maintained at a pressure no more than that required to give the eye its natural firmness, is subjected to an excessive amount of pressure. As a result, permanent damage occurs to the delicate structures inside the eye and results in loss of vision and sometimes blindness. When children are born with this condition, it is referred to as "congenital glaucoma," and when it comes on during the first few months of life, it is called "infantile glaucoma."

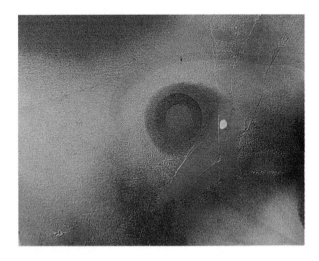

Right: Robert Travis, Visual Jazz-Theban Entry, 1984, acrylic on canvas, 21 1/2 × 27 3/4. Copyright © ART OF THE EYE, and FORECAST PUBLIC ARTWORKS.

Myopia is commonly referred to as nearsightedness, or the ability to focus only on objects near the eye. Hyperopia is farsightedness, or the ability to focus only on objects at a distance.

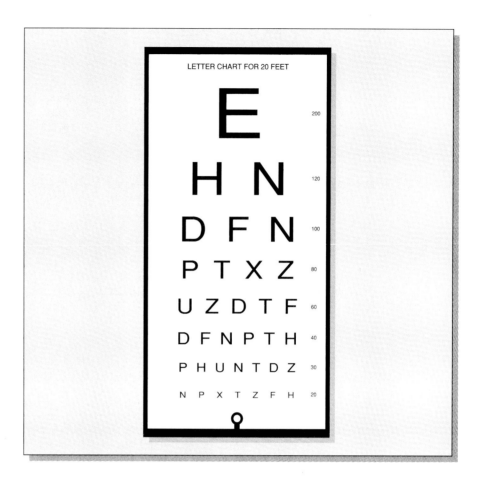

Figure 11.3
The Snellen chart.
Courtesy of the National Society to Prevent Blindness. Reprinted with permission.

and cognitive development; (c) psychomotor skills; and (d) academic achievement. The assessment of academic achievement should include an evaluation of concept development, braille and print reading, listening skills, social interaction and leisure skills, and functional living skills including daily living skills, orientation and mobility, and community and vocational skills (Scholl, 1986).

Due to the relatively small number of children with visual impairments and the variability in their characteristics, examiners find few norm-referenced assessment instruments specifically for this population. In addition, the norms of most existing standardized measures were not developed including samples of learners with visual impairments. However, selected subtests and items that are not visually dependent may be useful for prescriptive purposes. Criterion-referenced instruments are appropriate for use with learners with visual impairments, as are teacher-made checklists, interviews, and direct observation.

Barraga and Morris (1980) developed the Program to Develop Efficiency in Visual Functioning. This instrument assesses visual functioning and offers 150 instructional programs to train functional visual skills. In the area of concept development and readiness skills, several tests are available for application with learners who have visual impairments. Among these is the tactile version of the Boehm Test of Basic Concepts (Caton, 1976). The Peabody Mobility Scales (Harley, Wood, & Merbler, 1981) assesses concept development in body image,

*T*able 11.2   Signs of Possible Eye Trouble in Children

Appearance

Crossed eyes

Red-rimmed, encrusted, or swollen eyelids

Inflamed or watery eyes

Recurring styes (infections) on eyelids

Behavior

Rubs eyes excessively

Shuts or covers one eye

Tilts head or thrusts head forward

Has difficulty with reading or other close-up work; holds objects close to eyes

Blinks more than usual or is irritable when doing close-up work

Is unable to see distant things clearly

Squints eyelids together or frowns

Complaints

Eyes itch, burn, or feel scratchy

Cannot see well

Dizziness, headaches, or nausea following close-up work

Blurred or double vision

Source: Copyrighted by the National Society to Prevent Blindness. Reprinted with permission.

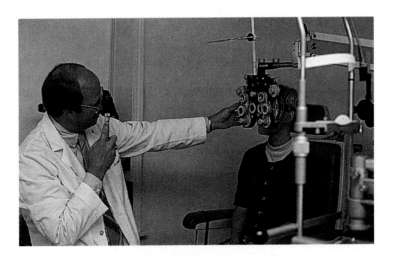

An optometrist measures an individual's visual acuity.

spatial relations, left-right discrimination, sound location, and tactile and olfactory discrimination. Mangold's Development Program of Tactile Perception and Braille Letter Recognition (1977) assess braille readiness skills.

Some achievement and diagnostic instruments are available in braille or large print. Among these are the Stanford Reading Achievement Test, the Stanford Diagnostic Reading Test, the Iowa Test of Basic Skills, and the Key Math Diagnostic Arithmetic Test. There are no adaptive behavior scales specifically designed for learners with visual impairment, but portions of the Vineland Adaptive Behavioral Scales and the AAMD Adaptive Behavior Scales are of assistance.

Providing a stimulating yet safe environment is a challenge for parents of learners with visual impairments.

The accurate assessment of learners with visual impairments is a collaborative venture including medical and educational professionals. As with all learners, emphasis must be placed on the learner's abilities and ways to accommodate the learner so that he or she has educational opportunities similar to those of his or her sighted peers.

Objective Three: To describe the impact of visual impairments on interactions in the home and classroom.

The Impact on Interactions in the Home and Classroom

One of the contextual factors related to young children with visual impairments that impacts on their development is that of the early relationships with caregivers. Simmons and Davidson (1985a) believe that the ways in which the primary caregiver mediates the environment with the child has a direct influence on how the child with a visual impairment learns about the world and thus develops. Problems in mediating the environment with children born with visual impairments challenge parents, as well as affecting the emotional relationship that the baby forms with the primary caregivers. Problems may occur in early bonding between the caregiver and child, contact with professionals, and the child's early exploring (Simmons & Davidson, 1985b). The primary caregivers of toddlers with visual impairments were found to provide highly directive input, offer relatively few descriptions, and initiate a greater proportion of discussion topics than the children, focusing almost exclusively on child-centered topics (Kekelis & Anderson, 1984).

Providing a stimulating, yet safe, home environment for young learners with visual impairments is a consistent challenge for families. Lang and Sullivan (1986) suggest that the environment should be designed to promote greater perception through vision or other senses, be safe, have decreased barriers to movement and integration, and promote increased interactions with various spatial elements, forms, and configurations.

Parents of learners with visual impairments have been found to be weak encouragers, or mere tolerators, or outright discouragers of sports-related experiences for their children, perhaps explaining the limited participation of children with visual impairments in such activities (Nixon, 1988a).

Both social-emotional support and support related to the care and education of the child with visual impairment should be provided to families of learners with

---

Box 11.1

Interacting with Learners With Visual Impairments

- When you initiate an interaction with the student, tell him or her your name. Tell the student when you are walking away.
- Ask the student if she or he needs help. If the student says yes, ask the nature of help needed.
- Serve as a "sighted guide" in new situations: Have the student grasp your arm above the elbow, walk half a step ahead with the student's left shoulder behind your right shoulder. In narrow areas, drop the guiding arm and tell the student to follow behind.
- Use "clock directions" as necessary (objects directly ahead are 12 o'clock, slightly to the right 1 o'clock, etc.).
- When an object is closer or farther away than usual, or if an object may be knocked over, guide the student's hand towards it and describe where it has been placed.
- Point out landmarks when the student first enters a room (i.e., teacher's desk, student's desk, shelves, windows, pencil sharpener). If something has been rearranged, report the new position to the student ■

Sources: American Foundation for the Blind, 1984; Corn & Martinez, 1985.

---

visual impairments. Successful support groups have been found to demonstrate three themes (Nixon, 1988b): (a) the support needs of different parents are met in different ways; (b) parents' perceived need for a support group varies at different stages in a child's life; and (c) professionals play a role in facilitating social support, organizational issues, and professional intervention.

In the Classroom

The placement of learners with visual impairments in the general education classroom may cause increased anxiety on the part of the teacher. The National Federation of the Blind (1991) provides the following guidelines and suggestions:

1. Learners with visual impairments can learn the same concepts that are taught other learners; the only difference is the method of learning.
2. Parents are used to helping their child get accustomed to new places and can provide guidance to the teacher in regards to orienting the child to the environment.
3. Children should be encouraged to join in active play; bumps and bruises last a few days, the negative effects of sheltering last a lifetime.
4. With few verbal additions, the soundtracks of movies and videos are sufficient in communicating information.
5. Knowledge of braille is not essential; a specially trained teacher would provide that instruction.
6. Additional hands-on direction may be necessary, but providing an individualized aide for the child is not necessary.
7. Learners with visual impairments should be disciplined in the same manner as their peers.

Box 11.1 provides a list of specific guidelines for teachers, students, and others interacting with learners with visual impairments in the classroom and school.

Unusual Task: Class Transcribes Braille

By Robert Kelly of the Post-Dispatch Staff

The first bell of the morning at Marissa High School in southeastern St. Clair County alerts nine students to begin working on what look like unusual typewriters.

The machines are, in fact, unusual—and so is the small class.

The students are learning to transcribe Braille texts for the blind on the machines, known as Perkins Braillers. And the class's two instructors say it could be the only high school class in the nation that gives credit to students for learning to produce Braille.

"As far as we have been able to determine—after checking with the Library of Congress, National Library Service for the Blind and with the National Braille Association—the Marissa High School is the only one in the United States teaching a full-credit course in Braille transcribing to high school students," said Victor Hemphill, 64, one of the instructors.

He and his brother, John, 63, are both certified by the Library of Congress to teach Braille transcription.

They started the high school class this fall after being given permission by the Marissa School Board last spring to organize the class. The Hemphill brothers, both widowers and both retired, agreed to volunteer their time at no charge to the school district.

"When we presented it to the School Board last March, it was a unanimous vote" to start the class, Victor Hemphill said. "The enthusiasm was tremendous."

The Hemphills also operate Volunteer Braille Services, Inc., out of a double-wide trailer near their home in Marissa. There, they produce hundreds of texts, documents and books in Braille, using computers that are programmed to print out embossed Braille transcripts.

If the Marissa School Board allows the Hemphills to have classes at the high school again next year, a second-year course in computer Braille transcription will be taught to students who successfully complete this year's class, the brothers said.

Superintendent William A. Gullick of the Marissa School District said he expected the board to react favorably to another year of Braille classes.

"Ultimately, we're hoping that there will be students here who will make careers out of this" Braille transcription, Gullick said. "I think it fits in with the fact that nationwide we're more aware of handicapped people and that they should fit into society."

Marissa High students now will get an elective class credit for passing the Braille transcription course.

The Hemphills hope the Illinois School Code will be amended to make the credit equivalent to a foreign language credit for college entrance requirements.

Victor Hemphill said state Sen. Ralph Dunn, R-DuQuoin, and state Rep. Terry Deering, D-Nashville, are expected to introduce a bill soon in the state Legislature to make the School Code change. Hemphill said a similar bill already has been passed with regard to learning American Sign Language.

Objective Four: To describe ways to mediate the environment for learners with visual impairments.

Mediating the Environment

Preschool

Researchers have suggested some specific ways to mediate the environment for preschoolers. With these strategies, preschoolers with visual impairment can experience many of the same activities as their peers with vision. When working with infants and toddlers with visual impairments, educators should focus on interventions to create, improve, or facilitate connections between children and some aspects of their environment. Davidson and Simmons (1984) describe three stages of each interaction: (a) providing access; (b) stimulating or guiding exploration; and (c) encouraging interpretation of the interaction. Proficiency in major motor areas, such as posture, balance, locomotion, coordination, and basic concepts (such as position in space) are necessary to facilitate orientation and mobility training as the child grows older (Palazesi, 1986). The use of social routines and language play can assist children in language development and independently initiating play activities (Rogow, 1983). Taped books with sound illustrations (that is, accurate

The most common way of learning Braille transcription has been correspondence courses through the Library of Congress, the Hemphills said.

But the need for Braille texts is so great that the brothers were looking for a new way to train transcribers, they said. Their 92-year-old mother, who once was Marissa's town librarian, had suggested that her sons approach the school district about a class.

"I stopped dead in my tracks and said, 'Why not?'" John Hemphill recalled.

Although the brothers were not related to a blind person, both learned Braille transcription years ago as a way to help the blind. Victor Hemphill later met his wife, who was blind, through his work with Braille.

Their interest in Braille has not flagged since both lost their wives. "We do nothing but this; we love it," Victor Hemphill said. "And we finance this out of our own pockets."

They are hoping to raise $135,000 for a permanent building for Volunteer Braille Services. The organization has a not-for-profit status, and donations are tax-deductible.

Donations may be sent to Volunteer Braille Services, Inc., P.O. Box 234, Marissa, Ill. 62257.

The Hemphills' students at the high school are finding the class interesting, but not necessarily easy.

"I've got everything pretty well down, except the spacing and hyphenating," said James Graham, 16, a junior. "It's a little bit harder than what I expected."

Sheryl Jones, 16, also a junior, said she found using the manual Braille transcriber to be simpler than using a regular typewriter. "I can do this pretty easily," she said.

Jones said she hoped to use her Braille transcription abilities later in life. "I learned about this class during the summer, and after reading about Helen Keller I've been interested in helping the blind," she said.

The class also is attended by Amelia Witte, who graduated from high school in 1979. She is the wife of the pastor of Faith Baptist Church in Marissa and had met the Hemphills at the church.

"I wanted to become a transcriber so I could work for them on a more permanent basis," Witte said. "When I get my certification, I'll be able to help them more.

"I'm enjoying it very much," she added. "It's a challenge."

Two full-time teachers at Marissa High also are taking the Braille course and plan to help the Hemphills teach it next year.

"Eventually, I'd like to teach other students Braille at the college level," said one of the teachers, Cinnamon Ernst, who teaches math, science, and social studies at the high school.

Emma Houshmand, who teaches art, said she was excited about learning Braille transcription to "expand my horizons."

Ernst and Houshmand said they were looking forward to teaching the Braille course next year. And Houshmand pointed out another plus to taking the course:

"It's offered right here in the [high school] building, and it's free" ■

Reprinted with permission of *St. Louis Post-Dispatch.*

narrative descriptions of graphics and photos) and tactile books stimulate learners with visual impairments (Larsen & Jorgensen, 1989). In addition, technological aids, such as sonar-sensory devices, can be used with infants and toddlers to help them avoid objects, increase reach, and explore near space (Humphrey, Dodwell, Muir, & Humphrey, 1988).

One particular area of concern when working with toddlers and preschoolers with visual impairments in the least restrictive environment involves problems perceived by the agency or center which in fact may be appropriate behaviors when the visual impairment is considered. Tait and Wolfgang (1984) give the example of mouthing objects, as children with visual impairments do to gain information, which is usually deemed unacceptable behavior for a 3-year-old. Tait and Wolfgang recommend that personnel be instructed in behaviors to be expected in children with visual impairments, ways to overcome passivity, and ways of establishing effective communication. A concern when working with toddlers and preschoolers with visual impairments in the least restrictive environment, that is, in general education classrooms, is staff misperceptions of how children with visual impairments interact with the environment and learn.

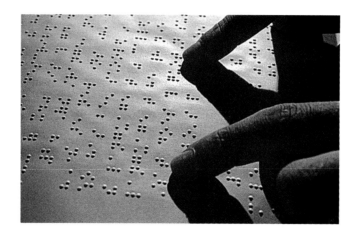

Braille is a private mode of communication for individuals with visual impairments.

School-Age Children

The most frequent services provided to learners with visual impairments in the public schools include professional development services, special intervention services, summer school programs, and books, equipment, and supplies (Harley & English, 1988). Matien and Curry (1987) report three sets of needs that must be addressed if schools are to provide services for learners with visual impairments:

1. Needs that can be met by adapting the curriculum
2. Needs that require changes in teaching method but not curriculum or objective
3. Needs that are the direct result of visual impairments that cause a lack of incidental learning

Specific educational interventions may be needed in the areas of communication, social skills, recreation, and career-oriented skills.

To facilitate the instruction of learners with visual impairments, the school may provide nonoptical aids, tactual aids, and auditory aids. Nonoptical aids include large print texts, bookstands to reduce postural fatigue, yellow acetate to improve the contrast between print and its background, broad-tip marking pens and pencils to increase the readability of print, and dimmer switches to allow the increasing and decreasing of light intensity. Among the tactual aids which can be provided in the classroom for learners with visual impairments are braille books, braillewriters, braille computers, slate and stylus sets, tactual globes and maps, abacus and similar counting frames, measuring devices, and various templates and writing guides. Two of the more essential auditory aids are the cassette tape recorder and recorded books. The tape recorder can be used for taking notes, recording home assignments, listening to assignments, and so on. Recorded or talking books can be used for study and leisure. There is an increasing number and variety of recorded books available through the Library of Congress and other institutions and organizations serving learners who are visually impaired.

Braille

Braille is a tactile system for reading and writing. The braille system is generally used by those whose vision limits their ability to read print. The braille letter is based on six cells, or potential positions for raised points. The braille alphabet is presented in Figure 11.4. There are various levels of braille writing, and in its

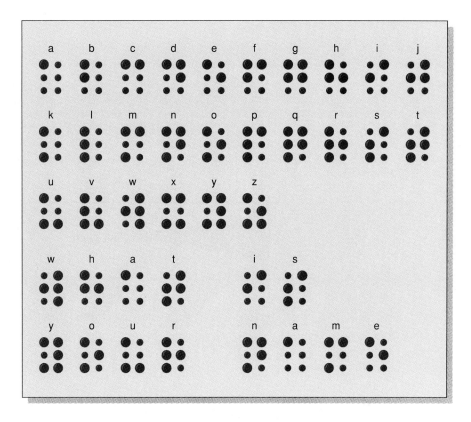

Figure 11.4
The braille alphabet.

simplest form each letter of each word is spelled out, much like the print on this page. In its more complex form, various letters and letter combinations are used to represent whole words. Braille is introduced to students with visual impairments at the same time that sighted students are introduced to reading and writing.

The use of braille has steadily decreased with the use of technological aids and alternative materials (Orlansky & Rhyne, 1981). Ferrante (1986) contends that braille remains an extremely useful tool for learners who are blind because (a) learners can make and read their own notes, giving them a private mode of communication, (b) personal and household objects can be labeled and identified, and (c) braille is concrete and can be reviewed, whereas audio materials cannot.

Braille is written with the aid of a braillewriter or a slate and stylus. The slate is a simple metal frame through which braille dots are punched with a stylus. The learner works from right to left, embossing the paper in the slate. When the paper is turned over, the message can be read by feeling the embossed dots from left to right. The slate and stylus are presented in Figure 11.5.

The braillewriter is used to type braille on paper. The braillewriter has six keys which correspond to the six dots in the braille cell. The keys are punched to emboss the paper. The braillewriter also has a space bar, back spacer, and line spacer. The braillewriter is presented in Figure 11.6.

Mobility and Orientation Training

Both orientation and mobility training are essential to learners with visual impairments and should be integrated throughout the curriculum. The purpose of mobility training is to teach learners to move, with safety, from one location to another.

Figure 11.5
A child using a slate and stylus.
Courtesy of American Printing House
for the Blind.

Orientation training teaches an individual about his or her position in the environment and that position relative to other objects in the environment. Both of these skills are essential to the independence of learners with visual impairments. Spatial-orientation training should be introduced no later than the primary grades (Feoktistove, 1987). Through discussion, modeling, physical prompting, and feedback, children can be taught to increase their gaze direction and sitting behavior, increasing positive perceptions of others towards them (Raver, 1987a; 1987b).

There are several aids available to facilitate orientation and mobility training, including sighted guides, the long cane, guide dogs, and electronic travel aids. Electronic aids are becoming increasingly common as their cost decreases and availability increases. The laser cane sends out three beams ahead of the traveler and allows the detection of obstacles straight ahead, at head height, and downward. The Sonicguide is used with the long cane. It sends out ultrasonic impulses from a transmitter mounted in an eyeglass frame and provides the traveler with information about direction, distance, and surface characteristics of objects. The Mowat sensor is a hand-held device which sends out a narrow beam of ultrasound. The beam reflects back, and the device vibrates and alerts the traveler to obstacles.

Figure 11.6
Examples of students using braillewriters.

Technological aids make print more accessible for some learners. Adaptive devices such as "beep balls" make sports accessible for learners with visual impairments.

Technological Aids

In recent years there have been several technological advances, in addition to those previously discussed in this chapter, which are of great assistance to learners with visual impairments. Among these are the Kurzweil Reader, the Opticon, devices that incorporate synthesized speech, the braille printer, the braille computer, and closed circuit television.

The Kurzweil Reader converts print directly into synthetic speech. When an open book is placed over a glass surface on the reader, a high-resolution camera scans the lines of print. The camera image is processed by a computer, which identifies the words and activates a speech synthesizer. Large community and university libraries frequently have readers available, and a new model for personal use is now available.

The Opticon (Optical to Tactile Converter) translates an image from a small camera into a vibrating image of the same shape that can be felt with the index finger. As the reader moves the camera along the line of print, words are read by feeling the letters.

Synthesized speech has been incorporated into many common items of great value to learners with visual impairments. Synthetic speech is available in watches, clocks, calculators, thermometers, and scales. Synthetic speech incorporated into computers provides the learner with visual impairments with valuable feedback.

The braille printer converts the printed word into braille. Closed circuit television allows for the enlargement of printed materials for learners with visual impairments.

Though strategies to mediate the environment for learners with visual impairments are many, and frequently specialized, teachers are typically supported through resource teachers, occupational therapists, and medical professionals. An effort should be made to present accommodations in as matter-of-fact a way as possible.

Nancy Luomala V-Focus Tilting Room, 1985, mixed media light box with movable panels, 23 1/2 × 12. Copyright © ART OF THE EYE, and FORECAST PUBLIC ARTWORKS. Double vision occurs when the eyes are misaligned and unable to look at the same object with both eyes simultaneously. As a result, objects are seen to be two separate places at the same time (diplopia) or, simultaneously, (confusion of images). Visually, this is an intolerable situation and the brain, is some cases, compensates for this by suppressing the visual information from eye or other.

Objective Five: To describe the impact of visual impairments on participation in the larger social systems—the school, community, and society.

The Impact on Participation in the School, Community, and Society

Children with visual impairments have lower educational aspirations than do children with sight and tend to have occupational expectations that are highly related to the type of training they receive at school (Kahn, 1986).

According to Willis, Groves, and Fuhrman (1979) visual impairments are one of the most difficult of the disabilities for a person without visual impairment to accept. In a review of literature on public attitudes towards people who are blind, Lowenfeld (1980) concluded that the general attitude that individuals who are blind are helpless and dependent persists. However, he suggests that this attitude is changing.

Society as a whole has responded to the unique needs of learners with visual impairments. Every state has free library services for those who, because of a physical or visual defect, cannot read ordinary print books. Special cassette machines and record players to use in listening to the taped or recorded reading materials are also loaned without cost. Recorded, braille, and large print reading matter can be mailed to and from learners with visual impairments free of charge if "Free Matter for the Blind" is written or stamped on the envelope or package (Finkelstein, 1989).

Summary

Because of the large amount of information most people gather through vision, it is often presumed that learners with visual impairments are less capable or have less potential than those who see. However, vision is only one source of information, and learners with visual impairments are as varied as any other group of individuals. Among learners with visual impairments, two large groups emerge: (a) those who are blind and require alternatives to print and visual materials, and (b) those who are partially sighted and may use print and visual materials with the help of large print, optical aids, technological aids, and education in use of residual vision.

Problems in mediating the environment for children born with visual impairments challenge parents as well as teachers. The placement of learners with visual impairments in the general education classroom may cause increased anxiety on the part of the teacher. To facilitate the instruction of learners with visual impairments, the school may provide nonoptical aids, tactual aids, and auditory aids. In addition, both orientation and mobility training are essential to learners with visual impairments and should be integrated throughout the curriculum.

Society has responded positively to the unique needs of learners with visual impairments. Every state has free library services for those who, because of a physical or visual defect, cannot read ordinary print books. Special cassette machines and record players for listening to the taped or recorded reading materials are also loaned without cost.

References

Abang, T. B. (1983). Blindism: Likely causes and preventive measures. *Journal of Visual Impairment and Blindness, 75,* 400–401.

American Foundation for the Blind (1984). *What do you do when you meet a blind person?* New York: Author.

Anderson, D. W. (1984). Mental imagery in congenitally blind children. *Journal of Visual Impairment and Blindness, 76,* 200–210.

Anderson, D., & Fisher, K. F. (1985). Nominal realism in congenitally blind children. *Journal of Visual Impairment and Blindness, 80,* 555–560.

Ashmead, D., Hill, E. W., & Talor, C. A. (1989). Obstacle perception by congenitally blind children. *Perception and Psychophysics, 46,* 425–433.

Barrage, N. C. (1986). Sensory perceptual development. In G. Scholl (Ed.), *Foundations of education for blind and visually handicapped children and youth.* New York: American Foundation for the Blind.

Barrage, N. C., & Morris, J. (1980). *Program to develop efficiency in visual functioning.* Louisville, KY: American Printing House for the Blind.

Bigelow, A. C. (1986). Blind children's concepts of how people see. *Journal of Visual Impairment and Blindness, 82,* 65–68.

Bigelow, A. C. (1987). Early words of blind children. *Journal of Child Language, 14,* 47–55.

Birns, S. L. (1986). Age at onset of blindness and development of space concepts: From topological to projective space. *Journal of Visual Impairment and Blindness, 82,* 577–582.

Caton, H.(1976). *Tactile test of basic concepts.* Louisville, KY: American Printing House for the Blind.

Civelli, L. (1983). Verbalism in young blind children. *Journal of Visual Impairment and Blindness, 77,* 61–63.

Cole, P., Jenkins, P., & Shott, C. T. (1985). Spontaneous expressive control in blind and sighted children. *Child Development, 60,* 683–688.

Corn, A. L., & Martinez, I. (1985). *When you have a visually handicapped child in your classroom: Suggestions for teachers.* New York: American Foundation for the Blind.

Davidson, I. F., & Simmons, J. N. (1984). Mediating the environment for young blind children: A conceptualization. *Journal of Visual Impairment and Blindness, 74,* 251–255.

Delta Gamma Foundation (1991). *Art of the eye: An exhibition on vision.* St. Louis, MO: Author.

Dodds, A. C., & Carter, D. D. (1983). Memory for movement in blind children: The role of previous visual experience. *Journal of Motor Behavior, 14,* 343–352.

Erin, J. N. (1986). Frequencies and types of questions in the language of visually impaired children. *Journal of Visual Impairment and Blindness, 80,* 670–674.

Erin, J. N. (1990). Language samples from visually impaired four-and five-year-olds. *Journal of Childhood Communication Disorders, 13,* 181–191.

Federal Register (1977). 42 (163), 42659–42688.

Feoktistove, V. (1987). Improvement of space orientation training of junior blind school-children. *Defektologiya,* No. 4, 60–64.

Ferrante, O. (1986). Why blind children should learn braille. *Journal of Visual Impairment and Blindness, 80,* 594.

Finkelstein, D. (1989). *Blindness and disorders of the eye.* Baltimore, MD: The National Federation for the Blind.

Grayson, D. (1984). *Facts about blindness and visual impairment.* New York: American Foundation for the Blind.

Harley, R. R., & English, W. H. (1988). Support services for visually impaired children in local day schools: Residential schools as a resource. *Journal of Visual Impairment and Blindness, 83,* 405–410.

Harley, R. K., Wood, T. A., & Merbler, J. B. (1981). *Peabody mobility scales.* Chicago: Stoelting.

Hirshoren, H., & Schnittjer, C. J. (1983). Behavior problems in blind children and youth: A prevalence study. *Psychology in the Schools, 20,* 197–210.

Humphrey, S., Dodwell, P., Muir, D. W., & Humphrey, D. E. (1988). Can blind infants and children use sonar sensory aids? *Canadian Journal of Psychology, 42* (2), 94–119.

Ittyerah, M., & Samarapungaven, A. (1989). The performance of congenitally blind children in cognitive developmental tasks. *British Journal of Developmental Psychology, 7* (2), 125–139.

Jan, J., Farrell, K., Wong, P. K., & McCormick, A. W. (1986). Eye and head movements of visually impaired children. *Developmental Medicine and Child Neurology, 28,* 286–293.

Kahn, M. N. (1986). Educational aspirations and occupational expectations of blind and normal children. *Perspectives in Psychological Research, 5* (2), 25–27.

Kekelis, L., & Anderson, E. (1984). Family communication styles and language development. *Journal of Visual Impairment and Blindness, 78,* 54–55.

Lang, M. A., & Sullivan, C. (1986). Adapting home environments for visually impaired and blind children. *Children's Environments Quarterly, 3* (1), 50–54.

Larsen, S., & Jorgensen, N. (1989). Talking books for preschool children. *Journal of Visual Impairment and Blindness, 83,* 118–119.

Leonhardt, M. (1990). Stereotypies: A preliminary report on mannerisms and blindisms. *Journal of Visual Impairment and Blindness, 84,* 216–218.

Mangold, S. S. (1977). *The Mangold developmental program of tactile perception and Braille letter recognition.* Castro Valley, CA: Exceptional Teaching Aids.

Matien, P., & Curry, S. (1987). In support of specialized programs for blind and visually impaired children. *Journal of Visual Impairment and Blindness, 81,* 7–13.

McConachie, H. (1990). Early language development and severe visual impairment. *Child Care, Health, and Development, 10,* 55–61.

Mereira, L. (1990). Spatial concepts and balance performance: Motor learning in blind and visually impaired children. *Journal of Visual Impairment and Blindness, 84,* 100–114.

National Association for the Visually Handicapped (1978). *The eye and your vision.* New York: Author.

National Federation of the Blind (1991). *The blind child in the regular preschool program.* Baltimore, MD: Author.

National Society to Prevent Blindness (1983). Home eye test gets a rousing send off. *Prevent Blindness News, 8* (1), 3.

Nixon, H. L. (1988a). Getting over the worry hurdle: Parental encouragement and the sports involvement of visually impaired children and youth. *Adapted Physical Activity Quarterly, 5,* 26–43.

Nixon, H. L. (1988b). Reassessing support groups for parents of visually impaired children. *Journal of Visual Impairment and Blindness, 82,* 271–278.

Orlansky, M. D., & Rhyne, J. M. (1981). Special adaptations necessitated by visual impairments. In J. M. Kauffman & D. Hallahan (Eds.), *Handbook of special education* (pp. 552–575). Englewood Cliffs, NJ: Prentice Hall.

Orwin, L. (1984). Language for absent things: Learning from visually handicapped children. *Topics in Language Disorders, 4* (4), 24–37.

Palazesi, M. A. (1986). The need for motor development programs for visually impaired preschoolers. *Journal of Visual Impairment and Blindness, 80,* 573–576.

Parsons, S. (1987). Locus of control and adaptive behavior in visually impaired children. *Journal of Visual Impairment and Blindness, 81,* 420–432.

Raver, S. (1987a). Training blind children to employ appropriate gaze direction and sitting behavior during conversation. *Education and Treatment of Children, 10,* 237–246.

Raver, S. (1987b). Training gaze direction in blind children: Attitude effects on the sighted. *Remedial and Special Education, 3* (5), 40–45.

Raver-Lampman, S. (1990). Effect of gaze direction on evaluation of visually impaired children by informed respondents. *Journal of Visual Impairment and Blindness, 84,* 87–90.

Rogow, S. (1983). Social routines and language play: Developing communication responses in developmentally delayed blind children. *Journal of Visual Impairment and Blindness, 77,* 1–4.

Rouse, M. W., & Ryan, J. B. (1984). Teacher's guide to vision problems. *The Reading Teacher, 38,* 306–317.

Scholl, G. T. (1986). What does it mean to be blind? In G. T. Scholl (Ed.), *Foundations of education for the blind and visually handicapped children and youth* (pp. 23–34). New York: American Foundation for the Blind.

Schwartz, T. (1983). Social cognition in visually impaired and sighted children. *Journal of Visual Impairment and Blindness, 77,* 377–381.

Scott, E. P. (1982). *Your visually impaired student: A guide for teachers.* Baltimore, MD: University Park Press.

Simmons, J. N., & Davidson, I. F. (1985a). Mediating the environment: A case study approach. *Child Care, Health, and Development, 11,* 185–207.

Simmons, J. N., & Davidson, I. F. (1985b). Perspectives on intervention with young blind children. *Child Care, Health, and Development, 11,* 183–185.

Tait, M. C., & Wolfgang, C. (1984). Mainstreaming a blind child: Problems perceived in a preschool day care program. *Early Child Development and Care, 13,* 135–137.

Ubiakor, F., & Otile, S. (1990). The self-concepts of visually impaired and normally sighted middle school children. *Journal of Psychology, 124,* 190–200.

U.S. Department of Education (1990). *Twelfth annual report to congress on the implementation of the Education of the Handicapped Act.* Washington, DC: Author.

Van Hasselt, V. (1983). Social adaptation in the blind. *Clinical Psychology Review, 3,* 87–102.

Van Hasselt, V. (1985). A behavioral analytic model for assessing social skills in blind adolescents. *Behavior Research and Therapy, 23,* 355–405.

Van Hasselt, V., Kazdin, A., & Hersen, M. (1986). Assessment of problem behavior in visually handicapped adolescents. *Journal of Clinical Child Psychology, 15,* 134–141.

Wilhelm, J. G. (1989). Fear and anxiety in low vision and totally blind children. *Education of the Visually Handicapped, 20,* 163–172.

Willis, D. J., Groves, C., & Fuhrman, W. (1979). Visually disabled children and youth. In B. M. Swanson & D. J. Willis (Eds.), *Understanding exceptional children and youth: An introduction to special education.* Chicago: Rand McNally.

12
Learners with Hearing Impairments

*O*bjectives

After completing this chapter, you will be able to:

1. describe the personal characteristics of persons with hearing impairments.
2. describe the identification and evaluation of learners with hearing impairments.
3. describe the impact of hearing impairment on interactions in the home and classroom.
4. describe ways to mediate the environment for learners with hearing impairments.
5. describe the impact of hearing impairment on participation in larger systems— the school, community, and society.

*K*ey Words and Phrases

American Sign Language (ASL)	interpreters
amplification	in-the-ear (ITE) hearing aids
behind-the-ear (BTE) hearing aids	otitis media
conductive loss	postlingual hearing impairment
cued speech	pragmatics
deaf	prelingual hearing impairment
fluctuating conductive hearing impairment	sensorineural loss
	speech audiometry
FM systems	speechreading
hard of hearing	TDD
hearing impairment	TTY
immitance	tympanogram

*D*EAFNESS, A HEARING LOSS, IS INVISIBLE. ALMOST NOTHING ABOUT ME ALERTS THE HEARING WORLD THAT something is amiss in my communication system. I say "almost" because there are actually two noticeable differences about me: I wear two hearing aids and I am always accompanied by a dog . . . I am not—and there are many like me—one of the aggressive militant disabled. I did not fight for my right to each job. I slunk away, eventually selecting a solitary style of employment based on another skill, writing. My selection is suitable to my temperament and my life as a writer, but such selectivity is hardly every disabled person's wish or choice. Most want to be out there, in there, involved, with people, part of the normality, that nine-to-five life that is sometimes a complaint but *always* the prerogative of anyone else.* ■

*From "Who Is Handicapped? Employees or Employers?" by Hannah Merker. Copyright ©1990 Hannah Merker. Excerpted by permission.

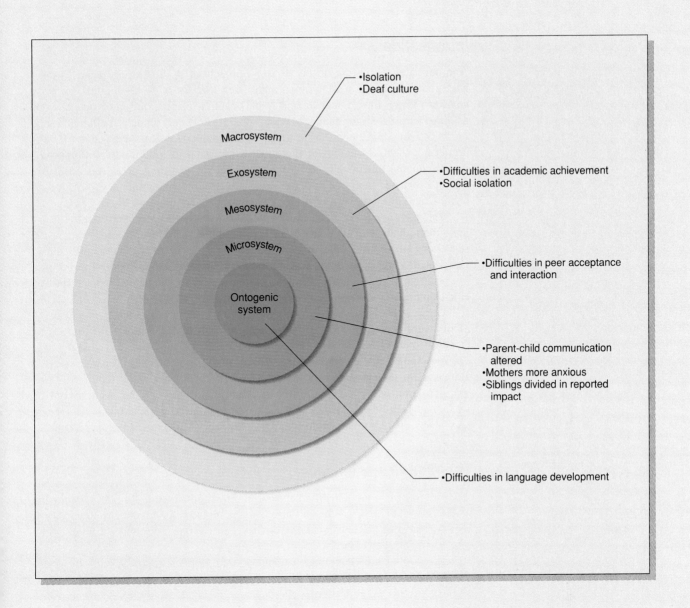

•Isolation
•Deaf culture

Macrosystem

Exosystem

•Difficulties in academic achievement
•Social isolation

Mesosystem

Microsystem

•Difficulties in peer acceptance
and interaction

Ontogenic
system

•Parent-child communication
altered
•Mothers more anxious
•Siblings divided in reported
impact

•Difficulties in language development

Introduction

Approximately 8 million of the 39.5 million school children in the United States have some degree of hearing impairment (Berg, 1987). In describing this group of children, Wray, Flexer, and Ireland (1988) caution that hearing impairment is not an either/or proposition; rather, hearing impairment occurs along a continuum ranging from being mildly hard of hearing to profoundly deaf. Ross and Calvert (1984) argue that 92 to 94 percnt of the entire population of individuals with hearing impairment are functionally hard of hearing and not deaf. In general, it is estimated that in every one thousand children, one is deaf, three or four are severely hard of hearing, and thirty have an educationally significant hearing loss (Ross, 1982).

The generic term **hearing impairment** includes both "deaf" and "hard of hearing." Individuals who are **deaf** have a hearing impairment that precludes successful processing of linguistic information through hearing with or without amplification. **Hard of hearing** individuals have hearing that is adequate for successful processing of linguistic information through hearing with amplification (Report of the Ad Hoc Committee to Define Deaf and Hard of Hearing, 1975).

During the 1990–91 school year, 59,312 learners with hearing impairments were served under the Individuals with Disabilities Education Act (U.S. Department of Education, 1992). Of these, about 27 percent were served in the regular classroom, 18.2 percent in the resource room, 31.7 percent in separate classes, 10.6 percent in separate schools, and 12.3 percent in residential facilities. Only more children who are visually impaired and deaf-blind children were served in residential facilities. Over half of the learners with hearing impairments completed secondary school with a diploma (U.S. Department of Education, 1990).

Objective One: To describe the personal characteristics of learners with hearing impairments.

Personal Characteristics

The groups of learners identified as hearing impaired are quite diverse. Any aspect of the personal characteristics of these learners involves the variations in their hearing mechanisms. An understanding of these variations can provide further insight into the personal characteristics of these learners.

A report of the Conference of Educational Administrators Serving the Deaf (Brill, MacNeil, & Newman, 1986) provided clarification of three important terms associated with the education of the deaf: prelingual hearing impairment, postlingual hearing impairment, and sensorineural loss. **Prelingual hearing impairment** is present at birth or occurs before the individual develops speech or language, which is generally at about 2 years of age. These learners require specialized services, which, as will be discussed in this chapter, require special curriculum and equipment. An ever increasing number of educational programs serve children with prelingual hearing impairment from birth to 3 years of age.

Postlingual hearing impairment occurs after the child has developed speech or language. Due to medical advances, the number of children with postlingual deafness is relatively small—approximately 5 to 10 percent of the hearing impaired population. These learners have educational needs that differ significantly from children with prelingual hearing impairment. They need assistance to maintain voice variations and idioms.

Sensorineural loss, which may occur at any time, is a result of a physical impairment of the inner ear, the peripheral hearing nerve, or other parts of the auditory system leading to the cortex of the brain and is, at present, irreversible.

Davis (1988) proposes several assumptions regarding the personal characteristics of learners with hearing impairments. First, students' hearing losses result in speech and language challenges of varying degrees, which in turn affect either academic achievement, social adjustment, or both. Second, schools present communicative demands that are particularly difficult for learners with hearing impairments. Communication is primarily verbal, persons speaking frequently do not face the person they wish to communicate with, schedules are maintained by bells, and audio and audiovisual aids are used frequently. In addition, if the unique needs of these students are not met, poor self-esteem and social isolation may occur.

Kretschmer and Kretschmer (1978) remind us that variations in communication development among learners with hearing impairments may be due to the restrictions placed on these individuals by their environments rather than the cognitive functions that result from their hearing impairments. Kretschmer and Kretschmer pose several possible scenarios regarding the communication development of persons with hearing impairments:

1. Language may be delayed because of a lack of cognitive experiences due to the hearing impairment.
2. The hearing impairment and the use of other means of communication (gestures, signs, finger spelling) may cause differences in development between learners who hear and those whose hearing is limited.
3. The language of learners with hearing impairments is dialectical in nature because English is a second language.
4. Any combination of the essentials of the three preceding scenarios may occur.

Any description of the characteristics of learners with hearing impairments must address the two groups of children involved: those who are hard of hearing and those with profound hearing impairments. In reference to communication, learners with profound hearing impairments have problems with the sound system of language, articulation, changes in pitch, and voicing. The speech of hard-of-hearing children is less affected in these areas. Though voice problems are less frequent, learners with mild hearing impairments have many misarticulations, consisting generally of consonant substitutions and distortions of sounds. Unlike learners with profound hearing impairments, hard-of-hearing learners do not misarticulate vowels, and their speech is typically intelligible.

In a study by Wolk and Schildroth (1986), teachers reported that 23 percent of the students with hearing impairments had unintelligible speech, 22 percent had speech that was marginally intelligible, and 10 percent were unwilling to speak in public. According to the teachers, 75 percent of the learners who were profoundly deaf did not have intelligible speech, and 14 percent of the learners with less severe hearing impairments had nonintelligible speech. Musselman (1990) found that most children with losses of 70–89 decibels developed some intelligible speech, those with losses of 90–104 decibels varied in the intelligibility of their speech, and few learners with losses greater than 105 decibels developed intelligible speech.

Vocabulary skills also differentiate learners with hearing impairments from individuals who can hear (Davis, 1988). On the average, children with hearing impairments seem to be delayed 2 to 3 years in vocabulary development. This may occur because learners with hearing impairments do not learn as much incidental vocabulary as do individuals without hearing impairments. In addition, they do not learn the slang use of words necessary for conversations among classmates and friends. Learners with hearing impairments, because they do not hear or do not hear well, are unable to use verbal models effectively and are frequently unable to profit from feedback offered by others in the environment.

Any degree of hearing impairment can put a learner at risk for reduced academic achievement (Davis, 1988). In a survey of 376 learners with hearing impairments in Iowa, Davis and associates (1982, 1986) reported that over a fourth of these children had repeated at least one grade. In addition, they were less accepted by peers, tended to be more aggressive, and had difficulty in making friends.

We must recognize that social adjustment is communication dependent. Social adjustment is grounded in interpersonal interactions such as talking, laughing, joking, and discussing. Learners with hearing impairments are challenged in environments such as their classroom, school, and community, all of which make a variety of communicative demands.

Young children with hearing impairments have been reported by their mothers to have more difficult temperaments, but no more behavior problems than young children who hear. Teachers also rated learners with hearing impairments as less well adjusted and more anxious than their peers without hearing impairments (Prior, Glazner, Sanson, & Debelle, 1988).

Children with hearing impairments have been found to be generally less assertive than their hearing peers (Macklin & Matson, 1985). They have been found to be more fearful of the unknown, injury, and small animals than are their hearing peers (King, Mulhall, & Gullone, 1989). Using a self-report procedure, Maxon, Brackett, and van der Berg (1991) found that learners with hearing impairments perceived themselves differently than did their hearing peers in verbal expression of emotions, verbal aggression, physical aggression, and interpersonal interaction. They suggested that these differences may be addressed through specific programming that emphasizes the language involved in appropriate interactions, as well as strategies for coping with anger and frustration through language.

Research findings on the self-concept of learners with hearing impairments are difficult to interpret because of the use of assessment instruments or procedures designed for hearing learners, which are inappropriate for those who are hearing impaired (Garrison & Tesch, 1978). The language demands in tests of self-esteem tends to lower the scores of learners who are hearing impaired. However, in one commonly used measure of self-esteem, Koelle and Convey (1982) found the scores of learners with hearing impairments to be inflated. Oblowitz, Green, and Heyns (1991) responded by developing a self-concept scale specific to learners with hearing impairments which appears sufficiently reliable and valid for further research. Nonverbal measures, such as drawing of the human figure, demonstrate comparable projective drawings between learners with hearing impairment and learners without hearing impairment (Cates, 1991).

Identification and Evaluation

Objective Two: To describe the identification and evaluation of learners with hearing impairments.

Public Law 94–142 defined deaf as "having a hearing impairment which is so severe that the child is impaired in processing linguistics information through hearing, with or without amplification, which adversely affects educational performance." Hard of hearing means "a hearing impairment, whether permanent or fluctuating, which adversely affects a child's educational performance but which is not included under the definition of deaf" (*Federal Register*, 1977, 300.5).

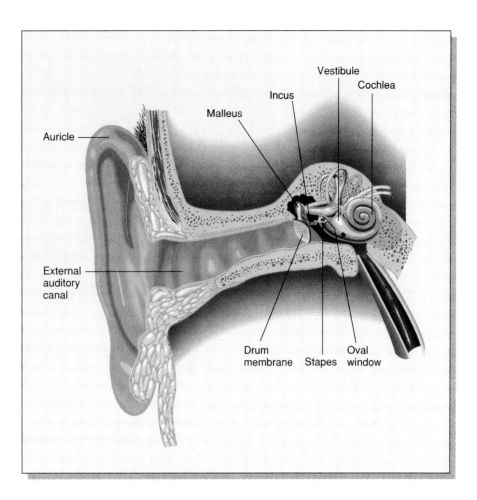

Figure 12.1
Internal and external structure of the ear.

Types and Degrees of Hearing Impairment

The primary types of hearing impairment are described by the location of the problem in the hearing mechanism. The ear is composed of three parts: the outer ear, the middle ear, and the inner ear. The outer ear includes the auricle (that part of the ear which protrudes from the side of the head, the only part of the hearing mechanism that is visible) and the external auditory canal. The auricle collects sound waves from the environment and channels them into the external auditory canal. The external auditory canal carries the sounds from the auricle to the tympanic membrane (the eardrum), which marks the beginning of the inner ear (see Figure 12.1).

Besides the tympanic membrane, the middle ear is composed of three small bones within an air-filled chamber. These bones, or ossicles, are called the hammer (malleus), anvil (incus), and stirrup (stapes). These bones conduct vibrations from the eardrum to the oval window, which connects the middle ear to the inner ear. **Conductive loss** is caused by impairment of the outer and middle ear that prevents the transfer of sound to the inner ear.

The two major components of the inner ear are the vestibular mechanism and the cochlea. The vestibular mechanism is concerned with the sense of balance. It is extremely sensitive to movement. The function of the vestibular mechanism is to

The goal of audiological evaluation is to determine the type and degree of hearing loss.

transmit information to the brain which enables an individual to determine his or her position in space, sense of balance, as well as acceleration and deceleration.

The cochlea is a crucial element of the ear. It is responsible for converting the mechanical energy received from the middle ear into electrical signals that are transmitted to the brain. The movement of the fluid in the cochlea stimulates hairlike cells. These cells are part of the auditory nerve. Sensorineural hearing impairments are associated with damage to the auditory nerve or the inner ear.

When the hearing mechanism is working efficiently, it converts sound waves to mechanical energy, then to fluid or hydraulic energy, and, finally, to electrical energy which stimulates the brain and thus permits the individual to hear.

To understand the evaluation of hearing, it is necessary to understand the concepts of sound, frequency, and loudness. Sound is produced by vibrations of molecules, through air, water, or another medium. Sound frequency is the number of variations of the medium per second. High frequencies are perceived through the hearing mechanism as high pitch, low frequencies as low pitch. Hertz (Hz) is the accepted unit of measurement for frequency. Individuals with normal hearing perceive sounds in the range of 20 Hz to 20,000 Hz.

Loudness or the intensity of sound is measured in decibels (dB). Loud sounds have a high dB measurement; soft sounds have a low dB measurement. A decibel range of 0 to 120 is used to measure how well an individual hears at different frequencies. A dB level of 125 or louder is generally painful to a human being. A normal hearing individual should hear sounds at the 0dB level.

Determining the type and degree of hearing loss is the first goal of audiologic evaluation (Maddell, 1990a). A basic audiologic evaluation includes air and bone conduction testing. Air conduction testing (the tones are presented through the regular channels which sound waves use to enter the hearing system) reveals the degree of hearing loss. Thresholds of decibel hearing level and designations for the severity of hearing loss are presented on Table 12.1.

The type of hearing loss is determined by the relationship between test results obtained with earphones (air conduction) and with a vibrator placed on the mastoid bone outside the ear (bone conduction). If there is a match between the bone conduction and air conduction measures, the hearing loss is considered to be sensorineural,

Table 12.1   Hearing Levels and Severity of Hearing Loss

Decibel Hearing Level	Type of Hearing Loss
25–50 decibels	Mild
40–55 decibels	Moderate
55–70 decibels	Moderate-Severe
70–90 decibels	Severe
> 90 decibels	Profound

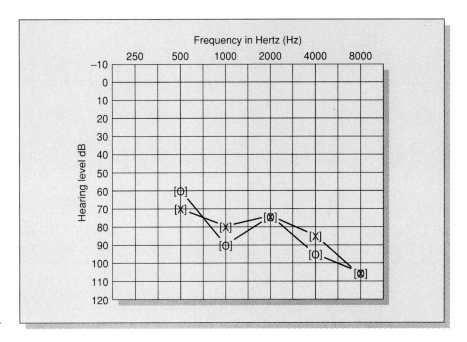

Figure 12.2
An audiogram for sensorineural hearing loss.

that is, caused by damage to the inner ear. If the bone conduction test is normal and the air conduction test indicates a hearing loss, then the loss is conductive, that is caused by damage to or blockage of the outer or middle ear. A mixed hearing loss, with both conductive and sensorineural losses, is also possible.

Many conductive hearing losses are treatable medically; most sensorineural losses are not. For this reason, medical evaluation is an important component of a comprehensive hearing evaluation (Maddell, 1990a).

Hearing levels are depicted on a chart called an audiogram. There are several conventions used in audiograms. For example, an "x" is used to depict air conduction levels in the left ear and an "o" is used to depict air conduction levels in the right ear. The intensity of sound is designated by decibels on one axis, and the pitch or frequency of the sounds, measured by Hertz, are along the horizontal axis. Levels which an individual hears with bone conduction are indicated with a "<" for the left ear and a ">" for the right ear. Air and bone conduction measures at the same level indicate a sensorineural loss, as depicted in Figure 12.2. The differences between air and bone conduction levels representative of a conductive loss are depicted in Figure 12.3.

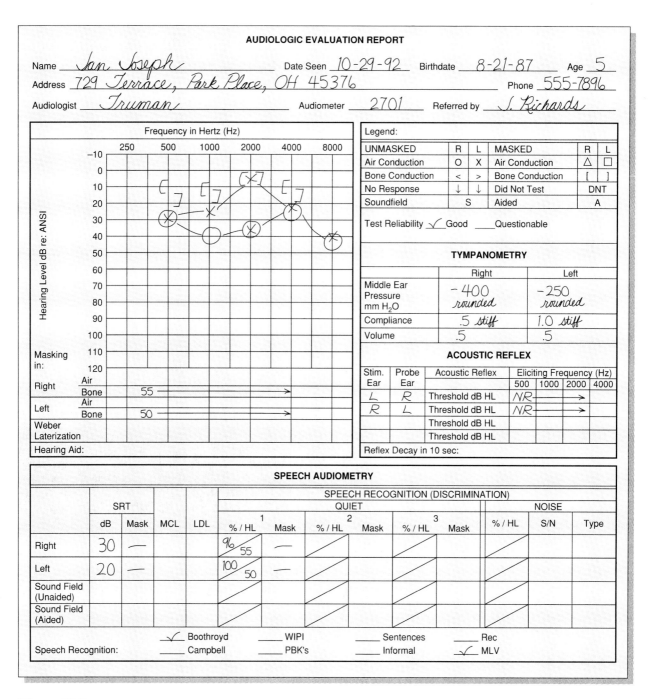

Figure 12.3

An audiologic evaluation report for conductive hearing loss.

One particularly challenging group of children are those with **fluctuating conductive hearing impairment.** The most common fluctuating conductive hearing loss is caused by **otitis media,** or middle ear infections (Webster, Saunders, & Bamford, 1984). Webster and associates report that fluctuating conductive hearing impairments have a serious effect on verbal-process and language dependent skills. Persistent otitis media has been related to underachievement in school. Webster and associates urge educators to give middle ear infection careful consideration as a contributing factor in children's developmental and learning difficulties.

Two additional assessments which are frequently used during an audiologic evaluation include (a) immitance, and (b) speech audiometry tests. **Immitance** testing includes the administering of a **tympanogram,** which measures the mobility of the eardrum, and acoustic reflex testing, which is used to confirm pure tone test results. Essentially, immitance testing provides information about the way in which the middle ear is working. **Speech audiometry,** the second test, determines how much speech an individual is able to understand. Maddell (1990b) suggests obtaining speech audiometry test results (a) at a low conversational level in a quiet environment, and (b) in an environment with competing noise. These test results are useful for educational programming and determining how well a learner may function in the classroom.

Communication Assessment

The second area of evaluation for learners with hearing impairments is communication skills. In 1978, Kretschmer and Kretschmer advocated the use of informal grammatical samplings as a component of the language evaluation for children with hearing impairments. Since that time, evidence has accumulated for the inclusion of all aspects of communication in context during assessment (Kretschmer & Kretschmer, 1988). This application of **pragmatics,** defined by Duchan (1988) as "the study of how linguistic, situational, or social contexts affect language use," has significantly changed the assessment process for learners with hearing impairments. According to Duchan, the evaluation of pragmatics includes (a) functional analysis (the intent of the communication); (b) conversational assessment (conversational turn taking, topic maintenance, and repairing communicative breakdowns); (c) conversational fine tuning (the style of communication); and (d) the nature of the individual's discourse.

Both formal and informal strategies may be used to assess an individual's language. Many agencies and schools may designate specific tests for use in evaluation. These tests, however, may not provide a comprehensive sampling of the child's language skills, may not be well standardized, may have very few items in each area to be used for teaching applications, or may not reflect current theoretical models of language (Moeller, 1988).

Ying (1990) argues that the ultimate purpose of evaluating the communication of learners with hearing impairments is to determine the learner's appropriate educational placement. For this reason, assessment must be made of the communicative demands placed on students in each potential placement. Individualizing, she argues, is necessary in selecting appropriate testing modifications, in interpreting the results obtained, and in designing programs.

The assessment of children with hearing impairments is a particular challenge. The pragmatic errors these children make bias assessment to such an extent that Ray (1989) urges that a multidisciplinary team approach should be in place during all assessment and evaluation activities with children with hearing impairments.

Objective Three: To describe the impact of hearing impairment on interactions in the home and classroom.

The Impact on Interactions in the Home and Classroom

Interactions in the Home

The learner's hearing impairment may have a significant impact on parent-child communication. Kenworthy (1986) found that the presence of a hearing impairment in a learner substantially alters the linguistic input the parent provides both at the interaction and the conversational level. Nienhuys, Horsborough, & Cross (1985) also found differences in the interactions of mothers and their preschool children with hearing impairments. Mothers of children with hearing impairments were found to address their children with verbalizations with lower cognitive complexity issues, and the mothers had more than twice the initiations than their children. All of the communication between parent and child, in one study, was imbedded in activities, with very little purely social communication observed (Brown, Maxwell, & Browning, 1990).

Further research has shown that these findings regarding mother-child interactions may, in fact, be related to the contexts in which they occur. Plapinger and Kretschmer (1991) reaffirm the didactic style of mother-child interaction as reported by other researchers in a clinic. In the home, however, mothers were very interactive and used dialogue more similar to that of mothers and hearing children. They suggest that without viewing interactions in a variety of contexts, parents of learners with hearing impairments may be viewed as nonfacilitative of their child's language development. Viewing interactions in a variety of contexts, over an extended period of time, may demonstrate that parents use a wide range of interaction styles with their children.

Parents of learners who are hearing impaired feel that their counseling needs regarding their child's hearing loss are not met (Martin et al., 1987). Parents feel the need for greater communication and a continuing relationship with the audiologist. This need for communication was also reported by McNeil and Chabessol (1984), who found that both mothers and fathers felt ignored during the diagnostic period and wanted greater and deeper communication with the professionals involved.

The mothers of children with hearing impairments were found to have elevated levels of anxiety, depression, and overall problem scores when compared with mothers of children with normal hearing (Prior, Glazner, Sanson, & Debelle, 1988).

In her study of the siblings of students with hearing impairment, Israelite (1985) found a mixed pattern of sibling reaction. The siblings were divided in their opinions as to the effects of the child with hearing impairments on relationships with their parents and in feelings of jealousy. The siblings who expressed positive feelings about their brother or sister with a hearing impairment tended to express positive opinions with regard to family relationships and social relationships. Conversely, siblings who were negative remained negative in all topics explored throughout the interview.

Interactions in the Classroom

Students spend at least 45 percent of the school day engaged in listening activities (Berg, 1987). Hearing is essential to classroom performance. The visual cues in the environment are not sufficient to allow learners with hearing impairments to compensate for their inability to hear. Though learners with hearing impairments may learn to speechread, many words look alike on the lips and cannot be discriminated without some kind of auditory information (Boothroyd, 1978).

Though children with hearing impairments may recognize that hearing loss is the cause of their problems in communicating in the classroom, they tend to not want other children to know they are hearing impaired (Davis, 1988). To avoid

The development of speechreading requires learners to follow the cues related to the message.

recognition, they may not ask for clarification, request changes in the classroom setting such as a better seat, or discuss adjustments in requirements with the teacher. In some situations, social isolation occurs because other children may find the learner with a hearing impairment's communication attempts either difficult to understand or slightly embarrassing.

Objective Four: To describe ways to mediate the environment for learners with hearing impairments.

Mediating the Environment

There appears to be no consensus in the field as to where and how to educate individuals with hearing impairments. In a national survey of 576 programs, King (1984) found that many educators combined different parts of various language instruction approaches rather than adhering closely to any single method. The type of symbol system to use and how to use the symbol systems varied greatly among the programs. The three most common methods of instruction and communication include (a) oral communication, (b) total communication, which involves simultaneous signing and oral communication, and (c) American Sign Language.

Northcott (1980b) states that the priority in the education of learners with hearing impairments is to ensure that all learners with usable hearing have the maximum opportunity to develop listening and oral skills, with the maximum opportunity to speak for themselves, to be understood, and to participate actively in

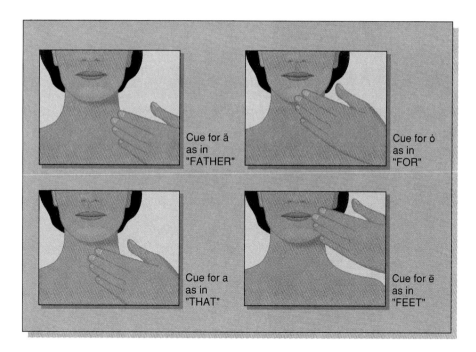

Figure 12.4
Cued speech (vowels).

decisions regarding their own lives and goals. It is important to support students in the use of their residual hearing. Children typically begin wearing hearing aids as early as possible to increase an awareness of environmental sounds (Sanders, 1982).

The development of **speechreading** requires learners to follow all the cues related to the message. Not only do many sounds vary in their visibility when spoken, but speech movements vary from individual to individual, making speechreading an extremely complex skill.

Cued speech is sometimes used to augment speechreading, helping the student to differentiate sounds that appear similar on the speaker's face when spoken (Nicholls & Ling, 1982). **Cued speech** is the use of hand cues which, together with speechreading, permit the visual identification of sounds. Consonants are represented by eight hand configurations, vowels by four configurations, and diphthongs represented by gliding from beginning to ending vowels (see Figures 12.4 and 12.5). Communicating through cued speech transmits a visual form of spoken sound patterns. Accuracy rates in reception of greater than 95 percent can be achieved by adding cued speech to speechreading.

Most parents initially select oral communication programs for their children (Northcott, 1980a). Before the mid-1960s, oral programs were the most prevalent programs, and, in many cases, signing was prohibited (Moores & Maestas y Moores, 1981). During this time, total communication programs emerged, with the development of a system called "signed English." In the signed English communication systems, the individual signs an equivalent for each word and diacritical marking.

American Sign Language (ASL) is a unique language which is the most common native language of deaf adults (Wilbur, 1979). ASL is not signed English, nor is it derived from spoken language, nor is it the same as the British sign language system. ASL word order is dissimilar from that of spoken English, and frequently

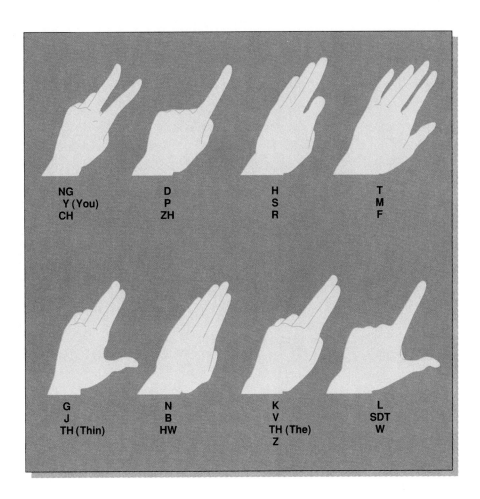

Figure 12.5
Cued speech (consonants).

signs are used that indicate concepts or groups of words rather than individual words. Variations in ASL, divergent signs, and "homemade" signs are used when the appropriate ASL sign is unknown, difficult to form, or nonexistent (Lewis, 1986). The American manual alphabet, which allows individuals to "fingerspell" words, is depicted in Figure 12.6.

In the middle of the manual communication continuum is what is commonly called Pidgin Sign English, which uses ASL signs in an English word order. This Pidgin Sign English (or PSE) may have more English characteristics in some settings, and more ASL characteristics in others. Typically, more fingerspelling is used in PSE than in ASL (Kyle and Woll, 1988).

With the continuum of communication strategies for learners with hearing impairment ranging from spoken English to ASL, another issue emerges. Depending on the context, learners with hearing impairments may "code switch," or change in one form of communication to another and back again (Kluwin, 1981). Code switching is a complex and pervasive part of the daily communication of individuals with hearing impairments. Kluwin (1981) suggested that code switching by teachers can serve to help children understand more complex concepts, by moving into whatever mode of communication is most readily understood.

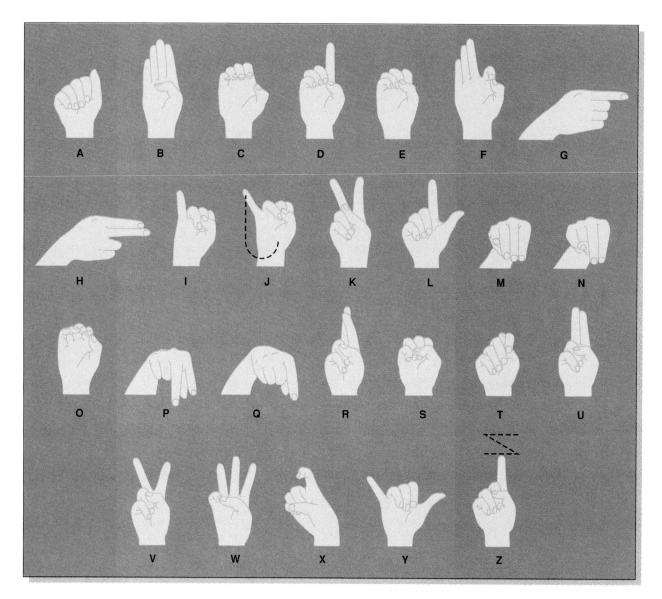

Figure 12.6
The American manual alphabet.

In an effort to evaluate the various forms of communication, Crittenden, Ritterman, and Wilcox (1986) found that in isolated tasks, such as a standardized receptive vocabulary test, communication modes using manual communication, including manual communication without mouth movement, total communication with audio, and total communication without audio, yielded performances significantly superior to those of oral communication with or without audio.

The Council on the Education of the Deaf (1976) formally stated that no single method of instruction or communication (including oral, total communication, or manual communication) can best meet the needs of all students with hearing impairments. The council's resolution indicated that:

1. A continuum of services, from assistance in the regular classroom to residential placement, should be available.

Children may communicate through signing.

2. The method of instruction should be available during the school day.
3. The child's program should be constantly monitored to assure that it is meeting his or her needs.

The courts, in attempts to define an appropriate public education, have also entered into decisions regarding the mode of communication to be used with learners who are hearing impaired (Katsiyannis, 1991). In one case in which parents desired placement in an oral program for their children, the hearing officer appointed under PL 94–142 procedures stated that the dominant view among scholars and practitioners in the profession is that total communication is an appropriate approach. This does not mean that the oral approach is inappropriate or comment on whether it might be more beneficial for a particular child, but that total communication is *one* appropriate approach (in re Jean Marie and Michelle Lyn H., 1979).

In an attempt to investigate the criteria used for placement of children with hearing impairments, Spear and Kretschmer (1987) found that among the team members involved, that is, administrators, psychologists, special education teachers, and audiologists, relatively different importance was given to different variables for placements (degree of impairment, learner and parent wishes, availability of services, etc.). A tendency towards more restrictive placements occurred among all teams.

Ross (1982) contends that hearing loss and other demographic variables aside, the more fully mainstreamed the average learner with hearing impairments, the better his or her academic achievements. Northcott (1980b) also suggests that less restrictive settings have the advantages of increased learning of coping skills, increased motivation, fewer unusual behaviors stemming from social isolation, and an enhanced understanding on the part of parents regarding their child's abilities. However, she suggests that daily competition and social problems may be difficult and, at times, challenging for some learners with hearing impairments.

In terms of social adjustment, Aplin (1987) found that children with sensorineural hearing losses who attended ordinary schools had significantly better levels of social adjustment and behavior than did their peers with hearing impairments who attended special schools. Yet, with an emerging emphasis among some groups for the recognition of a "Deaf culture," residential settings are gaining more attention.

There has been a trend in the last decade towards more naturalistic interventions with children with hearing impairments. Wood and Wood (1984) investigated the relationship between teacher control of conversations and children's initiative and fluency in communication. As teachers changed their conversational style to

This child is wearing a body aid because of hearing impairment.

increase personal contributions, students responded with increased initiative and mean length of turn. When teachers refrained from questioning them, children had more opportunities for spontaneous contributions and were more willing to take advantage of them.

Fisher, Monen, Moore, and Twiss (1989) posited a reverse mainstreaming approach to increase the social integration of children with and without hearing impairments. Three interventions were in place with hearing students: signing class, novel play equipment, and a buddy system. These interventions significantly increased the interaction among the children with or without hearing impairments.

Interpreters

Interpreters may support learners with hearing impairments in the general education setting. **Interpreters** are hearing individuals who communicate spoken language, usually through one of the manual or signed systems, to the learner who is hearing impaired. Interpreters may depart from the exact words of the speaker, and may paraphrase, define, or further explain what the speaker is communicating. Quigley and Paul (1984) contrast interpreting with translating, which is providing the verbatim signed equivalent of the speaker's oral communication.

Since 1964, the National Registry of Interpreters for the Deaf has maintained a list of certified interpreters (Levine, 1981). These interpreters may communicate what has been said in some form of sign language or fingerspelling or may inaudibly repeat the message more slowly and with clearer enunciation so that speechreading is facilitated (Northcott, 1984). Interpreters may also convert the signs of the learner who is hearing impaired into English for hearing listeners.

FM broadcast hearing aids are commonly worn by children with hearing impairments.

The interpreter should be positioned so that the learner with hearing impairments can see both the speaker and the interpreter. In addition, teachers frequently provide educational interpreters with vocabulary lists, lesson outlines, study guides, and other materials to help them in explaining materials to the learner with hearing impairments.

Amplification and Other Technological Ways to Mediate the Environment

Amplification is not a cure for a hearing impairment; it simply increases the intensity or loudness of some sounds, augmenting the individual's residual hearing while the amplification device is in place. The selection and use of appropriate amplification may be the single most important tool available for the learner with hearing impairments (Ling, 1984). Maddell (1990b) indicates that the main purpose of this amplification is to permit the learner to use her or his residual hearing to perceive speech. She contends that the characteristics of the learner and the communication environment are the basis of choice regarding the amplification system, but that nearly all children with hearing impairments will benefit from classroom use of FM amplification in addition to personal amplification, because even the best classroom is not a good acoustic environment.

An **FM** (frequently modulated) **system** is a wireless amplification system in which speech is transmitted from a microphone, worn by a teacher, via FM radio signals to an FM receiver worn by the student (Maddell, 1990b). In the classroom, there are several advantages of FM systems over individual hearing aids:

1. Problems that emerge as a result of distance from the speaker, noise in the classroom, and poor classroom acoustics are managed.
2. The signal is more intense than that arriving directly at the child's ear through a hearing aid.
3. Significantly more auditory information is available.

Maddell believes that an FM system will benefit every learner with a hearing impairment.

In addition to FM systems, individual amplification systems, or hearing aids, are used by some learners with hearing impairments. Maddell (1990a) describes several types of individual amplification. These personal amplification systems are presented in Figure 12.7. **Behind the ear (BTE) hearing aids** are the most

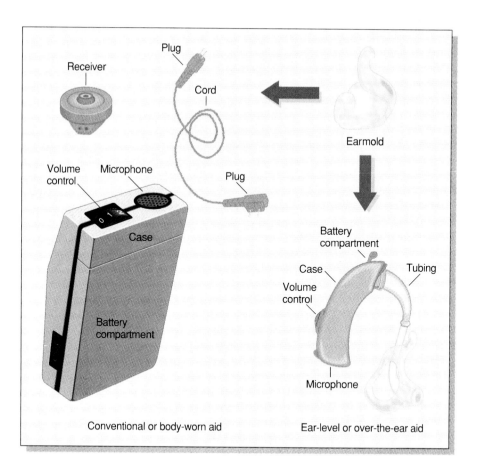

Figure 12.7
Amplification devices.

common for children, can be easily adjusted, and are compatible with FM systems. **In-the-ear (ITE) hearing aids,** popular with adults, are not good choices for children, because children grow rapidly and several expensive remakes may be necessary. Body-worn amplification, with the microphone on the chest, makes it possible to make the hearing aid louder with less interference, making it useful for children with severe and profound losses. Contralateral routing of offside sound (CROS) aids include a microphone behind both ears, making the wearer aware of sounds from either side, although the signals are routed to the better ear.

A recent technological advance used by some persons with profound hearing impairments is the cochlear implant. This implant requires a surgical procedure during which an internal electromagnetic coil, with an electrode which extends to the cochlea of the inner ear, is placed in the mastoid bone, behind the external ear. Another coil is fitted to the skull over the internal coil. A microphone, worn on the clothing, transmits sounds from the environment to the cochlear nerve through the implant. The implant does not enable the person to understand speech but it does enable the individual to distinguish some environmental sounds. In addition, with therapy, the learner may learn to differentiate some speech sounds and thus facilitate speechreading and communication (Schein, 1984; Brill, MacNeil, & Newman, 1986).

Objective Five: To describe the impact of hearing impairment on participation in larger social systems—the school, community, and society.

The Impact on Participation in the School, Community, and Society

Learners with Hearing Impairments in School

In a review of research related to the language learning of children with hearing impairments in classrooms, though much remains unknown, the ways in which students with hearing impairments cope with educational demands is very similar to that of their peers with learning disabilities (Weiss, 1986).

The strategies used by learners with hearing impairments are similar to those of their hearing peers. For example, Andrews and Mason (1991) found that when "reading between the lines," that is, understanding the multiple meanings of words and idioms, learners with hearing impairments described ways of understanding reading material from the context similar to those strategies used by their peers. However, learners with hearing impairments used some strategies, such as rereading and background knowledge, more frequently than students who could hear.

Learners with Hearing Impairments in the Community

In a study which assessed the independent behavior of children with hearing impairments, those children as well as children with normal hearing demonstrated equivalent independent social behaviors in areas of motor development, personal living, and community living. Significant discrepancies were identified between expected skills and the students' abilities to independently deal with money and its value, and social and communication skills (Klansek-Kyllo & Rose, 1985).

In recent years technology has facilitated the community functioning of learners with hearing impairments. Among these supports are closed caption television, computer-assisted instruction, videodiscs, the telecommunication device for the deaf (**TDD**), and the teletypewriter (**TTY**) and printer.

Closed caption television allows the learner with hearing impairments to see in subtitles the dialogue being presented verbally through the television's sound system. Closed captioned films for instruction and entertainment are available through many libraries in the United States. Converters that allow the television set to receive closed captioned programs are readily available for less than $200. In the very near future all television sets with a 13″ screen or larger will have a converter built into the set.

Both computer-assisted instruction and instructional videodiscs allow learners with hearing impairments to interact in a learning setting without auditory demands. The TDD system permits the sending, receiving, and printing of written messages by persons with hearing impairments through thousands of stations in the United States.

The use of telephone communication remains a major obstacle for learners who are hearing impaired; even with the use of amplification, many hearing aid users report difficulty understanding speech over the telephone (Rodriguez, Meyers, & Holmes, 1991). The TTY allows a person with hearing impairment to communicate by telephone. Typed letters are converted to electric signals through a modem. The signal is transmitted through the telephone line and converted back to a typed message by the receiver's telephone.

Closed caption television allows the learner with hearing impairments to read the dialogue being presented verbally.

In the Americans with Disabilities Act of 1990 (Public Law 101–336) it was mandated that communications companies that provide telephone services to the general public must offer intrastate and interstate telephone relay services to individuals who use telecommunications devices for the deaf (TDDs), voice telephones, or similar devices 24 hours a day, 7 days a week, at regular rates by July 26, 1993. This legislation will have significant impact on the ability of individuals with hearing impairments and speech impairments to communicate for social, family, and business purposes.

Learners with Hearing Impairments in Society

Luetke-Stahlman and Luckner (1991) describe "ethnic Deaf adults" as those who view themselves as members of the Deaf community. Capitalizing the word deaf signifies membership in the Deaf community. Padden and Humphries (1988) argue that the Deaf culture is not simply a support system among persons with a similar physical condition, but that it is a historically created and actively transmitted culture. It has its own humor, heroes, clubs, publications, fraternal organizations, churches, and theater groups. The primary identifying characteristic of the group, they argue, is its language, or manual communication. Persons who are members of the Deaf culture tend to associate with other members of the culture both in personal and business activities (Walker, 1986). Wilcox and Corwin (1990) suggest that the experiences of a deaf child in the Deaf culture is a form of indoctrination or enculturation into that culture.

Special Services: Bethany Deaf Church Dedicated

By Christine Bertelson

Ten years, $80,000 and the work of many hands went into the making of Bethany Deaf Church in Kirkwood.

Not to mention a broken ankle suffered by its pastor, the Rev. Thomas F. Lovis, during construction.

On Sunday, Lovis gathered his flock in a renovated American Legion Hall, at 310 East Argonne Drive, to dedicate the new sanctuary.

Bethany Deaf Church is one of only a handful of deaf churches in the United States, according to church secretary Erin H. Roach.

"Many hearing churches have interpreters for the deaf, who have to sit in a special area," Roach said. "Here we have a speaker for the hearing, but our services are primarily for the deaf culture."

All but a handful of Bethany's 60-member congregation are deaf, said Roach, who is not deaf. In some families both parents are deaf, but they have hearing children. In others, the opposite is true. All of Bethany's services, including the Sunday school for adults and children and the taped music, are signed.

Bethany's congregation is about 15 years old, but it has been at its present location only since March. It formerly was housed at Bethany Baptist Church on South Outer 40 Road in Chesterfield.

The Deaf Church is loosely affiliated with the Southern Baptist Conference. Because of its special mission, it operates more like a non-denominational church, Roach said.

The dedication Sunday featured an emotional performance by a religious singing group from Louisville, Ky., the Deaf Opportunity Outreach. The group performs at deaf churches all over the country and is supported by grants and donations, according to its president, Vesta Bice.

To music thundering from loud-speakers near the altar, the group of men and women performed a lyrical hand ballet—sing-signing along with those in the pews.

Behind them, a simple wooden cross set in a pink alcove was the only adornment at the altar. The plain white walls make it easier to follow the flutter and swoop of talking hands.

The Rev. Arnold Austin of Baker, La., delivered the sermon, signing with an unmistakable, exaggerated and emotional rhetorical style that marked him as a Southern evangelist.

Lovis concluded the service by asking his parishioners to pray with him in a circle at the altar.

"We feel more like we are a family here," said Lovis, a retired Post-Dispatch printer. "It's something the [hearing] world doesn't understand" ∎

Reprinted with permission of St. Louis Post-Dispatch.

Summary

There are approximately 8 million children with hearing impairments in the United States. Learners with hearing impairments are generally classified into two groups: hard of hearing and deaf. Learners who are deaf have difficulties with the sound system of language which has a significant impact on interaction and functioning in a hearing society. They also have difficulties in the areas of articulation, changes in pitch, and voicing. Learners who are hard of hearing are less affected in these areas but do have voice problems. This group exhibits misarticulations, substitutions, and distortions of sound. Learners who are hard of hearing have difficulties with the sound system of language and, as a consequence, vocabulary. The learner who is deaf has great difficulty learning voiced language. In a social context, learners with hearing impairments are generally found to be less assertive and more fearful than are their peers with normal hearing.

The learner with hearing impairments has difficulty in social interaction and communication. In that approximately one-half of the typical learner's school day is devoted to listening activities, it is extremely difficult for the learner with a hearing impairment to understand all of the information being communicated in the environment. Though considerable controversy exists as to how to mediate the environment for learners with hearing impairments, the Council on the Education of the Deaf (1976) formally states that no single method of instruction or communication can best meet the needs of all students with hearing impairments. Programming must be individualized in response to the needs of the individual within the context in which the learner is functioning or will function.

References

Andrews, J. F., & Mason, J. M. (1991). Strategy usage among deaf and hearing readers. *Exceptional Children, 57,* 536–545.

Aplin, D. Y. (1987). Social and emotional adjustment of hearing-impaired children in ordinary and special schools. *Educational Research, 29,* 56–64.

Berg, F. S. (1987). *Facilitating classroom listening: A handbook for teachers of normal and hard-of-hearing students.* Boston: College-Hill Press/Little, Brown.

Boothroyd, A. (1978). Speech perception and severe hearing loss. In M. Ross & T. G. Giolas (Eds.), *Auditory management of hearing-impaired children* (pp. 117–144). Baltimore, MD: University Park Press.

Brill, R. G., MacNeil, B., & Newman, L. R. (1986). Framework for appropriate programs for deaf children: Conference of Educational Administrators Serving the Deaf. *American Annals of the Deaf, 131,* (2), 65–76.

Brown, S. H., Maxwell, M., & Browning, L. D. (1990). Relations in public: Hearing parents and hearing impaired children. *Journal of Childhood Communication Disorders, 13* (1), 43–61.

Cates, J. A. (1991). Comparison of human figure drawings by hearing and hearing impaired children. *The Volta Review, 93,* 31–39.

Council on the Education of the Deaf (1976). *Resolution on individualized educational programming for the hearing impaired.* Washington, DC: CED.

Crittenden, J. B., Ritterman, S. I., & Wilcox, E. W. (1986). Communication mode as a factor in the performance of hearing-impaired children on a standardized receptive vocabulary test. *American Annals of the Deaf, 131,* 356–360.

Davis, J. (1988). Management of the school age child: A psychosocial perspective. In F. H. Bess (Ed.), *Hearing Impairment in Children* (pp. 401–416). Parkton, MD: York Press.

Davis, J., Elfenbein, J., Lansing, C., & Dixon, E. (1982). Experiences with mainstreaming: The view from the other side. Paper presented at the American Speech-Language Hearing Association Annual Convention, Toronto.

Davis, J., Elfenbein, J., Schumn, R., & Bentler, R. (1986). Effects of mild and moderate hearing impairments on language, educational, and psychosocial behavior of children. *Journal of Speech and Hearing Disorders, 51,* 53–62.

Duchan, J. (1988). Assessing communication of hearing-impaired children: Influences from pragmatics. *Journal of Rehabilitative Audiology* (Monograph Supplement), *21,* 19–40.

Federal Register (1977). 42 (163), 42478.

Fisher, A., Monen, J., Moore, D. W., & Twiss, D. (1989). Increasing the social integration of hearing-impaired children in a mainstream school setting. *New Zealand Journal of Educational Studies, 24,* 189–204.

Garrison, W. M., & Tesch, S. (1978). Self-concept and deafness: A review of the research literature. *The Volta Review, 80,* 457–466.

In re Jean Marie and Michelle Lyn H., (1979). *EHLR, 401,* 330.

Israelite, N. K. (1985). Sibling reaction to a hearing impaired child in the family. *Journal of Rehabilitation of the Deaf, 18,* 1–5.

Katsiyannis, A. (1991). Communication methods for hearing-impaired students: The role of the judiciary. *The Volta Review, 93,* 97–101.

Kenworthy, O. T. (1986). Caregiver-child interaction and language acquisition of hearing-impaired children. *Topics in Language Disorders, 6* (3), 1–11.

King, C. (1984). National survey of language methods used with hearing impaired students in the United States. *American Annals of the Deaf, 129,* 311–316.

King, N., Mulhall, J., & Gullone, E. (1989). Fears in hearing impaired and normally hearing children and adolescents. *Behavior Research and Therapy, 27* (5), 577–580.

Klansek-Kyllo, V., & Rose, S. (1985). Using the scale of independent behavior with hearing-impaired students. *American Annals of the Deaf, 130,* 533–537.

Kluwin, T. (1981). The grammaticality of manual representations of English in classroom settings. *American Annals of the Deaf, 127,* 417–421.

Koelle, H. W., & Convey, J. J. (1982). The prediction of the achievement of deaf adolescents from self-concept and locus of control measures. *American Annals of the Deaf, 127,* 769–778.

Kretschmer, R. R., & Kretschmer, L. W. (1978). *Language development and intervention with the hearing impaired.* Baltimore, MD: University Park Press.

Kretschmer, R. R., & Kretschmer, L. W. (1988). Communication competence and assessment. *Journal of Rehabilitative Audiology* (Monograph Supplement), *21,* 5–17.

Kyle, J. G., & Woll, B. (1988). *Sign language: The study of deaf people and their language.* New York: Cambridge.

Levine, E. (1981). *The ecology of deafness.* New York: Columbia University Press.

Lewis, M. A. (1986). South Carolina develops reference manual of preferred instructional signs. *Counterpoint, 6* (1), 16.

Ling, D. (1984). *Early intervention for hearing impaired children: Oral options.* San Diego: College Hill Press.

Luetke-Stahlman, B., & Luckner, J. (1991). *Effectively educating students with hearing impairments.* New York: Longman.

Macklin, G. F., & Matson, J. L. (1985). A comparison of social behaviors among nonhandicapped and hearing impaired children. *Behavioral Disorders, 11* (1), 60–65.

Maddell, J. R. (1990a). Audiological evaluation of the mainstreamed hearing-impaired child. In M. Ross (Ed.), *Hearing-impaired children in the classroom* (pp. 27–44). Parkton, MD: York Press.

Maddell, J. R. (1990b). Managing classroom amplification. In M. Ross (Ed.), *Hearing-impaired children in the classroom* (pp. 95–118). Parkton, MD: York Press.

Martin, F. N., George, K. A., O'Neal, J., & Daly, J. A. (1987). Audiologists' and parents' attitudes regarding counseling of families of hearing-impaired children. *ASHA Reports Series, 29* (2), 27–33.

Maxon, A. B., Brackett, D., & van der Berg, S. A. (1991). Self perception of socialization. The effects of hearing status, age, and gender. *The Volta Review, 93,* 7–17.

McNeil, M., & Chabessol, D. J. (1984). Paternal involvement in the programs of hearing-impaired children: An exploratory study. *Family Relations Journal of Applied Family and Child Studies, 33* (1), 119–125.

Merker, H. (1990). Who is handicapped? Employee or employer? *Shhh, 11* (4), 3–4.

Moeller, M. P. (1988). Combining formal and informal strategies for language assessment of hearing-impaired children. *Journal of Rehabilitative Audiology* (Monograph Supplement), *21,* 73–100.

Moores, D. G., & Maestas y Moores, J. (1981). Special adaptations necessitated by hearing impairments. In J. Kauffman & D. Hallahan (Eds.), *Handbook of special education.* Englewood Cliffs, NJ: Prentice Hall.

Musselman, C. R. (1990). The relationship between measures of hearing loss and speech intelligibility in young deaf children. *Journal of Childhood Communication Disorders, 13* (2), 193–205.

Nicholls, G. H., & Ling, D. (1982). Cued speech and the reception of spoken language. *Journal of Speech and Hearing Research, 25,* 262–269.

Nienhuys, T. G., Horsborough, K. M., & Cross, T. G. (1985). A dialogic analysis of interaction between mothers and their deaf or hearing preschoolers. *Applied Psycholinguistics, 5* (2), 131–139.

Northcott, W. (1980a). Freedom through speech: Every child's right. *The Volta Review, 83,* 162–181.

Northcott, W. (1980b). *Implications of mainstreaming for the education of hearing impaired children in the 1980s.* Washington, DC: Alexander Graham Bell Association for the Deaf.

Northcott, W. (1984). *Oral interpreting: Principles and practices.* Baltimore, MD: University Park Press.

Oblowitz, N., Green, L., & Heyns, I. de V. (1991). A self-concept scale for the hearing-impaired. *The Volta Review, 93,* 19–29.

Padden, C., & Humphries, T. (1988). *Deaf in America: Voices from a culture.* Cambridge, MA: Harvard University Press.

Plapinger, D., & Kretschmer, R. (1991). The effect of context on the interactions between a normally-hearing mother and her hearing-impaired child. *The Volta Review, 93,* 75–85.

Prior, M. R., Glazner, J., Sanson, A., & Debelle, G. (1988). Research note: Temperament and behavioral adjustment to hearing impaired children. *Journal of Child Psychology and Psychiatry and Allied Disciplines, 29* (2), 209–216.

Quigley, S., & Paul, P. (1984). *Language and deafness.* San Diego, CA: College Hill Press.

Ray, S. (1989). Context and the psychoeducational assessment of hearing impaired children. *Topics in Language Disorders, 9* (4), 33–44.

Report of the Ad Hoc Committee to Define Deaf and Hard of Hearing (1975). *American Annals of the Deaf, 120,* 509–512.

Rodriguez, G., Meyers, C., & Holmes, A. (1991). Hearing aid performance under acoustic and electromagnetic coupling conditions. *The Volta Review, 93,* 89–95.

Ross, M. (1982). *Hard of hearing children in the regular classroom.* Englewood Cliffs, NJ: Prentice Hall.

Ross, M., & Calvert, D. R. (1984). Semantics of deafness revisited: Total communication and the use and misuse of residual hearing. *Audiology, 9,* 127–145.

Sanders, D. A. (1982). *Aural rehabilitation* (2nd ed.). Englewood Cliffs, NJ: Prentice Hall.

Schein, J. D. (1984). Cochlear implants and the education of deaf children. *American Annals of the Deaf, 129,* 325–332.

Spear, B., & Kretschmer, R. E. (1987). The use of criteria in decision making regarding the placement of hearing impaired children. *Special Services in the Schools, 4* (1–2), 107–122.

U.S. Department of Education. (1990). *Twelfth annual report to Congress on the implementation of the Education of the Handicapped Act.* Washington, DC: Author.

U.S. Department of Education (1992). *Fourteenth annual report to Congress on the implementation of the Individuals with Disabilities Education Act.* Washington, DC: Author.

Walker, L. A. (1986). *A loss for words: The story of deafness in a family.* New York: Harper & Row.

Webster, A., Saunders, E., & Bamford, J. M. (1984). Fluctuating conductive hearing impairment. *AEP: Association of Educational Psychologists Journal, 6* (5), 6–19.

Weiss, A. L. (1986). Classroom discourse and the hearing impaired child. *Topics in Language Disorders, 6* (3), 60–70.

Wilbur, R. B. (1979). *American sign language and sign systems.* Baltimore, MD: University Park Press.

Wilcox, S., & Corwin, J. (1990). The enculturation of Bomee: Looking at the world through deaf eyes. *Journal of Childhood Communication Disorders, 13,* 63–71.

Wolk, S., & Schildroth, A. N. (1986). Deaf children and speech intelligibility: A national survey. In A. N. Schildroth & M. A. Karchmer (Eds.), *Deaf children in America* (pp. 139–159). San Diego, CA: College Hill Press.

Wood, H. A., & Wood, D. J. (1984). An experimental evaluation of the effects of five styles of teacher conversation on the language of hearing impaired children. *Journal of Child Psychology and Psychiatry and Allied Disciplines, 25* (1), 45–62.

Wray, D., Flexer, C., & Ireland, J. (1988). Mainstreaming hearing-impaired children: Typical questions posed by classroom teachers. *Hearsay* (Fall, 1988), 76–79.

Ying, E. (1990). Speech and language assessment: Communication evaluation. In M. Ross (Ed.), *Hearing-impaired children in the classroom* (pp. 45–60). Parkton, MD: York Press.

4

Learners Who Vary in Their Learning Styles and Rates

13
Learners Identified as Learning Disabled

14
Learners with Mild or Moderate Mental Retardation

15
Learners with Mild Disabilities

16
Learners with Severe and Multiple Disabilities

17
Learners Who are Gifted, Talented, or Creative

*L*EARNERS WHO VARY FROM PEERS' LEARNING STYLES AND RATES ARE GENERALLY IDENTIFIED AS A RESULT OF THE mismatch between expectations and demands in classrooms and the cognitive abilities and styles they demonstrate. As Futrell (1986) observes, schools today generally reflect an organizational model that was appropriate to nineteenth century industry, with few opportunities for cooperation and support. Marshall (1988) describes work-oriented classrooms in which the teacher sets the standards for work completion, monitors and evaluates performance, and manages the classroom with the primary thrust of "doing work." These classrooms emphasize the differences rather than similarities between learners who vary in their learning styles and rates from their peers.

Sapona and Phillips (1993), in a description of ideal schools for learners who vary in their styles and rates, discuss a classroom environment in which there is a community of learners. In this community, each member is encouraged to be actively involved and engaged in the learning process. Variations in students' learning styles and developmental levels are not seen as "problems." Such variations are seen to provide opportunities for sharing diverse means of working through complex problems and exploring a variety of interest areas and perspectives. In recognition of the wide range of developmental levels demonstrated even by learners who are not identified as disabled, we can suggest that rather than making the learner fit the system, the system should fit the learner.

In this section, we explore the various developmental contexts of learners identified as learning disabled, and those with mild or moderate mental retardation. Learners with both mild and severe disabilities are discussed. The section concludes with a discussion of learners who challenge the system in a unique way, with their unusual talents and abilities. Throughout these discussions, we would urge you to keep in mind the similarities of these learners to their peers rather than the variations ∎

References

Futrell, M. H. (1986). Restructuring teaching: A call for research. *Educational Researcher. 15* (10), 5–8.

Marshall, H. H. (1988). Work or learning: Implications for classroom metaphors. *Educational Researcher, 17* (9), 9–16.

Sapona, R. H., & Phillips, L. J. (1993). Classrooms as communities of learners: Sharing responsibility for learning. In A. M. Bauer (Ed.), *Children who challenge the system* (pp. 63–88). Norwood, NJ: Ablex.

Chapter

13

Learners Identified as Learning Disabled

*O*bjectives

After completing this chapter, you will be able to:

1. describe the personal characteristics of learners identified as learning disabled.
2. describe the identification and evaluation of learners identified as learning disabled.
3. describe the impact of learning disabilities on interactions in the home and classroom.
4. describe ways to mediate the environment for learners identified as learning disabled.
5. describe the impact of learning disabilities on participation in larger social systems—the community and society.

*K*ey Words and Phrases

attention deficit hyperactivity disorder (ADHD)

cognitive behavior modification

curriculum-based assessment

d-amphetamine (Dexedrine)

holistic communication based approaches

learning disabilities

methylphenidate (Ritalin)

social skills training

strategies training

tutoring

*T*HE PURPOSE OF EDUCATION IS TO DEVELOP TALENTS, NOT TO REINFORCE WEAKNESSES. AS TEACHERS, YOU SHOULD not waste precious instructional time in an attempt to identify the academic shortcomings of your students. Some problems that are burdensome in childhood may be sidestepped in adulthood. For example, the learning disabled child who does not do well in physical education classes may choose to forsake athletic pursuits as an adult. However, no individual may ignore his or her talents. Consequently you should not discount the abilities of your students. (David Quinn, an adult identified as a child as learning disabled, describing the implications of his experiences in special education, 1984, p. 297.) ■

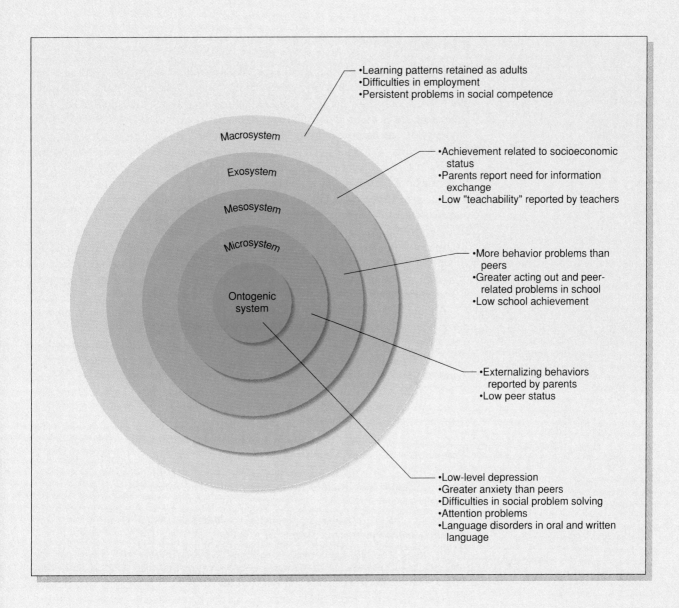

Macrosystem
• Learning patterns retained as adults
• Difficulties in employment
• Persistent problems in social competence

Exosystem
• Achievement related to socioeconomic status
• Parents report need for information exchange
• Low "teachability" reported by teachers

Mesosystem
• More behavior problems than peers
• Greater acting out and peer-related problems in school
• Low school achievement

Microsystem
• Externalizing behaviors reported by parents
• Low peer status

Ontogenic system
• Low-level depression
• Greater anxiety than peers
• Difficulties in social problem solving
• Attention problems
• Language disorders in oral and written language

317

Introduction

Working with learners identified as having learning disabilities represents the largest and fastest growing field in special education (Torgesen, 1991). During the 1990–91 school year, learners identified as learning disabled accounted for 49.1 percent of the learners in special education. Between the 1989–90 and 1990–91 school years, the number of 6- to 21-year-old individuals identified as learning disabled increased 4.0 percent. Between the 1976–77 and 1990–91 school years, the number of learners identified as learning disabled increased over 170 percent (U.S. Department of Education, 1992). During the 1990–91 school year, over two million learners were served as learning disabled; this number represents approximately 4.0 percent of all the learners between 6 and 21 years of age. During the 1989–90 school year, the percentage of learners classified as learning disabled ranged from 1.69 percent in Georgia to 6.8 percent in Rhode Island. Though approximately 20 percent of these students were served in regular classes, approximately 60 percent were served in resource rooms, and almost 21 percent were served in separate classes within the public schools (U.S. Department of Education, 1990).

Although the field of learning disabilities has a relatively brief history, emerging in the early 1960s, learners who demonstrated "congenital word blindness" were identified as early as 1917 (Hinshelwood, 1917). Over the past three decades, learning disabilities have been described in many ways, ranging from a "dysfunction of the brain" (Johnson & Myklebust, 1967), to a category of disability derived to explain the growing number of reading failures (Sleeter, 1984), to a developmental lag in movement through the preoperational, concrete operational, and formal operational stages of Piagetian development (Fakouri, 1991). Though questions have emerged related to the validity of identifying large numbers of learners as learning disabled, a large number of learners were identified and the preponderance of programs seems to demonstrate that the concept of learning disabilities has been socially accepted, politically protected, clinically assumed, and educationally endorsed.

Wood (1991) suggests that problems related to the identification of learners identified as learning disabled occur in part through a lack of consonance between definitions of learning disabilities and identification criteria. She contends that a total picture of the student's functioning is necessary, rather than simply identifying a discrepancy between achievement and abilities or school failures. Yet as Ysseldyke and Algozzine (1983) argue, discussions over what to call these students and who they are sidetracks educators from the question of how to serve this large group of children who need support.

Poplin (1988) argues strongly for a holistic or constructivist perception of learning disabilities, suggesting that the context must be considered in all interventions. She contends that applying a "reductionist" perspective can put limits on learners who are already challenged by an insensitive system. Considering the learner in the context of a community of learners in the area of reading, for example, would emphasize developing a strategic concept of reading rather than to decode the sound-symbol relationship. In mathematics, rather than completing a speed drill, instruction would emphasize applying computation to daily situations from the beginning of the instructional process.

Learners identified as learning disabled bring many challenges to the instructional setting, including variations in the way in which they learn to read, write, use language, and engage in mathematics. These challenges and variations, however, are highly individualized.

Personal Characteristics

In a clinical-psychological investigation of the characteristics of learners identified as having **learning disabilities,** Cohen (1986) argues that these learners are more heterogeneous than homogeneous. However, several common characteristics emerged: (a) problems in working and learning; (b) chronic, low-level depression and relatively high, free-floating anxiety; and (c) unconscious concerns about self and others. In addition to higher anxiety, Rodriguez and Routh (1989) report greater peer-nominated depression among learners identified as learning disabled when compared to their peers.

Social and Behavioral Competence

McConaughy (1986) studied parent reports of social competence and behavior problems among learners identified as learning disabled. Among boys 12 to 16 years of age, there were significantly more behavior problems among learners identified as learning disabled than among their nonidentified peers. Boys identified as having learning disabilities received significantly lower scores on all social competence scales, including participation in activities, social contact with organizations and friends, school performance, and total social competence.

Though learners identified as learning disabled may be less socially competent than their peers and may function socially at a lower developmental level, the most marked differences may occur in peer conflict situations (Carlson, 1987). Healey (1987) suggests problems in social interactions may be due to difficulties in defining interpersonal problems, thinking of alternative solutions, anticipating consequences, articulating sequenced problem solving, and demonstrating sensitivity to social causes and others' perspectives.

Using teacher reports, learners identified as learning disabled have been found to demonstrate more acting out, distractibility, and problems with peer relationships (Bender & Golden, 1988). These students may not "tune in" to learning situations (Reiff & Gerber, 1990). Teachers suggested that problems in physical competence may also contribute to the peer acceptance of learners identified as learning disabled (Margalit, Raviv, & Pahn-Steinmetz, 1988).

The self-concept of learners identified as learning disabled has been related to the setting in which they receive services (Beltempo & Achille, 1990). Learners identified as learning disabled in restrictive placements such as the special classroom demonstrated and retained the lowest self-concepts throughout the school year. Those in partial placement with inclusion demonstrated higher self-concepts at the beginning and end of the academic year. Girls were found to demonstrate poorer self-concepts than boys.

In a longitudinal, 3-year study, McKinney (1989) found that learners identified as learning disabled demonstrate a persistent pattern of classroom behavior that distinguishes them from nonidentified peers. These problems include attention problems, conduct and classroom management problems, and withdrawn-dependent behavior. Identified learners with attention and conduct problems demonstrated poorer academic outcomes than those of their nonidentified peers. When compared with their classmates, learners identified as learning disabled are more likely to be off-task and to be interacting with teachers (McKinney and Speece, 1983).

As with all learners, generalizations related to social skills must be viewed with caution. Not all learners identified as learning disabled experience peer difficulties, and girls may be more at risk than boys for peer problems (laGreca, 1987).

Language

In a study of 242 eight- to twelve-year-old children with learning disabilities, Gibbs and Cooper (1989) found that a speech, language, or hearing problem was exhibited by 96.2 percent of the students. Among the students exhibiting difficulties, language problems were found in 90.5 percent, articulation disorders in 23.5 percent, and voice disorders in 12 percent. However, only 6 percent of the students were receiving the services of a speech-language pathologist.

Terrell (1990) reports that in preschool, children are frequently labeled as "language disordered"; however, in school, these same children are labeled "learning disabled." He contends that though their language issues remain, the language disorders "go underground" because of the issue of reading and overriding concern for academic problems.

Language problems frequently associated with learning disabilities include (a) trouble with word meanings; (b) off-target responding; (c) inaccurate word selection; (d) difficulty with word finding; (e) neologisms (invented words); (f) topic closure; (g) use of immature grammatical structures; and (h) disorganization (Candler & Hildreth, 1990). Olson, Wong, and Marx (1983) found that in a situation in which students were taught a board game, learners identified as learning disabled demonstrated communication patterns which varied from their nonidentified peers. Learners identified as learning disabled used fewer adjectives and prepositions and asked fewer questions than their peers. In addition, learners identified as learning disabled used fewer organizational strategies and planned ahead less than normal achieving learners during communication in a semistructured task. Learners identified as learning disabled performed more poorly than did their peers on tasks that involved the use of metaphoric language (Lee & Kamhi, 1990). In conversation, learners identified as learning disabled demonstrate a greater rate of communication breakdowns than that of their peers (MacLachlan & Chapman, 1988). Figure 13.1 shows one learner's expression of what it's like to communicate in ways different from one's peers.

In written language, those identified as learning disabled differ from their peers in syntax and number of grammatical errors (Johnson & Grant, 1989). Thomas, Englert, and Gregg (1987) found both quantitative and qualitative differences between learners identified as learning disabled and their peers in writing performance. Those identified as learning disabled had significantly more difficulty sustaining their expository writing efforts; their errors suggested a reliance on the knowledge-telling strategy as a basis for expository writing. Although adolescents identified as learning disabled had a rudimentary knowledge of story form, their knowledge was less well developed than that of their nonidentified peers (Vallecorsa & Garris, 1990). The writing of identified adolescents was also marked by less coherence and less fluency.

Attention

Attention deficit disorders have been described in the literature since 1930s. Using current concepts, the early term "minimal brain dysfunction" referred to children identified as having learning disabilities, hyperactivity, distractibility, impulsivity, and emotional and social problems. Now, learning disabilities are a presumed neurological disorder with impact on the processes involved in the understanding or use of spoken or written language characterized by an imperfect ability to listen, think, speak, read, write, spell, or do mathematics (Silver, 1990). **Attention deficit hyperactivity disorder** (ADHD) is a presumed neurological disorder that impacts

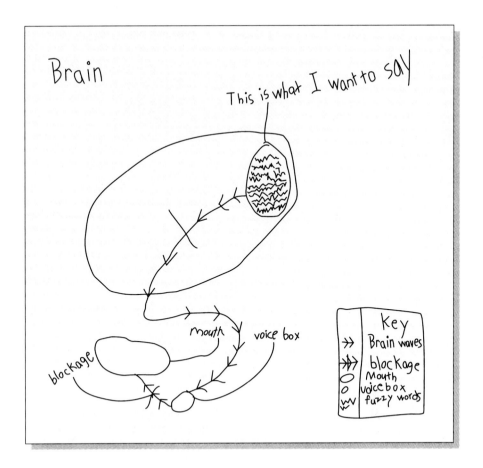

Figure 13.1
"This is what I want to say." Drawing by a learner identified as learning disabled to describe his processing problem.

Children with short attention spans find the classroom a challenging learning environment.

***T*able 13.1   DSM-III-R Criteria: Attention Deficit Hyperactivity Disorder**

A. A period of 6 months or more during which at least eight of the following symptoms are present:
    1. Has difficulty remaining seated.
    2. Often fidgets with hands or feet or squirms in seat.
    3. Has difficulty playing quietly.
    4. Often talks excessively.
    5. Often shifts from one uncompleted activity to another.
    6. Has difficulty sustaining attention to tasks and play activities.
    7. Has difficulty following through on instructions from others (not due to oppositional behavior or failure of comprehension).
    8. Is easily distracted by extraneous stimuli.
    9. Often interrupts or intrudes on others (e.g., butts into games).
    10. Often blurts out answers to questions before they have been completed.
    11. Has difficulty awaiting turns in games or group situations.
    12. Often engages in physically dangerous activities without considering possible consequences (not for the purpose of thrill seeking) (e.g., runs into street without looking).
    13. Often loses things necessary for tasks or activities at school or at home.
    14. Often does not seem to listen to what is being said to him or her.
B. Onset before the age of 7 years.
C. Does not meet the criteria for pervasive developmental disorder.

American Psychiatric Association: *Diagnostic and Statistical Manual of Mental Disorders,* Third Edition, Revised, Washington, DC, American Psychiatric Association, 1987.

on the ability to control motor activity level, to determine which external stimuli are relevant or not relevant, and to reflect before acting (Shaywitz & Shaywitz, 1988).

The revised Diagnostic Statistical Manual of the American Psychiatric Association (American Psychiatric Association, 1987) eliminated the distinction between attention deficit disorder with and without hyperactivity because there is little empirical evidence supporting any differences. Rather than ADD and ADDH, attention deficit hyperactivity disorder is described, with a wide range of manifestations. The DSM-III-R criteria for attention deficit hyperactivity disorder are listed in Table 13.1. At least eight of these symptoms must be apparent for the diagnosis.

Studies of the relationship between learning disabilities and attention deficit disorders demonstrate that between 15 and 20 percent of children and adolescents with learning disabilities will also have ADHD (Silver, 1980; Halperin, Gittelman, Klein, & Rudel, 1984). Other researchers maintain, however, that the majority of learners identified as learning disabled demonstrate attention problems (Epstein, Bursuck, & Cullinan, 1985).

Using the current federal definition of learning disabilities, ADHD is an associated disorder but not a learning disability. As a consequence, children identified as having ADHD who are not learning disabled are not served in school programs for learners with learning disabilities (Silver, 1990). Yet, Eliason and Richman (1988) found that attentional problems account for 30 percent of the behavior problems among these learners.

Though children were originally felt to outgrow ADHD, current evidence suggests that the impulsivity and concentration problems related to the disorder persist into adulthood. Wender (1987) indicates that the primary symptoms that persist include attention problems, impulsivity, mood swings, disorganization and inability to complete tasks, and low stress tolerance. Barkley and associates (in press) concur, indicating that between 30 and 70 percent of children diagnosed as having ADHD continue to have either the full syndrome or some significant residual symptoms into young adulthood.

A "notice of inquiry" was included in Public Law 101–476 (The Individuals with Disabilities Education Act of 1990) which requires the Secretary of Education to solicit public comment regarding the appropriate components of an operational definition of attention deficit disorder. This appears to be an initial step in clarifying the concerns of parents and professionals with regards to this disorder and its place within services for individuals with disabilities.

Achievement

Learning disabilities are typically recognized as a discrepancy between ability and achievement (Rhodes & Dudley-Marling, 1988). However, judgments with regard to underachievement are difficult, and they may not discriminate between those students with learning disabilities and those who are underachieving or demonstrating low achievement. Identification as learning disabled tends to be limited to learners performing significantly below grade level. Though some exceptionally bright students with learning disabilities may be functioning at grade level, the effort and energy they apply to this "typical" level of achievement may be great and stressful.

Results of studies indicate that school psychologists may have difficulty discriminating reliably between students in the lowest quartile of academic achievement and children identified as learning disabled (Epps, Ysseldyke, & McGue, 1984). Rhodes and Dudley-Marling (1988) suggest that the only characteristic that separates groups of learners with learning disabilities from learners who are underachieving is the degree of underachievement. McLeod (1983) goes as far as suggesting that students with learning disabilities are a subset of underachievers.

Objective Two: To describe the identification and evaluation of learners identified as learning disabled.

Identification and Evaluation

The federal definition of learners with learning disabilities which appears in guidelines published in the *Federal Register* (1977), states:

> ". . . children with learning disabilities" means those children who have a disorder in one or more of the basic psychological processes involved in understanding or in using language, spoken or written, which disorder may manifest itself in imperfect ability to listen, think, speak, read, write, spell, or to do mathematical calculations. Such disorders include such conditions as perceptual handicaps, brain injury, minimal brain dysfunction, dyslexia, and developmental aphasia. Such terms do not include children who have learning problems which are primarily the result of visual, hearing, or motor handicaps, of mental retardation, of emotional disturbance, or of environmental, cultural, or economic disadvantage (p. 65083).

Many professionals consider this definition to be exclusionary, that is, that it defines what a learning disability is *not* rather than what it is.

According to the *Federal Register,* learners could be determined by a multidisciplinary team to have a learning disabilities if:

a. The child does not achieve commensurate with his or her age and ability levels in one or more of the following areas when provided with learning experiences appropriate for the child's age and ability levels: oral expression, listening comprehension, written expression, basic reading skill, reading comprehension, mathematics calculation, or mathematics reasoning.

b. The team finds that a child has a severe discrepancy between achievement and intellectual ability in one or more of the same areas listed in the preceding statement (p. 65083).

Learners could not be identified as learning disabled if the discrepancy between ability and achievement is the result of a hearing, visual, or motor disability, mental retardation, emotional disturbance, or environmental, cultural, or economic disadvantage.

The Interagency Committee on Learning Disabilities (1987) presented a report to Congress which identified four basic concerns related to the federal definition:

1. Learning disabilities are not clearly described as a heterogeneous group of disorders.
2. The persistence of learning disabilities through adulthood is not recognized.
3. The definition does not clearly indicate that there are inherent alterations in the way information is processed.
4. The potential for other disabling or environmental conditions to co-occur with learning disabilities is not recognized.

Hammill (1990) argues that the National Joint Council on Learning Disabilities definition represents the broadest current consensus on definition in the field. The NJCLD definition states that:

> Learning disabilities is a general term that refers to a heterogeneous group of disorders manifested by significant difficulties in the acquisition and use of listening, speaking, reading, writing, reasoning, or mathematical abilities. These disorders are intrinsic to the individual, presumed to be due to central nervous system dysfunction, and may occur across the life span.
>
> Problems in self-regulatory behaviors, social perception, and social interaction may exist with learning disabilities but do not in themselves constitute a learning disability.
>
> Although learning disabilities may occur concomitantly with other handicapping conditions (for example, sensory impairment, mental retardation, serious emotional disturbance) or with extrinsic influences (such as cultural differences, insufficient or inappropriate instruction), they are not the result of those conditions or influences (NJCLD Memorandum, 1987).

Though many states use a formula to describe the discrepancy between aptitude and achievement, Dangel and Ensminger (1988) found that about half of the learners assessed who did not demonstrate a discrepancy adequate for state eligibility were placed in special education classes on the basis of the judgement of the multidisciplinary team.

Assessment

The assessment of learners identified as learning disabled remains as problematic as the definition itself. Gelzheiser (1987), for example, argues for an emphasis on support for all challenging students on the basis of classroom needs, rather than on numbers of students identified as learning disabled. Early identification of learning disabilities remains a serious challenge. Preschool screening instruments lack rigor and generally have not been validated (Satz & Fletcher, 1988).

Ysseldyke, Thurlow, Graden, Wesson, Algozzine, and Deno (1983) summarized several issues related to learners identified as learning disabled. In 5 years of research, they could find no reliable psychometric differences between students labeled learning disabled and those who were perceived to be low achievers. In addition, identification as "learning disabled" depended on the criteria used, with different children being identified depending on the definition applied. If a child moved to a different school district, she or he may no longer be identified as learning disabled.

Algozzine (1991) argues that problems related to the identification of learners as learning disabled begin at the point of referral. The first problem, he suggests, is teachers' reasons for referral. For example, the new move towards "excellence" in education increases the likelihood that low-performing students will be referred as potentially disabled and appropriate for special education services. The second problem includes the high rate of referral, with a shortage of individuals well prepared and certified to conduct the necessary evaluations. The third problem is that over 90 percent of students referred are tested, and over 70 percent of those tested are then placed in special education programs.

Though current practice seems to involve searching for discrepancy between measured ability and performance, Algozzine (1991) proposes alternative means of assessment to guide the instruction of learners identified as learning disabled. He suggests **curriculum-based assessment.** This assessment approach includes direct observation and analysis of the learning environment, analysis of the processes used by students in approaching tasks, examination of students' products, and control and arrangement of tasks for the student. In his emphasis on curriculum-based instruction, Algozzine reminds us that "time spent looking for definitions, tests, or criteria is not time spent teaching students" (p. 53).

Objective Three: To describe the impact of learning disabilities on interactions in the home and classroom.

The Impact on Interactions in the Home and Classroom

Interactions in the Home

In an exploration of parents' perceptions of their children's adjustment problems, Konstantereas and Homatidis (1989) found that parents of learners identified as learning disabled reported externalizing behavior, such as fighting and acting out, as more stressful than internalizing behaviors such as withdrawal and daydreaming. Boys were rated by both parents as significantly more problematic and stressful than girls. Mothers who were younger and fathers with a lower self-concept were found to report greater child adjustment problems. Although mothers did not differ from fathers in rating children's behavior, they reported greater stress in response to them.

The academic and occupational outcomes of learners identified as learning disabled has been related to the socioeconomic status of the family. O'Connor and Spreen (1988) found that 28 percent of the variance among learners' outcomes was related to the fathers' socioeconomic status. This relationship held across groups of children with learning disabilities, whether hard and soft neurological or no neurological findings were reported.

In addition to socioeconomic status, Switzer (1990) reports four commonly observed factors in families with learners identified as having learning disabilities who were perceived to be high functioning: the families of these children accepted the learning problems, engaged with the child around achievement, and were consistent and explicit in their discipline. The child's role in the family was related to the child's success.

The teachers of learners identified as learning disabled perceived the parents of these children to have needs in excess of those they used or requested (Simpson, 1988). Parents' greatest reported need was that of information exchange.

Participation in parent group sessions has been found to increase parents' acceptance of their child being identified as learning disabled, and to increase their awareness of the potential impact of their behavior on the child (Omizo, Williams, & Omizo, 1986).

Interactions in the Classroom

The classroom status of learners identified as learning disabled has often been judged to be low. However, as Wiener (1987) urges, peer status must not be viewed as a unidirectional relationship between peer status and social skills. Peer status of these learners must be seen as an outcome of reciprocal interactions between learners identified as learning disabled and their teachers and peers. The source of peer relationship problems must be viewed as problems of both partners (Forman, 1987), and learners identified as learning disabled cannot be assumed to earn low esteem because of their limited social strategies.

The peer acceptance of learners identified as learning disabled has not been related to achievement or intelligence; rather, ratings by peers reveal that most learners identified as learning disabled are accepted by their classmates, and that acting out and withdrawn behaviors are related to peer rejection (Kistner & Gatlin, 1989). Wiener, Harris, and Shirer (1990), however, found that learners identified as having learning disabilities were less popular, due to difficulties with prosocial skills rather than because they exhibit negative social behavior.

Zigmond, Kerr, and Schaeffer (1988), using observational data, depicted the learner identified as learning disabled as a passive learner who comes to class ill-equipped for the lesson, goofs off during about 40 percent of class time, fails to follow teachers' procedural directions, avoids giving information, and seldom volunteers. Though this seems to focus on negative classroom behaviors, Zigmond and associates also found that in one-task behaviors, compliance rates to procedural requests, response rates to informational requests, asking questions, and making unsolicited, content-appropriate comments, learners identified as learning disabled did not significantly differ from their nonidentified peers.

Teachers, in rating the "teachability" of learners identified as learning disabled and nonidentified peers, report less positive ratings on identified students' school-appropriate behavior (Bender, 1986). In addition, they report a greater frequency of classroom problem behaviors (acting out, distractibility, and immaturity) among identified learners. Teachers also appear to view the problem behaviors of students identified as having learning disabilities as a major determinant of adaptive behavior in the classroom (Bender & Golden, 1989). Teachers rated learners identified as learning disabled as having significantly more difficulty than their peers in terms of frustration tolerance, adaptive assertiveness, and global adjustment (Toro, Weissberg, Guare, and Liebenstein, 1990).

Objective Four: To describe ways to mediate the environment for learners identified as learning disabled.

Mediating the Environment

The majority of learners identified as learning disabled are served in resource rooms (McNutt, 1986). Thurlow, Ysseldyke, Graden, and Algozzine (1983) find that more opportunities for differentiated instruction, particularly in reading, occurs in resource rooms, though no real differences were noted in the amount of time students were actively engaged in instruction when comparing resource rooms with general

*T*able 13.2   Strategy for Maintaining Attention in Class

SLANT —
S — sit up
L — look at the teacher
A — act interested
N — nod when you understand
T — take part in discussions

education classrooms. In a critical analysis of resource rooms, Wiederholt and Chamberlain (1989) report great variability in terms of what occurs in resource rooms.

As indicated earlier, most learners identified as learning disabled are educated to some extent within general education. In one study, the extent to which students remained in general education, however, was determined one-third of the time by the data generated by the battery of assessment instruments rather than by observational or behavioral data (Vance, Bahr, Hubert, & Ewer-Jones, 1988).

Cognitive behavior modification (also called metacognitive training or cognitive behavior management) has been used in working with alleviating social skill problems of learners identified as learning disabled. In cognitive behavior modification, learners are taught (a) to recognize and define the problem that exists, (b) to identify alternative courses of action and likely consequences, (c) to select an adequate problem solution, (d) to carry out the solution through instructions, modeling, reinforcement, peer feedback, and other ways, and (e) to evaluate the effectiveness of the solution attempted (Cullinan, Epstein, & Lloyd, 1991). Cognitive behavior modification has been used successfully in content area instruction as well as in improving social skills (Ross & Braden, 1991).

Most research applying cognitive strategies with learners identified as learning disabled has focused on self-monitoring (Rooney & Hallahan, 1985). This approach is useful in that it stresses self-initiative, engages the learner, and seems appropriate in managing distractibility and impulsivity (Hallahan & Kauffman, 1988).

Learning strategies are one form of cognitive behavior modification frequently used with learners identified as learning disabled. These approaches focus on helping the learner acquire content through **strategies training** (Mercer, 1988). Derry (1990) describes a learning strategy as the complete plan one formulates for accomplishing a learning goal, whereas a learning tactic is described as any individual processing technique one uses in service of the plan. Strategies build on mental processes such as focusing attention, building schema (developing a mental outline or plan), comprehension monitoring, and idea elaboration.

Strategy instruction involves selecting a strategy, such as paraphrasing reading material, and teaching it directly to the learner to increase his or her comprehension. The strategy in itself is taught, but the application is restricted to the task for which it is applied. In this way, content and strategy are learned at the same time (Mercer, 1988). A sample strategy for maintaining attention in class is presented in Table 13.2.

Larson and Gerber (1987) found that among adjudicated delinquent adolescents identified as learning disabled, those given metacognitive training showed significant improvements in quantity of negative behavior reports, staff ratings on rehabilitation achievement, and institutional living unit phase level promotions.

Teachers learn about their students through observation.

Metacognitive programming is an educational program structured to assist learners in planning, implementing, and evaluating approaches to learning and problem solving. Although both those identified as learning disabled and those not identified who received cognitive training significantly improved their behavior, on every variable the learners identified as learning disabled had a greater proportion of learners improve. Parallel improvement in metacognitive skills and significant correlations between social metacognitive scores and indicators of effective behavior supported the notion that social metacognition was the "mechanism" of change and that social metacognition mediates over social behavior in novel contexts without specific cuing from the environment.

Social skills training also uses cognitive behavior modification techniques. One of the most widely used social skills training techniques typically involves five steps: (1) instruction; (2) demonstration in self or using others; (3) imitation; (4) feedback; and (5) practice (Cartledge & Milburn, 1986). Role playing is frequently used to assist students in learning and practicing the technique.

School survival skills and classroom survival skills are often taught through structured learning experiences, much in the same way as social skills training is implemented. However, the focus of these group training sessions is on those skills needed to survive in school. McGinnis and associates describe thirteen classroom survival skills, including listening, asking for help, saying "thank you," bringing materials to class, following instructions, completing assignments, contributing to discussions, offering to help adults, asking questions, ignoring distractions, making corrections, finding something to occupy time, and setting goals (McGinnis, Goldstein, Sprafkin, & Gershaw, 1984). Silverman and associates describe three groups of school survival skills, including behavior control, teacher-pleasing behaviors, and study skills (Silverman, Zigmond, & Sansone, 1981). Small group instruction, role playing, and challenge activities are used to practice the skills. Four methods of instruction are utilized: presentation, practice, mastery in isolation, and mastery in context.

Small group instruction allows for social skills to be introduced.

Tutoring   In a review of empirical studies of **tutoring** or one-on-one instruction, involving learners identified as learning disabled, Scruggs and Richter (1988) found that these learners can and do learn in tutoring situations. However, there was little data to support social benefits to the tutors or tutees. Though tutoring supports learners in passing their classes, remaining in school, and addressing immediate problems, it generally serves as a short-term solution (Alley & Deshler, 1979). The use of tutoring also may increase the learner's dependence on the resource room. Special education teachers, particularly at the secondary level, may not be adequately trained in content areas to support learners in tutoring sessions.

Medication   Medication is helpful to many children identified as demonstrating ADHD (Wender, 1987). The use of medication requires a physician with specific knowledge about children and youth with such behavioral issues and psychogenic medication, usually a psychiatrist. Wender suggests that parents and professionals may be hesitant to use medication because (a) it indicates a physical, and therefore perhaps persistent rather than developmental, problem; (b) treatment seems artificial, controlling rather than addressing the behavior; and (c) parents fear the child will become dependent on the medication both physically and psychologically.

The most commonly used medication for learners identified as having ADHD are stimulants, including **methylphenidate (Ritalin)** and **d-amphetamine (Dexedrine).** Approximately two-thirds of the children and youth identified as having ADHD respond to these medications by becoming calmer, less active, more attentive, and easier to manage. The duration of these medications is short-lived (about 4 hours for Ritalin, 6 hours for Dexedrine). Side effects include loss of appetite and sleeplessness. Medication must be carefully monitored by the physician with teachers and parents documenting the learner's behaviors.

According to Wender (1987), when medication is effective, it produces a dramatically effective response. The effects of stimulant medication on children identified as having ADHD have been reported as (a) improved peer perceptions of the child (Henker & Buhrmester, 1989), (b) increased academic performance (Tannock, Schacher, & Carr, 1989), and (c) improved task performance (Milich & Lichet, 1989).

Practicing the writing process may improve the quality of students' writing.

Though medical strategies for the treatment of ADHD have been criticized, efforts to increase the attention of individuals through alternative strategies have not been particularly successful. However, Gordon, Thomason, Cooper, and Ivers (1991) did find a response cost program (that is, a loss of the reinforcer occurs as a result of inappropriate behavior) for increasing attention temporarily effective, but results dissipated when the program was not enforced.

Holistic Communication Based Approaches

Holistic communication based approaches emerged in response to the failure of traditional, mechanics-driven direct teaching strategies to increase the writing skills of learners identified as learning disabled. Holistic approaches refer to those in which persons and processes are seen as a whole and treated in such a manner rather than the parts being treated separately. Vallecorsa, Ledford, and Parnell (1991) describe the use of the process approach to writing, as described by Graves (1983), for learners identified as learning disabled. In this studio approach, writing is presented as an activity in which errors are to be expected and serve as ways to learn. Writing is seen as a process involving planning, multiple drafts, editing, and revising. Rules of grammar, punctuation, capitalization, and spelling are taught as needed within the context of composing. Students are given extensive opportunities to write so that they will have multiple means of practicing the writing process.

Teaching writing as a process appears to help learners identified as learning disabled improve the maturity of their writing and their vocabulary level (Bos, 1988). It has been demonstrated to have a positive impact on the length and overall quality of students' compositions (Roit & McKenzie, 1985).

*T*able 13.3   Procedures for Reciprocal Teaching

1. Begin by discussing why a task may be difficult, the importance of strategies, and the conditions for using strategies.
2. Introduce, define, and provide the rationale for the strategy.
3. Practice the strategy in family situations.
4. Teacher checks the learners' use of the strategy before the dialogue begins.
5. Learners apply the strategy to increasingly difficult aspects of the tasks and are supported by the teacher.
6. Teacher engages in dialogue with students and models the use of strategies by thinking out loud.
7. Learners comment on the model, clarify, make predictions, and answer questions.
8. Responsibility for the dialogue is shifted from the teacher to the learners through guided practice.
9. Teacher monitors performance and provides additional instruction and modeling when necessary.

(Palincsar & Brown, 1984; 1986).

In addition to compositions, dialogue journals have been used to increase the writing fluency of learners identified as learning disabled (Gaustad & Messenheimer-Young, 1991). In this process, the student writes in his or her journal and the teacher reads and responds. This written conversation reinforces the tenet that written work is in itself communication, rather than merely a mechanical skill.

A well-documented holistic approach to reading instruction is presented by Palincsar and Brown (1986). This "reciprocal teaching" approach engages students in a dialogue between the teacher and students. Instruction begins at the point where it is required to support the learner in the next step needed to complete the task, and faded so that learners are challenged to apply the strategy. The steps involved in using reciprocal teaching are summarized in Table 13.3.

Learners have been found to generalize this strategy over time and settings (Brown & Palincsar, 1987).

Technological Aids   Recent advances in technology may assist in the instruction of learners identified as learning disabled. Such technologies, in all probability, will have a greater impact on instruction in the future. Of greatest assistance to learners identified as learning disabled, at present, appears to be computer-assisted instruction. Kneedler (1984) suggests that computer-assisted instruction can be used for (a) drill and practice, and (b) learning style modification. Ellis and Sabornie (1986) find that educational software may take any of the following formats: (a) drill and practice, (b) tutorials, in which the computer serves as teacher, (c) games, to promote problem solving, (d) simulations, (e) problem solving, and (f) word processing. They report good results when computer-assisted instruction supplements rather than replaces teacher instruction.

Objective Five: To describe the impact of learning disabilities on participation in larger social systems—the community and society.

The Impact on Participation in the Community and Society

Learners identified as learning disabled appear to retain their learning patterns through adulthood (Kroll, 1984). These learning problems have a continued impact on their lives, demonstrated through lower employment rates and income than the general population, difficulties in locating and holding jobs, and their remaining home far beyond their teenage years. The persistence and pervasiveness of learning disabilities throughout an individual's life, and inappropriate adult diagnostic

Vocational education prepares adults for the working world.

procedures, are emerging as such essential issues that the National Joint Committee on Learning Disabilities has issued a position paper with a "call to action" in response to the problem (National Joint Committee on Learning Disabilities, 1987).

In a survey of adults identified as learning disabled, the results describe individuals with ongoing specific problems in education, employment, and psychosocial functioning who aspire to learn more about themselves and their learning disabilities (Malcolm, Polatajko, & Simons, 1990). In another study, many of the characteristics of learning disabilities, including low motivation, distractibility, self-concept problems, emotional instability, and lack of organization, were found to persist through adulthood (Buchanan & Wolf, 1986). While many of the adults in this study described themselves as lacking motivation, they tended to be unusually persistent in efforts to achieve their goals.

Employment

Adults identified as learning disabled, though generally optimistic about future career success, voiced frustration regarding previous jobs and admitted employment-associated anxieties (Kokaska & Skolnik, 1986). In a large-scale, national needs assessment, a comparison across all need areas indicated that service providers and consumers identified vocational needs involving securing an appropriate job and vocational rehabilitation services as the most critical need area of adults identified as learning disabled, with secondary areas of concern including poor self-concept, lack of self-understanding, and lack of self-acceptance (Hoffman, Shelton, Minskoff, & Sautter, 1987). Michaels (1989) notes that employers may need to become more flexible in supervisory styles when working with these adults.

Social competence is viewed as the most serious vocational adjustment of adults identified as learning disabled (Cartledge, 1987). Due to persistent vocational problems, Smith (1988) believes that educational interventions should be targeted on the demands of adulthood and adaptation to adult roles, that is, work. DeBettencourt, Zigmond, and Thornton (1989) however, found that in comparison with their same-age peers who also dropped out of secondary education, learners identified as learning disabled did not vary in how they fared in their employment. However, identified learners were more likely to drop out of school and demonstrated lower age competency levels.

Post-Secondary Education

Involvement in extracurricular activities while in high school, the use of community resources, intelligence, and reading and mathematic grade equivalent scores were found to be important factors that differentiated between learners identified as learning disabled who chose to participate in post-secondary education during the year after high school and those who did not (Miller, Snider, & Rzonca, 1990). Bursuck, Rose, Cowen, and Yahaya (1989) explored the nature of services available for learners identified as learning disabled who engaged in post-secondary education. Ninety percent of the responding members of the Association of Handicapped Student Service Programs institutions indicated that they provided taped textbooks, tape recordings of lectures, notetakers, and modified exam procedures. Most of the institutions also had special services including academic advisement, tutoring, counseling, advocacy, and progress monitoring. Seventy-seven percent had reading remediation, 82 percent offered written language remediation, 78 percent offered remedial math, and 86 percent offered remedial study skills. Few schools monitored whether or not their students identified as learning disabled were graduated.

Three factors have been associated with how services are provided to post-secondary learners identified as learning disabled (Nelson & Lignugaris-Kraft, 1989). First, differences in program emphasis and service delivery reflected differences in program objectives, from supporting students in classes to remediating basic skills. The provision of remedial services or support services often reflects differences in the expected entry-level skills of students. Second, the mission of the college influenced services, by providing opportunities ranging from preparation for high school equivalency to noncredit courses. Finally, the amount of funding allocated was associated with how services were delivered.

According to McGuire and Shaw (1987), the learner identified as learning disabled who chooses to pursue college work should identify the post-secondary program which best meets his or her needs. Three major components should be explored, including (a) the characteristics of the students, (b) the characteristics of the institution, and (c) the characteristics of the support program available for individuals identified as learning disabled. They state, however, that the proper gathering of information to make appropriate decisions takes time, and that both students and parents should be actively involved throughout high school in planning for the most appropriate educational program to prepare the student for post-secondary study.

Summary

Over the past three decades, learning disabilities have been conceived in many ways, ranging from a "dysfunction of the brain" (Johnson & Myklebust, 1967), to a category of disability derived to explain the growing number of reading failures (Sleeter, 1984), to a developmental lag in movement through the preoperational and concrete operational stages, to the formal operational stages of Piagetian development (Fakouri, 1991). In this chapter questions related to the validity of identifying large numbers of learners as learning disabled is explored, as well as the impact of learning disabilities in the school and home. The constructivist view is presented and discussed as consistent with systems theory.

Learners identified as learning disabled are the largest and fastest growing group of learners with disabilities. However, these learners are far more heterogeneous than homogeneous. These learners have common problems in (a) working and learning; (b) chronic, low-level depression and relatively high, free-floating anxiety; and (c) unconscious concerns about self and others. In terms of social and behavioral abilities, learners identified as learning disabled may have difficulty in peer relationships. These learners often have a speech, language, or hearing problem, manifested both in oral and written communication.

The definition of learning disabilities has long been controversial. Early identification of learning disabilities remains a serious challenge. The use of standardized measures is giving way to curriculum based assessment, and an emphasis on what the learner knows.

The progress demonstrated by learners identified as learning disabled has been related to socioeconomic status. In the classroom, peer status is usually poor. Teachers' acceptance of the learners is related to their perception of how difficult the learner is to teach.

Most learners identified as learning disabled are served in resource rooms. Cognitive behavior management, tutoring, and medication are all used to mediate the environment. Two emerging trends in intervention include holistic communication based approaches and technological aids.

Learners identified as learning disabled retain their learning patterns through adulthood. Difficulties in employment may result from their challenges in the area of social competence.

References

Algozzine, B. (1991). Decision-making and curriculum-based assessment. In B. Y. L. Wong (Ed.), *Learning about learning disabilities.* (pp. 40–55). San Diego, CA: Academic Press.

Alley, G., & Deshler, D. (1979). *Teaching the learning disabled adolescent: Strategies and methods.* Denver, CO: Love.

American Psychiatric Association (1987). *Diagnostic and statistical manual of mental disorders* (3rd ed., revised). Washington, DC: Author.

Beltempo, J., & Achille, P. A. (1990). The effect of special class placement on the self-concept of children with learning disabilities. *Child Study Journal, 20* (2), 81–103.

Bender, W. N. (1986). Teachability and behavior of learning disabled children. *Psychological Reports, 59* (2, Pt. 1), 471–476.

Bender, W. N., & Golden, L. B. (1988). Adaptive behavior of learning disabled and non-learning disabled children. *Learning Disability Quarterly, 11* (1), 55–61.

Bender, W. N., & Golden, L. B. (1989). Prediction of adaptive behavior of learning disabled students in self-contained and resource classes. *Learning Disabilities Research, 5,* 45–50.

Bos, C. (1988). Process-oriented writing: Instructional implications for mildly handicapped students. *Exceptional Children, 54,* 523–527.

Brown, A. L., & Palincsar, A. S. (1987). Reciprocal teaching of comprehension strategies. In J. Borkowski & J. D. Day (Eds.), *Intelligence and cognition in special children: Comparative studies of giftedness, mental retardation, and learning disabilities.* New York: Ablex.

Buchanan, M., & Wolf, J. S. (1986). A comprehensive study of learning disabled adults. *Journal of Learning Disabilities, 19* (1), 34–38.

Bursuck, W. D., Rose, E., Cowen, S., & Yahaya, M. A. (1989). Nationwide survey of postsecondary education services for students with learning disabilities. *Exceptional Children, 56,* 236–245.

Candler, A. C., & Hildreth, B. L. (1990). Characteristics of language disorders in learning disabled students. *Academic Therapy, 25,* 333–343.

Carlson, C. I. (1987). Social interaction goals and strategies of children with learning disabilities. *Journal of Learning Disabilities, 20,* 306–311.

Cartledge, G. (1987). Social skills, learning disabilities, and occupational success. *Journal of Reading, Writing, and Learning Disabilities, 3* (3), 223–239.

Cartledge, G., & Milburn, J. F. (1986). *Teaching social skills to children* (2nd ed). New York: Pergamon.

Cohen, J. (1986). Learning disabilities and psychological development in childhood and adolescence. *Annals of Dyslexia, 36,* 287–300.

Cullinan, D., Epstein, M. H., & Lloyd, J. W. (1991). Evaluation of conceptual models of behavioral disorders. *Behavioral Disorders, 16* (2), 148–157.

Dangel, H. L., & Ensminger, E. E. (1988). The use of a discrepancy formula with LD students. *Learning Disabilities Focus, 4,* 24–31.

DeBettencourt, L. U., Zigmond, N., & Thornton, H. (1989). Follow-up of postsecondary-age rural learning disabled graduates and dropouts. *Exceptional Children, 56,* 40–49.

Derry, S. J. (1990). Remediating academic difficulties through strategy training: The acquisition of useful knowledge. *Remedial and Special Education, 11* (6), 19–31.

Eliason, M. J., & Richman, L. C. (1988). Behavior and attention in LD children. *Learning Disability Quarterly, 11,* 360–369.

Epps, D., Ysseldyke, J. E., & McGue, M. (1984). "I know one when I see one"—Differentiating LD and non-LD students. *Learning Disability Quarterly, 7,* 89–101.

Epstein, M. H., Bursuck, W., & Cullinan, D. (1985). Patterns of behavior problems among the learning disabled: Boys aged 12–18, girls aged 6–11, and girls aged 12–18. *Learning Disability Quarterly, 9,* 43–54.

Fakouri, M. E. (1991). Learning disabilities: A Piagetian perspective. *Psychology in the Schools, 28,* 70–76.

Federal Register (1977). 42, 65082–65085.

Forman, E. A. (1987). Peer relationships of learning disabled children: A contextualist perspective. *Learning Disabilities Research, 2* (2), 80–90.

Gaustad, M. G., & Messenheimer-Young, T. (1991). Dialogue journals for students with learning disabilities. *Teaching Exceptional Children, 23* (Spring), 28–30.

Gelzheiser, L. M. (1987). Reducing the number of students identified as learning disabled: A question of practice, philosophy, or policy? *Exceptional Children, 54,* 145–150.

Gibbs, D. P., & Cooper, E. B. (1989). Prevalence of communication disorders in students with learning disabilities. *Journal of Learning Disabilities, 22* (1), 60–63.

Gordon, M., Thomason, D., Cooper, S., & Ivers, C. L. (1991). Nonmedical treatment of ADHD/hyperactivity. *Journal of School Psychology, 29,* 151–159.

Graves, D. (1983). *Writing: Teachers and children at work.* Exeter, NH: Heineman.

Hallahan, D. P., & Kauffman, J. M. (1988). *Exceptional children: Introduction to special education* (4th ed.). Englewood Cliffs, NJ: Prentice Hall.

Halperin, J. M., Gittelman, R., Klein, D. F., & Rudel, R. G. (1984). Reading disabled hyperactive children: A distinct subgroup of attention deficit disorder with hyperactivity. *Journal of Abnormal Child Psychology, 12,* 1–14.

Hammill, D. D. (1990). On defining learning disabilities: An emerging consensus. *Journal of Learning Disabilities, 23,* 74–84.

Healey, K. N. (1987). The price of social ineptitude in learning disabled children: The challenge ahead. *Journal of Reading, Writing, and Learning Disabilities International, 3,* (2), 149–160.

Henker, B., & Buhrmester, D. (1989). Does stimulant medication improve the peer status of hyperactive children? *Journal of Consulting and Clinical Psychology, 57,* 545.

Hinshelwood, J. (1917). *Congenital word blindness.* London: Lewis.

Hoffman, F., Shelton, K. L., Minskoff, E. H., & Sautter, S. W. (1987). Needs of learning disabled adults. *Journal of Learning Disabilities, 20* (1), 43–52.

Interagency Committee on Learning Disabilities (1987). Learning disabilities: A report to the U.S. Congress. Bethesda, MD: National Institutes of Health.

Johnson, D. J., & Grant, J. O. (1989). Written narratives of normal and learning disabled children. *Annals of Dyslexia, 39,* 140–158.

Johnson, D., & Myklebust, H. R. (1967). *Learning disabilities: Educational principles and practices.* New York: Grune and Stratton.

Kistner, J. A., & Gatlin, D. (1989). Correlates of peer rejection among children with learning disabilities. *Learning Disability Quarterly, 13,* 133–140.

Kneedler, R. D. (1984). *Special education for today.* Englewood Cliffs, NJ: Prentice Hall.

Kokaska, C. J., & Skolnik, J. (1986). Employment suggestions from LD adults. *Academic Therapy, 21,* (5), 573–577.

Konstantereas, M. M., & Homatidis, S. (1989). Parental perception of learning-disabled children's adjustment problems and related stress. *Journal of Abnormal Child Psychology, 17,* 177–186.

Kroll, L. G. (1984). LD's: What happens when they are no longer children? *Academic Therapy, 20* (2), 133–148.

laGreca, A. M. (1987). Children with learning disabilities: Interpersonal skills and social competence. *Journal of Reading, Writing, and Learning Disabilities International, 3* (2), 167–185.

Larson, K. A., & Gerber, M. M. (1987). Effects of social metacognitive training for enhancing overt behavior in learning disabled and low achieving delinquents. *Exceptional Children, 54,* 201–211.

Lee, R. F., & Kamhi, A. G. (1990). Metaphoric competence in children with learning disabilities. *Journal of Learning Disabilities, 23,* 476–482.

MacLachlan, B. G., & Chapman, R. S. (1988). Communication breakdowns in normal and language learning disabled children's conversation and narration. *Journal of Speech and Hearing Disorders, 53* (1), 2–7.

Malcolm, C. B., Polatajko, H. J., & Simons, J. (1990). A descriptive study of adults with suspected learning disabilities. *Journal of Learning Disabilities, 23* (8), 518–520.

Margalit, M., Raviv, A., & Pahn-Steinmetz, N. (1988). Social competence of learning disabled children: Cognitive and emotional aspects. *Exceptional Children, 35* (3), 179–189.

McConaughy, S. H. (1986). Social competence and behavioral problems of learning disabled boys aged 12–16. *Journal of Learning Disabilities, 19,* 101–106.

McGinnis, E., Goldstein, R. P., Sprafkin, R. P., & Gershaw, N. J. (1984). *Skillstreaming the elementary school child.* Champaign, IL: Research Press.

McGuire, J. M., & Shaw, S. F. (1987). A decision making process for the college-bound student: Matching learner, institution, and support program. *Learning Disabilities Quarterly, 10,* 106–111.

McKinney, J. D. (1989). Longitudinal research on the behavioral characteristics of children with learning disabilities. *Journal of Learning Disabilities, 22* (3), 141–150.

McKinney, J. D., & Speece, D. L. (1983). Classroom behavior and the academic progress of learning disabled students. *Journal of Applied Developmental Psychology, 4* (2), 149–161.

McLeod, J. (1983). Learning disability is for educators. *Journal of Learning Disabilities, 16,* 23–24.

McNutt, G. (1986). The status of learning disabilities in the states: Consensus or controversy. *Journal of Learning Disabilities, 19,* 291–293.

Mercer, C. D. (1988). *Students with learning disabilities.* Columbus, OH: Merrill.

Michaels, C. A. (1989). Employment: The final frontier. *Rehabilitation Counseling Bulletin, 33* (1), 67–73.

Milich, R., & Lichet, B. G. (1989). Attention deficit hyperactivity disordered boys' evaluations of and attributions for task performance on medication versus placebo. *Journal of Abnormal Child Psychology, 98,* 280.

Miller, R. J., Snider, B., & Rzonca, C. (1990). Variables related to the decision of young adults with learning disabilities to participate in postsecondary education. *Journal of Learning Disabilities, 23,* 349–354.

National Joint Committee on Learning Disabilities (1987). Adults with learning disabilities: A call to action. *Journal of Learning Disabilities, 20,* 172–175.

Nelson, R., & Lignugaris-Kraft, B. (1989). Postsecondary education for students with learning disabilities. *Exceptional Children, 56,* 246–265.

O'Connor, S. C., & Spreen, O. (1988). The relationship between parents' socioeconomic status and education level, and adult occupational and educational achievement of children with learning disabilities. *Journal of Learning Disabilities, 21,* 148–153.

Olson, J. L., Wong, B. Y. L., & Marx, R. W. (1983). Linguistic and metacognitive aspects of normally achieving and learning disabled children's communication process. *Learning Disabilities Quarterly, 6,* 289–304.

Omizo, M. M., Williams, R. E., & Omizo, S. A. (1986). The effects of participation in parent group sessions on child-rearing attitudes among parents of learning disabled children. *Exceptional Children, 33,* 134–139.

Palincsar, A. S., & Brown, A. L. (1984). Reciprocal teaching of comprehension fostering and comprehension monitoring activities. *Cognition and Instruction, 1,* 117–175.

Palincsar, A. S., & Brown, A. L. (1986). Interactive teaching to promote independent reading from text. *Reading Teacher, 39,* 771–777.

Poplin, M. S. (1988). The reductionist fallacy in learning disabilities: Replicating the past by reducing the present. *Journal of Learning Disabilities, 21,* 389–400.

Quinn, D. (1984). Perspective from the other side: A message of hope for learning disability teachers and students. *Learning Disability Quarterly, 7,* 295–298.

Reiff, H. B., & Gerber, P. (1990). Cognitive correlates of social perception in students with learning disabilities. *Journal of Learning Disabilities, 23,* 260–262.

Rhodes, L. K., & Dudley-Marling, C. (1988). *Readers and writers with a difference.* Portsmouth, NH: Heinemann.

Rodriguez, C. M., & Routh, D. K. (1989). Depression, anxiety, and attributional style in learning disabled and nonlearning disabled children. *Journal of Clinical Child Psychology, 18,* 299–304.

Roit, M., & McKenzie, R. (1985). Disorders of written communication: An instructional priority for LD students. *Journal of Learning Disabilities, 18,* 258–260.

Rooney, K. J., & Hallahan, D. P. (1985). Future directions for cognitive behavior modification research. *Remedial and Special Education, 6,* 46–51.

Ross, P. A., & Braden, J. P. (1991). The effects of token reinforcement versus cognitive behavior modification on learning-disabled students' math skills. *Psychology in the Schools, 28,* 247–256.

Satz, P., & Fletcher, J. M. (1988). Early identification of learning disabled children. *Journal of Consulting and Clinical Psychology, 56,* 824–829.

Scruggs, T. E., & Richter, L. (1988). Tutoring learning disabled students: A critical review. *Learning Disability Quarterly, 11*, 274–286.

Shaywitz, S. E., & Shaywitz, B. E. (1988). Attention deficit disorder: Current perspectives. In J. F. Kavanagh & T. J. Truss, Jr. (Eds.), *Learning disabilities: Proceedings of the national conference* (pp. 369–423). Parktown, MD: York Press.

Silver, L. B. (1980). The relationship between learning disabilities, hyperactivity, distractibility, and behavior problems. *Journal of the American Academy of Child Psychiatry, 20*, 385–397.

Silver, L. B. (1990). Attention deficit-hyperactivity disorder: Is it a learning disability or related disorder? *Journal of Learning Disabilities, 23*, 394–397.

Silverman, R., Zigmond, N., & Sansone, J. (1981). Teaching coping skills to adolescents with learning problems. *Focus on Exceptional Children, 13* (6), 1–20.

Simpson, R. L. (1988). Needs of parents and families whose children have learning and behavior problems. *Behavioral Disorders, 14*, 40–47.

Sleeter, C. (1984). Why is there learning disabilities? A critical analysis of the birth of the field in its social context. Paper presented at the annual meeting of the American Educational Research Association, Chicago, IL.

Smith, J. O. (1988). Social and vocational problems of adults with learning disabilities: A review of the literature. *Learning Disabilities Focus, 4*, 46–58.

Switzer, L. B. (1990). Family factors associated with academic progress for children with learning disabilities. *Elementary School Guidance and Counseling, 24*, 200–206.

Tannock, R., Schacher, R. J., & Carr, R. P. (1989). Dose-response effects of methylphenidate on academic performance and overt behavior in hyperactive children. *Pediatrics, 84*, 648.

Terrell, B. Y. (1990). Some thoughts on language-learning disabilities and the preschool child. *Hearsay* (Spring-Summer), 58–59.

Thomas, C. C., Englert, C. S., & Gregg, S. (1987). An analysis of errors and strategies in the expository writing of learning disabled students. *Remedial and Special Education, 8* (1), 21–30.

Thurlow, M. L., Ysseldyke, J. E., Graden, J., & Algozzine, B. (1983). What's special about the special education resource room for learning disabled adolescents? *Learning Disability Quarterly, 6* (3), 283–288.

Torgesen, J. K. (1991). Learning disabilities: Historical and conceptual issues. In B. L. Wong (Ed.), *Learning about learning disabilities,* (p. 3–31). San Diego, CA: Academic Press.

Toro, P. A., Weissberg, R. P., Guare, J., & Liebenstein, N. L. (1990). A comparison of children with and without learning disabilities on social problem solving skill, school behavior, and family background. *Journal of Learning Disabilities 23*, 115–120.

U.S. Department of Education (1990). *Twelfth annual report to Congress on the implementation of the Education of the Handicapped Act.* Washington, DC: Author.

U.S. Department of Education (1992). *Fourteenth annual report to Congress on the implementation of the Individuals with Disabilities Education Act.* Washington, DC: Author.

Vallecorsa, A. L., & Garris, E. (1990). Story composition skills of middle-grade students with learning disabilities. *Exceptional Children, 57*, 48–54.

Vallecorsa, A. L., Ledford, R. R., & Parnell, G. G. (1991). Strategies for teaching composition skills to students with learning disabilities. *Teaching Exceptional Children, 23* (2), 52–54.

Vance, L. K., Bahr, C. M., Hubert, T. J., & Ewer-Jones, B. (1988). An analysis of variables that affect special education placement decisions. *Journal of Learning Disabilities, 21*, 444–447.

Wender, P. (1987). *The hyperactive child, adolescent, and adult.* New York: Oxford University Press.

Wiederholt, J. L., & Chamberlain, S. P. (1989). A critical analysis of resource programs. *Remedial and Special Education, 11* (1), 22–31.

Wiener, J. (1987). Peer status of learning disabled children and adolescents. *Learning Disabilities Research, 2,* 62–79.

Wiener, J., Harris, P. J., & Shirer, C. (1990). Achievement and social-behavioral correlates of peer status in LD children. *Learning Disability Quarterly, 13,* 114–127.

Wood, D. M. (1991). Discrepancy formulas and classification and identification issues that affect diagnoses of learning disabilities. *Psychology in the Schools, 28,* 219–225.

Ysseldyke, J. E., & Algozzine, B. (1983). LD or not LD: That's not the question! *Journal of Learning Disabilities, 16,* 29–31.

Ysseldyke, J. E., Thurlow, M. L., Graden, J. L., Wesson, C., Algozzine, B., & Deno, S. L. (1983). Generalizations from five years of research on assessment and decision making: The University of Minnesota Institute. *Exceptional Education Quarterly, 4* (1), 75–93.

Zigmond, N., Kerr, M. M., & Schaeffer, A. (1988). Behavior patterns of learning disabled and non-learning disabled adolescents in high school academic classes. *Remedial and Special Education, 9* (2), 6–12.

Chapter

14

Learners with Mild or Moderate Mental Retardation

After completing this chapter, you will be able to:

1. describe the personal characteristics of learners with mild or moderate mental retardation.

2. describe the identification and evaluation of learners with mild or moderate mental retardation.

3. describe the impact of mild or moderate mental retardation on interactions in the home and classroom.

4. describe ways to mediate the environment for learners with mild or moderate mental retardation.

5. describe the impact of mild or moderate mental retardation on participation in the larger social systems of the community and society.

*K*ey Words and Phrases

basic concepts	moderate mental retardation
deviance disavowal	normalcy fabrication
educable mental retardation	profound mental retardation
mental retardation	severe mental retardation
mild mental retardation	trainable mental retardation

ONE OF THE MOST SIGNIFICANT FACTORS WHICH MUST BE RECOGNIZED AS INFLUENCING THE INTERACTIONS OF mentally retarded individuals is their stigmatized identity. Retarded and nonretarded persons alike seek to present themselves as competent relative to the requirements or expectations operating in the social situation in which they are participating, as competent members of their society. For those who have been ascribed a special status by society specifically on the basis of their perceived incompetence, however, the problem of presenting a demeanor of competence becomes particularly salient. Virtually every social interaction in which they participate is affected by their awareness of the stigma attached to incompetence and their attempts to disguise or disavow it. In their interactions, such individuals often have a hidden agenda. They are not only trying to convey information, ask a question, or participate in a conversation, they are trying to protect their self-esteem by demonstrating competence or disguising incompetence. (Kiernan and Sabsay, 1993, p. 145) ∎

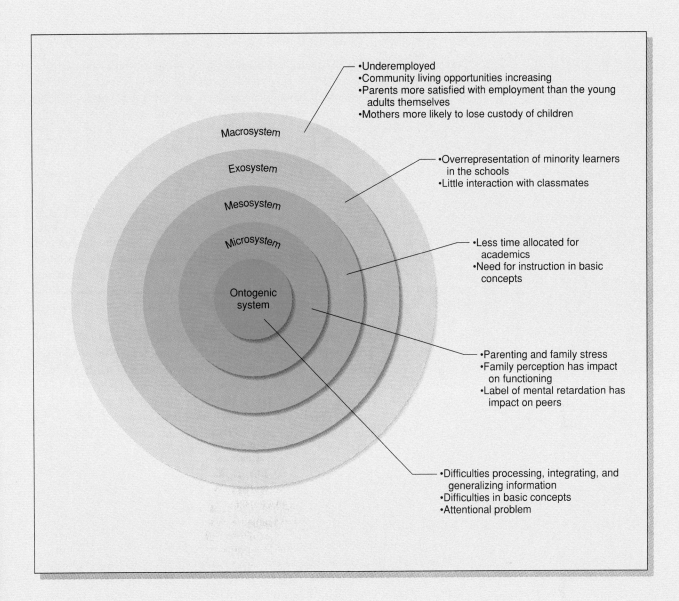

Macrosystem

•Underemployed
•Community living opportunities increasing
•Parents more satisfied with employment than the young
 adults themselves
•Mothers more likely to lose custody of children

Exosystem

•Overrepresentation of minority learners
 in the schools
•Little interaction with classmates

Mesosystem

•Less time allocated for
 academics
•Need for instruction in basic
 concepts

Microsystem

Ontogenic
system

•Parenting and family stress
•Family perception has impact
 on functioning
•Label of mental retardation has
 impact on peers

•Difficulties processing, integrating, and
 generalizing information
•Difficulties in basic concepts
•Attentional problem

Introduction

Forness and Kavale (1984) contend that the education of those with mental retardation has historically served as a catalyst for resolution of major issues in special education. Through efforts of parents and professionals working with individuals with mental retardation, issues such as zero reject education, early intervention, the misuse of intelligence testing, the pejorative effects of labeling, the efficacy of special classes, mainstreaming, and parental participation in special education placement emerged.

The number of learners with mental retardation receiving services in public schools has consistently decreased since the 1976–77 school year, with a total decrease of over 39.0 percent or approximately 320,000 students between 1976–77 and 1990–91 (U.S. Department of Education, 1992). In 1990–91, mental retardation, representing 12.0 percent of all learners with disabilities, was the third largest classification of student disabilities, following learning disabilities and speech and language impairment. In 1976–77, by contrast, learners with mental retardation accounted for 24.9 percent of all learners with disabilities and was the second largest group of disabled learners, following only those with speech and language impairment.

During the 1989–90 school year, learners with mental retardation represented approximately 1.2 percent of the total population of learners from 6 to 17 years of age. In 1989, approximately one-half million students with mental retardation were served in special education programs (U.S. Department of Education, 1990). About 96 percent of these students with mental retardation are classified as mildly or moderately mentally retarded (Baroff, 1986), and they are discussed in this chapter. The remaining 4 percent of students with mental retardation are classified as severely or profoundly mentally retarded, and they are discussed in Chapter 16, Learners with Severe and Multiple Disabilities. According to Grossman (1983), the generally accepted prevalence of mental retardation in the United States is 3 percent, though estimates range from 1 to 3 percent.

The decrease in the number of learners identified as mentally retarded may be due to the reclassification of some of the children previously served as mentally retarded as learning disabled or developmentally disabled. In addition, the criteria for identification of mental retardation have become more exclusive, with the cut-off score for tested intelligence quotient being lowered to 70 in 1973 and the co-requisite of deficits in adaptive behavior added in 1983. In addition, the emphasis on more valid evaluation of learners from diverse cultures who previously may have been identified as mentally retarded may contribute to decreased numbers of learners in this category.

Learners with mental retardation are served in various instructional settings, including general education classes (5.9 percent), resource rooms (22.4 percent), separate classes (58.9 percent), separate schools (11.3 percent), and residential centers, home, and hospital settings (1.6 percent). Of those learners with mental retardation leaving formal education in the 1989–90 school year, 59 percent received diplomas or certificates of completion and approximately 41 percent reached the maximum age for services, dropped out, or left for unknown reasons (U.S. Department of Education, 1992).

Box 14.1

Characteristics of Individuals with Down Syndrome

Down syndrome, a group of chromosomal abnormalities, occurs in approximately two in every one thousand live births. The condition was originally referred to as mongolism by J. Langdon Down in 1866. More than fifty characteristics have been identified, including:

small skull with flat back of the head
slanting, almond-shaped eyes
flat-bridged nose and ears slightly smaller than average
small mouth with protruding, fissured tongue
shortness of stature
stubby hands
too little muscle tone
varied levels of mental retardation

All types of chromosomal abnormalities which cause Down syndrome result in an extra chromosome on the twenty-first pair of chromosomes, or trisomy 21. In some individuals who have "mosaicism," some cells may have 46 chromosome cells and others 47. These individuals may have normal intelligence and few abnormal characteristics (Koch & Koch, 1974; LeJeune, Gauter, & Turpin, 1963) ▪

Objective One: To describe the personal characteristics of learners with mild or moderate mental retardation.

Personal Characteristics

Etiology

The etiology, or causes, of mental retardation include several factors, few of which are considered to be the single and sufficient cause of the disability. Among the possible causes of mental retardation are (Smith & Luckasson, 1992):

- biological factors
- infections and poisons (toxins)
- injury
- socioeconomic and environmental factors

Mental retardation caused by biological factors includes Down syndrome, Tay-Sachs disease, phenylketonuria (PKU), and tuberous sclerosis, among others. Down syndrome is the result of an extra chromosome which attaches to the twenty-first pair of chromosomes causing mental retardation and other specific characteristics, described in Box 14.1. Tay-Sachs disease is a metabolic disorder which affects the processing of fats and results in mental retardation. The child's life expectancy is approximately 4 years. PKU is a metabolic disorder which affects the processing of protein and results in mental retardation. PKU can be controlled with a specialized diet; early diagnosis and intervention are essential (see Box 14.2 for further information). Tuberous sclerosis is a progressive neurological disorder which results in mental retardation accompanied with multiple disabilities.

Box 14.2

Phenylketonuria (PKU)—An Example of Successful Early Intervention

Phenylketonuria (PKU) is an autosomal recessive inborn error of metabolism. Children with PKU are usually normal at birth, since prenatally the nutrients they ingest are already metabolized through the umbilical cord. Through universal blood test screening 24 to 48 hours after birth, the disorder may be diagnosed and treatment begun. If PKU is found, the infant is placed on a low phenylalanine diet, based on synthetic formula (phenylalanine is present in almost all proteins). The diet is the sole nutrient these infants receive.

Because phenylalanine is toxic only to developing brain tissue, treatment can cease or be relaxed when brain development is complete. Common practice is to return the child to normal food at about age 8, though some research suggests that longer dietary treatment may be helpful. Though the diet may prevent mental retardation, children with PKU may have learning disabilities with particular problems in perception (Brown, 1986; Brunner, Jordon, & Berry, 1983). For children who have been treated through the diet, the average adult tested intelligence quotient is about 90; for those who receive no treatment, severe mental retardation occurs by 3 years of age ■

There are many infections and toxins that can cause mental retardation. Three viruses that may result in mental retardation are rubella, meningitis, and measles. Alcohol, tobacco, and other drugs (cocaine, crack, and heroin) used by the mother during pregnancy may cause various degrees of mental retardation. Children who live in older housing or housing being rehabilitated may ingest leaded paint; lead poisoning occurs most frequently in 1- to 5-year-old children who ingest leaded paint. Far lower levels of lead ingestion than earlier assumed may cause neurological problems and subsequent mental retardation. Lead levels below that which cause severe brain damage may cause more subtle behaviors and learning disabilities (Blouin, Blouin, & Kelly, 1983).

Mental retardation can be the result of traumatic brain and head injury. Injuries during the birth process may also result in mental retardation. The level of retardation is related to the location and extent of the injury.

Socioeconomic and environmental factors may also contribute to mental retardation. Menolascino and Stark (1988) found the major factor in 75 to 80 percent of the persons with mild mental retardation, without an organic basis, to be poverty. The many factors which accompany poverty that may contribute to mental retardation include poor sanitation, unsafe housing, lead-based paints, poor nutrition, and inadequate and insufficient child care.

Characteristics

Among the ways in which learners with mental retardation vary from their peers are cognition, language, and behavior and social skills. These factors have impact on social judgment, the development of learned helplessness, persistence in using ineffective strategies, outerdirectedness, self-concept, and transition.

Cognitive Skills   Perhaps the most readily recognized characteristics of learners with mild or moderate mental retardation are those related to cognitive skills. Processing information may be less automatic for learners with mild or moderate mental retardation, and problems may emerge in integrating or generalizing processes

Even low levels of lead ingestion may cause mental retardation.

or information (Ashman, 1983). When deeper levels of cognitive processing are required, learners with mild or moderate mental retardation become progressively slower in processing and manipulating information (Schultz, 1983). As learners demonstrate more severe mental retardation, they expend more energy towards coding and processing information.

Ellis and Wooldridge (1985) found that learners with mental retardation retain pictures better than words when processing more complex and abstract information. Problems emerge in changing from one mode of processing to another, for example, from pictures to written word or spoken word to written word.

Nelson and Cummings (1984) administered the Boehm Test of Basic Concepts to learners with mental retardation and nonidentified peers. This test is designed to measure the mastery of basic concepts assumed to be necessary for verbal instructions and early school achievement (Conoley & Kramer, 1989). The test consists of fifty relational concepts (for example, front, below, fewest). It is used by the classroom teacher for identifying (a) individual children whose overall level of concept mastery is low and who therefore may need special attention, and (b) individual concepts with which large numbers of children in a class may be unfamiliar. It may be used to evaluate the receptive vocabulary of young school-aged children (McLoughlin & Lewis, 1990). Using the Boehm test, Nelson and Cummings found that of the fifty concepts tested, four were missed by more than 75 percent of the primary children with mental retardation tested. Between 25 and 49 percent of these children missed 17 concepts. A total of 29 concepts were misunderstood by more than one-fourth of the sample they tested. Among the basic concepts of which

High interest activities typical of their age peers support the learning of individuals with mental retardation.

these learners failed to demonstrate an understanding were above, always, beginning, between, and separated. By comparison, only three of the fifty concepts were missed by more than 25 percent of the nonidentified second graders who served as a standardization group.

Learners with mental retardation frequently demonstrate difficulties in paying attention. Brooks and McCauley (1984) state that attentional difficulties, such as attending sufficiently to the task at hand for an adequate period of time, may contribute to these learners' challenges in developing cognitive skills.

Language   Beitchman and Peterson (1986) suggest that many of the adaptive behavior problems in children were mental retardation may be due to problems in language and communication strategies. Learners with mental retardation have been found to focus more on the formal, sequential processes of language than do their nonidentified peers (Abbeduto & Nuccio, 1991).

Though learners with mental retardation are proficient in simpler contexts, they become more challenged in terms of topic maintenance and other pragmatic skills when the number of speakers, number of utterances, and degree of appropriateness of the speakers' responses changes (Koetting & Rice, 1991). In addition, learners with mental retardation have difficulty identifying the emotional state of other persons in complex situations and settings (Sternina, 1990). For example, individuals with mental retardation may continue to sit next to a child on the bus who is continually making fun of them.

In research with adults with mild and moderate mental retardation, Kernan and Sabsay (1993) found that in context, learners with mental retardation understand and produce stories that are essentially the same in structure as those produced by persons who are not identified as disabled. In generating stories, they found that learners with mental retardation are well able to recognize the main points, judge the importance and relevance of information, and make inferences based on prior knowledge. Kernan and Sabsay contend that when understood in the context of the social situation in which it occurs, the communication of learners with mental retardation often demonstrates sensitivity and creativity not otherwise recognized.

Social and Emotional Characteristics   Learners with mild or moderate mental retardation demonstrate more behavioral and emotional problems than do their peers (Polloway, Epstein, & Cullinan, 1985). Weiss (1981) believes that learners with mild or moderate mental retardation may also demonstrate "learned helplessness," that is, a perception that behavior and its outcomes are independent of each other. Feedback from professionals and peers may suggest to these learners that some tasks are simply too difficult to try. As a response, learners may exhibit deterioration in applying strategies when compared to their peers. In the future, with early intervention and appropriate instruction, learned helplessness may become less evident among learners with mental retardation (Polloway and Smith, 1983). Perhaps related to learned helplessness is a greater incidence of the symptoms of depression among adolescents with mild mental retardation (Reynolds & Miller, 1985).

Learners with mental retardation may demonstrate a less positive real and ideal self-image than do their peers (Leahy, Balla, & Zigler, 1982). Negative self-statements, withdrawal, and an apparent lack of motivation may be related to their less positive self-image.

Social Interaction   Though often perceived to demonstrate "deficiencies of social intelligence" (Greenspan, 1979) individuals with mental retardation, among themselves, share four "focal concerns" which demonstrate social sensitivity (Turner, 1983), as follows:

1. A need for affiliative relationships, a need to belong, to have friends, to become engaged in romantic involvements.
2. The desire to find refuge from prevailing negative attitudes, pejorative labels, and unfavorable social comparisons of "being retarded" through deviance disavowal.
3. The need for social harmony and to repair conflicts.
4. The needs to avoid boredom and to seek some novelty and stimulation.

Kernan and Sabsay (1993) write that, in addition to these four focal concerns, learners with mental retardation, as a result of their disability and the reaction of others to that disability, lack knowledge and experience in certain areas. To deal with this lack of knowledge and experience, learners with mental retardation use a variety of strategies. In terms of **deviance disavowal,** Kernan and Sabsay report **normalcy fabrication,** which is the telling of stories concerning some aspect of personal life in which the teller claims to have had some experience that he or she has not actually had. The stories present the teller as leading a life more normal and less restricted than the life he or she actually lives. For example, an individual who lives in a group home and receives few visits may have pictures of his "wife" and "children" in his wallet, and he may share stories about what the family did over the weekend. These stories are often presented following some event that has threatened or damaged the teller's self-esteem. For example, stories about Christmas shopping, carolling, and receiving large and multiple presents may follow the teller's remaining in the group home over the holidays as others visited their families.

Another challenge in social interactions among learners with mental retardation is described by Graffam (1985). He indicates that adults with mental retardation place little belief in the concept of chance or accident, so that if a problem occurs regarding social relations, a responsible party is sought. So, when a speaker presents a problem, someone is usually "blamed." This blaming, though often accepted by peers who are also mentally retarded, causes stress in social interactions among others.

According to Coffman and Harris (1980), learners with mental retardation exhibit "transition shock" when entering new and unfamiliar settings. Transition shock is characterized by a generalized disorientation, regression, and emotional stress. The learner may exhibit cuing problems, value discrepancies, physical and emotional feelings of dissatisfaction, adjustment problems, and inappropriate emotional responses.

Objective Two: To describe the identification and evaluation of learners with mild or moderate mental retardation.

Identification and Evaluation

McLean and Snyder-McLean (1988) describe four critical features that are relatively consistent among the various definitions of **mental retardation.** First, the problem is developmental, that is, not the result of immediate trauma, and it is manifested throughout the developmental period. Second, the problem is "mental" in that it reflects impairments in general intellectual functioning. Third, mental retardation is pervasive, in that the learner's ability to function in all activity spheres is affected. Finally, mental retardation is fully defined only when adaptive functioning, including independent self-care behaviors, language development, self-direction, and socialization, are considered.

The definition of mental retardation used in Public Law 94–142 is the definition originally adopted by the American Association on Mental Retardation in 1973. In 1983, this definition was modified to include a greater emphasis on adaptive behavior. According to the AAMR definition, mental retardation is

> significantly subaverage general intellectual functioning existing concurrently with deficits in adaptive behavior and manifested during the developmental period (Grossman, 1983, p. 11).

Intellectual functioning is generally measured by at least one individually administered intelligence test, and "significantly subaverage" is generally accepted to be two standard deviations below the mean (that is, 70 or below). Deficits in adaptive behavior are viewed as problems in attaining the cultural and age standards in personal independent, learning, or social responsibility. The developmental period is usually assumed to occur between conception and the learner's 18th birthday. The AAMR definition is essentially the same as that adopted by the American Psychiatric Association and presented in the *Diagnostic and Statistical Manual of Mental Disorders,* third edition, revised (American Psychiatric Association, 1987).

Polloway (1985) contends that the adaptive behavior of learners who may be identified as mentally retarded should be evaluated in a variety of contexts, and not just in the school. He believes that by emphasizing adaptive behavior and allowing some flexibility in cut-off scores on intellectual testing, learners with mental retardation are more likely to receive the services they need.

Wodrich and Barry (1991) surveyed a random sampling of school psychologists regarding the ways in which learners with mental retardation were identified. The Weschler Intelligence Scales were the most frequently used tool for describing intelligence quotient scores, which, with adaptive behavior scale scores, were rated as the most influential in identification and placement decisions. Of social behavior scales, the Vineland Adaptive Behavior Scales were the most commonly used.

Gold (1980) states that there are several assumptions implicit in the AAMR definition which in itself puts a limit on the potential of the individuals labeled mentally retarded. He points out that the AAMR definition assumes that intelligence, as defined by tests, is permanent and that defined intelligence is sufficiently general to describe a learner's potential or functioning. The AAMR definition assumes that a definable "developmental period" exists for all people, and that it is somehow meaningful to catalogue individuals according to their tested intelligence and tested adaptive behavior. Finally, Gold notes that the definition assumes that retardation is most meaningfully conceptualized as a phenomenon existing within the individual rather than the contexts in which the individual functions.

Gold proposes the following alternative definition:

> Mental retardation refers to a level of functioning which requires from society significantly above average training procedures and superior assets in adaptive behavior, manifested throughout life.
>
> The mentally retarded person is characterized by the level of power needed in the training process required for him to learn, and not by limitations in what he can learn.
>
> The height of a retarded person's level of functioning is determined by the availability of training technology and the amount of resources society is willing to allocate and not significant limitations in biological potential.

Gold's definition places the limitations imposed by retardation within the cultural and social contexts in which the individual functions.

From a systems perspective, mental retardation may be defined as the social role to which the individual is assigned, and assumes, within the ecological contexts in which he or she functions. According to Mercer (1973), an individual with mental retardation, from the social systems perspective, is one who "occupies the status of mental retardate and plays the role of mental retardate in one or more of the social systems in which he participates" (p. 27). This may be an explanation for the fact that many children classified as mildly mentally retardation may be classified as such during the school year and during the school day. However, these children may function within the normal limits of their cultural groups prior to entering and leaving the school system and before and after the school day. These children were referred to as the "six-hour retarded child" in the report of the President's Committee on Mental Retardation (1970).

Reschley (1988) describes the overrepresentation of learners who are members of minority cultural, ethnic, or linguistic groups in classes for learners with mild mental retardation. During the early 1970s and 1980s, there was extensive placement-bias court litigation, which included efforts to address problems in the role of intelligence tests in the classification and placement decision-making process, the correctness of assertions concerning the nature of mild mental retardation, and conclusions regarding the effectiveness of special education programs for learners with mild mental retardation. The National Academy of Sciences, through a panel comprised of leading scholars in academic disciplines, minority social scientists, and legal, mental health, and test-development experts, developed several recommendations for reform related to the overrepresentation of learners from minority cultures in programs for learners with mild mental retardation. These reforms included such actions as emphasizing prereferral interventions, increasing the emphasis on adaptive behavior in the identification process, and placing an emphasis on instruction rather than on the placement setting.

While recognizing the great diversity within the various levels of mental retardation, the American Association on Mental Retardation has, nevertheless, grouped persons with mental retardation into four levels: mild, moderate, severe, and profound. Persons with **mild mental retardation** have a tested intelligence quotient of between 50–55 and 70. These persons typically master basic academic skills, independent functioning, and living independently as adults. Learners with **moderate mental retardation** demonstrate intelligence quotients between 35–40 and 50–55 on standardized measures, and usually acquire self-help, communication, social, and some occupational skills. Learners with **severe mental retardation** and **profound mental retardation** require close life-long supervision. These learners may learn self-help skills, and those with severe mental retardation may learn simple vocational skills.

For educational purposes, prior to the current emphasis on individualized programming and inclusion, learners with mental retardation were often classified as educable, trainable, and severe/profound. Learners with mild mental retardation are referred to as having **educable mental retardation** and are typically served in special education programs with inclusion in general education. Learners with moderate mental retardation are referred to as having **trainable mental retardation** and are served primarily in special education programs. However, these learners are being increasingly included in general education programs. With the increasing emphasis on the inclusion of learners with mental retardation into general education classrooms and schools, the reliance on the classifications (educable, trainable, and severe/profound) for placement and programming purposes has been dramatically reduced in most school districts.

Objective Three: To describe the impact of mild or moderate mental retardation on interactions in the home and classroom.

The Impact on Interactions in the Home and Classroom

Interactions in the Home

Ysseldyke and associates (1991) report that the home environments of students classified as having educable mental retardation were less conducive to academic achievement than those of their nonidentified peers, particularly in the area of stress and valuing of education. According to Turnbull and Turnbull (1986), a child with mental retardation may cause family stress which may result in negative reactions of guilt, grief, denial, overprotection, and avoidance.

The well-being of families with young children with mental retardation is significantly related to the child's behavior and well-being. In addition, the child's behavioral characteristics are significantly related to the child's progress as perceived by the parents (Dunst, Trivette, Hamby, & Pollock, 1990). Orr, Cameron, and Day (1991) found that a family's perceptions of the birth or diagnosis of a child with mental retardation are the most significant factors in their ability to cope with the child and the resulting circumstances.

Positive outcomes have been reported for integrating students with mental retardation on general education.

Blacher and Bromley (1990) reviewed the literature on the placement of learners with mental retardation out of their biological homes. They found that out-of-home placements appeared to relate to social support available to the family, parent-child attachment, overall family adjustment, specific child characteristics, and the family's needs and resources.

Even when available, Salisbury (1990) found a low level of use of respite care across all levels of children's retardation. Though the child's level of functioning was found to have an impact on parent depression, social support, and personal well-being, Salisbury found a significant discrepancy between families' need for respite care and its use. Requests for community living services for young adults with mental retardation were found by Black, Molaison, and Smull (1990) to be more related to characteristics of the young adult or to desire for the young adult to be out of the home for day activities than a desire to promote the young adult's independence.

An emerging out-of-home placement option for learners with mental retardation is adoption. Glidden (1990) investigated the long-term adjustment of families who have adopted children with mental retardation. Positive outcomes were reported for almost all of the 567 children placed adoptively.

Interactions in the Classroom

Ysseldyke and associates (1991) found that students served in classes for the educable mentally retarded, when compared to their nonidentified peers, had less time allocated to academic activities and more to free time. McWhirter, Wilton, Boyd, and Townsend (1990) report that more individualized learning activities were implemented when the learners were in general rather than special education classes.

Van Bourgondien (1987) studied the effects of socially inappropriate behaviors and the label "in a special class for the retarded" on the attitudes and behavior of 8- to 9-year-old and 12- to 13-year-old girls in general education. The results indicated that a child's social behaviors had a significant effect on the attitudes and behaviors of peers, while the label "in a special class for the mentally retarded" did not. Neither behavior nor labels affected the peers' performance as teachers of the target child. Older children and children who were acquainted with a child in special education were more positive in their attitudes.

Even after an instructional program related to friendship awareness, learners with mental retardation had little interaction with students who were not identified as mentally retarded. When interactions did occur among the children during lunch and recess, they were brief and inconsistent (Fritz, 1990).

Mediating the Environment

Objective Four: To describe ways to mediate the environment for learners with mild or moderate mental retardation.

Polloway and associates (1991) argue that with changes in the population of learners with mental retardation and the discouraging findings in follow-up studies on adult outcomes of education interventions, curriculum must be modified to reflect students' long-term needs. They propose that the profession adopt an attitude of recognizing "subsequent environments." Using this approach, primary attention will be given to variables that may influence vertical and horizontal transitions for these students.

Primary aged children with mental retardation have significant deficits in their understanding of basic concepts (Nelson, Cummings, & Boltman, 1991). **Basic concepts** are those concepts related to size, position, order, and sequence on which other cognitive processes are based. These learners need to have multiple examples of concepts and represented application of these concepts. Concepts should be produced in everyday activities, using pictures, commands, and cues to enter the abstract level.

Less intrusive strategies, that is strategies which are less remarkable in the general education classroom, are emerging for learners with mental retardation. Engaging peers in the education of these learners and using cognitive behavior modification strategies call little negative attention to the learner. The possibilities of technological aids are just beginning to be explored.

Peer Tutoring

Peers have been found to be helpful as mediators for learners with mental retardation. Vacc and Cannon (1991), for example, studied the use of cross-age tutoring in mathematics education with elementary school students with mental retardation. The results of the tutoring program indicated that these learners' mathematics skills increased. The teachers involved in the tutoring program evaluated it as a positive learning activity and evaluated all participants' academic and/or social achievement as increasing as a result of the tutoring session. In classwide peer tutoring, the rates and accuracy of learners' responses to academic tasks and performance on weekly spelling tests both increased. Students also increased their retention of spelling words.

Box 14.3

Classwide Peer Tutoring
(as described by Maheady, Sacca, and Harper, 1988).

Peer support, cooperative learning, and group contingencies may be used in combination to support students' learning. The following process was explored by Maheady and associates in the implementation and evaluation of classwide peer tutoring:

1. Weekly study guides were developed collaboratively by general and special educators through (a) examining the weekly content during 40 minute consultation sessions and generating lists of instructional objectives, (b) developing a series of comprehension questions and appropriate responses, and (c) having the study guides reviewed by another individual for accuracy and clarity.
2. New classroom materials were introduced each week via 1–2 days of teacher lecture/discussion followed by assigned readings and homework. During the remainder of the week, 20–30 minutes of peer tutoring were involved. The classroom was divided into two teams by drawing colored squares. Team membership was the same for 2 weeks. Teams competed for the highest point totals in social studies. The teacher randomly paired students within each team.
3. Teachers and students were trained through role-play sessions. In-class supervision was also conducted. Bonus points were awarded to tutors for displaying "good tutoring" behaviors of (a) clear and accurate dictation of questions, (b) appropriate use of error corrections procedures, (c) contingent and accurate delivery of points for correct responses, and (d) use of praise and supports.
4. Quiz responses also earned points. Each correct response on each student's quiz earned the team 5 points. Weekly results were posted, and bonus points rewarded extra efforts.

The procedures resulted in immediate and systematic increases in the weekly social studies test performance of both the learners with disabilities and those without disabilities ▪

The peer tutors reported positive evaluations of the process and perceived positive social and self-esteem changes (Mallette, Harper, Maheady, & Dempsey, 1991).

Several variables must be taken into consideration for the effective implementation of peer tutoring programs with learners with mild or moderate mental retardation. First, the instructional objective must be measurable. In addition, time must be available for the program. Tutors must be selected and trained, and both the tutor and tutee must be engaged in the evaluation process (Krouse, Gerber, and Kauffman, 1981). An example program of classwide peer tutoring is described in Box 14.3.

Gottlieb and Leyser (1981) used team cooperative learning experiences to facilitate the social mainstreaming of learners with mental retardation. This was an effort to change the classroom climate from one emphasizing rewards based on competition to rewards based on achievement. The cooperative learning teams were heterogeneous and included learners with mental retardation. The teams' primary function was to prepare its members through peer tutoring. This approach resulted in reduced failure and increased success for the learners with mental retardation.

*T*able 14.1   Generalization Strategies

1. Fade reinforcers in the original setting, while increasing the power of reinforcement in new settings.
2. Vary directions, cues, and supports.
3. Modify materials.
4. Vary responses and response time.
5. Move from single to many stimuli, adding distractors and increasing the abstract level of the stimuli.
6. Vary the setting.
7. Vary instructors.

(Vaughn, Bos, and Lund, 1986)

Cognitive Behavior Modification

Cognitive behavior modification techniques, including self-instruction and self-recording, have been used with success with learners with mental retardation. A six-step self-instruction package for use with learners with mental retardation was developed by Burgio, Whitman, and Johnson (1980). The steps in the program are as follows:

1. The learner asks, "What does the teacher want me to do?"
2. The learner decides the nature of the task in response to the above question.
3. The learner determines the sequential order of the steps required to complete the assigned task.
4. The learner reinforces his or her personal success.
5. Using self-cues, the learner stays on task and ignores distractions.
6. The learner decides how she or he will cope with possible failure.

Using these procedures, Burgio and associates produced direct and generalized changes in the behavior of learners with mental retardation on printing and mathematics tasks. In addition, learners' off-task behaviors decreased. In oral reading tasks, Rose (1984) found simple self-instructional techniques to be effective with learners with mild mental retardation.

Self-recording has been used successfully with learners identified as mildly and moderated mentally retarded in increasing both on-task behavior and productivity (McCarl, Svobodny, & Beare, 1991). In self-recording, learners are trained to observe and document their personal behaviors. Sugai and Rowe (1984) used self-recording procedures to increase the in-seat behavior of a learner with mild mental retardation.

An ongoing challenge with learners with mild or moderate mental retardation is the generalization of skills taught in one setting to another setting. Vaughn, Bos, and Lund (1986) suggest several strategies that increase the likelihood that skills will generalize. These strategies are summarized in Table 14.1.

Technological Aids

Technology has also emerged as a means of mediating the environment for learners with mental retardation. Parette (1991) contends that technology can (a) support educational activities, (b) provide, restore, or extend a learner's physical abilities, and (c) provide opportunities for greater participation in the mainstream of society. Gardner and Bates (1991) report that learners with mental retardation positively evaluated the use of computers. The learners reported that they found computers attractive, and that using computers increased their confidence, self-esteem, and ability to learn some tasks.

In an innovative use of technology, Flexer, Millin, and Brown (1990) found that when using sound field FM amplification of the teacher's speech (see Chapter 12, Learners with Hearing Impairments, for an explanation of this technology), learners with mental retardation were more relaxed and responded more quickly to the teacher's directions. With only a 10 decibel amplification, primary-level children increased their accuracy and performance on tasks related to verbal communication.

Social Skills Training

Thomas (1980) reviewed the application of Goldstein's Social Skills Curriculum with learners with mental retardation. The curriculum is based on the assumption that learners with mental retardation can solve social problems through reasoning. It uses direct instructional methods and stresses "survival" tasks and competencies. In a review of the instructional techniques applied in several social skills training programs, Davis and Rogers (1985) found that active rehearsal in combination with other instructional techniques is more effective than instruction, reinforcement, and demonstration alone. They found the most frequently applied and most successful training procedures are a combination of visual instruction, practice, and contingent reinforcement.

Instructional Strategies

Instructional strategies that have been used with learners with mental retardation include sequential prompting and individualized instruction. When using sequential prompting, teachers should provide learners with "just enough" support to ensure success, but not so much that the learner's personal resources are not challenged. The steps to sequential prompting are as follows (Schloss, 1986):

1. Identify the target behavior.
2. Determine the sequence of tasks to be completed to attain the objective.
3. Determine the prompts that may be applied to assist the learner.
4. Determine the possible sequence of prompts that may be used.
5. Implement the instructional program beginning with the least obtrusive prompt.

Among the prompts that may be selected for implementation of sequential prompting are physical guidance, modeling, vocal prompting, and graphic prompts. The teachers, prior to implementation, must determine how the prompts will be faded.

Teachers should individualize instruction in response to the learner's style and rate. Among the modifications that may be made in an effort to individualize instruction for learners with mental retardation are (a) slowing the pace of the lesson, (b) shortening the length of instructional practice sessions, (c) breaking down instructional objectives into subobjectives, and (d) simplifying instruction, that is, teaching each concept separately (Darch & Thorpe, 1978).

'Their Spirit Lifts Them'
The dancers of Images in Motion are mentally retarded but movement has made them eloquent

By Lou Ann Walker

David L. Edwards does not look like a dancer. With his squarish body and stocky legs, wearing cut-off sweatpants, what he really resembles is a Samurai warrior. But when the music starts, David is transformed. Head erect, the motion of his arms and hands elegant, he has the grace and poise of a Nureyev. Smiling, he does a stylish rhythmic triplet across the dance floor: bold step, shuffle, shuffle, then launches into his routine.

"All right!" calls out Patricia Fulton, the company director, clapping after David's final bow. He grins as Jeanine Meyer, a fellow dancer, gives him a hug. David Edwards, 44, who dances professionally with the dance troupe called Images in Motion, has Down syndrome. Off the dance floor, his words are virtually impossible to understand. But when he dances, David communicates eloquently through movement.

All of the members of Images in Motion, based in Boulder, Colo., are mentally retarded. How they became such accomplished dancers in three short years and how Patricia Fulton, 43, came to establish the company is an extraordinary saga of will and determination.

In 1986, Fulton was teaching dance at a private studio to a small group of mentally retarded adults when one of them, Donald Meskimen, now 48, told her they wanted to perform. Fulton was dubious. Their skills were so basic, she felt it couldn't work. Parents of retarded children kept telling her audiences wouldn't be sensitive enough. But the dancers were willing to take a chance.

The first dress rehearsal was a disaster. The dancers were tired. Costumes weren't ready. At the beginning of the actual performance, dancers looked nervously to the wings for cues. Their heads were down, their shoulders hunched forward.

Yet people watching in the audience that evening could sense something special was happening. At the end, the audience came onstage to join the encore. "For that moment," Fulton says, "we were all speaking the same language."

There are five members in Images' core company: Kam Burns, 29, wears his hair stylishly with a long tendril in back and often sports rock-concert T-shirts; Judy Johnson, 46, a short, rounded woman, is deeply religious; Jeanine Meyer, 32, slender and sandy-haired, is slightly reserved; Donald Meskimen is bearded and dark-haired. Three have Down syndrome. Some have multiple handicaps, and several are flat-footed. The IQs of the dance company members range from about 30 to 60. These five all live at Carmel House, an adult residence, where they lead very busy lives. Still, when they began dancing, they seemed to find new purpose.

Fulton started with the basics. "People who don't think retarded people can remember things just haven't broken those tasks down into their components," she points out. At first, the group memorized all the dances. Then one day, Kam asked David and Donald: "Do you want to be a high shape or a low shape?" Fulton suddenly realized they were experimenting with the concept of shape, that they were able to *understand* the ideas she was presenting. "They are creative people," she says. "There is so much inside them. I'm giving them a vocabulary to express themselves."

"It's a movie in my mind," says Donald, who is legally blind.

"I love to dance," Jeanine says simply.

After that first performance, the dancers began working hard, but early bookings were scarce. Fulton insisted that Images dancers be appreciated as artists. Once, before a performance with a visiting ballet company, Fulton was discussing choreography when a shocked manager said, "You mean you want *our* dancers to dance with *them?*" Fulton immediately canceled.

The sliding-scale fee dancers pay for classes covers studio rental and costumes. The dancers are paid for performances, and several say they'd like to give up their sheltered workshop jobs to work full-time as dancers.

Fulton choreographs each number so performers can use their special skills. One dancer, for example, is able to slide across the room in one direction but not in the

Langone (1981) argues for an ongoing, diligent effort to provide relevant instruction to learners with moderate mental retardation. He suggests that teachers ask themselves questions such as:

- Where do my students go at the end of the day?
- Where will my students be in several years?
- What skills will my students need to live in the community?
- How can I include daily activities to address these skills?

other. Fulton uses only classical or folk music. Rock causes the dancers to withdraw into themselves or begin repetitive motions.

Dance students at colleges in the area often help Fulton with rehearsals and then appear, along with her, in performances. Most of the dances express an idea through movement. For example, in one piece, dancers walk hurriedly across the stage, never meeting each other's eyes, making the point that people often ignore each other in our society. In another, troupe members and volunteers cavort in bright red, green and blue bags zipped up all around. At the end, when performers unzip their bags, the audience is astonished to realize how no one had guessed who was or wasn't disabled.

Preparing for an upcoming performance, a rehearsal moves quickly. "I'll work the tape recorder!" Kam says. Fulton, blond and lithe, wearing sweat pants and a blue shirt, directs.

"All right, ladies," she calls, as Judy and Jeanine practice with 6-foot yellow fans to ethereal pan flute music. Kam has been developing a dance around a 4-foot-high beam, which he'll do with Fulton. He runs across the floor and leaps over the end of the beam. "No, that's not right," he says, gently correcting Fulton. "It's got to be like this." His own leaping grows bold.

Like true dancers, the members of Images in Motion have learned improvisation. Last year, during a

performance, David and Fulton were doing a duet amidst other dancers who finished too soon. David calmly extended his arms and improvised. "I didn't teach him that," Fulton says. "I never know what's going to happen, and it gives me apoplexy in one way. But, in another, that's what I live for."

Marda Kim, founder and director of The Colorado Dance Festival, one of the three top dance festivals in the U.S., invited Images to perform in 1988. "I cried," she says. "Their performance was one of the most incredible at our festival. These dancers become so beautiful when they dance. It's almost as if their spirit lifts them."

The success of Images demonstrates how much people can accomplish if given a chance. After each performance, there's a reception so dancers can meet the public. "I was always so afraid of these people before," one woman admitted. "Now I'm not."

The dancers have changed too. "I think it has done her a world of good," says Jeanine Meyer's mother, Velna M. Meyer. "She's more outgoing now." The dancers also have developed grace and self-assurance. Their concentration has improved. One group hired the company to do peer teaching with other disabled people.

The development of Images in Motion has marked a resurgence in Patricia Fulton's life too. A ballerina since age 7 and the picture of blooming health, Fulton actually has been terribly ill for the last two

decades. Unexplained debilitating headaches, severe abdominal pain and later convulsions forced her to leave her teaching job at Texas Woman's University. A doctor of clinical ecology finally diagnosed her problem as environmental illness: Her body had become extremely sensitive to food additives, dyes, chemicals and exhaust fumes. While lying in bed struggling to recover, she had a dream: to unleash the expressiveness in mentally retarded people. And she realized perhaps that the safest place for her was a dance studio. It took the dreams of the dancers to create the company she now directs.

Four years ago, Fulton met and married Thomas Mennitt, a computer expert. Mennitt videotapes the company, tracking the metamorphosis of each dancer.

At a recent rehearsal, Donald Meskimen, the first who had asked to perform, speaks up. At the next performance he wants to make an announcement to the audience. "This is what I feel when I dance," Donald says firmly. "I feel special. And I'm happy" ∎

Reprinted with permission from "Their Spirits Lift Them" by Lou Ann Walker in *Parade*, January 6, 1991. Copyright © 1992.

Objective Five: To describe the impact of mild or moderate mental retardation on participation in the larger social systems of the community and society.

The Impact on Participation in the Community and Society

Though many learners with mild mental retardation live independently in the community, a continuum of supported living environments is an increasingly available option for those who need assistance. Among these options are mentor or "special friend" programs, in which the individual lives independently with occasional visits, phone calls, or other contacts with a support person; supervised apartments, in which the individual lives in one of several units in a building, with either live-in or

Some citizens with disabilities live independently with others.

hourly supervisors; and group homes, which usually accommodate between five and ten persons and may be managed by houseparents or hourly employees. Though there has been difficulty locating these housing alternatives in some communities, the general population appears to be understanding and accepting of them.

Changes have occurred in order to help learners with mental retardation have a more typical "home" experience. Howard (1990) analyzed how changing the structure of group homes and reducing the unnecessary regimentation (for example, ordering bedspreads and blankets bulk so that they are all identical) could create a more "normal" home environment. She claims that the needs of parents and staff to "get things done" or to "stay on schedule" often obstructed the learners' ability to become more independent and more adult in their behavior patterns. Parents and staff members became uncomfortable in many situations when the residents themselves took the responsibility for some personal decisions.

Finding and keeping gainful employment is also a challenge for learners with mental retardation. The employment rates of persons with mental retardation are low. In a statewide survey of the employment rates of learners with mental retardation who graduated from high school between 1980 and 1984, Hasazi, Gordon, Roe, Hull, Finck, and Salembier (1985) found that only 41 percent of the graduates were employed full- or part-time in the competitive job market.

Hill, Seyfarth, Banks, Wehman, and Orelove (1987) used a mail survey to study parents' attitudes about the working conditions of their adult sons and daughters with mental retardation. In their sample, there was low interest in specific improvements in the working conditions of their children, particularly in increased wages. Most of the parents indicated a positive attitude toward work for their children, but only 12 percent reported a preference for competitive employment. Young adults with mental retardation, however, were not happy with their work experiences. In an interview study, Szivos (1990) found that the learners themselves described work in the sheltered work environment as boring and frustrating. When asked why they did not seek another job, four reasons emerged: unusual position, perceived incompetence, nonavailability of jobs, and fear of discreditation.

Mothers with mental retardation have been found to be more likely to lose custody of their children to human service agencies than are those mothers who are not identified as mentally retarded. Tymchuk and Andron (1990) found that child removal frequently occurred if the mother had a problem in addition to her retardation, or if she was unwilling to attend and actively participate in a training program, or if she did not have someone who could provide support. Many mothers with mental retardation who provide good care to their children live with a relative who shares child-care responsibilities.

Riordan and Vasa (1991) studied the accommodations made for and participation of learners with mental retardation in religious organizations. They found that clergy were aware of few persons with disabilities in their congregations and were not very active in providing accommodations or services to parents and families of these individuals or the individuals themselves. Though some church-oriented programs were available for children, the number of proactive accommodations and programs for individuals with mental retardation decreased as the learners became older.

Summary

The majority of learners with mental retardation, those with mild or moderate mental retardation, are discussed in this chapter. The field of mental retardation has served as a catalyst for other areas of special education. However, there are decreasing numbers of learners identified as mentally retarded.

The etiology of mental retardation is a complex issue. Possible causes include biological factors, infections and poisons (toxins), and injury. These learners may present problems in processing information, attention, and language development. A particular difficulty arises in the area of generalization, that is, applying skills learned in one setting to another setting.

The definition of mental retardation has three components, including generalized below average cognitive functioning, concomitant problems in social adaptability, and occurrence during the developmental period. There is, however, an overrepresentation of learners who are members of minority cultural, ethnic, or linguistic groups in classes for learners with mild mental retardation. This overidentification is related to the ways in which learners are identified and assessed.

The home environments of students classified as educable mentally retarded were less conducive to academic achievement than those of their nonidentified peers. In addition, the nature of the educational placement of learners with mental retardation may have an impact on their educational outcomes.

Several effective strategies have emerged for learners with mental retardation. The use of peer tutoring can support learners in less restrictive environments. In addition, cognitive behavior modification and technological aids may assist them in the general education classroom. Social skills training has emerged as a consistent instructional need for these students.

Greater opportunities are developing for learners with mental retardation to live in their community. Supported living assists individuals in living as independently as possible. Challenges remain, however, in that learners with mental retardation usually face limited employment opportunities. In addition, learners with mental retardation, as parents, are more likely to lose the right to parent their children than parents who are not identified as having this disability.

References

Abbeduto, L., & Nuccio, J. B. (1991). Relation between receptive language and cognitive maturity in persons with mental retardation. *American Journal on Mental Retardation, 96,* 143–149.

Ashman, A. F. (1983). Exploring the cognition of retarded persons: A brief report. *International Journal of Rehabilitation Research, 6,* 355–356.

Baroff, G. S. (1986). *Mental retardation: Nature, cause, management* (2nd ed.). New York: Hemisphere.

Beitchman, J. H., & Peterson, M. (1986). Disorders of language, communication, and behavior in mentally retarded children: Some ideas on their co-occurrence. *Psychiatric Clinics of North America, 9,* 689–698.

Blacher, J., & Bromley, B. E. (1990). Correlates of out-of-home placement of handicapped children: Who places and why? *Journal of Children in Contemporary Society, 21,* 3–40.

Black, M. M., Molaison, V. A., & Smull, M. W. (1990). Families caring for a young adult with mental retardation: Service needs and urgency of community living requests. *American Journal on Mental Retardation, 95,* 32–39.

Blouin, A. G., Blouin, J. H., & Kelly, T. C. (1983). Lead, trace, mineral intake, and behavior of children. *Topics in Early Childhood Special Education, 54,* 249–262.

Brooks, P. H., & McCauley, C. (1984). Cognitive research in mental retardation. *American Journal of Mental Deficiency, 88,* 479–486.

Brown, R. T. (1986). Etiology and development of exceptionality. In R. T. Brown & C. R. Reynolds (Eds.), *Psychological perspectives on childhood exceptionality* (pp. 181–229). New York: Wiley.

Brunner, R. L., Jordon, M. K., & Berry, H. K. (1983). Early treated PKU: Neuropsychologic consequences. *Journal of Pediatrics, 102,* 381–385.

Burgio, L. D., Whitman, T. C., & Johnson, M. R. A. (1980). A self-instructional package for increasing attention behavior in educable mentally retarded children. *Journal of Applied Behavior Analysis, 13,* 3–7.

Coffman, T. L., & Harris, M. C. (1980). Transition shock and adjustments of mentally retarded persons. *Mental Retardation, 18,* 3–7.

Conoley, J. C., & Kramer, J. J. (1989). *The tenth mental measurements yearbook.* Lincoln, NE: Buros Institute of Mental Measurements.

Darch, C. B., & Thorpe, H. W. (1978). An intervention strategy for teachers of the mildly handicapped. *Education and Training of the Mentally Retarded, 13* (1), 29–36.

Davis, R. R., & Rogers, E. S. (1985). Social skills training with persons who are mentally retarded. *Mental Retardation, 23* (4), 186–196.

Dunst, C. J., Trivette, C. M., Hamby, D., & Pollock, B. (1990). Family systems correlates of the behavior of young children with handicaps. *Journal of Early Intervention, 15,* 204–218.

Ellis, N. R., & Wooldridge, P. W. (1985). Short-term memory for pictures and words by mentally retarded and nonretarded persons. *American Journal of Mental Deficiency, 89,* 622–626.

Flexer, C., Millin, J. P., & Brown, L. (1990). Children with developmental disabilities: The effect of sound field amplification on word identification. *Language, Speech, and Hearing Services in Schools, 21,* 177–182.

Forness, S. R., & Kavale, K. A. (1984). Education of the mentally retarded: A note on policy. *Education and Training of the Mentally Retarded, 19,* 239–245.

Fritz, M. F. (1990). A comparison of social interactions using a friendship awareness activity. *Education and Training in Mental Retardation, 25,* 352–359.

Gardner, J. E., & Bates, P. (1991). Attitudes and attributions on use of microcomputers in school by students who are mentally handicapped. *Education and Training in Mental Retardation, 26,* 98–105.

Glidden, L. M. (1990). The wanted ones: Families adopting children with mental retardation. *Journal of Children in Contemporary Society, 21,* 177–205.

Gold, M. W. (1980). An alternative definition of mental retardation. In M. W. Gold (Ed.), *"Did I say that?" Articles and commentary on the Try Another Way system.* Champaign, IL: Research Press.

Gottlieb, J., & Leyser, Y. (1981). Facilitating the social mainstreaming of retarded children. *Exceptional Education Quarterly, 1* (4), 57–70.

Graffam, J. (1985). About ostriches coming out of communist China: Meanings, functions, and frequencies of typical interactions in group meetings for retarded adults. In S. Sabsay, M. Platt, et al., *Social setting, stigma, and communicative competence: Practice and beyond, 6,* 9–40.

Greenspan, S. (1979). Social intelligence in the retarded. In N. R. Ellis (Ed.), *Handbook on mental deficiency research: Psychological theory and research* (2nd ed.). Hillsdale, NJ: Lawrence Erlbaum Associates.

Grossman, H. (1983). *Classification in mental retardation.* Washington, DC: American Association of Mental Deficiency.

Hasazi, S. B., Gordon, L. R., Roe, C. A., Hull, M., Finck, K., & Salembier, G. (1985). A statewide follow-up on post-high school employment and residential status of students labeled "mentally retarded." *Education and Training of the Mentally Retarded, 20* (6), 222–224.

Hill, J. W., Seyfarth, J., Banks, P. D., Wehman, P., & Orelove, F. (1987). Parent attitudes about working conditions of their adult mentally retarded sons and daughters. *Exceptional Children, 54,* 9–23.

Howard, M. (1990). "We don't have no say in our lives anymore": An anthropologist's study of group home life for adults with mental retardation. *Adult Residential Care Journal, 4* (3), 163–182.

Kernan, K. T., & Sabsay, S. (1993). Discourse and conversational skills of mentally retarded adults. In A. M. Bauer (Ed.), *Children who challenge the system* (pp. 145–184). Boston: Ablex.

Koch, R., & Koch, K. (1974). *Understanding the mentally retarded child: A new approach.* New York: Random House.

Koetting, J. B., & Rice, M. L. (1991). Influence of the social context on pragmatic skills of adults with mental retardation. *American Journal on Mental Retardation, 95,* 435–443.

Krouse, J., Gerber, M. M., & Kauffman, J. M. (1981). Peer tutoring: Procedures, promises, and unresolved issues. *Exceptional Education Quarterly, 1* (4), 107–115.

Langone, J. (1981). Curriculum for the trainable mentally retarded . . . or "What do I do when the ditto machine dies?" *Education and Training of the Mentally Retarded, 16,* 150–154.

Leahy, R. L., Balla, D., & Zigler, E. (1982). Role-taking, self-image, and imitativeness of mentally retarded and nonretarded individuals. *American Journal of Mental Deficiency, 86,* 372–379.

LeJeune, J., Gautur, M., & Turpin, R. (1963). Study of the somatic chromosomes of nine mongoloid idiot children. In S. H. Bayer (Ed.), *Papers on human genetics* (pp. 238–240). Englewood Cliffs, NJ: Prentice Hall.

Maheady, L., Sacca, M. K., & Harper, G. F. (1988). Classwide peer tutoring with mildly handicapped high school students. *Exceptional Children, 54,* 52–59.

Mallette, B., Harper, G. F., Maheady, L., & Dempsey, M. (1991). Retention of spelling words acquired using a peer-mediated instructional procedure. *Education and Training in Mental Retardation, 26,* 156–164.

McCarl, J. J., Svobodny, L., & Beare, P. L. (1991). Self-recording in a classroom for students with mild to moderate mental handicaps: Effects on productivity and on-task behavior. *Education and Training in Mental Retardation, 26,* 79–88.

McLean, J. E., & Snyder-McLean, L. (1988). Application of pragmatics to severely mentally retarded children and youth. In R. L. Schiefelbusch & L. L. Lloyd (Eds.), *Language perspectives* (pp. 255–289). Austin, TX: Pro-Ed.

McLoughlin, J. A., & Lewis, R. B. (1990). *Assessing special students* (3rd ed.). Columbus, OH: Merrill.

McWhirter, J., Wilton, K., Boyd, A., & Townsend, M. A. (1990). Classroom interactions of mildly intellectually disabled children in special and regular classrooms. *Australia and New Zealand Journal of Developmental Disabilities, 16,* 39–48.

Menolascino, F. J., & Stark, J. A. (Eds.). (1988). *Preventive and curative intervention in mental retardation.* Baltimore, MD: Paul H. Brookes.

Mercer, J. (1973). *Labelling the mentally retarded.* Berkeley: University of California Press.

Nelson, R. B., & Cummings, J. A. (1984). Educable mentally retarded children's understanding of the Boehm Basic Concepts. *Psychological Reports, 154,* 81–82.

Nelson, R. B., Cummings, J. A., & Boltman, H. (1991). Teaching basic concepts to students who are educable mentally handicapped. *Teaching Exceptional Children, 23* (2), 12–15.

Orr, R. R., Cameron, S. J., & Day, D. M. (1991). Coping with stress in families with children who have mental retardation: An evaluation of the double ABCX model. *American Journal on Mental Retardation, 95,* 444–450.

Parette, H. P. (1991). The importance of technology in the education and training of persons with mental retardation. *Education and Training in Mental Retardation, 26,* 165–178.

Polloway, E. A. (1985). Identification and placement in mild mental retardation programs: Recommendations for professional practice. *Education and Training of the Mentally Retarded, 20,* 218–221.

Polloway, E. A., Epstein, M. H., & Cullinan, D. (1985). Prevalence of behavior problems among educable mentally retarded students. *Education and Training of the Mentally Retarded, 20,* 3–13.

Polloway, E., Patton, J. R., Smith, J. D., & Roderique, T. W. (1991). Issues in program design for elementary students with mild retardation: Emphasis on curriculum development. *Education and Training in Mental Retardation, 26,* 142–150.

Polloway, E. A., & Smith, J. D. (1983). Changes in mild mental retardation: Population, programs, and perspectives. *Exceptional Children, 50,* 149–159.

President's Committee on Mental Retardation (1970). *The six-hour retarded child.* Washington, DC: U.S. Government Printing Office.

Reschley, D. J. (1988). Minority MMR overrepresentation and special education reform. *Exceptional Children, 54* (4), 316–323.

Reynolds, W. M., & Miller, K. L. (1985). Depression and learned helplessness in mentally retarded and nonretarded adolescents: An initial investigation. *Applied Research in Mental Retardation, 6,* 295–306.

Riordan, J., & Vasa, S. F. (1991). Accommodations for and participation of persons with disabilities in religious practice. *Education and Training in Mental Retardation, 26,* 151–155.

Rose, T. L. (1984). The effects of previewing on retarded learners' oral reading. *Education and Training of the Mentally Retarded, 19* (1), 49–53.

Salisbury, C. L. (1990). Characteristics of users and nonusers of respite care. *Mental Retardation, 28,* 291–297.

Schloss, P. J. (1986). Sequential prompt instruction for mildly handicapped learners. *Teaching Exceptional Children, 18* (3), 181–184.

Schultz, E. E. (1983). Depth of processing by mentally retarded and MA matched nonretarded individuals. *American Journal of Mental Deficiency, 88,* 307–313.

Smith, D. D., & Luckasson, R. (1992). *Introduction to special education: Teaching in an age of challenge.* Boston: Allyn & Bacon.

Sternina, T. Z. (1990). Mentally retarded children's comprehension of another person's emotional state. *Soviet Psychology, 28,* 89–104.

Sugai, G., & Rowe, P. (1984). The effects of self-recording on out-of-seat behavior of an EMR student. *Education and Training of the Mentally Retarded, 19* (1), 23–28.

Szivos, S. E. (1990). Attitudes to work and their relationship to self-esteem and aspirations among young adults with a mild mental handicap. *British Journal of Mental Subnormality, 36,* 108–117.

Thomas, M. A. (1980). Strategies for problem solving: A conversation with Herbert Goldstein. *Education and Training of the Mentally Retarded, 15* (3), 216–223.

Turnbull, A. P., & Turnbull, H. R. III. (1986). *Families, professionals and exceptionality: A special partnership.* Columbus, OH: Merrill.

Turner, J. L. (1983). Workshop society: Ethnographic observations in a work setting for retarded adults. In K. T. Kernan, M. J. Begab, & R. B. Edgerton (Eds.), *Environments and behavior: The adaptation of mentally retarded persons* (pp. 147–171). Baltimore, MD: University Park Press.

Tymchuk, A. J., & Andron, L. (1990). Mothers with mental retardation who do or do not abuse or neglect their children. *Child Abuse and Neglect, 14,* 313–323.

U.S. Department of Education (1990). *Twelfth annual report to Congress on the implementation of the Education of the Handicapped Act.* Washington, DC: Author.

U.S. Department of Education (1992). *Fourteenth annual report to Congress on the implementation of the Individuals with Disabilities Education Act.* Washington, DC: Author.

Vacc, N. N., & Cannon, S. J. (1991). Cross-age tutoring in mathematics: Sixth graders helping students who are moderately handicapped. *Education and Training in Mental Retardation, 26,* 89–97.

Van Bourgondien, M. E. (1987). Children's responses to retarded peers as a function of social behaviors, labeling, and age. *Exceptional Children, 53,* 432–439.

Vaughn, S., Bos, C. S., & Lund, K. A. (1986) . . . . But they can do it in my room: Strategies for promoting generalization. *Teaching Exceptional Children, 18* (3), 176–180.

Weiss, J. R. (1981). Learned helplessness in black and white children identified by their schools as retarded and nonretarded. *Developmental Psychology, 17,* 499–508.

Wodrich, D. L., & Barry, C. T. (1991). A survey of school psychologists' practices for identifying mentally retarded students. *Psychology in the Schools, 28,* 165–171.

Ysseldyke, J. E., Thurlow, M. L., Christenson, S. L., & Muyskens, P. (1991). Classroom and homelearning differences between students labeled as educable mentally retarded and their peers. *Education and Training in Mental Retardation, 26,* 3–17.

15
Learners with Mild Disabilities

*O*bjectives

After completing this chapter, you will be able to:

1. describe the personal characteristics of persons with mild disabilities.
2. describe the identification and evaluation of learners with mild disabilities.
3. describe the impact of mild disabilities on interactions in the classroom.
4. describe ways to mediate the environment for learners with mild disabilities.
5. describe the impact of mild disabilities on participation in the larger social systems of the school, community, and society.

*K*ey Words and Phrases

collaborative consultation   school survival skills
high prevalence disabilities   teacher assistance teams
noncategorical

*I*T TAKES JACOB A LONG TIME TO PUT HIS THINGS AWAY. HE EXHIBITS SOME CONFUSION ABOUT WHERE THEY BELONG. Do I point out to him that it would be easier if he sat near the place where the books are kept, instead of in the corner where he has to walk past the other children to get them? . . . Or, by so doing am I emphasizing his disabilities, making too important the amount of time he is taking to do these things? . . . I have so many questions. Among them is: Why have I received no guidance from the specialists who may *know* what would be best for me to do?" (A kindergarten teacher describing her concerns about managing a learner with mild disabilities in her classroom, Heitz, 1989.) ■

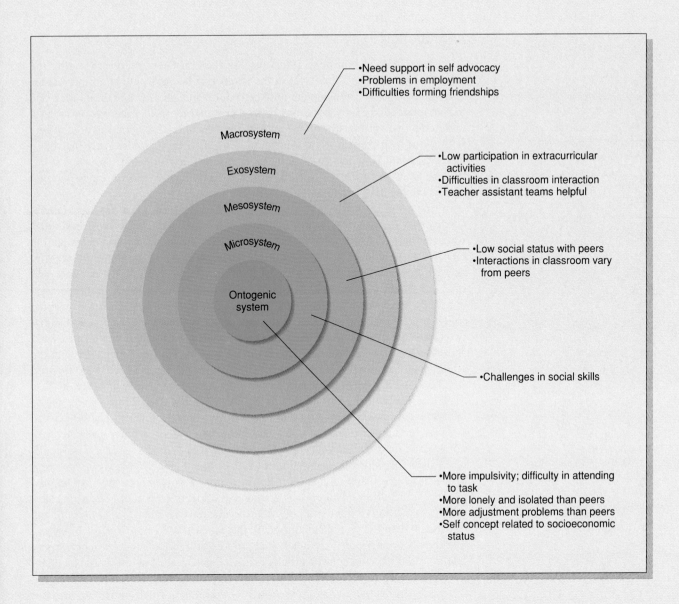

• Need support in self advocacy
• Problems in employment
• Difficulties forming friendships

Macrosystem

• Low participation in extracurricular
  activities
• Difficulties in classroom interaction
• Teacher assistant teams helpful

Exosystem

Mesosystem

• Low social status with peers
• Interactions in classroom vary
  from peers

Microsystem

Ontogenic
system

• Challenges in social skills

• More impulsivity; difficulty in attending
  to task
• More lonely and isolated than peers
• More adjustment problems than peers
• Self concept related to socioeconomic
  status

Introduction

Algozzine and Korinek (1985) discuss the consistent increases during the 5-year period from 1978 to 1982 in the number of learners with "high prevalence disabilities," that is, learners with mild behavior disorders, learning disabilities, and mental retardation. They write that these data could mean that there is an increasingly effective system to provide specialized educational experiences to students failing to profit from general education. However, they also suggest that these increases could be evidence of an increasingly ineffective system, in which it has become more profitable and socially desirable to find more students either learning disabled or mentally retarded.

In an effort to classify patterns of individual differences prior to school failure, Cooper and Speece (1990) studied children in the first grade before any disabilities were formally identified. They examined the role classroom environments play in modifying the course of school failure. They posited that young children who entered school without a diagnostic label do not "catch" a disability as one would catch a biophysiological disorder; rather, they bring with them as yet unspecified cognitive, behavioral, linguistic, and affective characteristics developed over time, which interact with the academic and social ecology. Cooper and Speece found that two classroom environments tended to be associated with school failure: (a) pencil and paper tasks, when the structure is diffuse and the teacher is engaged with the whole class, as in spelling tests, and (b) pencil and paper tasks, with focused structure, and a disengaged teacher, as in working independently on seatwork.

Historically, learners with mild handicaps have been served in a wide variety of structures; however, research does not clearly support any one service delivery system over another (Kauffman & Pullen, 1989). In a study of forty special education classes for students with different categorical classifications of mild disabilities, Algozzine, Morsink, and Algozzine (1988) found few differences in the extent to which teacher communication patterns, learner involvement, and instructional methods were different in classes containing students classified as learning disabled, behaviorally disordered, or educable mentally retarded. Regardless of the categorical identification of the program, there was a low occurrence of behaviors related to working with individuals and groups, little use of convergent/divergent inquiry, little development of problem-solving skills, and few efforts to facilitate generalization or the transfer of learning. Algozzine and associates found that instruction for learners who are identified as educable mentally retarded, learning disabled, or behaviorally disordered is more similar than different, though teachers of learners identified as educable mentally retarded modified the instruction to meet individual learner needs about half as frequently as teachers of learners with other disabilities.

If we assume that the individuals with mild disabilities are those served within general education classes, we find that during the 1989–90 school year, approximately 31.5 percent of learners with all disabilities were maintained in general education classes and about 37.6 percent were maintained in general education classes with the support of resource rooms (U.S. Department of Education, 1992). The percentage of learners in each of the disability areas served in general education or in general education with resource room support is presented in Table 15.1.

Table 15.1   Percentage of Learners Identified in Each Disability Area and Served in General Education Classes or Resource Rooms

Disability Area	Percent of Learners Served	
	General Education	Resource Room
Specific learning disabilities	20.7	56.1
Speech and language Impairments	76.8	17.7
Mental Retardation	6.7	20.1
Behavioral Disorders	14.9	28.5
Hearing Impairments	27.0	18.2
Multiple disabilities	5.9	14.3
Orthopedic Impairments	29.6	18.9
Other Health Impairments	31.2	22.3
Visual Impairments	39.3	23.7
Deaf-Blindness	8.0	16.3

Includes learners 6 to 21 years of age; preschoolers are not reported categorically.

Source: U.S. Department of Education, 1992.

Objective One: To describe the personal characteristics of learners with mild disabilities.

Personal Characteristics

Learners with mild disabilities are assumed to demonstrate academic achievement lower than that of their peers. However, remediating academic areas has not been demonstrated to meet the needs of all of these students. Sabornie and Beard (1990) state that special education practitioners have come to realize that learners with mild disabilities demonstrate social challenges in their everyday lives.

Social Emotional Characteristics

Sabornie and Beard (1990), summarizing the findings of current research regarding the social competence of learners with mild handicaps, characterize these learners as (a) having low social status among their peers, (b) participating in few extracurricular activities, (c) being dissatisfied with their social lives, (d) having fewer friends, and (e) being more lonely and isolated than their peers.

In a comparison of three subgroups of learners with mild handicaps (that is, learning disabilities, mild mental retardation, behavioral disorders) using a teacher rating scale, Gresham, Elliott, and Black (1987) found a significant difference between all of the mildly disabled subgroups and a matched sample of typical students. No differences, however, were found between the subgroups of learners with mild disabilities. Analysis revealed that three-fourths of the learners with mild disabilities could be correctly classified on the basis of teacher-rated social skills. In another study, Hutton and Roberts (1983) found that learners who were mildly handicapped were reported to have significantly more problem behaviors than their typical peers. This finding was supported by the work of Cullinan and Epstein (1985), who found that all groups of learners with mild disabilities had

Learners with behavioral disorders demonstrate more disruptive behaviors than their peers.

more adjustment problems than their peers. Learners with behavioral disorders usually demonstrated more problems than did other learners with mild disabilities. In some age groups learners with behavioral disorders and learning disabilities did not differ.

Though the three largest categories of learners with mild disabilities may be similar in many ways, Maheady, Maitland, and Sainato (1984) found that they varied in their interpretation of social interactions. In clinical observations of learners with mild learning disabilities, mild behavioral disorders, and mild mental retardation, total behavior ratings revealed significant differences among the groups. The most challenged in social interactions were, understandably, the learners with behavioral disorders. These results were supported by the findings of Epstein and Cullinan (1984), who again found significant differences among the three groups of learners regarding behavior.

The self-concept of learners identified as mildly disabled who are served in special education has been found to be comparable to the self-concept of their typical peers; lower self-concepts, however, were found among those with mild disabilities totally integrated into general education classes (Coleman, 1983a, 1983b). Coleman suggests that this variation in self-concept is due to the social comparison learners with mild disabilities make when associating with their typical peers.

In 1985, Coleman continued his study of self-concepts of learners with mild disabilities, and included the variables of socioeconomic status and achievement. He found that higher achievers reported higher self-concept scores than did low achievers. In addition, learners from lower socioeconomic status homes demonstrated higher self-concepts than their peers from higher socioeconomic status homes.

Nonacademic activities may provide an alternative path to achievement and self-esteem for many learners with mild disabilities. Murtaugh (1988), in an investigation of nonacademic activities, found that learners with mild disabilities were much less likely than their general education peers to be seriously involved in

Many factors influence the motivation and academic functioning of learners.

activities outside of school. Individual case studies demonstrated that the involvement in activities provides students means to demonstrate their abilities and talents in ways not usually afforded by their school achievement.

As learners with mild disabilities grow older, they continue to vary from their peers. In an ethnographic study of typical adolescents and adolescents with mild disabilities, an account was obtained about the life of each student, both in the home and among friends outside the home. Murtaugh and Zetlin (1988) found that autonomy is achieved through a gradual process of negotiation during high school. Learners with mild disabilities generally lagged behind their general education peers in breaking away from the family. While about three-fourths of the typical learners made significant gains toward increased freedom, less than half of the learners with mild disabilities had negotiated less parental supervision. However, most of the learners with mild disabilities were satisfied with the amount of independence they had gained.

Language

Natsopoulos and Zeromeritou (1990) investigated the use and knowledge of language structures of learners with mild disabilities. They found no real problem in the use of syntactic information to process semantic information, in that typical learners of equivalent verbal mental age used the same processes as learners with mild disabilities. However, learners with mild disabilities were more challenged than were their typical peers when asked to describe the processes they applied to manipulate information.

It appears that learners with mild disabilities in the general education classroom vary from typical peers quantitatively rather than qualitatively. The instructional characteristics of both groups are similar with regard to frequency, intensity, and duration (Bauer & Shea, 1989). Learners with mild disabilities tend to be more impulsive, and exhibit attentional problems in the areas of focusing, vigilance, and selectivity. Their temperamental patterns tend to differ from those of general education students with regard to activity level, distractibility, adaptability, responsiveness, and mood. They tend to be more cautious when approaching new activities. Motivational problems are related to their failure expectations, outer-directedness or reliance on others, learning set (that is, their basic approach to learning a new skill), and difficulty transferring what they have learned from one situation to another. Needless to say, these unique characteristics are not exhibited by all learners with mild disabilities who are served in general education classrooms. According to Mehring and Colson (1990), among the many factors which influence the motivation and academic functioning of learners with mild disabilities are (a) anxiety, (b) self-concept, (c) teacher expectations, (d) the learning process, (e) goal structure, and (f) incentives for learning.

Objective Two: To describe the identification and evaluation of learners with mild disabilities.

Identification and Evaluation

The categories used in special education for students with mild disabilities are not reliable or valid as indicators of the services or forms of services individuals receive (Reynolds, Wang, & Walberg, 1987). In an examination of the relationship between state level financial and demographic characteristics and variability in the identification and degree of mainstreaming of learners with mild disabilities, Noel and Fuller (1985) found that much of the variance among states in terms of numbers of identified learners with mild disabilities and the use of special rather than mainstreamed placement was accounted for by the amount of financial resources that states and local districts commit to education, the state's minority enrollment, and the number of children living in or at the poverty level.

Though the long-standing belief has been held that, in most cases, we are unable to determine the cause of mild disabilities, Smith (1989) found that many of these problems are due to medically identifiable syndromes. Rather than "cultural familial" or unknown in origin, Smith suggested that fetal alcohol effects, chromosomal abnormalities, multiple anomaly syndromes, phenylketonuria, Tourette syndrome, and several other genetic syndromes may be the cause of mild disabilities.

Difficulties in differentiating learners with mild disabilities from those who demonstrate low achievement is a consistent problem in special education. The primary difference that has emerged in differentiating these two groups of learners is that learners who are mildly disabled scored significantly lower in achievement than did their low-achieving peers (Shinn & Marston, 1985). Aksamit (1990) believes that there is an apparent overidentification of learners as disabled, and that changes in teaching, school organization, and staffing approaches might enhance the education of at-risk children and reduce the numbers labeled as disabled. Learners from minority cultures and ethnic groups are particularly at risk for misidentification.

The use of standardized assessment instruments with learners with mild disabilities has been continually problematic. Intelligence quotient scores, for example, are no longer perceived to be as stable as once assumed. Bauman (1991) found that children initially tested before 8 years of age had a significant loss in intelligence quotient scores at a later age. This loss was particularly strong among those learners whose initial test scores approached the mean (100) on the verbal subtest of the Wechsler Intelligence Score for Children (Revised).

Maheady, Algozzine, and Ysseldyke (1984) argue that many of the academic difficulties for which learners are referred may be directly attributable to problems in the learning environment. They recommend the use of a functional assessment perspective that involves assessing a child's performance in the context of the existing learning environment.

The Impact on Interactions in the Classroom

Objective Three: To describe the impact of mild disabilities on interactions in the classroom.

In a study of teachers' classroom interactions with learners with mild disabilities, learners with mild disabilities were found to receive fewer teacher questions and were provided with less teacher feedback than their typical peers (Alves & Gottlieb, 1986). Teacher-student interactions between teachers and learners with mild disabilities vary from teacher interactions with their typical peers in the frequency of interactions (learners with mild disabilities had fewer), frequency and quality of feedback (typical learners received more feedback and it was more intense), and the proportion of behavioral interventions (more were employed with learners who were mildly disabled) (Thompson, Vitale, & Jewett, 1984).

Beattie and Calhoun (1986) found that learners who are mildly disabled did not participate appropriately in the classroom, and they were poor users of verbal and written communication skills. Learners who are mildly disabled varied from their peers in study and organizational skills, communication skills, and social skills such as class participation, handling criticism, and test taking (Calhoun & Beattie, 1987).

Mediating the Environment

Objective Four: To describe ways to mediate the environment for learners with mild disabilities.

Coleman, Pullis, and Minnett (1987) argue that the current research base on the education of learners with mild disabilities with regard to mainstreaming is problematic. They suggest that further research is needed which (a) provides a longitudinal analysis and assessment across environments, (b) uses multitrait-multimethod strategies, and (c) weaves a complex pattern from the personal, peer, family, and school factors involved.

Data suggesting that teacher certification made little difference in instruction or achievement caused Marston (1987) to question whether a categorical service delivery model for learners with mild disabilities is appropriate. O'Sullivan, Marston, and Magnusson (1987) found no differences in the instructional behavior of teachers with various categorical certifications. Jenkins, Pious, and Peterson (1988) also found that similarities in instructional level and learning rates are greater than differences in the categorical programs for learners with mild disabilities.

Several services have been used with learners with mild disabilities. These include remaining in general education, consultation, resource room services, and self-contained programs.

Preschool

Jenkins, Speltz, and Odom (1985) contrasted the effects of integrated and segregated preschool programs for young learners with mild disabilities and found that the learners in both programs made significant gains across the year. The learners

---

Box 15.1

Adapting Textbooks for Use with Learners with Mild Disabilities

Meese (1992) presented three general areas in which textbooks can be adapted for use by learners with mild disabilities in general education classrooms. These areas, and related techniques, include the following:

Modify the textbook by
highlighting information
tape recording text segments
using an alternative, high-interest, low-vocabulary text

Alter instructional procedures by
teaching students how to use the textbook's structure
helping students preview the chapter or section
providing advance organizers for the student
teaching key words, phrases, or other critical vocabulary

Teach textbook reading strategies such as
self-questioning about the main idea, summaries, and themes
reading actively
making study cards ■

---

in integrated special education programs, however, scored significantly higher in terms of changes in their social play. The amount of time the learners spent with typical peers had no pervasive effect on the learners' development.

Services in General Education

There has been little longitudinal analysis and assessment comparing students' learning in mainstreamed or more restrictive environments (Coleman, Pullis, & Minnett, 1987). O'Sullivan, Ysseldyke, Christenson, and Thurlow (1990) explored the learning opportunities in general education classes for learners with mild disabilities. They found that learners with mild disabilities in general education classes, when contrasted with their ability peers in special education classes, were actively engaged and responding a lower proportion of time. However, because less time was spent overall in special education classes for reading, the absolute time spent engaged or responding was approximately the same in both types of classes. However, they found that learners with mild disabilities had fewer opportunities to learn when they were in general education classes.

In a study of general education teachers' perceptions of educational program modifications made for learners with mild disabilities, simple modifications were found to be common (Munson, 1986). However, there were significant negative relations between general education teachers' age and years of teaching experience, and the number of modifications reported for learners with mild disabilities. Examples of modifications for using textbooks and for solving arithmetic problems are presented in Boxes 15.1 and 15.2.

Salend and Lutz (1984) surveyed general and special educators to determine the skills and competencies needed by learners with mild disabilities for success in general education classrooms. They found that three general areas of competency were necessary: (1) positive peer interaction, (2) ability to follow rules, and

---

Box 15.2

Self-Monitoring in Arithmetic

The complex sequences involved in computation may be a challenge for learners with mild disabilities. Frank and Brown (1992) suggest using self-monitoring strategies to help students remember the steps that must be followed during computation. They suggest using the following steps to develop a personal self-monitoring strategy for a student:

1. Analyze the steps needed to successfully complete the task. For example, for addition, in which column should the student begin? Under which column should the student write the sum?
2. Write down the steps in a clear, concise sequence.
3. Create a mnemonic to help the student remember the steps (for example, for addition, **SASH**—**S**tart in the one's column, **A**dd, **S**hould I carry, **H**ave I carried correctly).
4. Model using the strategy; use it verbally at the board, write the steps near problems, etc.
5. Fade the supports as the student begins to use the strategy independently ■

Box 15.3

Helping Students with Mild Disabilities Become Organized

Students with mild disabilities may need additional supports to help them develop organizational skills. Shields and Heron (1989) suggest several strategies to help students become more organized (and maintain organization):

Provide students with a visual representation of what must be learned, what tasks need to be accomplished, and the time frame.

Teach students to use an assignment log. This log can be coordinated with a two-pocket work folder, in which one pocket is labeled "completed" and the other "to be completed."

Set up a workstation for the student which signals academic engaged time.

Color code assignments; red flags can mean due immediately, yellow for due tomorrow, and green for due in the near future.

Provide "guided notes" which include a list of key terms, definitions of the terms, and comprehension questions ■

---

(3) appropriate work habits. In the area of positive peer interaction, learners needed to be able to work effectively with others, respect the feelings of others, avoid fighting and stealing, engage in cooperative play, and share materials and equipment. Specific class rules to be adhered to included remaining quiet while others are speaking, using appropriate language, and telling the truth. Appropriate work habits needed to function successfully in the general education classroom are following directions, seeking assistance when appropriate, initiating assignments independently, attending to and persisting at tasks, and attending class regularly. Several strategies for helping learners with mild disabilities become organized are presented in Box 15.3.

Peer Tutoring

Classwide peer tutoring has been suggested as an effective strategy for learners with mild disabilities. Implementation of peer tutoring has been associated with increases of approximately eighteen points on social studies examinations of learners with mild disabilities (Maheady, Sacca, & Harper, 1988). In addition, the implementation of classwide peer tutoring has been found to reduce failing grades. In one study, learners with mild disabilities received no grades below a C.

Collaborative Consultation

West and Idol (1990) write that **collaborative consultation,** can support learners with mild disabilities. Consultation is effective in (a) preventing learning and behavioral problems, (b) remediating these problems, and (c) coordinating instructional programs.

The purpose of collaborative consultation is to have the special and general educator work as a team to develop specific management and instructional interventions for learners with mild disabilities and other difficult-to-teach learners who are served in the general classroom (Pugach & Johnson, 1988). Through consultation, the general educator is provided assistance in the identification, intervention, and evaluation of learner behavior.

In an effort to overcome the barriers to true collaborative consultation caused by differences in the professional roles and functions of the general and special educators, Pugach and Johnson have reconceptualized collaborative consultation on four dimensions:

1. Consultation should be a reciprocal process and involve mutual interaction among all professionals in the school.
2. Consultation should result in the development of independent problem-solving skills by the general educator.
3. Consultation should be a routine part of the function of all professionals in the school.
4. A common language should be used in consultation communications which does not emphasize the specialized language used in special education or other professions.

Teacher Assistance Teams

The **teacher assistance team,** whose members include teachers, school administrators, and professionals in psychology, social work, and special education, has been suggested as a strategy for maintaining learners with mild disabilities in the general education program (Hayek, 1987). As a prereferral support system, the teacher assistance team can be of aid to students who are not eligible for special education services due to the mildness of their disability and to students who though eligible for special education services can be maintained in the general education classroom with services from the general education teacher.

The teacher assistance team is "a teacher-centered instructional alternative support system" (Hayek, 1987). By engaging in problem-solving activities, the members of the team generate ideas, methods, techniques, and activities and develop a plan to assist the teacher in efforts to maintain the learner in the mainstream.

In addition to reducing the number of unnecessary referrals to special education, the teacher assistance team is an excellent in-service training or staff development device for teachers and administrators unfamiliar with specialized instructional and management interventions. Team activities facilitate open communication among general and special educators and other support personnel.

Of course, the teacher assistance team cannot function without the general education teacher who willingly agrees to participate and implement the interventions developed by the team. In addition to the teacher, membership in the team may include the school principal, psychologist, social worker, and specialized instructional personnel, including the special educator. Membership in the team is fluid and will vary from case to case and from setting to setting. It should be clearly understood by the members of the team that the team is not a special education strategy but rather a way to prevent referral to and placement in special education services.

Prior to referral to the teacher assistance team, the teacher should implement and document the interventions that have been used to assist the learner in the general education classroom. If these interventions have not been effective, then the teacher confers with the principal and, together, they determine the need for referral to the teacher assistance team. The teacher then completes the proper forms and follows the accepted procedures to convene the team. When the team meets, the teacher presents his or her major concerns about the child and the team engages in collaborative problem-solving activities, leading to recommended interventions. The teacher implements the interventions for a predetermined period of time and documents implementation and results. If the interventions are not effective, then the team is reconvened to develop additional interventions, or refer the learner to special education for a diagnostic evaluation.

Resource Room Programming

Resource room programs are reportedly the most widely used educational service delivery system for learners with mild disabilities. In their national survey of state departments of education, Friend and McNutt (1984) found that the resource room was indeed the most frequently used alternative to the general education classroom setting for learners with mild disabilities. This is reaffirmed by the data presented in Table 15.1.

There are essentially two types of resource room services: categorical and noncategorical. The categorical resource room serves learners from one disability classification, that is, learners identified as learning disabled, educable mentally retarded, *or* behaviorally disordered. The **noncategorical** resource room serves learners from several disability classifications. Teachers in noncategorical resource rooms usually hold multiple certifications in areas such as learning disabilities, behavioral disorders, and mild mental retardation.

The amount of time the learner spends in the resource room varies greatly depending on each learner's IEP. The learner may spend from as little as one or two instructional periods daily to one-half of the school day in the resource room.

In a survey study involving general education teachers, Chiappone (1984) found that almost 90 percent of the teachers stated that some student needed resource room services and that such services contributed to not only the learner's progress but the overall functioning of the school.

Wiederholt, Hammill, and Brown (1978) discuss the advantages of the noncategorical resource room. These advantages are as follows:

1. Learners can benefit from both the services of the resource room and the regular class.
2. The special education resource room teacher can devote more time to assisting the learners than either the special or general education teacher.
3. Resource room programs are less costly to operate than special classes.
4. Because learners with mild disabilities are accommodated in the resource room, the development of more severe secondary problems may be avoided.
5. Flexible scheduling permits remediation in the general education class by the general education teacher with support from the resource room teacher in addition to the services provided in the resource room. With flexible scheduling, programs can be changed quickly.
6. Because the resource room can serve the majority of learners with disabilities in the school, the special class can be reserved for services for more severely involved learners.
7. Due to broad experiences with the instructional and management problems of many learners, the resource room teacher can serve as an "in-house" consultant for other school personnel.
8. The noncategorical resource room avoids the use of labels and thus the stigma associated with labels.
9. Because the noncategorical resource room does accommodate learners from several categories of disabilities, the probability that the learner is served in the neighborhood school is increased.
10. Because placement is an individual school decision, less time is consumed between referral and placement for services.
11. Because diagnostic evaluation and specialized examinations are done at the school's request, specialists can devote more time to the functions for which they are trained.

Special Class Programming

One argument for separate special education classes for learners with mild disabilities is a presumed need for intensive instruction in which there is a relatively small student-teacher ratio. However, in their study of state-recommended student-teacher ratios for learners with mild disabilities, Thurlow, Ysseldyke, and Wotruba (1989) found extreme variation in state teacher-student ratios. In addition, significant discrepancies were noted between ratios specified in states' guidelines and ratios reported by the U.S. Department of Education in its annual reports to Congress. It cannot be assumed that assignment to special education provides lower teacher-student ratios.

In an international study contrasting separate and integrated programming for learners with mild disabilities, de Noronha and de Noronha (1984) found, in an analysis of 8 years of programming, that learners in integrated programs achieved more academically, physically, and socially than did learners in separate programs.

Gresham (1984) reports that learners with mild disabilities are often better accepted by their typical peers if they remain in segregated classes rather than being "integrated" into the mainstream school environment. He argues that the main goals of mainstreaming should shift from being academic in nature, to emphasizing peer acceptance, teacher acceptance, and positive peer interaction.

Powerful interventions take place in the community in addition to school activities.

As a result of an analysis of fifty research studies, Carlberg and Kavale (1980) conclude that special classes had a significantly less positive impact on learners with behavioral disorders and learning disabilities when compared to general education classes. They statistically demonstrate that special class placement is inferior to regular class placement with reference to the benefits derived by the learner.

Social Skills Programming

An overriding concern for learners with mild disabilities is that of providing programming in social skills or, in some cases, what are referred to as **school survival skills.** Schaeffer, Zigmond, Kerr, and Farra (1990) state that instruction in school survival skills must be a part of the special education agenda if learners with mild disabilities are to succeed in school and, eventually, work. These critical skills, according to Zigmond, Kerr, Brown, and Harris (1984) include:

1. Going to class daily.
2. Being on time.
3. Bringing necessary materials to class.
4. Turning in work on time.
5. Interacting with teachers without "backtalk."
6. Reading written and following oral directions.

The effectiveness of instruction in these skills is significantly enhanced if parents reinforce the lessons learned in school at home.

Objective Five: To describe the impact of mild disabilities on participation in the larger social systems of the school, community, and society.

The Impact on Participation in the School, Community, and Society

Putnam (1987) suggests that the most powerful interventions for learners with mild disabilities take place in the community-at-large as well as in the schools. These interventions require a cooperative and trusting working relationship between the school, the student's home, and the community. Secondary school counselors may serve to support the transition from school to work, through involvement in vocational planning and training in social skills, the coordination of services, and consultation with other professionals on progress and outstanding needs (Rose, Friend, & Farnum, 1988).

Learners with mild disabilities may need to learn skills to become their own advocates in the community. Sievert, Cuvo, and Davis (1988) demonstrated the effectiveness of a program that taught young adults with mild disabilities (1) to discriminate whether or not possible violations of legal rights occurred, and, if so, (2) to role-play how to deal with these violations. Learners who completed the program showed marked increases in their knowledge of their personal rights, community responsibilities, human services, and consumer rights.

In a study utilizing participant observation, Zetlin and Hosseini (1989) spent one year studying six young adults with mild disabilities the year following their graduation from high school. All students reported that they were glad to have graduated. Five of the students were less than satisfied with the special education program and their experiences during high school. These adult learners experienced problems with typical peers, whose friendship they preferred. All six of the learners received only minimal vocational skills. After graduation they went to junior college, but they took unchallenging courses. In addition, they were all unwilling to acknowledge their disabilities and the complications their particular problems presented towards normative achievements. Though challenged in their participation in the community, all of the learners shied away from support services designated for the developmentally disabled as soon as they shed their special education label. These adult learners floundered from job to job, expressed discontent and frustration, but were at a loss to plan for the future and maintained an unrealistic appraisal of their skills.

Fardig (1985) also found that little specific vocational training was available to rural learners with mild disabilities. Okolo and Sitlington (1988) suggest that this low participation of learners with mild disabilities in vocational programs is related to several factors, including (a) the level of independence required in vocational programs, (b) reading and writing skills required, (c) primary modifications needed for effective participation, such as extra assistance or additional time, (d) lack of staff training for work with learners with disabilities, (e) minimal staff involvement regarding decisions in placements of learners with disabilities, and (f) low staff comfort level with individuals with mild disabilities.

In an interview study conducted 6 years after graduation, Scuccimarra and Speece (1990) reported that most of their respondents relied on self, family, and friend networks to secure employment. Most of the adults were single, resided at home, and were in primarily unskilled, semi-skilled, or service positions. Scuccimarra and Speece state that these findings are consistent with 30 years of data documenting low-level employment for learners with mild disabilities.

Edgar (1988), paraphrasing Finn (1986), writes that special education for learners with mild disabilities had three primary purposes in the area of skills

Learners with mild disabilities contribute to the community.

preparation. Special education should teach skills needed to function by preparing learners with skills to (a) function in the social system in which they live, (b) lead personally fulfilling lives, and (c) prepare for the next phase of their life, whether it be higher education or employment. In an extensive analysis of the research, Edgar concludes that learners with mild disabilities have more difficulty finding employment than do their peers. Learners labeled mildly mentally retarded do less well in the area of employment than any other subgroups. Females do less well than males. The positions obtained by learners with mild disabilities are low-paying and lack fringe benefits. There is little evidence to support the conclusion that differential education impacts on future employment. However, special education graduates have greater success finding employment than dropouts.

Summary

In this chapter, we discussed learners with mild disabilities. We discussed our concern with the consistent increase in the number of learners being identified as mildly learning disabled, mildly behaviorally disordered, and mildly mentally retarded. Consideration was given to the discussion of providing categorical or non-categorical services for this group of learners. Research does not support the need for categorical services. The type of certification held by the teacher appears to have little influence on the instructional methods applied with learners who have mild disabilities. It was noted that during the 1989–90 school year the U.S. Office of Education reported that 69.1 percent of learners with disabilities were served either full- or part-time in the general education classroom. Though learners with mild disabilities present academic challenges to teachers, these learners also present significant social-emotional challenges.

Though research data is limited, it appears that a broad range of instructional and management interventions may be applied to facilitate the education and socialization of learners with mild disabilities. These interventions include: preschool services, modified instruction in the general education classroom, peer-tutoring, collaborative consultation, teacher assistance teams, prereferral interventions, resource room programs, and special class instruction. Social or survival skills instruction appears to be essential to the effective functioning of learners with mild disabilities. This need for support continues when learners leave the school and enter the workplace and community. Assistance through vocational training, higher education, and socialization to adulthood are needed.

References

Aksamit, D. (1990). Mildly handicapped and at-risk students: The graying of the line. *Academic Therapy, 25* (3), 277–289.

Algozzine, B., & Korinek, L. (1985). Where is special education for students with high prevalence handicaps going? *Exceptional Children, 51,* 388–394.

Algozzine, B., Morsink, C. V., & Algozzine, K. M. (1988). What's happening in self-contained special education classrooms. *Exceptional Children, 55,* 259–265.

Alves, A. J., & Gottlieb, J. (1986). Teacher interactions with mainstreamed handicapped students and their nonhandicapped peers. *Learning Disability Quarterly, 9* (1), 77–83.

Bauer, A. M., & Shea, T. M. (1989). *Teaching exceptional students in your classroom.* Boston: Allyn & Bacon.

Bauman, E. (1991). Stability of WISC-R scores in children with learning difficulties. *Psychology in the Schools, 28,* 95–100.

Beattie, J. R., & Calhoun, M. L. (1986). Participating in the high school mainstream: Communication skills of mildly handicapped adolescents. *High School Journal, 70* (1), 40–45.

Calhoun, M. L., & Beattie, J. (1987). School competence needs of mildly handicapped adolescents. *Adolescence, 22,* 555–563.

Carlberg, C., & Kavale, K. (1980). Efficacy of special versus regular class placement for exceptional children: A meta-analysis. *Journal of Special Education, 14,* 295–309.

Chiappone, A. D. (1984). Regular class teachers' attitudes toward resource rooms. *Remedial and Special Education, 5* (4), 47–48.

Coleman, J. M. (1983a). Handicapped labels and instructional segregation: Influences on children's self-concepts versus the perceptions of others. *Learning Disability Quarterly, 6,* 3–11.

Coleman, J. M. (1983b). Self-concept and the mildly handicapped: The role of social comparisons. *Journal of Special Education, 17* (1), 37–45.

Coleman, J. M. (1985). Achievement level, social class, and the self-concepts of mildly handicapped children. *Journal of Learning Disabilities, 18,* 26–30.

Coleman, J. M., Pullis, M., & Minnett, A. M. (1987). Studying mildly handicapped children's adjustment to mainstreaming: A systemic approach. *Remedial and Special Education, 8* (6), 19–30.

Cooper, D. H., & Speece, D. L. (1990). Maintaining at-risk children in regular education settings: Initial effects of individual differences and classroom environments. *Exceptional Children, 57* (2), 117–127.

Cullinan, D., & Epstein, M. H. (1985). Adjustment problems of mildly handicapped and nonhandicapped students. *Remedial and Special Education, 5* (2), 5–11.

de Noronha, Z. E., & de Noronha, M. (1984). Integrate or segregate? *School Psychology International, 5* (3), 161–165.

Edgar, E. (1988). Employment as an outcome for mildly handicapped students: Current status and future directions. *Focus on Exceptional Children, 21* (10), 1–8.

Epstein, M. H., & Cullinan, D. (1984). Behavior problems of mildly handicapped and normal adolescents. *Journal of Clinical Child Psychology, 13* (1), 33–37.

Fardig, D. B. (1985). Postsecondary vocational adjustment of rural, mildly handicapped students. *Exceptional Children, 52,* 115–121.

Finn, C. E. (1986). A fresh option for the noncollege-bound. *Phi Delta Kappan, 68* (4), 234–348.

Frank, A. R., & Brown, D. (1992). Self-monitoring strategies in arithmetic. *Teaching Exceptional Children, 24* (2), 52–54.

Friend, M., & McNutt, G. (1984). Resource room programs: Where are we now? *Exceptional Children, 51* (2), 150–155.

Gresham, F. M. (1984). Social skills and self-efficacy for exceptional children. *Exceptional Children, 51* (3), 253–261.

Gresham, F. M., Elliott, N., & Black, F. L. (1987). Teacher-rated social skills of mainstreamed mildly handicapped and nonhandicapped children. *School Psychology Review, 16* (1), 78–88.

Hayek, R. A. (1987). The teacher assistance team: A prereferral support system. *Focus on Exceptional Children, 20* (1), 1–7.

Heitz, T. (1989). How do I help Jacob? *Young Children,* (November), 11–15.

Hutton, J. B., & Roberts, T. (1983). Factor structure of problem behavior for mildly handicapped and nonhandicapped students. *Psychologistical Reports, 52* (3), 703–707.

Jenkins, J. R., Pious, C. G., & Peterson, D. L. (1988). Categorical programs for remedial and handicapped students: Issues of validity. *Exceptional Children, 55* (2), 147–158.

Jenkins, J. R., Speltz, M. L., & Odom, S. L. (1985). Integrating normal and handicapped preschoolers: Effects on child development and social interaction. *Exceptional Children, 52,* 7–17.

Kauffman, J. M., & Pullen, P. (1989). An historical perspective: A personal perspective of our history of service to mildly handicapped and at risk students. *Remedial and Special Education, 10,* 12–14.

Maheady, L., Algozzine, B., & Ysseldyke, J. E. (1984). Minority overrepresentation in special education: A functional assessment perspective. *Special Services in the Schools, 1* (2), 5–19.

Maheady, L., Harper, G. F., & Sacca, K. (1988). A classwide peer tutoring system in a secondary, resource room program for the mildly handicapped. *Journal of Research and Development in Education, 21,* 76–83.

Maheady, L., Maitland, G., & Sainato, D. (1984). The interpretation of social interactions by mildly handicapped and nondisabled children. *Journal of Special Education, 18,* 151–159.

Maheady, L., Sacca, M., & Harper, G. F. (1988). Classwide peer tutoring with mildly handicapped high school students. *Exceptional Children, 55,* 62–59.

Marston, D. (1987). Does categorical teacher certification benefit the mildly handicapped child? *Exceptional Children, 53,* 423–431.

Meese, R. L. (1992). Adapting textbooks for children with learning disabilities in mainstreamed classrooms. *Teaching Exceptional Children, 24* (3), 49–54.

Munson, S. M. (1986). Regular education teacher modifications for mainstreamed mildly handicapped students. *Journal of Special Education, 20,* 489–502.

Murtaugh, M. (1988). Achievement outside the classroom: The role of nonacademic activities in the lives of high school students. *Anthropology and Education Quarterly, 19,* 382–395.

Murtaugh, M., & Zetlin, A. G. (1988). Achievement of autonomy by nonhandicapped and mildly learning handicapped adolescents. *Journal of Youth and Adolescents, 17* (5), 445–460.

Natsopoulos, D., & Zeromeritou, A. (1990). Language behavior by mildly handicapped and nonretarded children on complement clauses. *Research in Developmental Disabilities, 11* (2), 199–216.

Noel, M., & Fuller, F. (1985). The social policy construction of special education: The impact of state characteristics on identification and integration of handicapped children. *Remedial and Special Education, 8* (3), 27–35.

Okolo, C., & Sitlington, P. L. (1988). Mildly handicapped learners in vocational education: A statewide study. *Journal of Special Education, 22,* 220–230.

O'Sullivan, P. J., Marston, D., & Magnusson, D. (1987). Categorical special education teacher certification: Does it affect instruction of mildly handicapped pupils? *Remedial and Special Education, 8,* 13–18.

O'Sullivan, P. J., Ysseldyke, J. E., Christenson, S. L., & Thurlow, M. L. (1990). Mildly handicapped elementary students' opportunity to learn during reading instruction in mainstream and special education settings. *Reading Research Quarterly, 25,* 131–146.

Pugach, M. C., & Johnson, L. J. (1988). Rethinking the relationship between consultation and collaborative problem-solving. *Focus on Exceptional Children, 21* (4), 1–8.

Putnam, M. L. (1987). Effective interventions for mildly handicapped adolescents in the home and the community. *Pointer, 31* (3), 19–24.

Rose, E., Friend, M., & Farnum, M. (1988). Transition planning for mildly handicapped students: The secondary school counselor's role. *School Counselor, 25,* 275–283.

Reynolds, M. C., Wang, M. C., & Walberg, H.J. (1987). The necessary restructuring of special and regular education. *Exceptional Children, 53* (5), 391–398.

Sabornie, E. J., & Beard, G. H. (1990). Teaching social skills to students with mild handicaps. *Teaching Exceptional Children,* 35–38.

Salend, S. J., & Lutz, G. L. (1984). Mainstreaming and mainlining: A competency based approach to mainstreaming. *Journal of Learning Disabilities, 17* (1), 27–29.

Schaeffer, A. L., Zigmond, N., Kerr, M. M., & Farra, H. E. (1990). Helping teenagers develop school survival skills. *Teaching Exceptional Children, 23* (1), 6–9.

Scuccimarra, D. J., & Speece, D. L. (1990). Employment outcomes and social integration of students with mild handicaps: The quality of life two years after high school. *Journal of Learning Disabilities, 23,* 213–219.

Shields, J. M., & Heron, T. E. (1989). Teaching organizational skills to students with learning disabilities. *Teaching Exceptional Children, 21* (2), 8–13.

Shinn, M., & Marston, D. (1985). Differentiating mildly handicapped, low-achieving, and regular education students: A curriculum-based approach. *Remedial and Special Education, 6* (2), 31–38.

Sievert, A. L., Cuvo, A. J., & Davis, K. (1988). Training self-advocacy skills to adults with mild handicaps. *Journal of Applied Behavior Analysis, 21,* 299–309.

Smith, S. M. (1989). Congenital syndromes and mildly handicapped students: Implications for special educators. *Remedial and Special Education, 10* (3), 20–30.

Thompson, R. H., Vitale, P. A., & Jewett, J. P. (1984). Teacher-student interaction patterns in mainstreamed classrooms. *Remedial and Special Education, 5* (6), 51–61.

Thurlow, M. L., Ysseldyke, J. E., & Wotruba, J. W. (1989). State recommended student-teacher ratios for mildly handicapped children. *Remedial and Special Education, 10,* 37–42.

U.S. Department of Education (1991). *Thirteenth annual report to Congress on the implementation of the Individuals with Disabilities Education Act.* Washington, DC: Author.

U.S. Department of Education (1992). *Fourteenth annual report to Congress on the implementation of the Individuals with Disabilities Education Act.* Washington, DC: Author.

West, J. F., & Idol, L. (1990). Collaborative consultation in the education of mildly handicapped and at-risk students. *Remedial and Special Education, 11* (1), 22–31.

Wiederholt, J. L., Hammill, D. D., & Brown, V. (1978). *The resource teacher: A guide to effective practice.* Boston: Allyn & Bacon.

Zetlin, A. G., & Hosseini, A. (1989). Six postschool case studies of mildly learning handicapped young adults. *Exceptional Children, 55,* 405–411.

Zigmond, N., Kerr, M. M., Brown, G. M., & Harris, A. L. (1984). *School survival skills in secondary school age special education students.* Paper presented at the meeting of the American Educational Research Association, New Orleans.

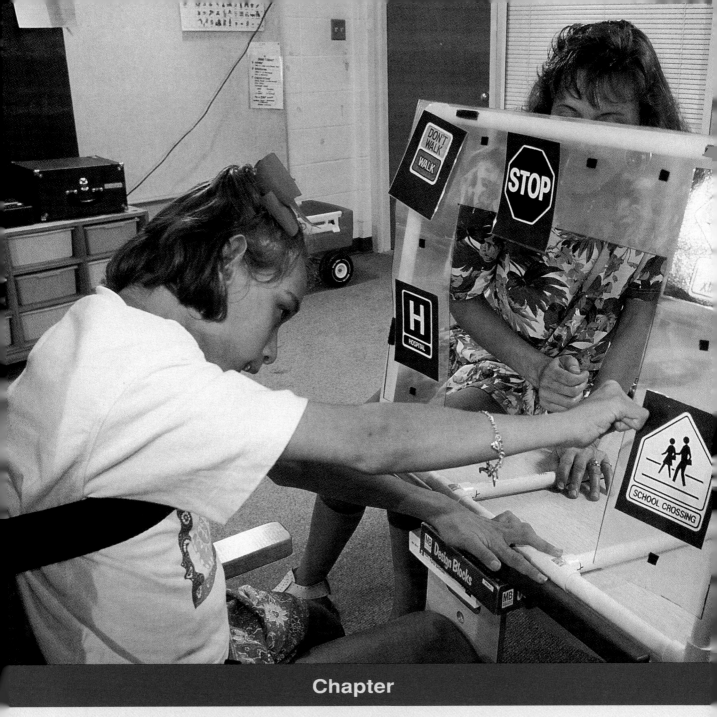

16

Learners with Severe and Multiple Disabilities

*O*bjectives

After completing this chapter, you will be able to:

1. describe the personal characteristics of learners with severe or multiple disabilities.
2. describe the identification and evaluation of learners with severe or multiple disabilities.
3. describe the impact of severe or multiple disabilities on interactions in the home and classroom.
4. describe ways to mediate the environment for learners with severe or multiple disabilities.
5. describe the impact of severe or multiple disabilities on participation in the larger social systems of the community and society.

*K*ey Words and Phrases

augmentative communication systems   multiple disabilities

autism   severe disabilities

dual sensory impairments

*T*HE LIVING QUARTERS FOR OLDER MEN AND WOMEN WERE, FOR THE MOST PART, GLOOMY AND STERILE. THERE WERE rows and rows of benches on which sat countless human beings, in silent rooms, waiting for dinner call or bed time. We saw resident after resident in "institutional garb." Sometimes the women wore shrouds—inside out.

We heard a good deal of laughter but saw little cheer. There were few things to be cheerful about. A great deal of the men and women looked depressed and acted depressed. Even the television sets, in several of the day rooms, appeared to be co-conspirators in a crusade for gloom. These sets were not in working order. Ironically, the residents continued to sit on their benches, in neat rows, looking at the blank tubes.

We observed adult residents during recreation, playing "ring-around-the-rosy." Others, in the vocational training center, were playing "jacks." These were not always severely retarded patients. However, one got the feeling very quickly that this is the way they were being forced to behave. (A description of an institution for individuals with mental retardation in the early 1960s from Blatt & Kaplan, 1966.) ■

● At The Seaside there is time, time for teaching a young child to use a spoon or fork, time for helping a child to learn to use a zipper, time to heal a wound—either of the body or the soul. But, at The Seaside, there is no time for tomorrow. There is a fight against inertia. Children must be helped today, for in too few tomorrows children become adults and residents become inmates.

At The Seaside, there is schooling. Some children attend school at the institution. The older and more capable youngsters attend school in the community—public school—with other children who are living at home. At The Seaside, it is not difficult to tell that this is an environment designed for children. The lawns are filled with swings and jungle gyms and bicycle paths. During Christmas

388

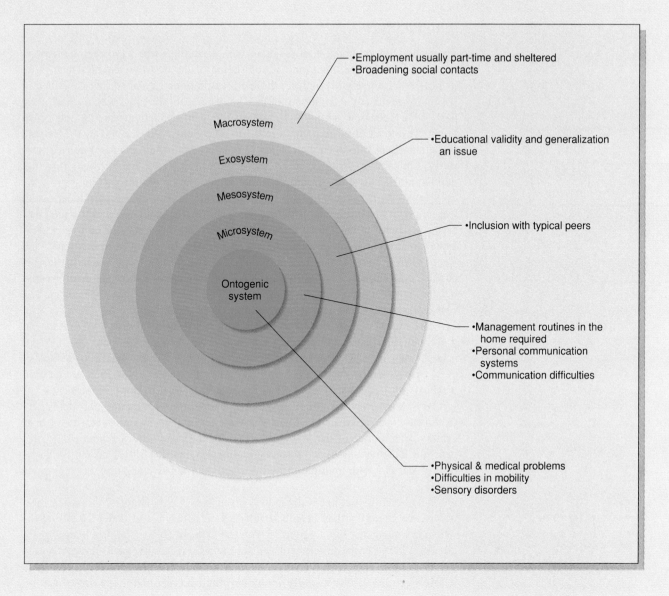

•Employment usually part-time and sheltered
•Broadening social contacts

Macrosystem

•Educational validity and generalization
  an issue

Exosystem

Mesosystem

Microsystem

•Inclusion with typical peers

Ontogenic
system

•Management routines in the
  home required
•Personal communication
  systems
•Communication difficulties

•Physical & medical problems
•Difficulties in mobility
•Sensory disorders

time, each room is decorated, welcoming Santa Claus and the spirit of Christmas. Rooms are clean and orderly. Furniture that adults use is designed for adults.

There are adult residents at The Seaside. However, they are not in the same dormitories, or programs, with the children. Adults have other needs and the following may illustrate how some of these are met.

One of our difficulties in photographing activities at The Seaside was our inability to take very many pictures of adult residents. There is a very good explanation for this. Most of the adults at The Seaside worked during the day—they are on institutional jobs or out in the community. Some, who could not be returned to their own homes, live in a work training unit. Here, they are together with friends and co-workers, under the supervision of a cottage mother and father. During the day they are on placement—working in the community—and in the evening they return to their "home" where they can receive special help and guidance in their successful attempts to integrate into normal communities and become contributing members of society. (A description of an experimental institution for the severely retarded in the early 1960s from Blatt and Kaplan, 1966.) ■

Introduction

There are, without doubt, no individuals with disabilities who have been more positively affected by the litigation and legislation of the past two decades than those identified as severely or multiply disabled. Institutions similar to that described in the first vignette at the beginning of the chapter are, for the most part, a thing of the past. Today, the few adults and children living in residential centers and group homes reside in environments similar to The Seaside described in the second vignette presented to open the chapter. Though the transition is not complete, these individuals have progressed, in great numbers, from institutions into the mainstream of the educational community and the community at large.

However, there remains an ongoing debate on the policy of educating all learners with disabilities. This debate has been fueled, in a large part, by the costs associated with providing educational services and disagreement among professionals regarding whether all students can profit from an education. Noonan and Reese (1983) contend that not only does the educability litigation reaffirm that equal   educational opportunity is valued and education is to be defined broadly, but that curricular approaches should be carefully examined for their efficiency, cost-effectiveness, and educational validity.

The number of learners identified with multiple disabilities increased and those with dual sensory impairments decreased between the 1989–90 and 1990–91 school years (U.S. Department of Education, 1992). During the 1990–91 school year, 97,625 learners between 6 and 21 years of age were classified as multiply disabled and 1,522 were classified as demonstrating dual sensory impairments.

Most learners with multiple disabilities or dual sensory impairments are served in separate special education classes, private and public facilities, and residential centers. A minority of the learners in each of the categories are being served in general education classes and resource room programs. Table 16.1 presents the percent of learners with multiple disabilities and dual sensory impairments in various placements.

Another low-incidence disability, discussed in this chapter, is autism. The prevalence of autism has been estimated to range from 4 to 5 per 10,000 births (Ritvo & Freeman, 1978) to 10 to 15 per 10,000 births (American Psychiatric Association, 1987). Most learners with autism are served in segregated programs (day schools, public and private institutions, and residential facilities). However, these learners are being increasingly integrated into public school special education programs and, in some cases, into regular classes with support services.

Objective One: To describe the personal characteristics of learners with severe or multiple disabilities.

Personal Characteristics

There is great variation among individuals with severe or multiple disabilities. These learners frequently have severe to profound mental retardation as well as one or more significant motor or sensory impairments. Orelove and Sobsey (1987) indicate that learners with severe or multiple disabilities often present two or more of these concerns:

physical and medical problems
restricted movement
skeletal deformities
sensory disorders
seizure disorders

***T*able 16.1**   Percentage of Learners in Various Placements
(6–21 years old)—1990–91 School Year

	Regular Class	Resource Room	Special Class	Public/ Private Facility	Public/ Private Residential	Home- bound
Dual Sensory Impairments	8.0	16.3	29.9	16.6	28.4	1.0
Multiple Disabilities	5.9	14.3	43.7	29.5	3.9	2.7

Source: U.S. Department of Education, 1992.

respiratory difficulties

the need for appropriate positioning and handling

the need for augmentative communication strategies

the need for a means to choose, that is, make personal decisions

Learners with Autism   In 1981, learners with autism were reclassified from "serious emotional disturbance" to "other health impaired" as a result of parent and professional efforts to emphasize the biological nature of the disorders. In Public Law 101–476 (the Individuals with Disabilities Education Act of 1990), autism was again reclassified as a separate category of disability. There is ongoing professional dialogue with regard to the personal characteristics of learners with autism. However, it is generally agreed that, in varying degrees, learners with **autism** demonstrate many of these characteristics (Simpson, 1992):

- difficulty relating to others and developing interpersonal relationships
- communication problems in both language and speech
- developmental delays in cognitive, social, and motor areas
- difficulties reacting appropriately to environmental events

Learners with autism, when compared to those with mental retardation and no identified disabilities, demonstrate less diverse play, particularly in spontaneous and cued symbolic play (Sigman & Ungerer, 1984).

The incidence of autism is three times greater in boys than in girls. Its occurrence is fifty times as great in siblings than in the general population (American Psychiatric Association, 1987). Autism was first described as a clinical syndrome by Leo Kanner in 1943. Kanner's use of the word "autism," which had prior to his work been used to describe a symptom of schizophrenia, contributed to confusion surrounding the biological nature of the disorder (Rutter, 1978). The American Psychiatric Association has attempted to clarify this issue by referring to these children as having a "pervasive developmental disorder." In recent research, many organic factors have been associated with autism, including maternal rubella during pregnancy, celiac disease, tuberous sclerosis, metabolic disorders, and genetic conditions such as fragile-x syndrome (Rutter & Schopler, 1985). However, none of these factors accounts for more than a very small number of cases; in most situations, the cause of the disability cannot be determined.

Based on advances in research, Prizant (1984) conceptualizes autism from a communication perspective. In order to describe the functioning of these individuals, he delineates three levels of communicative functioning and the behaviors

_T_able 16.2 Communicative Functioning of Learners with Autism (Prizant, 1984)

Level of Communication	Description	Behaviors
Preintentional/early intentional	Active exploration of the environment; no direct signals or gestures; in early intentional begins direct signals, and develops ways to communicate which only significant other can understand; shows some persistence in signalling	Stereotypic manipulation of objects; orients to stimuli in the environment; inconsistent response to others' speech; in early intention will manipulate adults' hands to perform specific tasks; moves adult physically to initiate action; may use echolalia with intent
Prelinguistic, intentional/ emerging linguistic	Clear concept of communication; uses conventional gestures; more persistent if communicative goals not met; in emerging linguistic uses some words or signs; increased word comprehension	Signals, vocalizes, uses echolalia for a variety of functions; later uses words; greater flexibility in use of echolalia
Intentional/linguistic	Language primary means of communicating; problems in nonliteral forms of language	Initiates and responds to verbal interactions; demonstrates primary problems in pragmatics

related to each levels (see Table 16.2). When autism is viewed from Prizant's communication perspective, much of the "bizarre" behavior of learners with autism take on or can be ascribed meaning.

Learners with Dual Sensory Impairments   Originally referred to as "deaf-blind," learners with **dual sensory impairments** have both visual and auditory disabilities. As a result of these complex disabilities, learners with dual sensory impairments present severe communication deficits as well as developmental and educational problems.

Ninety-four percent of learners classified as dual sensory impaired have some residual hearing and/or vision (Fredericks & Baldwin, 1987). Andrews (1989) states that the essential issue with these learners is to facilitate their use of residual vision and hearing. However, he cautions against overestimating the value and use that a learner with dual sensory impairments can make of these senses. There are special problems related to these learners. For example, because of lack of feedback from the infant, there is poor mother-child bonding and parental overprotection.

Objective Two: To describe the identification and evaluation of learners with severe or multiple disabilities.

Identification and Evaluation

Public Law 94–142 and its amendments do not include a definition of the term **severe disabilities.** One of the more widely used definitions is that of the Bureau of Education for the Handicapped (U.S. Office of Education, 1975):

> Severely handicapped children are those who because of the intensity of their physical, mental, or emotional problems, need educational, social, psychological, and medical services beyond those which are traditionally offered by regular and special education programs, in order to maximize participation in society and self-fulfillment. Such severely handicapped children may possess severe language or perceptual-cognitive

Age appropriate activities support improved quality of life for learners with severe disabilities.

deprivations and evidence a number of abnormal behaviors including failure to attend to even the most pronounced stimuli, self-mutilation, manifestations of durable and intense temper tantrums, and the absence of even the most rudimentary forms of verbal control. They may also have extremely fragile physiological conditions (Sec. 121.2).

According to an analysis by Dollar and Brooks (1980), three criteria for identification as severely handicapped emerge from this definition. First, severe disabilities must be present. Second, an intense educational program with a wide range of resources is necessary. Finally, the focus of educational programs must be towards independent functioning.

In 1990, The Association for Persons with Severe Handicaps (TASH) proposed an alternative definition for severe disabilities which refers to level, duration, and supports needed by the individual. In addition, the definition considers the goals and outcomes of service. TASH defines persons with severe disabilities as:

> . . . individuals of all ages who require extensive, ongoing support in more than one major life activity in order to participate in integrated community settings and to enjoy a quality of life that is available to citizens with fewer or no disabilities. Support can be required for life activities such as mobility, communication, self-care, and learning, as necessary for independent living, employment, and self-sufficiency (Lindley, 1990, p. 1).

Another working definition of individuals with severe disabilities includes those who "have a significant functional discrepancy in: (1) general developmental disabilities, (2) caring and looking after themselves, (3) expressing thoughts, ideas, and feelings, (4) responding to environmental stimuli, and (5) interacting socially with chronological-age peers" (Brimer, 1990, p. 15).

Learners with **multiple disabilities,** as defined by Public Law 94–142 and its amendments, are those learners with

> . . . concomitant impairments (such as mentally retarded-blind, mentally retarded-orthopedically impaired, etc.) the combination of which causes such severe educational problems that they cannot be accommodated in special education programs solely for one of the impairments.

*T*able 16.3   Diagnostic Criteria for Infantile Autism from the DSM-III R, APA 1987

a. Onset before 30 months of age.

b. Pervasive lack of responsiveness to other people (autism).

c. Gross deficits in language development.

d. If speech is present, peculiar speech patterns such as immediate and delayed echolalia, metaphorical language, and pronominal reversal.

Learners with dual sensory impairments are not included in this group. Rather, they are identified as deaf-blind, with the term defined as "concurrent hearing and visual impairments, the combination of which causes such severe communication and educational problems that they cannot be accommodated in special education programs for either the deaf or blind student" *(Federal Register,* 1977).

The Federal Register does not provide a definition of autism, but refers to it as ". . . an autistic condition, which is manifested by severe communication and other developmental and educational problems." The American Psychiatric Association (APA), in the *Diagnostic and Statistical Manual of Mental Disorders* (3rd edition-revised, 1987), refers to autism as a "pervasive developmental disorder" including (a) qualitative impairment in reciprocal social interaction, (b) impairment in communication and imaginative activity, and (c) restricted range of interest and activities. The APA provides criteria for the diagnosis of autism which are presented in Table 16.3.

In a description of the process used by the APA committees in determining the criteria for the diagnosis of autism, Denckla (1986) reports that social impairment was felt by some to be the core characteristic of the disorder. In addition, communication skills, both verbal and nonverbal, must also be impaired for the diagnosis of autism. The presence of repetitive, ritualistic behaviors, in and of themselves, were not felt to establish a diagnosis of autism, but, when present with social and communicative impairments, provide diagnostic confirmation.

Students with severe and multiple disabilities are particularly susceptible to discriminatory assessment practices (Sigafoos, Cole, & McQuarter, 1987). In a study of the types of tests used with these students, there was found to be a lack of technically adequate norm-referenced tests which are appropriate. Generally, school systems do not select tests on the basis of technical adequacy. In addition, they found that criterion-referenced assessment and adaptive behavior measures are used rather infrequently.

Standardized tests are not appropriate for learners with severe disabilities in that they are not designed for them, they do not include these learners in the standardization sample, scoring does not allow for adaptive motor or language responses, and changes in behavior may be too small to be measured on standardized instruments (Linehan, Brady, & Hwang, 1991). In the alternative ecological approach, the teacher, family, and related service personnel determine the practical and functional skills needed in the home, school, community, and vocational setting. Linehan and associates found that ecological assessment reports generated higher expectations among professionals.

Based on his and others' previous work, Brown (1987) suggests that in order to appropriately assess learners with severe and multiple disabilities, a person's daily activities should be broken down into a series of routines composed of different core skills. An emphasis on routines for these learners reflects the complex competencies needed to function as independently as possible in the community. These routines can be grouped within four domains: personal management, vocational/ school, leisure, and mobility. The most appropriate strategy for this type of assessment is observation of the learner in the natural environment. In addition, parent or caregiver interviews are helpful in acquiring specific information regarding skills.

Snell and Grigg (1987) specify a strategy for assessment, grounded in an ecological inventory of the activities in which the learner engages and the skills required within those activities:

1. Specify the curriculum domains. Rather than traditional academic categories, these domains represent the major life areas, lead to practical skills, and emphasize movement towards independence.
2. Analyze the environments and subenvironments in which the activities occur.
3. Assess the subenvironments for the relevant activities performed there, rather than identifying every possible activity. Emphasis is on those activities necessary for basic acceptable performance.
4. Examine the activities to isolate the skills required. Each skill is then broken down into meaningful units.

An emerging area is the assessment of biobehavioral states of students with profoundly disabling conditions. Guess, Mulligan-Ault, Roberts, Struth, Siegel-Causey, Thompson, Bronicki, and Guy (1988) describe biobehavioral states as the general state of alertness and responsiveness described in the literature about infants. In discussing learners with profound disabilities, Guess and associates expressed a concern that program schedules were followed regardless of student receptivity or responsiveness, though the students may have had very severe neurological, physical, and/or sensory impairments, been susceptible to a variety of acute illnesses, or been heavily medicated. They suggest that in working with these learners, understanding the patterns or clusters of periods during which the learner "shuts down" to external sensory or social stimulation is essential. By using a variation of the Neonatal Behavioral Assessment Scale (Brazelton, 1973), Struth and Guess (1986) describe six biobehavioral states: asleep/inactive; asleep/active; drowsy; awake/inactive/alert; awake/active/alert; and crying/agitated. It is important, however, to collect biobehavioral data over longer durations of the day, to describe possible intrastudent fluctuations in their state conditions which can then be compared on an across-day basis.

A comprehensive assessment approach is needed for learners with autism (Simpson, 1992). The approach is multidisciplinary and uses both formal and informal assessment techniques. The areas recommended for assessment are (a) cognitive skills; (b) family and environmental behaviors, (c) neurological, sensory-motor, and medical difficulties, (d) social and behavioral abilities, and (e) the curriculum (preacademic, academic, vocational, self-help, communication, and independent living).

Objective Three: To describe the impact of severe or multiple disabilities on interactions in the home and classroom.

The Impact on Interactions in the Home and Classroom

In the Home

Though management of daily household tasks and child care routines in families with adopted children with severe disabilities was not identified as stressful, interactions with school, medical personnel, and other professionals were extremely stressful for all families interviewed (Todis & Singer, 1991). Medical crises and

A Camp That Cares

When Jeffrey Erlanger was 10, his parents, Pam and Howard Erlanger of Congregation Beth El in Madison, Wisconsin, enrolled him as a camper at the UAHC's Olin-Sang-Ruby Union Institute in Oconomowoc. Today, Jeffrey, 21, is a counselor at the camp and a merit scholarship student at Madison's Edgewood College, majoring in journalism.

Jeffrey, a quadriplegic, lost the use of both arms and legs in infancy.

The Erlangers' decision to send Jeffrey to the Olin-Sang-Ruby camp led to the creation of an unusual program—an annual Kallah that enables Jewish families with disabled children to spend three days together at the camp to discuss mutual problems, enjoy recreational activities such as waterfront sports and horseback riding, and just hang out and have fun.

The Kallah was organized in 1984 by camp director Gerard W. Kaye with the help of Pam Erlanger, a professional occupational therapist. Held every August at the Union Institute camp, it is attended by between 10 and 15 families from various parts of the Midwest. Some 20 teenage members of temple youth groups from NoFTY and CFTY sign on as volunteer Kallah counselors—Jeffrey Erlanger himself was one—and receive an intensive orientation on working with the disabled. The teens are supplemented by college students and adult occupational and physical therapy professionals.

The Kallah is jointly sponsored by the Olin-Sang-Ruby camp and Keshet, a 200-member support group for Jewish families with disabled children. Disabilities run the gamut from visual impairment to serious learning disabilities to diseases such as muscular dystrophy. In fact, most of the children in the Keshet program suffer from multiple handicaps.

"As important as the Kallah is for the disabled youngsters," says Kaye, "it's no less so for their parents and brothers and sisters who rarely have a chance to enjoy a simple family vacation."

Another key aim is to make available to the disabled youngsters activities that normally would be denied them, such as horseback riding or taking their wheelchairs onto a pontoon boat. "No activity at the Kallah is off limits for a child because of a disability," he says.

For the temple youth teens who serve as volunteer Kallah counselors, the experience can be profound. "Many self-involved kids soon discover in themselves previously untapped wells of sensitivity," the camp director explains.

But the greatest impact is on the disabled youngsters themselves and their families. The opportunity to give and receive emotional support and practical advice can be an extraordinary experience, says Pam Erlanger. Equally important, she adds, is the chance for parents to have a mini-vacation

"within a family context," secure in the knowledge that their children are being well cared for.

Jeffrey Erlanger observes that serving as a Kallah counselor gave him an opportunity to help disabled children, just as he himself had been helped, by giving them a sense of reassurance and determination. "Because of my own disability," he says, "I could honestly tell the younger disabled kids that they are capable of achieving a lot more than they may have hoped or even dreamed of."

As a camper, Jeffrey was able for the first time to establish ongoing relationships with children who were not disabled. "In school I could never do that," he says. "The other kids did not exactly make fun of me, but they found it hard to be my friend because they thought I was different. But at camp, I had something in common with the non-disabled kids—Judaism and the fact that we were all campers together."

Jeffrey contends that the annual Kallot give other disabled children the same chance, even if only for three days. "Camping helped change my life," he says. "Perhaps it can help change their lives, too." ■

Reprinted with permission from *Reform Judaism*, published by the Union of American Hebrew Congregations, New York.

behavior problems were seen by the families as time-limited sources of stress; dealing with service providers and "figuring out the system," however, were chronic problems. Household management routines, medical and hygiene routines, time away from the family, and social support from other families with special-needs children were viewed as ways of coping with difficulties.

In interviews with twenty-eight families whose children had dual sensory impairments, Giangreco, Cloninger, Mueller, Yuan, and Ashworth (1991) found that parent concerns clustered around a "good life" for their children, as well as their experiences with fear, frustration, and change. Parents expressed the frustrations that "dealing with schools can be tough" and that the sheer number of professionals working with their children is hectic and an invasion of their privacy. Parents viewed themselves as their child's case-manager, though professional case managers can be helpful.

In a review of twenty-seven studies of parental attitudes on the deinstitutional- ization of a family member, Larson and Lakin (1991) found that in the studies in which the family member was still institutionalized, families indicated general opposition to deinstitutionalization. In those studies in which the family member had already moved to the community, parents who had retrospectively reported lower levels of satisfaction with earlier institutional placement reported lower levels of opposition to deinstitutionalization and high levels of satisfaction with community settings.

There was considerable research, prior to Public Law 94–142, on the reasons that individuals with severe and multiple disabilities were placed in out-of-home residential services. In 1991, Bromley and Blacher, as part of a parent interview study of out-of-home placement, reviewed the literature and concluded that parents have three major areas of concerns when placing a child out-of-home. Their con- cerns focused around the child's characteristics, family characteristics, and lack of supportive services. Child characteristics related to out-of-home placement included behavior problems and severe levels of mental retardation. Family charac- teristics were related to daily stress, parental health, marital status, and family size. The availability of supportive services such as help in the home, babysitters, and respite care also influenced the decision to place an individual out-of-home. In their study of sixty-three parents (primary caregivers) of individuals with severe disabili- ties between the ages of 2 and 16, Bromley and Blacher found that the decision to place was not based on one factor but influenced by a number of factors working together. Of the twenty factors that emerged, the five most influential were (1) day- to-day stress, (2) the child's level of functioning and potential for future learning, (3) the child's behavior, (4) the feelings of nondisabled siblings, and (5) the spouse's attitude toward placement. The availability of supportive services was not found to be essential in the decision to place children out-of-home.

Parent involvement has been correlated significantly with many factors reflect- ing the home and quality of parenting (Meyers & Blacher, 1987). Overall family adjustment and the level of the mother's education have been correlated to parent involvement. Schools reportedly provided some respite for parents, and many par- ents felt they did gain techniques and skills for better working with their child through their involvement. When compared to mothers of children with milder dis- abilities, some mothers of learners with severe or multiple disabilities were able to identify as many communication cues as those of infants with milder disabilities, perhaps because they adapted to their infants' disabilities and were more able to interpret their behavior (Yoder & Feagans, 1988).

Parents of learners with dual sensory impairments need practical help, advice, and resources, including contact with other parents who had similar experiences. They frequently need information on hearing aids (Andrews, 1989).

In the Classroom

Chadsey-Rusch (1990), using narrative recording procedures, studied the social interactions of secondary-aged students with severe disabilities by observing ten students attending a junior high school campus. She found that these students were involved in more task-related than non-task-related interactions, and that they were

Students use technology to communicate.

engaged more with teachers than with their peers. In addition, these adolescents were dependent on contrived or additional cues and feedback rather than those which naturally occurred in the school or vocational settings.

Schnorr (1990) studied how part-time mainstreaming of a learner identified as moderately mentally retarded was understood by his first grade classmates. The partially mainstreamed student was assigned to a special class for learners with moderate and severe disabilities for the remainder of the school day. While in the first grade room he followed the cues of the other first graders quite well in routine situations, such as waiting in line, playing a game, and following directions. In discussions with the first graders, Schnorr found that they identified themselves as first graders and in Ms. _____'s class. The mainstreamed student was not really regarded by the first graders as a member of the class, but as a visitor who "comes and goes." The mainstreamed student was perceived as someone who has no grade, no teacher to speak of, whose desk is empty most of the day, who gets his own stickers instead of the typical reward system, rather than as a first grader like themselves. Schnorr concluded that for this student, being a part-time first grader was a different, rather than briefer, experience.

General education adolescents who were integrated with peers with severe disabilities reported several benefits related to their relationships with classmates with disabilities (Peck, Donaldson, & Pezzoli, 1990). The general education students indicated that their experiences improved their self-concept, increased their growth in social cognition, increased their tolerance of others, reduced their fear about others' differences, and increased their interpersonal acceptance and friendships. These students, however, reported that they had difficulty and felt uncomfortable in dealing with the challenging behaviors demonstrated by the learners with severe disabilities.

In a study of students in second through sixth grade, Condon, York, Heal, and Fortschneider (1986) found that girls were more accepting than boys and that respondents in the same school as the students with severe disabilities were more

Reaction encourages learners to participate to the best of their ability.

accepting than those in a different school. Older respondents were more tolerant than younger students, but this increased acceptance appeared to dissipate when contact between students stopped.

York, Vandercook, Macdonald, Heise-Heff, and Caughey (1992), in an analysis of questionnaires regarding integration, reported that almost all of the classmates of learners with severe or multiple disabilities reported that integration is a good idea, and made comments such as "they need to be around normal people" and "it teaches her more stuff." Special educators, general educators, and classmates all reported perceived positive changes, particularly in social and communication skills.

In a study contrasting peer-tutoring and "special friends" interactions, Cole, Vandercook, and Rynders (1988) found that peer tutoring interactions tended to be lopsided, with nonidentified students watching, teaching, and helping. Interactions with "special friends" were more reciprocal, though some distinct imbalance was apparent. Special friend relationships were closer to best friends, whereas peer tutors were more like teacher-students. Students who were engaged in the "special friends" program attended a training session where they learned rules and roles, how to play, how to communicate, what is a friend, why integration, what is a prosthesis, how does a disabled person live, and similar issues.

Objective Four: To describe ways to mediate the environment for learners with severe or multiple disabilities.

Mediating the Environment

The overall goal of education for learners with severe and multiple disabilities is the development of "functional" skills, that is, skills which can be used in the immediate and future domestic, vocational, community, and recreation/leisure environments. "Educational programs are future-oriented in their efforts to teach skills and behaviors that will enable students with severe handicaps to be as independent and productive as possible after they leave school" (Heward & Orlansky, 1992, p. 433).

Variables which must be considered when designing a curriculum for learners with severe or multiple disabilities are: (a) functionality, (b) chronological age-appropriateness, (c) varying levels of participation, (d) encouragement of decision-making, (e) facilitation of communication, (f) vocational training, and (g) development of recreation and leisure skills. A functional curriculum includes skills that are useful and productive to the learner in the real environment in which the learner functions or will function in the future. It is essential that curricular activities be age-appropriate for the learner rather than either contrived or appropriate for persons of a younger age. Activities should encourage the learner to participate to as great an extent as possible. Caregivers are cautioned not to assume the decision-making responsibilities of learners with severe and multiple disabilities. These learners should be provided with the means and encouraged to make personal decisions and express personal preferences. Communication skills, either verbal, gestural, or through augmentative communication aids, are essential to learners with severe disabilities. Finally, employment-related and recreation and leisure skills are important to the present and future dignity and self-concept of learners with severe and multiple disabilities.

Inclusion in the general school community has emerged as a major trend in the education of learners with severe or multiple disabilities. York and Vandercook (1990) suggested several change strategies to generate a more unified and inclusive system of education for learners with severe and multiple disabilities. First, they argue for natural proportions, that is, the distribution of learners with severe or multiple disabilities in school which reflects their diversity in the larger community. The second principle is one of natural supports, that is, using persons typically available in a given environment who can provide assistance to an individual with disabilities. For example, the teacher and classmates are natural supports to a learner with or without disabilities. In addition to these guiding principles, York and Vandercook suggest several change strategies, summarized in Table 16.4, to facilitate the development of inclusive school environments.

An ongoing concern regarding the educational programs for learners with severe and multiple disabilities is that of educational validity. Voeltz and Evans (1983) write that educational validity is a concept which addresses these measurement questions:

1. Has behavior change occurred as a function of the educational intervention?
2. Did the educational intervention occur as specified in the treatment plan?
3. Is the resultant behavior change meaningful, that is, beneficial for the learner now and in the future, and considered to be valuable by those in the learner's natural environment?

By addressing these questions, the internal, educational, empirical, and social validity of an intervention are addressed.

Learners with severe and multiple disabilities have several unique concerns that require mediation. These concerns include physical management and handling, including proper lifting, carrying, positioning, feeding, toileting, and dressing (Campbell, 1987). The goal of any physical management procedure is to allow the

***T*able 16.4**   Change Strategies to Facilitate the Development
of Inclusive School Environments

A. Identify and recruit collaborators in the process
    1. develop a planning team to provide direction and leadership
    2. organize task forces or work groups
B. Communicate with all members in the school community
    1. communicate with all faculty; provide a vision
    2. communicate with students; involve and educate students
    3. communicate with parents; invite them in
C. Conduct an inventory of life within the school community
    1. study student life
    2. study faculty life
    3. study the general community's involvement
D. Share space
    1. integrate general education homerooms
    2. integrate general education classes

---

student to perform independently as many parts of a task as possible. In this way, the learner not only gets to practice selected movements, but the amount of physical stress on the individual teaching or caring for the learner is reduced.

Leisure activities are also an essential part of programming for learners with severe or multiple handicaps. Moon and Bunker (1987) summarize the need of leisure programming to (a) increase community integration, (b) reduce inappropriate behaviors, and (c) increase skills in other areas.

Communication is an essential part of the program for learners with severe and multiple disabilities. Communication instruction should occur in the individual's natural environment, throughout the day, as an ongoing process. Kaiser, Alpert, and Warren (1987) describe "child-directed modeling" as one strategy to develop communication skills. In this process, the teacher first focuses his or her attention on what the student is interested in or gets the student to attend to something the teacher wishes to discuss. When the teacher has control over the object and can manipulate the object being discussed, he or she presents a model for the learner to imitate. If the student imitates the model, the learner is immediately verbally praised and the requested material is offered. If the learner does not attempt to imitate the model or performs an unrelated response, the teacher establishes joint attention again and presents the model again.

During communication programming, the environment must be arranged to increase the rate of requests and communicative interactions. Objects and events of interest must be available. Snack and lunch as well as free play situations may be used for facilitating the development of communication.

Augmentative Communication   When learners do not demonstrate the ability to use speech effectively, **augmentative communication systems** may be necessary. As Miller and Allaire (1987) suggest, these systems may be based on gestures or sign language systems, or they may require an aid of some sort. Aided systems vary

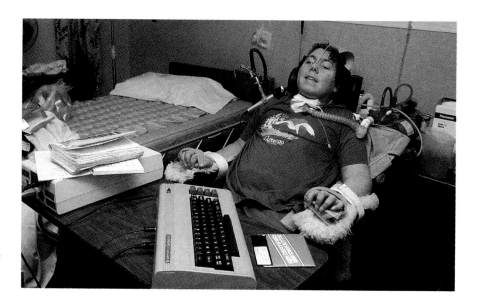

Communication systems may be necessary for learners who are challenged in verbal communication.

with regard to the type of motor response needed (whether it be to point, to blink an eye or to press a button). Systems may include language boards or other electronic aids. Objects, photographs, pictures, rebus systems, or written words may be incorporated into these systems.

Whenever augmentative and alternative communication applications are involved, professionals should consider (a) the need for life-long management, family and peer involvement, and current information about available options, and (b) the need for a well-coordinated interdisciplinary team that is able to treat other problems that may coexist (Mirenda & Mathy-Laikko, 1989). Bryen and McGinley (1991) suggest that even in using a system as common as sign language, professionals should ask:

1. Do significant others have the needed sign language competence to be effective models?
2. Does the learner use sign language to communicate with peers?

In addition, when working with learners with physical handicaps such as cerebral palsy, positioning becomes a significant part of the communication intervention (McEwen & Lloyd, 1990).

"Gentle Teaching"   Gentle teaching, a method grounded in interpersonal interactions, is suggested by McGee, Menolascino, Hobbs, and Menousek (1987) as a way to work with learners with severe and multiple disabilities. The goals of this methodology are to teach learners three basic interactional processes: (a) that the presence of the teacher signals safety and security; (b) that teachers' words and contact are inherently rewarding; and (c) that participation yields reward. Gentle teaching is based on interactional equity, in which there is fairness and equality between caregivers and persons with special needs.

Several supportive strategies are used in gentle teaching. Ignoring is used to remove the power of the undesirable behaviors demonstrated. Interruption is used to refocus toward more desirable behaviors. Redirection is used to communicate "do this instead." Each of these supports is faded as the learner becomes more successful and finds the interaction with the teacher more rewarding. Examples of these strategies are provided in Box 16.1.

Box 16.1

Supportive Strategies of "Gentle Teaching"

Strategy	Incident	Action Taken
Ignoring	Learner throws popcorn during snack	Teacher continues to eat snack and increases attention to learners eating appropriately
Interruption	Learner throws popcorn during snack	Teacher touches learner's hand gently, asks, "Would you like something to drink?"
Redirection	Learner throws popcorn during snack	Teacher touches learner's hand gently, states, "Popcorn stays on the table or goes into your mouth" and praises immediately upon appropriate response ■

(McGee, Menolascino, Hobbs, & Menousek, 1987)

Learners with Autism   In recognition of the communicative issues of learners with autism, Biklen and Schubert (1991) studied the effects of a method called facilitated communication. Through using physical supports, providing initial successful training, and maintaining the students' focus, they used computer supported communication. Typing at the computer, the learners with autism with whom they worked demonstrated a surprising level of literacy and numeracy skills. Biklen and Schubert hypothesize that it is perhaps far easier and less complex for these learners to use this augmentative communication system than to speak.

According to Simpson (1992), effective programs for learners with autism should use age-appropriate and functional curriculum strategies. Professionals should be sensitive to the multiple needs of these learners, and they should utilize the expertise of a multidisciplinary team. Efforts should be made to present activities that are meaningful in the present and future environments in which the learner with autism functions.

As with all learners discussed in this chapter, community-based instruction is essential for learners with autism. To the maximum extent possible, instruction should take place in the environments in which the learner with autism functions or will function in the future, such as the home, places of employment, stores and shopping centers, restaurants, theaters, and recreation facilities.

Learners with Dual Sensory Impairments   Until federal legislation founded regional model centers for learners with dual sensory impairments in 1968, learners with dual sensory impairments were usually educated in private residential schools or remained at home or in residential facilities. Beginning in 1983, states were provided federal funds to develop programs for learners with dual sensory impairments.

Nearly all learners with dual sensory impairments (about 94 percent) have either residual hearing or residual sight (Michael & Paul, 1991). Working with these learners is complicated by the fact that relatively few data are available concerning the enhancement of residual vision and hearing of young learners with dual sensory impairments. Specialized services in modes of communication, functional sensory training, and orientation and mobility are essential to support these learners.

Downing and Eichinger (1990) suggested several instructional and curricular strategies for learners who are deaf-blind in integrated settings. They suggested the enhancement of visual and auditory stimuli because most students identified as deaf-blind have some residual vision, or hearing, or both. The clearest information, however, is provided by tactile input, which is not meant to replace either visual or auditory information, but increases the amount of information available to the learner. Efforts to increase visual and auditory skills should occur within a meaningful context.

Learners with dual sensory impairments require small instructional groups. In these groups, cooperative learning strategies can be used to develop essential social skills such as turn-taking and accommodating to social interactions. Throughout all activities, the principle of partial participation should be applied. That is, students with severe disabilities who may not be totally independent in a given activity should be given the opportunity to learn those steps of which they are capable. However, Curtis (1982) found that over a 4-year period, communication among his sample of learners with dual sensory impairments was found to be unchanged and adjustment and learning had deteriorated. Other researchers argue that the outcome is likely to be better than earlier predictions presumed (Freeman, Goetz, Richards, & Groenveld, 1989).

Transdisciplinary Teams   Due to the complexity of the educational challenges regarding learners with severe or multiple disabilities, Lyon and Lyon (1980) argue for a transdisciplinary team approach. This approach involves a joint, team effort to meet the learner's needs. Through role release, two or three members of the team share general information regarding their individual expertise, duties, and responsibilities. Each team member teaches the other team members to make specific teaching decisions within his or her area of expertise. Each professional trains other team members to perform specific skills within his or her area of expertise. The teacher emerges as the actual implementer of much training, with other team members providing training, skill development, education, and support. The schematic in Figure 16.1 depicts the differences between the traditional interdisciplinary team and the transdisciplinary team.

Objective Five: To describe the impact of severe or multiple disabilities on participation in the larger social systems of the community and society.

The Impact on Participation in the Community and Society

As Bellamy reminds us (1985), learners with severe and multiple disabilities require ongoing support throughout their lives. Employment of learners identified as severely and multiply disabled is a particular challenge. In their study of the employment status of 117 transition-age young adults with moderate, severe, or profound mental retardation, Wehman, Kregel, and Seyfarth (1985) found that 88 percent were unemployed, with only 14 of the 117 holding competitive jobs. Wage accumulation was seriously limited. Nearly 80 percent of the young adults had received no rehabilitation services.

Kennedy, Horner, and Newton (1989), in a study of the social contacts of adults with severe and multiple disabilities, found that the 23 participants in their study engaged in regular social contact with people other than those with whom they interacted due to proximity. Some participants engaged in social contacts only

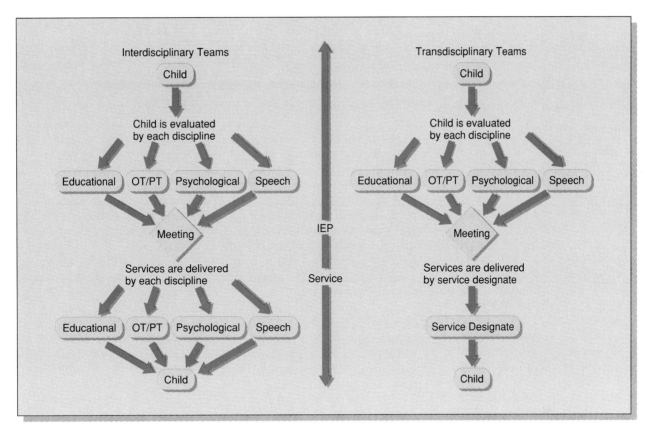

Figure 16.1
Interdisciplinary and transdisciplinary teams.

Individuals with severe disabilities participate
in ongoing social contacts.

The National Parks
In search of access for all . . . disabled face fewer barriers to enjoying America's scenic wonders

By Wendy Roth and Michael Tompane
Universal Press Syndicate

In the wilderness, we all are physically challenged.

Whether hiking a backcountry trail, shooting the rapids or setting up camp under the stars, we must consider our physical abilities as well as preparations for a rewarding experience.

In the United States, our most precious wilderness settings are in national parks—treasures kept in trust for all. They afford each of us, including those with disabilities, the opportunity to remain in touch with our natural heritage.

With the passage of the Americans With Disabilities Act in 1990, the United States has recognized the rights of those with mobility problems, visual and hearing impairments, and developmental problems.

The National Park Service was the first federal agency to make accessibility a matter of policy. While much remains to be done, people with disabilities can explore many of the national parks.

We set out to visit a selection of wilderness treasures and evaluate their accessibility—for people with mobility problems, families with young children and senior citizens. We also noted opportunities for deaf and blind visitors.

Because we think wilderness is best enjoyed in undeveloped surroundings, we did not limit our journeys to automobile drives.

Michael, who does not have a disability, has been a backpacker on primitive wilderness trails. He began hiking in the national parks at age 8 with his father.

Wendy walked many of this country's natural trails until 10 years ago. During the past 18 years, since her early 20s, she has lost voluntary movement in her legs, hands and upper body because of multiple sclerosis. She uses an electric wheelchair and requires assistance when traveling.

On our journey, we drove more than 32,000 miles, stayed at more than 100 campsites and visited 45 parks. The resulting book, *Easy Access to National Parks* (Sierra Club Books), encourages people with disabilities to visit them.

Initially, we were concerned that many parks would not have adequate access. For example, we planned not to visit Chaco Culture National Historical Park. Having visited Chaco Canyon several years earlier, Michael thought the prehistoric pueblo dwellings would not give Wendy access to the Anasazi ruins. At the urging of a ranger in a nearby park, however, we decided to visit Chaco.

Although Wendy did get to Pueblo Bonito, the largest ruin in the park, it is not fully or legally accessible. Only the beginning portion of the trail is what we term fully accessible, one that meets the Uniform Federal Accessibility Standards.

From the parking lot, a paved path leads to the ruin's outer wall. It soon became steep and narrow, however, forcing us to retrace our steps. We entered Pueblo Bonito's central plaza through the other end of the trail, Michael assisting Wendy over the soft dirt to keep her chair from getting stuck.

Big Bend National Park in Texas has only a few short trails with wheelchair access. We began to wonder whether Big Bend, with its abundant desert wildlife, would be only a "windshield experience," a park viewed exclusively from inside an automobile. We could not even find a trail to the Rio Grande.

Then we learned that Big Bend River Tours guides visitors of differing abilities on eight-hour raft trips from Lajitas, Texas, through the park's Santa Elena Canyon. We started along banks lush with desert life, then entered the narrow canyon, with 1,500-foot walls. With the wheels popped off and the wheelchair frame securely strapped to the rubber raft's seat, Wendy felt like Cleopatra on her Nile barge.

The tour climaxed with our shooting the white-water rapids at the "Rockslide." Twisting through the roiling river and diving perilously close to midstream boulders, the raft seemed close to capsizing. In hindsight,

once a week, while others participated in activities with companions daily. One problem which emerged in their data, however, was the limited number of companions who remained a part of the participant's social sphere for more than a few months. Family members were the most stable companions, but it was rare for a participant to have contact with anyone other than his or her family for more than 18 months.

In a national survey of the community involvement of persons with severe disabilities, Aveno (1989) found that individuals with severe disabilities spend more time in employment or day activities, using health care services, walking or wheelchair strolling for pleasure, and using of parks or zoos than do their nondisabled peers.

though, it was a thrilling and safe experience.

In addition to rafting, park experiences can include canoeing, boating, scuba diving and horseback riding.

One unique opportunity is the sit-ski program at Badger Pass in Yosemite National Park, Calif. Sit skis are designed for skiers with paralysis of the lower body. They sit in a kayaklike device and control the ski with upper-body movement and short poles.

Yosemite's famous valley features 8 miles of paved trails, and most of the developed facilities and trails are at least moderately accessible. At the west end of Lake Tenaya, we stood where Ansel Adams and Edward Weston took famous photographs.

Farther north, in Olympic National Park, Wash., another rewarding trail is Madison Falls Trail, designed for accessibility by everyone, including wheelchair users. The 200-foot asphalt trail ends at an observation platform overlooking Madison Falls, which tumbles 100 feet down a basalt cliff.

Less than 200 miles northeast of Olympic in North Cascades National Park, Happy Creek Trail is an elevated boardwalk that gives visitors a squirrel's-eye view of the forest.

If the trails in the Pacific Coast parks are not challenging enough, visit Haleakala National Park on the Hawaiian island of Maui. It is a hugh shield volcano rising 10,020 feet above sea level. At lower elevations, the rocks-and-roots trail through the tropical woods is a real test of chair control.

The major attraction, however, is the rim of the crater, with a moderately accessible path at Puu Ulaula Summit. While wheelchair users may need assistance in certain areas, asphalt makes it pretty free-wheeling. On a clear day, it's easy to see why the early Hawaiians called Haleakala the "House of the Sun." On a cloudy day, it's still overwhelming.

Park visits need not be confined to developed facilities; people with disabilities can enjoy primitive areas, too. Ranger Steve Eide, who has a spinal cord injury, led us along Cascade Lake at Yellowstone National Park in Wyoming. Eide, who uses a manual wheelchair, negotiated logs and gentle hills into a meadow where bison graze. The trail has significant barriers but, for athletic or skillful wheelchair users, this can be an exhilarating experience.

Families with young children, senior citizens and visitors with mobility problems can use many of the boardwalks through Yellowstone's geothermal areas to view geysers, bubbling mud and hot springs.

On our travels, the sights were only a part of our fascination with the parks. We met many interesting people—people with and without apparent disabilities.

Parents often pushed young children in strollers behind us, assuming that strollers could go where Wendy could. Other wheelchair users shared with us their satisfaction in being able to travel park trails. We went canoeing with an expert canoeist, a triple amputee, and we shared paths with people who have vision and hearing impairments.

Several parks have sign-language interpretation for deaf visitors. On our visit to Theodore Roosevelt National Park in North Dakota, a ranger interpreted her tour of the Maltese Cross Cabin built by Roosevelt. The future U.S. president used it while hunting and raising cattle in the Dakotas.

While a great task remains to improve accessibility everywhere, opportunities in the parks clearly abound. Recreation and contact with nature can be great healers and should be available to all ■

Summary

In this chapter, low incidence disabilities, that is, severe and multiple disabilities, dual sensory impairments, and autism, were discussed. It was noted that these learners, who just a few decades ago were either not served or served in restrictive settings, have made dramatic strides in inclusion in the community and general education classroom.

Learners with severe and multiple disabilities are an extremely heterogenous group. Standardized assessment instruments have scant validity and reliability in efforts to assess the strengths and needs of these learners. A comprehensive ecological approach for assessment was proposed as the most practical and useful basis for programming.

The impact of severe and multiple disabilities on the home and classroom is substantial. Parents experienced stress when conducting everyday household and childcare tasks and extreme stress when interacting in behalf of their children with school, medical, and other professionals.

Integration of these learners into general education was found to be of value to both the learners with disabilities and their nonidentified peers. General education students, for the most part, were found to accept learners with severe and multiple disabilities and stated that they profited from the experience of associating with them.

To effectively mediate the environment in behalf of learners with severe and multiple disabilities, it is recommended that they be integrated into natural environments in proportion to their numbers in the general population and provided the natural supports available in those environments. Valid educational programs must be provided for these learners which are responsive to their physical management and handling, leisure, communication, and vocational needs.

Learners with severe and multiple disabilities require life-long support systems. There is a continuing need for vocational training, rehabilitation, and employment services. Learners were found to have limited social contacts with friends, other than family members, and their circle of friends was quite restricted.

References

American Psychiatric Association (1987). *Diagnostic and statistical manual of mental disorders* (3rd ed., revised). Washington, DC: Author.

Andrews, A. K. (1989). Meeting the needs of young deaf-blind children and their parents. *Child Care, Health, and Development, 15,* 195–206.

Aveno, A. (1989). Community involvement of persons with severe retardation living in community residences. *Exceptional Children, 55,* 309–314.

Bellamy, T. (1985). Severe disability in adulthood. *Newsletter of the Association for Persons with Severe Handicaps, 11* (1), 6.

Biklen, D., & Schubert, A. (1991). New words: The communication of students with autism. *Remedial and Special Education, 12,* 46–57.

Blatt, B., & Kaplan, F. (1966). *Christmas in purgatory: A photographic essay on mental retardation.* Boston: Published and distributed under the auspices of a group of parents and friends of the mentally retarded.

Brazelton, T. B. (1973). *Neonatal behavior assessment scale.* Philadelphia, PA: Lippincott.

Brimer, R. W. (1990). *Students with severe disabilities: Current perspectives and practices.* Mountain View, CA: Mayfield Publishing.

Bromley, B. E., & Blacher, J. (1991). Parental reasons for out-of-home placement of children with severe handicaps. *Mental Retardation, 29* (5), 275–280.

Brown, F. (1987). Meaningful assessment of people with severe and profound handicaps. In M. Snell (Ed.), *Systematic instruction of persons with severe handicaps* (3rd ed.), 30–63.

Bryen, D. N., & McGinley, V. (1991). Sign language input to community residents with mental retardation. *Education and Training of the Mentally Retarded, 26,* 207–213.

Campbell, P. (1987). Physical management and handling procedures with students with movement dysfunction. In M. Snell (Ed.), *Systematic instruction of persons with severe handicaps* (3rd ed.), 174–188.

Chadsey-Rusch, J. (1990). Social interactions of secondary-aged students with severe handicaps: Implications for facilitating the transition from school to work. *Journal of the Association for Persons with Severe Handicap, 15,* 69–78.

Cole, D. A., Vandercook, T., & Rynders, J. (1988). Comparison of two peer interaction programs: Children with and without severe disabilities. *American Educational Research Journal, 25,* 415–439.

Condon, M. E., York, R., Heal, L. W., & Fortschneider, J. (1986). Acceptance of severely handicapped students by nonhandicapped peers. *Journal of the Association for Persons with Severe Handicap, 11,* 216–219.

Curtis, M. S. (1982). Study of behavioral change in 40 severely multi-sensorily handicapped children. *International Journal of Rehabilitation Research, 5,* 550–551.

Denckla, M. B. (1986). New diagnostic criteria for autism and related behavioral disorders: Guidelines for research protocols. *Journal of the American Academy of Child Psychiatry, 25,* 221–224.

Dollar, S., & Brooks, C. (1980). Assessment of severely and profoundly handicapped. *Exceptional Education Quarterly, 1,* 87–91.

Downing, J., & Eichinger, J. (1990). Instructional strategies for learners with dual sensory impairments in integrated settings. *Journal of the Association for Persons with Severe Handicap, 15,* 98–105.

Federal Register (1977), *42,* 42659–42688.

Fredericks, H. D., & Baldwin, V. (1987). Individuals with dual sensory impairments: Who are they? How are they educated? In L. Goetz, D. Guess, & K. Stremel-Campell (Eds.), *Innovative program design for individuals with dual sensory impairments* (pp. 3–14). Baltimore, MD: Paul H. Brookes.

Freeman, R. D., Goetz, E., Richards, D., & Groenveld, H. (1989). Blind children's early emotional development: Do we know enough to help? *Child Care, Health, and Development, 15,* 3–28.

Giangreco, M. F., Cloninger, C. J., Mueller, P. H., Yuan, S., & Ashworth, S. (1991). Perspectives of parents whose children have dual sensory impairments. *Journal of the Association for Persons with Severe Handicap, 16,* 14–24.

Guess, D., Mulligan-Ault, M., Roberts, S., Struth, J., Siegel-Causey, E., Thompson, B., Bronicki, G. J. B., & Guy, B. (1988). Implications of biobehavioral states of the education and treatment of students with the most profoundly handicapping conditions. *Journal of the Association for Persons with Severe Handicap, 13,* 163–174.

Heward, W. L., & Orlansky, M. D. (1992). *Exceptional children: An introductory survey of special education* (4th ed.). New York: Merrill.

Kaiser, A. P., Alpert, C. L., & Warren, S. F. (1987). Teaching functional language: Strategies for language intervention. In M. Snell (Ed.), *Systematic instruction of persons with severe handicaps* (3rd ed.), 247–272.

Kennedy, C. H., Horner, R. H., & Newton, J. S. (1989). Social contacts of adults with severe disabilities living in the community: A descriptive analysis of relationship patterns. *Journal of the Association for Persons with Severe Handicap, 14,* 190–196.

Larson, S. A., & Lakin, K. C. (1991). Parent attitudes about residential placement before and after deinstitutionalization: A research synthesis. *Journal of the Association for Persons with Severe Handicap, 16,* 5–38.

Lindley, L. (1990). Defining TASH: A mission statement. *TASH Newsletter, 16* (8) (August), 1.

Linehan, S. A., Brady, M. P., & Hwang, C. (1991). Ecological versus developmental assessment: Influences on instructional expectations. *Journal of the Association for Persons with Severe Handicap, 16,* 146–153.

Lyon, S., & Lyon, G. (1980). Team functioning and staff development: A role release approach to providing integrated educational services to severely handicapped students. *Journal of the Association for the Severely Handicapped, 5,* 250–263.

McEwen, I. R., & Lloyd, L. L. (1990). Positioning students with cerebral palsy to use augmentative and alternative communication. *Language, Speech, and Hearing Services in the Schools, 21,* 14–21.

McGee, J. J., Menolascino, F. J., Hobbs, D. C., & Menousek, P. E. (1987). *Gentle teaching: A nonaversive approach to helping persons with mental retardation.* New York: Human Sciences.

Meyers, C. E., & Blacher, J. (1987). Parents' perceptions of schooling for severely handicapped children: Home and family variables. *Exceptional Children, 43,* 441–449.

Michael, M. G., & Paul, P. V. (1991). Early intervention for infants with deaf-blindness. *Exceptional Children, 57,* 200–211.

Miller, J., & Allaire, J. (1987). Augmentative communication. In M. Snell (Ed.), *Systematic instruction of persons with severe handicaps* (3rd ed.), 273–298.

Mirenda, P., & Mathy-Laikko, P. (1989). Augmentative and alternative communication applications for persons with severe congenital communication disorders: An introduction. *AAC: Augmentative and Alternative Communication, 5,* 3–13.

Moon, M. S., & Bunker, L. (1987). Recreation and motor skills programming. In M. Snell (Ed.), *Systematic instruction of persons with severe handicaps* (3rd ed.), 214–244.

Noonan, M. J., & Reese, R. M. (1983). Educability: Public policy and the role of research. *Journal of the Association for Persons with Severe Handicap, 9,* 8–15.

Orelove, F. P., & Sobsey, D. (1987). *Educating children with multiple disabilities: A transdisciplinary approach.* Baltimore, MD: Paul H. Brookes.

Peck, C. A., Donaldson, J., & Pezzoli, M. (1990). Some benefits nonhandicapped adolescents perceive for themselves from their social relationships with peers who have severe handicaps. *Journal of the Association for Persons with Severe Handicap, 15,* 241–249.

Prizant, B. M. (1984). Assessment and intervention of communicative problems in children with autism. *Communicative Disorders, 9,* 127–142.

Ritvo, E. R., & Freeman, B. J. (1978). National Society for Autistic Children: Definition of the syndrome of autism. *Journal of Autism and Childhood Schizophrenia,* 162–169.

Rutter, M. (1978). Diagnosis and definition of childhood autism. *Journal of Autism and Developmental Disorders, 8,* 139–161.

Rutter, M., & Schopler, E. (1985). Autism and pervasive developmental disorders: Concepts and diagnostic issues. Paper prepared for the NIMH Research Workshop.

Schnorr, R. F. (1990). "Peter? He comes and goes . . ." : First graders' perspective on a part-time mainstream student. *Journal of the Association for Persons with Severe Handicap, 15,* 231–240.

Sigafoos, J., Cole, D. A., & McQuarter, R. J. (1987). Current practices in the assessment of students with severe handicaps. *Journal of the Association for Persons with Severe Handicap, 12,* 264–273.

Sigman, M., & Ungerer, J. A. (1984). Cognitive and language skills in autistic, mentally retarded, and normal children. *Developmental Psychology, 20,* 293–302.

Simpson, R. L. (1992). Children and youth with autism. In L. M. Bullock (Ed.), *Exceptionalities in children and youth* (pp. 168–195). Boston: Allyn & Bacon.

Snell, M. E., & Grigg, N. C. (1987). Instructional assessment and curriculum development. In M. Snell (Ed.), *Systematic instruction of persons with severe handicaps* (3rd ed.), 64–109.

Struth, J., & Guess, D. (1986). *Implications of biobehavioral states for the education and treatment of persons with severe and profound handicaps.* Unpublished manuscript. University of Kansas, Lawrence.

Todis, B., & Singer, G. (1991). Stress and stress management in families with adopted children who have severe disabilities. *Journal of the Association for Persons with Severe Handicap, 16,* 3–13.

U.S. Department of Education (1992). *Fourteenth annual report to Congress on the implementation of the Individuals with Disabilities Education Act.* Washington, DC: Author.

U.S. Office of Education (1975). Estimated number of handicapped children in the United States, 1974–75. Washington, DC: Bureau of Education for the Handicapped.

Voeltz, L. M., & Evans, I. M. (1983). Educational validity: Procedures to evaluate outcomes in programs for severely handicapped learners. *Journal of the Association for Persons with Severe Handicap, 8,* 3–15.

Wehman, P., Kregel, J., & Seyfarth, J. (1985). Transition from school to work for individuals with severe handicaps: A follow-up study. *Journal of the Association for Persons with Severe Handicap, 10,* 132–136.

Yoder, P. J., & Feagans, L. (1988). Mothers' attributions of communication to prelinguistic behavior of developmentally delayed and mentally retarded infants. *American Journal on Mental Retardation, 93,* 36–43.

York, J., & Vandercook, T. (1990). Strategies for achieving an integrated education for middle school students with severe disabilities. *Remedial and Special Education, 11* (5), 6–16.

York, J., Vandercook, T., Macdonald, C., Heise-Heff, C., & Caughey, E. (1992). Feedback about integrating middle-school students with severe disabilities in general education classes. *Exceptional Children, 58,* 244–259.

17

Learners Who Are Gifted, Talented, or Creative

Objectives

After completing this chapter, you will be able to:

1. describe the personal characteristics of learners identified as gifted, creative, or talented.
2. describe the identification and evaluation of learners identified as gifted, creative, or talented.
3. describe the impact of giftedness, creativity, or talent on interactions in the home and classroom.
4. describe ways to mediate the environment for learners identified as gifted, creative, or talented.
5. describe the impact of giftedness, creativity, or talent on participation in the larger social systems of the school, community, and society.

Key Words and Phrases

acceleration
Cinderella complex
creative
enrichment
gifted

gifted imposter phenomenon
mentor
talented
underachievement

PROGRAMS FOR ABLE STUDENTS SIMPLY DID NOT EXIST IN MY SCHOOL. I ALWAYS KNEW I LEARNED FAST BECAUSE I GOT my work done before everyone else most of the time, and I always felt the teachers were mad at me for doing this. I learned to not work so fast. I remember getting into trouble lots of times, mostly for talking or for disturbing other students around me. My sixth-grade teacher even rapped me on the knuckles once with a long wooden stick, which made me very angry and embarrassed. If only science class hadn't been so boring with so much sitting and lecturing, I might not have been doodling on my assignment sheet and bothering my neighbors.

You see, I didn't understand why I got into trouble so much, or why I began to dislike school, or why I felt I never fit in. I only felt alienated, different from my teachers and my classmates, and basically incompetent nine months of the year. (Carol Woodin Boyce, a resource teacher for the gifted, in a letter to a student, 1991, p. 10) ■

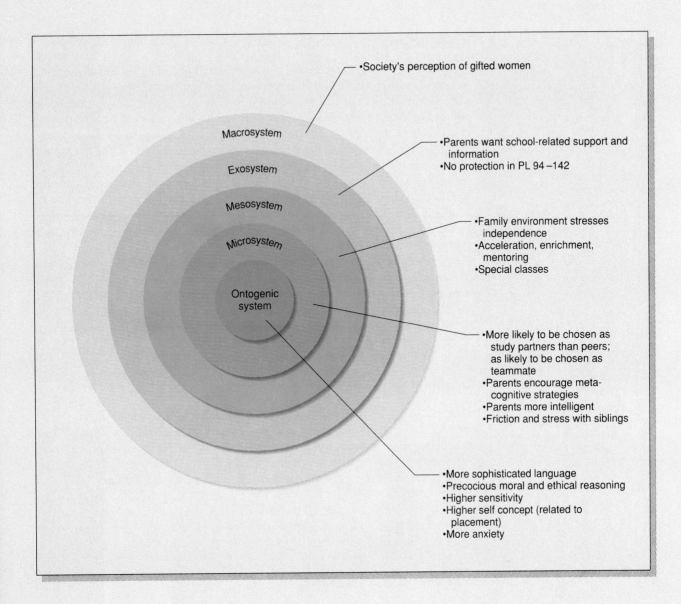

•Society's perception of gifted women

Macrosystem

Exosystem

Mesosystem

Microsystem

Ontogenic
system

•Parents want school-related support and
information
•No protection in PL 94 –142

•Family environment stresses
independence
•Acceleration, enrichment,
mentoring
•Special classes

•More likely to be chosen as
study partners than peers;
as likely to be chosen as
teammate
•Parents encourage meta-
cognitive strategies
•Parents more intelligent
•Friction and stress with siblings

•More sophisticated language
•Precocious moral and ethical reasoning
•Higher sensitivity
•Higher self concept (related to
placement)
•More anxiety

Introduction

Sapon-Shevin (1987) suggests that two assumptions underlie educational programming and the identification of learners who are gifted and talented. First, learners who are gifted and talented are assumed to represent an empirically identifiable population. Second, the needs of this population are assumed to be significantly different from those of children in general. Current definitions of learners who are gifted, creative, or talented limit the identified population to 3 to 5 percent of the general population. These limitations lead to severe restrictions on the selection of learners to be served, and, in addition, charges of elitism (VanTassel-Baska, Patton, & Prillaman, 1989). Marjoram (1986) supports a widening of the definition of giftedness and urges its application to the top 10 percent of the population, with a reconceptualization of education on youth services, open learning, and flexible study opportunities throughout the learner's life.

Salkind (1988) argues that learners who are gifted and talented are exceptional in the same sense of the word as those defined within Public Law 94–142 and that mandated services would be appropriate for this population. While well-designed gifted programs can provide appropriate education for children, those that respond to the mandates in an effort only to quiet the demands of parents and advocates will simply be "costly frills" (Dettmer, 1988).

Objective One: To describe the personal characteristics of learners who are gifted, creative, or talented.

Personal Characteristics

Learners who are gifted and talented, though an extremely heterogeneous group, may be confronted with unique developmental challenges (Hilyer, 1988). These predictable developmental crises may include (a) society's contradictory treatment of learners who are gifted and talented, (b) labeling, (c) more rapid development, (d) heightened sensitivity or over-sensitivity, (e) a discrepancy between intellectual and social skills, (f) unrealistic goals or expectations, (g) perfectionism, (h) stress, anxiety, and depression, and (i) difficulty dealing with failure and success. These crises are perhaps even more significant for gifted females, the highly gifted, gifted learners from various cultures, and gifted learners who underachieve.

Socioemotional Development

In a study of self-concept, self-esteem, and peer relations, Janos, Fung, and Robinson (1985) found that 40 percent of the children who were gifted and talented thought of themselves as different and demonstrated self-esteem scores significantly lower than those who did not see themselves as different. Coleman and Fults (1983), however, suggest that studies related to the self-concept of children who are gifted and talented must take into account the learner's educational placements. Because children judge their capabilities in relation to others in their immediate environment, and that judgment is governed by the similarities between individuals, learners in separate programs for the gifted and talented may report a lower self-concept than similar children in integrated programs.

Other studies of self-concept support the heterogeneity of this group. Maddux, Scheiber, and Bass (1982) found that students who were gifted and talented tended to have higher self-concepts, and, in one grade (the sixth), children in a segregated program had demonstrated higher self-concepts than their nonidentified peers. They found no evidence that identification or placement in segregated or integrated programs resulted in lower self-concept scores among learners who are gifted and

Students who are gifted or talented are often more anxious in class situations.

talented. Girls presented stronger self-concepts than boys on three self-concept measures in another study (Loeb & Jay, 1987). Forsyth (1987) found no significant difference between children who are gifted and talented and peers in self-concept, but children who are gifted and talented were found to be more anxious. In yet another study, children who are gifted and talented and in integrated programs demonstrated higher scores for academic self-concept and similar scores in social and physical self-concept when compared to their peers (Schneider, Clegg, Byrne, & Ledingham, 1989).

Coleman and Fults (1985) examined the influence of instructional segregation on the self-concepts of children who are gifted and talented. All of the learners had robust self-concepts, yet demonstrated higher self-concept scores prior to being placed in the segregated program. Coleman and Fults argued that the reduction in heterogeneity of ability in gifted classrooms forces some learners to see their abilities in a less favorable light. Students who are at the lower end of the distribution of children who are gifted and talented were most affected. This study supported earlier findings (Coleman & Fults, 1982) in which the measure of self-concept decreased on placement in a segregated program and increased when the students reentered general education. These findings support the issue of the developmental context; children's development is influenced by the program that they attend and the peers with whom they interact.

When the content of the self-esteem measure is academically oriented, children who are gifted and talented report higher self-esteem (Eccles, Bauman, & Rotenberg, 1989). Though learners who are gifted and talented were found more likely to be chosen as study partners, they were about as likely to be chosen as a friend or teammate. Depending on the criteria and context, peer acceptance of learners who are gifted and talented may vary.

Roeper (1982) describes several roles learners who are gifted and talented may assume to cope with their emotions. She describes

1. the perfectionist, who combines early omnipotence with later conscience development.
2. the child-adult, who combines the feeling of omnipotence with an unrealistic goal of total independence.

3. the winner of the competition, who combines feelings of omnipotence with a desire to achieve over others.
4. the exception, in whom the feeling of omnipotence remains an overpowering force that deters normal growth.
5. the self-critic, who is fixated on conscience development.
6. the well-integrated, who proceeds through the typical developmental social emotional phases.

Though no one particular child may be completely described as being in one category, these roles may describe some of the approaches children who are gifted and talented use to cope with their emotions.

When presented with psychosocial dilemmas and open-ended questions, learners who are gifted and talented were found to be more likely to express internal attributions, heightened sensitivity to the protagonist's dilemmas, and a precocious moral and ethical reasoning (LeVine & Tucker, 1986). These findings suggest that learners who are gifted and talented may analyze and react uniquely to stressful situations and may demonstrate a unique sensitivity and distress. These findings concur with Su's (1982) research which reported no differences between learners who are gifted and talented and their peers in emotional stability, but found stronger reactions to anger and sadness among learners who are gifted and talented.

The incidence of psychological problems among children who are intellectually gifted has been found to be comparable to the regularly achieving population (Gallucci, 1988). However, it must be recognized that learners who are gifted and talented do have personal concerns. Galbraith (1985) interviewed 400 learners and summarized their concerns as evolving around being gifted, feeling different and unaccepted, peer relationships, parent and teacher expectations, and world problems.

Language Development

Children who are gifted and talented have been found to demonstrate higher scores on measures of receptive language than their peers (Chermak & Burgerud, 1983). Guilford, Scheurle, and Shonburn (1981) also found that learners who are gifted and talented demonstrated advanced receptive language operations in auditory memory and memory for linguistic information. Though the measure they used did not demonstrate significantly greater expressive language when comparing learners who are gifted and talented and their peers, Guilford and associates felt that the gifted learners were able to bring more complex and deep language structures and rules to completion in comprehension and verbal syntax.

Cognitive Development

By definition, learners who are gifted exhibit advanced cognitive skills. These learners are intellectually capable and learn to speak fluently at an early age. Research by Carter (1984) using Piaget's stages of development found that learners who are gifted and talented demonstrated all operations earlier than did children with normal ability. Davis and Rimm (1985) found among the cognitive characteristics of the gifted and talented: good comprehension, good problem-solving skills, and ease in recognizing cause-and-effect relationships. These learners participate at an early age in reading, writing, mathematics, music, and artistic endeavors. They are capable of retaining and manipulating extraordinary quantities of information. They are analytic thinkers, capable of manipulating abstract concepts and acting intuitively.

Talented learners often excel in art, music, or leadership.

Identification and Evaluation

The terms gifted, creative, and talented are used throughout this chapter to describe that heterogeneous group of individuals who demonstrate unique ability, skills, talents, leadership, or creativity. In general usage, **gifted** refers to the academically gifted, those learners whose tested intelligence quotients are within the superior range and who perform exceptionally in academic areas. In reference to school, gifted learners are generally two or more grade levels ahead of their typical peers in achievement. Those judged to be **creative** are capable of expressing unique and novel ideas, solutions, and products; they excel in divergent thought processes. Learners who are **talented** exhibit special abilities, aptitudes, and accomplishments in various areas, such as art, music, leadership, or theater.

Public Laws 94–142, 99–457, and 101–476 mandate appropriate public education for all children with disabilities; those who are gifted, creative, or talented are not protected by these laws. However, the federal government recognized this group of learners in the Gifted and Talented Children's Education Act of 1978 (Purcell, 1978). In this legislation, this group of learners are defined as:

> children, and whenever applicable, youth, who are identified at the preschool, elementary, or secondary level as possessing demonstrated or potential abilities that give evidence of high performance responsibility in areas such as intellectual, creative, specific academic, or leadership ability, or in the performing and visual arts and who by reason thereof require services or activities not ordinarily provided by the school. (Sec. 902.)

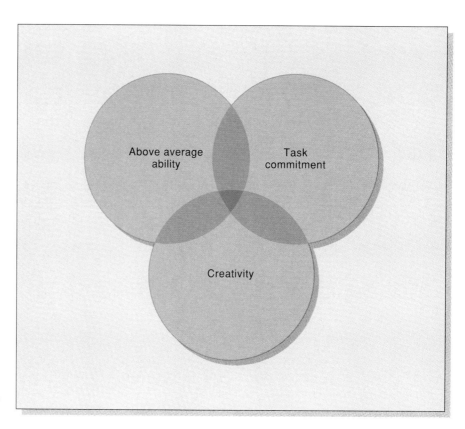

Figure 17.1
Renzulli's definition of giftedness.
From "What Makes Giftedness? Re-examining a Definition" by J. Renzulli, 1978, Phi Delta Kappan, *60 (3), p. xx. Used with permission.*

Renzulli (1978) offered a broader definition which has been accepted by some factions within the field of gifted education. He defines giftedness as a condition that results when creativity, task commitment, and above average ability are brought to bear on a field of learning. This definition brings together the several dimensions of giftedness (see Figure 17.1). It requires that all learners be given expanded opportunities to demonstrate creativity or talent, with a subgroup then continuing for advanced work on the basis of their performance and interest.

Both the federal and Renzulli definitions of giftedness differ significantly from the original definitions offered by Terman (1954) and his contemporaries. Their definitions employed intelligence quotients as the indicators of giftedness. They were applied at a time when society was greatly concerned with academic performance and enamored with intelligence tests. Terman originally suggested that gifted learners were those who received an intelligence quotient of 140 or above on the Stanford-Binet Intelligence Test. Later, the academically talented were defined as those receiving an intelligence quotient of 115 or more on the Stanford-Binet or a similar score on another instrument. At this time, students who are gifted were placed into the subcategories of academically talented (IQ above 116), gifted (IQ above 132), and highly gifted (IQ above 148) (Gallagher, 1985). Both the federal and Renzulli definitions are broader and make a concerted effort to include learners who are talented and creative as well as academically gifted. In addition, the definitions are an effort to respond to the identification of learners who are gifted in ways not generally recognized by the majority culture and learners who are not easily identified as gifted and talented. They are, as definitions, more democratic and more appropriate for application in American schools.

Karnes and Koch (1985), in an exploration of the status of the definition of giftedness, found that ten states used a form of the federal definition, and two used variations of Renzulli's definition. In seventeen states, "gifted" with no inclusion of "talented" is used, and in five others, the term "intellectually gifted" is applied. Twenty-eight states use the term "gifted and talented," though only three defined "talented." Only twenty states indicated that those identified as gifted and talented are to be provided services beyond general education.

Because Public Law 94–142 and its amendments provide no protection for students who are gifted and talented, state legislation regarding this population is permissive rather than mandated. In *Roe vs. the Commonwealth of Pennsylvania* (1986) the courts determined that due process and "stay put" do not apply to programs for learners who are gifted and talented. The issue of contention for potential participants in these programs, then, is whether the criteria for eligibility is appropriate. Courts have, to this point, deferred to educational agencies in their implementation of programs for children who are gifted and talented (Rothstein, 1990).

Birch (1984) argues that identifying children who are gifted, creative, or talented should focus on assessment and education, with the application of curriculum imbedded processes. When general education classroom teachers and teachers of learners who are gifted and talented were asked to describe preferred criteria for referral for gifted programs, Schack and Starko (1990) reported an emphasis on criteria, learning quickly and easily, and initiating one's own learning. As teachers' experience with learners who are gifted and talented increased, a higher percentage of teachers chose intelligence quotient test scores as a basis for referral. Schack and Starko recommended the role of general education teacher as "talent scout" in seeking out learners not identified by other means.

Lowenstein (1982) assessed the accuracy of teachers in primary and secondary schools in determining which children are gifted and talented. Teachers' perceptions were compared with scores on individually administered intelligence tests. Results showed that there was a greater tendency for all teachers to overrate rather than underrate children as gifted and talented at the primary school level and that there were relatively fewer students at the secondary level assessed by teachers and psychologists as being gifted, creative, or talented. In addition, there was a strong tendency for teachers at the secondary school level to underrate children. More girls were overrated by teachers in both primary and secondary schools, and more boys were underrated. Lowenstein concludes that though they are able to identify a certain number of children as gifted, creative, or talented, teachers generally underrate and overrate the performance of children on the basis of academic achievement.

The use of intelligence tests with learners who are gifted and talented has been controversial. Robinson and Chamrad (1986), however, believe that much of this controversy derives from professionals using tests in ways they were not designed to be used. They suggest that many of the criticisms of intelligence tests are based not on the tests themselves but on unrealistic expectations that they will accomplish what they were never intended to accomplish. Conventional intelligence tests have been shown to present problems in terms of cultural bias. Alternatives, such as assessing learning ability, have been suggested (Tyerman, 1986).

Feldhusen, Asher, and Hoover (1984) presented an alternative procedure for the identification of giftedness, talent, or creativity. They contend that the identification process should begin as a program process. First, the program goals and types of youth to be served should be outlined, followed by the development of nomination and assessment procedures. Next, individual differentiation should take

More than 2 percent of all individuals with disabilities are gifted.

place, followed by an evaluation and validation of the identification, that is, are the learners for whom the program is designed those who are being identified and served?

Betts and Neihart (1988) provide further insights into the question of how to identify the gifted, talented, and creative by studying learner profiles. After conducting observations, interviews, and reviewing the literature, they developed six profiles of learners who are gifted and talented. The profiles include:

1. Successful students.
2. Underground learners, who have not and do not wish to be identified.
3. Divergently gifted students, who demonstrate their abilities in ways which are not necessarily recognized by the school.
4. Dropouts.
5. Double-labeled students, that is, those who demonstrate a disability as well as giftedness, talent, or creativity.
6. Autonomous learners, who are usually identified as intellectually gifted and successful in school.

Identification of Gifted and Talented Learners

Gifted Learners with Disabilities   Professionals are beginning to focus on the challenges presented by learners who are both disabled and gifted. The disability, which often masks the learner's giftedness, may be a learning disability, hearing or visual impairment, communication problem, physical disability, or other disability. Whitmore and Maker (1985) estimate that more than 2 percent of the disabled population is gifted and talented.

Children with learning disabilities who are also gifted and talented may not be identified for services for either exceptionality, in that they may appear to be functioning within the average range and neither their giftedness nor their learning disabilities are recognized (Suter & Wolf, 1987). Such children may demonstrate a combination of success and failure which challenge teacher's stereotypes that gifted children are good at everything and that children with learning disabilities are only of average intelligence (Yewchuk, 1983). A particular challenge for teachers is to recognize the learning disability when the learner excels in some other area of learning or performance.

Minner (1990) found that teachers were significantly less likely to refer learners who have learning disabilities to programs for children who are gifted and talented. In a study using identical behavioral vignettes and descriptions, students labeled physically disabled were more likely to be described as gifted than those labeled learning disabled (Minner, Prater, Bloodworth, & Walker, 1987). According to Chermak and Burgerud (1983), children with learning disabilities who are gifted and talented did not perform as well as their peers who are gifted and talented on three measures of receptive language. Learners with learning disabilities who are gifted and talented may be defensive regarding their strengths and weaknesses, independent in their ways of thinking and problem-solving, and perplexed regarding their own weaknesses (Yewchuk, 1985). Yewchuk and Bibby (1989) suggest that educational programs work towards helping these learners develop a strong self-concept and an accurate assessment of personal strengths and weaknesses.

Children with learning disabilities who are gifted and talented tend to have lower self-concepts than their peers who are gifted and talented. In addition, a relationship has been found between lower self-concepts and the level of hyperactivity or social interaction these learners demonstrate. Because these learners are not failing, few are reported by their parents or general education teachers as having learning problems (Waldron, Saphire, & Rosenblum, 1987).

Brown-Muzino (1990) lists the issues regarding learners with learning disabilities who are gifted and talented as follows:

a. Assessment: in addition to the assessment administered to all children, for these children additional concerns of perfectionism, feelings of inadequacy, unrealistic goals, hypersensitivity, demand for adult attention, and intolerance should be evaluated.
b. Early intervention: specifically aimed at preventing underachievement.
c. Flexible placements: designed to respond to individual needs, because traditional "gifted programs" may not meet the needs of these students.
d. The use of strategies: positive reward systems and ways to increase a personal awareness of strengths and weaknesses should be used.

Students who are gifted and talented and have visual impairments have problems similar to those learners who are gifted and talented and learning disabled. Corn (1986) contends that the obstacles to the identification of these children include (a) stereotypic expectations related to persons with visual handicaps, (b) developmental delays, (c) incomplete information, and (d) a lack of opportunity to display superior abilities. In a similar manner, learners with hearing impairments may present information deficits due to their hearing impairment, learners with communication disorders may present problems in expressive language, and so on. Learners who are gifted and talented and have physical disabilities have been helped greatly through advances in technology, such as the personal computer and augmentative communication devices, for instance.

Gifted Learners Who Are Culturally or Socioeconomically Disadvantaged   Two neglected subgroups of learners who are gifted and talented are (a) individuals who may not actualize their potential because they are from cultural backgrounds which

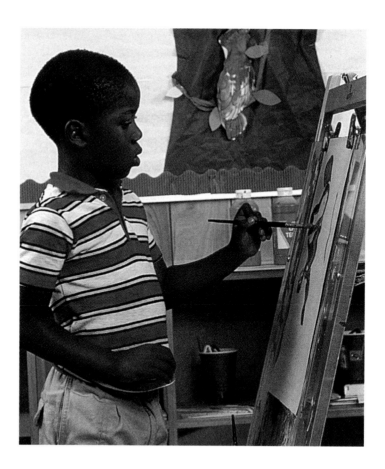

Learners who are gifted and talented need contact with more challenges.

differ from the mainstream culture, and (b) individuals who are socially and economically disadvantaged (VanTassel-Baska, Patton, & Prillaman, 1989). Deschamp and Robson (1984) conceptualize "gifted disadvantaged" students as:

1. high-achieving students in disadvantaged areas; with little contact with other more capable students, they may not be challenged or presented opportunities.
2. underachievers, whose teachers may not recognize their potential or who may be in systems which do not intervene.
3. high-achieving students from ethnic groups who have difficulty reconciling language and value differences between home and school.
4. high-achieving students from socioeconomically or culturally diverse groups who have difficulties in the school-home cultural mismatch.

In addition, the latter group of learners who are gifted and socioeconomically disadvantaged may demonstrate giftedness or talent in ways which are not generally understood and accepted by the majority culture. Programming for these students includes focusing on maintaining their ethnic identity, cultural enrichment, counseling, parent support services, and career education (Rimm, 1985).

A study commission by the Secretary of Education cited four conditions which must be considered if the needs of learners who are gifted and disadvantaged are to be met:

1. Learners from minorities represent 30 percent of the public school population but less than 20 percent of the learners selected for gifted programs.

2. Learners from low-income backgrounds represent 20 percent of the school population but only 4 percent of the learners performing at the 95th percentile or above on standardized tests.
3. Seniors in high school who are from disadvantaged families (in which the mother did not complete high school) are over 50 percent less likely to have participated in programs for the gifted and talented than their more advantaged peers.
4. Disadvantaged students are far less likely to be enrolled in academic programs to prepare them for college and are about half as likely to take courses in advanced math and science than are more advantaged students (U.S. Department of Education, 1989).

Interventions for learners who are gifted and disadvantaged should demonstrate the following generic characteristics (VanTassel-Baska, Patton, & Prillaman, 1989):

- Early and systematic assessment
- Parent involvement
- Effective school strategies, for example, time on task, school leadership
- Experiential and hands-on learning approaches
- Activities that allow for self-expression
- Mentors and role models
- Community involvement
- Counseling efforts that address the issue of cultural values as well as facilitating talent development

Underachieving Learners Who Are Gifted and Talented   Those learners who are gifted and talented yet do not achieve to their potential, usually referred to as "underachievers," are not a homogeneous group. As a group, these learners demonstrate a significant discrepancy between ability and achievement. The factors that influence their achievement are often situation specific and highly variable (Gonzalez & Hayes, 1988). Whitmore (1986) contends, however, that the school experience may be hazardous to the mental health and achievement motivation of young learners who are gifted and talented. Her work with children identified as underachievers, based on these learners' perceptions of the school experience, suggests that patterns of special socialization needs, personality attributes and emotional conflict, and low motivation are facets of classrooms which have a damaging effect on the achievement and performance of learners who are gifted and talented.

According to Rimm (1985), accurate measures to determine **underachievement** are not available. He suggests assessing trends in behavior patterns to identify underachieving learners. The patterns of behaviors to be analyzed include (a) competition, (b) responsibility, (c) self-control, (d) interpersonal communications, and (e) respect. A parent report is suggested to obtain information on these five patterns. The characteristics of underachievement in the area of competition are: bossiness, blaming others, avoiding competition, and depression. In the area of responsibility, the characteristics are seeking assistance with home assignments, postponing long-term projects, and trying to please perfectionist parents. The negative correlations to achievement were parent generosity, a close and somewhat dependent maternal relationship, conforming to peers, and being able to convince parents to change their minds. In the area of communication, the underachiever had a maternal emphasis on school. Finally, the underachievers were found to tend to have a tendency to "talk back" or be disrespectful.

In a study comparing learners who were achievers and those who were perceived to be underachievers, Dowdall and Colangelo (1982) found underachievers to be less socially mature, have more emotional problems, demonstrate more antisocial behavior, and have a lower self-concept. Underachievement was found to be primarily a male phenomenon. The major characteristics of underachievers who are gifted and talented are summarized in Table 17.1.

Major emphasis of programs for underachievers is on changing their counterproductive behaviors to productive behaviors. Whitmore (1980) urges the application of six principles when working with these learners. First, pressure should be reduced by deemphasizing grades and competition. Nonconforming behavior that does not interfere with programming should be tolerated. Second, the student's motivation should be analyzed to pair strengths and weaknesses with their likes and dislikes. Third, independent activities that emphasize choice and self-evaluation should be used. Fourth, instruction in social skills and effective leadership should be provided. Fifth, activities should reward both long- and short-term goals. Finally, students should be assisted in developing a rational understanding of their personal limitations and emphasize self-control over personal behavior and its consequences.

Girls and Young Women Who Are Gifted or Talented

Though they may perceive themselves as more scholastically competent than either boys who are gifted or talented or regularly achieving girls (Li, 1988), girls who are gifted and talented are confronted with a series of challenges in efforts to meet their potential. During elementary school, the interests of girls are more similar to the interests of boys who are gifted or talented than to the interest of their normal ability peers. However, by the time they reach adolescence, young women who are gifted or talented develop lower career aspirations than those of young men who are gifted and talented (Kerr, 1985). This change in aspirations occurs at approximately 14 years of age. At this time, young women are confronted with socialization patterns toward passivity and dependence.

According to Kerr, there are both internal and external reasons for the underachievement of females who are gifted or talented. External causes include sexism and a lack of resources. Women receive fewer graduate fellowships and receive lower salaries. In addition, they remain primarily responsible for child care, frequently performing what has been termed a "second shift." Because they frequently must balance professional interests and higher education with traditional sex roles, women who are gifted or talented are said to be "cultural underachievers," (Davis & Rimm, 1985) that is, they are forced to achieve at less than their potential due to their culturally relegated role as primary parent and home manager.

Personal causes of underachievement in girls and young women include two unique socialization patterns: (a) the **gifted imposter phenomenon** (a personal belief that one is not truly as successful as others believe, and that this lack of success will be discovered), and (b) the **Cinderella complex** (waiting to be rescued from personal responsibilities by a male partner). According to Silverman (1986), women who achieve with a high degree of excellence combine the beliefs, values, behaviors, and expectations of both males and females. Facilitating the potential of females who are gifted and talented requires early identification, avoiding overprotection, fostering independence, ability grouping which permits the expression of abilities and talents without fear, retaining high expectations, academic and career counseling, appropriate role models and mentors, and social-emotional support.

Table 17.1   Characteristics of Underachievers Who Are Gifted or Talented

Patterns related to achievement

poor performance on tests
at or below level in basic skills
daily work incomplete or poorly done
discrepancy between oral and written communication
little academic initiative

Patterns related to cognition

superior retention and comprehension when interested
large repertoire of facts
many interests, areas of expertise
interests are frequently rigid

Patterns related to personality

creative and imaginative
persistently dissatisfied with work
avoids new tasks to prevent imperfect performance
self-critical, with poor self-esteem
self-selects home projects
rationalizes and denies failure
impulsive emotional responses
immature
external locus of control
perceives environment as threatening
uncooperative, autonomous

Patterns related to social interaction

distrustful of overtures of affection
productive in groups
sensitive towards self and others
few friends
belligerent, intolerant, critical
low sense of personal and social work
perceives self as alienated and unlikable

Patterns related to school behaviors

withdrawn or aggressive in class
dislikes drill, practice, rote learning, memorization
distractible, difficulty focusing and attending
negative attitude towards school
difficult to motivate, reinforce, discipline
procrastinates
frequently absent, malingers
disorganized, poor study habits, little persistence

Sources: Whitmore, 1980; Gallagher, 1975; Shoff, 1984; Mamchur, 1982; Seeley, 1985; Rimm, 1984; Blackburn
& Erickson, 1986; with the assistance of Faye Wagner.

Gifted Learners from Various Cultures

If consideration is to be given to learners from various cultures, a multicultural perspective must be included in the identification process (Schlesinger, 1987). Diversity within cultures, as well as the search for data from multiple sources and an awareness of the different types of behavior manifested by learners from differing cultural backgrounds who are gifted and talented must be considered (Frasier, 1987). Language may also emerge as an issue among Hispanic children, in that poor test performance limits referral to programming for learners who are gifted and talented (deBernard, 1985).

In their comparison of behavioral ratings of Anglo and Hispanic children who are gifted and talented, Argulewicz, Elliott, and Hall (1982) found significant ethnic differences in the areas of learning and motivation, with Anglo students being rated higher. No significant differences were found between the two groups in the areas of creativity and leadership. The use of this type of measure may, depending on the criteria used, result in the exclusion of Hispanic learners, by nature of their culture.

In their exploration of behavior rating scales, Elliott and Argulewicz (1983) found that differences between Anglo and Hispanic learners did not appear to be educationally significant. In addition, when they analyzed the data by socioeconomic status, there again were no significant differences. They contend that behaviors indicative of intellectual giftedness are similar across socioeconomic status and ethnic background, but support the position that ethnic, sex, grade, and socioeconomic status differences should be considered in the development of local and national norms.

In working with learners who are gifted and talented from various cultures, support in developing a bond between parents and school may be necessary, especially to assure parents that the development of the learner's abilities and the preservation of family and community values are addressed in the gifted program (Colangelo, 1985).

Technology has contributed to meeting the needs of migrant children who are gifted and talented. Hamilton (1984) describes the Migrant Student Record Transfer System, which allows students who have been identified as gifted and talented in one district to be immediately eligible for services when moving to another district. With over 672,000 active files, the program assists migrant students from being lost in the system and helps them to consistently receive the programming needed to meet their potential. In addition, programming specific for "high potential minority youth," such as the Skills Reinforcement Project (Lynch & Mills, 1990) which involves Saturday classes and a residential summer program, have been found to make significant differences in these learners' ability to match the achievements of their Anglo peers.

Very Young Children Who Are Gifted and Talented

Children who are gifted and talented are frequently identified at very early ages. In a study of children identified between 3 and 5 years of age, parents reported early verbal expression skills, an unusual curiosity level, and long attention spans (Creel & Karnes, 1988). Perhaps of most interest was the finding that in retrospect, 96.3 percent of the fifty-three sets of parents interviewed supported a specialized gifted preschool program on at least a half-day basis.

It is difficult to recognize a truly gifted preschool child.

As is true among older children who are gifted and talented, there are multiple factors beyond tested intelligence quotient that have an impact on the young child's skill performance and adaptation to social and nonsocial situations (McGuffog, Feiring, & Lewis, 1987). Among young children, however, it is at times difficult to differentiate children who have had a multitude of experiences and opportunities and have a broad base of general knowledge from young children who are truly gifted and talented.

Objective Three: To describe the impact of giftedness, creativity, or talent on interactions in the home and classroom.

The Impact on Interactions in the Home and Classroom

The majority of families with children who are gifted and talented experience moderate levels of adaptation and cohesion, suggesting that having a child who is gifted and talented in the home is not necessarily associated with extreme patterns of family functioning (West, Hosie, & Mathews, 1989). Family relationships may be affected, however, in the areas of the tempo of family interactions, family system makeup, sibling self-perceptions, and collective attitudes toward the giftedness (McMann & Oliver, 1988). Children who were creatively gifted have been shown to have family environments that stress independence, are less child-centered, and exhibit tense family relationships and more negative affect, resulting in motivation to attain power. Academic achievers came from cohesive, child-centered families with strong parent-child identification (Olszewski, Kulieke, & Buescher, 1987). Families with a child who is gifted and talented have been shown to demonstrate higher levels of adjustment in problem solving, communication, roles, and affective responsiveness (Mathews, West, & Hosie, 1986).

Parents   Parents may experience stress associated with the increased demands of parenting children who are gifted and talented, and they may have a particular challenge in working with daughters who are gifted and who are confronted with stereotyping by their peers (Shaughnessy & Neely, 1987). Though all of the parents

Cornell and Grossberg (1989) interviewed acknowledged thinking of their children as gifted, over one-fourth of them reported not using the term "gifted" in reference to their children. The families with parents who used the term were more achievement oriented and provided less freedom for expression of individual feelings.

In comparison with the general population, fathers of children who are gifted and talented were found to be more intelligent, independent, aloof, assertive, and tense (Fell, Dahlstrom, & Winter, 1984). In the same study, mothers tended to be more intelligent and independent, as well as conscientious, persistent, and more calculated and controlled in their approach to life as members of the general female population.

Braggett, Ashman, and Noble (1983) analyzed the type of support and assistance sought by parents of children who are gifted and talented. The parents (a) wanted to understand their childrens' development in terms of giftedness, intellectual ability, social-emotional development, and motivation; (b) were anxious that their children proceed at their own pace and avoid boredom; and (c) searched for enrichment activities. The parents consistently expressed the desire that their children, though gifted, be "normal." Parents of children who are gifted and talented tend to spend more time with their child on school-related activities, report unconditional love for their child, and encourage independence (Karnes, Swedel, & Steinberg, 1984).

Parent recognition of their child's uniqueness and special needs may help the child avoid social and emotional issues. Sebring (1983) advised parents to value the individuality of their child and, while approving accomplishments, show acceptance of failure. He urges that these children be helped to enjoy being a child, while being provided opportunities for choices and decision-making which teaches them responsibility. Parents' awareness of resources such as school staff, other parents, organizations, and literature is helpful in meeting the continuing needs of children who are gifted and talented (Conroy, 1987).

When engaged in problem-solving tasks, the mothers of young children who are gifted were significantly more likely to encourage metacognitive strategies such as predicting consequences than mothers of average children who provided more direct solutions to problems (Moss & Strayer, 1990). High self-esteem has been associated with the degree to which children who are gifted and talented viewed their mothers as likely to explain reasons for disciplining them (Enright & Rusicka, 1989).

Nontraditional Families and Families Representing Various Cultures   Gelbrich and Hare (1989) found that living in a single parent home negatively affected the school achievement of children who are gifted and talented, with boys more affected than girls.

Families in rural areas are presented with a unique set of challenges related to their children who are gifted and talented. These families may need specific help in overcoming obstacles that inhibit creativity in children, including additional parent education (Strom & Johnson, 1989b).

Strom and Johnson (1989a), in their work with Hispanic parents, found that Hispanic parents were more likely to join their children in play, expressed a higher level of comfort during these periods, and assigned more importance to play than did their Anglo counterparts. Anglo parents reported more favorable perceptions towards their child's creativity, control, and teacher-learning activities.

Siblings   Labeling one child in a family as gifted or talented may have significant impact on the whole family system. Cornell (1983) found that in the majority of families with children in gifted programs, at least one parent did not perceive the child as gifted. Those parents who did perceive their child as gifted expressed pride in the child and described a closer parent-child relationship to their gifted child in comparison to his or her siblings. The siblings of children who are gifted and talented were significantly less well-adjusted than other children, and were significantly less careful of social rules, less outgoing, more easily upset, more shy, and more frustrated. Adjustment problems were found to occur primarily in general education students who were perceived as less gifted than their siblings by their parents (Cornell & Grossberg, 1986).

Siblings of children who are gifted and talented perceived themselves as happier about their gifted sibling's participation in accelerated programs than the gifted child perceived their siblings to be (Colangelo & Brower, 1987a). Siblings of children who are gifted and talented reported friction and pressure when the gifted child was the older (Grenier, 1985). Large age gaps appeared to be beneficial to the sibling relationship, with highest scores for general positive relationship demonstrated between siblings who were more than 3 years apart in age. Siblings are typically fairly close in their tested intelligence quotients to their gifted sister or brother, although giftedness in a second child may be difficult to identify due to behavioral differences relative to first and second born children (Silverman, 1986). Ballering and Koch (1984) report that children who are gifted and talented were more likely to assign a negative affect to their relationships with their regular education siblings. As the child's intelligence quotient score increased, his or her perceptions of positive affect in relations with a gifted sibling decreased.

Colangelo and Brower (1987b), in a study of the long-term effects of the gifted label on siblings, found that though nonlabeled siblings scored significantly lower on academic self-concept, they did not differ from their siblings identified as gifted and talented on general self-esteem, and, in fact, scored higher in the areas of personality adjustment and endurance.

Mediating the Environment

Objective Four: To describe ways to mediate the environment for learners who are gifted, creative, or talented.

The range of educational alternatives needed to respond to the varied needs of learners who are gifted and talented is rarely available within a school system (Cox & Daniel, 1984). The possible exception to this assertion is a few major urban school systems.

Preschool

The early identification and programming for children who are gifted and talented has generated a broad range of concerns. Johnson (1983) contends that preschool learners who are gifted and talented are in a double-jeopardy situation because they are a minority and, historically, there have been few gifted programs for young children. Kitano (1985) describes issues related to parents' expectations and children's confidence and self-concepts in programs specifically for those who are gifted and talented.

It is difficult to identify young children who are gifted and talented by administering standard instruments such as intelligence and achievement tests. Such instruments are generally inappropriate for use with young children. In addition, the fact that young children develop rapidly and unevenly during preschool renders formal testing difficult. Perhaps the most effective methods of identification are direct observations of the child's functioning and parent nominations.

Johnson (1983) suggests that an enriched, child-responsive preschool environment that affords opportunities for all children to demonstrate and develop the gifts specific to them would meet the educational and affective needs of children who normally would have been identified as gifted or who would have been overlooked. Karnes and Johnson (1987) also found that when programming to enhance divergent, convergent, and evaluative thinking skills was in place, both preschool children identified as gifted and talented and their nonidentified peers made gains in cognitive and creative functioning.

Early school entry has been suggested for young learners who are gifted and talented. Gallagher (1986) argues that administrative convenience should give way to developmental appropriateness in providing early admittance to school and other educational options for young children. Maddux (1983) maintains, however, that unless schools change so that children receive instruction from which they are ready to profit, early school entry will not address the needs of young children who are gifted and talented, or, in fact, other children.

Acceleration and Enrichment

Two ways of mediating the environment for learners who are gifted and talented include acceleration and enrichment. **Acceleration** refers to moving through the curriculum rapidly. **Enrichment** refers to the addition of activities to enhance the curriculum. Horowitz and O'Brien (1986) stated that the evaluation of these two approaches and information on how best to mediate the instructional environment remain insufficient for professionals who plan, implement, and evaluate such programs. In addition, they argue that knowledge about the developmental course of giftedness remains sparse, and that there is little information on the impact of acceleration, enrichment, or other strategies on intellectual, social, and personality processes in learners who are gifted and talented over the life span.

Acceleration   Acceleration options for children who are gifted and talented include early school entrance, fast-paced or accelerated classes, extra course load, ungraded classes, or summer programs (Sisk, 1988). Sisk argues that acceleration is appropriate for most learners who are gifted and talented because they are usually advanced in overall development and successful when accelerated. Advanced achievement, high motivation, and a healthy self-concept are essential for this strategy.

In a survey of the attitudes of coordinators of gifted programs, school psychologists, principals, and teachers towards early admission and acceleration, Southern, Jones, and Fiscus (1989) found consistently conservative attitudes towards the value of acceleration as an appropriate intervention for young children. Though there were few negative reactions, even the group most favorably disposed toward acceleration, the coordinators of gifted programs, viewed the strategy as potentially hazardous to the child's development.

The primary purpose of acceleration is to speed up the educational development of budding professionals so that they will be in a position to make an impact on society when they reach a creative peak in their mid-twenties. Among the most

Box 17.1

"Let's Build a Sailboat"

Learners who are gifted and talented are usually assumed to be intellectually gifted and have exceptional achievement. However, learners may also be talented in other areas, such as leadership, planning, and construction. Forster (1990) describes the use of projects to facilitate the development of secondary school students' problem-solving skills and creativity. Projects can support students' learning by sharpening their planning skills and helping them effectively use their resources. He provides five questions to focus attention on whether or not a project would be appropriate for learners who are gifted and talented:

1. Does the project challenge learners cognitively and affectively?
2. Does the project have a "student monopoly" on decision-making?
3. Does the project measure experience gained through participating?
4. Does the project allow students to follow decisions with actions?
5. Does the project use self-regulation and self-evaluation?

Students were presented the task "Let's build a sailboat." Class was arranged into crews, and students wrote journals of what they expected to accomplish and how they planned to accomplish it. Basic plans were provided, but students were "turned loose" in planning, building, and testing their craft. Students used brainstorming, computers, models, spreadsheets, and other strategies to build their boats. Through the task, students in groups recognized the individual strengths of "crew" members, the need for a division of labor, how each of them varied in their abilities, and that leadership and cooperation themselves are talents ∎

common strategies for acceleration are early admission to kindergarten, first grade, junior and senior high school, and college; grade-skipping; and telescoping 3 years of academic work into 2 years (Davis & Rimm, 1985). Credit by examination and correspondence courses are also acceleration options. According to Pantus (1984), popular thought with regard to the social and emotional harm to students who have been accelerated has not been demonstrated in the professional literature.

Enrichment   Enrichment programs are designed to provide learners who are gifted and talented with additional experiences without placing them in a higher grade. This model has been criticized as simply adding more to the traditional learning context rather than modifying it and making it more responsive to the needs of the students (Kirschenbaum, 1984). Enrichment may take the form of classroom enrichment activities, consulting teacher services, pull-out and resource room programs, honors classes, special courses and seminars, independent study, research projects, special classes and schools, and community contributions such as mentoring programs (Eulie, 1983).

In-classroom enrichment activities are generally provided by the general education class teacher who may or may not have specific training in the education of learners who are gifted and talented. Such activities may include special projects and assignments, studying more advanced materials than the other members of the class, assisting the teacher, or serving as a laboratory assistant (see Boxes 17.1 and 17.2 for sample projects). In a few school systems, a consulting teacher is available to assist the regular class teacher in programming for learners who are gifted and

Box 17.2

Storytelling

Young children who are creative or talented can build a greater awareness of themselves as creative individuals with valuable messages through storytelling. Sasser and Zorena (1991), in their "tell me a story" project, focused their students' efforts on real issues and problems. Students, through being urged to tell a story, could explore a wide range of subjects according to their interests.

Students were given basic guidance, but researched, organized, and wrote their stories independently. Though the students were familiar with research and writing a presentation, "Tell me a story" required them to include a performance component. Emphasizing the performance aspect increased students' reevaluation, editing, and polishing of their work. Research skills were required; the story could not be told without a solid foundation and adequate supporting details. Stories involved:

the beginning of the earth—one student interviewed a local geology professor as part of her research

town history

the remembrance of a grandparent, grounded in a historical event ■

---

talented. Pull-out or resource room programs allow the learner who is gifted and talented to leave the regular class and attend programs with their peers under the supervision of a specially trained teacher.

Honors classes and special courses and seminars allow the learners who are gifted and talented to interact in a learning environment with gifted peers and to engage in the study of various topics of interest in some depth. Such activities are generally under the supervision of specially trained teachers or experts in the study topic.

Special Classes and Schools

Special schools, sometimes called magnet schools (schools of performing arts, schools of science and technology, classical academies), expose the student to in-depth exploration of their specific areas of giftedness or talent under the supervision of specially trained teachers and in the company of peers. Such schools also provide the student with the general knowledge and skills common to an education in the regular classroom and school.

Evans and Marken (1982) assessed the cumulative impact of special class in the public school on sixth through eighth grade students identified as gifted and talented. A battery of psychological and behavioral measures were used to assess five areas of functioning. Data were analyzed to determine any main effects of the program, sex, and grade on the five measures. No main effects of class placement were observed. As a group, females reported stronger intellectual achievement responsibility and self-perceived congeniality than did males. Males in special classes held somewhat less positive attitudes towards school and teachers, as well as weaker commitment to classroom. Overall, females showed a more positive school orientation.

A mentor can help a child succeed.

Mentoring Programs   A **mentor** provides individualized assistance to learners who are gifted and talented through his or her own expertise and time. Gray (1984) described two model mentoring programs, a helping relationship model and a four-phase mentoring model. In the helping relationship model, the community mentor plans, initiates, and directs activities based on background information from the learner and the teacher. The mentor then solicits the learner's reaction to the plan and, together, they discuss and modify it to respond to the learner's specific needs. Next, the student and mentor, contributing equally, conduct the activity. As the learner's contribution increases, the mentor's influence decreases. During the final phase of the program the learner functions independently.

The four-phase mentoring model is more directive than the helping relation model. First, the mentor writes a proposal. Second, the proposal is presented to potential students, who participate in writing a mutually agreed upon plan of action. Next, the mentor shares his or her personal expertise with the student. Finally, the activity is completed by the student and presented to the student's peers.

Management and Curriculum   Jones (1983) contends that the manner in which teachers approach classroom management has a significant effect on learners who are gifted and talented. He maintains that learners who are gifted and talented are sensitive to disruptive environments and that their unique needs require a particular style of classroom leadership to enhance their personal and academic potential. The classroom environment is critical because it must offer the student variety, stimulation, and challenge (Wyatt, 1982).

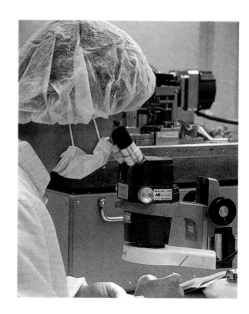

Society perceives women as less able to make major decisions and less serious about their careers.

Inadequate feedback and the lack of reward for originality which frequently occur in classroom assessment and testing procedures may challenge learners who are gifted and talented (Smith, 1986). The typical testing and examination procedures used in classrooms may have a harmful effect on the student's attitudes and intrinsic motivation. A differentiated curriculum, which (a) promotes higher thinking processes, (b) employs teaching strategies that accommodate both curriculum content and individual learning styles, and (c) provides special grouping arrangements appropriate for particular children may enhance the development of learners who are gifted and talented (George, 1990).

Objective Five: To describe ways the impact of giftedness, creativity, or talent on participation the larger social systems of the school, community, and society.

The Impact on Participation in the School, Community, and Society

Popular theories about the social and emotional harm to learners who are gifted and talented caused by rejection by peers and the social isolation of accelerated programs are not supported in the literature (Paulus, 1984). Students who are gifted and talented rated positively their gifted programs as well as the gifted label. A significant impact on positive ratings included the use of computers, independent study, and increased contact with teachers in small group discussions and lab activities (Midgett & Olson, 1983).

Reviewing the history of programming for learners who are gifted and talented may provide some insight into society's perceptions of these learners. Johnson (1986), in her review, indicates that in the early twentieth century, learners who were gifted and talented were identified primarily by their ability to excel on tasks measured by intelligence tests. These early programs focused on accelerating students through existing academic content. During the 1920s, enrichment became the preferred practice. By the 1950s however, researchers began to recognize the limitations of intelligence testing, and, as reflected in current definitions, the concept of ability and its various aspects is now the focus.

Myths around giftedness continue to plague learners who are gifted and talented. Roedell (1986) suggests that these myths, unrealistic expectations, pressure to perform, constant criticism or praise, pressures to conform, and challenges in making friends and dealing with peers remain for these learners.

Society's perception of women who are gifted and talented is a significant challenge for these learners. As late as 1979, attorneys in a Sears Roebuck and Company sex discrimination suit argued that women do not want better paying jobs and cannot handle stress, competition, or risk. The historical and accepted perception remains that women are not really suitable candidates for leadership (Tell, 1987). Historically, women are perceived as a powerless group, as is reflected in discrepancies in salaries and the numbers of females in executive positions or with doctorates (Curcio, Morsink, & Bridges, 1989).

Summary

Learners who are gifted, creative, or talented comprise approximately 3 to 5 percent of the population. Many professionals suggest that present definitions and assumptions with regard to the gifted artificially limits the number of learners identified as gifted, creative, or talented. Some believe that this population of learners is closer to 10 percent of the school age population.

Though an extremely heterogeneous group, learners who are gifted, creative, and talented are distinguishable from other learners in the areas of social-emotional development, language development, and cognitive development. Initially, services for learners within this heterogeneous group focused exclusively on the academically talented. With the development of broader definitions of giftedness, talent, and creativity, the number of students within this population expanded dramatically. Emphasis in identification is placed on the demonstration of unique abilities, skills, talents, leadership abilities, and creativity. Greater attention is given to identifying and serving gifted, talented, and creative individuals who are disabled, socioeconomically disadvantaged, members of diverse cultures, females, very young children, and underachievers.

Society's response to individuals who are gifted, talented, and creative is mixed. On the one hand, society appears to appreciate the gifted and desire their skills and abilities; on the other, society tends to resist providing programs and services. Society appears confused in its reaction to women who are gifted, talented, and creative. It provides them with fewer opportunities than their male counterparts, including fewer fellowships, lower salaries, and fewer employment opportunities.

References

Argulewicz, E. N., Elliott, S. N., & Hall, Robert. (1982). Comparison of behavioral ratings of Anglo-American and Mexican-American gifted children. *Psychology in the Schools, 19* (4), 469–472.

Ballering, L. D., & Koch, A. (1984). Family relations when a child is gifted. *Gifted Child Quarterly, 28* (3), 140–143.

Betts, G. T., & Neihart, M. (1988). Profiles of the gifted and talented. *Gifted Child Quarterly, 32,* 248–253.

Birch, J. W. (1984). Is any identification procedure necessary? *Gifted Child Quarterly, 28* (4), 157–161.

Boyce, C. W. (1991) Dear Sam. *Gifted Child Today, 14* (4), 10.

Braggett, E. J., Ashman, A., & Noble, J. (1983). The expressed needs of parents of gifted children. *Gifted Education International, 1* (2), 80–83.

Brown-Muzino, C. (1990). Success strategies for learners who are learning disabled as well as gifted. *Teaching Exceptional Children, 23* (1), 10–12.

Carter, K. R. (1984). Cognitive development in intellectually gifted: A Piagetian perspective. *Roeper Review, 1* (3), 180–184.

Chermak, G. D., & Burgerud, D. M. (1983). Receptive language of gifted and learning disabled-gifted children. *Exceptional Children, 30* (3), 226–229.

Colangelo, N. (1985). Counseling needs of culturally diverse gifted students. *Roeper Review, 8* (1), 33–35.

Colangelo, N., & Brower, P. (1987a). Gifted youngsters and their siblings: Long-term impact of labeling on their academic and personal self-concepts. *Roeper Review, 10* (2), 101–103.

Colangelo, N., & Brower, P. (1987b). Labeling gifted youngsters: Long-term impact on families. *Gifted Child Quarterly, 31* (2), 75–78.

Coleman, J. M., & Fults, B. A. (1982). Self-concept and the gifted classroom: The role of social comparisons. *Gifted Child Quarterly, 26* (3), 116–120.

Coleman, J. M., & Fults, B. A. (1983). Self-concept and the gifted child. *Roeper Review, 5* (4), 44–47.

Coleman, J. M., & Fults, B. A. (1985). Special-class placement, level of intelligence, and the self-concepts of gifted children: A social comparison perspective. *Remedial and Special Education, 6* (1), 7–12.

Conroy, E. H. (1987). Primary prevention for gifted students: A parent education group. *Elementary School Guidance and Counseling, 22* (2), 110–116.

Corn, A. L. (1986). Gifted students who have a visual handicap: Can we meet their educational needs? *Education of the Visually Handicapped, 18* (3), 71–84.

Cornell, D. G. (1983). Gifted children: The impact of positive labeling on the family system. *American Journal of Orthopsychiatry, 53* (2), 322–335.

Cornell, D. G., & Grossberg, I. N. (1986). Siblings of children in gifted programs. *Journal for the Education of the Gifted, 9* (45), 253–264.

Cornell, D. G., & Grossberg, I. N. (1989). Parent use of the term ''gifted'': Correlates with family environment and child adjustment. *Journal for the Education of the Gifted, 12* (3), 218–230.

Cox, J., & Daniel, N. (1984). Comprehensive programs for able learners. *Gifted, Creative, and Talented, 32,* 47–53.

Creel, C. S., & Karnes, F. A. (1988). Parental expectancies and young gifted children. *Roeper Review, 11* (1), 48–50.

Curcio, J., Morsink, C., & Bridges, S. (1989). Women as leaders. *Educational Horizons, 67* (4), 124–130.

Davis, G. A., & Rimm, S. B. (1985). *Education of the gifted and talented.* Englewood Cliffs, NJ: Prentice Hall.

deBernard, A. E. (1985). Why Jose can't get in the gifted class: The bilingual child and standardized reading tests. *The Roeper Review, 8* (2), 80–82.

Deschamp, P., & Robson, G. (1984). Identifying gifted-disadvantaged students: Issues pertinent to system-level screening procedures for the identification of gifted children. *Gifted Education International, 2* (2), 92–99.

Dettmer, P. (1988). Mandated gifted programs: Panacean or problematic? *Journal for the Education of the Gifted, 12* (1), 14–28.

Dowdall, C. B., & Colangelo, N. (1982). Understanding gifted students: Review and implications. *Gifted Child Quarterly, 26* (4), 179–183.

Eccles, A. L., Bauman, E., & Rotenberg, K. J. (1989). Peer acceptance and self-esteem in gifted children. *Journal of Social Behavior and Personality, 4* (4), 401–409.

Elliott, S. N., & Argulewicz, E. N. (1983). Use of behavior rating scale to aid in the identification of developmentally and culturally different gifted children. *Journal of Psychoeducational Assessment, 1* (2), 179–186.

Enright, K. M., & Rusicka, M. F. (1989). Relationship between perceived parental behaviors and the self-esteem of gifted children. *Psychological Reports, 65* (1), 931–937.

Eulie, J. (1983). Wanted: A program for gifted and talented that meets individual district needs. *Thrust, 12* (May–June), 36–38.

Evans, E. O., & Marken, D. (1982). Multiple outcome assessment of special class placement for gifted students: A comparative study. *Gifted Child Quarterly, 26* (3), 126–132.

Feldhusen, J. F., Asher, J. W., & Hoover, S. M. (1984). Problems in the identification of giftedness, talent, or ability. *Gifted Child Quarterly, 28* (4), 149–151.

Fell, L., Dahlstrom, M., & Winter, D. C. (1984). Personality traits of parents of gifted children. *Psychological Reports, 54*, 383–387.

Forster, B. R. (1990). Let's build a sailboat: A differentiated gifted education project. *Teaching Exceptional Children, 22* (4), 40–43.

Forsyth, P. (1987). A study of self-concept, anxiety, and security of children in gifted, French Immersion, and regular classes. *Canadian Journal of Counselling, 21*, 153–156.

Frasier, M. M. (1987). The identification of gifted Black students: Developing new perspectives. *Journal for the Education of the Gifted, 10*, 155–180.

Galbraith, J. (1985). The eight great gripes of gifted kids: Responding to special needs. *The Roeper Review, 8* (1), 15–18.

Gallagher, J. J. (1985). *Teaching gifted children* (3rd ed.). Boston: Allyn & Bacon.

Gallagher, J. J. (1986). The need for programs for young gifted children. *Topics in Early Childhood Special Education, 6* (1), 1–8.

Gallucci, N. T. (1988). Emotional adjustment of gifted children. *Gifted Child Quarterly, 32*, 273–276.

Gelbrich, J. A., & Hare, E. K. (1989). The effects of single parenthood on school achievement in a gifted population. *Gifted Child Quarterly, 33* (3), 115–117.

George, D. (1990). The challenge of the able child. *Cambridge Journal of Education, 20* (2), 175–182.

Gonzalez, J., & Hayes, A. (1988). Psychosocial aspects of the development of gifted underachievers: Review and implications. *Exceptional Children, 35* (1), 39–51.

Gray, W. A. (1984). Mentoring gifted, talented, creative students on an initial student teaching practicum: Guidelines and benefits. *Gifted Education International, 2*, 121–128.

Grenier, M. E. (1985). Gifted children and other siblings. *Gifted Child Quarterly, 29* (4), 164–167.

Guilford, A., Scheurle, J., & Shonburn, S. (1981). Aspects of language development in the gifted. *Gifted Child Quarterly, 25*, 159–163.

Hamilton, J. (1984). The gifted migrant child: An introduction. *Roeper Review, 6* (3), 146–147.

Hilyer, K. (1988). Problems of gifted children. *Journal of the Association for the Study of Perception, 21*, 10–26.

Horowitz, F. D., & O'Brien, M. (1986). Gifted and talented children: State of knowledge and directions for research. *American Psychologist, 41*, 1147–1152.

Janos, P., Fung, H. C., & Robinson, N. M. (1985). Self-concept, self-esteem, and peer relations among gifted children who feel "different." *Gifted Child Quarterly, 29* (2), 78–82.

Johnson, L. G. (1983). Giftedness in preschool: A better time for development than identification. *Roeper Review, 5* (4), 13–15.

Johnson, S. (1986). Who are the gifted? A dilemma in search of a solution. *Education of the Visually Handicapped, 18* (2), 54–70.

Jones, V. (1983). Current trends in classroom management: Implications for gifted students. *Roeper Review, 6* (1), 26–30.

Karnes, F. A., & Koch, S. F. (1985). State definitions of the gifted and talented: An update and analysis. *Journal for the Education of the Gifted, 8* (4), 285–306.

Karnes, M. B., & Johnson, L. J. (1987). Training for staff, parents, and volunteers working with young gifted children, especially those with disabilities and from low-income homes. *Young Children, 44,* 49–56.

Karnes, M. B., Swedel, A., & Steinberg, D. (1984). Styles of parenting among parents of young gifted children. *Roeper Review, 6* (4), 232–235.

Kerr, B. A. (1985). Smart girls, gifted women: Special guidance concerns. *Roeper Review, 8* (1), 30–33.

Kirschenbaum, R. J. (1984). Examining the rationale for gifted education. *Roeper Review, 7,* 95–97.

Kitano, M. K. (1985). Issues and problems in establishing preschool programs for the gifted. *Roeper Review, 7* (4), 212–213.

LeVine, E. S., & Tucker, S. (1986). Emotional needs of gifted children: A preliminary, phenomonological view. *Creative Child and Adult Quarterly, 11* (3), 156–165.

Li, A. (1988). Self-perception and motivational orientation in gifted children. *Roeper Review, 10,* 175–180.

Loeb, R. C., & Jay, G. (1987). Self-concept in gifted children: Differential impact in boys and girls. *Gifted Child Quarterly, 31* (1), 9–14.

Lowenstein, L. F. (1982). Teachers' effectiveness in identifying gifted children. *Gifted Education International, 1* (1), 33–35.

Lynch, S., & Mills, C. J. (1990). The Skills Reinforcement Project (SRP): An academic program for high potential minority youth. *Journal for the Education of the Gifted, 13* (4), 364–379.

Maddux, C. D. (1983). Early school entry for the gifted: New evidence and concerns. *Roeper Review, 5,* 15–17.

Maddux, C. D., Scheiber, L. M., & Bass, J. E. (1982). Self-concept and social distance in gifted children. *Gifted Child Quarterly, 26* (2), 77–81.

Mamcnur, C. (1982). The reluctant learner. A paper presented at the annual meeting of NCTE. ERIC document 219761. Washington, DC: ERIC.

Marjoram, T. (1986). Better late than never: Able youths and adults. *Gifted Education International, 4* (2), 89–96.

Mathews, F. N., West, J. D., & Hosie, T. W. (1986). Understanding families of academically gifted children. *Roeper Review, 9* (1), 40–42.

McGuffog, C., Feiring, C., & Lewis, M. (1987). The diverse profile of the extremely gifted child. *Roeper Review, 10* (2), 82–89.

McMann, N., & Oliver, R. (1988). Problems in families with gifted children: Implications for counselors. *Journal of Counseling and Development, 66* (6), 275–278.

Midgett, J., & Olson, J. (1983). Perceptions of gifted programming. *Roeper Review, 5,* 42–44.

Minner, S. (1990). Teacher evaluations of case descriptions of LD gifted children. *Gifted Child Quarterly, 34* (1), 37–39.

Minner, S., Prater, G., Bloodworth, H., & Walker, S. (1987). Referral and placement recommendations of teachers toward gifted handicapped children. *Roeper Review, 9,* 247–249.

Moss, E., & Strayer, F. F. (1990). Interactive problem-solving of gifted and non-gifted preschoolers with their mothers. *International Journal of Behavioral Development, 13* (2), 177–197.

Olszewski, P., Kulieke, M. J., & Buescher, T. (1987). The influence of the family environment on the development of talent: A literature review. *Journal for the Education of the Gifted, 11* (1), 6–28.

Pantus, P. (1984). Acceleration: More than skipping grades. *Roeper Review, 7* (2), 98–100.

Purcell, C. (1978). *Gifted and talented children's education act of 1978, Congressional Record.* Washington, DC: Government Printing Office.

Renzulli, J. S. (1978). What makes giftedness? Reexamining a definition. *Phi Delta Kappan, 65,* 180–184.

Rimm, S. (1985). How to reach the underachievement. *Instructor, 95* (1), 73–76.

Rimm, S. (1985). Identifying underachievers: The characteristics approach. *Gifted, Creative, and Talented, 41,* 2–5.

Robinson, N. M., & Chamrad, D. L. (1986). Appropriate use of intelligence tests with gifted children. *Roeper Review, 8* (3), 160–163.

Roedell, W. C. (1986). Socioemotional vulnerabilities of young gifted children. *Journal of Children in Contemporary Society, 18,* 17–29.

Roeper, A. (1982). How the gifted cope with their emotions. *Roeper Review, 5* (2), 21–24.

Rothstein, L. F. (1990). *Special education law.* New York: Longman.

Salkind, N. J. (1988). Equity and excellence: The case for mandating services for the gifted child. *Journal for the Education of the Gifted, 12* (1), 4–13.

Sapon-Shevin, M. (1987). Giftedness as a social construct. *Teachers College Record, 89* (1), 39–53.

Sasser, E., & Zorena, N. (1991). Storytelling as an adjunct to writing: Experiences with gifted students. *Teaching Exceptional Children, 23* (2), 42–44.

Schack, G., & Starko, A. J. (1990). Identification of gifted students: An analysis of criteria preferred by preservice teachers, classroom teachers, and teachers of the gifted. *Journal for the Education of the Gifted, 13,* 346–363.

Schlesinger, B. (1987). Considerations in the identification of the talented child from non-English speaking backgrounds. *Gifted Education International, 4* (3), 160–162.

Schneider, B. H., Clegg, M. R., Byrne, B. M., & Ledingham, J. E. (1989). Social relations of gifted children as a function of age and school program. *Journal of Educational Psychology, 81* (1), 48–56.

Sebring, A. D. (1983). Parental factors in the social and emotional adjustment of the gifted. *Roeper Review, 6* (2), 97–99.

Seeley, K. (1985). Facilitators for gifted learners. In J. Feldhusen (Ed.), *Towards excellence in gifted education.* Denver: Love.

Shaughnessy, M. F., & Neely, R. (1987). Parenting the prodigies: What if your child is highly verbal or mathematically precocious? *Creative Child and Adult Quarterly, 11,* 7–20.

Shoff, H. G. (1984). The gifted underachiever: Definitions and identification strategies. ERIC Document 252092. Washington, DC: ERIC.

Silverman, L. K. (1986). Parenting young gifted children. *Journal of Children in Contemporary Society, 187,* 73–87.

Sisk, D. A. (1988). The bored and disinterested gifted child: Going through school lockstep. *Journal for the Education of the Gifted, 11,* 5–18.

Smith, D. J. (1986). Do tests and examinations alienate the gifted student? *Gifted Education International, 4* (2), 101–105.

Southern, W. T., Jones, E. D., & Fiscus, E. D. (1989). Practitioner objections in the academic acceleration of gifted children. *Gifted Child Quarterly, 33,* 29–35.

Strom, R., & Johnson, A. (1989a). Hispanic and Anglo families of gifted children. *Journal of Instructional Psychology, 16* (4), 164–172.

Strom, R., & Johnson, A. (1989b). Rural families of gifted preschool and primary grade children. *Journal of Instructional Psychology, 16* (1), 32–38.

Su, C. W. (1982). A study on the development of basic emotions of gifted children and adolescents. *Bulletin of Educational Psychology, 15,* 67–84.

Suter, D. P., & Wolf, J. S. (1987). Issues in the identification and programming of the gifted/learning disabled child. *Journal for the Education of the Gifted, 10* (3), 227–237.

Tell, D. (1987). Disparity or discrimination? *Society,* (Sept./Oct.), 4–16.

Terman, L. (1954). The discovery and encouragement of exceptional talent. *American Psychologist, 9,* 221–230.

Tyerman, M. J. (1986). Gifted children and their identification: Learning ability not intelligence. *Gifted Education International, 4* (2), 81–84.

United States Department of Education (1989). No gifted wasted: Effective strategies for educating highly able, disadvantaged students in mathematics and science. Washington, DC: Government Printing Office.

VanTassel-Baska, J., Patton, J., & Prillaman, D. (1989). Disadvantaged gifted learners at risk for educational attention. *Focus on Exceptional Children, 22* (3), 1–15.

Waldron, K. A., Saphire, D. G., & Rosenblum, S. A. (1987). Learning disabilities and giftedness: Identification based on self-concept, behavior, and academic patterns. *Journal of Learning Disabilities, 20,* 422–427.

West, J. D., Hosie, T. W., & Mathews, F. N. (1989). Families of academically gifted children: Adaptability and cohesion. *School Counselor, 37* (2), 121–127.

Whitmore, J. R. (1980). *Giftedness, conflict and underachievement.* Boston: Allyn & Bacon.

Whitmore, J. R. (1986). Preventing severe underachievement and developing achievement motivation. *Journal of Children in Contemporary Society, 18* (3–4), 119–133.

Whitmore, J. R., & Maker, C. J. (1985). *Intellectual giftedness in disabled persons.* Rockville, MD: Aspen.

Wyatt, F. (1982). Responsibility for gifted learners: A plea for the encouragement of classroom teacher support. *Gifted Child Quarterly, 26* (3), 140–143.

Yewchuk, C. R. (1983). Learning disabled/gifted children: Characteristic features. *Mental Retardation and Learning Disabilities, 11* (3), 218–233.

Yewchuk, C. R. (1985). Gifted/learning disabled children: An overview. *Gifted Education International, 3* (2), 122–126.

Yewchuk, C. R., & Bibby, M. A. (1989). The handicapped gifted child: Problems of identification and programming. *Canadian Journal of Education, 14* (1), 102–108.

5

A Look Toward the Future

18

Issues, Trends, and Directions

Chapter

18
Issues, Trends, and Directions

*O*bjectives

On completing this chapter, you should be conversant with:

1. issues, trends, and directions emerging from the current dialogue about inclusion of learners with identified disabilities in general education.
2. issues, trends, and directions emerging from the current dialogue about educational reform.
3. issues, trends, and directions emerging from the current dialogue about educability and the cost/benefit of special education services.
4. issues, trends, and directions emerging from the current dialogue about early intervention for young children at risk.

*K*ey Words and Phrases

children at risk
cost/benefit
educability
General Education Initiative

inclusion
integration
zero-reject philosophy

*I*T IS EASY FOR US AS A NATION TO GIVE LIPSERVICE TO THE NEED FOR EDUCATIONAL REFORM, BUT FREQUENTLY SCHOOLS are the beneficiaries of far more rhetoric than resources. Even at best, efforts to turn rhetoric into reality too often focus on students who are able to learn the most with the least investment. . . As with any effective school reform, we must seek to alter not just the curriculum but the climate and structure of the educational experience offered these children (Edelman, 1990, p. ix) ■

Children with disabilities can get involved in activities.

Objective One: To be able to discuss issues, trends, and directions emerging from the current dialogue about inclusion of learners with identified disabilities in general education.

Introduction

There are many issues confronting general education and special education during the next decades. Several of these issues, such as assessment, identification, and cultural diversity, have been discussed in the various chapters of the text. In this chapter, four overriding issues which must be addressed conjointly by general and special educators, as well as the general population, are discussed. The resolution of these issues will have a significant impact on the future of both special and general education and the role and functions of those working with learners with disabilities. Of greater significance, the resolutions of these issues will impact on the lives, present and future, of learners with disabilities. The issues selected for review and discussion are: (a) inclusion, (b) educational reform, (c) educability, and the cost/benefits of special education, and (d) early intervention for young children at risk.

Inclusion

Madeline Will (1986), as assistant secretary for the United States Office of Special Education and Rehabilitative Services, recommended that the major focus for change in special education be to include learners with identified disabilities in general education. She urged that a major step toward inclusion is "to have building-level administrators empowered to assemble appropriate professional and other resources for delivering effective, coordinated, comprehensive services for all students based on individual educational needs rather than eligibility for special education programs" (p. 312). Through Will's efforts, and those of other policy-making professionals, the **General Education Initiative (GEI)** (initially referred to as the Regular Education Initiative or REI) emerged.

Several factors have contributed to the formulation of the GEI. These include (a) the dramatic rise in the number of learners identified as mildly disabled, though research has demonstrated a large overlap between students who are identified and those who are low achievers, (b) the finding that once students are placed in pull-out special education programs, they tend to stay there for a substantial period of time, and (c) the large number of students who "fall through the cracks" and do not receive the services they need (Gersten & Woodward, 1990).

Davis (1989) expressed the concern that the debate over inclusion of learners with disabilities in general education has largely taken place in university-based special education departments rather than in the public schools. This lack of participation of general educators may be a primary reason why the movement may fail. Davis suggests that the issue of inclusion of learners with disabilities requires more substantial involvement of special and general educators at the local school district level. In addition, he argues that there have been few efforts to involve students themselves in the design, implementation, and evaluation components of their personal educational program. Davis suggests that the general education debate is really about how schools can better serve learners who require special attention, interventions, and support systems, to enjoy a better quality of education, personal, social, and vocational life in the future.

The GEI is fueled by two parallel efforts: (1) the inclusion of learners with severe disabilities into partial participation in the general classroom curriculum, and (2) retaining students with mild disabilities in general education classrooms and reducing pull-out programs (Sailor, 1991).

Inclusion of Learners with Severe Disabilities

Sailor (1991) writes that most recently, the emphasis in the literature regarding the inclusion of learners with severe disabilities has shifted from a discussion of integration to inclusion models that exemplify the placement of these learners in the general education classroom, with some program time in other environments. **Inclusion** is the philosophy that all students, regardless of disability, are a vital and integrated part of the general education system. Special services may be delivered in and outside of the general education classroom. **Integration,** on the other hand, refers only to the placement of individuals with disabilities in educational programs serving their peers. The basic components of inclusion are:

1. All students attend the school to which they would be assigned if they had no disability.
2. There are no more or no fewer learners with disabilities in a single school than would be found districtwide.
3. A **zero-reject philosophy** would be in place (that is, no student could be excluded from receiving educational services, regardless of the disability).
4. Placements would be age and grade appropriate, with no self-contained special education classes.
5. Cooperative learning and peer instruction would be used in general instruction.
6. Special education supports would be provided in the integrated environment.

These components require that school be seen as a unified place with a shared responsibility for learners with or without disabilities.

According to Lipsky and Gartner (1992), full inclusion requires the development and implementation of the "new" school or the reconceptualization of the construct of schooling. Such reconceptualization of schooling recognizes that to be successful, all students, including those presently labeled as disabled, must be enabled "to become effective workers in the production of their own learning." The "new" school will (a) demonstrate respect for students, (b) actively engage students in learning, (c) prepare students for a lifetime of learning, (d) recognize, early in the learning process, that the failure of the student is a failure of the school to meet the student's needs and effectively engage the student in the work of learning, and (e) develop an effective partnership with both parents and the community.

Lieberman (1992), in a discussion of inclusion of learners with severe disabilities, cautions against oversimplification of the changes which must occur in the classroom, school, and community for effective integration:

> Can a severely mentally disabled child be fully integrated in regular classrooms, in the school, in the community, on the street, in all manner of social gathering? Yes. Absolutely yes. It must be given careful consideration by thoughtful, committed people who are making decisions based on the best interest of individuals. This is what public policy must be, not extremist, fanatical rhetoric that deals in a reality that exists in the minds of its subscribers.
>
> The day the standard for education becomes meeting the individual needs of all children, all disabled and handicapped children can be in the regular classroom (p. 24).

Retaining Learners with Mild Disabilities in General Education

The GEI assumes that, under certain service delivery models, learners with mild disabilities would do better in mainstreamed educational programs than in pull-out, resource room, or separate classroom programs (Reynolds, Wang, & Walberg, 1987). It is recognized, however, that general education teachers may not be ready to meet the needs of learners with mild disabilities without some support. Two models of teacher support are provided in Boxes 18.1 and 18.2. An alternative service delivery model, the General Education Collaboration Model (Simpson & Myles, 1990), is described in Box 18.3.

Current Perceptions of the GEI

In a mailed questionnaire study designed to explore teachers' perceptions of the GEI, Gans (1987) found that special educators, who depend on their own interpretations of the integration needs of general educators, are likely to misconstrue the needs of general educators with regard to the GEI. In addition, the willingness of the general educators to participate in the GEI tended to be shaped by variables linked with nonaffective personal and career characteristics and procedural classroom concerns. General educators expressed dissatisfaction with their personal skills in working with learners with mild disabilities in their classrooms.

In their discussion of the GEI for learners with mild disabilities, Carnine and Kameenui (1990) write that there are three possible future directions: (a) accept the status quo, (b) dismantle the current system, as it pertains to the mildly disabled, and thus leave more and more students to the remnants of failed educational reforms, or (c) extend the support provided to special education teachers and students to other teachers who have a majority of at-risk students.

Garver-Pinhas and Schmelkin (1989) report significant differences among general education teachers, special education teachers, and general and special education administrators in attitudes towards mainstreaming. The most striking differences among the groups occurred regarding academic and administrative concerns. Classroom teachers exhibit the least positive attitudes regarding academic concerns,

---

Box 18.1

Supporting Teachers through Peer Collaboration

Johnson and Pugach (1991) suggest a structured problem-solving process, peer collaboration, to assist classroom teachers in developing and implementing interventions for learners with disabilities. This four-step collegial dialogue involves (Pugach & Johnson, 1989):

1. Clarifying questions. The initiating teacher brings a brief written description of the program and responds to questions from the peer teacher about all aspects of the problem.
2. Summary. The initiating teacher develops (a) a description of the pattern of the student's behavior, (b) the teacher's response, and (c) the identification of variables over which the teacher has control.
3. Interventions and predictions. Teachers generate at least three interventions, using the information from the preceding step. The initiating teacher predicts potential outcomes for each of the three potential interventions.
4. Evaluation. An evaluation plan is developed, and a meeting is set for approximately 2 weeks following the beginning of the collaboration process to assess the effectiveness of the intervention.

As a result of peer collaboration, teachers became more tolerant of the students with special needs. Teachers were able to generate a variety of interventions to address classroom strategies, and over 86 percent of the strategies were effective. The use of a structured, reflective process was helpful in supporting teachers' development of ways to meet students' individual needs ■

Box 18.2

The Consultation Process

The consultation process typically has three steps (Johnson & Bauer, 1992):

1. Problem identification. The consultant works with the teacher to identify the problem; this process usually includes observations in the teacher's classrooms and a series of discussions.
2. Strategy development. A series of potential strategies is considered, and an implementation plan is developed which includes (a) the problem description, (b) strategy description, (c) time for implementation, (d) a plan for monitoring progress, (e) a plan to determine if the problem is resolved, and (f) the date for a follow-up or review meeting.
3. Implementation. The consultee proceeds with the plan indicated.

Several barriers may inhibit the success of collaboration. These may include (Johnson, Pugach, & Hamitte, 1988):

incongruence between the views of the general and special educator regarding appropriate and acceptable strategies

giving advice rather than using collaborative problem-solving, which may lead to dependency and blaming

credibility conflicts, in which the classroom teacher may consider the consultant unrealistic or the consultant may consider the classroom teacher less than committed

confused problem ownership, in which the consultant takes on more responsibility than the classroom teacher in identifying problems ■

Box 18.3

The General Education Collaboration Model

One comprehensive model for inclusion of learners with mild disabilities is the General Education Collaboration Model (Simpson & Myles, 1990). This model assumes that:

- General educators are responsible for teaching; special educators provide support and resources to enhance student success.
- Social and academic interactions in the general education classroom benefit everyone.
- Students, parents, and school personnel prefer inclusion to segregated programs.
- Most general educators are willing and able to serve students with mild to moderate disabilities in general education classrooms.

The essential elements of this model, which all need to be in place for success, include:

- Flexible departmentalization, that provides for coordination of services, communication, and control through shared responsibility and decision-making.
- Program ownership, with general educators assuming responsibility for the students, with the expectation that they will have full participation in the decision-making process and appropriate support.
- Identification and development of supportive attitudes of both the individuals with whom students with disabilities and youth interact and their unidentified peers.
- Student assessment as a measure of program effectiveness, including assessment of achievement, self-concept, and social integration.
- Classroom modifications that support mainstreaming, including reduced class size, the use of consultation, in-service programs, the use of paraprofessionals, provision of planning time, and availability of support services.

The General Education Collaboration Model recognizes that general education teachers should not be expected to "go it alone," even with consultative assistance. Rather, through structural changes such as class size, additional training, and planning time, general education teachers are assumed to be able to manage learners with disabilities in their classrooms ■

---

followed by special education teachers. Principals and special education administrators report more positive attitudes. Distrust is apparent in the findings, with special educators stating that they do not believe principals would give the support needed by learners with disabilities.

In an innovative study of the attitudes of the general public (377 adults at a shopping mall), Berryman (1989) found generally favorable attitudes towards the concept of integrating learners with disabilities into the general education classroom. The individuals surveyed were most favorable toward students with speech disorders and chronic medical problems, and least favorable toward students with disruptive behavior.

Strategies Used in the GEI Hawkins, Doueck, and Lishner (1988) found that when teachers were provided training in proactive classroom management, interactive teaching, and cooperative learning, low achievers showed more favorable attitudes towards math, more bonding to school, greater expectations for continuing schooling, and less serious misbehavior as measured by suspensions and expulsions than a control group.

Box 18.4

Teacher Assistance Teams

Teacher assistance teams are school-based problem-solving units used to assist teachers in developing intervention strategies. A team usually consists of a core group of three elected faculty members representing various grade levels or content areas who assist other teachers. The classroom teacher who is requesting help serves as a fourth and equal member of the team. The membership of the team may vary by building and specific teacher needs. Teams may include principals, special educators, or parents (Chalfant & Pysh, 1989).

The teacher assistance team model provides a way for teachers to meet and engage in positive, productive, collaborative problem-solving (Chalfant & Pysh, 1981). Teachers may request help in analyzing and understanding classroom problems, managing an individual student, dealing with an entire class, modifying the curriculum, or preparing for a parent conference.

Teacher empowerment is the underlying assumption of teacher assistance teams. In this way, they are an essential part of prereferral interventions. Through teacher empowerment, teacher assistance teams are differentiated from (a) special education child study teams responsible for screening, and (b) traditional multidisciplinary teams responsible for the diagnostic evaluation and placement process required by Public Law 94–142. Rather than these student-oriented, mandated processes, teacher assistance teams are teacher-oriented, and function as a way to complement both general and special educators, not as a substitute for special education services or as part of the referral process (Chalfant & Pysh, 1989) ■

In the effort to support all learners in the general education setting, cooperative professional development may be appropriate as an adjunct to or substitute for consultation (Glatthorn, 1990). Cooperative professional development involves small teams of special education and general education classroom teachers and uses a variety of approaches to enhance their mutual and professional growth.

Prereferral intervention has emerged as a supportive strategy to maintain learners in general education. Pugach and Johnson's (1989) prereferral intervention is typically classified as (a) informal, school-based, problem-solving teams with (b) consultation on the part of special education teachers. Prereferral intervention may be viewed as a progressive strategy because it (a) acknowledges the limitations of the existing, cumbersome, resource-intensive diagnostic and identification procedures specified in Public Law 94–142; (b) is based on the redistribution of the special education resources to more immediate problem-solving and far greater interaction with general education; (c) recognizes the absence of other assistance for teachers; and (d) adds credence to the notion that classroom teachers are likely to need problem-solving strategies for many students for whom referral is not and will never be a viable option. Graden (1989) argues that prereferral intervention, however, is not really a "new" service, but a form of consultation. As more collaboration and consultation occurs in a school, the need for consultation increases. Two models to support prereferral intervention, the teacher support team and the mainstream assistance team, are described in Boxes 18.4 and 18.5.

Schumaker and Deshler (1988) caution that wholesale application of the GEI is a gross oversimplification of the changes that need to occur in special education. Miller (1990) contends that, in view of current knowledge about school improvement, efforts to make the GEI viable must include classroom teachers and special educators engaging in meaningful dialogue. They need to observe each other at

Box 18.5

Mainstream Assistance Teams

Mainstream assistance teams (Fuchs, Fuchs, Bahr, Reeder, Gilman, Fernstrom, & Roberts, 1990) provide support to teachers for students who are difficult to teach, with the assumption that improvements in on-task behavior and academic productivity will reduce the likelihood of referral. Embedded in behavioral consultation, three phases of activities are conducted: preintervention, intervention, and postintervention.

Preintervention Activity In this first phase, the consultant assists the teacher in identifying and defining the problem. Classroom behavior is observed, using interval recording, observation with peers, and computing the percentages of problem behavior of both the identified student and two same-gender randomly selected peers. Peer behavior is measured to provide a frame of reference for the teacher and consultant in setting goals. In addition, five samples of the student's work are collected and evaluated in terms of amount and accuracy.

In the second part of this phase, the long-term goal for the problem behavior is selected and short-term objectives are generated. The teacher meets with the student to identify and describe the problem behavior and to develop a written contract regarding the behavior.

Intervention Activity In this phase the student's progress on daily goals as designated in the contract are documented. On an individual monitoring sheet the student is responsible for responding to a self-talk question, such as "Did I do my work without fiddling in my desk?" After 2 days of joint monitoring, the student assumes self-reporting of the behavior. Reinforcement and supports are gradually faded. After the desired behaviors are consistent in the first classroom, they are generalized to an additional setting.

Postintervention Activity In a meeting with the consultant, the teacher and consultant determine whether the goal of the intervention has been achieved. If the goal is met, fading continues. If the goal was not met, the teacher and consultant may continue with the original intervention, change the goal, change the intervention, or change the goal and intervention. Additional consultation sessions may be planned at this time ■

work and practice and master new ways of doing business in school. She argues a site-based approach, in which each faculty develops its own approach to implementing the initiative. Teachers should be given the opportunity to provide leadership, and should be engaged in the dialogue, reflection, and observation. Finally, teachers and administrators need to form networks and partnerships that extend beyond the school, into the community.

Objective Two: To be able to discuss issues, trends, and directions emerging from the current dialogue about educational reform.

Educational Reform

It is difficult to discuss the GEI and inclusion without addressing the current dialogue about educational reform. Indeed, most proponents of the GEI (Reynolds, Wang, & Walberg, 1987; Sapon-Shevin, 1987; Stainback & Stainback, 1984; Will, 1986) call for dissolution of the present dual system in public schools (general education and special education), and the development of a single system which would allow for more effective and appropriate education of all students.

As Eisner (1991) suggests, there are many "comfortable habits" in place in the schools, which may have been historically grounded, but which have little

Time is spent changing classes in many schools.

relevance in terms of learning. For example, in a typical school, students may shift from teacher to teacher yearly, and may change subjects, location, and teacher every 50 minutes during any given day. Subject matter is fragmented, and the incentive-driven system teaches students to strive for grades rather than learning. Schools and teachers are rewarded for achievement (as measured by a standardized test) rather than addressing the needs of the learner. As Gideonse (1990) reports, however, children and youth of the same age display great variation in motivation, cultural norms, performance, ability, and other instructionally relevant variables. Individual learning styles and means of expression alternative to print and verbal skills (such as art, music, movement, mathematics) are not addressed. The existing structures of "school" fail to account or acknowledge these differences, which are essential in the complex society that exists outside the school.

The structure of instruction has driven not only practice but research regarding that practice. For example, Anderson, Brubaker, Alleman-Brooks, and Duffy (1985), in their examination of one school-related structure (seatwork), suggest that the structure is useful in engaging students in a task so that they do not need the teacher's attention for a predictable period of time. However, they found that students who needed the most instruction in reading were actually the ones who got the least because of their lack of understanding for completion of the work. Rather than questioning its very existence, Anderson and associates offered a suggestion for the productive use of seatwork. Teachers using seatwork should ask if it contributes to learning or addresses basic questions with regard to the purpose of "reading" as a means of communication.

Duffy (1982), in his exploration of what really happens in classrooms, found that the existing, accepted structures of school to place incredible constraints on the actions of the teacher. Beyond pacing and grouping, few instructional decisions were in the hands of teachers. Teachers contended with limited amounts of freedom and flexibility, as well as resource shortages. The reality of classroom instruction included explicit mandates to use a particular basal textbook in a particular way, a professional evaluation based on how well individual teachers adhered to the prescribed procedures, and an accountability system based on how well individual teachers' students did on standardized tests (Duffy, Roehler, & Putnam, 1987). Teachers experienced curricular restraints, through following traditional basal reading instruction in which metalinguistic skills are presented as automatized procedures. Teachers reported instructional constraints, arguing that their professional preparation did not assist them in their practice. Teacher described constraints related to the classroom and school milieu, in terms of grouping patterns, class sizes, time allocation, and schedules. And, they described organizational constraints, in which daily classroom and schoolwide routines emerge as survival patterns rather than patterns to enhance learning (Duffy & Roehler, 1986).

In a national survey of teachers (Genevie & Zhao, 1988), 79 percent of the teachers reported that they feel frustrated with administrative practice and school structures. In addition, teachers reported that they are rarely recognized for their expertise and performance.

Sailor (1991) believes that the shift in emphasis from efforts to improve curriculum and instruction to the total reorganization of school and district-level governance systems presents a "window of opportunity" for the emergence of a shared educational agenda which holds potential for innovative programming for all students. He summarizes four common considerations of school restruction as (a) increasing school autonomy, (b) employing site-based management and shared decision-making, (c) infusion and coordination of categorical resources, and (d) community participation in the life of the school. Reynolds, Wang, & Walberg (1987) describe what they refer to as the necessary restructuring of special and regular education. They argue that the categories used in special education are not valid indicators of particular forms of education. They assert that the use of categorical education is expensive and inefficient, and causes much disjointedness in school programs.

Reform may not always support all learners. In a discussion of "America 2000," one of many blueprints for national educational reform, Sindelar, Watanabe, McCray, and Hornsby (1992) warn that educational reform may improve schools' report cards but it may also exclude students who are low achieving and difficult to manage. In the press to maximize achievement, special education and the students it serves may be eased out of the educational mainstream.

Educability and the Cost/Benefit of Special Education

Objective Three: To be able to discuss issues, trends, and directions emerging from the current dialogue about educability and the cost/benefit of special education.

The issue of the **educability** (that is, the capacity for learning) of all children is one which has evolved since 1975 when the mandates of Public Law 94–142 were imposed. Issues related to the nature and characteristics of an appropriate education have become interwoven with issues of the **cost/benefit** of special education.

Early enthusiasm related to educability is represented by statements by Fredericks and associates (1975), who maintained that "every child, regardless of handicapping condition, can learn. If a child is not learning, the fault lies not with the child but with the environment" (p. 1). Sailor and Haring (1977) wrote that "educators cannot provide a program and merely expect students to respond or be failed. A tremendous responsibility is placed on the educator" (p. 70). At that time, it was assumed that if we could manage the environment appropriately, we could teach the child (Shea & Bauer, 1987).

Noonan and Reese (1984) report that the policy of educating all learners with disabilities has come under attack because of two factors: (a) the costs associated with providing educational services, and (b) disagreement among professionals concerning whether all learners with disabilities can indeed profit from an education. By the end of the 1970s some professionals became skeptical of our ability to put the concept of education for all into practice (Ellis, 1979; Bailey, 1981; Rainforth, 1982; Hotte & associates, 1984). Kauffman and Krouse (1981) questioned whether education was taking place in classrooms for learners with severe disabilities. They characterized education as "more than mere exposure to program: it refers to a student's acquisition of socially significant behaviors as a result of instruction" (p. 53). However, Baer (1981) maintained that a student could not be declared ineducable until all known teaching techniques have been tried and failed entirely, a task he perceives as impossible within the learner's lifetime. He suggests that "the cost of truthfully affirming a child to be unteachable is not less than the cost of continuing to attempt teaching the child" (p. 67). Noonan, Brown, Mulligan, and Rettig (1982) clarified the discussion by asserting that the question of educability was a smokescreen for the real issue of whether different individual capabilities warrant the assumption that human lives have differing degrees of worth.

According to Shea and Bauer (1987), the issue of educability is difficult to discuss on a purely intellectual and objective plane. We are not dealing solely with economic, political, administrative, and bureaucratic issues when we discuss the "ideal of educability." We are attending to a basic philosophical question—the meaning of humanness. It would, it appears, be unwise to permit economic, political, administrative, and bureaucratic questions to usurp personal and professional responsibilities with regard to education of individuals with disabilities. As professionals, we have not completed the task of developing effective and potentially effective teaching technologies and strategies. We have not completed research in the education of learners with severe disabilities.

Costs   School districts often argue that the basis for their unwillingness to provide an education for some learners with severe disabilities is cost. However, limits on the cost of related services have been made by the courts. In the case of *Board of Education versus Rowley* (1982), the definition of appropriate education does not require "potential maximization." Rather, education was determined to provide the "basic floor of opportunity." The cost of psychological services and counseling was at issue in the case of *Max M. versus the Illinois State Board of Education.* The decision in this case placed limits on the amount of reimbursement, even when counseling and psychological services are related to education.

Benefiting from an Education   Court decisions with regard to an individual's ability to "benefit from education" are based in the Fourteenth Amendment to the U.S. Constitution, that is, equal protection under the law. According to Rothstein (1990), in decisions such as these, the courts take two factors under consideration: (1) "the importance of the right at issue," and (2) "whether the person claiming a denial of equal protection is a member of a class of individuals who are or should be entitled to special consideration" (p. 53). In the case of *Timothy W. versus the Rochester School District,* the first factor was conceded—the right to an education was an important factor. The decision was based on the second factor, as to whether Timothy is a member of a class of individuals who are or should be entitled to special consideration. In *Timothy W. versus the Rochester School District,* a serious blow to the Public Law 94–142 mandate for education for *all* learners was nearly struck. In this case, the court based its decision on the findings of the Rowley case,

The courts consider two factors for determining if an individual with disabilities will benefit from general classrooms.

that is, that the law does not guarantee that disabled students' individualized instruction will maximize their potential, but rather that it will provide services that are adequate for the students' educational need. A brief summary of this case, representative of the "right to education" cases, follows.

The Case of Timothy W   Timothy W., born on December 8, 1975, was 2 months premature and weighed 4 pounds. He was transferred from the hospital in which he was born to another hospital shortly after birth due to respiratory difficulties. In the second hospital, he had intracranial bleeding, hydrocephalus, and seizures. He was cared for and discharged 3 months later, with a shunt implanted to drain excess cranial fluid. At this time, he was diagnosed as severely developmentally retarded with suspected hearing and visual impairments. The child's physical and mental development were slow. He received physical and occupational therapy and other services at a developmental center during the 1979–80 school year.

In February, 1980, the pupil evaluation team of the Rochester School District attempted to determine if Timothy was eligible for special education services under the Education for Handicapped Children Act, Public Law 94–142. The team reviewed all available documents, reports, and observations, and in March, 1980, determined that Timothy was not eligible for services in the district program because of his inability to benefit from special education.

Soon after being refused public school services, Timothy entered services provided by the New Hampshire Department of Health and Welfare. His "Individualized Service Plan" included medical care, physical therapy, tactile stimulation, feeding therapy, and respite care. When reassessed for eligibility in 1983, the school district's evaluation team failed to reach a decision and requested additional neurological evaluations.

During the due process hearings following these decisions, a hearing officer ruled that Timothy was, in fact, qualified for special education, on the basis that special education law entitled "all handicapped children" to education regardless of the severity of the handicap. Inquiry as to whether the child might benefit from special education was ruled to be irrelevant.

The school district appealed the decision, and the federal district court asserted that the hearing officer was in error and that the law applied only to those children who could benefit from an education. The district court claimed it was not the intent of Congress to provide special education for children who cannot benefit from that education. The court concurred with the district court's assertion and concluded that no such mandate was intended by Congress in Public Law 94–142, and that an initial determination of the ability of the individual with disabilities to benefit from education is requisite to the provision of service.

The parent appealed the decision of the federal district court. The United States Court of Appeals, First Circuit, reversed the decision of the district court and found that Congress clearly intended to provide public education for every handicapped child, unconditionally and without exception, regardless of the severity of the handicap. In addition, the court of appeals found that the most severely handicapped children were to get priority attention, although no educational benefit was guaranteed and potential for such benefit was not prerequisite.

The decision of the court of appeals was appealed to the United States Supreme Court. On November 27, 1989, the Supreme Court refused to review the case of Timothy W., thus letting stand the First Circuit Court's decision that the Education of Handicapped Children Act mandates a **zero-reject** philosophy which entitles all disabled children to receive a free appropriate public education regardless of the nature or severity of their disabling conditions (CRR Publishing Company/LRP Publications, 1989).

The First Circuit Court's decision is binding in four New England states and Puerto Rico. If future rulings in other circuit courts disagree with the First Circuit Court then the Supreme Court may address the issue of eligibility in the future.

Objective Four: To be able to discuss issues, trends, and directions emerging from the current dialogue about early intervention for young children at risk.

Early Intervention

According to Slavin (1989), in discussions of **children at risk** we are referring to those who are "unlikely to graduate." Davis and McCaul (1990) present alarming statistics regarding learners at risk:

One million students drop out of school each year.
On any given night there are at least 100,000 homeless children.
Fifteen percent of graduates of urban high schools read at less than the sixth grade level.
Almost 10 million children have no source of regular medical care.

Davis and McCaul describe the primary indicators of learners at risk as (a) poverty, (b) minority cultural or ethnic group identity, (c) non-English or limited English background, (d) specific family configurations such as single parent households. The biological and environmental risk factors selected by two or more states, as summarized by Harbin and Maxwell (in press), are presented in Table 18.1.

According to data of the United States Department of Education (1991), 250,000 infants and toddlers were served in early intervention programs in December, 1989. In addition, a total of 388,625 children between the ages of 3 and 5 received special education and related services in December, 1989, an increase of 30,000 over the previous years. In 1990, thirty-four states had mandatory legislation requiring a free appropriate public education for learners 3 through 5 years of age, and an additional thirteen states will have mandated programming in the 1991–92 school year.

***T*able 18.1**   Risk Factors Selected by States for Identifying
Children as At Risk Under IDEA, Part H

Biological Risk Factors Selected by Two or More States

birthweight of less than 1500 grams

birthweight of less than 1000 grams

chemically dependent mother

mother exposed to medications known to cause brain damage to fetus

extended neonatal intensive care stay (7 or more days)

ventilator support for 48 hours or more

abnormalities in tone

neonatal or perinatal seizures

small for gestational age

birth trauma/infection/disease

traumatic illness/acute life threatening event

lead poisoning/toxic substances

growth deficiency/nutritional problems

prematurity (less than 32 weeks)

birth/neonatal complications

significant medical problems

prenatal infections (CMV, rubella, AIDS)

respiratory distress with or without prolonged mechanical ventilation

asphyxia with or without neurological complications

sensory impairments

failure to thrive

history of substance abuse/maternal drug use

feeding dysfunction

ventilator dependent/technology dependent

intraventricular hemorrhage grade III or IV

congenital infections (i.e., neonatal meningitis)

parent health problems

central nervous system lesion or abnormality

periventricular leukomalacia

Apgar score between 0 and 3 at 5 minutes

positive maternal HIV

severe chronic illness

catastrophic infections, traumatic illness, or serious accident known to affect the central nervous system

abnormal neurological exam

brain infections/disease

near drowning

diabetic mother

Early intervention programs are grounded in two fundamental assumptions: (a) developmental plasticity, and (b) cost effectiveness (Ysseldyke, Algozzine, and Thurlow, 1992). Unless these assumptions are accepted, early intervention efforts are unreasonable.

Slavin (1990) argues that prevention of putting children at risk should begin at the onset of pregnancy. Health problems, such as lead poisoning and poor nutrition,

*T*able 18.1   (Cont.)

Environmental Risk Factors Selected by Two or More States

parent or caretaker with disability or health problems

child abuse or seriously disturbed relationship between parent and child

high level of family disruption

parental or familial substance abuse/chemical dependency

parental age less than 15

low income/economic disability

parents lack of high school education

family member with a disability

lack of routine well-child care

substantiated abuse or neglect in the home

parental retardation or mental illness

homeless or transient family

home environment lacks adequate physical resources

inability to perform parenting due to impairment in psychologial or interpersonal functioning

limited maternal and family care/social support

poor nutrition

adolescent parent

severe parenting risk including parents' mental or developmental disability or substance abuse

no well-child care by 6 months of age

parent less than the age of 16

lack of prenatal care

parental concern about development

accidents/environmental toxins

poor parent-infant attachment

foster care or in other alternative living arrangement

lack of parenting skills

developmental disability of parent which interferes with caregiving

mother-infant separation

parental chronic illness limiting caregiving ability

deviation from the norm in behavior or interpersonal relations

can be alleviated, increasing children's readiness. Research has begun to demonstrate the positive effects of preschool participation on such outcomes as high school graduation and delinquency (Berrueta-Clement, Schweinhart, Barnett, Epstein, & Weikart, 1984). There is growing evidence that a combination of prevention and early intervention programs, intensive support in first grade, and improved classroom practices at all grade levels can substantially reduce the number of students who are at risk for school failure or special education.

Any effort at providing early intervention for young children who are at risk must be centered in the family rather than the child (Dunst, Trivette, & Deal, 1988). The social systems perspective, as discussed throughout this text, perceives the family as a social unit within several nested contexts. In view of this perspective, Dunst and his associates define intervention as "the provision of support (i.e.

Early intervention programs are needed to keep students in school and out of trouble with the juvenile authorities.

resources provided by others) by members of a family's informal and formal social network that either directly or indirectly influences child, parent, and family functioning" (p. 5). The goal of intervention is the empowering of the family to respond effectively to circumstances which impact on it by using its strengths. Project Head Start, established in 1965, was the first nationally based attempt to provide early intervention. An essential part of Project Head Start is parent involvement and participation in decisions regarding the program.

Means and Knapp (1991) suggest several curricular principles in working with young children at risk:

- Focus on complex, meaningful problems, rather than breaking tasks into small skills.
- Embed instruction on basic skills in the context of global tasks.
- Make connections with students' out-of-school experience.
- Apply instructional strategies such as modeling and thinking strategies, encouraging multiple approaches, providing scaffolding to enable students to accomplish complex tasks, and making dialogue the major medium for teaching and learning.

The Perry Preschool Program (Schweinhart and Weikart, 1980) is one early intervention program for children at risk that has been documented to have an impact on the learners involved. In this cognitively oriented program, parents were visited in their homes 1½ hours each week, and children attended preschool 5 half-days every week. Materials used in the classroom and homes (parents were encouraged to structure household activities and to include the children in accomplishing the tasks) provided the children with the opportunity to experience the environment, classify objectives, learn about the size and order of objects, and understand temporal and spatial relationships. School records and interviews compiled over a 15-year period demonstrated that students who had been in this preschool program were 21 percent less likely to report that they had been arrested by age 19 than were control students. Sixty-five percent of the Perry Preschool graduates had graduated

Head Start programs encourage children to focus on attention and completion of activities, two skills essential to successful school performance.

or were still in school, as opposed to 45 percent of the control group. During interviews, children with the preschool experience were more willing to talk to parents about school, spent more time on homework, and had a higher self-rating of school ability than did members of the control group.

Four Head Start programs in Louisville, Kentucky, served as the site for research conducted by Miller and Bizzell (1983). These four programs used various methods, including a Montessori program, a direct instruction program, traditional preschool, and a program based on the formation of basic concepts. Strong and continuing program effects were indicated for boys who attended the Montessori program, possibly because the materials focused on attention and completion of activities, two skills essential to successful school performance.

Stallings and Stipek (1986) suggest that summaries of the long-range effects of preschool programs for children at risk imply that family involvement activities support positive attitudes toward school and in turn support children in feeling successful enough in school to continue to graduation.

Though efforts to serve young children at risk were initiated in 1964 with Head Start legislation, other legislative enactments have extended and expanded programming into the 1990s. In 1968, legislation was enacted to assist in the development of demonstration centers to serve preschool children and their families. Also, in 1968, "child find" was initiated and states were required to submit plans and timetables for serving all children and youth with disabilities from birth to 21 years. In 1972, it was mandated that not less than 10 percent of national enrollment opportunities be allotted to learners with disabilities. This 10 percent allocation was modified from national to state enrollment opportunities in 1975. In addition, in 1975, funding was provided to serve children with disabilities from ages 3 to 5 years. In 1986, incentive funds were provided to serve infants and toddlers, as an initiation of programming for these children was to be phased in between 1987 and 1991. In 1991, demonstration and outreach programs were funded, technical assistance was directed towards specific groups, social work services were included as interventions, and training and dissemination requirements established (Ysseldyke, Algozzine, and Thurlow, 1992).

Summary

In this final chapter, we have presented four overriding issues whose resolution will have a significant impact on the future of learners with disabilities, special education, and general education. The issues discussed were (a) inclusion, (b) educational reform, (c) educability and the cost/benefit of special education, and (d) early intervention for children at risk.

The inclusion of learners with disabilities in general education is occurring and accelerating as indicated by the ever-increasing numbers of children with mild disabilities remaining in the general education classroom, both full- and part-time, and the increasing numbers of learners with severe disabilities being integrated into the schools and associating with nondisabled peers. Obviously, the task of full inclusion is far from complete.

In the 1990s educational reform is sweeping the nation. It is the topic of discussion in mass media, among politicians, in business forms, and in the community, universities, and public schools. Its eventual form is as yet indistinct, but literally hundreds of demonstration projects are occurring through the nation. As advocates for individuals with disabilities, our greatest concern with the reform movement and the movement towards excellence in education is its consequences for learners with disabilities. Will those with disabilities be an essential and integral part of the movement, or will they remain outside of the mainstream of change and return to the pre-Public Law 94–142 years?

The debate with regard to educability and the cost/benefit of special education has consumed much time and energy over the past several years. The major question in this issue appears to be the "innate worth of human life." It will be unfortunate if we allow economic and political issues to determine who shall and shall not be given the opportunity for an education and, thus, an improved quality of life.

We have made great strides, as a profession and society, in the past few years in providing services for young children at risk. Programs are now serving children from birth to school entry. In this task, special educators are not working alone but in concert with medical, social service, and other helping professionals, and especially in concert with parents who are essential to the early development of their children. Though the data is limited, there are indications that programs for children at risk will improve school attendance and learning and decrease the number of children classified as disabled. With increased services to children at risk and increased prenatal care for all parents, then perhaps we shall see a dramatic decrease in the numbers of children in special education in the next generations.

As we conclude this text, it remains apparent that the job of special education and special educators is far from complete. We have much work to do before all children and youth with disabilities are served.

References

Anderson, L. M., Brubaker, N. L., Alleman-Brooks, J., & Duffy, G. G. (1985). A qualitative study of seatwork in first-grade classrooms. *The Elementary School Journal, 86,* 123–140.

Baer, D. M. (1981). A hung jury and a Schottish verdict: "Not proven." *Analysis and Intervention in Developmental Disabilities, 1,* 91–98.

Bailey, J. S. (1981). Wanted: A rational search for the limiting conditions of habilitation in the retarded. *Analysis and Intervention in Developmental Disabilities, 1,* 42–52.

Berrueta-Clement, J. R., Schweinhart, I. J., Barnett, W. S., Epstein, A. S., & Weikart, D. P. (1984). *Changed lives.* Ypsilanti, MI: High/Scope Educational Research Foundation.

Berryman, J. D. (1989). Attitudes of the public towards educational mainstreaming. *Remedial and Special Education, 10,* 44–49.

Board of Education v. Rowley (1982). 458 U.S. 176.

Carnine, D. W., & Kameenui, E. J. (1990). The General Education Initiative and children with special needs: A false dilemma in the face of true problems. *Journal of Learning Disabilities, 23,* 141–144, 148.

Chalfant, J. C., & Pysh, M. V. D. (1981). Teacher assistance teams: A model for within-building problem solving. *Counterpoint, 2* (November).

Chalfant, J. C., & Pysh, M. V. D. (1989). Teacher assistance teams: Five descriptive studies on 96 teams. *Remedial and Special Education, 10* (6), 49–58.

CRR Publishing Company/LRP Publications (1989). *Education for the handicapped law report.* Supplement 255, December 15, 1989. Summary and analysis: Supreme Court refuses to review Timothy W.

Davis, W. E. (1989). The Regular Education Initiative debate: Its promises and problems. *Exceptional Children, 56,* 440–446.

Davis, W. E., & McCaul, E.J. (1990). *At risk children and youth: A crisis in our schools and society.* Orono, ME: Maine Department of Educational Services, University of Maine.

Duffy, G. G. (1982). Fighting off the alligators: What research in real classrooms has to say about reading instruction. *Journal of Reading Behavior, 14* (4), 357–373.

Duffy, G. G., & Roehler, L. (1986). Constraints on teacher change. *Journal of Teacher Education, 37,* 55–58.

Duffy, G. G., Roehler, L. R., & Putnam, J. (1987). Putting the teacher in control: Basal reading textbooks and instructional decision making. *The Elementary School Journal, 87,* 357–366.

Dunst, C. J., Trivette, C., & Deal, A. (1988). *Enabling and empowering families: Principles and guidelines for practice.* Cambridge, MA: Brookline Books.

Edelman, M. W. (1990). Preface. In J. Knitzer, Z. Steinberg, & B. Fleisch, *At the schoolhouse door.* New York: Bank Street College of Education (p. ix).

Education for the Handicapped Law Report (1989). Supreme Court refuses to review Timothy W. Supplement 255, December 15, 1989, SA 265–266, and Supplement 244, June 30, 1989, SA 393–406.

Eisner, E. (1991). Should America have a national curriculum? *Educational Leadership, 49* (2), 76–81.

Ellis, N. R. (1979). The Partlow case: A reply to Dr. Roos. *Law and Psychology Review, 5,* 15–49.

Fredericks, H. D., Baldwin, V. L., Grove, D. N., Riggs, C., Furey, V., Moore, W., Jordan, E., Gage, M., Levak, L., Alrik, G., & Wadlow, M. (1975). *A data based classroom for the moderately and severely handicapped.* Monmouth, OR: Instructional Development Corporation.

Fuchs, D., Fuchs, L., Bahr, M., Reeder, P., Gilman, S., Fernstrom, P., & Roberts, H. (1990). Prereferral intervention to increase attention and work productivity among difficult-to-teach pupils. *Focus on Exceptional Children, 22* (6), 1–8.

Gans, K. D. (1987). Willingness of regular and special educators to teach students with handicaps. *Exceptional Children, 54,* 41–45.

Garver-Pinhas, A., & Schmelkin, L. P. (1989). Administrators' and teachers' attitudes toward mainstreaming. *Remedial and Special Education, 10,* 38–43.

Genevie, L., & Zhao, X. (1988). *The Metropolitan Life survey of the American teacher.* New York: Louis Harris.

Gersten, R., & Woodward, J. (1990). Rethinking the Regular Education Initiative: Focus on the classroom teacher. *Remedial and Special Education, 11* (3), 7–16.

Gideonse, H. D. (1990). Organizing schools to encourage teacher inquiry. In R. F. Elmore (Ed.), *Restructuring schools: The next generation of educational reform* (pp. 97–124). San Francisco: Jossey-Bass.

Glatthorn, A. A. (1990). Cooperative professional development: Facilitating the growth of the special education teacher and the classroom teacher. *Remedial and Special Education, 11,* 28–34, 50.

Graden, J. L. (1989). Redefining "prereferral" intervention as intervention assistance: Collaboration between general and special education. *Exceptional Children, 56,* 227–231.

Harbin, G. L., & Maxwell, K. (in press). Status of the states' progress toward developing a definition for developmentally delayed: Report #2. Chapel Hill, NC: Carolina Institute for Child and Family Policy, University of North Carolina.

Hawkins, J. D., Doueck, H. J., & Lishner, D. M. (1988). Changing teaching practices in mainstream classrooms to improve bonding and behavior of low achievers. *American Educational Research Journal, 35,* 31–50.

Hotte, R. A., Monroe, H. J., Philbrook, D. L., & Scarlata, R. W. (1984). Programming for persons with profound mental retardation: A three year retrospective study. *American Journal of Mental Deficiency, 22* (2), 75–78.

Johnson, L. J., & Bauer, A. M. (1992). *Meeting the needs of special students: Legal, ethnical, and practical ramifications.* Newberry Park, CA: Corwyn.

Johnson, L. J., & Pugach, M. C. (1991). Peer collaboration: Accommodating students with mild learning and behavior problems. *Exceptional Children, 58,* 454–461.

Johnson, L. J., Pugach, M. C., & Hamitte, D. J. (1988). Barriers to effective special education consultation. *Remedial and Special Education, 9,* 41–47.

Kauffman, J. M., & Krouse, J. (1981). The cult of educability: Searching for the substance of things hoped for, the evidence of things not seen. *Analysis and Intervention in Developmental Disabilities, 1,* 53–60.

Lieberman, L. M. (1992). Preserving special education . . . for those who need it. In W. Stainback & S. Stainback (Eds.), *Controversial issues confronting special education: Divergent perspectives.* Boston: Allyn and Bacon (pp. 13–25).

Lipsky, D. K., & Gartner, A. (1992). Achieving full inclusion: Placing the student at the center of educational reform. In W. Stainback & S. Stainback (Eds.), *Controversial issues confronting special education: Divergent perspectives.* Boston: Allyn and Bacon (pp. 3–12).

Means, B., & Knapp, M. S. (1991). Introduction: Rethinking teaching for disadvantaged students. In B. Means, C. Chelemer, & M. S. Knapp (Eds.), *Teaching advanced skills to at-risk students* (pp. 1–26). San Francisco: Jossey-Bass.

Miller, L. (1990). The Regular Education Initiative and school reform: Lessons from the mainstream. *Remedial and Special Education, 11* (3), 17–22.

Miller, L., & Bizzell, R. (1983). Long term effects of four preschool programs: Sixth, seventh, and eighth grades. *Child Development, 54,* 727–741.

Noonan, M. J., Brown, F., Mulligan, M., & Rettig, M. A. (1982). Educability of severely handicapped persons: Both sides of the issue. *TASH Journal, 7,* 3–12.

Noonan, M. J., & Reese, R. M. (1984). Educability: Public policy and the role of research. *Journal of the Association for Persons with Severe Handicaps, 9,* 8–15.

Pugach, M. C., & Johnson, L. J. (1989). Prereferral interventions: Progress, problems, and challenges. *Exceptional Children, 56,* 217–226.

Rainforth, B. (1982). Biobehavioral state and orienting: Implications for educating profoundly retarded students. *TASH Journal, 6,* 33–37.

Reynolds, M. C., Wang, M. C., & Walberg, H. J. (1987). The necessary restructuring of special and regular education. *Exceptional Children, 53,* 391–398.

Rothstein, L. F. (1990). *Special education law.* New York: Longman.

Sailor, W. (1991). Special education in the restructured school. *Remedial and Special Education, 11* (6), 8–22.

Sailor, W., & Haring, N. G. (1977). Some current directions in education of the severely/multiply handicapped. *AAESPH Review, 2,* 3–86.

Sapon-Shevin, M. (1987). The national education reports and special education: Implications for students. *Exceptional Children, 53,* 300–307.

Schumaker, J. B., & Deshler, D. D. (1988). Implementing the Regular Education Initiative in secondary schools: A different ball game. *Journal of Learning Disabilities, 21,* 36–42.

Schweinhart, L., & Weikart, D. (1980). *Young children grow up: The effects of the Perry Preschool Program on youths through age 15* (Monograph #7). Ypsilanti, MI: High/Scope Educational Research Foundation.

Shea, T. M., & Bauer, A. M. (1987). Education for all children: Evolution and devolution of a concept. Edwardsville, IL: Southern Illinois University (unpublished manuscript).

Simpson, R. L., & Myles, B. S. (1990). The General Education Collaboration Model: A model for successful mainstreaming. *Focus on Exceptional Children, 23* (4), 1–10.

Sindelar, P. T., Watanabe, A. K., McCray, A. D., & Hornsby, P. J. (1992). Special education's role in literacy and educational reform. *Teaching Exceptional Children, 24* (3), 38–41.

Slavin, R. E. (1989). Students at risk of school failure: The problem and its dimensions. In R. Slavin, N. Karweit, & N. Madden, (Eds.), *Effective programs for students at risk* (pp. 3–19). Boston: Allyn & Bacon.

Slavin, R. E. (1990). General education under the Regular Education Initiative: How must it change? *Remedial and Special Education, 11* (3), 40–50.

Stainback, S., & Stainback, W. (1984). A rationale for the merger of special and regular education. *Exceptional Children, 51,* 102–111.

Stallings, J. A., & Stipek, D. (1986). Research on early childhood and elementary school teaching programs. In M. C. Wittrock (Ed.), *Handbook of research on teaching* (3rd ed.) (pp. 727–753). New York: Macmillan.

Timothy W. v. Rochester School District (1987–88). EHLR Dec. 559:580 (DNH 1988).

United States Department of Education (1991). *Thirteenth annual report to Congress on the implementation of the Individuals with Disabilities Education Act.* Washington, DC: Author.

Will, M. (1986). Educating children with learning problems: A shared responsibility. *Exceptional Children, 52,* 311–314.

Ysseldyke, J. E., Algozzine, B., & Thurlow, M. L. (1992). *Critical issues in special education* (2nd ed.). Boston: Houghton Mifflin.

Glossary

The chapter in which these key words first appear is indicated in brackets following the definition.

acceleration   moving through the curriculum at a more rapid pace [17]

accommodation   adaptation or adjustment [1]

Acquired Immune Deficiency Syndrome (AIDS)   a fatal viral disease transmitted through intimate sexual contact, contaminated blood or blood products, contaminated needles and syringes, and from mother to child; no known cure is available [10]

adapted physical education   physical education designed for the successful participation of learners with disabilities [10]

Adoption Assistance and Child Welfare Act of 1980 provided subsidies for families adopting special needs children; mandated state procedures for promptly terminating parents' rights when appropriate to facilitate permanency for children [6]

African American   an American whose ancestry includes individuals native to Africa [8]

aggression   behaviors that assault another individual [7]

American Sign Language (ASL)   the native language most frequently used among persons with hearing impairments; it is not the signed equivalent of English [12]

Americans with Disabilities Act (1990)   mandates equal accommodations for individuals with disabilities in all businesses, public facilities, and transportation systems and bans discrimination [3]

amblyopia   "lazy eye" [11]

amplification   increasing volume [12]

appropriate education   that education which allows an individual to achieve commensurate with peers [3]

Anglo   the white middle-class culture [8]

Appalachian   an individual whose ancestry includes individuals native to the Appalachian region [8]

articulation   production of speech sounds [9]

articulation disorders   difficulties with producing the sound system of oral language or speech; also known as phonological disorders [9]

Asian American   an American whose ancestry includes individuals native to Asia [8]

astigmatism   a condition marked by variations in the cornea that result in blurred vision [11]

attention deficit hyperactivity disorder   a clinical disorder marked by difficulties in focusing and often concomitant hyperactivity [13]

augmentative communication systems   systems that serve as an alternative to spoken language, including gestures, sign language systems, or mechanical or technological aids of some sort [16]

augmentative systems   systems used to support communication [9]

autism   a developmental disorder apparent before 30 months of age and demonstrated by a pervasive lack of responsiveness to other people and communicative disorders [16]

basic concepts   those concepts related to size, position, order, and sequence, on which other cognitive processes are based [14]

behavior   the expression of the dynamic relationship between the individual and the environment [1]

behavioral disorders   learners who, in the school environment, vary from their peers in terms of interaction, and whose challenging behaviors persist despite interventions typically used in general education [7]

behavioral perspective   a point of view from which the individual's behavior is seen as being maintained by stimuli in the immediate environment in which the individual functions [1]

behind-the-ear (BTE) hearing aids   hearing aids that fit behind the learner's ear [12]

biophysical perspective   a point of view which emphasizes neurological and other organic factors as the cause of the individual's behavior [1]

blind   a visual impairment requiring alternatives to print and visual materials [11]

cascade of services   the range of placement options available to learners with disabilities [3]

cancer   a group of diseases of unknown cause which produce abnormal cell growth [10]

cataracts a clouding of the lens of the eye [11]

catheterization insertion of a tube into the urethra to drain urine from the bladder [10]

cerebral palsy a dysfunction of the neurological motor system [10]

child abuse physical or mental injury or sexual abuse of a child under the age of eighteen by a person responsible for the child's welfare under circumstances which indicate that the child's health or welfare is harmed or threatened [6]

Child Abuse Prevention and Treatment Act of 1975 provided mechanisms for the reporting and prevention of child abuse and neglect; included legal definitions of child abuse and neglect [6]

child maltreatment child abuse and neglect [6]

child neglect failing to provide for the physical, medical, emotional, or educational needs of a child by an individual responsible for the child's welfare [6]

children at risk children who, without intervention, may be identified as disabled due to family, developmental, or medical history, physical characteristics, life circumstances, or environmental factors; also preschoolers younger than 3 years of age who, though not labeled, are suspected of having disabilities [18]

Cinderella complex the tendency to wait to be rescued by a male partner [17]

Civil Rights Act of 1963 banned discrimination in education [5]

cluttering running together sounds, words, and phrases, producing rapid, jumbled speech [9]

cognition the process of knowing and thinking [9]

cognitive behavior modification strategies in which the learner overtly and eventually covertly practices a set script for addressing problems [13]

collaboration the participation of equal partners in the solution of problems [4]

collaborative consultation consultation in which the special and general educator work as a team, as equal partners [15]

collaboration in the school community activities in which family members serve as volunteers or paraprofessionals [4]

collaborative support for school programs activities that support the in-class program of the learner with disabilities [4]

communication sharing understanding [9]

compensatory education a model of education that provides for "making up" or compensating for weaker skills or ability [2]

conductive loss hearing loss caused by damage to the outer or middle ear [12]

congruence match or goodness of fit [1]

context setting [1]

cost/benefit the relationship between the expense of a service and the gain derived from the service [18]

creative capable of expressing unique and novel ideas, solutions, and products [17]

criteria of the least dangerous assumption the belief that assumptions made regarding individuals should be those least intrusive and least limiting [4]

criterion-referenced evaluation evaluation which focuses on the learner's mastery of specific skills [3]

cued speech a set of hand cues, which, together with speech reading, permit visual identification of spoken sound [12]

curriculum-based assessment assessment grounded in the curriculum and materials in which the learner receives instruction [13]

cystic fibrosis a disease of the pancreas marked by abnormally thickened mucus and other glandular secretions [10]

d-amphetamine (Dexedrine) a stimulant sometimes used in the treatment of attention deficit hyperactivity disorder; brand name Dexedrine [13]

deaf learners unable to process auditory linguistic information [12]

depression a dysphoric mood or loss of pleasure that lasts at least two weeks [7]

development the continual adaptation or adjustment of the individual and the environment to each other

deviance disavowal efforts made by a learner with a disability to reject differences attributed to their disability [14]

diabetic retinopathy aneurisms in the retinal capillary blood vessels due to diabetes [11]

Diagnostic and Statistical Manual of Mental Disorders the manual for the classification system of mental disorders developed by the American Psychiatric Association [7]

diagnostic evaluation the process of studying a learner and the learner's developmental contexts to determine the nature of the problem if, in fact, there is a problem [3]

diagnostic evaluation team the group of individuals from various disciplines responsible for the evaluation of learners [3]

disability a reduction in function [2]

disfluency stuttering and cluttering [9]

disturbed behaviors behaviors that occur across settings [7]

disturbing behaviors behaviors that are person, setting, or task specific [7]

dual sensory impairments concurrent hearing and visual disabilities, the combination of which causes such severe communication and educational problems that they cannot be accommodated in special education programs for either deaf or blind students [16]

ecology   the study of the relationship of humans with their environment [1]

ecological context   the setting in which an individual develops [1]

educability   capable of benefitting from schooling [18]

educable mental retardation   the education term for mild mental retardation [14]

Education of the Handicapped Act of 1983   authorized grants and contracts to strengthen and coordinate education, training, and related services to assist youth with disabilities in the transition from school to community [5]

enrichment   additional activities that enhance the typical curriculum [17]

epilepsy   a condition marked by seizure disorders [10]

etiology   cause [1]

ethnicity   membership in a group of people who share a unique social and cultural heritage that is transmitted from one generation to the next [8]

exceptional learner   learners perceived to vary from peers [1]

exosystem   those settings which do not involve the developing individual directly, but may impact on the individual [1]

expressive language   language for developing and sending messages [9]

externalizing behaviors   behaviors directed outward, such as stealing, lying, disobedience, and fighting [7]

fetal alcohol syndrome   a birth defect caused by maternal alcoholism, which causes prenatal and/or postnatal growth retardation, central nervous system damage, and a set of common facial characteristics [6]

fluctuating conductive hearing impairment   the fluctuating hearing loss that may occur as a consequence of otitis media [12]

FM systems   a wireless amplification system in which speech is transmitted from a microphone via frequency modulated radio signals to a receiver worn by the learner [12]

foster care   substitute care placement which is typically licensed and regulated by state human services agencies [6]

General Education Initiative   the professional field's efforts to increase the inclusion of learners with disabilities in general education programs [3]

generalization   the demonstration of a behavior in a context in which it was not directly taught [5]

gentle teaching   a method grounded in interpersonal interactions for working with learners with severe and multiple disabilities [16]

gifted   usually refers to learners who are intellectually or academically within the superior range [17]

gifted imposter phenomenon   a personal belief that one is not truly as successful as others believe, and that this lack of ability will be discovered [17]

glaucoma   increased pressure in the eye [11]

handicap   disadvantage that results from a disability that limits or prevents fulfillment of a role [2]

hard of hearing   learners who have hearing losses that still permit them to process auditory information [12]

hearing impairment   all learners whose hearing is not typical for their age and culture [12]

heart condition   any of a number of conditions which may cause cardiac malfunction [10]

hemophilia   a genetically transmitted disease marked by problems with blood coagulation [10]

high prevalence disabilities   mild handicapping conditions such as educable mental retardation, learning disabilities, and mild behavioral disorders [15]

Hispanic   persons of all races whose cultural heritage is related to the use of the Spanish language and the Latino culture [8]

holistic communication-based approaches   intervention strategies which involve instruction in reading and writing as communication in context [13]

human immunodeficiency virus (HIV)   a virus that affects the immune system and impairs the individual's ability to fight infections; develops into AIDS [10]

hydrocephaly   a condition in which fluid accumulates in the ventricles of the brain [10]

hyperkinesis   hyperactivity [13]

hyperopia   far sightedness [11]

immitance   audiologic testing which includes typanometry and acoustic reflex testing [12]

inclusion   the philosophy that all students, regardless of disability, are a vital and integral part of the general education system; special needs services addressing the IEP goals and objectives of students with disabilities may be rendered in or out of the general education classroom [3]

individual-referenced evaluation   evaluation that focuses on the learner's progress over time [3]

Individualized Family Service Plan   a year-long plan of services and outcomes for the family of a child with a disability who is younger than 3 years of age [3]

Individualized Education Program   a year-long plan of the services and activities conducted with a learner with a disability [3]

information-giving activities   activities in which the family is the passive recipient of information [4]

information-sharing activities   activities in which the family shares and receives information [4]

integration placement of individuals with disabilities in the same facilities as their age peers

internalizing behaviors behaviors directed inward, such as physical complaints, phobias, social withdrawal, and fearfulness [7]

interpreter one who explains the meaning of oral English in one of several signing systems, and explains signing in English [12]

in-the-ear (ITE) hearing aids hearing aids that fit in the learner's ear [12]

juvenile diabetes a metabolic disorder caused by inadequate production of insulin [10]

juvenile rheumatoid arthritis a chronic childhood disorder marked by joint inflammation [10]

language the ability to communicate complex ideas through an organized system of meaning [9]

language disorders deviant or delayed development of comprehension and/or the use of the signs and symbols of a spoken, written, or other symbol system [9]

lead poisoning neurological damage resulting from the ingestion of toxic levels of lead [10]

learning disabilities a general term that refers to a heterogeneous group of disorders manifested by significant difficulties in the acquisition and use of listening, speaking, reading, writing, reasoning, or mathematical abilities [13]

least restrictive environment the environment in which the learner can succeed which is most typical of that in which his or her peers are educated [3]

levels system an organizational framework within which various behavior management interventions are applied to shape behaviors [7]

life space interview a technique in which the teacher and student interact in a guided interview with the aim of developing appropriate student responses to incidents in the environment; developed by Redl [7]

low achiever a learner whose achievement is below that of her or his peers [15]

mainstreaming participation of learners with disabilities with their typical peers [3]

macrosystem the majority culture's belief system [1]

macular degeneration a breakdown of the macula, the central part of the retina [11]

mentor an established individual in a profession or field who serves as a model [17]

medical model an evaluation and treatment model that focuses on the issues, concerns, and disabilities of the individual [2]

mesosystem interrelationships between two or more settings [1]

mental retardation generalized subaverage intellectual functioning, concurrent with problems in adaptive behavior, which occurs before 18 years of age [14]

methylphenidate (Ritalin) a stimulant frequently used in treatment of attention deficit hyperactivity disorder; brand name Ritalin [13]

microsystem immediate interpersonal relationships [1]

migrant persons who move frequently, following employment opportunities [8]

mild mental retardation retardation indicated by intelligence quotients on standardized tests of about 50 to 70 [14]

milieu an individual's environment or developmental context [1]

minority any group with unequal access to power [8]

moderate mental retardation retardation indicated by intelligence quotients on standardized tests of about 20 to 50 [14]

morphology the smallest units of meaning [9]

multiple disabilities concomitant disabilities (such as mentally retarded-blind, mentally retarded-orthopedically impaired, etc.) the combination of which causes such severe educational problems that they cannot be accommodated in special educational programs designed solely for working with one of the impairments [16]

muscular dystrophy a group of diseases characterized by the wasting and progressive weakness of skeletal muscles [10]

myopia nearsightedness [11]

Native American a descendant of the indigenous population of the Americas [8]

neural tube defect spina bifida; a defect of the spinal column in which the spine fails to close properly around the column of nerves it is designed to protect [10]

noncategorical programs that serve learners from more than one disability area [15]

nonparticipation the option to not be involved in an activity [4]

norm the standard [1]

norm-referenced evaluation evaluation that compares students' performance with the performance of others [3]

normalcy fabrication a story, told by an individual with a disability, to appear more competent or "normal" [14]

nystagmus rapid and uncontrolled eye movements [11]

occupational therapy therapy designed to support the development of work, recreation, and self-care skills [10]

ontogenic system personal characteristics [1]

orthopedic disability a physical disability that challenges mobility, managing body functions, and social interactions [10]

orthotic a device to enhance the partial functioning of a part of the body [10]

otitis media middle ear infection [12]

parent training   activities to increase parents' knowledge and skills [4]

partially sighted   unable to use print and visual materials without the help of large print, optical aids, technological aids; usually requires education in the use of residual vision [11]

peripheral vision   seeing by means of the outermost portions of the eye, i.e., the corner of the eye [11]

Perkins Vocational Education Act of 1973   provided for vocational services for individuals with disabilities; required client involvement in the design and delivery of services [5]

phonemes   the written representation of speech sounds [9]

phonology   the sound system of language [9]

physical impairment   a disability involving physical functioning [10]

physical therapy   therapy designed to increase strength, endurance, and range of motion [10]

placement   the assignment of a learner to a specific program [3]

possible fetal alcohol effects   a group of mild birth defects caused by maternal use of alcohol, usually involving prenatal and/or postnatal growth retardation and central nervous system damage [6]

postlingual hearing impairment   a hearing impairment occurring after the development of language [12]

pragmatics   the social, communicative consideration of language [9, 12]

prelingual hearing impairment   a hearing impairment present prior to the development of language [12]

prenatal drug and alcohol exposure   fetal exposure to drug and alcohol of any kind or amount by the mother's use during pregnancy [6]

prereferral activities   those activities conducted in the general education classroom by the general education teacher to address the individual needs of a learner prior to referral for evaluation for special education services [3]

profound mental retardation   the most severe degree of mental retardation, with intelligence quotients on standardized tests below the 20 to 25 range; persons with profound mental retardation require life span care and supervision [14]

prosthetics   artificial replacements for missing body parts [10]

psychoeducational perspective   a point of view that emphasizes the primary cause of the individual's behavior as being dynamic intropsychic phenomena [1]

Public Law 94–142   The Education for All Handicapped Children Act (1975); required a free, appropriate public education for all learners [3]

Public Law 99–457   Amendments to PL 94–142 which included permissive legislation for services for learners 0–2 and required preschool programming for learners 3–5 years of age [3]

Public Law 101–336   Americans with Disabilities Act (ADA); bars discrimination; mandates equal accommodations for individuals with disabilities in all businesses, public facilities, and transportation [3]

Public Law 101–457   Amendments to PL 94–142, called the Individuals with Disabilities Education Act; provided for a transition planning for all learners 16 or more years of age and person first language [3]

receptive language   language for receiving messages [9]

reciprocal association   mutual effects of the individual and the environment [1]

referral   the process for initiating the diagnostic evaluation of a learner [3]

Rehabilitation Act of 1973   assured the civil rights of individuals with disabilities [3]

related services   those services required so that an individual may profit from special education [3]

retinitis pigmentosa   an inherited condition that begins with a loss of night vision and leads to gradually decreasing peripheral vision [11]

retinopathy of prematurity   an abnormal proliferation of blood vessels in the eye, causing scar tissue and bleeding and detachment of the retina [11]

school survival skills   skills necessary for successful interactions with teachers, for example being on time, bringing materials, doing assignments [15]

scoliosis   a lateral curve of the spine [10]

screening   activities to identify learners at risk for further study [3]

seizure disorders   a disorder represented by any of various types of seizures; epilepsy [10]

semantics   the meaning of individual words, and their relationship with each other [9]

sensorineural loss   hearing loss caused by damage to the neurological hearing system [12]

seriously emotionally disturbed   the label used in federal law for learners identified as behaviorally disordered [7]

severe disabilities   intense physical, mental, or emotional problems which require education, social, psychological, and medical services beyond those that are traditionally offered by general and special education programs [16]

severe mental retardation   an extensive degree of mental retardation; persons with intelligence quotients on standardized instruments in the 20–25 to 35–40 range; require life span care and supervision [14]

sickle cell disease   a genetically transmitted disease marked by chronic anemia and sickle-shaped red blood cells [10]

social skills training   specific interventions, usually involving problem solving, aimed at increasing the ability of learners to interact with others [13]

social systems perspective   a point of view from which the individual is seen as developing in a dynamic relationship with and as an inseparable part of the social contexts in which the individual functions over the life span [1]

special education   a subsystem of regular education, responsible for the education of learners with disabilities [1]

speech   the vocal system of language [9]

speech audiometry   a measure of a person's aural detection of speech [12]

speech disorders   impairments in the production of oral or spoken language [12]

speechreading   the process of following environmental cues related to a message and recognizing speech movements produced by another individual [12]

spina bifida   a congenital condition marked by a defect of the spinal column in which the spine fails to close properly (see neural tube defect) [10]

spinal cord injury   an injury to the neural column; the extent of injury varies from case to case [10]

stage theory   the theory that family members progress through a set pattern of reactions to the birth or diagnosis of a member with a disability [4]

stereotypies   repetitive, inappropriate social behaviors such as rocking, swaying, and head posturing [11]

stigma   an attitude towards others that discredits them in some manner [4]

strabismus   crossed eyes (internal) or eyes which look outward (external) [11]

strategies training   the teaching of specific strategies to complete academic tasks [13]

stuttering   a disruption in the timing of speaking [12]

substitute care   the placement of children for rearing with other than the biological parents [6]

symbols   representations [9]

syntax   the rule system for constructing sentences [9]

talented   exhibiting special abilities, aptitudes, and accomplishments in various areas [17]

talipes   the turning of a foot towards the midline of the body; often referred to as "clubfoot" [10]

teacher assistance teams   teacher-centered instructional alternative support systems [15]

token economy   an exchange system that provides individuals or groups whose behavior is being changed with immediate feedback cues of the appropriateness of their behavior [7]

trainable mental retardation   the educational term for learners with moderate mental retardation [14]

transactional model   the development of the child is seen as the product of the continuous interactions of the learner and the experiences provided by the caregivers in the social context [9]

transactions   an interaction in which each participant is altered by the other [1]

transition   the movement from one system or service to another [5]

transition services   services to facilitate the individual's movement between educational and other service programs, from home to school, between school programs, from school to work, advanced training, or postsecondary education [3]

traumatic brain injury   injury to the brain which impairs functioning [10]

TDD   telecommunication device for the deaf; a teletypewriter connected to a telephone system that allows persons with hearing impairments to communicate [12]

TTY   teletypewriter; a device connected to a telephone which allows communication between persons with hearing and persons with hearing impairments [12]

tutoring   one-on-one or small group teaching of materials used in the learner's other instructional settings [13]

tympanogram   a test of the function of the eardrum [12]

underachiever   a learner who demonstrates a significant discrepancy between ability and performance [17]

visual acuity   ability to distinguish small spatial separations or intervals between portions of a visual field; sharpness, distinctiveness [11]

visual impairment   a generic term for any of several conditions which limit vision [11]

visually handicapped   having sight limited in any way and to such an extent that special services are required [11]

Vocational Education Act of 1963   mandated 10 percent of the funds allocated to vocational education for programs for persons with disabilities [5]

voice disorders   difficulties in the resonant quality of speech [9]

Wild Boy of Aveyron   Itard's student, and the subject of an historically significant study of the treatment of a learner with mental retardation and autism [2]

zero reject philosophy   the philosophy that no student may be excluded from receiving educational services, regardless of the disability [18]

Credits

Chapter 1

Opener: © Paul Conklin/Photo Edit; p. 10 left: © Jane Williams/Unicorn Stock Photos; p. 10 right: © Robert Brenner/Photo Edit; p. 10 bottom: © Bob Daemmrich/Stock Boston; p. 11 left: © S. Feld/H. Armstrong Roberts; p. 11 right: © Jeff Greenberg/Unicorn Stock Photos

Chapter 2

Opener: © P. Reininger/Unicorn Stock Photos; p. 19: © M. Grecco/Stock Boston; p. 21: © Anheuser-Busch; p. 22: © Deborah Davis/Photo Edit; p. 23: © Dale Wilson/First Light, Toronto; p. 32: © Camerique/H. Armstrong Roberts

Chapter 3

Opener: © Tony Freeman/Photo Edit; p. 39: © Paul Conklin/Photo Edit; p. 40: © Tony Freeman/Photo Edit; p. 42: © Camerique/H. Armstrong Roberts; p. 43: © Daneve Leigh Bunde/Unicorn Stock Photos; p. 50: © Tony Freeman/Photo Edit; p. 54: © Jeff Greenberg/Unicorn Stock Photos

Chapter 4

Opener: © James Shaffer; p. 77, 80, 81: © James Shaffer; p. 88: © Melanie Carr/Zephyr Pictures; p. 90: © Martin R. Jones/Unicorn Stock Photos; p. 91: © Cleo Freelance Photo

Chapter 5

Opener: © James Shaffer; p. 100, 103: James Shaffer; p. 105: © M. Dwyer/Stock Boston; p. 111: © Jean Higgens/Unicorn Stock Photos

Chapter 6

Opener: © Deneve Leigh Bunde/Unicorn Stock Photos; p. 118: © Richard Hutchings/Photo Edit; p. 120: © James Shaffer; p. 121: © Charles Gupton/Stock Boston; p. 125: © Chris Boylan/Unicorn Stock Photos; p. 129: © Tom McCarthy/Photo Edit

Chapter 7

Opener: © Rhoda Sidney/Stock Boston; p. 150, 152: © James Shaffer; p. 157: © Jeff Dunn/The Picture Cube; p. 160: © Cleo Freelance Photo; p. 166: © Arthur Sirdofsky

Chapter 8

Opener: © James Shaffer; p. 177: © Mark Gibson; p. 180: © Alan Oddie/Photo Edit; p. 182: © Jeffrey Aaronson/Network Aspen; p. 191: © Frank Siteman/Light Source Stock; p. 196: © Paul Conklin/Photo Edit

Chapter 9

Opener: © L. L. T. Rhodes/Devaney Stock Photos; p. 211: © Bob Coyle; p. 212: © Elena Rooraid/Photo Edit; p. 216: © Nathan Benn/Stock-Photo; p. 221: © Seth Resnick/Light Source Stock; p. 223: © Bill Aron/Photo Edit

Chapter 10

Opener: © Tony Freeman/Photo Edit; p. 233: © Tony Freeman/Photo Edit; p. 242: © Greg Greer/Unicorn Stock Photos; p. 244: © MacDonald Photography/Unicorn Stock Photos; p. 246: © Tony Freeman/Photo Edit; p. 248: © Kenneth Karp/Omni Photo Communications; p. 249 bottom left: © Paul Conklin/Photo Edit; p. 249 top right: © Tony Freeman/Photo Edit; p. 249 top left: © Robert Brenner/Photo Edit; p. 249 bottom right: © Robert Brenner/Photo Edit; p. 250: © Art of the Eye and Forecast Public Artworks

Chapter 11

Opener: © Todd Karol/First Light, Toronto; 11.2A, B, C, D, E,© Art of the Eye and Forecast Public Artworks; p. 271: © Martha McBride/Unicorn Stock Photos; p. 272: © Alan Oddie/Photo Edit; 11.5: © Zefa-U.K./H. Armstrong Roberts; p. 276: © Tony Freeman/Photo Edit; 11.6A: © James Shaffer; 11.6B: © Martin R. Jones/Unicorn Stock Photos; p. 280 left: © Rhoda Sidney/Photo Edit; p. 280 right: © Bob Daemmrich/Stock Boston

Chapter 12

Opener: © Kenneth Kapp/Omni Photo Communications; p. 297: © Cleo Freelance Photo; p. 298: © David Young-Wolff/Photo Edit; p. 301: © Stephen McBrady/Photo Edit; p. 302: © David Young-Wolff/Photo Edit; p. 303: © Cary Wolinsky/Stock Boston; p. 306: © Jeff Dunn/Stock Boston

Chapter 13

Opener: © J. Myers/H. Armstrong Roberts; p. 321: © Tony Freeman/Photo Edit; p. 328, 329: © James Shaffer; p. 330: © Esbin Anderson/Omni-Photo Communications; p. 332: © Melanie Carr/Zephyr Pictures

Chapter 14

Opener: © James Shaffer; p. 347: © Tony Freeman/Photo Edit; p. 348: © David Young Wolff/Photo Edit; p. 353: © Richard Hutchins/Photo Edit; p. 360: © Gaye Hilsanrath/Picture Cube

Chapter 15

Opener: © Gale Zucker/Stock Boston; p. 372: © Eric R. Berndt/Unicorn Stock Photos; p. 373: © Tony Freeman/Photo Edit; p. 381: © Stephen Frisch/Stock Boston; p. 383: © James Shaffer

Chapter 16

Opener: © Bob Daemmrich/Stock Boston; p. 393: © Paul Conklin/Photo Edit; p. 398: © Linda Dufurrend/Grant Heilman Photo; p. 399: © James Shaffer; p. 402: © Peter Bates/Picture Cube; p. 405: © Devaney Stock Photos

Chapter 17

Opener: © Jeffrey Aaronson/Network Aspen; p. 417: © Myrleen Ferguson Cate/Photo Edit; p. 419: © Jeffrey Aaronson/Network Aspen; p. 422: © Seth Resnick/Light Sources Stock; p. 424: © Bachmann/Stock Boston; p. 429: © James Shaffer; p. 435: © David Young Wolff/Photo Edit; p. 436 top left: © Michael Newman/Photo Edit; p. 436 top right: © Julie Houck/First Light, Toronto; p. 436 bottom: © Mark E. Gibson

Chapter 18

Opener: © Dennis MacDonald/Unicorn Stock Photos; p. 447, 454: © James Shaffer; p. 457: © John Newbauer/Photo Edit; p. 461: © Tony Freeman/Photo Edit; p. 462: © James Shaffer

Name Index

Subject Index